BY YOUR COMMAND
The Unofficial and Unauthorised Guide to
Battlestar Galactica

Volume Two
The Reimagined Series

BY YOUR COMMAND
The Unofficial and Unauthorised Guide to
Battlestar Galactica

Alan Stevens and Fiona Moore

Volume Two
The Reimagined Series

First published in the UK in 2015 by
Telos Publishing Ltd

www.telos.co.uk

This edition 2015

Telos Publishing Ltd values feedback. Please e-mail us with any comments you may have about this book to: feedback@telos.co.uk

ISBN: 978-1-84583-922-2

By Your Command: The Unofficial and Unauthorised Guide to Battlestar Galcactica: *Volume 2: The Reimagined Series* © 2014, 2015 Alan Stevens and Fiona Moore

Foreword © 2014 Matthew Bennett

Index by Ian Pritchard

The moral right of the authors has been asserted.

British Library Cataloguing in Publication Data.
A catalogue record for this book is available from the British Library.

This book is sold subject to the condition that it shall not by way of trade or otherwise, be lent, resold, hired out or otherwise circulated without the publisher's prior written consent in any form of binding or cover other than that in which it is published and without a similar condition including this condition being imposed on the subsequent purchaser.

Dedication

To Theodore
'Tsi-Nan-Fu'

and

To Jaffa
'Face-Plant'

CONTENTS

So Say We All?: Authors' Introduction — 9
Foreword — 12

I Have Seen Earth: Revival Efforts 1994-2001 — 13
The DeSanto/Singer Proposal — 17

Reimagined Battlestar Galactica: Credits — 23
Reimagined Battlestar Galactica: Background and Production — 62
1 - Battlestar Galactica: The Miniseries (Parts One and Two) — 74
Season One 2004-2005 — 91
2 - 33 — 95
3 - Water — 101
4 - Bastille Day — 107
5 - Act of Contrition — 113
6 - You Can't Go Home Again — 120
7 - Litmus — 125
8 - Six Degrees of Separation — 131
9 - Flesh and Bone — 136
10 - Tigh Me Up, Tigh Me Down — 143
11 - The Hand of God — 149
12 - Colonial Day — 155
13 - Kobol's Last Gleaming (Parts One and Two) — 162
Season Two: 2005-2006 — 172
14 - Scattered — 176
15 - Valley of Darkness — 182
16 - Fragged — 187
17 - Resistance — 194
18 - The Farm — 200
19 - Home (Parts One and Two) — 205
20 - Final Cut — 215
21 - Flight of the Phoenix — 221
22 - *Pegasus* — 227
23 - Resurrection Ship (Parts One and Two) — 234
24 - Epiphanies — 242
25 - Black Market — 249
26 - Scar — 255
27 - Sacrifice — 260
28 - The Captain's Hand — 266
29 - Downloaded — 272
30 - Lay Down Your Burdens (Parts One and Two) — 279
Season Three: 2006-2007 — 289

31 - The Resistance/Crossroads (Parts One To Ten)	293
32 - Occupation	298
33 - Precipice	304
34 - Exodus (Parts One and Two)	310
35 - Collaborators	318
36 - Torn	324
37 - A Measure of Salvation	331
38 - Hero	338
39 - Unfinished Business	344
40 - The Passage	349
41 - The Eye of Jupiter	354
42 - Rapture	360
43 - Taking a Break From All Your Worries	366
44 - The Woman King	373
45 - A Day in the Life	379
46 - Dirty Hands	384
47 - Maelstrom	390
48 - The Son Also Rises	397
49 - Crossroads (Parts One and Two)	403
Season Four: 2008-2009	412
50 - Razor	418
51 - He That Believeth in Me	429
52 - Six of One	436
53 - The Ties That Bind	443
54 - Escape Velocity	451
55 - The Road Less Travelled	459
56 - Faith	464
57 - Guess What's Coming to Dinner?	470
58 - *Sine Qua Non*	477
59 - The Hub	484
60 - Revelations	490
61 - Sometimes a Great Notion	496
62 - The Face of the Enemy	503
63 - A Disquiet Follows My Soul	509
64 - The Oath	516
65 - Blood on the Scales	523
66 - No Exit	530
67 - Deadlock	538
68 - Someone to Watch Over Me	544
69 - Islanded in a Stream of Stars	551
70 - Daybreak (Parts One, Two and Three)	556
71 - The Plan	576
72 - Blood and Chrome	585

Caprica	593
Merchandise and Legacy	610
Index by Title	615
About the Authors	618

So Say We All?
Authors' Introduction

Before we begin the book, we would like briefly to outline our approach to *Battlestar Galactica*. As people who have become fans of both the original and the reimagined series (and willing to acknowledge that *Galactica 1980* at least has some merit), we intend to celebrate *Battlestar Galactica* in all its diverse televisual incarnations, and to show the connections, homages and interplay between the various interpretations of the story of a space-borne exodus in search of Earth.

Writing books that cover the 1978, 1980 and 2003-2013 series has thrown up a unique set of challenges. For the first volume our main concern was to track down behind-the-scenes information that contextualised the series for the modern reader, given that over 30 years had passed since the making of the programmes. In this second book, however, we have found ourselves in the opposite situation, with so much information about the 2003-onwards series available at the time of writing via blogs, websites, news services and recorded interviews with cast and crew that the problem has been instead to figure out what should be included, and what left for our readers to discover through other sources. This has made for a corresponding shift in emphasis in the content of the two volumes, with the first leaning more heavily on production details than the second. However, in both volumes we have aimed to focus on the series' main strength: its development of strong continuing narratives and character arcs. For consistency's sake, we are using the same episode numbering system as we did in Volume 1, allocating each story a number rather than using the studio's own production code system. However, unlike Volume 1, 'base star' and 'base ship' will be rendered as composite words, to bring them in line with the reimagined series, apart from in the review of the Singer/DeSanto pilot story, in which the relevant terminology is as in the original series.

For reasons of space we have chosen to focus on the televised or webcast series, covering the comic-book, game and novel spin-offs in overview essays. In order that the volume on the reimagined series can be enjoyed both before and after viewers have become aware of its various plot twists, we have included footnotes designated as 'SPOILER SECTION' in cases where subsequent revelations cast a new light on earlier episodes. All production and season overview essays will contain spoilers. For the sake of clarity, the term 'deleted scene' refers to a scene which does not appear at all in the transmitted version of an episode (though it may have been recorded, and may be available to view on one or more DVD and Blu-ray releases or as an online extra), while the term 'extended scene' refers to extra material that was cut from the transmitted version, but appears as a deleted scene or has been reinstated as part of the DVD/Blu-ray cut of the episode. When giving credits for episodes on which two

SO SAY WE ALL? AUTHORS' INTRODUCTION

or more writers worked, we will follow the WGA screenwriting credit policy, such that '&' denotes writers who have worked on a script together, and the word 'and' denotes writers who have worked on a script consecutively. Although the series was made mainly on videotape, we will also be using the term 'film' in the loose sense, to denote recording more generally.

As with our earlier Telos Publishing books, *Liberation: The Unofficial and Unauthorised Guide to Blake's 7* and *Fall Out: The Unofficial and Unauthorised Guide to The Prisoner*, we do not here propose to have the 'last word' on a series as dynamic and long-lived as *Battlestar Galactica*. We do hope to be able to contribute a guide that will be interesting, analytical and thought-provoking – and occasionally, given our 'unofficial and unauthorised' designation, challenging received wisdom – as we, through both volumes, trace the evolution of the series from its 1970s origins to the present day.

We would like to acknowledge the help of, in no particular order: Matthew Bennett, Paul Winter, Nick Lewis, Ilana Rain, Shawn O'Donnell, Alex Lewczuk, Andy Swinden and Ben Keywood from Galaxy 4 in Sheffield, Leah Cairns, Michael Angeli, Jim Smith, Mark Oliver, Jane and Robert Moore, Bronwen Moore and David Clark, David Howe and Stephen James Walker at Telos, and all the many people who work tirelessly to make draft scripts, production information, concept art and so forth available to fans, particularly on the websites named below, all of which we would encourage our readers to visit. Special thanks are due to Marcel Damen for allowing us to see advance copies of interviews for his website www.galactica.tv, and for providing us with rare series-related material.

The main books consulted for this guide have been: *Somewhere Beyond the Heavens: The Battlestar Galactica Unofficial Companion* (2006, Imprint) by David Criswell and Richie Levine, *Frak You!: The Ultimate Unauthorized Guide to Battlestar Galactica* (2007, ECW Press) by Jo Storm, *Finding Battlestar Galactica* by Lynnette Porter, David Lavery and Hillary Robson (2008, Sourcebooks Inc), *Battlestar Galactica: Investigating Flesh, Spirit and Steel* edited by Roz Kaveney and Jennifer Stoy (2010, I B Tauris & Co), *The Science of Battlestar Galactica* by Patrick Di Justo and Kevin R. Grazier (2010, Wiley Publishing) and the various volumes of *Battlestar Galactica: The Official Companion* (2005-9, Titan Books) by David Bassom and Sharon Gosling. Although we have consulted far too many websites and forums to be able to acknowledge them all, our key sources have been: www.battlestarwiki.org, www.battlestargalactica.com, scifi.com, galactica.tv, www.colonialfleets.com, www.byyourcommand.net, www.battlestarfanclub.com, Colonial Defence Forces (www.cdfcommand.com), Galactica Sitrep (www.galacticasitrep.blogspot.com), www.kobol.com, www.bearmccreary.com, www.annelockhart.com, www.richardhatch.com, The Chief's Deck (community.livejournal.com/aarondouglas), John Laroque's document archive for the reimagined series (members.tripod.com/john_larocque/tns/archive.html), Maureen Ryan's blog (featuresblogs.chicagotribune.com/), the website for Propworx, the auction house that handled the official auctions of *Battlestar Galactica*-related material (www.propworx.com), and the satirical website

WikiFrakr (wiki.frakr.com).

Finally, a brief word on the title of this book. The most obvious reason for choosing 'By Your Command' is that it is the only phrase that appears in all three series of *Battlestar Galactica* and its spinoffs. However, the phrase also evokes themes common to all of televised *Battlestar Galactica*: the nature of totalitarianism, the legitimacy of command, the question of when to submit to authority and when to resist it, and the way in which the characters of all series ultimately find themselves following the plans of divine beings.

Foreword
Matthew Bennett

Connection. It was the first word that crossed my mind when I returned to my office after meeting the gracious and brilliant authors of this book, Fiona Moore and Alan Stevens.

We had met in a steamy coffee shop in Toronto only a few days after Christmas. There was snow on the ground, and even though we were talking about a television series that had been completed more than four years before, I suddenly realised how strongly I was still connected to it.

My thoughts turned to a day I will remember forever. It was my birthday and I was sat in my trailer in Vancouver at the North Shore Studios waiting for the crew to set up another shot for a new miniseries I had been cast in, called *Battlestar Galactica*. We were several days into the shoot and I had a feeling that something incredible was happening. I had watched the original series as a boy and now I was part of its rebirth ... the 'reimagining' of *Battlestar Galactica*, and while I knew that what we were creating was going to be special, I didn't realise how special it would ultimately turn out to be.

I can reference my role on *Battlestar Galactica* as a catalyst for many things in my life. It gave me work, travel, it's taken my career to unexpected places, but the greatest thing it's allowed me is to be in a position to meet some amazing people, and for me, that has been the greatest gift ... the connections I have experienced.

I count myself incredibly fortunate to have been indelibly connected to such a groundbreaking television series that has meant so much to so many, and I am constantly amazed by the people who approach me, sometimes for photos or autographs, but mostly just to talk about *Battlestar Galactica*, a series that has had a profound effect on them as well.

I have found that for many, the series brought them into a worldwide community of like-minded viewers who thought of *Battlestar Galactica* as 'their show'. And as I think about it now, if you are a fan of a series it somehow does belong to you in a unique way ... as much as it does to the actors who have played on it ... we are all connected to it.

To all of the fans who have watched, and to all of the fans who are reading this incredible companion, I thank you for your interest, dedication, and for the connections we have shared.

Peace and love to all.

Matthew Bennett
Aka Aaron Doral ... Cylon #5

I Have Seen Earth: Revival Efforts (1994-2001)

For about 15 years after the final episode of *Galactica 1980*, *Battlestar Galactica* fans were limited to the occasional new comic or tie-in novel for series-related material. (For a brief review of this subject, see Volume 1.) However, repeats of the original series on the Sci-Fi Channel in 1993-4 and 1996-7 sparked interest in a revival, culminating in the 2003 reimagined *Battlestar Galactica*.

Novel Ideas: Richard Hatch's Revival Efforts

According to battlestargalactica.com, Richard Hatch announced in 1994 that he had written 'a trilogy' of scripts for a new *Battlestar Galactica*. The chronology of this is debatable, as in the book *Somewhere Beyond the Heavens* Hatch has also been quoted as saying that he was inspired to mount a revival effort after going to a *Star Trek* convention in Pasadena in 1995 and being impressed by the fan interest in *Battlestar Galactica*. Either way, in 1996 Hatch announced that he was in talks with Universal over a revival, which he compared to the *Star Trek* movies of the late 1970s to 1990s. Hatch continued his campaign throughout the late 1990s, building on the success of his series of *Battlestar Galactica* spin-off novels (which he appears to have seen as a template for the series, saying of them 'I ... wanted to lay out a possible vision for bringing back this series with the original characters intact, and a new generation of their children born in space'). This culminated in a self-funded and self-produced proof-of-concept trailer called *Battlestar Galactica: The Second Coming*.

The Second Coming, executive-produced, co-scripted (with Sophie LaPorte) and co-directed (with Jay Woelfel) by Hatch, was, according to Hatch's website, begun in 1998 and completed in 1999. The trailer is just over four minutes long and is of perhaps surprisingly high quality, with good costumes, effects and make-up, and effective use of CGI, with space sequences featuring both updated and original spacecraft. It seems to hold to Hatch's assertion that his concept involved 'adding to, not subtracting from, the original look of the show'. It features, as well as Hatch returning as Apollo, Terry Carter as President Tigh, Jack Stauffer as Bojay and George Murdock as Doctor Salik. It also has the last screen appearance of John Colicos, who died in 2000, as Baltar (the production's science adviser, Doctor Kevin Grazier, would later act as consultant on the reimagined series). Count Iblis, played in the original series by Patrick Macnee, is here portrayed by Richard Lynch, who had played *Galactica 1980*'s recurring villain Xaviar. Continuity related to Hatch's books includes a new, red-jacketed flight uniform, and the presence of a Lieutenant Troy, played by Mickalean McCormick. The trailer was shown at science-fiction conventions around the turn of the millennium, and is still possible to track down online today.

Lost Civilisations: Battlestar Atlantis

Hatch's activities appear to have left Glen Larson slightly bemused, as he was also involved in a revival attempt at the same time, and a certain amount of rivalry existed between the two efforts, with Larson pointing out in the 2000 *Sciography* documentary that as Hatch did not have the rights to the series, his efforts were wasted. Although there are some reports that the two talked about working together, they appear to have operated in parallel. Larson's interest in such a project was first indicated in 1994, at the Fifteen Yahren Reunion convention, when he announced that he was doing a four-hour revival story with the Fox Network. The latter idea ultimately came to nothing; subsequently, Larson announced that the movie rights for *Battlestar Galactica* had reverted to his own production company, and that he intended to use them to develop a motion picture that would first reintroduce Commander Cain and the battlestar *Pegasus*, and then tell the story of the lost battlestar *Atlantis*, which carried the Thirteenth Tribe to Earth at the time of the exodus from Kobol. Todd Moyer, director of the film *Wing Commander* (1999), was named as producer and Mike Finch as writer of the screenplay. Larson put out a simple 30-second long trailer, consisting of a title card and some animation sequences, in August 1999, announcing a movie release for Christmas 2000, but nothing has been seen since.

Slightly Foxed: The DeSanto/Singer Proposal

In August 2001, Studios USA, who had purchased Universal's TV section, greenlit a *Battlestar Galactica* revival spearheaded by Tom DeSanto and Bryan Singer, producer and director respectively of the 2000 film *X-Men*. (Singer is also known for producing, among others, the acclaimed films *The Usual Suspects* (1995) and *Apt Pupil* (1998), and the TV series *House*.) Fox was to be the screening network.

This project was initially planned as a May 2002 'event TV movie' directed by Singer, which, if it did well, would serve as a backdoor pilot for an autumn 2002 TV series. Production got to an advanced stage, with Vipers and sets being constructed.[1] However, the terrorist attacks of 11 September 2001 resulted in production being halted for about a month, as during this time most entertainment companies were concerned about producing films and programmes featuring bombs, wars, terrorists or related themes. During this hiatus, a conflict emerged with Singer's schedule for *X-Men 2*, meaning that he had to withdraw from the project, and Fox then announced that they would be doing Joss Whedon's *Firefly* instead.

---

1 Further details are given in the next chapter.

DeSanto subsequently approached other networks with the concept, including the Sci-Fi Channel, but to no avail.

Imagine All the People: The Eick/Moore Reimagined Series

Around the time that Fox lost interest in the DeSanto/Singer proposal, in November 2001, the President of Studios USA, David Kissinger, approached David Eick, who was Senior Vice-President of Original Series Development for USA Cable, and who had worked in various capacities on, among others, *Hercules: The Legendary Journeys*, *Xena: Warrior Princess* and *American Gothic*, to spearhead a *Battlestar Galactica* revival. This would be under the auspices of Studios USA and would run on the Sci-Fi Channel. Eick agreed in December 2001, and subsequently approached Ronald D Moore to participate in the project.

Moore was then best known for his work on the *Star Trek* franchise. A *Star Trek* fan from an early age, he got his start as a writer when a friend arranged for him to visit the set of *Star Trek: The Next Generation* in 1987 and he handed a finished script to the studio tour guide. Despite the informality of this approach, he was invited to pitch for the series and ended up as a staff writer, working on a number of episodes for the various series, as well as on two of the *Next Generation* films, *Star Trek: Generations* (1994) and *Star Trek: First Contact* (1996). He also worked on, among others, *Roswell*, *Mission Impossible II* (2000), and *The Dead Zone*. Moore was at the time keen to get away from the *Star Trek* concept. This motivation strongly informed the development of the revived *Battlestar Galactica* series as an earthy universe lacking aliens but featuring active divine intervention, and explains why Moore said that he was very much taken with the original *Battlestar Galactica* pilot, 'Saga of a Star World', describing it as having 'the darkest premise of any pilot I've ever seen'. He has said that he was also inspired by the terrorist attacks of 11 September 2001 and the possibility of exploring, through the apocalyptic concept of *Battlestar Galactica*, how people behave when their worlds change.

The studio reverted back to Universal at this time, after the sale of Studios USA to Vivendi Universal, and the revival was officially announced on 2 April 2002, with Moore named as showrunner, Eick as executive producer, and Breck Eisner (later to be replaced by Michael Rymer) as director. In shades of the DeSanto project, Moore was commissioned to write a four-part miniseries as a backdoor pilot, although, as he was also acting as executive producer on the critically-acclaimed (if ultimately unsuccessful) series *Carnivàle*, he was not present during the shooting of this.

The somewhat awkward term 'reimagining' was applied to the new *Battlestar Galactica* in publicity by the Sci-Fi Channel, to emphasise that the series was more a conceptual than a straight remake. According to Moore (in an interview quoted in *Somewhere Beyond the Heavens*), he and Eick decided early on to do the series as a reboot rather than a continuation, which the studio and network accepted unproblematically, and the rumours of 'epic battles being waged behind the scenes' over whether the series was to be a remake or a prequel 'are completely and utterly false'. In *The Official Companion*, Moore says that he briefly considered doing a continuation series but decided that it wasn't viable in today's marketplace – although the fact that DeSanto's proposal had been for a continuation series would undoubtedly have also been a factor.

This decision understandably upset a lot of the original cast (Moore, in *Somewhere Beyond the Heavens*, said 'I think it hit a lot of them like a slap in the face') as well as many fans of the original series, who felt particularly irked by the fact that, after 25 years of patient campaigning for a continuation of their favourite series and finally achieving that goal in the DeSanto project, it was promptly abandoned in favour of a proposal that appeared, superficially at least, to change most of original *Battlestar Galactica*'s best-loved elements. Their feelings were summed up by Richard Hatch, who said, 'I had fought for seven, almost eight, years to bring back the original show. I had put tens of thousands of my own dollars and incredible amounts of energy and time into convincing the networks to bring back the original series ... The greatest, and most painful, realisation for me was that regardless of my personal feelings and efforts, I had to come to terms with the fact that I didn't own *Battlestar*'. The term GINO, 'Galactica in Name Only' (a nickname apparently derived from the political pejorative RINO/DINO, 'Republican/Democrat in Name Only') emerged in fandom to describe the series. Early interviews with Moore, Eick and the new series' principal cast members often come across as somewhat defensive in consequence, and frequently contain veiled attacks on the original series and its fandom, which unfortunately does not help their position. However, DeSanto himself at the time urged fans to give the series a chance, saying that he saw a lot of similarities between his ideas and theirs.

As will be indicated in the season overviews and episode reviews later in this book, the differences between the two series are not quite as radical as some people on both sides of the issue have claimed. Eick has stated: 'The first step in the process of any remake or sequel is ... the true acknowledgment of whatever genius, origin or starting point led you to want to revive the material in the first place. We have seen what has happened when these fundamental ingredients are treated in too cavalier a fashion'. While the reimagined series has a post-millennial take on them, the elements that made the original such a strong programme are all present and run through the episodes to the end of the story.

BY YOUR COMMAND: VOL 2

The DeSanto/Singer Proposal

0 – BATTLESTAR GALACTICA

WRITERS: Billy Brown and Dan Angel

SYNOPSIS: The Fleet have found an asteroid rich in minerals and water, and have established two settlements: one a mining colony, the other, orbiting it and held in position by two gravitational stabilisers, a domed residential area called New Caprica. No Cylons have been seen in 25 years. The President, Mara, wants to decommission the battlestar *Galactica* in order to fund the expansion of the Arts and Commerce Centre, and strongarms its commander, Orin, adopted son of Apollo, into agreeing. Orin's daughter, a schoolteacher named Leda, has as a pupil a young girl named Astraea, who experiences mysterious fits and is believed by the mining community to be a prophet. Orin's sons, pilots Elias and Ash, who are rivals for the affections of fellow pilot Raina, quarrel over Elias's decision to leave military service; they try to settle it with an off-log flying competition but end up crashing their Vipers onto a remote asteroid. In doing so, they discover a Cylon base star. As they have only one functional Viper, Elias flies back to warn the Fleet, with the Cylons in pursuit. The warriors are rapidly outgunned by the Cylons, who order them to surrender and submit for transport to the planet Cylon. Orin and Elias come up with a plan to destroy the base star by loading two of the new Colonial craft, the Scorpions, with explosives and aiming them at one of the stabilisers, propelling New Caprica into the base star. Ash shows up in a captured Raider to join the battle. Leda rescues Astraea and her brother Kai from the mining colony and takes them to the *Galactica*. As the Fleet heads off to resume the search for Earth, Raina is concerned by an apparent gap in Ash's memory. Meanwhile, on the planet Cylon, a meeting takes place among the Cylons' governing council: a body of cyborgs, which includes the missing pilot Apollo.

ANALYSIS: The most successful revival attempt before the actual reimagined series was Bryan Singer and Tom DeSanto's proposed sequel. What follows is based on a second-draft script of the pilot dated 22 October 2001, and published interview material with Tom DeSanto.[2]

---

[2] Some of DeSanto's later descriptions of the plot have interesting differences from the draft script, chiefly in that he mentions using the *Galactica*'s guns rather than the Scorpions to destroy the stabiliser, suggesting he is thinking of either an earlier or later treatment.

THE DESANTO/SINGER PROPOSAL

Cardboard Boxey: Continuity with the Original Series

Like most of the proposed revivals, the Singer/DeSanto version is explicitly a sequel to the original series. Starbuck and Boomer (both now Colonels) feature as characters, as would Apollo have done in the episodic series. A character named Colonel Tiburon is present, who seems to fulfil the same function as Colonel Tigh. As well as Apollo's adopted son from the original series, Boxey, now going by the name of Orin, commanding the battlestar, Starbuck's daughter Raina becomes the subject of a love triangle. The Council of Twelve still exists, and includes among its numbers the improbably named Hathor (who, despite having been named after the cow-headed Egyptian goddess of fertility, is male) and Lepus (who is suitably rabbit-like in demeanour).

Orin is stated to be 45, and the Cylons to have not attacked in 25 years, meaning that, if we assume Boxey to have been between six and eight in the original series, it is set between 37 and 39 years after the original; tragically, he seems to have grown up into a rather dull stick-in-the-mud. The *Galactica* appears to have had a redesign, as the landing bay now has doors that open and close; Cylon craft, likewise, now require the pilot to stick a forearm in a jack, like an ignition key, in order to operate them. The Republic of New Caprica is the official name of the new colony, which is an artificial cone-shaped structure encased in a dome, held above the asteroid on which the mining colony is located, through the use of two gravity stabilisers; there is a sort of *Metropolis*-like class tension established between the inhabitants of New Caprica and the miners, though the miners' children appear to attend school on New Caprica.

DeSanto has also indicated in an interview in *Somewhere Beyond the Heavens* that he had planned a detailed storyline involving the battlestar *Pegasus* and its commander, Cain. The *Pegasus* would have re-encountered the Fleet and then been lost again in its final battle with the Cylons, 23 years before the pilot. (The chronology and details of the final encounter with the Cylons differ slightly in DeSanto's account from those in the draft script used as a reference here.) At that point, Cain's daughter Sheba would have rejoined its crew. In the episodic series, the *Pegasus* would have returned with Sheba in command, only to be lost yet again; DeSanto mentions that he had spoken to Anne Lockhart about having her reprise the role of Sheba. There was also an idea of revealing, in the episodic series, that Starbuck's love interest Cassiopea had given up on him, married fellow pilot Bojay, and joined the *Pegasus* crew. *Galactica 1980* seems to have been largely ignored (bar the detail that Boxey is a nickname rather than a real name); but very few fans would have had a problem with it being written it out of the continuity. DeSanto also mentions that they wanted Jane Seymour's character to return, through the device of having her original series character, Serina, come back as one of the lightship people, the advanced alien race who periodically aided the humans' rag-tag fleet.

DeSanto has provided an explanation for the cyborg Cylons who appear briefly at the end of the pilot: that, in a reframing of the original series, the mechanical Cylons turned on their lizard creators because their programming, to bring order to the universe, caused them to attack anything with free will; their Imperious Leader was the last surviving lizard Cylon, who had chosen to be injected with 'nano technologies' that destroyed his free will and allowed him to join the machine. Baltar, the human traitor who joined the Cylons in the original series, would have injected himself with the same machines after the Cylons' final battle with the humans, out of a fear that 'the Cylons were turning against him and he was starting to lose his usefulness'. (Again, DeSanto's account differs slightly from the draft script, in which the Cylons do not fight a final battle with the humans, but simply disappear.) When the experiment was proved successful, this would have been used to develop other such beings.

This concept works well with the original series' backstory for the Cylons as outlined in 'War of the Gods'; specifically, that the lizard Cylons, fearful of the humans, asked the advanced being Count Iblis for his help, and the price was their transformation into a mechanical race. The cyborg Cylons in the pilot script say 'to the Second Cylon Dynasty and the destiny of consciousness', and Orin says that after the Cylons disappeared, the humans 'found evidence that they began to fight among themselves'; as consciousness and free will, as defined here, are linked, this all suggests that their absorption of humans is leading, as in the reimagined series, to a new development in which the Cylons start to generate free will and to challenge each other. While this is an interesting post-hoc rationalisation for many of the original series' concepts, it does not totally fit with what we have seen before, as on several occasions the original series Cylons displayed individuality, initiative, free will, humour and a complex internal *realpolitik*.

The story that we have is, not surprisingly, based largely on the original series pilot 'Saga of a Star World', featuring as it does politicians who are complacent and/or venal assuming that the Cylons are no longer a threat and working against the military; the final third of 'Saga of a Star World' has the Fleet considering abandoning their exodus and settling on a planet. There are other similarities, including a pair of male leads, one of whom is strait-laced and the other impetuous and hedonistic, a scene where two pilots accidentally stumble upon the Cylons about to ambush the unsuspecting humans; and a blended family at the core of the story. Ash does a wing-waggling manoeuvre to identify his Raider as Colonial, an idea clearly taken from the original series story 'The Hand of God'. Orin's reference to the Cylons fighting among themselves is in line with a deleted scene from the *Galactica 1980* story 'The Night the Cylons Landed', in which Doctor Zee speculates that the creation of humanoid Cylons would lead to the development of human-like passions and thus to internal conflict.

There are some continuity differences from the original series, however. The terminology has changed from the Colonial units to Earth ones (years rather than yahrens, for instance), and the term 'ag-ship' is used instead of agroship. Prostitutes seem to be low-status workers in contrast to the respectable 'socialators' of the original. It is stated that Orin has never fought in a battle or personally killed a Cylon; however, if the last Cylon attack came when he was

20, and he joined the service around the age of 18, this raises the question of what he spent the two intervening years doing. In the pilot, it is repeatedly indicated that Earth is a myth that most people don't believe in, but in the original series its existence is firmly established as a fact in several episodes. Orin refers to people being 'captured or killed' by the Cylons in the attacks on the Colonies, but the Cylons in the original series did not take prisoners. (DeSanto indicates that this was a set-up, as those left behind on the Colonies would have been the source of humans to convert. However, since the idea of converting the humans came about only due to Baltar experimentally injecting himself with the 'nano technologies', this would mean that the Cylons had spent two years pursuing the rag-tag fleet and ignoring the humans left behind on the Colonies, who DeSanto estimates made up '99 percent of the population'.) The script also comes across as less gender-egalitarian than either the original series or the reimagined one; while it does have a female pilot, a female president, and two (rather undeveloped) female bridge crew characters, women are otherwise characterised as schoolteachers, wives or 'slinky babes' who flirt with pilots in entertainment arcades.

Looking Forward: Similarities to the Reimagined Series

There are also several resemblances to the reimagined series, although these appear to be down to the fact that both teams were working from the same source material, the original series, as well as to the use of SF archetypes and clichés in both productions. The DeSanto/Singer pilot, like the Moore/Eick series, features a love triangle involving two pilot brothers, one of whom doesn't actually want to be a pilot, and a third, female, pilot; and a military family where the father insists that his sons join the armed forces regardless of their own feelings about it. Both stories begin with the *Galactica* facing decommissioning. Mara is a ruthless female president who, if anything, makes the reimagined series' Roslin look liberal and cuddly, and Orin's daughter Leda is, like Roslin (and Athena in the original series), a schoolteacher. Astraea, like Hera in the reimagined series, is a child with special powers, and her prophecies are similar to those of the Hybrids. A hiatus on a world called New Caprica, and a plotline involving discontented labourers organising a union, anticipate storylines in in Season Three of the reimagined series, and both series involve a resource crisis over water. The humanoid Cylons of the reimagined series are actual synthetic beings rather than converted humans, but the concept is similar. The Cylon Raiders (a term used in both this pilot and the reimagined series, but never the original), like their reimagined series counterparts, 'hang from the underside' of the basestar. On a production level, there were plans to film the series in Canada to save on costs.

Night of the Lepus: Good and Bad aspects of the Pilot

The story has a few good lines, such as Starbuck's 'Initiate the docking sequence.

I'll initiate the ass-kissing sequence', as the President comes aboard *Galactica*. DeSanto has also said that he wanted to address the feeling he had that people were losing purpose and focusing on materialism, reflected in Starbuck's remark 'When I was [Elias's] age ... we could dream of being heroes. I guess now the dream is to make a fortune on New Caprica'. A sequence where an overworked doctor, confronted with Hathor insisting on immediate treatment for a minor wound, offers him a pill to alleviate the pain, which turns out to be a laxative, is wickedly funny.

Some of the politics are also quite interesting to observe. New Caprica is a deeply unequal society, and Mara is a ruthless character who clearly supports this, as her ostensible reason for cutting the military budget is to fund the expansion to the Arts and Commerce Centre rather than to further social programmes. She endorses the expensive 'Black Squadron' project to develop the Scorpion fighters, but tells Orin to keep it secret; she then uses the fact that he has an 'overspend' in his budget to justify decommissioning the *Galactica*, knowing that he can't explain the reason for the overspend in public. Although she claims that she is trying to hold together a fragile coalition, the fact that she is able, when she desires, to shout down the rest of the Quorum indicates that, in fact, she rules most aspects of society, and her attacks on the military are thus not actually sops to Hathor and Lepus as she claims, but in fact her own attempts to undermine the last remaining source of opposition to her.

There are a few problematic aspects. While the characters in the story are recognisable archetypes, this is not necessarily a bad thing, as the same could be said of many in the original and reimagined series. However, the female characters tend to fall into some rather unfortunate stereotypes (the ruthless female politician, the doting wife, the girl who plays her two lovers off against each other), and the only left-wing character, Florian, a union organiser who is dating Leda, is an uncaring bastard, baiting Astraea mercilessly in an attempt to prove to the miners that she is not a prophet, and he is conveniently killed in the Cylon attack. Orin is said not to like Florian, which suggests, since Orin otherwise does not show much in the way of emotional intelligence, that Orin is either prejudiced against the working class or anti-union, neither of which make him look very sympathetic. The returning characters, Starbuck, Boomer and Apollo, are all marginalised in favour of the far less interesting new characters, mainly the unpleasant Orin and his rather overindulged children.

Although the idea of a politician trying to weaken the military through budget cuts is plausible, the story is rather vague on what 'decommissioning' the *Galactica* and/or the Vipers involves. The society looks insanely nepotistic, with Orin casually stating that Ash, who is up for review, is sure to get a promotion, and with neither of his sons anticipating any comeback for taking Vipers out on an unauthorised joyride (and, since we learn that Elias got another pilot killed in a similar stunt, it is surprising that Ash goes along with this). Mara is quite formal and distant with Orin, which is surprising since we then learn that she went to school with Orin's wife. (The fact that Orin's wife later dies in the attacks suggests a set-up for a rebound romance between him and Mara.) The original series' Fleet contained only about 6,000 people, meaning that the New Caprica system must contain about 30,000 people at most, but it is continually treated as a much larger society. It is stated that there have been no training flights on the Scorpions, which raises the question of how they managed to design them.

There are some very stilted lines, such as Orin's 'I'm so sorry for trying to make you [Elias] be like Ash. It's one of the many ways I've been a fool' and Elias's response, 'I know I questioned our family's tradition. But from the moment I saw what they did to New Caprica, everything changed'. Some of the dialogue and description also seems inadvertently to refer to Orin's testicles, as when Mara says, 'I take it I'll be seeing your boys today', and later when Orin is said to be 'absentmindedly clicking the toy's balls against each other … He looks at the balls again, then back out the window, then back at the balls – an idea just beginning to form in his mind'. Possibly there is a hidden metaphor whereby Orin, castrated by the female president, regains his manhood through his daring gambit against the Cylons.

There are some awkward technical terms, such as 'digital binocs' and 'cloaking mechs'. Some of the physics in the episode is also problematic, such as a description of the glass of a Viper cockpit 'imploding' (although the vacuum is surely outside, not inside, the glass). The colony being illuminated by a series of giant mirrors, one of which, when knocked out of alignment, becomes a 'death ray' burning unlucky colonists, draws on Hermann Oberth's 1929 proposal for an early space weapon; however, like Oberth, the writers do not take into account the fact that the focal length of a mirror that size would prevent it from concentrating the sun's light in the required manner.

Despite its problems, it is possible that the DeSanto/Singer pilot might have developed into an effective programme. However, as it stands, its main role is as an important middle step between the original show of the 1970s and the commissioning of the reimagined series.

Reimagined *Battlestar Galactica* Credits

Please note: Where a number or numbers appear in brackets after a person's name in the listing below, this indicates the story or stories on which that person was credited. Information regarding the credits for the 'Battlestar Galactica: The Resistance'/'Crossroads' and 'Battlestar Galactica: The Face of the Enemy' webisodes has been obtained from blog.scifi.com/battlestar/ and imdb.com.

PRODUCTION TEAM

Developed by:
Ronald D Moore

Based on the Series *Battlestar Galactica*
Created by:
Glen A Larson

Executive Producers:
Ronald D Moore (1-71)
David Eick
Jane Espenson (62, 71)
Michael Taylor (71, 72)
Jonas Pate (72)

Co-Executive Producers:
Toni Graphia (2-30)
Mark Verheiden (19-30, 32-61, 63-70)
Michael Angeli (32-61, 63-70)
Jane Espenson (50-61, 63-70)
Michael Taylor (50-61, 63-70)

Producers:
Harvey Frand (1-31, 61-71)
William Kendall (31)
Bradley Thompson (31-49)
David Weddle (31-49)
Michael Rymer (32-61, 63-70)
Ron E French (50-71)
Paul M Leonard (72)
Clara George (72)

REIMAGINED *BATTLESTAR GALACTICA* CREDITS

Supervising Producers:
Harvey Frand (32-60)
Michael Taylor (32-49)
Bradley Thompson (50-61, 63-70)
David Weddle (50-61, 63-70)

Co-Producers:
Bradley Thompson & David Weddle (14-30)
Sian McArthur (71)
Paul M Leonard (23-30, 32-71)
Maril Davis (62)
Michael D Gibson (72)
Erin Smith (72)

Consulting Producer:
Glen A Larson
Mark Verheiden (14-19)

Associate Producers:
Paul M Leonard (1-22)
Trisha Brunner (23-30, 32-35)
James Halpern (35-61, 63-70)
Andrew Seklir (50-71)
Sian McArthur (31, 50-71)
Gregg Tilson (61-71)
Maril Davis (71)

Producer/Post Production Work:
Paul M Leonard (31, 62)

Line Producer:
Ron E French (1-30, 32-49)

Story Editors:
David Weddle & Bradley Thompson (2-13)
Carla Robinson (14-30)
Anne Cofell Saunders (32-49)

Executive Story Editor:
Joel Thompson (14-30)

Assistant to Mr Moore:
Maril Davis (2-30, 32-70)

24

Assistant to Mr Eick:
James Halpern (2-30, 32-34)
Adam J Karp (66-71)

Assistant to Mr Olmos:
Joseph Ferguson (71)

Assistant to the Producers:
Weatie Rosenlehner (1)
Debbie Forbes (2-13)
Sian McArthur (14-49)
Tara Strauss (72)
Morgan Reynolds (72)
Amy Morrison (72)

Assistant to the Director:
Craig Anderl (1)

Staff Writer:
Carla Robinson (2-13)

Directors of Photography:
Joel Ransom (1)
Stephen McNutt ASC, CSC (2-30, 32-71)
John Drake (31)

Production Manager:
Ron E French (1-30, 32-35)
Boris Ivanov (31, 62)
Chris Rudolph (36-49)
Wayne Rose (50-71)
Erin Smith (72)

First Assistant Directors:
Peter Dashkewytch (1)
Wayne Rose (2, 4, 6, 8, 10, 11, 13-15, 19, 20, 23, 25, 27, 30, 32, 33, 35-38, 40-42, 44, 49)
Lee Knippelberg (3)
John Mavrogeorge (5, 7, 9, 11, 12)
Rachel Leiterman[3] (16-22, 24, 26, 28, 29, 43, 45, 48, 69, 72)
Craig Matheson (19)
Shirley-Anne Parsons (31)
Alexia S Droz (31)

---

3 Name given as 'Letterman' in 69.

REIMAGINED *BATTLESTAR GALACTICA* CREDITS

Patricia Dyer Walden (34)
Michael Shandley (39, 40, 47, 50, 52, 54-68, 70, 71)
Brad Jubenvill (46)
Stacy Fish (51, 53, 62)

Second Assistant Directors:
Brad Jubenvill (1)
Derek Thomson (2-10, 12, 13)
Sara Irvine (11)
Michael Shandley (14-30, 32-38, 41-46, 48, 49)
Mindy Heslin (31)
Alexia Droz (39, 40, 47)
Michelle Dutka (39, 40)
Kit Marlatt (50-57)
Kate Weiss (58-61, 63-70)
Jody Ryan (71)
Gary Hawes (72)

Third Assistant Directors:
Sara Irvine (1, 5, 6, 8-10, 12, 13)
Michael Johannson (2-4)
Sean Osmack (7, 11)
Troy Scott (14-30, 32-49, 63-71)
Jennifer Carpenter (19)
Ashley Bell (50-61)
Haylee Thompson (72)

Co-Third Assistant Director:
Marian Koprada (71)

Trainee Assistant Director:
Marian Koprada (50-52, 63-70)
Bob Rogers (53-61)
Shaun Moskie (72)

'A' Camera Operator:
Ryan McMaster (1, 22-30, 32-61, 63-71)
Joel Guthro (2-22)
Kevin Hall (62)
Mike Wrinch (72)

Series Cinematography by:
Ryan McMaster (62)

Director of Photography:
Lukas Ettlin (72)

BY YOUR COMMAND: VOL 2

'A' Camera Operator/Steadicam:
Tim Spencer (62)

'B' Camera Operator/Steadicam:
Lou Gruzelier (1)
Tim Spencer (2-30, 32-61, 63-71)
Ryan Purcell (72)

'A' Camera First Assistant:
Cory Budney (1)
Chris Thompson (2-5, 14-30, 32-61, 63-71)
Ivan Muldonado (6-13)
Shannon Abbott (31)
Richard Egan (62)

'B' Camera First Assistant:
Richard Eagan (1)
Ryan S Gillard (2-30)
Mikil Rullman (32-35)
Robb Devitt (36-61, 63-71)

Camera First Assistants:
John Seale (72)
Cory Budney (72)
Brendan Chalmers (72)
Nick Watson (72)

'A' Camera Second Assistant:
Richard Porta (2-13, 18-22)
Robb Devitt (14-17)
Colin Mullin (23-30, 32-61, 63-71)
Thomas Billingsley (71)
Chris Moone (62)

'B' Camera Second Assistant:
Mark Weinhaupl (1)
Robb Devitt (2-13, 18-30)
Richard Porta (14-17)
Chris Rothfelder (30)
Jose Lau (32-61, 63-71)
Thomas Billingsley (71)

Camera Second Assistants:
Kyle Brown (72)
Mike Sharky (72)
Sean Esler (72)

REIMAGINED *BATTLESTAR GALACTICA* CREDITS

'C' Camera Operator:
Tenzin Lhalungpa (72)

Camera Trainee:
Frank Gelbrich (1)
Kyle Brown (2-4)
Nick Lamb (5-8)
Ryan Nazar (9, 10)
Alex Guld (11-13)
Shannon Abbott (14-17)
Jason Haycock (18, 19)
Cherie Korol (20-22)
Katie Matheson (23-28)
Norm Li (29, 30)
Brandy Pagani (32-49)
Amy Hanbyol (50-52)
Adam Braverman (53-61)
David Patterson (63-65)
Thomas Billingsley (66-70)
Masayo Tadaka (72)

Assistant Chief Lighting Technician:
Tim Heller (62)

2nd Unit Director of Photography:
John Drake (36-61, 63-71)
Mark Berlet (72)

2nd Unit Camera Operator:
Grizz Salzl (72)

2nd Unit Camera 1st Assistant:
Ted Smith (72)

2nd Unit Camera 2nd Assistant:
Scott Cozens (72)

2nd Unit Digital Imaging Tech:
Clint Paglaro (72)

2nd Unit Playback Operators:
Lawrence Lau (72)
Tom Chen (72)

2nd Unit On-Set Costumers:
Ardyth Cleveland (72)
Danise Lee (72)

2nd Unit 1st Assistant Make-up:
Candice Stafford (72)
Trish Porter (72)

2nd Unit 1st Assistant Hair:
Charlene Dunn (72)

2nd Unit 2nd Assistant Hair:
Paula Demille (72)

2nd Unit On-Set Dresser:
Charlie Schrodt (72)

2nd Unit On-Set Props:
Mike Love (72)

2nd Unit Gaffer:
Vincent Uytdehaag (72)

2nd Unit Best Boy Electric:
Derek Saari (72)

2nd Unit Lamp Ops:
Cory Hodson (72)
Lawrence James (72)

2nd Unit Key Grip:
Ozzy Sawatski (72)

2nd Unit Best Boy Grip:
Virgil Dean (72)

2nd Unit Dolly Grip:
Troy Bassett (72)

2nd Unit Grip:
Dean Lavoie (72)

2nd Unit Script Supervisor:
Claudia Morgado (72)

REIMAGINED *BATTLESTAR GALACTICA* CREDITS

2nd Unit Location Production Assistant:
Josh Pickens (72)

2nd Unit Background Wrangler:
Dale Bredeson (72)

2nd Unit First Aid:
Violet Barisoff (72)

Still Photography:
Carole Segal (34-61, 63-72)
Eike Schroter (72)

HD Technician:
Mike Sankey (14-30, 32-61, 63-71)

Gaffer:
Don Saari (1, 3-30)
Jeff Trebenski (2, 32-61, 63-71)
Guy Patterson (31)
Blair McDonald (62)
Mark Berlet (72)

Best Boy Electric:
Jeff Trebenski (1, 3, 4-30)
Fred Boyd (2)
Paul Bougie (31)
Bill Dawson (32-49)
Rick Dean (50-61, 63-71)
Jeff Boudier (62)
Vincent Uytdehaag (72)

Genny Operator:
Murray Chysyk (2-61, 63-70)
Derek Saari (71)
Bill Tennant (72)

Lamp Operator:
Blair McDonald (31)
Bryce Dickson (62)
Nigel Niessen (62)
Doug Reynolds (62)
Marc Daunais (71)
Irwin Figueira (71)
David C Innes (71)
Craig Riley (72)

Shamus Whiting-Hewlett (72)
Darryl Laval (72)

Rigging Gaffer:
Mike Dube (1)
Guy Patterson (14-30, 32-61, 63-71)
Oliver Hajdu (72)

Rigging Best Boys:
Ron Baran (50-61, 63-71)
Blair McDonald (71)
Pete Smith (71)
Shem Ellis (72)

Board Operator:
Paul Akehurst (71)
Dave Riley (72)

Rigging Lamp Operator:
Maria Stanborough (50-61, 63-65)

Key Grips:
Harvey Fedor (1)
Curt Griebel (2-30, 32-61, 63-71)
Mark Leiterman (31)
James Vinblad (62)
Steve Sherlock (72)

Grips:
Tom Evans (62)
Jesse Oliver (62)

Best Boy Grips:
Anthony Creery (1)
Ian Smith (2)
Bruce Beaulac (3-13)
Neil McBride (14-22)
Budd Legree (23-30, 32-61, 63-71)
Dave McKinlay (31)
Ron Baran (31)
Peter Webster (62)
Jeff Bzowy (72)

Dolly Grips:
Michael Iwan (1)
Darin Wong (2-22)

REIMAGINED *BATTLESTAR GALACTICA* CREDITS

Jordan Neifer (2-29, 32-61, 63-71)
Trevor Williams (23-28)
Ross Newcomb (29, 30)
Phillipe Palu (30)
James Vinblad (32-61, 63-70)
Tracy Nixon (62)
Darcy Booth (71)
Micah Dance (72)
Arron Johnson (72)
Bernie Young (72)

Company Grips:
James Vinblad (71)
Ross Newcomb (71)
Andreas Carmona (71)
Brock Miller (72)

Rigging Key Grip:
David Neveaux (1)
Andrew Mackie (50-61, 63-71)
Mike Lemmers (72)

Rigging Grip:
Adam Bunz (72)

Leadman Set-up:
Budd Legree (2-22)
Andrew Mackie (10, 23-30, 32-49)
Mike Carpenter (9, 11, 12)

Supervising Art Director:
Doug McLean (1-30, 32-61, 63-71)

Art Directors:
Ken Rabehl (1)
Ivana Vasak (1)
Tyler Harron (72)

Second Art Director:
Joanna Dunn (72)

Assistant Art Directors:
Margot Ready (1)
Ken Rabehl (2-30)
Ivana Vasak (2-30, 32-61, 63-71)
Peter R Stratford (32-57)

Ricado Sandoval (50-61, 63-70)
Andy Amoroso (72)

Art Department Coordinator:
Michael Corrado (2-6)
Lynn Snedden (6-30, 32-61, 63-71)

Storyboard Artist:
David Maclean (50-61, 63-71)

Illustrator:
Ken Rabehl (72)
John Gallagher (72)

Graphic Designer:
Simon Gore (72)

Art Department Assistant:
Chad Kerychuk (72)

Set Designer:
Mark Soparlo (71)
Joseph Wolkosky (72)

Set Decorators:
Shirley Inget (1)
Jonathan Lancaster (2-61, 63-72)

Co-Decorator:
Jamie Jonasson (50-61, 63-71)

Assistant Set Decorators:
Terry Ewasiuk (1)
Perry Battista (2-30)
Jamie Jonasson (32-49)
Paul Burton (50-61, 63-71)
Brad McMurray (72)

Set Decorator Buyers:
Roger Dole (1)
Fresca Dappen (1)
Felipe Barragan (2-30)
Myron Ruth (32-49, 72)

Lead Dresser:
Barry W Brolly (1)

REIMAGINED *BATTLESTAR GALACTICA* CREDITS

Toni Soragnese (14-22)
Ocea Ringrose (23-30)
Mark Prior[4] (32-61, 63-71)
Anthony Chruszcz (72)

2nd Lead Dresser:
Clayton Allan (50-61, 63-70)

Set Decorator Coordinator:
Paul Burton (14-30, 32-49)

On Set Dressers:
Mark Wood (1)
Paul Burton (2-13)
Maurice Woodworth (14-22, 31, 62)
Colin Meacham (22-61, 63-71)
Lisle Fehlauer (31)
Glenn MacDonald (72)

Dressers:
Michael Bethune (1)
Ian Langmann (1)
Marc Green (71)
Tony Soragnese (71)
Maurice Woodworth (71)
Lisle Fehlauer (71)
Andrea Dance (71)
Melissa Dutchak (72)
John Werner (72)

Set Wireman:
Les Wilson (71)

Construction Coordinator:
Chris Claridge (1-30, 32-61, 63-71)
Dave R Dague (72)

Construction Foremen:
Andrew 'Rowly' Rowland (1, 50-61, 63-71)
Jim Hayes (2-30, 32-61, 63-71)
Rob Moser (50-61, 63-71)
William Morrill (72)

---

4 Name given as 'Mark Pryor' 32-49.

Lead Carpenters:
Wolfgang Mueller (72)
Chris Rodgers (72)
Jerry Frigault (72)

Scenic Carpenters:
James Polkinghorne (72)
Rob MacArthur (72)
Darius Staniszewski (72)
Cameron Senum (72)
Bruce Wallace (72)
Robert Newbold (72)

Carpenter Helpers:
Colin Fotherby (72)
Steve Williams (72)

On Set Carpenter:
Matt Clancy (23-64)
Eric Hargreaves (65-71)

Tool Maintenance:
Mirek Scheller (72)

Stage Lead:
Doug Ham (71)

Paint Coordinator:
Sean Lavoie (23-30, 32-61, 63-71)
Ben Wildeman (72)

Foreman:
Vern Lavoie (50-61, 63-71)

Lead Paint:
Noel Burke[5] (23-30, 32-60, 63-71)
Rory Sulllivan (71)
Sean Wynia (72)

Scenic Artist:
Ray Alley (71)

On Set Painter:
Dave Pirie[6] (23-30, 32-61, 63-71)

---

5 Credited as 'Noel Burke Gaffney' on episode 71.

REIMAGINED *BATTLESTAR GALACTICA* CREDITS

Property Masters:
Dan Sissons (1)
Ken Hawryliw (2-30, 32–61, 63-71)
Brent Lane (62)
Jim Pate (72)

Assistant Property Master:
Gerri L Crawford (72)

Assistant Props Master On Set:
Brad Shemko (72)

1st Assistant Props on Set:
David Goodman (50-61, 63-71)

1st Assistant Props:
Tony Germinario (1, 32-36)
Max Matsuoka (1)
Don McGill (2-7)
Nina Polkinghorne (2-8)
Santino Barile (8, 9, 11-13, 50-61, 63-71)
Alex Kutschera (10)
Mike Love (14-28, 31)
Lance Johnson (14-22)
Sacha Moiseiwitsch (23-30, 32-49)
Chuck Newson (29, 30)
Glenn Hilworth (31, 62)
Gerry Thompson (31, 62)
Rob Stecky (31, 37-49, 62)

Prop Buyers:
Lance Johnson (71)
David Asmodeus (71, 72)

Props Assistant:
Paxton Downard (72)

Props Maker:
Derek Pineo (1)

Props Truck:
Tasha Moth (71)

---

6 Credited as 'David Pirrie' 50-71.

Armourer:
Robert Fournier (72)

Sound Mixers:
Ruth Huddleston (1)
Rick Bal CAS[7] (2-30, 35, 37-61, 63-72)
Mark Noda (31)
Wayne Finucan (32-34, 36)
Matt Willoughby-Price (62)

Boom Operators:
Wayne Williams (1)
Matt Willoughby-Price (2-13)
Greg Hewett (14-30, 32-61, 63-72)
Keith Henderson (31)
Tony Wyman (31, 62)

Sound Assistant:
Greg Hewitt (2-12)
Naan Speiss (13, 50-61)
Graham Timmer (14-30)
Matt Willoughby-Price (32-49, 63-72)
Naan Pollock (71)

Stunt Coordinator:
Mike Mitchell (1-30, 50-61, 63-70)
Duane Dickinson (14-30, 32-49)
Rick Pearce (64, 70, 71)
Gerald Paetz (71)
Jeff Ong (72)

Assistant Stunt Coordinator:
Duane Dickinson (2-13)

Stunt Riggers:
Alister King (71)
Chad Sayn (71)

Special Effects Coordinators/Supervisors:
Stewart Bradley (1)
Andy Chamberlayne (2-30, 32-61, 63-71)
Allistair Collis (31, 62)
Kevin J Andruschak (31, 62)

---

[7] Name given as 'Ric Bal' on 37, 38.

REIMAGINED *BATTLESTAR GALACTICA* CREDITS

Rob Carter (62)
Bill Ryan (72)
Ron Kozier (72)

Special Effects Co-Coordinator:
Terry Sonderhoff (1)

Assistant Special Effects Coordinator:
Bill Ryan (71)

Special Effects Best Boy:
Bill Ryan (14-30, 32-61, 63-70)
Jason Dolan (72)

Special Effects Assistants:
Philip Jones (2, 4-13)
Ron Seida (2-30, 32-65)
Murray Cambell (2-15)
Stacey Goodman (7-30, 32-49)
Robert Carter (16-30, 32-71)
Robert Tomsic (50-70)
Kevin Andruschak (66, 67-71)
Chris Link (71)

Costume Designer:
Deborah Everton (1)
Glenne Campbell (2-72)

Assistant Costume Designer:
Cory Burchell (1)
Glenna Owen (2-30, 50-61, 63-68)
Cali Newcomen (14-30, 32-49)
Andrea Hiestand (32-49)
Katherine Wigzell (69-72)

Costume Coordinator:
Andrea Hiestand (50- 61, 63-70)
Linda Leduc (71)
Charron Hume (72)

Costume Supervisor:
Debbie Douglas (1)
Pamela Cameron (2-30, 32-49)
Keith Parent (31, 50-61, 63-71)
Katherine Wigzell (62)

Costumer:
Lauren M Walker (31, 62)
Charron Hume (31)
Kathy Linder (72)

Set Costumer:
Charron Hume (62)
Paulette Nelson (62)

Extras Costumer:
Kathy Linder (71)

Background Costumer:
Ardyth Cleveland (72)

Truck Costumer:
Soo McLean (71)

Prep Costumer:
Andrea Hiestand (71)

Costume Cutter:
Olga Tsernova (71)
Janet Dundas (72)

Make-Up Artist:
Bev Keigher (1)
Patricia Murray (2-30, 32-61, 63-71)
Lise Kuhr (2-9)
Ankara Eden (31, 62, 71)
Shauna Magrath (62)
Rebecca Lee (72)

Mary McDonnell's Make-Up:
Michelle Hrescak (1-70)

1st Assistant Make-Up:
Hayley Miller (14-30, 32-61, 63-70)
Shauna Magrath (31)
Leslie Graham (62)
Vincenza Celetano (71)
April Boyes (72)

2nd Assistant Make-Up:
Ankara Eden (50-61, 63-70)
Liz Raman-Nair (31, 62)

REIMAGINED *BATTLESTAR GALACTICA* CREDITS

Prosthetic Make-up Designer:
Todd Masters (72)

Hair Stylists:
Gerald Gibbons (1-30, 32-61, 71)
Forest Sala[8] (8, 9, 63-70)
Gene Kendall (62)
Anne Carrol (71)
Janice Rhodes (72)

1st Assistant Hair Stylist
Roy Siddick[9] (14-22)
Wayne Russell (23-30, 32-61)
Jamie McKay (31, 62)
Bev Sewers (62)
Anne Carroll (63-70)
Janet Sala (71)
Codey Blair (72)

2nd Assistant Hair Stylist:
Dean Scheck (50-61)
Rene Dombroski (63-70)
Gene Kendall (71)
Wayne Russell (71)

Canadian Casting by:
Coreen Mayrs CSA
Heike Brandstatter

USA/Los Angeles Casting by:
Robert Ulrich CSA (1-71)
Eric Dawson CSA (1-71)
Carol Kritzer CSA (1-71)
Anya Colloff (72)
Amy McIntyre Britt (72)

Casting Associate:
Hannah Cooper (50-56)
Sibby Kirchgessner (57-61, 63-70)

Los Angeles Casting Associate:
Corbin Bronson (1)

---

[8] Name given as 'Forrest Salla' on episodes 8 and 9.
[9] Name given as 'Roy Sidick' on episodes 20-22.

Canadian Casting Coordinator:
Errin Clutton (1-13)
Robin Stone (14-22)

Casting Coordinators:
Garrett McGuire (72)
Amy Nygaard (72)

Canadian Casting Assistant:
Liz Van Assum (1-13)

Casting Assistant:
Laura Obenaus (72)

Extras Casting:
James Forsyth (1-30)
Lisa Ratke (32-61, 63-72)

Extras Casting Assistants:
Tim MacArthur (71)
Jennifer Melchiorre (71)

Background Wrangler:
Dale Bredeson (72)

Production Designer:
Richard Hudolin (1-71)
Brian Kane (72)

Production Coordinator:
Cara Rogers (1-13)
Jennifer Tanami-Hendricks (14-30)
Rhiannon Charles (32-49)
Melissa Barrie (50-71)
Fawn McDonald (72)

1st Assistant Production Coordinators:
Jennifer Tanami/Tanami-Hendricks (1-13)
Nicole Shizuka Oguchi (1-13)
Rhiannon Charles (14-30)
Chaunce Drury (32-49, 72)
Genevieve West (50-52)
Jill Christensen (53-57)
Jill McQueen (58-61)
Laura Livingstone (63-71)

REIMAGINED *BATTLESTAR GALACTICA* CREDITS

2nd Assistant Production Coordinators:
Qadesh Markowski (14-30)
Tim Bennett (32-49)
Melina Morokhovich (50-61)
Nicole Stojkovich (63-71)

2nd Unit Production Coordinator:
Nicole Florian (50-61)
Hon Lui (63–69, 71)

Office PA:
Kelsey Chobotar (72)

Production Assistants:
Tanis Hofmann (2-13)
Tim Bennett (2-13, 22-30)
Anthony Alvaro (14-21, 23-30)
Justin McGowan (14-21, 32-42)
Paul Redekopp (32-49)
Brodie Louie (43-49)
Otto Mak (50-52)
Andrea Palmer (50-52)
Helen Murrey (53-56)
Stuart Blackie (53-60)
Jessica Sawaf (57-61, 63-71)
Keith McQuiggan (59-61, 63-71)
Michael Bishop (62)

Script Supervisor:
Corey Jones (1, 4, 5, 7-22, 35, 38, 40-61, 63-72)
Beth Mercer (2, 3, 6)
Linda Strathdee (23-30, 62)
Carol Green-Lundy (31)
Claudia Morgado (32-34, 36, 37, 39)

Script Coordinator:
Ryan Mottesheard (2-30, 32-70)
David Reed (71)

Writers' Assistant:
Robert J Thissen (2-13)
Kevin Fahey (14-30, 32-49)
David Reed (50-61, 63-70)
Ben McGinnis (62, 71)

Science Advisor:
Kevin Grazier (2-71)

Military Tech Advisor:
Ron Blecker (14-30, 32-49, 51-61, 63-64)
Thomas Potter (72)

Production Accountant:
Laurie Boyle (1-30, 32-61, 63-72)

1st Assistant Accountant:
Carol Bailey (1-13)
Reva Clavier (14-30, 32-61, 63-71)
Kathy Davis (72)

Accounts Payable:
Reva Clavier (72)

Payroll Accountant:
Shaun McKay[10] (1, 9-19, 32-61, 63-71)
Reva Clavier (2-8)
Dave Hoodless (19-30)
Vicki Egilson (72)

2nd Assistant Accountant:
Tony Lort (32-61, 63-71)

Accounting Clerks:
Natalie Kangropool (2-8)
Tom McAlley (2-13)
Tony Lort (9-30)
Dave Hoodless (14-19)
Rosemarie Martin (14-30, 32-61, 63-71)
Jennifer Lloyd (19-30)
Kathy Candiago (32-49)
Ola Mota (32-61, 63-70)
Julia Tanner (50-61)
Sheri Buckham (71)
Sandi Envik (72)

Unit Manager:
Craig Forrest (1-8)
Lorne Davidson (9-13)

---

10 Name spelled 'Shawn' in miniseries.

REIMAGINED *BATTLESTAR GALACTICA* CREDITS

Boris Ivanov (31, 62)
Geoff Teoli (72)

Location Manager:
Kent Sponagle (1-30, 32-61, 63-71)

Assistant Location Manager:
John Alexander (1)
Tisha Simpkins (14-29)
Bonny Northcott (30)
Devin Senft (32-61, 63-71)

Location Scout:
Bonny Northcott (23-30, 32-48)
Dave Tamkin (50-61, 63-70)

Location Assistants:
John Alexander (1)
Tisha Simpkins (2-13)
Bonny Northcott (10-13)
Trevor Brokop (10-13)
Dale Bredeson (14-24)
Kelly Boulding (14-22)
Barbara Copp (14-27)
Jessica Feskun (23-30, 32-48, 50-57)
Scott Black (23, 24)
Jay Law (25)
Jonathon Watson (26-30, 32-45)
Michael Bender (28)
Nathan Conchie (29, 30)
Stacey Campbell (30, 50-57)
Jennifer Lawson (32-45)
Jeff Hardy (46-49)
Marc Leveille (46-49)
Coco Molloy (49)
Sue Meckenzie (49)
Ian Cairns (50-61, 63-70)
Adrian Lysenko (58-61, 63-70)
Julian Marles (58-61, 63-70)
Jeff Meagher (62)
Stephanie Brown (71)
Jessica Campbell (71)
Esther Kang (71)

Transportation Coordinator:
Bill Janssen (1-30, 32-61, 63-71)
Robin Csibi (72)

Transportation Captains:
Ranj Jawant (1-13)
James Michalchuk (1)
Mitch Lafleur (2-30)
Lawrence Albright (14-30)
Ron Lacroix (32-49)
Steve Siegel (32-61, 63-70)
Brian Whitlock (71)
Gord Chitty (71)
Dale Miller (72)

Supertruck:
Don Emond (72)

Super Star Driver:
Paul Antonic (72)

Cast Driver:
Manfred Rossdeutscher (72)

Utility Driver:
Russ Henrichsen (72)

Set Dec Driver:
George Fennell (72)

Construction Driver:
Al Voth (72)

Catering:
Tivoli Moving Picture Caterers (1-30, 32-61, 71)
Michael Levy (50)
Mint Movie Picture Catering Inc. (63-70)
Edible Planet (72)

Chef:
Resho Ollek (50)
Ingrid Severson (72)

Assistant Chefs:
Gabrielle Pirocchi (50)
Rachel Ziegler (50)

REIMAGINED *BATTLESTAR GALACTICA* CREDITS

Kelly Densmore (72)

2nd Assistant Chefs:
Jane Quennell (72)
Maili Dinim (72)

Medic/Craft Services:
Ron Grey (1-13)
Peter Conway (14-22)
Michael Campbell (23-30, 32-60, 63-71)
Tim Gunderson (31)
Glenne Moore (62)

First Aid:
Rahni Gill (72)

Security Captain:
Tracey Motherwell (72)

Stand-Ins:
Surya Kellar (72)
Tanya Champoux (72)
Paul Puzzella (72)

Second Editor:
Sondra Watanabe (1)

Main Title Theme by:
Richard Gibbs

Original Music by:
Richard Gibbs (1, 3, 4)
Bear McCreary (2, 5-71)

Additional Music by:
Bear McCreary (1, 3, 4)
Aaron Roethe and Brandon Roberts (71)

Original Score Produced by:
Bear McCreary and Steve Kaplan (70-72)

Conducted by:
Bear McCreary

Orchestrated by:
Brandon Roberts (70, 71)

Additional Orchestrations:
Jeremy Levy (70)
Jordan Siegel (71)

Music Preparation:
Mark Cally (70, 71)

Additional Engineers:
Lawrence Schwarz (70, 71)
Tom Brissette (70, 71)
Theo Mack (71)

Scoring Coordinator:
Aaron Roethe (70, 71)
Jonathan Ortega (72)

Executive Scoring Assistant:
Amanda Pettit (71)

Scoring Assistants:
Jonathan Ortega (70, 71)
Michael Beach (70-72)
Brendon McCreary (70, 71)
John W Snyder (70, 71)
Georgia Bennett-Ramseur (72)
Andy Harris (72)
David Matics (72)
Kevin Porter (72)
Nate Underkuffler (72)

Score Recorded at:
Warner Bros Eastwood Scoring Stage (70)
The Bridge Recording Studio (72)

WB Score Recordist:
Greg Dennen (70)

The Bridge Score Recordist:
Milton Gutierrez (72)

WB Scoring Tech:
Ryan Robinson (70)

WB Stage Crew:
Richard Wheeler Jr (70)

REIMAGINED *BATTLESTAR GALACTICA* CREDITS

WB Stage Coordinator:
Jamie Olvera (70)

The Bridge Scoring Assistants:
Andy Zisakis (72)
Greg Ching (72)

The Bridge Stage Coordinator:
Vicki Giordano (72)

Orchestra Contractors:
Sandy DeCrescent (70)
Peter Rotter (70, 72)

Performed by:
The Hollywood Studio Symphony (70, 72)

Featured Soloists:

Vocals:
Raya Yarbrough
Brendan McCreary (72)

Duduk, Bansuri, Ethnic Woodwinds, Flute:
Chris Bleth (70–72)

Electric Sitar:
Steve Bartek (72)

Electric Violin:
Paul Cartwright (70-72)

Irish Whistle and Bagpipes:
Eric Rigler (70)

Biwa:
Doctor Kitajima (70)

Erhu, Yialli Tanber:
Martin St Pierre (70, 71)

Acoustic and Electric Guitars:
Steve Bartek (70, 71)
Ira Ingber (70, 71)

BY YOUR COMMAND: VOL 2

Acoustic Guitars:
Brandon Roberts (70)

Electric Guitars:
Mike Keneally (72)

Electric Bass:
John Avila (70, 71)

Drum Kit:
Nate Wood (70)

Percussion:
M B Gordy (70-72)
Jonathan Ortega (72)

Piano, Harmonium:
Bear McCreary (70, 71)

Hurdy Gurdy, Keyboards:
Bear McCreary (72)

Violins:
Julie Gigante (70, 72)
(Concert Master)

Katia Popov (70, 72)
Eunb-Mee Ahn (70)
Robert Anderson (70)
Darius Campo (70)
Roberto Cani (70)
Paul Cartwright (70)
Kevin Connolly (70)
Nina Evtuhov (70)
Lorenz Gamma (70, 72)
Henry Gronnier (70)
Tamara Hatwan (70)
Peter Kent (70)
Natalie Leggett (70)
Phillip Levy (70)
Marina Mamukian (70)
Serena McKinney (70)
Helen Nightengale (70)
Joel Pargman (70)
Searmi Park (70)
Sara Parkins (70)

REIMAGINED *BATTLESTAR GALACTICA* CREDITS

Neil E Samples (70)
Tareza Stanislav (70)
Lisa M Sutton (70, 72)
Irina Voloshina (72)
Jessica Guideri (72)
Lorand Lokuszta (72)
Radu Piepta (72)

Violas:
Andrew Duckles (70)
Robert Brophy (70)
Thamas Diener (70)
Matthew Funes (70)
Pamela Goldsmith (70)
Shawn Mann (70)
Victoria Miskolczy (70)
David Walther
Thomas 'Dirty Brahms' Lea

Violoncelli:
Steve Erdody (70, 72)
Antony Cooke (70)
Christine Ermacoff (70)
Paula Hochhalter (70)
Dennis Karmazyn (70)
Jennifer Lee Kuhn (70)
Victor Lawrence (70)
Andrew Shulman (70, 72)
Jacob Szekely (70, 72)

Contrabass:
Michael Valerio (70)

Orchestral Engineer:
Robert Fernandez (1-22)
Steve Kaplan (23-70)

Score Mixer/Scoring Engineer:
Steve Kaplan
Laurence Schwartz (72)
Tom Brissette (72)

Orchestration:
Edward Trybek (72)
Henri Wilkinson (72)

Music Coordinator:
Jason Ruder (5-13)

Vocalists:
Mamak Khadem & Deborah Dietrich (1)

Music Editors:
Jordan Corngold (1)
Gordon Fordyce (2, 3, 4)
Jason Ruder (2, 3, 5, 6-13)
Steven McCroskey (14)
Michael Baber (15-72)

Visual Effects Supervisor:
Gary Hutzel

Technical Director:
Trevor Adams (31, 61)

Head of Technology:
Jeremy Lang (72)

Visual Effects Coordinator:
Michael Gibson (2-13)
Blaine Lougheed (14-28)
Jonathan MacPherson (23-30)
Ross Woo (32-49)
Greg Behrens 50-71)

Visual Effects Editor:
Eric Lea (22-30, 32-72)

Assistant VFX Editor:
Mary Pritchard (72)

CGI Supervisor:
Doug Drexler (14-30, 32-72)

Visual Effects Assistant:
Blaine Lougheed (2-13)
Ross Woo (14-30)

Visual Effects by:
BSG In-House Visual Effects (26, 32-72)
Zoic Studios (1-5, 12-15, 19-24, 28-30)
ENIGMA Studios Inc (6-8)

REIMAGINED *BATTLESTAR GALACTICA* CREDITS

Atmosphere Visual Effects (9-11, 16-18, 23, 25, 27, 30)

Additional Visual Effects by:
ENIGMA Studios Inc (2-5, 12)
Atmosphere Visual Effects (7, 8, 13, 19, 21, 24, 26, 32-42)
Zoic Studios (6, 8, 9, 11, 23, 26)
BSG In-House Visual Effects (27, 28, 30)
Jose A Perez (50)
Alain Rivard (50)
John Allardice (50)
John Teska (50)
Jamie Clark (50)
Gabe Koerner (50)
Ralph Maiers (50)
Derek Ledbetter (50)
Mark Devlin (50)
Michael Kaelin (50)
Jon Greenhalgh (50)
Hailey Murray (50)
Lifeline Character Animation Ltd. (50)
Paranoid Delusions Inc. (50)
Meshweaver (50)
Forrec Group (50)
Ravenwood Entertainment (50)

CGI Artists:
Adam 'Mojo' Lebowitz (26, 29, 30, 32-71)
Rob Bonchune (32-61, 63-71)
Sean M Jackson (32-61, 63-71)
Kyle Toucher (42-61, 63-72)
Aram Granger (50)
James Ford (50-61, 63-65)
Michael Davidson (51-61, 63-71)
Derek Ledbetter (62)
Jesse Mesa Toves (70-72)
David Morton (70-72)
James Allan May (70, 71)
Kojo Kuramura (70)
Neal Sopata (72)
Douglas Graves (72)
Kevin Quattro (72)
Niall Booker (72)
James Hibbert (72)
Daksh Pandhi (72)
Alice Ries (72)

BY YOUR COMMAND: VOL 2

Richard Livingston (72)

Head of Technology:
Jeremy Lang (72)

CGI/Comp Artist:
Aram Granger (50)

CGI Character Animator:
Timothy Albee (32-49)

CGI Modeller:
Alain Rivard (26)
Pierre Drolet (32-71)

Junior CGI Artist:
Michael Davidson (32-50)

VFX PA:
Kelly Whitfield (71)

VFX Post Coordinator:
Ross Woo (50)

Senior VFX Compositor:
Aurore de Blois (50-61)

CGI Office Coordinator:
Jack Marshall (32-49)

VFX Set Coordinator:
Greg Behrens (32-49)

VFX Consultant:
Kelly Lee Myers (26, 28-30, 32-45)

Lead VFX Compositors:
Heather McAuliff (72)
Derek Ledbetter (72)

VFX Compositors:
Aurore de Blois (26, 28-30, 32-49)
Melissa Best (26, 28-30, 32-45)
Nina Yoon (31, 42-49, 62)
Steve McLeod (32-49)
Chris Wood (45-61)

REIMAGINED *BATTLESTAR GALACTICA* CREDITS

Heather McAuliff (50-61, 63-71)
Derek Ledbetter[11] (50-61, 63-71)
Michael Ross-Lang (62, 70)
Ryan Schroer (62, 70, 71)
Jeffery L Sargent (70)
Randy Little (71)
August Coleman (72)
Jesse Siglow (72)
Sarah Grieshammer (72)
Ryan C Schroer (72)
Arthur Vail III (72)
Patrick Murphy (72)
Alberto Ludena (72)
John Cornejo (72)
Anthony D'Agostino (72)
Eric McAvoy (72)
Philip A Sisk (72)

Render Coordinator:
Manuel Choi (62, 70-72)

Render Assistants:
Farrah L Welch (62, 70, 71)
Jeffery Quinn (70)
Matt Boardman (72)
Aine Graham (72)
Shane Hoffman (72)

Coordinator Assistant:
James Ledwell (70)

VFX Production Assistants:
Jeff Quinn (50-60)
Kelly Whitfield (50-61)
Rob Tobin (51-60)

Composite Office Coordinator:
Anthony Alvaro (32-61)

Digital Logistics Coordinator:
Jeremy Lang (50-71)

---

11 Name given as 'Dereck Ledbetter' on 51-60.

BY YOUR COMMAND: VOL 2

Digital Supervisor:
Emile Edwin Smith (1)

Digital Imaging Technician:
Tracy Sim (31)
Jim Bach (62)
Dave Kurvers (72)

CG Supervisor:
Lee Stringer (1)

Compositing Supervisor:
Patti Gannon (1)

Pre-Visualisation:
Paul Maples (1)

Visual Effects Producer:
Kristen Leigh Branan (1)
Michael D Gibson (24, 25, 27-30, 32-40, 42-46, 50-61, 63-72)

Senior Visual Effects Coordinator:
Cordell Wynne (1)
Michael D Gibson (2-23, 26, 34-35, 41, 47-49)
David Takemura (50-72)

Visual Effects Coordinators:
Chris Tucker (72)
Kelly Whitfield (72)
Blair Scott (72)
Willis Lombard (72)

VFX Data Wranglers:
Kennedy Shah (72)
Jed Glassford (72)

Edited by:
Dany Cooper (1, 2, 5, 8, 11, 13, 23)
Jacques Gravett (3, 6, 9, 12, 16, 17, 21, 24, 27, 30, 33, 36, 42, 45, 48)
Andrew Seklir ACE (4, 7, 10, 13, 14, 19, 23, 25, 28, 30, 32, 35, 38, 43, 45, 47, 49, 50, 61, 62, 67-72)
Annette Davey (15, 18, 22, 23, 26)
Michael S Stern (20)
Michael O'Halloran (26, 31, 39, 52, 55, 59, 62, 63, 67, 69, 70)
Bert Glatstein ACE (29)
Ian Kezsbom (31, 62)

REIMAGINED *BATTLESTAR GALACTICA* CREDITS

Tim Kinzy (31, 49, 50)
Anthony Redman ACE (34, 37, 40, 44, 46)
Julius Ramsay (41, 44, 46, 49, 51, 54, 57, 60, 64, 66, 70)
Gib Jaffe (53, 56, 58)
Michael Lim (62, 71)
Harry Jierjian (62)
Stewart Schill (65, 67, 68)
Eric Lea (72)
Ron Rosen (72)

Assistant Editors:
Mark Levine (1)
Jason Dale (1)
Greg D'Auria (2-13)
Harry Jierjian (2-13, 16, 17, 20, 21, 24, 27, 30, 31)
Mark Tuminello (9-13)
Christine Kim (14, 19, 20, 23, 25, 28, 30)
Michael O'Halloran (15, 18, 22, 23, 26, 29, 31, 33, 36, 42, 45, 48)
Sue Len Quon (23)
Tim Kinzy (31, 32, 35, 38, 41, 43)
Ian Kezsbom (31, 34, 37, 40, 44, 46, 52, 55, 59)
Shaheed Qaasim (44, 46, 49, 51)
Michael Lim (50, 51, 54, 57, 60, 64, 70)
Ben Stokes (53, 55, 56, 58)
Beth Barnette (61, 65, 68, 70)
Matthew Gilna (62, 70, 71)
Melissa Lawson (63, 67, 69, 70)
Paul M Leonard (72)

Additional Editing by:
Jacques Gravett (39)
Julius Ramsay (39, 61)
Tim Kinzy (43, 47)
Andrew Seklir (45, 69)
Michael O'Halloran (61)
Michael Lim (66)

Main Title design by:
Andrew Seklir (2-30, 32-61, 63-70)

Sound Editorial Services by:
Anefx, Inc. (1-30, 32-72)

BY YOUR COMMAND: VOL 2

Supervising Sound Editor:
Jack Levy (1-17, 19, 20, 22-24, 26, 28, 30, 32-72)
Daniel Colman MPSE (18, 21, 23, 25, 27, 29, 30, 31, 38-72)

Sound Designer:
Daniel Colman MPSE

Dialogue Editor:
Vince Balunas (1-30, 32-72)
Greg Stacy (72)

ADR Supervisor:
Frank John Nolan (1)

ADR Editor/Additional Editorial:
Chris Boyett (1-16)
Sara Bencivenga (72)

Sound Editor:
Jeff Brunello (1)

Foley Recordists:
Matthew Manselle (72)
Sam Lewis (72)

Foley Editor:
Sam Lewis (72)

Foley Artists:
Doug Madick (2-30, 32-72)
Richard Partlow (70, 72)

Foley Mixer:
Sam Lewis (70)

Additional Sound Design:
George Johnsen (50)

Sound Re-recording Provided by:
Todd Sound

Re-Recording Mixers:
Kevin Burns (1-13)
Todd Orr (1-13)
Michael Olman, C A S (14-16, 18-30, 32-71)
Kenneth Kobett, C A S (14-30, 32-71)

REIMAGINED *BATTLESTAR GALACTICA* CREDITS

Jeffrey P Kloth (31)
Peter S Reale (17)
John Cook (72)
Peter Nussbaum (72)

Re-Recording Engineer:
Whitney Purple (72)

Post Production Supervisor:
Trisha Brunner (2-22)
Gregg Tilson (23-30, 32-60)
Ian 'Maddog' Maddox (61-71)

Post Production Coordinator:
Gregg Tilson (2-22)
Dan Delaney (32-48)
Ian Maddox (49-60)
Bettina Zachariah Treviranus (61-71)

Post Production Assistants:
Dan Delaney (23-30)
Ian Maddox (39-48)
Bettina Zachariah (50-60)

Post Production Accounting:
R C Baral & Co, Inc. (1)

Post Production Facility:
Modern Videofilm, Inc. (1-30, 32-49)

Colour Timer:
Joe Finley (1-14, 19-22)
Dan Judy (15-19, 23-25, 49)
Kim Schneider (26-30, 39, 41-48, 49, 52)
George Cvjetnicanin (32-38, 40, 72)
Ron Nichols (50, 51, 53-71)

Title Artist:
Amy D'Alessandro (70, 71)
Jacqueline LeFranc (72)

Inferno Artists:
O T Hight (70, 71)
Richard Hiltzik (70, 71)

BY YOUR COMMAND: VOL 2

Computer/Video Playback Coordinator:
Ross Framo (14-30, 32-61, 63-72)
Lawrence Lau (62)
Sheryes Mithawala (62)

Playback Coordinator:
Scott Steyns (72)

Assistant Playback Coordinator/PB Operator:
Shreyas Mithaiwala (50)

Animator/PB Operator:
Lawrence Lau (50, 72)

PB Operator:
Tom Chen (50)

PB Designer:
Scott Higgs (50)

2nd Unit PB Operator:
Brent Barratt (50)

Video Playback Services by:
West Media Film and Post (2-30, 32-61, 63-71)

Post Production Online Services Provided by:
Level 3 Post (70, 71)
Universal Digital Services (72)

Post Production Supervisor:
Brooke Murphy (70, 71)
Susan Gosstrom (72)

Online Editors:
Christopher Currall (70, 71)
Rick Piccini (70, 71)
Andrew Ralston (72)

Avids Provided by:
Magneto Digital Post (2-13)

Filmed at:
Vancouver Film Studios (2-72)

REIMAGINED *BATTLESTAR GALACTICA* CREDITS

Consultant:
Jerry Hultsch (14-30, 32-61, 63-71)

R&D TV Logo by:
Jerry Hultsch (5-13)

Studio Executive:
Richard Rothstein (31)

Studio Executive in Charge of Production:
Todd Sharp (31, 62)

Network Executives:
Mark Stern and Erik Storey (31)

News Footage Provided by:
AP Archive/Sky News (70)

Stock Footage Provided by:
Getty Images (70)
Universal Studios (70)
Warner Bros. (70)
Footage Bank (70)

REGULAR CAST

Commander/Admiral William Adama/Husker – Edward James Olmos (1-30, 32-54, 56-61, 63-71)
President Laura Roslin – Mary McDonnell (1-30, 32-54, 56, 57, 59-61, 63-70)
Lieutenant/Captain Kara Thrace/Starbuck – Katee Sackhoff (1-15, 17-24, 26-28, 30, 32-47, 49-61, 63-70)
Captain/Major/Commander Leland Joseph 'Lee' Adama/Apollo – Jamie Bamber (1-28, 30, 32-61, 63-70)
Doctor/Vice-President/President Gaius Baltar – James Callis (1-25, 28-30, 32-45, 46, 48-57, 59- 67, 69, 70)
Number Six – Tricia Helfer (1-20, 22-25, 28-30, 32-38, 40-61, 63-71)
Lieutenant Sharon Valerii/Boomer/Athena/Number Eight – Grace Park (1-27, 29-30, 32-34, 36-42, 44, 45, 47-53, 55-71)
Colonel Saul Tigh – Michael Hogan (1-36, 38-45, 47-55, 57, 58, 60-71)
Billy Keikaya – Paul Campbell (1-17, 19-25, 27)
Crew Chief/Specialist Galen Tyrol – Aaron Douglas (1-24, 26, 28-49, 51-55, 57, 60, 61, 63-71)
Petty Officer Second Class/Lieutenant Anastasia 'Dee' Dualla – Kandyse McClure (1-6, 8-28, 30, 32-34, 37-45, 47-49, 51, 52, 57, 58, 60, 61)
Lieutenant Felix Gaeta – Alessandro Juliani (1-6, 8, 10-24, 26-28, 30, 32-45, 47-49,

51-53, 55-57, 60-65)
Specialist Callandra 'Cally' Henderson/Henderson Tyrol – Nicki Clyne (1-4, 7, 8, 11-18, 21-24, 28, 30-36, 39, 41, 42, 44-46, 48, 49, 53, 57, 70)
Lieutenant/Captain Karl Agathon/Helo – Tahmoh Penikett (1-15, 17-24, 26, 29, 30, 32-42, 44, 45, 47-49, 51-53, 55-57, 59-61, 63-65, 68-70)
Lieutenant Alex Quartararo/Crashdown – Samuel Witwer (2, 3, 5-7, 11, 13-16)
Ensign Samuel T Anders/Longshot – Michael Trucco (17, 18, 29, 30, 32-35, 39, 41-43, 47-49, 51-57, 60, 61, 64-71)

Reimagined Battlestar Galactica: Background and Production

The reimagining of *Battlestar Galactica* entailed a number of decisions being taken regarding the degree to which the series premise and characters needed to be changed, as well as developments in design and production.

Everything Old is New Again: Changes to the Series

The main difference between the two series has to do with the nature of the Cylons. Rather than an empire-building lizard race who were turned into machines through a pact with the devil, they are now a mechanical slave race created by humans, who rebelled, leading to a war that has been over for 40 years at the start of the reimagined series. This also casts the Cylons straight away as victims, and the humans as oppressive slave-owners. The Cylons worship a warlike patriarchal god, who does not appear to have any direct connection to Count Iblis (the mysterious demonic being who was instrumental in the development of the original-series Centurians[12]). They also include models that are human in appearance, to a greater degree than the humanoid Cylons featured in *Galactica 1980*, being, like the replicants of *Blade Runner* (1982), virtually indistinguishable from humans down to the cellular level. This idea was originally employed in the reimagined series as a measure to save on CGI costs, but rapidly became a key driving feature. Their population also consists of a large number of copies of a few models, which recalls the clone race from the original series story 'The Gun on Ice Planet Zero' (as does the somewhat enthusiastic sexuality of certain female Cylon models).

The human characters now have conventional first name-surname nomenclature, with the more exotic names of the original series becoming pilot call-signs. The Lords of Kobol are worshipped as gods, with the same names as the Greco-Roman pantheon. (Moore says he was inspired in this by the original series' drawing on classical names.) Rather than being included in the service as an emergency measure, women pilots are an unchallenged feature of the

---

12 For the sake of clarity, we will be using the spelling 'Centurian' when referring to the Cylons from the original series and *Galactica 1980*, when the name was alternately given as 'Centurian' and 'Centurion', but using the latter when referring to the reimagined series, in which, although 'Centurian' occasionally appears in draft scripts, including '33' and 'Kobol's Last Gleaming', the spelling appears to have been standardised in official documents as 'Centurion'.

military from the outset, and Moore repeatedly emphasises in his podcasts[13] that he wanted to give the series a gender-egalitarian feel; although, as will be noted in relation to individual episodes, he does not always succeed in this.

Approximately 50,000 people in 64 ships survive the destruction of the Colonies, as opposed to the 6,000 in 221 ships mentioned in the original series story 'Greetings from Earth'. As the reimagined series was aimed at the adult market, Boxey's role is reduced to a cameo, and the cute robot Muffit the daggit written out entirely: Moore, referring to the fact that Muffit was played by a costumed chimpanzee, facetiously said 'I couldn't do that to a chimp'.

In other, minor changes, Pyramid is now a basketball-like sport and Triad a card game. (Moore confesses in a podcast that he mixed the two up.) The six-sided cards for Triad are based on the Pyramid cards in the original series, and Moore says that they indirectly inspired the cutting of corners on papers as a distinctive aspect of the reimagined series. As in the original series, the main unit of currency, the 'cubit', appears as a rectangular metal coin, but reimagined-series cubits have their corners clipped, and are complemented by the use of paper currency. Although 'frack' is retained as an all-purpose swear word (shortened to 'frak' to make it a genuine four-letter word), the distinctive time/distance vocabulary of the original is lost, and the exotic fauna (daggits, equelluses, etc) replaced with more mundane Earth equivalents (dogs, horses, etc). 'Felgercarb', a scatological expletive in the original, becomes a brand of toothpaste. As well as Vipers, the Fleet boasts a new type of ship, the Raptor, a two-man craft capable of carrying passengers or cargo, and have dual uses as shuttles and as scout craft. The Vipers now have manoeuvring jets as well as thrusters, and the Combat Information Centre (CIC) is now deep within the vessel rather than dangerously positioned at its surface and behind a vulnerable window.

There are also, however, a large number of similarities between the original and reimagined series. In the documentary *Battlestar Galactica: The Lowdown*, actor Edward James Olmos observes that the new series is basically the same as the 1978 version, and only the appearance is different. The symbolic use of the number 12 continues, with 12 Cylon humanoid models being added to the humans' 12 Colonies and Council/Quorum of Twelve. The names of the planets are broadly similar (with a few slight differences, such as 'Aerilon' replacing 'Aeries' and 'Gemenon' replacing 'Gemoni'). The Gemonese remain the religious hardliners. The reimagined series also makes use of the original series' utilitarian, grungy aesthetic. Many of the ships in the Fleet are openly based on original-series ones (with the effects department containing several unabashed original-series fans). Tylium is still the main fuel, processed on refinery ships.

---

13 During the series' run, podcasts by Moore (with occasional guests) and others were made available on the Sci-Fi Channel's website for interested fans to download and listen to as episode commentaries. These were later made available on the series' DVD releases as commentary tracks, although some DVDs also include specially-recorded commentaries.

REIMAGINED *BATTLESTAR GALACTICA*: BACKGROUND AND PRODUCTION

The military rank structure is taken wholesale from the original series.

The technology of *Galactica* is more or less the same, with the ship being based on aircraft carriers. There are only one or two minor differences, for instance that the landing deck is open at both ends (presumably so that a ship coming in too fast can fly on through and not crash into the wall), and these ends consist of 'pods' that extend and retract rather than, as in the original, being static, with the opening protected by a semi-permeable force field.

Thematically, the series again draws on American adventure stories, particularly *Moby-Dick*, with its sense of destiny, the guidance of a God, and central figures obsessed with a death wish. The time in which the series is set is initially left deliberately ambiguous, but is resolved by the end of the final story, 'Daybreak'.

Moore and Eick, in public statements, remain ambivalent about the merits of series' title. Moore comments that the brand *Battlestar Galactica* has amazing name recognition, but carries a lot of baggage with it. However, in our opinion, if it caused any difficulties at all, these probably had more to do with audiences being bored of conventional space-opera in general than with any negative associations from the original series. Moore's dominating concern regarding the series is apparently to differentiate it from the *Star Trek* franchise; whenever he refers disparagingly to 'other sci-fi series' in his podcasts, he is more often than not implicitly referencing *Star Trek*, as most of *Battlestar Galactica*'s supposed 'innovations' (documentary-style footage, focus on characterisation, realistic military culture and lack of technobabble) are in fact firmly grounded in other series such as *Firefly*, *Babylon 5*, *Space: Above and Beyond* and *Farscape*. Moore also admits that he drew on the British series *Space: 1999* as part of his inspiration: this is clearly the case, as *Battlestar Galactica* likewise features inexplicable occurrences, quasi-mystical phenomena, and a central romance between two older authority figures. *Battlestar Galactica*'s religious system appears to have been drawn from *Xena: Warrior Princess*, a series co-developed by David Eick, which featured deities loosely based on the Greek pantheon, who are eventually replaced by one loosely based on the Judeo-Christian God, all of whom actively interfere in the affairs of mortals. Although no writer appears willing to admit to it, the series also shows clear influences from *V*, which revolved around an embattled resistance fighting alien oppression, and featured a hybrid child who would unite the warring races. Moore also produced a two-page document that was widely circulated among cast and crew, entitled 'Battlestar Galactica: Naturalistic Science Fiction – or Taking the Opera out of Space Opera'. While it is debatable how much the series did actually, as is sometimes claimed, 'reinvent' hard SF television in the USA, it certainly did the most to bring the innovations developed in such series as *Firefly* and *Farscape* to a wider audience.

Going for Starbucks: The Characters

One of the most controversial decisions of the new series was the regendering of Starbuck. The various changes in gender, ethnicity and, in some cases, species, of

Boomer, Tigh, Athena and Cain all seem to have incurred much less comment – something that Boomer/Athena actress Grace Park has gone on record as saying was a surprise to her. Katee Sackhoff introduces herself in the series documentary *Battlestar Galactica: The Lowdown* by saying 'Hi, I'm Katee Sackhoff. I play Starbuck – deal with it'.

Although this will be discussed in more detail in subsequent articles, Kara 'Starbuck' Thrace is, at the start of the series, very much like her original-series counterpart, the main differences being her deep religious faith and her gender. This last does, however, change the way she relates to other characters – for instance allowing her relationships with both the Adama brothers and with Baltar to become sexual. It also affects the way her behaviour is viewed by fans and critics – for example, her maintaining two sexual relationships at the same time has been roundly condemned, whereas similar behaviour on the part of the original Starbuck was seen simply as 'roguish'. Sackhoff herself has noted that there are many similarities between her portrayal of the character and her predecessor Dirk Benedict's.

Moore has defined his reasons for regendering the character as wanting to avoid the 'rogue pilot with a heart of gold' cliché, and also to avoid direct comparison with Dirk Benedict's portrayal. Benedict himself, however, was not won over, and was initially a vocal opponent of the new series precisely because of this change, writing an essay for *Dreamwatch* (May 2004) entitled 'Starbuck: Lost in Castration' to express his outrage over what he saw as the feminisation of the character.

Gaius Baltar has some differences to his original-series counterpart, being a celebrity scientist (unfortunately, also, fulfilling the science-fiction cliché of the general-purpose scientist who knows about all disciplines from computer technology to biochemistry), although he remains a charming but narcissistic man and shares his predecessor's talent for political spin. As per the original series' cast of treacherous Brits, he is played by an English actor. (Although Apollo actor Jamie Bamber is also British, he adopts a convincing American accent throughout.) Unlike original-series Baltar, however, he does not make a conscious and deliberate alliance with the Cylons; instead his hubris and self-obsession are exploited by Caprica-Six (who in a sense fulfils the role of Baltar's treacherous assistant Karibdis from the original series, although she is acting not on Baltar's behalf, but directly for the Cylons). Reimagined Baltar is also somewhat more comedic than the original, which is apparently down to actor James Callis's own ideas about how to play the character. A final key difference is that, in the reimagined series, nobody realises he is a traitor until midway through the second season.

The reimagined Saul Tigh has changed from a charismatic, continuously competent officer to an alcoholic, darkly funny man who is at his best under pressure, with a new first name evoking a sinner in need of a Damascene conversion. (The draft script for the initial miniseries, underlining the analogy, gives his name as 'Paul'.) In this case, Moore's intention was to work against the loyal-executive officer (XO) stereotype found in the *Star Trek* series, and instead

REIMAGINED *BATTLESTAR GALACTICA*: BACKGROUND AND PRODUCTION

bring in something closer to the flawed-XO character seen in many war films. In particular, he says he was inspired by Otto Preminger's film *In Harm's Way* (1965), which had Kirk Douglas as the flawed second-in-command of a submarine. Moore discusses Tigh's backstory extensively in the podcast for 'Tigh Me Up, Tigh Me Down'. Briefly, this is that Tigh is a war veteran who worked his way up through the ranks to become an officer, then became a pilot and flew combat missions, but, at the end of hostilities, found himself discharged, working on a civilian freighter and drinking himself to death before meeting Adama, who – as detailed in 'Scattered' – got him back into the service.

Lee 'Apollo' Adama is also characterised as almost the diametric opposite of his original-series character, being a solitary type who does not get along with his father (although he does have some similarities with Skyler, the cold and emotionally-withdrawn prototype in Larson's original concept, who eventually became the warm, family-focused Apollo in the 1978 series). Moore, in the podcast for 'Final Cut', says that Lee was a test pilot who (as the character was developed) had enlisted out of a sense of obligation and duty, but had a dream of leaving the service and going to run a bar. Over the course of the series, the character would find his true vocation as a politician, but only after a long and rather circuitous journey.

The change in Apollo's character reflects a couple of significant shifts since the time of the original series. Whereas the 1970s Apollo was in a sense the embodiment of his elderly father Adama's will, performing the action scenes that he could not, the post-millennial Adama is much less sure of himself and his mission, leading to a correspondingly unsure son. In addition, modern audiences find the idea of a sexagenarian action hero much less problematic than those of earlier decades, making Apollo's physical role redundant. Athena was originally excluded from the line-up of characters because Moore could not see a place for her (presumably because the series already had a number of strong female warriors, and a heterosexual female Starbuck made the character's love-interest role redundant), but appears from Season Three onwards in a considerably different form.

Commander William Adama, in the reimagined series, is no longer an astute paranoid. Although he is clever, it requires President Roslin to pull him back from doing a Commander Cain-style last-ditch stand against the Cylons following the attacks on the Colonies. His marital situation is also more problematic than the original series implied; he is divorced from a woman he married largely out of convenience (see 'Scattered') and it is implied that his son Zak's death may have been the final straw for the relationship.

One innovation in the reimagined series is the introduction of a generally credible voice for the politician characters (in contrast to their portrayal in the original series, save for the occasional exception such as Siress Tinia). President Laura Roslin's views are presented on an equal basis with Adama's, rather than relegated to being one of a chorus of antagonistic voices. Moore is quoted in *Somewhere Beyond the Heavens* as saying 'The tension between the military and the civilian leadership is a natural and, for the most part, healthy aspect of a democracy, and the reality of a *Galactica* world demands that the president has a strong role, not simply relegated to the caricature of the "weak-willed" president that the wise military minds must constantly overcome'. Roslin also appears to have taken over Adama's original-series role as religious leader.

Another positive development in the reimagined series is the addition of a number of regularly-appearing well-developed minor or supporting characters, civilian and military support staff – such as Tyrol's deck crew, Roslin's aides Billy Keikeya and Tory Foster, and the priest Elosha – who give the sense of a genuine ongoing and diverse community among the Fleet.

A character idea that fell by the wayside early on had to do with Boomer's relationship with Tyrol. Originally, according to a statement by Moore quoted on John Laroque's webpage, Boomer was a male character and Tyrol a female character of inferior rank, but Moore felt this made the power dynamics too conventional. Moore considered having Boomer as a young female pilot who winds up in a relationship with an older enlisted man, leading to complications as, although he is senior in age, she is his superior officer.[14] However, when casting Tyrol, Eick and director Michael Rymer decided Aaron Douglas was the best choice, which made the dynamic more egalitarian as he is visibly closer to Grace Park in age. Boomer was not to have been a Cylon at first; according to Moore, Eick suggested this as a twist with which to end the miniseries. The series bible's entry on her character begins, rather charmingly, 'Sharon's first memory is that of crawling across the artificial grass in her backyard toward the family cat, Mr Perkles. It's a vivid memory … It's also completely fake'.

Casting the Net: The Performers

The actors approached to play Adama and Roslin were Edward James Olmos and Mary McDonnell, both of whom the writing team had had in mind when developing the characters. Alternatives under consideration in the event that they turned the roles down included, in the case of Adama, Chris Cooper, Tom Skerritt, Sam Elliott and Powers Boothe, and, in the case of Roslin, Susan Sarandon, Alfre Woodard and Kathleen Quinlan. Fortunately, however, both accepted.

Olmos is a well-known Hispanic actor and political activist with an extensive stage and screen career, taking in experimental theatre, the cult detective series *Miami Vice* (winning an Emmy and a Golden Globe award for his performance) and the crucial role of the enigmatic Gaff in *Blade Runner*, a film from which the reimagined *Battlestar Galactica* extensively borrowed. Rymer says that his work was reviewed by Olmos before the actor agreed to take the part.

McDonnell is an award-winning stage actress who achieved international fame for her role in *Dances with Wolves* (1990) and appeared in two films that had

---

14 Presumably, the fact that the ship is being decommissioned and her crew stood down is the reason why the highest-ranking member of the technical staff is only an NCO.

REIMAGINED *BATTLESTAR GALACTICA*: BACKGROUND AND PRODUCTION

a clear influence on the reimagined *Battlestar Galactica*: *Independence Day* (1996) and *Donnie Darko* (2001). She had initial doubts about appearing in an SF series, but was convinced partly because she found the role appealing, and partly because of her respect for Olmos, who had already agreed to do it at the time she was approached.

Aside from Olmos and McDonnell, other cast members underwent auditions, leading to some interesting decisions. Grace Park was originally up for the part of Dualla, and then became one of four candidates for the part of Starbuck. Aaron Douglas similarly auditioned for the part of Apollo and then for Gaeta before getting the role of Tyrol. Michael Trucco, who also auditioned for Apollo (originally conceived of, in Eick's turn of phrase, as more of a 'beefcake' role), wound up playing resistance leader Sam Anders later on, in part because Eick came to feel that the series needed more 'beefcake' men.

Tricia Helfer was famously a risky choice to become a *Battlestar Galactica* regular. She had been a model prior to this and had only a few minor acting roles. She got the audition because she knew the series' casting director. Eick, however, insisted she be cast as Number Six. While the network took some convincing, they were ultimately impressed enough to make her a central feature of their marketing campaigns. Olmos advised Helfer to base her portrayal of the Cylon on the replicants of *Blade Runner*, which proved astute. The actress's naturally dark hair was bleached for the role, but this caused so much damage that subsequently changed to a blonde wig. She continued her association with the modelling world while working on *Battlestar Galactica*, hosting *Canada's Top Model* and appearing naked in the February 2007 issue of *Playboy*.

Katee Sackhoff, similarly, was almost passed over for Starbuck because Eick felt she looked too feminine, and also because the directors were looking for someone in her mid-thirties (where Sackhoff, at the time of the miniseries, was 23). She took the part seriously, and in fact voiced concerns about Starbuck's smoking habit as the series went on, as she was aware that she was becoming a role model for young women. Her achievements were recognised with a Saturn Award in 2006. During breaks from *Battlestar Galactica*, she also appeared in Eick's doomed *Bionic Woman* remake.

Michael Moriarty of *Law and Order* fame was initially considered for Tigh, as was Donnelly Rhodes (a Canadian actor, best known for his work on *The Young and the Restless* and *Soap*, who was ultimately cast as Doc Cottle), but the part went to Michael Hogan, a prominent Canadian character actor.

Aaron Douglas, a Canadian recognised for his appearances in *X-Men 2*, *Taken* and *Smallville*, was a controversial choice for Tyrol since, as noted, the character was originally to have been much older. The role was considerably expanded due to Moore being impressed by Douglas's ad-libbing abilities. By contrast, Crashdown appears to have been originally intended as a major figure – actor Sam Witwer says that the role was described to him as a 'male version of Katee Sackhoff's Starbuck' and as resembling Han Solo – but was ultimately much less prominent and much less heroic.

Jamie Bamber (full name James St John Bamber Griffith), the actor ultimately cast as Lee 'Apollo' Adama, is a London-born Cambridge graduate best known in the UK for playing Archie Kennedy in ITV's *Hornblower* series (and, since *Battlestar Galactica*, for Matt Devlin in *Law and Order: UK*). He is an active sportsman, making the 'Fat Lee' arc in Season Three deeply ironic. In order to increase the supposed familial resemblance between them, Olmos wore blue contact lenses (as he did in *Blade Runner*), and Bamber dyed his hair darker.

The other prominent British actor in the series, James Callis in the role of Baltar, is best known internationally for playing Tom in the *Bridget Jones* film series, and also works as a director. According to him, the casting brief for Baltar read 'Please present all ethnicities'. Another actor up for the part was Canadian Matthew Bennett, who eventually wound up as Doral. Callis thought about playing the character with an American accent, but Eick told him to keep his British accent; the actor later commented 'The Americans don't want to be seen as bad so [Baltar] has to be someone else'. Nonetheless, he won a Saturn Award for best supporting actor, a Peabody Award and an American Film Institute award for the role of Baltar.

Other roles were filled mainly by Canadian and, in some cases, American character actors (exceptions being Kandyse McClure, who is South African, and later Lucy Lawless, a New Zealander). Grace Park, a Korean North American, was born in Los Angeles but lived most of her life in Vancouver; she has a degree in psychology from UBC and, like Tricia Helfer, had done modeling work prior to getting into acting. Tahmoh Penikett, cast as Karl Agathon, is the son of the former premier of the Yukon Territory. Vancouver-based Alessandro Juliani is a singer as well as an actor, and was chosen to play Gaeta on the recommendation of Eick's wife.

Bush Leagues: Neoconservatism and Reimagined Battlestar Galactica

Whereas the original series reflects the pro-neoconservative mood toward the end of the Carter Administration, the reimagined series takes its political cues from the twilight of modern neoconservatism, during its final rallying phase around the start of the second Iraq War. Consequently, the reimagined series has a much more pessimistic take on this philosophy than its predecessor. The post-11 September 2001 nature of the reimagined series is often remarked upon; whereas the original presented a strong Fleet leadership with a clear idea of where they were going, the reimagined series presents us with a Fleet leadership who are confused, angry, prone to lashing out or removing civil liberties, and inclined to make up stories to give the public hope rather than aim for something they truly believe in. (Adama, in the reimagined series, does not believe Earth exists, but uses it as a fiction to keep the Fleet together while they search for an acceptable substitute.) There are obvious echoes here of the US government's behaviour in the era of the War on Terror. It is also significant that fantasy-based television was undergoing a revival in the USA at the time, providing, as well as a form of escapism, a 'safe space' in which to explore and question the recent drastic changes to American society. Much as the USA was questioning its identity in the wake of the 9/11 attacks, so *Battlestar Galactica* questions the validity of ongoing political discourses.

While the reimagined series still presents a very pro-military, authoritarian set-up, Moore argues that it does so in a less certain way, saying in his podcast for 'Sacrifice': 'The show is at its most effective when it presents complicated motivations and complex ideas and just lets the audience draw their own conclusions, rather than force-feed them ... in a very television way by saying "Well, clearly the right thing to do is what the Captain's done."' Elsewhere, he says, 'The show doesn't really have a political agenda in that [it] is neither liberal nor conservative in the way those labels are thrown about in the soundbite era of demagoguery that currently passes for political discourse in this country ... I do see the show as an opportunity to raise questions in the minds of its audience and ask them to think, which is something of a rarity in these days when politics seems to be about stoking emotionalism and finding simple-minded slogans to stand in for actual answers to complex problems'. Although Moore's repeated protestations of political neutrality seem disingenuous, it is true that the series is less certain of the benefits of a neoconservative philosophy, in line with the more anti-political mood of the early 21st Century.

Both series also draw on the ideas and imagery of apocalyptic Christianity. This is in keeping with the religious shift in American politics since the late 1970s; following the Carter Administration's use of religion as a political motivator, appeals to faith have become a key part of any American political campaign, and the War on Terror is frequently constructed as a thinly-veiled clash between Christianity and Islam. However, while both series also couch their divine characters in science-fiction language, the emphasis is slightly different; in keeping with the interest in von Däniken (who argued, most famously in his book *Chariots of the Gods*, that aliens have visited Earth in the past and influenced human development) in the 1970s, the original series has its gods as particularly advanced aliens, whereas the reimagined series, following the interest in virtual reality and psychology of the 1980s and 1990s, instead suggests that the messengers from God who appear may be virtual creatures or projections. However, the reimagined series does eventually return to its roots, making it clear, at the very end, that its God is indeed an alien.

Somewhere Beyond Vancouver: Series Production

Vancouver was chosen as a location for filming the series primarily because it is cheaper than the USA and, as it has hosted many other American TV and film series, has an extensive infrastructure. The miniseries was filmed at Lions' Gate Studios and nearby locations (scouted with the aid of the Vancouver Film Commission), while the episodic series relocated to the nearby Vancouver Film Studios. Richard Hudolin, the production designer, had worked on the first five seasons of *Stargate SG-1* and on the 1996 *Doctor Who* TV movie. Gary Hutzel, heading up the visual effects team, was a cinematographer whose credits included *Star Trek: The Next Generation* and *Star Trek: Deep Space Nine*. He recruited award-winning effects house Zoic, who had previously worked on *Firefly* and *Buffy the Vampire Slayer*, and would later work on, among many others, *Terminator: The Sarah Connor Chronicles*, *Dollhouse*, *Breaking Bad* and *Banshee*. A number of inside jokes crept into the effects work, with, for instance, production team members' names appearing on the Vipers, which have their pilots' names and call-signs stencilled on the side.

Hutzel and Hudolin worked closely together to ensure that design elements were consistent, for instance having the exterior ribbing of the *Galactica* reflected in the interiors. The sets were huge, floor-to-ceiling affairs, giving a sense of scale. Where back-projection was used in the original, green-screen and CGI, which are much less costly and time-consuming, were used for the reimagined series. Moore also insisted on a handheld-camera, documentary feel (which is at times effective and at other times simply confusing), and this necessitated the construction of an entirely new camera rig so as to film cockpit sequences in 'wobblecam'. However, an early idea to film the battle sequences silently to reflect the fact that there is no sound in space went by the wayside as being too distracting, replaced instead by muted sound. Another key distinction of the series is its consistent use of light and colour filters to make the planet locations look different from each other and give them an alien feel.

The general atmosphere of the *Galactica* remains broadly the same as in the original series, it being deliberately based on aircraft carriers and submarines, in line with the space-opera tradition of using spaceships in more or less the same way as sailing ships. Other real-life craft were used as conceptual models for other vessels, *Colonial One*, for instance, being based on commercial airliners. Eick and Moore told the effects crew to keep the design of *Galactica* and the Vipers similar to the 1978 versions. The Sci-Fi Channel, however, rejected production illustrator Eric Chu's initial design for *Galactica* on the grounds that it was *too* close to the original. Chu then went for a 1950s look, and the combination evolved into the final version, which in Moore's estimation retained the same basic 'alligator on skis' look of the original. CGI supervisor Lee Stringer says that elements of the original *Galactica* model were also duplicated and incorporated into the new ship. The Viper Mark II looks very much like the 1978 version, including the predominantly green computer displays, but with a yellow muzzle-flash and percussive firing noise, reminiscent of the older Viper seen in the original-series episode 'The Long Patrol'.

The series' design generally combines futuristic and retro elements, with clunky phones that resemble miniature field telephones and 1930s-style microphones in the Quorum chamber mixing with the *2001*-inspired design of the *Colonial One* interior and the streamlined Viper Mark VII. This type of approach has generally proved successful in screen science fiction in general, as series that aim for a futuristic look (e.g. *Star Trek: The Next Generation*) tend to date quite quickly, while those that go for a more retro feel (e.g. *Star Wars* (1977)) usually age better. Lee Stringer has stated that the effects team put a lot of work into making the CGI models look realistically used and worn.

REIMAGINED *BATTLESTAR GALACTICA*: BACKGROUND AND PRODUCTION

The new Cylon Centurions are similar in design to the originals but more streamlined, making it obvious that there is no actor inside. Eric Chu, who designed them, incorporated elements of a hooded Angel of Death into the design, at Hutzel's suggestion; the guns built into the arms were Eick's idea. The redesigned Cylon Raiders, which are clearly now cyborgs rather than piloted ships, look suspiciously like some of those seen in Hatch's *Battlestar Galactica: The Second Coming* trailer. Hudolin says that they were given an organic, 'muscular' look to reflect the idea that they lie somewhere between Centurions and humanoids; the incorporation of the 'head' with its scanning eye was another Eick suggestion. The metal shutter that raises and lowers over the scanning eye was clearly influenced by that of the robot Gort from *The Day the Earth Stood Still* (1951). Chu says that Zoic's baseship design was inspired by electron microscope images of plant and animal life, in a call-back to *Blade Runner*'s aesthetic ethos, where the city resembles the electron microscope image of a snake scale. Zoic's animators, rather than use motion capture, developed a 'Cylon movement' incorporating human and robotic movement patterns.

The new Colonial flight-suits incorporate reptilian elements into their design, picking up on the name 'Viper' as well as recalling the idea that the Cylons, in the original series, were once a reptile race. (Here, of course, the humans are the Cylons' creators.) The helmets look like stylised snake heads, and the backs of the costumes are ribbed like reptile scales.

Another distinctive aspect of the Colonial aesthetic is the use of hexagons rather than circles, and paper and screens having clipped corners to give them a similarly polygonal look. The Viper craft movement is modelled less on aircraft and more, following the lead of *Babylon 5*, on Newtonian physics. The series' military adviser, Ron Blecker, held a boot camp for the actors playing military characters, to teach them appropriate drill and procedure, and this was also something of a bonding experience for the participants.

The music for the miniseries was composed by former Danny Elfman bandmate Richard Gibbs, who was given a rough cut that Michael Rymer had temp-tracked both with music from the movies *The Last Temptation of Christ* (1988) and *Solaris* (2002) and with Japanese taiko drumming. Fittingly, the finished music reflects the early-2000s fondness for world music-inspired scores, with a lot of percussion and Southeast Asian instruments combined with Celtic vocals. As Gibbs had only three weeks in which to score the miniseries, he engaged Bear McCreary as an assistant.

The series was written in a kind of semi-planned fashion, with certain elements being left open to development and improvisation, giving it a more structured feel than episodic series, but also allowing greater freedom to the writers than on the more rigidly-structured *Babylon 5*. The writing team were also open to suggestions and improvisations from actors to some extent, although not completely: in a documentary on the Season 4.5 box set, Callum Keith Rennie says that the Cylon actors were not given the full Cylon backstory. Moore also engaged in a certain amount of strategising as regards the network, providing them with dumbed-down scripts for approval and then cutting out the unnecessary lines when actually in production. The writers also drew freely on a number of classic and popular films, in particular *Blade Runner*, *Aliens* (1986), *Independence Day*, *Black Hawk Down* (2001), *The Matrix* trilogy and the *Godfather* trilogy, while also showing a clear debt to such series as *The Prisoner*, *The West Wing* and the uneven space-marines drama *Space: Above and Beyond*. Individual episodes frequently contain homages to well-known movies such as *Easy Rider* (1969) and *Jaws* (1975).

The miniseries faced a particularly difficult genesis, not from a production point of view so much as from an audience reception point of view. Eick's decision to throw out all (or almost all) of the material from Singer's original pilot and start again resulted in a rumour that the Sci-Fi Channel had forced this decision, which was not in fact the case. Moore had also assumed that the fan community would be happy with the return of the show in whatever form, and was surprised by the negative reaction to the news that it would be a 'reimagining' rather than a continuation. He tried going online and connecting with fans, with little success; eventually things came to a head when Olmos, angered by the hate mail he was receiving, told the press that fans of the original series should not watch the new one as it would only upset them. Although the network were not happy about this (their intention, according to Eick, was to make the series distinct from contemporary space-operas rather than from its predecessor), it generated a lot of positive publicity for the series, causing Moore and Eick to repeat the line frequently in their own promotional material. This, however, had the unfortunate effect of causing some people to view the two series as completely distinct (save for sharing a title), when, as will be discussed throughout this book, in fact they are strikingly similar in design, concept and sociopolitical leanings.

The reimagined *Battlestar Galactica* thus takes a faithful but not slavish approach to its predecessor, developing certain themes and techniques in light of technological and social developments in the intervening 30 years while still remaining a military drama focused around neoconservative politics and religious questions.

BATTLESTAR GALACTICA: THE MINISERIES

1: *Battlestar Galactica*: The Miniseries (Parts One and Two)

FIRST TRANSMISSION DATE: 8 and 10 December 2003 (USA)

WRITERS: Ronald D Moore and Christopher Eric James

BASED ON A TELEPLAY[15] BY: Glen A Larson

DIRECTOR: Michael Rymer

CREDITED CAST: Callum Keith Rennie (Leoben Conoy); Matthew Bennett (Doral); Barclay Hope (Transport Pilot); Lorena Gale (Elosha); Conner Widdows (Boxey); John Mann (CAG); Michael Eklund (Prosna); Haili Page (Cami); Alonso Oyarzun (Socinus); Ty Olsson (Captain Kelly); Ron Blecker (Launch Officer); Ryan Robbins (Armistice Officer); Tim Henry (Doctor); Dwesi Ameyaw (Liner Captain); Brenda McDonald (Old Woman); Suleka Mathew (Reporter); Erin Karpluk (Woman #1); Jenn Griffin (Woman #2); B J Harrison (Woman #3); Moneca Delain (Blonde Woman); Zahf Paroo (Man #1); Robert Lewis (Man #2); Denzal Sinclaire (Man #3); Nadine Wright (Chantara); Michael Soltis (Chantara's Husband); Fred Keating (Junior Reporter); Lymari Nadal (Giana); Biski Gugushe (Pilot #1); Nahanni Arntzen (Pilot #2); Nogel Vonas (Pilot #3); Ryan Nelson (Pilot #4)

KNOWN UNCREDITED CAST: Mike Mitchell (Desperate Man)

SYNOPSIS: The Cylons, created by humans as a labour force for the Twelve Colonies, rebelled, engaged in a war with humanity and then, following the declaration of an armistice, disappeared. Forty years later, the crew of the battlestar *Galactica* conduct the vessel's decommissioning ceremony, and Doctor Gaius Baltar, celebrity scientist, learns that his girlfriend is in fact a new type of Cylon, one of 12 models that resemble humans and are capable of downloading their consciousnesses into new bodies upon death. She has used the access Baltar has given her to Colonial military computer systems to compromise the Colonial defences, including using Baltar's Command Navigation Program (CNP) to render their warships helpless. *Galactica* survives and fights back, as, being an older vessel, her computers are not networked and the CNP program was never loaded into them. Secretary of Education Laura Roslin, the most senior surviving

---

15 'Teleplay' normally denotes a script adapted from someone else's story idea, so its use here is arguably inaccurate.

politician, is declared President. The crew of one of *Galactica*'s Raptors, Helo and Boomer, land on Caprica and rescue a few survivors, and Helo gives up his seat so that Baltar can be saved. Roslin, assisted by Viper pilot Captain Apollo, gathers surviving civilian vessels, while Adama puts out a general call for all remaining Colonial military craft to regroup at Ragnar Anchorage. There they meet a strange man, Leoben Conoy, who also proves to be a Cylon and is killed by Adama. Roslin's Fleet go to Ragnar, but, in doing so, are forced to abandon all vessels incapable of travelling at faster-than-light speeds. Roslin and Adama clash over what to do next, but eventually Roslin wins the day, and the survivors strike out looking for a new home. Adama, at a memorial service for the dead, says that the Fleet will go in search of the planet Earth, home of the lost Thirteenth Tribe. Later, to Roslin, he reveals that he does not believe it exists, but that the Fleet needs hope. Baltar identifies Aaron Doral, a PR man, as a Cylon, and he is abandoned on Ragnar. When other humanoid Cylons come to find Doral, we learn that Boomer herself is also a Cylon.

ANALYSIS: The reimagined series' first outing is arguably not as powerful as the original series' opener 'Saga of a Star World', being too long, unevenly paced and characterised, and somewhat self-conscious about its relationship to the original series. However, one can see in it elements of the much stronger drama it would become, and glimpses of how the post-9/11 aesthetic affects the reimagined series in much the same way that the neocon aesthetic affected the original.

A Mini Adventure: The Storyline

The three-hour miniseries (which has no official title) was screened over two nights in December 2003. It appears to have changed little in essence over its development. The draft script dated 7 October 2002 that circulates on the internet differs mainly in details – chiefly the presence of a few mercifully-deleted info-dump sequences (some of which were filmed but abandoned), and extra scenes setting up a familial relationship between Boxey, Sharon and Tyrol (again, some of which were filmed). The draft script also confusingly suggests that the humans are living on Kobol as well as on the Colonies; this probably stemmed from a misunderstanding of 'Saga of a Star World', either taking the concept that the planets are the Twelve Colonies of Kobol to indicate that Kobol itself is still inhabited, or else picking up on a continuity error in the first part of the original serial, in which a news broadcast refers to the peace negotiations taking place on the 'star Kobol'. Key developments which were relatively late additions included the idea that Sharon is a Cylon, and the scene in which Six kills a baby (the latter of which was introduced so late in the day that it does not appear in the draft script).

The early scenes on *Galactica* are well done, efficiently introducing and setting up the central characters with an iconic continuous tracking shot that starts off following Thrace on her run through the ship, then moves off to

BATTLESTAR GALACTICA: THE MINISERIES

'follow' the press pack and various members of the crew: Starbuck and her anti-authoritarian attitude, Tigh with his drinking problem, Chief Tyrol and his deck crew with their down-to-earth perspective on events, efficient Gaeta and charismatic Adama. The press pack, led by Aaron Doral, here to witness *Galactica*'s rededication as a military museum, also provides a natural way of establishing the current situation and the basic worldbuilding behind the story.

The programme effectively gives a strong sense of build-up in its first third, with the use of captions to indicate rapid changes of location and time. The background detail throughout is striking (for instance the implication that the Armistice Officer is Boxey's father), and this alone invites multiple viewings. The story also contains a series of parallels that are subtly built up: Tigh's dilemma about whether or not to sacrifice the crewmen trapped in the burning flight pod parallels Roslin's decision to sacrifice the ships without jump capabilities, for instance. Baltar's denial over his role in the destruction of the Colonies similarly parallels Adama's denial over his role in his son Zak's death in a Viper accident two years earlier, with Apollo accusing his father of having pushed Zak to become a pilot even though he was not suited for the job, and also the humans' denial of their culpability in the creation of the Cylons. Significantly, Baltar began dating Six two years earlier, about the time when relations began to break down within the Adama family. A speech by Adama where he talks about humanity refusing to take responsibility for what they have done is clearly influenced by his conversation earlier with Apollo, in which the latter accused him of failing to own up to his role in Zak's death; and the draft script contains a stage direction indicating that Adama should be thinking of that conversation at this point.

The middle third is slightly more uneven, with a few jarring elements. Helo's self-sacrifice, unwittingly made on behalf of the man actually responsible for the whole catastrophe, is not very convincing, as it seems a bit too strong-jawed space-hero to fit well with the stark realism for which the miniseries is otherwise aiming. The sudden random death of deckhand Prosna is also far less affecting than intended, as the audience hasn't really had much time to get to know him as a character. Even writer Ronald D Moore admits that the apparent destruction of *Colonial One*, followed by the reveal that Apollo has employed a bit of technobabble ('I just used the hyperdrive to manipulate the energy coils') to save it, is preposterous.

The ending of the story is much stronger. The irony that Baltar accuses Doral of being a Cylon simply to provide a plausible story for how he came to find the Cylon device in CIC, and yet Doral turns out to *be* a conscious Cylon agent, is well conveyed. The revelation that Adama does not in fact know where Earth is, and is simply using the myth as a means of building solidarity, reinforces the miniseries' themes of uncertainty and seeking direction, and also gives the Fleet's military commander a cynical, slightly manipulative attitude toward belief, which will be challenged by subsequent events. Although the story was originally to have made it explicit that Baltar was the one who left the note reading 'There are only 12 Cylon models' for Adama, the final version is ambiguous; which, as Moore remarks in his commentary, is more effective (although the question is finally resolved in 'The Plan').

The now-iconic 'So say we all' scene, where Adama rallies the troops at the memorial service, arose in part through improvisation. Originally, Adama was to have made a stirring formal speech following Elosha's service; however, Edward James Olmos and Lorena Gale discussed the scene (which was the first one Olmos filmed) intensively prior to shooting and concluded that the idea of the commander of the ship following a funeral with a speech was inappropriate, and instead decided to play it as a spontaneous act on Adama's part. The repeated 'So say we all', picking up on the concluding line of Elosha's prayer, was a complete ad-lib, and the cast's cheers at the end were also spontaneous. The story's climax thus illustrates the blend of planning and improvisation that is both a strength of, and sometimes a problem for, the series.

Sex with Six: The Cylons

The reimagined series' Cylons, while clearly harking back to the 1978 versions (as indicated by the original-series Centurian and basestar model in *Galactica*'s museum[16] and the original-series Centurian specifications, designated 'Cylon Centurian Model 0005', read by the Armistice Officer), have a few developments. Chief among these is the key role played by human-appearing Cylons, which featured briefly in *Galactica 1980* and might, according to a proposal document of questionable authenticity, have appeared in *Battlestar Galactica*'s unmade second season, but which never played a major role in the original series. They are flesh and blood throughout, albeit with silica relays in their brains, synthetic chemicals in their make-up that are detectable upon cremation, and spines that glow red during sex – a concept that David Eick, bizarrely, asserts he came up with as a homage to the glowing eyes of the originals. The idea of Cylons being able to download their consciousness at death into a new body is also new to the televised series (though not to the books, as the concept appears in Richard Hatch's original novels), with the further plot point that the process can be blocked, leading to total death for the Cylon in question.

As noted, Moore has said that the decision to focus on humanoid Cylons was initially taken to reduce costs, but that the writing team then found that the metaphorical and narrative possibilities of having human-like Cylons were particularly interesting to explore; however, the idea of having there be a limited number of Cylon models meant that the final scene of the miniseries, with a procession of Sixes, Leobens and Dorals walking through Ragnar Station, was the most difficult to film. Given the Cylons' reinvention as analogues to terrorists, infiltrating Colonial society to destroy it from within, it is also no surprise to learn that they comprise both conscious fifth-columnists and 'sleeper

---

16 Although the Centurian display makes two further appearances, in the 'Razor' webisodes and in 'Daybreak', sharp-eyed viewers will observe that the display, and the Cylon in it, looks slightly different each time.

agents' programmed to believe themselves human.

The Cylons are chiefly represented here by the woman we come to know as Number Six – a deliberate reference to *The Prisoner,* and to the Nexus-6 androids of *Blade Runner.* Six is well characterised, with an alien scientific curiosity: the sequence in which she examines the baby in a way suggesting she is totally unfamiliar with children is nicely sinister, as is her question to the Armistice Officer, 'Are you alive? … Prove it', in an echo of *Dune*'s 'Are you human?' Her killing of the baby is unexplained – though as we later learn that the Cylons cannot, as far as they know, have children, there is a poignant significance to her choice of victim. Although she murders the child casually, we see her afterwards looking first anguished, then resigned, indicating how she feels about her mission on Caprica: although she knows she must carry it out, she has come to love Baltar. The Cylons' collective motivation in continuing to pursue the human Fleet is established at the end of the second part: that if they do not, they believe, the remnant of the humans will return one day and seek revenge.

We also discover a few things about Cylon faith. Cylons can be religious, and are, in contrast to the pantheistic humans, monotheists. A speech by Leoben to Adama also indicates that they see a theological justification for their actions against humans: that God made a mistake, and, having withdrawn his favour from his first creation, established the Cylons as the new chosen people. This emphasis on theology as a rationale for their attacks again links the Cylons with the religiously-inspired terrorism of the early 21st Century. Although their obsession with fertility, which is a feature of the series, does not appear in the finished miniseries, the draft script contains a scene in which Boxey asks Sharon if she has children, and she replies that she is infertile. The colour red is also associated with Cylons; their spines aside, the Armistice Station Six, the Head Six and the Doral model are all depicted wearing red at some point.

The miniseries also establishes the concept of the 'head characters' which will return, like the dead characters in the earlier HBO drama *Six Feet Under,* as a major aspect of the series. In the miniseries they are represented by Head Six, the vision of Six who appears to Baltar repeatedly from his rescue by Boomer onwards. Moore has said that he did this initially because he enjoyed the interaction between the characters so much that he wanted it to continue. In doing so, however, he established one of the series' driving mysteries. Two explanations are presented here for the phenomenon: Baltar's, that she is an hallucination brought on by the stress of recent events, and hers, that a Cylon chip has been implanted in his head. The miniseries deliberately never comes down on the side of one explanation or the other (although Rymer told James Callis to play it as if it were the latter); as Moore notes in his commentary, Head Six imparts no information that Baltar couldn't figure out on his own, though he, Eick and Rymer all agree that the fact that, when Baltar walks out of frame, she remains on screen suggests something otherworldly. Callis voiced the theory around this time that she was a supernatural being or someone from another plane of existence. Although she herself speaks mostly 'in character', as if she is the Six who was Baltar's lover on Caprica, she says 'Honestly, I don't know' when asked what the Cylon device is; which, since Baltar's lover carried one in her handbag, suggests they are not the same person. Her line 'I want you to love me ... God is love' provides an early hint that perhaps she may be connected to a higher being.

The Mask of Apollo: The Characters

The establishment of the series' characters is slightly uneven. Generally speaking, the ones who are closest to their original series forebears are the strongest (for instance Starbuck, Adama and Baltar), while attempts to change the formula are more hit and miss (the reimagining of Tigh as a surly drunk works, while turning Apollo into an angsty, non-heroic type simply leaves a void in the story), as are the original characters (Laura is strongly characterised, for instance, while Helo is initially very much a heroic stereotype).

Baltar's selfishness and sexual proclivities are firmly highlighted as the character's defining flaws; the series bible also notes, as backstory, that he is part of a movement of young scientists who, now that the Cylon threat is a thing of the past, are engaged in reviving and developing computer network technology and artificial intelligence. Although Six says that he must have suspected something was odd about her interest in the defence computers, she asserts that he ignored it due to his inflated sense of ego. However, that selfishness may well become his strength, as his assertion to Head Six, 'I am not on anybody's side!', places him between the humans and the Cylons, in a position to bridge the two.

Olmos's Adama is stoic, autocratic and not used to being argued with, but given to moments of emotion that are subtly underlined, in this story at least, by the fact that, while he is impeccably turned out, his quarters are a mess. His paternal relationship with Starbuck is highlighted by the two sharing a call-and-response that is clearly some sort of inside joke ('What do you hear?' 'Nothin' but the rain'. 'Then grab your gun and bring in the cat'.). This will be repeated at certain points in the series, and the draft script states that these exchanges 'date back to a common experience in flight school'.[17]

There is also a slightly abortive reintroduction of the character of Boxey. Here he is again an orphan with a Dorothy Hamill haircut, but about six years older than the original. The initial idea was to have him, Sharon and Tyrol form a kind of blended family along the lines of Apollo, Boxey and Sheba in the original, but this was later put aside as the series developed in different ways. The concept survives, however, in several scenes in the draft script available on the internet, and in one filmed scene available on the Region 1 DVD, in which Tyrol houses Boxey in the officers' quarters in a bunk formerly occupied by a dead pilot; an idea Boxey finds somewhat depressing. The draft

---

17 The final response is not fixed; variations in the series include 'Boom, boom, boom!', 'Wilco!' and 'Aye-aye, sir!'

script also has him as much younger (about six years old, like the original) and makes it plain that he is the son of the Armistice Officer, which in the final version is apparent only to those who make the connection between Boxey and the Armistice Officer's family photos.

The reimagined Tigh is set up early on as a source of black humour when Doral, passing him by, says 'You'll see things [on the *Galactica*] that look odd or even antiquated ... Hello ...' underlining that Tigh is indeed both. Tigh's difficult relationship with his wife is introduced through Starbuck's comments in a card game sequence, and later we see Tigh burning the right eye out of a picture of her in a red dress (both of which are, in hindsight, strong foreshadowings of what will happen to the Tighs' relationship in later seasons). Significantly, when Tigh freezes over what to do about the people trapped in the port flight pod, he looks briefly to Adama, suggesting that he draws strength from his relationship with his commander. The Tigh-Starbuck confrontation at the end is also one of the single strongest scenes in the miniseries, in part because of Michael Hogan's performance, with his cheek twitching to indicate how difficult apologising to Starbuck is for Tigh, and in part because of Starbuck's unexpected response, defying cliché by rejecting Tigh's overtures. (The equivalent scene in the draft script conversely involves Starbuck seeking out Tigh to tell him she thinks he made the right call during the fire, and that he should not blame himself for the deaths, and as such is far less powerful.) Tigh's reaction – he is first seen throwing out the bottle of alcohol in his desk, and then later staring pensively at the retrieved bottle – underlines that, while brave and aware of his flaws, he is also consumed by his own weaknesses.

The reimagining of Apollo is at this point less successful, as he comes across as angst-ridden and directionless, his opposition to his father verging on the film cliché. It is worth noting, however, that we see the seeds of the character's later development in his continued searching for a direction, his uneasy friendship with Starbuck, and his attraction to politics. The series bible has him as assigned to test pilot school, but by the final version this idea has been dropped. His estrangement from his father dates from Zak's death; again, though, we are still in cliché territory, revisiting the familiar idea of the career-driven paterfamilias alienating his family through his devotion to his work. There is an irony in that Adama's pressuring of his sons to become Viper pilots may have killed Zak, but, under the circumstances of the holocaust, it has saved Apollo's life; a fact that cannot be lost on either of them.

The most prominent of the new characters is Laura Roslin, an ex-teacher and Secretary for Education who becomes President, all the other cabinet ministers having perished in the attack and she having survived merely by virtue of the fact that she was attending the *Galactica*'s decommissioning ceremony. Roslin takes command very believably – a natural leader who has hitherto not been given a chance to show it. However, as Eick points out in the commentary, Mary McDonnell delivers such words as 'Cylon' and 'combat' with a slight uncertainty, indicating that the character is unfamiliar with her role and figuring it out as she goes along (and indeed Michael Rymer notes that she initially played it far too uncertain, and that he had to encourage her to be slightly more heroic). We also see the character learning from her experiences: when the Cylons launch warheads at the Fleet, Roslin decides not to jump to safety, and the Fleet is saved from destruction only by Apollo's using an electromagnetic pulse to disable the warheads and fool the Cylons into thinking there has been a nuclear explosion. However, Roslin clearly realises that her choice was the wrong one (and also that the deception with the EMP will work only once), and this informs her later decision to follow Apollo's advice and sacrifice the ships without faster-than-light (FTL) travel capabilities.

Roslin's cancer, introduced at the outset, clearly gives her the courage to continue; as she has already come to terms with the possibility that she may be dying, she can cope with outside catastrophe. Beyond this, however, it does strike a slightly problematic note, in that it comes across as an attempt to make the character 'interesting' at this juncture rather than as something flowing naturally from her situation. It also seems unoriginal, recalling Serena's plight in the initial cut of 'Saga of a Star World' (where she suffered from pluton poisoning incurred during the Cylon attack on Caprica), and *The West Wing*, which featured a president keeping a progressive illness secret from his staff and the electorate.

Other new characters are more poorly developed. The fact that Helo was not intended to be a recurring character shows, as he has almost no personality at all, bar the hint that he may be an ex-smoker (indicated by the fact that he sucks a lollipop during the card game). Tahmoh Penikett revealed in an interview that the extent of the development he was given at this stage was that Helo was a man with a permanent tan and an eye for the ladies, which did not sit well with him. Sharon, also, is rather underdeveloped: the gradual removal of the original idea that she should be an inexperienced rookie pilot (the last vestige, a sequence in which she nearly crashes her Raptor, was deleted in the final editing process) has left her with only two character points, namely that she is a Cylon, and that she is sleeping with Chief Tyrol.

There is a hint in the actors' performances that Cally rather fancies Tyrol, though he is indifferent to her, and is slightly jealous of Boomer. This would have been further developed in a deleted scene in which Cally confronts Tyrol about his relationship with Boomer, reminding him of the potential conflict of interest in sleeping with a superior officer; and it would be elaborated upon in the series itself.

The miniseries also sets up a tension – personal, political and sexual – between Adama and Roslin. Adama clearly has difficulty accepting civilian authority, and Roslin, for her part, plays power games with him, making Adama wait for an audience until Billy has finished making his report, and then immediately asking Adama if he intends to declare martial law, anticipating the type of military-dominated scenario seen in the original series. In the end, they make an agreement – which will prove to be a fateful one – to keep military and civilian spheres separate. This symbolises the tension between military and civilian worldviews that will be one of the series' driving forces, and also reflects the writers' desire to avoid the scenario that emerged as the original series wore on, whereby the Quorum served simply as interchangeable, unreasonable antagonists to Adama's natural leadership; although it has to be said that this is at the cost of a sense of focused heroism.

Another significant difference from the original series is that Adama does indeed initially intend to expend all his resources in an all-out counterattack on the Cylons, and it is Roslin who voices the position taken by Adama in the original series, that they must acknowledge that this is pointless and that Adama's responsibility is instead to retreat and protect the remnants of the human race. Apollo's initial support for Roslin also stems as much from her tacit opposition to his father's philosophy as from her being brave enough to admit that the war is lost.

New and Different Flavour? Worldbuilding and Relationship with the Original Series

From the outset, the miniseries distances itself from the original series. Differences include that the war with the Cylons ended over 40 years earlier, rather than being an ongoing conflict as in the original; *Galactica* is no longer a ship on active service, but one that was built in the early days of the conflict and is now redundant; and whereas the original series only mentions eight battlestars, the miniseries states there were 12 constructed during the Cylon War (one for each Colony), and there are now an unknown number. (We hear a report that 30 battlestars were lost in the initial attack on the Colonies, which wiped out a quarter of the Fleet, suggesting that there were about 120 battlestars.) *Galactica,* which again represented Caprica, is being decommissioned – hence the general laxity of discipline aboard the vessel – and turned into a museum (leading to a dry exchange between Starbuck and Tyrol: 'Why can't we use the starboard launch?' 'Because it's a gift shop now'). This turns out to be, as well as a good excuse for *Galactica*'s retro look, an explanation for its survival: as the Cylons can infiltrate networked computers, an old and decommissioned ship will be unaffected.

Faster-than-light travel is, as the series bible notes, 'a misnomer', as it is here envisioned as a kind of tessering: a 'jumping' from one point in space to the next through the folding of space itself. Although Raptors have FTL capabilities, Vipers do not. Other battlestars named are the *Atlantia,* the *Triton,* the *Columbia* and the *Solaria;* all of these were also names of battlestars in the original series except for the last, which may be a nod to *Solaris* (2002), the soundtrack of which was influential on the music of *Battlestar Galactica.* The *Galactica* has not jumped in over 20 years; an unfortunately deleted exchange from the draft script has Tigh remarking, 'Probably rats living in the FTL relays', and Adama replying, 'Hope not. Hate the smell of burned rat'. Unlike the Viper Mark II's, the Viper Mark VII's newer computers are vulnerable to the Cylon attacks, but Gaeta states that he will have the deck crew retro-fit them to make them usable in future encounters.

Despite all these differences, the story does have a number of clearly deliberate parallels with the original series. In the DVD commentary, Moore acknowledges that the scene introducing Starbuck, in which she is shown to be a successful Triad player and an anti-authoritarian, is a deliberate homage to the equivalent character's introduction in 'Saga of a Star World'. We also have the narration of the destruction of the Colonies through news reports, the mobbing of a Raptor by angry refugees demanding rescue; and a pilot (here, Starbuck) flying through clouds in space to discover a previously-unsuspected army of Cylons. The Cylon basestars (which, as in the original series, are referred to interchangeably as 'basestars' and 'baseships') really are star shaped, although the draft script refers to them as having the two-flattened-cones shape of the originals; they also bear a slight resemblance to the Ship of Lights from the original series.

The Cylon Raiders fire ammunition with a blue flare, and the Vipers ammunition with a reddish flare, in a clear visual reference to the lasers of the original-series craft. The sequence involving the crew having to smother fires on *Galactica*'s port side, featuring the difficult decision to sacrifice some crew members for the good of the ship, is conceptually related to the original-series episode 'Fire in Space', and Head Six has a clear antecedent in John from 'Experiment in Terra', a being from a more enlightened race whom only Apollo could see, and who acted as a kind of spirit guide to the pilot.

A character with a Cylon transmitter implanted in the head featured in the original draft of 'Fire in Space' by Michael Sloan. The Mark II Vipers are described as far back as the draft script as 'virtually identical in design to the 70s TV series'. The names of the Colonies are broadly the same, and the religion (which here includes female priests) similarly based on a von Däniken myth of external origin: in a knowing nod to the original series' title sequence and premise, Adama announces that the first line of the sacred scrolls is 'Life here began out there'. Leoben's remark 'Suspicion and distrust – that's military life, isn't it?' couples the original series' sense of paranoia and mistrust with a less pro-military stance, indicating the miniseries' simultaneous indebtedness to, and yet freedom to break away from, the original series.

There are also a few jokier homages to the original series. Aside from the visible presence of an original-series Centurian and basestar model in the museum, the Armistice Officer's Cylon technical sheet is one relating to the 1978 programme (with a reference to 'yahrens', the original-series' word for a year, being visible to the sharp-eyed), and he also has a document entitled Cimtar Peace Accord (in a reference to the abortive signing of a peace accord at the moon Cimtar in the original series). Two children wearing original-series Cylon masks and wielding toy swords are briefly visible in the background in the scene where Baltar and Six go for a walk prior to Six meeting her unknown contact. The TV programme *The Spotlight* plays an arrangement of the original series' theme tune as a fanfare before Baltar's interview, and the Viper flyby at the decommissioning ceremony is also to an arrangement of said theme.[18] When Jackson Spencer discovers that his Viper is not responding, he orders 'Jolly, take over', suggesting that there is a Lieutenant Jolly in the new series as well, albeit one who promptly perishes horribly in flames. The Botanical Cruiser is also clearly modelled on the original series' agroships, raising expectations that it will become part of the Fleet, which are then unexpectedly dashed (although, by the televised series, another has quietly appeared). At the end of the story, one of the Sixes says 'By your command', in the first repetition of the earlier Cylon catchphrase in the reimagined series; this was suggested by Moore's friend Breen Frazier, a writer on *Roswell*, in a script review that Moore requested from him at the height of the controversy about the reinvention of the series.

Although they are few in number, some details about life in the reimagined Colonial society emerge. As noted, the pilots' familiar names, such as Starbuck and Apollo, are now call-signs; Adama's, we learn, was 'Husker'. While Eick and Moore, in their commentary, emphasise that they wanted to avoid the original series' alien terms (such as 'lexon', a unit of weight), a few new ones are introduced, such as 'DRADIS', the name of a radar-like detection system, and the distress call 'Krypter, krypter, krypter'. In what will become a recurring problem with the series, the fact that at least some of the survivors of the bombardment ought to be suffering from radiation sickness is completely ignored. Although we learn little about Caprican society here, we do discover that it has the death penalty for treason. The ship carrying Laura Roslin, *Colonial Heavy 798*, changes its name to *Colonial One* when she becomes President, much as the call sign Air Force One is used in the modern USA for any Air Force plane carrying the President. The phrase 'So say we all', apparently the Colonial version of 'Amen', will rapidly become a reimagined series catchphrase; it sounds slightly totalitarian, in an early hint that Colonial society is far from a benevolent democracy.

A few concepts introduced in the miniseries will become more significant as the series develops. An exchange between Adama and Tigh – 'They better start having babies'. 'Is that an order?' 'Maybe, before too long' – foreshadows upcoming conflicts between individual freedom and the needs of the collective. Baltar's throwaway description of the Centurions as 'walking chrome toasters' is the first instance of a metaphor that will run and run; as well as mocking the Cylon appearance, it has connotations of scorching or incineration. The prison ship, which will become of increasing importance in the first season, is introduced here (significantly, in light of later events, with the news that the captain is considering executing the prisoners to save resources; Roslin's decision to countermand this will have repercussions for

---

18 According to Bear McCreary's blog, the theme music of the original series is the 'Colonial Anthem'. It is indeed used in the reimagined series much as a national anthem would be; however, it must have been composed prior to the unification of the Colonies, as it features briefly in an episode of *Caprica*, 'Gravedancing'.

the next four seasons). Head Six's exposure of the Cylon device in CIC also points to further developments, raising the questions of why the Cylons placed it there (perhaps to ensure that the *Galactica* was spared?) and why she should want the humans to remove it.

After the Gold Rush: 9/11 and Late Neoconservatism

Like the original, the new series is firmly located within its political context. Where 'Saga of a Star World' was a confident assertion of a right-wing position in the light of an improving economy and the final stages of the Cold War, the miniseries comes across as less certain of its message, more like a story seeking a direction, reflecting the shaken mindset of the American public after the 9/11 attacks. Following outside political events, the characters spend the miniseries stumbling about in shock; gradually, over the next four years, they will develop a coherent narrative for the events of the disaster and achieve a new position. Randomness is a continual theme, with unexpected equipment failures and a missile hitting the *Galactica* simply because Starbuck is unable to shoot it down in time. Rather than reacting with stoic heroism, Tyrol panics and loses control when confronted with the realities of combat, with Adama, the veteran, having to tell him to pull himself together. The destruction of the Colonies and its immediate aftermath looms much larger in the storyline of the miniseries than in 'Saga of a Star World', with the helplessness of the outnumbered and immobilised Colonial pilots during the 'turkey-shoot' sequence extensively dwelled upon. All of this is consistent with the state of mind of a country that sees itself as under attack; and the return of the original series' philosophy of sacrificing the few for the many, however painful, acknowledges the realities of a country at war.

The miniseries also has religious overtones, harking back to the original series but also indicative of the strong role of evangelical Christianity in post 9/11 America. Baltar's sexual relationship with Six, original-sin-style, is the downfall of humanity (and there is a direct cut from Baltar having sex with Six to Boomer having sex with Tyrol, drawing parallels between the two relationships).[19] Originally, there was to have been a sequence in which the Armistice Officer eats an apple before the arrival of Six, with obvious Garden of Eden symbolism. A small pagan element does creep in, though, in the similarity of the name of Ragnar Anchorage to Ragnarok.

The Cylons, similarly, have undergone a shift from Soviet analogues, representing a powerful rival empire, toward al-Qaeda analogues, a mysterious shadowy threat that the Colonials essentially brought upon themselves through negligent, selfish actions. Although Moore says that he liked the idea of the monotheist Cylons attacking the polytheist humans as a kind of parallel to the

---

19 SPOILER SECTION: The conception of Hera in Series One, and her subsequent significance, means that sex is also the redemption of both the human and Cylon races.

rise of monotheism in the West (and thus, since the Cylons are at this point the bad guys, as a kind of oblique swipe at Christian hegemony), the image of the enemy as devotedly monotheistic religious fundamentalists is a visible allegory of American images of extreme Islamists. At this point in the series the Cylons come across not so much as individuals as a sinister, unknowable force. At the same time, however, they reflect contemporary fears of overdependence on technology: the idea of the Cylons shutting down the electrical systems on the Vipers has echoes of the Y2K scares of the late 1990s, as well as of the potential destructive impact of electromagnetic pulses and of terrorist attacks through the internet. On a more visual level, the reporting of the attacks on the Colonies echoes the news coverage of the 9/11 attacks, and the flag-draped coffins on the *Galactica* toward the end of the story easily evoke news images of bodies returning from Iraq and Afghanistan.

Adama's speech at the decommissioning ceremony sets out the ethos of *Battlestar Galactica* as a post-9/11 series. He accuses humans of refusing to recognise their role in provoking the Cylon attacks, echoing arguments of the time that America was in part responsible for its own situation through its contradictory foreign policy, which in previous eras included actually supporting the Taliban and, at various times, the Iraqi and Iranian regimes. Leoben's assertion that humanity is 'not a pretty race', and that they are 'only one step away from beating each other with clubs like savages', is driven home sharply by the sequence shortly thereafter in which Adama kills him brutally with a makeshift club, and further indicates that the series will be somewhat critical of the reaction to 9/11. Leoben's line 'Sooner or later the day comes when you can't hide from the things you've done' sums up the series' position: the Cylon attacks are explicitly retributive, and the humans must acknowledge their own guilt before they can move on.

Documentary Style: Writing and Technical Production

The script was written by Ronald D Moore, but credited to Moore and 'Christopher Eric James', a pseudonym for Glen Larson (apparently after Larson's sons), on the grounds that Moore felt that the story owed too great a debt to 'Saga of a Star World' not to acknowledge. The draft script, although broadly similar to the final, indicates that the series was originally to have featured action sequences done, 24-style, in split screen, which the draft says would form a 'signature' look. In the final version, the same sequences are presented as more conventional mock-documentary action montages, which in fact work much better and give the series a more immediate, less gimmicky feel. The one thing lost by the change is that the split-screen version contains footage of Dualla visiting the morgue and paying her respects to Prosna, preceding the scene in which she meets Billy in the corridor and kisses him passionately, which puts her actions in a different context.

The decision to go for a mock-documentary style was apparently made at a very early stage in the series' development, and the idea is taken to such extremes as having a piece of CGI debris 'hitting' the 'camera' during the Armistice Station scene. While effective, the style is not quite as original as is often claimed; leaving aside the fact that the mock-documentary style is a hallmark of such well-known post-millenial TV series as *The Office*, *Firefly* had made extensive use of a handheld camera effect, including in space sequences prefiguring *Battlestar Galactica*'s 'wobblecam-in-space' battle scenes.

Another ultimately discarded aspect of the draft script was that the Armistice Officer was to have been shown ageing over the many years of his visits to the Armistice Station; these sections were in fact recorded, but for time reasons cut down to a single sequence with the Armistice Officer as an older man. The time spent hiring and making up a young actor, Ryan Robbins, to look progressively older was thus wasted (although it did allow Robbins to return as Charlie Connor, a very different character, in Season Three). David Eick reportedly wanted Dirk Benedict to play the Armistice Officer, feeling that having him die at the start of the new series would set an appropriate tone, but Benedict declined. (By contrast, Richard Hatch was initially considered for the ongoing role of Elosha.) The Armistice Station sequence was itself a fairly late addition to the story, which originally began with the sequence of Starbuck jogging, but the writing team felt that a better initial dramatic hook was needed.

Principal photography on the miniseries was done between 1 April and 12 June 2003, which, according to James Callis, was seven months after the cast auditions. The Caprica City sequences were filmed in Burnaby, BC, with the Ragnar Anchorage sequences being shot at a disused potash silo and a sugar mill (where, David Eick says, the fumes were so bad that the crew wore surgical masks) and the *Colonial One* hold sequences inside a ferry. Few problems arose, despite the absence of Ronald D Moore (who, as noted above, was working on *Carnivàle*);. However, tensions erupted when the network objected to the level of violence in the fight between Adama and Leoben, which had been re-choreographed at Olmos's suggestion from a fairly conventional punch-up to a brutal conflict in which Adama beats Leoben to death with a flashlight. A heated discussion between the network and the production team resulted in a compromise in which most of the violence was retained but certain shots were redone.

In other respects, the network was apparently quite supportive of the miniseries. They contributed extra money when its budget was exhausted and the team were considering scrapping the scenes of Adama and Leoben discussing philosophy in the corridors of Ragnar Station in favour of a straight police drama-style interrogation scene between the two; and later they willingly gave up some advertising time when the finished edit exceeded its slot duration slightly even after extensive cuts (which Eick puts down to the writer's unfamiliarity with the mock-documentary style, which runs slower than traditional space-opera in the *Star Trek* mould).

The miniseries was directed, after the original director Breck Eisner left, by Michael Rymer, an Australian whose previous credits include *Queen of the Damned* (2002) and who had worked with David Eick on an unmade pilot for

Studios USA. The key factor in his appointment was apparently that he also directed *Angel Baby* (1995), a low-budget film about the mentally handicapped, which Eick felt had a humanity that the production team wanted to capture. Rymer appears to have been a crucial influence on casting and design; and Moore and Eick would subsequently engage him to direct key episodes of the series that followed.

The effects were done by Zoic, with extra work carried out by Vancouver-based studio Atmosphere. The original director's cut envisaged the inclusion of 600 effects sequences, with the budget only allowing for 100; in the end, the team and the network compromised on 300, though the team particularly felt the loss of a sequence in which Apollo leads a missile away from *Colonial One* and takes his Viper into planetary atmosphere, and repeatedly commented that they wanted to restage this for the series. (A version with crude placeholder effects can be found on the Region 1 DVD release.)

Rymer contributed the idea of indicating jumps with a vertigo-zoom effect, but this would be dropped after the miniseries: as Moore puts it in the podcast for 'Guess What's Coming to Dinner', 'In the miniseries, we did the jumps inside the ship with the characters, and we did that sort of zoom-in-pull-out thing, that Rymer did, and we never did it again ... After that we kind of got rid of the idea that there was anything special about the jumps; they just kind of happened'.

The miniseries shows influences from a number of other areas. The sequence where Roslin's doctor tells her she has cancer and his words are drowned out by the roar of the ship taking off is a filmic representation of the way the mind goes blank when confronted with traumatic information, as used in the scene in the David Lynch movie *Mulholland Drive* (2002) where two characters encounter a horrifying figure outside Winkie's restaurant. Richard Gibbs's incidental music (which Rymer requested that he make 'Kubrickian') is very Polynesian/world music-influenced, recalling similar scores to *Firefly*, *Farscape* and *Babylon 5*'s less-influential spin-off *Crusade*, although Gibbs also stated that he wanted to work in subtle homages to Stu Phillips's original-series score.

The influence of the original *Star Wars* trilogy is also apparent, in the staticky sound of the pilots' radio transmissions and the general aesthetic of the ship: high-tech but old and grungy. The slang term 'toaster' for a humanoid android first appears in *Alien 3* (1992). The opening sequence, in which Armistice Station is destroyed, recalls the beginning of *Babylon 5*'s first episode, 'Midnight on the Firing Line', in which a Centauri space station is attacked. The idea of the Colonial craft being incapacitated by a computer virus is indebted to *Independence Day*, as is the cut sequence of Apollo leading a missile away from *Colonial One*, going down to the surface of a planet and travelling through a ravine. The aesthetic on *Colonial One*, meanwhile, is an obvious visual nod to the shuttle sequences of *2001: A Space Odyssey* (1968).

Roslin's situation is paralleled to Lyndon B Johnson's, with her swearing-in being a deliberate reference to Johnson's on Air Force One after John F Kennedy's death; and the destruction of the Botanical Cruiser (itself an obvious nod to *Silent Running* (1972), the Garden of Eden and the original series) is based on the Johnson campaign's scaremongering 'daisy' television commercial, featuring a girl innocently playing as nuclear destruction looms. Roslin herself has obvious parallels with both John F Kennedy and Franklin D Roosevelt, American Presidents who had illnesses or disabilities that they concealed, wholly or partly, from the public.

Head Six's relationship with Baltar is heavily indebted to the central conceit of *Blithe Spirit* (1945), in which a man is haunted by the ghost of his former wife, who engages him in racy banter. The sequence where Helo and Sharon deploy decoys to lure Cylon missiles away from their Raptor is loosely based on a similar manoeuvre used in *Crimson Tide* (1995), a film that will be continually referenced in the series: other examples in the miniseries include Kara Thrace's run through *Galactica*, which recalls a scene in the film where Denzel Washington's character goes for a jog through the corridors of a submarine, and the abovementioned fire-fighting sequence, which appears to have been drawn in part from one in the film where a fire breaks out in the submarine's galley.

There are also one or two noteworthy errors or details to watch out for. Tigh, viewing the picture of Adama with his sons, somewhat anachronistically exclaims 'Jesus!' (apparently an ad-lib by the actor that found its way into the final version). Canadians and Canadophiles can have fun playing spot-the-Vancouver-area-location in the Caprica sequences; fans of Canadian music might also recognise the actor playing *Galactica*'s original CAG (Commander Air Group), Jackson Spencer, as John Mann, lead singer and songwriter for the folk-indie band Spirit of the West. Ron Blecker, the series' military adviser, has a brief cameo as a launch officer. The correct pronunciation of some later-familiar names and words has not been established yet (with 'DRADIS' 'Leoben' and 'Gaeta' being particularly variable; Sagittaron is also pronounced 'Sagittarion' here). The *Serenity*, the ship from *Firefly*, is visible in the sky over Caprica at one point. The photo of Adama with his children, which does not feature in the draft script, is a rather badly photoshopped image including the visibly cut-and-pasted head of someone who looks distinctly like the Fonz from *Happy Days* (and nothing at all like the actors who would later play the younger Adama in the 'Razor' flashback sequences and in 'Blood and Chrome'). Likewise, the photographs of Zak and of the as-yet-unnamed Mrs Tigh depict different people from the actors who would subsequently portray them. Two relatives of cast and crew also turn up in minor roles: Edward James Olmos's wife portrays the refugee who asks Apollo if he has news of her husband in the Colonial service (whose story will later form a key subplot of the telemovie 'The Plan'), and David Eick's wife Jenny Birchfield-Eick stands in for Mrs Tigh in the Colonel's photograph.

Although an initial test screening had the miniseries performing poorly, with the audience saying they couldn't identify with the characters, the premiere, when broadcast on the Sci-Fi Channel, had strong ratings on its first night and, in a rare occurrence, even better ones on the subsequent night. It ultimately proved to be the most-watched original cable TV miniseries of the year, and critical response was also good.

In summation, the miniseries is less powerful than it could have been; Ronald D Moore seems at this point not to have had a firm grip on either what the original programme was about or where he would like to go with the new series. However, certain aspects, principally the ending, give an indication of the much stronger episodic series that is to follow.

Season One: 2004-2005

Although the miniseries had been successful, an episodic series was originally deemed unaffordable by both Universal and the Sci-Fi Channel, the early budget estimates being so high that, according to Eick in *The Official Companion*, 'The chairman of the studio said flat out, "It's over! Forget about it. Move on. Stop bugging me!"'. Then, however, Britain's Sky TV network, which was looking to invest in the production of high-profile American shows, signed a co-production deal with Universal, providing the necessary money. Renewal was officially announced on 10 February 2004, and filming on the first season began on 19 April 2004 and continued for the next five months.

The series' production moved from Lions' Gate Studios to stages G, H and I at Vancouver Film Studios, and followed an eight-day-per-episode shooting schedule. The interior *Galactica* corridor set was broken up to fit the new location, so a continual-loop tour of the set, as seen in the opening to the miniseries, became impossible. The CIC set gained a second level in the episode 'Tigh Me Up, Tigh Me Down', so as to allow for a sequence in which Roslin looks down upon Adama from above. Location filming was done in the Vancouver area. The house used as Baltar's residence in the miniseries was unavailable, so a different but similar-looking building was used. Where the miniseries had been shot on 35mm film, the episodic series moved to high-definition (HD) video instead, which would also be the case for its spinoffs. According to director Marita Grabiak, interviewed in *Finding Battlestar Galactica*, whereas on some series the visual effects department works independently of the directors, on *Battlestar Galactica* the directors were much more involved, having several meetings with the team as the effects took shape.

One key change from the miniseries was the departure of Richard Gibbs, who passed up the chance to score the episodic series in order to concentrate on his film work. Gibbs did however develop the series' theme tune, working from a temp track consisting of a Sanskrit chant and a piece of music by Peter Gabriel, and also scored two early episodes, 'Water' and 'Bastille Day', so that his stylings would overlap with those of his successor Bear McCreary and thereby ensure consistency. McCreary had assisted Gibbs on the miniseries, and followed his drum-heavy, world-music-influenced style while also providing a flavour of Colonial classical music (in 'Tigh Me Up, Tigh Me Down') and popular dance tunes (in 'Colonial Day'). A McCreary-reworked version of the theme went out on the series' US broadcasts, but Gibbs's original remained on the UK broadcasts. The lyrics are the Sanskrit Gayatri Mantra, translating more or less as 'We meditate on the glory of that Being who has produced this universe; may He enlighten our minds'.

The series also gets for the first time a title sequence, in the form of a brief set of captioned images explaining the Cylon backstory for viewers, followed by several recap clips (chosen by the head writer and editor) and then, to the sound of the theme music, a further selection of clips recapping the destruction of the Colonies, the swearing-in of Roslin and the departure of the Fleet. The sequence also includes a quick montage of images from the episode that is to follow (a very 1970s idea that, according to Moore, was inspired by *Space: 1999*'s 'This Episode' sequences). These 'precaps' are essentially meaningless dramatic images that tell the viewer nothing about the episode except in hindsight, but do serve to whet the appetite for the story to come. The episodes conclude with a series of short animated segments in which cartoon avatars of Eick and Moore attempt to kill each other in various over-the-top ways, based on *Mad* magazine's *Spy vs. Spy* cartoons; these were suggested by Eick and animated by his friend Jerry Hultsch.

One key difference between the original and the reimagined series is that the new version features far fewer trips to other planets or to other ships of the Fleet. (Plans for the latter were shelved to keep down the costs of new sets; the main ship visited outside of *Colonial One* is *Cloud 9*, which looks like a park and was thus depicted through location filming rather than set-building.) However, the setting of storylines on Caprica and, later, Kobol, provides for outdoor locations and breaks up the industrial imagery of *Galactica*. Eick has also stated that one of the reasons for keeping the fantasy sequences set in Baltar's house was to provide an additional location.

A few other differences from the original series include Kobol being a lush forested planet rather than a desert world, and the reasons for the exodus from Kobol being considerably vaguer than the technological/ecological catastrophe of the original, hinting that it was down to humans rebelling against the gods. The team also draw upon but cleverly reverse a common trope of 1970s drama (which, to be fair, never appeared in original *Battlestar Galactica*), in featuring in the Caprica sequences a drawn-out story of a vulnerable man being stalked by a predatory woman.

Although the original series did have story arcs, the arc format is much more prominent in the reimagined series, with very few episodes being stand-alone. The writing team were influenced by *Hill Street Blues* to develop a three-tier arc structure consisting of series arcs, multi-episode arcs and episode arcs: the series bible, elaborating on this, says 'Series Arcs run through the life of the show ... Multi-Episode Arcs allow us to spend 2-4 episodes dealing with a specific crisis ... and the Episode Arcs provide closed-end narratives for each show'.[20] Moore felt this was a risky but worthwhile strategy, saying in the podcast for 'The Eye of Jupiter', 'We don't do the same show every week. And I think that's one of the strengths of the show. I think it's also one of the dangers of the show. 'Cause there is an element to the audience that very strongly wants to watch the same show every week ... so I think when you're doing a series like this you are riding the line between challenging and surprising ... and also worrying about getting

---

20 Spelling as in the original document.

in the way of the audience's comfort'. The arced nature of the storytelling may, however, have contributed to encouraging the viewing public to regard the series as less *Star Trek* and more *The West Wing*.

The Caprica-set storyline was a late addition. Originally Helo was not to have appeared again after giving up his seat to Baltar, but Moore was so impressed by Penikett's performance, and by the number of people who came up to him and Eick at the premiere saying how much they had liked Helo and asking what would happen to him next, that he was written into the series. (The character Racetrack, introduced in 'Kobol's Last Gleaming', was similarly intended to be a short-lived one, but was also retained because Eick and Moore liked actress Leah Cairns's performance.) Unfortunately, the lateness of this change is very visible, with the Caprica-set segments showing little development for quite a long time, and with Helo unfortunately coming across as a very underwritten character for most of Season One.

On the Fleet, Boomer was originally not to have suspected her Cylon nature as soon as she does, but the idea of moving this development to an earlier point in the series came up during planning for the second episode, 'Water'. One abandoned storyline would have had Lee, upon becoming Laura's advisor, beginning a May-December romance with her (as hinted at in the miniseries, and also echoing the abandoned idea of Tyrol and Boomer having an intergenerational romance), leading to a rivalry between father and son Adamas. In the end it was decided not to follow this line of thought, the focus shifting instead to the initial tension and gradual formation of a partnership between Roslin and Adama.

In developing and publicising the series, Eick and Moore continued to draw on the document 'Battlestar Galactica: Naturalistic Science Fiction or Taking the Opera out of Space Opera'. This was dubbed the series' 'manifesto' by Olmos, who claims that reading it was what got him interested. The document was written as a sales piece, setting out the goals of the show, telling the network what the creative team planned to do with it and explaining how, in their view, it differed from other SF shows. It reads in part like Eick working through his concerns that the title *Battlestar Galactica* would prove off-putting to post-millennial viewers, and Moore working through his issues about *Star Trek*. It states that the series will avoid 'stock characters, techno-double-talk, bumpy-headed aliens, thespian histrionics and empty heroics', and underlines its hand-held, documentary feel.

While it is questionable how far the series really did avoid all of the listed taboos (it certainly had its share of technobabble; Alessandro Juliani recalls that he would frequently write his more technical lines on the set in erasable marker), and indeed how typical these are of telefantasy series in general, it did seem to do a good job of giving the cast and crew a sense of unified purpose. Olmos in particular famously asserted that he would leave if the series included aliens, saying, 'If I ever see a three-eyed or four-eyed creature coming at me, that will be it for Adama – I'm going to faint and he will die of a heart attack!' The actor emphasised instead that the series should keep a dystopian urban feel, saying,

'The only way I can get involved with this ... is if we walk into the world that *Blade Runner* opened, and we continue to walk in through that space'.

Although, as per the conflict with fans before the miniseries aired, Moore's commentaries and interviews continue to be fairly negative regarding the original series, he begins to acknowledge the series' debt to its predecessor in an increasingly positive fashion. Certainly the connection between the two series is still present even in small details; writer Bradley Thompson confesses that he and his co-writer David Weddle kept copies of *The Iliad* and *The Odyssey* in the office to look through for ancient Greek names, continuing the pin-in-the-classical-dictionary tradition of the original, and the painting of the First Cylon War seen in Adama's quarters – supposedly by fictional artist Monclair but actually painted by assistant art director Ken Rabehl – recalls, as well as old lithographs and war paintings, the Cylon War artwork that featured in the introductory section of the telemovie version of 'Experiment in Terra'.

As part of Sky's deal with Universal, the first season actually premiered in the UK, on Sky One, rather than in the USA, where broadcasts followed on the Sci-Fi Channel. While the reimagined series did not gain the hugely impressive ratings of the original series, airing as it did on cable and satellite and being aimed at a narrower audience, it garnered a lot of critical praise from all quarters, Moore commenting, 'It is a continual source of fascination that the show is cited by publications as diverse as the [right-wing] *National Review* and the [left-wing] *New York Times* as not only worthy viewing, but also as supposedly espousing views similar to those found on their own editorial page'. The first season thus achieved a strong international start for the reimagined series.

2: 33

FIRST TRANSMISSION DATE: 18 October 2004 (UK)

WRITER: Ronald D Moore

DIRECTOR: Michael Rymer

CREDITED CAST: Alonso Oyarzun (Socinus)

SYNOPSIS: The Fleet is under siege, with Cylon attacks coming every 33 minutes. After 236 attacks, the pilots and crew are at breaking point from lack of sleep and general stress. Doctor Amarak, a passenger on the civilian craft the *Olympic Carrier*, contacts the President saying that he has important information regarding how the Cylons were able to defeat Colonial defences. This alarms Baltar. When the *Olympic Carrier* fails to make the next jump, and the Cylons also fail to arrive at the 33 minute mark, Head Six implies this is the action of God. Baltar rejects this, at which point the *Olympic Carrier* returns. Baltar, terrified, obeys Head Six's commands to put his fate in the hands of God, and the *Olympic Carrier* is destroyed by the Vipers on suspicion that it has been infiltrated by Cylons, after it triggers a radiological alarm. On Caprica, Helo encounters a woman he thinks is Boomer (actually another Cylon of the same model), and they flee together, observed by a Number Six.

ANALYSIS: '33' is one of the single most praised episodes of 21st Century *Battlestar Galactica*. A large number of writers, actors and production staff cite it as their favourite; it won a Hugo Award for the Best Short-form Dramatic Presentation (2005); and Moore himself says in the podcast for 'Occupation', that it 'was just a standout episode in my mind and one that I think that we've never quite matched in a lot of ways'. Certainly it marks a strong start to the first season.

Counting to None: Storyline and Themes

Following the events of the miniseries, the Fleet now find themselves subjected to repeated Cylon attacks (the one taking place in the pre-credits sequence is the two hundred and thirty-seventh). These are seemingly intended to wear the crew down and get them making mistakes, though at this stage in the series we cannot be sure if this is the true, or only, motivation; the Cylons remain a sinister, unknown and unknowable force, and the attacks may equally be a test, a form of torment, an attempt to force the humans' pace on their way to Earth (as, although the Cylons ultimate goal is to exterminate the humans, the series bible indicates, with echoes of *Galactica 1980*, that the Cylons have an interest in the humans finding Earth as well), or something more metaphysical.[21] The lack of information, and randomness of the events, generates a sense of mounting confusion, tension and panic among both characters and audience. This is intensified by the use of captions indicating how many hours the crew have gone without sleep, while the precise timing of the attacks reinforces the mechanical, robotic side of the Cylons. The Cylons' not attacking for over 45 minutes after the loss of the *Olympic Carrier* furthers the panic rather than alleviates it, raising the questions of why the pause has come then and there, whether or not there is a connection with the *Olympic Carrier*, and what they are planning.

The *Olympic Carrier*'s story, one of the most powerful and grim in the series, develops this theme of random versus seemingly-random action. The disappearance, reappearance and destruction of the ship bearing Doctor Amarak, the man who could possibly betray Baltar's role in the destruction of the Colonies, is not explained within the episode. Is it a power game by Cylons who have, as Head Six postulates, taken over the ship? Is it a coincidence, with Baltar's delusions causing him to interpret it as directed events? Or is it really, as Head Six also states, God's punishment for Baltar's lack of faith, followed by a reward for his renewed confession of belief? It could even be a combination of these – the Cylons acting as the agents of God's will, for instance – or something else entirely: the fact that the Cylons cease pursuit once the *Olympic Carrier* is destroyed would seem to confirm Head Six's assertion that it was the means by which they were tracking the Fleet. We don't even know at the end of the story whether Doctor Amarak really was on the ship, or whether this has all been a Cylon deception to gain access to the President and/or discredit Baltar. The mechanical behaviour of the pilots on stimulants suggests that the incident is, whether by accident or design, blurring the boundary between human and machine. (Even by the end of the series, when the various roles of the political and the metaphysical are explained in greater detail, the question of what precisely happened on the *Olympic Carrier* will not be fully resolved.)

The incident raises another issue besides Baltar's crisis of faith. Although the original intention was to make it plain there were civilians still on the *Olympic Carrier* (the 22 June 2004 draft script explicitly stating that Apollo was to see 'the faces of the civilian passengers ... pressed against the windows, looking right at him'), '33' itself leaves this ambiguous. While Apollo's decision to fire on the ship is taken in the light of his not having seen anyone at the windows, this does not mean there is no-one on board. This fact clearly occurs to the pilots as well, as they are reluctant to fire on the vessel even after the order has been given. The emotional and social repercussions of the decision to follow the order are plain in the Adamas's subsequent exchange, 'I gave the order. That is my responsibility'. – 'I pulled the trigger. That's mine'. In war, all are culpable, and

---

21 An explanation will later be provided in 'The Plan'.

following orders is as deliberate an act as giving them.

This also raises again the question of whether or not humans are worth saving, in confirming Leoben's assertion that they will happily attack each other given the right circumstances. Baltar, notably, is willing to allow a shipful of people to be killed to save his own life and/or reputation. Finally, if Head Six is correct and God is ultimately responsible for the incident, then it does not cast the divine being in a particularly good light either.

Thematically, '33' picks up on the religious imagery introduced in the miniseries. Although Moore has said that the number 33 was picked at random[22], it can also be seen as another subtle example of Christian symbolism in *Battlestar Galactica*, as 33 was the age at which Jesus is traditionally said to have been crucified. The Six on Caprica asks Helo the same question that she, or her cohort, asked the Armistice Officer – 'Are you alive?'– and kisses him, again raising the question of what it is to be alive and sentient. Head Six raises the idea that 'procreation is one of God's commandments', introducing the viewer to the Cylon obsession with reproduction for the first time, and suggests that she and Baltar will have a child together, bringing in the idea that the two species' destinies are genetically and spiritually linked.

Good Hunting: Characterisation and Continuity

The characterisations established in the miniseries are re-established and developed in '33'. Starbuck takes Apollo to task for being 'too nice' as a leader, and, significantly, does so by telling him not to use the greeting 'Be careful out there' with the pilots, but rather, 'Good hunting'. As the former is a catchphrase borrowed from *Hill Street Blues*, and the latter from *Das Boot* (1981), Starbuck is also subtly indicating the fact that the military, unlike the police, are there to fight rather than to protect; a distinction that becomes blurred in later seasons, to dramatic effect. Baltar, meanwhile, hones his ability to hold conversations simultaneously with real people and with Head Six. ('Have you always been able to multitask like this?' she asks him, interested.) Following on from the series of difficult decisions Roslin faced in the miniseries, here she is the one who officially authorises the destruction of the *Olympic Carrier*. Tigh, meanwhile, is not drinking and asserts that the pressure of the past few days has made him feel 'more alive than I have in years', answering, in part, the question of why Adama would keep a disruptive alcoholic on staff as XO: although he comes adrift under normal circumstances, he thrives under crisis conditions.

A deleted scene exists in which Adama and Roslin debate the case of a ship, the *Tauranian Traveler*, that wants to break away from the Fleet. Roslin asserts that the vessel should not be allowed to leave, as losing the people it carries

---

22 On the other hand, Moore has also indicated, in the podcast for 'The Passage', that the number three has a dramatic power for him, which may explain both the 33-minute intervals in this story and the frequent recurrences of threes and 33s in the rest of the series.

would further reduce the population and compromise the Fleet's survival prospects. Adama counters that any captain who thinks he can do better on his own is welcome to try it, but nonetheless orders the alert fighters to make three close passes by the ship, as a hint – bringing up the perennial *Battlestar Galactica* tension between the needs of the many and the rights of the few.

In the draft script, an ultimately deleted exchange in which Adama and Tigh discuss the possibility of dividing the Fleet and making multiple jumps before a later rendezvous, has Tigh raise the objection that without enough cartographic information they could wind up jumping into the heart of a star. This appears to have stemmed from the idea in the miniseries that the Fleet has now jumped past the 'Red Line', beyond which it is unsafe to go. The series bible explains that this is because, while the ships arrive at their destination instantaneously, they must plot the jump on the basis of information that has travelled to them at the speed of light; therefore, the more distant the system to which they are jumping, the more out-of-date the information they have about it.

This episode introduces the running survivor count that will continue (with occasional meaningful interruptions) until the very end of the series. While we will not be remarking on the survivor count unless it is relevant to the story, it is worth noting that the count is 50,298 initially and 47,973 at the end of the episode. The story also establishes a total of 64 ships in the Fleet (only 41 made the rendezvous at Ragnar Anchorage, suggesting that a few stragglers have been picked up since then); and the Cylon ship is referred to as a 'basestar', indicating, again, that this is a recognised alternate term for 'baseship'. Six days have passed since the miniseries, according to the date count regarding Helo's adventures on what the captions describe as 'Cylon-Occupied Caprica'; Helo has been staving off radiation sickness with pills from the medical kit he took from the Raptor in the miniseries. On the *Galactica*, the bruise Tigh sustained when Starbuck hit him during the miniseries has healed and Adama's cut from his fight with Leoben is no longer stitched.

There have been few personnel changes between the miniseries and this episode. The two notable ones are the absence of Boxey (who will appear only once more in the series outside of deleted scenes) and the introduction of the ominously-named pilot Crashdown, Boomer's new ECO (Electronic Countermeasures Officer), who is described by Boomer as a 'refugee from *Triton*' and sports a *Battlestar Triton* shoulder patch.

Despite the fact that the existence of humanoid Cylons is ostensibly a secret, rumours are spreading, with both Starbuck and Crashdown joking about it; Starbuck suggests, presciently, that Boomer is holding up better than anyone else in the squadron because she's a Cylon.

Perpetual September: Original-Series and Outside References

This story again develops the 9/11 references of the miniseries. The sequence where Dualla attempts to trace some people, presumably family or friends, who she believes were lost in the attacks, and posts their pictures on a wall where many others have done likewise, recalls contemporary images of people trying to trace 9/11 survivors and/or putting up impromptu memorials to victims of the attack. We also see, on the wall of the pilots' briefing room, a black-and-white photo of a kneeling man[23], which the pilots all touch for luck as they leave. Later, another copy of the photo appears on *Colonial One*. According to Moore on his blog, this was inspired by a famous picture of firefighters raising the flag at Ground Zero in New York, and was intended to be the Colonial equivalent: 'A snapshot taken in the moment that becomes a symbol of the day they can never forget and of all they had lost'. In a deleted scene, Roslin is presented with her copy of the photo, along with a card that says it was taken on the roof of the Capitol Building on Aerilon during the attack; the inscription on this copy reads 'Lest we Forget', which Moore says is a reference to the John Wayne film *She Wore a Yellow Ribbon* (1949).

Elsewhere, the Gerry Anderson connections in this story are not limited to the new, *Space: 1999*-inspired episode-preview sequence during the opening credits: the story is generally reminiscent of *Captain Scarlet*, which features a mysterious alien force whose goal is apparently to manipulate the humans into causing as much destruction to their own side as possible. The birth that sounds a note of hope at the end of the episode takes place on the *Rising Star*, named after a leisure ship in the original *Battlestar Galactica* series.

I'll Sleep When I'm Dead: Story and Production

The production goes out of its way to bring across the impact of sleep deprivation and stress on the crew. Olmos consulted a sleep deprivation expert to find out the main symptoms, and Michael Rymer (who had been brought in by Eick and Moore deliberately in order to smooth the transition between the miniseries and the episodic series) told the actors to choose one symptom to focus on, to bring home the effects more clearly to the audience. Several cast members also reportedly went without sleep for a time before filming, so as to play their scenes more realistically. Rymer's camerawork, with out-of-focus shots mimicking the way vision blurs when one is tired, highlights the sense of fatigue, and Baltar's memories/visions of his life on Caprica, with their bright, sunlit quality, contrast with the grim greyness of his present life in the Fleet. As a side note, the *Olympic Carrier* ship is in fact based on a rejected design for *Colonial One*. A sequence in the draft script where Cally begins to panic and Tyrol comforts her by saying 'It's gonna be all right' is revised in the final version to have Tyrol saying 'Cally? ... Shut up', showing a less kindly side to the Chief.

The scenes on Caprica are, however, rather weak. As the decision not to kill off Helo was a last-minute one, his scenes with Sharon were written late in the day, and they come across very much as an afterthought. Furthermore, the scene where a Six walks up with a Centurion to watch Helo and Sharon escape, while

---

23 The man in the image is first assistant director Wayne Rose.

effective from a directorial point of view, is highly implausible, as had Helo so much as glanced back he would have seen her. The sequence where Helo is chased by Centurions is perhaps too visually reminiscent of action in *The Terminator* (1984), particularly when a partially-destroyed Centurion tries to attack him.

Caprica sequences aside, though, '33' is a powerful episode by any standards, with its mysterious and impenetrable foe, its unanswered religious and moral questions, and the general sense that the enemy is as much humanity's own failings as any outside force.

3: Water

FIRST TRANSMISSION DATE: 24 October 2004 (UK)

WRITER: Ronald D Moore

DIRECTOR: Marita Grabiak

KNOWN UNCREDITED CAST: Leo Li Chiang (Tattooed Pilot)

SYNOPSIS: On *Galactica*, Boomer awakes from a catatonic state to find herself dripping with water in a maintenance room. She discovers explosives missing from the small-arms locker and tells Chief Tyrol, but is afraid to report the loss to the master-at-arms, as she will have to explain the circumstances that led her to learn they are missing. Before either she or Tyrol can do anything, however, there is an explosion in *Galactica*'s port-side water tanks, which causes a catastrophic venting of water into space. Adama orders a search for nearby planets with water. Boomer locates one, but also discovers a bomb on board her Raptor, and finds that she is unable to speak to tell her new ECO, Crashdown, about the water until she touches the bomb. Returning to *Galactica*, she tells Tyrol to look for a fault in her Raptor, knowing he will find the explosive device. Meanwhile, Baltar stalls on building the Cylon detector, while on Caprica, Helo and Sharon pick up a Colonial Fleet signal and follow it.

ANALYSIS: 'Water' is where the first season really gets going, building on themes established in '33' to deliver strong subtexts (albeit the result more of clever editing than of writerly intention) and pacy dialogue, with good character development and use of symbolism throughout.

The Life Aquatic: Water Imagery and Boomer

Water imagery is present throughout the story. The first thing we see is the water dripping off *Galactica*-Boomer where she sits, as if mesmerised, in the storage area. (Although this is unstated, she has clearly just returned from swimming in the tanks to plant the bombs.) Elsewhere, we see Tigh carefully marking finger-widths on his bottle of alcohol to ration out the contents (later recalled by Adama's suggestion that they celebrate the discovery of water with 'a drink'), and continuous rain during the Caprica sequences where we learn that Helo is running out of radiation pills. Baltar's visions, always a counterpoint to his life in the Fleet, have Head Six speaking to him from a jacuzzi while he stands on his porch looking out over a body of water.

3: WATER

In a deleted scene, rendered in the 4 May 2004 draft of the script as follows, Baltar outlines why the bomb had to be placed within the tank: 'Fluid accretion dynamics. Water's an incompressible medium. Set off an explosion underwater, a shock wave forms. In this case, the shock waves from multiple simultaneous explosions were focused and combined in such a way as to *amplify* the effect. This resulted in enormous pressures which were directed against the exterior hull which had already been weakened by a nuclear explosion'. Tyrol also says, 'I don't know how any human being could survive the pressures inside that tank even wearing a suit'. It is a shame this scene was deleted, as it not only explains why Boomer had to dive into the tank to set up the bombs, but also uses the water imagery to outline the paranoia underlying the narrative, the shockwaves destroying the tank symbolising the accusations and repercussions tearing the Fleet apart.

The story develops the tensions of the previous episode, as paranoia mounts on the *Galactica* about the presence of a potential fifth column in their midst. Roslin voices the fear that once word gets out about the humanoid Cylons, it will lead to witch-hunts where people start accusing each other of being Cylons on the flimsiest pretexts – another reference to real-world reactions following 9/11 as well as to similar historic cases such as the persecution of alleged Communists during the McCarthy era in the USA. These tensions form the heart of the Boomer storyline as, disturbed by having apparently stayed out all night without realising it, she confides her strange situation to Tyrol and states her fear that, having been found in a compromising scenario with no memory of how she got there, people will believe she is a Cylon agent (implying that she herself suspects she is one). Tyrol, for his part, tries to come up with alternative explanations and assures her that he won't let anything happen to her. However, the suggestion that Boomer may be an unwitting traitor will inform their relationship from this point onwards.

Boomer's Cylon side is explored both symbolically and in performance. Her dialogue with Tyrol as they investigate the water tank breaches recalls Baltar's conversations with Head Six, in that it is full of double meanings and personal signals. Cally's smile and headshake as Boomer and Tyrol disappear together into the storage area references an idea shown in the miniseries' deleted scenes that their relationship is the worst kept secret on the ship. The relationship also gives them an appropriate cover for their investigation into what happened, since everyone clearly attributes their secrecy and use of personal codes to their sneaking around to have clandestine sex. This again links Cylons with themes of sex and sexuality; and Boomer's being found dripping wet at the start of the story also provides imagery of sex and birth and, as we will later see, of the Cylon resurrection technology.

While Boomer to some extent takes advantage of Tyrol's closeness to her, ensuring that he and no-one else finds the bomb on her Raptor by suggesting that he, and he alone, fix a problem with her injection pyros, Tyrol is clearly a willing participant in covering for Boomer, claiming he found the bomb during maintenance so as to draw suspicion away from her. As Boomer would have been the victim of the bomb's explosion, the inference most people would make is that someone else put it on the Raptor.

The sequence at the story's climax where Boomer sees that her scans have detected water on the planet but is unable to articulate it until she touches the armed bomb on the ship, is significant. Boomer appears here to be warring against her Cylon side, with her hand drifting toward the detonator as she struggles to say the words; a little time after she reports that she has found water, she is able to switch the bomb off. The bomb is probably there to detonate if Crashdown spots water first, and Boomer groping for it is her Cylon side attempting to prevent her human side from getting the better of it and revealing that there is water – a theory supported by a deleted scene recorded for 'The Plan'. This is the first indication that the Boomer/Sharon models can, and will, fight their Cylon heritage to side with the humans.

Roslin Rising: Politics and the Adamas

Elsewhere, the repercussions from the *Olympic Carrier* incident are still being felt. In particular, Lee Adama is having nightmare flashbacks to the event and holding conversations about the philosophy of leadership with his father: Lee argues that as leaders, they have a responsibility to question their own decisions, whereas his father says that leaders do what they have to do, and live with the result for the rest of their lives. At the end of the episode, Lee repeats his father's position to Roslin, and she tells him about an incident where President Adar made a decision to send in some marines on Aerilon (the events are alluded to rather than discussed in detail, but it is implied to be some kind of well-known crisis); she says that Adar considered this a mistake but never admitted so publicly.

These discussions foreshadow future political events in the series. The theme of leaders having to take difficult decisions and facing negative repercussions will recur again and again, particularly for Roslin, although the story about Adar most closely prefigures events in Tigh's storyline. We also see here the continuation of Lee Adama's slow attraction toward politics and away from the military, as he finds himself drawn toward Roslin as an oppositional voice to his father's and she encourages this attraction, asking him to serve as her personal military advisor. Although the series still focuses on the conflict between Lee and Commander Adama, it is hard to see Lee as a conventionally heroic figure, as he appears to spend most of his time searching for a direction. There are also sexual overtones to his attraction to Roslin, in an echo of the abandoned 'May-December romance' storyline. The distinction between civilian and military forces, established in '33', is also reiterated by Adama: 'There's a reason why you separate the military and the police. One fights the enemies of the state, the other saves and protects the people. When the military does both … then the enemies of the state tend to become the people'. This reminds the audience of the civilian-military tension throughout the series.

3: WATER

Join the Army, Be a Man: Character Development

Following on from this idea that not all the 'military' characters are devoted to a militaristic ideology, we learn in this episode that Gaeta is not a career soldier; he studied genetics at university and plans to use his military service to get a grant to allow him to do graduate work on this subject. This may provide a background for his later difficulties in dealing with the hardships on the Fleet, even though here he is sufficiently imbued with military protocol that, when Roslin asks him to guess at the cause of the explosions, he hesitates to do so until Adama gives him a direct order. His assignment as Baltar's assistant first shows his tendency to be attracted on a personal level to charismatic intelligent male leaders; and Baltar's attempts to get rid of him also indicate that he has a habit of being attracted to people who will take advantage of, or even betray, his idealistic principles. Baltar, in turn, is shown to simultaneously enjoy and be discomfited by others' attempts to hero-worship him. He, for his part, turns out to be rather good at poker. This parallels Baltar's personal situation, in which he has to find a plausible reason why he cannot now detect Cylons in the Fleet when he was able to identify Doral so quickly in the miniseries (he pleads a lack of physical resources), and also provides a pretext for the start of his infatuation with Starbuck.

The theme of developing relationships and attractions on the Fleet is mirrored elsewhere in the story, as Billy attempts, with hilarious ineptitude, to develop a relationship with Dualla, and as Helo and Caprica-Boomer, in the only really noteworthy development in the Caprica storyline this episode, start getting downright flirtatious with each other. Adama insists on full protocol ceremonies every time Roslin comes aboard *Galactica*, which she puts up with because she thinks it makes him happy; then Lee lets her know that Adama is doing it because he thinks it will make her feel more presidential, in an amusing comedy of manners. (In a deleted scene, this is elaborated on slightly, with Adama revealing to Tigh and Apollo that he wants her to feel presidential not only as a courtesy, but to keep her from giving the military too much grief.) The two leaders also begin what will be a series-long bonding over a shared love of literature, as Adama gives Roslin a book; its title, *Dark Day*, being symbolic of recent events.

Continuity and Worldbuilding

On the continuity front, we learn that *Galactica* has a near-perfect water recycling system, giving them enough water to last for several years, but that other ships in the Fleet do not and thus have to bleed supplies off the flagship. This makes sense, as a military ship might be expected to spend long periods in space, out of reach of supply lines, while civilian craft would not necessarily be constructed to do so. Raptors, rather than Vipers, are sent out to look for planets with water, fitting with the idea that they are essentially scout ships. The pilots are now gambling for alcohol as well as cubits, and Baltar is also able to put up items of clothing as a stake (winning a new jacket), as the economy on the Fleet begins a slide toward barter. Caprica-Sharon has a Raptor, suggesting that, with Boomer being a member of the Colonial Fleet, the Cylons were able to send out others of her model to spread sedition and commandeer equipment.

The episode continues the references to the original series. The plotline itself, along with mentions of civilian unrest due to rationing and Baltar's own fear that they will run out of food as well as water, all recall the original series' stories about lack of resources. Roslin's predecessor, President Adar, who was mentioned in the miniseries, has the same name as the President in 'Saga of a Star World', and, although cigars are not called 'fumarellos', they are said to be made of 'fumarello leaf', reconciling old and new series terminology. Finally, Baltar's Cylon detector has some conceptual resemblances to the genetic testing system from the original series episode 'The Man with Nine Lives', and raises similar issues about the ethical problems of results disclosure.

Story and Production

From a production point of view, the episode now opens with a textual preamble about the development and motivation of the Cylons, before the recap and pre-credits sequence. This conceptually resembles the preamble at the start of the miniseries, but abbreviates the Cylon backstory and briefly explains the presence of human-like Cylons and sleeper agents. Director Marita Grabiak, who is also known for work on *Lost*, *Firefly*, *Angel*, *Buffy the Vampire Slayer*, *Alias* and *ER*, continues Rymer's technique of using the lighting on the ship to add to the sense of tension, giving the sequences on the decks a grainy, overexposed, headache-inducing look.

In terms of story development, *The Official Companion* indicates that Moore originally toyed with the idea of focusing the episode on a paper shortage, which seems a strange one (although the idea will return in 'The Passage' in a quip by Tigh about how the Fleet survivors have stopped eating paper due to a just such a shortage). This story is particularly noteworthy for having a large number of deleted or edited-down scenes. Of the excised material, only a couple of scenes involving Boxey would have contributed much of substance, indicating that the child is developing a role as a black marketeer. However, given the actor's poor performance, they also suggest a reason why the character and related storylines were axed.

Although the cuts improve the story, making it tighter and requiring the audience to deduce what exactly is going on, Moore was unhappy with them at the time, saying 'I was always uncomfortably aware of the "cheats" involved; that is, dropped scenes, the internal cuts to scenes that made a hash of some of the logic I tried to lay out, the half-expressed thoughts, the missing emotional beats, etc'. By the time of his commentary for 'Razor', however, Moore would be acknowledging that deleting such scenes can indeed improve a story, as, although they are not there, the actors have them in mind as they perform other material – and this is of course also true for the writer and production team.

Lee's flashback, in the 4 May 2004 draft of the script, has him seeing the faces of the people he killed on the *Olympic Carrier*, but this was changed to a less melodramatic sequence of him remembering the moment he pressed the trigger, in keeping with the ambiguity in the final filmed version of '33' as to who, if anyone, was on board.

The 4 May 2004 draft is very similar to the story as recorded, with most of the omitted material surviving as deleted scenes. One noteworthy difference is the draft's inclusion of an early sequence where Gaeta looks slightly askance at Baltar's jacket, which is stated to be too small for him, and Baltar explains that it's borrowed – which, taken with his later putting that garment up as a stake in the poker game, indicates that he's not above gambling with other people's property. Also noteworthy is a line ultimately removed from Roslin's discussion with Adama about riots breaking out on the Fleet, which has Adama saying 'Fifteen people throwing high-priced wine bottles is not a riot'. If left in, this would have detracted from the story by suggesting first that resources are not all that scarce for certain elite members of the Fleet, and secondly that Adama is perfectly happy to allow that situation to continue. Also in the draft, Dualla at one point addresses the *Virgon Express* as the *Tauranian Traveler*, suggesting that the troublesome vessel from the deleted scenes of '33' was to have made a return appearance.

'Water' may thus suggest a writing and production team who are still experimenting with the format, characters and narrative style of the series, but it is, if anything, a stronger episode for it, with plotlines and themes neatly dovetailing while not talking down to the audience.

BY YOUR COMMAND: VOL 2

4: Bastille Day

FIRST TRANSMISSION DATE: 24 November 2004 (UK)

WRITER BY: Toni Graphia

DIRECTOR: Allan Kroeker

CREDITED CAST: Connor Widdows (Boxey); Richard Hatch (Tom Zarek); Alonso Oyarzun (Socinus); Pat Adrien Dorval (Wilkens); Ron Selmour (Seaborne); Matthew Bennett (Aaron Doral); Brent Stait (Mason); Graham Young (Marine #1); Curtis Hicks (Marine #2); Colby Johannson (Flat-Top)

KNOWN UNCREDITED CAST: Scott Nicholson (Starke/Stunt Con #6); Guy Bews (Stunt Guard #1); Lou Bollo (Stunt Guard #2); Duane Dickinson (Stunt Guard #3); Tony Morelli (Stunt Con #1); Ernest Jackson (Stunt Con #2); Gaston Howard (Stunt Con #3); Scott Atea (Stunt Con #4); Simon Burnett (Stunt Con #5); Gerald Paets (Stunt Con #7) ; Charles Andre (Stunt Marine); Dave Hospes (Lee Adama Stunt Double); Leo Li Chiang (Tattooed Pilot)

SYNOPSIS: The Fleet needs to recover the water they have found, and Adama suggests offering the men on board the prison ship *Astral Queen* the chance to earn their freedom through working on this task. Apollo, accompanied by Billy, Dualla and Cally, goes to the ship to request volunteers, but they are taken hostage during a rebellion led by noted political prisoner Tom Zarek. Adama, Tigh and Starbuck plan a military operation to retake the ship, while Apollo endeavours to talk Zarek round to a peaceful solution, realising over the course of their conversation that Zarek in fact desires martyrdom at the hands of the military. As the Marines storm the ship, Apollo convinces Zarek that political negotiation is the wiser, and braver, path, and the standoff is concluded with the prisoners taking charge of the ship, and agreeing to organise the workforce for the water detail. Adama confronts Baltar over his failure to build a Cylon detector; Baltar, prompted by Head Six, requests, and receives, a nuclear warhead in order to complete the project.

ANALYSIS: 'Bastille Day' develops concepts drawn from the original-series story 'The Gun on Ice Planet Zero' to explore further the political tensions of the reimagined series, and to introduce one of its most memorable and ambiguous characters, Tom Zarek.

4: BASTILLE DAY

Long Walk to Freedom: Tom Zarek and His Ambitions

The role of Zarek was given to the original series' Apollo, Richard Hatch; an actor who still looks very good for his age and exudes enormous charisma. (It is ironic that his first scene is with the still-rather-uncharismatic Lee 'Apollo' Adama.) Zarek inspires not only the loyalty of the prisoners but also that of at least one guard (who assists in their escape). He is described in the 12 May 2004 draft script as 'handsome to a fault'. Zarek is a skilled political artist, who in his conversations with Lee is capable of reading between the lines to pick up on the tension between Adama and Roslin, and, later, to correctly interpret Adama's request for negotiation as a bid to buy time to get his men into position. Roslin characterises him as someone with a keen understanding of the value of image, who refused to give in to President Adar's demand that he apologise for his actions and forswear violence, even to gain a full pardon, although she herself has a stake in presenting Zarek as a negative figure.

Zarek also seems to put his political activities above his followers' lives, courting martyrs to the cause, although it is uncertain how much of this is motivated by idealism and how much by narcissism. He appears to weep when the hostage crisis ends, but the reason behind his tears remains unexplained. It might be relief at the end of the standoff, regret at having had to make concessions and deny himself his moment of martyrdom, or a sudden recognition of the burden of responsibility that is now incumbent upon him, or perhaps all of the above.

Zarek and his actions are controversial from the start. While he is said by Billy to have been fighting the oppression of Sagittarons by the other 11 colonies, Dualla, who disagrees with his cause and methods, reminds Billy that she herself is a Sagittaron. It is not insignificant that the two initial champions of Zarek's cause, Billy and Lee, are Capricans from a privileged background Zarek himself picks up on, implying that Lee is a bourgeois liberal who will gladly read his book at university but is less tolerant when the oppressed actually fight back.

The 12 May 2004 draft script has a line from Billy stating that no-one ever proved that Zarek was actually responsible for the crime for which he was imprisoned, namely blowing up a building. Lee's reaction to Zarek's tactics might have been attributable to him believing Zarek to be a non-violent revolutionary who was framed by the government. Without it, however, it seems that Lee is aware of Zarek's terrorist activities and objects simply because he himself is now on the receiving end. The cut line also would have added an interesting twist to Roslin's story about how Zarek refused Adar's offer of a pardon on condition that he 'apologise and give up violence': in other words, to gain his pardon, Zarek would have had to admit he was legitimately convicted when that was not in fact the case.

Although Zarek is correct in arguing that Roslin's rule is technically illegitimate, he disregards the fact that to call an election at this juncture would throw the Fleet into chaos. His reference to 'the first day of a new era' recalls both Pol Pot's Year Zero and Germany's *Stunde Null* ('zero hour', referring to the establishment of the new nation in the wake of World War II). Mason, a prisoner who attempts to rape Cally, appears to represent Zarek's dark side; someone who wants attention and will turn violent when he doesn't get it. Zarek defends Mason by saying that society is to blame for his actions, but he is nonetheless excusing abusive behaviour.

The Zarek storyline also shows up Roslin's weaknesses as a politician. Although at the start of the story she is anxious to ensure the prisoners' rights (as in the miniseries, when she stopped the captain of the *Astral Queen* from throwing his charges overboard to save resources), by the end of it she is taking a hard line, in an indication that her political positions may be situational. She clearly recognises in Zarek a potential rival for power, and this informs the way she talks about him. She confides the truth about her illness to Lee, but insists on keeping it secret from the others on the grounds that she doesn't want the Fleet to lose hope through the news. This reflects her understanding, throughout the hostage crisis, that public opinion is a strong political weapon. Seen in the company of other politicians, then, Roslin's ruthless side comes to the fore.

Shoot First, Negotiate Later: The Military

The military, however, are not much better, with Adama apparently believing the prisoners irredeemable, even after his son points out that the ones aboard the *Astral Queen* were being taken to parole hearings. (The fact that the *Astral Queen* was not designed for long journeys has also, it is implied, exacerbated the situation among the prisoners.) Lee, meanwhile, takes the position that the prisoners should be allowed to earn their freedom through hard work, which, although more humane, is slightly sanctimonious and, as the hostage crisis indicates, does not take into account the interests of the prisoners.

The theme of conflict between the civilian and military worldviews is here developed through the father and son tension between the Adamas. Although Lee is continuing his slow attraction to politics, ultimately being the one to negotiate the settlement with the prisoners, he still attempts to exist in both worlds, as illustrated by an exchange where his father tells him, 'Every man has to decide for himself which side he's on', he replies, 'I didn't know we were picking sides', and Adama says, 'That's why you haven't picked one yet'. However, Adama also warns that living in two worlds is impossible, telling him, 'I have nothing to say to the personal representative of the President', then, when Lee replies, 'I'm still your head pilot', adding, 'I have nothing to say to him, either'. Zarek echoes this in a piece of dialogue added by Moore, in which he first likens Lee to Apollo, son of Zeus, a Lord of Kobol who was both a warrior and a healer, but then states that no human being can incorporate such contradictory principles, and that Lee must choose between them. Lee's indecisiveness thus serves as an indicator of the way in which the Fleet is becoming polarised between contradictory principles.

Other ongoing storylines are also developed. Tigh's alcoholism is presented here as common knowledge, with Cally visibly trying not to laugh (and failing) as he conducts a meeting while drunk. In an ironic counterpoint, Tigh then berates Boomer for keeping a secret 'everyone knows'– her affair with Tyrol, naturally, although an unwitting reference to her status as a Cylon agent can be inferred by the audience as well – and tells her to stop it for the good of ship discipline. Finally, Starbuck confronts Tigh over his flaws in a scene reversing their exchange at the end of the miniseries, during which she admits that she has failings and Tigh counters that the difference between them is that whereas his flaws are personal, hers are professional: as shown early in the episode, Tigh, whatever his failures as a human being, is capable of acting as a competent XO even when drunk, whereas Starbuck's mixing of her personal and professional lives is destructive to all concerned.

Elsewhere, Billy's attempts to woo Dualla go from farce to black comedy, as his scheme for spending more time with her leads to them being taken hostage on the prison ship (Dualla is impressively sanguine about all this); and Starbuck has evidently realised that Baltar is interested in her and willing to encourage the interest, though she is still clearly unhappy about his beating her at cards in the previous story. Boxey makes his one and only appearance in the episodic series, getting in a good line when Tigh asks, 'Where's your mommy?' and he replies, 'Dead. Where's yours?'

Effective Detector: The Cylons and Baltar

Another theme is articulated in the discussion between the two Cylon observers on Caprica. Six expresses regret for Caprica's destruction, while Doral argues that the humans would have destroyed themselves anyway (and it has to be said that events on the Fleet are not doing much to counter the Cylon image of humans as brutal and id-driven). When Six says, 'We're the children of humanity. That makes them our parents in a sense', Doral replies that parents have to die so that children can progress; an idea that, it transpires, forms the basis for the human-Cylon conflict.

Baltar, for his part, attempts to prevaricate again when Adama confronts him over his failure to produce a Cylon detector, but Head Six, realising that Baltar cannot keep bluffing the Commander, sets him on the road to developing one, even having him demand (and get) a nuclear warhead from Adama to form part of the system. The way Callis plays the scene suggests that he really does need the warhead for the detector, and that his subsequent explanation is in fact the truth, as he reasons what role radioactive materials play in the process. It still, however, remains ambiguous as to whether Head Six is his subconscious working through the process of constructing the detector, a Cylon agent manipulating him into doing their bidding, or the instrument of a plan by an unknown outside force; or, indeed, all three.

Crime and Punishment: Continuity and Worldbuilding

We learn a few details about the political and justice systems on the Colonies.

Hard labour is apparently an accepted punishment for prisoners (in an early indication that Colonial society has some rather illiberal aspects), and they have fixed-term elections and a pantheon that appears so far to be virtually identical to that of the ancient Greeks. Zarek's remark, 'If we're not free then we're no different than Cylons', is either an allusion to the Cylons' previous status as slaves, or else a disparagement of the enemy as robots lacking in individuality.

As well as the links to 'The Gun on Ice Planet Zero', this episode brings up Lee Adama's interest in legal matters, paralleling the fact that the original-series Apollo studied law and in 'Murder on the *Rising Star*' acted as a defence attorney. Zarek's use of the phrase 'the holocaust' to describe the destruction of the Colonies is a link to the original series' use of the term as well as its wider resonances in the contemporary world. The image of the prisoners in magenta jumpsuits recalls those of modern American prisoners in transport sporting bright orange uniforms. Tigh wishes Starbuck 'Good hunting' when she goes off with the marines as a sniper, in another association of this phrase with the military faction on the Fleet.

Hatching the Plot: Writing and Production

The story was written by Toni Graphia, co-executive producer on *Battlestar Galactica* between 2004 and 2006. She and staff writer Carla Robinson came up with the name 'Tom Zarek'. They had wanted a religious-sounding first name for the character and originally considered 'Peter', but the change to 'Thomas' – necessitated, according to Graphia, by the legal department's objections to their first choice – is an improvement, as that name carries connotations of doubt and questioning. Moore has said that he had wanted a prison-ship story from the outset, and had written the reference to the *Astral Queen* into the miniseries as a deliberate set-up. Cally was originally intended to die in the episode, but survived instead as the writing team were wary of portraying female characters as victims.

Alan Kroeker, the director, was a veteran of *Star Trek*: *Deep Space Nine*, *Voyager* and *Enterprise*, as well as of *Roswell* and *Firefly*. He contributes a number of clever touches, such as the use of multiple shots of prison doors opening to convey a sense of the scale of the *Astral Queen*. The episode was filmed partly at the Port Mann power station in Vancouver, and is the only one in the first season to reflect the original, ultimately too costly idea of having a number of stories set on different ships in the Fleet.

Richard Hatch was first approached by Moore at a convention and asked if he would be willing to play a role in the reimagined series, to which he responded that he would if the part was right. He says that he subsequently accepted the role of Zarek without reading the script or discussing the fee, simply on the strength of Moore's description of the character as a kind of Nelson Mandela figure (which is perhaps not the most accurate real-world analogy). Although Jamie Bamber (not unsurprisingly) expressed initial misgivings that casting his predecessor was simply a gimmicky in-joke, it proved to be an inspired move, Hatch's presence providing a bridge with the original series and its fan community. Hatch said of the role, 'I felt that although his character was very idealistic, he obviously had multiple agendas going on inside of him in terms of what he believes and what he is willing to fight and die for'.

The story contains a notable continuity change: in the miniseries, the *Astral Queen* is implied to be a liner transporting in its hold 500 prisoners *en route* to a penal station, but by this episode, the vessel has become a purpose-built prison ship, the number of prisoners has risen to 1,500 and their destination has changed to parole hearings. The inconsistencies are covered by having Paul Campbell redub his lines from the miniseries for the recap clip, with suitable alterations made. Zarek's prison number, 893893, is a multiple of 47, the repetition of which number in *Battlestar Galactica* apparently continues an in-joke originating with *Star Trek*'s writing team[24]. In visual terms, the sharp-eyed may spot that the *Astral Queen* model is the same as that of the prison barge in the original series.

Differences between the 12 May 2004 draft and the final version include a note in the character list reading 'Leoben – OMITTED; Doral – INCLUDED', suggesting Doral's part was originally taken by Leoben. Removed from Kara's briefing to the pilots were a couple of too-jokey lines in which she clowns around with Boxey. More problematically, a line where Lee refers to Zarek's organisation as the Sagittaron Freedom Movement was cut, meaning that Dualla's later reference to 'the SFM' is unexplained on screen. There are also a couple of interesting changes in stage directions: Tyrol and Cally were originally to have responded to the sight of Tigh's drunkenness with polite smiles rather than covert humour; and, in the sequence where Six is ranting at Baltar, it was stated that 'for a brief moment Six suddenly seems twisted', possibly implying that she may be demonic.

'Bastille Day' highlights the themes of polarisation, freedom versus constraint, and the danger of secret-keeping, as well as continuing the production team's referencing of, but differentiating themselves from, the original *Battlestar Galactica* series.

---

[24] The origins of the in-joke apparently lie in the fact that one of the *Star Trek: The Next Generation* writing team attended Pomona College, California, where a mathematician wrote a 'joke proof' in 1964 that all numbers were equal to 47, leading to the formation of a '47 society' for the promotion of 47 as the perfect random number.

5: Act of Contrition

FIRST TRANSMISSION DATE: 8 November 2004 (UK)

WRITERS: Bradley Thompson & David Weddle

DIRECTOR: Rod Hardy

CREDITED CAST: Lorena Gale (Elosha); Donnelly Rhodes (Doctor Cottle); Jill Teed (Sergeant Hadrian); Tobias Mehler (Zak Adama); Colby Johannson (Flat Top); Bill Meilen (Caprica Cleric); Bodie Olmos (Constanza/Hot Dog); Luciana Carro (Katraine/Kat); Terry Chen (Perry/Chuckles)

SYNOPSIS: An accident on the *Galactica*'s hangar deck kills or wounds a large number of pilots, necessitating the training of new recruits, or 'nuggets'. Starbuck is tasked with this assignment, which leads her to recall her relationship with Zak Adama, and how, as his trainer, she passed him in basic flight training despite knowing he was unready. Consequently she is particularly hard on her charges, finally refusing to teach them. Adama finds out the truth about her having passed Zak, and angrily orders Starbuck to reinstate the trainees to flight status. When a training session is interrupted by a Cylon attack, a suicidal Starbuck attempts to take on the entire Cylon patrol by herself, but trainee Hot Dog comes to her rescue. Starbuck's Viper is damaged in the attack, and she crash-lands on a nearby moon. Meanwhile, President Roslin opts for an alternative cancer therapy, intending to take a drug called Chamalla extract; and on Caprica, Helo and Sharon find a bunker stocked with food and medical supplies.

ANALYSIS: This episode is the first to be contributed by David Weddle and Bradley Thompson, a writing team that will become crucial to the series' development, and the first to mark the start of a *de facto* two-part story (though it is not officially designated as such). It is a Starbuck-focused adventure picking up on the backstory established in the miniseries of her relationship with the Adama family.

Never Marry a Pilot: Starbuck, Zak and the Adamas

The story was conceived, right from the very first draft dated 30 April 2004, as a nonlinear narrative loosely linked to a series of regressive/nesting flashbacks experienced by Starbuck as she fights to regain control of her damaged Viper. The flashbacks start with a recall of the events following Flat Top's thousandth landing, then go further back to the events surrounding Zak's funeral, and then to Starbuck's relationship with Zak. Somewhat to its detriment, however, this sequence of flashbacks is also intercut with events Starbuck could not have seen (for instance Roslin's visit to Doctor Cottle, Lee's conversation with his father, and the unfolding story on Cylon-Occupied Caprica). Early drafts had the pilot's face being obscured during the 'contemporary' scenes, meaning that the viewer would not have learnt it was Starbuck, and understood the context of the flashbacks, until the final sequence; this conceit wouldn't have added much to the story. The fact that Starbuck is seen to eject from the Viper twice might be taken as a suggestion that what at first appears to be a 'contemporary' sequence is actually itself a flashback, but as there is no other evidence to support this, we have to assume that it is a directorial/narrative conceit done for dramatic reasons.

The focus of the story is Starbuck, and the destructive consequences of her inability (observed by Tigh in 'Bastille Day') to keep her personal and professional lives separate. The fact that she was Zak's lover as well as his flight instructor led to her clearing him as a pilot when her professional instincts told her not to. This incident now causes her to go too far the other way with the new pilots, driving them too hard out of guilt over Zak's death. There is a deep irony when Adama tells Starbuck, 'Just give them the attention and professionalism you gave my son, and they'll be one hell of a squadron'. A deleted scene exists where Lee tries to get Starbuck to talk about her grief over the accident on the hangar deck, and she refuses, indicating her inability to work through tragic events and move on. This will be seen more and more as a key aspect of her character's motivation as the series explores her background.

However, we also see the positive side of this. When Hot Dog breaks formation to try to save her from her own self-destructive impulses as she faces down eight Cylon Raiders alone, Starbuck acts to defend and save the new pilot. Tigh's complimentary remark after Starbuck resumes training the new pilots – 'I'll be damned. What's got into Starbuck? She actually sounds like a real instructor for a change' – also indicates that Starbuck is capable of great things when she is able to focus her energies in an appropriate direction.

The 30 April 2004 draft opened with Kara having an alcohol-fuelled casual sexual encounter with Lee, rendered awkward when she cries out Zak's name at the point of climax. This was mercifully dropped by the 17 May draft, but will later re-emerge, more successfully, in 'Kobol's Last Gleaming', as the basis for her encounter with Baltar.

Adama's finding out about Starbuck's role in Zak's death is also a key development in their relationship. At the start of the story, Adama tells Starbuck, 'I love you like a daughter' (and since she was engaged to Zak at the time of his death, there is also a loose familial connection between them), and they are familiar enough with each other that she can tell embarrassing stories about him in the presence of his son. When he learns, accidentally, about her responsibility for Zak's death, however, he says 'Walk out of this cabin while you still can', His grief over his son's death and, presumably, his anger over Starbuck's lack of professionalism undermine his feelings toward her. The intercutting of her free-fall through the atmosphere with the events taking place in the episode draws a parallel between her loss of control over her Viper and her despair at being cut loose by Adama. The rift between them will clearly influence what happens in the second part of the story.

The question of who is ultimately responsible for Zak's death is resolved, in *An Inspector Calls* fashion, by pinning the blame on three people: Adama for pushing Zak too far, Starbuck for passing him against her better judgment, and, under the surface, Zak himself for having an unrealistic desire to be a pilot to please his father rather than standing up to him, as Lee is beginning to do, and insisting on an alternate career.

Requiem: Themes of Death

The themes of death are echoed in the episode's subplots. The irascible chain-smoking ship's medic Doc Cottle is introduced in this story, as Roslin begins to face up to her own fatal illness. The revelation that Roslin's mother died of a similar cancer, and that Roslin was thus more than usually irresponsible in letting five years pass between scans, suggests that Roslin was afraid of the possibility of death. Cottle's quip 'For what it's worth ... I would seriously consider prayer', when Roslin inquires about alternative treatments, proves an ironic foreshadowing of the fact that her choice of the Chamalla extract treatment will turn out to have strong religious implications for the Fleet.

The celebration for Flat Top also shows the more fatalistic side of the military culture, as the cart in which he is wheeled about looks disturbingly like a coffin, and we get yet another sequence involving flag-draped coffins subsequently. The preparations Starbuck and Apollo make for the celebration involve the accidental spilling of red paint, symbolising blood, as they write the numeral '1000' on a pilot's helmet. The number of dead during the Flat Top incident is put at 13 (an unlucky number) and the number of wounded at seven (a lucky number, presumably in that they are still alive). Helo and Sharon, who are now on Day 14 of their stay on Cylon-Occupied Caprica, comment on the fact that someone built and stocked a shelter, then died before they could use it, although the sight of Six wafting by in the rain, keeping an eye on them, suggests that the Cylons may have established it for them to find, and left the signal to draw them there, for as yet unknown reasons.

Flattening Flat Top: Continuity and Worldbuilding

In terms of story development, the Fleet is still occupied with 'water manoeuvres', following on from the previous episode. Baltar's card games with the pilots are evidently becoming a regular occurrence, and Gaeta is now taking part and apparently enjoying them, suggesting Baltar is a bad influence on the officer. We learn that Adama served on the *Atlantia* as a Viper pilot, that he and Starbuck have both served on the *Galactica* together for over two years,

5: ACT OF CONTRITION

and (in the sequence where Starbuck meets her charges for the first time) that *Galactica*, unlike her original-series incarnation, does not have a flight simulator. This episode also marks the first actual named appearance of *Galactica*'s master-at-arms, Hadrian (referred to, though not by name, in 'Water'), who will play a key role in 'Litmus'. Various drafts of the story have Hadrian playing a larger role, and a deleted scene was filmed in which she questions Tyrol about why he personally investigated Boomer's report of a fault and found the bomb, foreshadowing sequences in 'Litmus' in which she investigates the events of 'Water', but not really in keeping with the rest of the story here.

The episode also provides a few details about the pilots' rituals and customs, chiefly that there are particular ceremonies involved in completing one's thousandth landing. The little call-and-response ditty the pilots sing during the celebration is rather racist from a Cylon point of view, and contains a previously-unheard slang term for them, 'tin cans'; given its reference to 'three little Cylons in the air', like the three-man Cylon craft seen in the original series and 'Razor', it probably dates from the Cylon War. The amusing subtext that the pilot's call-signs have ironic aspects also starts to become evident, as Flat Top is, effectively, flattened, and Hot Dog is not only a daredevil, but also a bit of a wiener and, as later events will show, an unlikely success with women.

As is still very much the norm at this stage, the story owes much to the original series, in particular the serial 'Lost Planet of the Gods'. Both feature Starbuck teaching a squadron of new pilots following the unexpected removal from service of a number of old ones, and Starbuck letting his/her personal feelings get in the way of being able to do the best job possible as an instructor. The training sequences are very similar to those in 'Lost Planet of the Gods', including having a manoeuvre interrupted by a Cylon attack, and having one of the students disobey orders and return to aid Starbuck. Both stories have similar themes about the legitimacy of leadership and when it is right to follow and when to disobey. In both series, Starbuck was involved with one of Adama's children (Athena in the original, Zak in the reimagined one). This story also sets up a multi-episode arc loosely based on *Galactica 1980*'s 'The Return of Starbuck'. The 'tin cans' slang term for Cylons also appears in the original series episode 'The Young Lords'.

Writing and Production

The story was heavily based on the series bible's entry for Starbuck. The decision to frame it around Starbuck crash-landing her Viper was taken by Moore, who also wrote the flashback scene featuring Adama's first meeting with Thrace. According to Thompson in *The Official Companion*, '[Originally] we planned to do the attrition phase of the Battle of Britain and show the *Galactica*'s pilots repeatedly getting shot up by the Cylons and dying'. However, as this proved too expensive to film, Moore suggested instead an incident based on one which happened aboard the USS *Forrestal* during the Vietnam War, in which the accidental detonation of a missile led to 132 deaths and 62 injuries (though it is worth pointing out that a similar incident does also occur on Ragnar Anchorage in the miniseries, where a munitions shell accidentally falls and explodes, albeit with no fatalities).

Writers Weddle and Thompson had worked with Moore before, on *Star Trek: Deep Space Nine*, and Moore says in the podcast for 'The Hand of God' that they were two of the first people he considered involving in the series. He elaborates in the podcast for 'Someone to Watch Over Me' that the pair came to a preview screening of the miniseries at the Directors' Guild of America, and got to talking with him at the event about how much they enjoyed it, leading to his inviting them to work on the series. Thompson is an amateur military historian with a strong focus on tactics and jargon, while Weddle has an interest in the work of Sam Peckinpah, having written a biography of the director called *If They Move, Kill 'Em*. Both of these interests fit with the ethos and, in part, visual style of the show.

Director Rod Hardy, an Australian whose previous credits include episodes of original-series producer, director and scriptwriter Donald Bellisario's naval series *JAG*, continues reimagined *Battlestar Galactica*'s interesting use of lighting; he shoots the flashback-within-a-flashback to Zak's funeral in washed-out colours, giving it an unreal, bleak look, where the flashback-within-a-flashback-within-a-flashback of Kara and Zak making love is lit in rich dark colours and blues, giving it a cool sensuality.

Changes between the draft and final versions are mostly fairly superficial. As well as the ones discussed above, they include a couple of different iterations to the conversation where the pilots play cards with Baltar and Gaeta. In the 17 May 2004 draft, Crashdown repeats a rumour that the Cylons blew up the water tanks, and Gaeta, picking up on the logic, says 'That means the Cylons know we'll need more water. Then all they'll have to do is–', implying that the Cylons will stake out planets with known water resources. In the 20 May draft, Crashdown responds to Gaeta's saying that even if a Cylon detector existed, he wouldn't talk about it, with 'You just did', whereas in the final version, Baltar quickly comes to Gaeta's rescue by diverting Crashdown onto another line of conversation. In the 30 April draft, when Zak says to Starbuck that he wants to ask her a question, instead of telling him straight away about his test results, she responds 'Yes, Zak … you were my first …', and in the 17 May draft this has changed to 'Yes, Zak, you're the worst I've ever had. The absolute worst in the history of the worst'. Early versions of the Cottle and Roslin scene have Roslin being much more aggressive, demanding that Cottle give her the treatment she wants, and also have Cottle ranting about how, given the rough-and-ready nature of medicine on a battlestar, she is lucky he has cancer-treating drugs available.

A very significant change, however, comes in the 30 April draft. This contains a brief scene where Sharon and Helo eat in the restaurant (described as a 'diner' at this stage), and the Bob Dylan-written and Jimi Hendrix-covered

5: ACT OF CONTRITION

song 'All Along the Watchtower' comes on the jukebox, at which point an extended stage direction reads:

And yes, gentle reader, it really is 'All Along the Watchtower' that's coming out of that jukebox (or at least something iconic and classic from American pop culture that is instantly recognisable to the audience). Not 'our version' of a classic, but the real deal ... How can these people on another planet be listening to Jimi Hendrix? What are we saying? Just as the audience begins to realise that the world of Galactica that they thought they knew may not be what it seems and just as they begin to wonder if we're out of our collective minds, the first hint of the true answer is heard: ELOSHA (prelap) 'All of this has happened before. And all of it will happen again'.[25]

The prelap leads into a scene where Elosha is advising Roslin to take comfort in those words. This indicates that the use of 'All Along the Watchtower' as a signifier of the circularity of events was present in the series from a very early stage.

Other things to watch out for in the screened version include Starbuck's mention of a manoeuvre called the Thorch Weave, possibly based on the real-life defensive manoeuvre the Thatch Weave, said to have been developed in WWII by US naval commander John S Thatch. Finally, in a minor inside joke, Doc Cottle was named after a family physician from David Weddle's childhood.

On the casting front, another Olmos relative makes it into the story, as Brendan 'Hot Dog' Costanza[26] is played by Edward James Olmos's son Bodie; ironically, given the focus of the story on Adama's sons. The photo of Zak in Kara's locker has changed from the miniseries to show Tobias Mehler, who will play him in the episodic series. Meanwhile Caroline Adama, who was briefly glimpsed in a background photo in the miniseries, is here played by a blonde supporting artist with her face shadowed by a heavy black veil, with the obvious intention that, if the character should be featured more prominently at a later date (which happens in the Season Three episode 'A Day in the Life'), all the team would have to do would be to ensure they got a blonde actress of approximately the right age and build. Luciana Carro, who plays the delightfully outspoken Louanne 'Kat' Katraine, is a fan of the original series, and reportedly brought her Xbox joystick with her into the audition to use as a Viper control pad.

---

25 'Prelap' is a screenwriting term, meaning that dialogue from the following scene precedes to the cut to that scene.
26 The spelling of this character's name in the series' credits is amazingly variable, with alternate renderings variously renaming the character 'Brenden', 'Hotdog' and 'Constanza'; the draft scripts usually render his name 'Brendan "Hot Dog" Constanza', though a draft of 'Torn', by Anne Cofell Saunders, does refer to him as 'Brenden "Hotdog" Constanza', indicating that even the writers are slightly confused.

'Act of Contrition' is the first episode to fall short of the high standard set by '33', being a somewhat unevenly-constructed narrative with a fairly heavy-handed treatment of the situation between Starbuck and the Adama family, though it still has many things for fans of the series to enjoy.

✓ 6: You Can't Go Home Again

FIRST TRANSMISSION DATE: 15 November 2004 (UK)

WRITER: Carla Robinson

DIRECTOR: Sergio Mimica-Gezzan

CREDITED CAST: Donnelly Rhodes (Doctor Cottle); Alonso Oyarzun (Socinus); Bodie Olmos (Constanza/Hot Dog)

SYNOPSIS: Following the events of the last episode, Starbuck ejects from her Viper and crash-lands, injuring herself, on a nearby moon. Finding a downed Cylon Raider, she climbs inside and figures out how it can be piloted. Meanwhile Adama searches obsessively for her, refusing to give up even after the point at which her oxygen supply must have expired. Starbuck, at the last moment, flies the Raider up to the Fleet, having painted 'STARBUCK' on the underside of its wings to let them know it is her. On Caprica, Sharon apparently vanishes during a raid by Centurions.

ANALYSIS: 'You Can't Go Home Again' concludes the narrative begun in the previous episode, and instigates a new story arc based around the captured Cylon Raider. Like 'Act of Contrition', it is not one of the best stories of the season, though it does explore some aspects of the philosophy of survival that underlies both original and reimagined series.

The Return of Starbuck: The Personal versus the Professional

This story focuses around the idea common to both series, that sometimes individuals must be abandoned for the good of the Fleet. This occurred in many episodes of the original, with Adama permanently abandoning Starbuck in *Galactica 1980*'s 'The Return of Starbuck', and was reintroduced in the miniseries, through Tigh's decision to abandon the crewmen trapped in the flight pod and Roslin's to abandon the ships without jump capability. In this story, however, the issue is problematised, with Adama and Apollo agitating to find Starbuck even after her oxygen is believed to have run out, Roslin, Baltar and Tigh objecting, and the entire Fleet grinding to a halt. From an audience point of view we know, intellectually, that Tigh and Roslin are right, but emotionally, we sympathise with the Adamas; and, from our omniscient perspective, we know that Starbuck is alive, so we want them to keep trying.

The theme from the previous episode of letting the personal override the professional continues. In particular, Adama's feelings of guilt over his falling-out with Starbuck (and, as Roslin observes, the fact that she is his and Apollo's last link to Zak), cause him to become obsessed with rescuing her, saying to Roslin 'Frak the odds, we're going to find her', and the patently untrue 'We leave no-one behind' (at which point Tigh looks a little worried). Possibly one of the reasons why Adama has previously been willing to indulge Starbuck in her own breaches of protocol is due to his own largely repressed tendencies in this direction. When Lee asks why they are doing this, Adama says, 'Kara was family. You do whatever you have to do. Sometimes you break the rules'; and when Lee asks if Adama would do the same for him, Adama replies 'If it were you ... we'd never leave'. Adama is thus clearly willing to let his personal feelings guide his professional decisions.

Lee is also pushing the pilots to the limit because of his feelings of guilt; he and his father, for a change, side with each other against Roslin, and, when Tigh challenges them, they move out of earshot to plot in whispers. The phrasing of Adama's line 'Get as many birds in the sky as possible and find our girl', speaks volumes, as does the conversation where Lee says he thinks that they have both come to terms with Zak's death and Adama replies, 'I haven't', implying that Lee is also fooling himself. Lee, for his part, accuses Tigh of letting his own personal life interfere with his professional life, accusing him of wanting to leave Starbuck behind because he dislikes her. However, when Adama relieves Tigh of duty, he goes, even though he would clearly love to argue; in obeying his superior officer despite his misgivings, he is still putting duty ahead of his personal feelings.

Roslin is particularly astute and intuitive in this story, figuring out that Lee is close to Kara in a way that he isn't to the other pilots, and reading the situation with him and his father correctly. She is also, however, ruthless in the way that she uses the knowledge, bluntly telling both men exactly why they are acting as they are, to shame them into behaving like proper military officers. Again, her actions are informed by her experience with the abandonment of the ships in the miniseries and the shooting down of the *Olympic Carrier* in '33'. Adama, though, is equally ruthless, continually invoking the agreement he made with Roslin in the miniseries by declaring the operation a 'military matter' and thus out of her jurisdiction. She stays on the *Galactica* when Adama finally agrees they should jump, clearly to make sure that they do so.

Baltar's decision to side with Roslin and Tigh is, significantly, encouraged by Head Six, suggesting either that his own selfishness is being justified through his visions (in a deleted line, she describes Baltar as having 'a passionate devotion to his own epidermis') or that Head Six is the articulator of a wider philosophy. (As the operation leaves the Fleet vulnerable, it seems unlikely in this story that she is operating on the Cylons' behalf, unless, of course, it is part of a broader strategy to sow dissent between the civilian and military factions.)[27] The scene in which Baltar converses with Head Six aloud and in front of Roslin is something of a weak point in the story, however, as normally such conversations are either held when he is alone or conducted through the use of double meanings (although it should be noted that some of the things Head Six does, such as her rustling the hospital curtain in 'Litmus' and her constant playing with Baltar's hair, must be invisible to outsiders, so possibly the same is true of the conversation here). There is a deleted scene where Head Six comments that, even at a time of crisis, Baltar is wondering what sex with Roslin would be like.

Staking out the Waterholes: Continuity and Worldbuilding

In continuity terms, Adama reasons that the Cylons currently don't know where the Fleet is and are staking out likely systems looking for it. The Fleet encounters a small recon patrol of Cylons, but no baseship, implicitly confirming that the *Olympic Carrier* was the means by which the Cylons were tracking it. The captured Raider proves, as hinted in the miniseries, to be a single organism built into a spaceship hull (not unlike the alien race called the Sky featured in Richard Hatch's *Battlestar Galactica* novel series). The flight suits are indicated as being able to act as life-support systems for short periods, as Starbuck uses hers to survive in a hostile environment. Starbuck, in the final scene, asks for 'a stogie', and Adama gives her his last one (indicating that she may soon be forced to give up smoking; the reference to it being his last does not appear in the 2 June 2004 draft script). She also asks Lee suggestively if he would like to give her a bath, continuing the frisson between the pair of them. Her question to the Raider, 'Are you alive?', while it makes sense in the context, is a direct allusion to Six's question to the Armistice Officer in the miniseries and to Helo in '33', and does not appear in the 2 June draft.

More minor points include the fact that Roslin's whiteboard has not yet been updated to indicate the deaths of the 13 pilots in the last episode. A couple of new expressions are introduced: 'bingo fuel' meaning almost out of fuel, and 'mark one eyeball' meaning observing with the naked eye. Kara likens Cylons to insects when, regarding the dead Raider, she muses, 'Even cockroaches have to breathe; how do you?' There is a brief deleted scene in which Doc Cottle describes the severity of Starbuck's knee injury to Adama, which, while unnecessary to the plot, does explain why she's out of commission as a pilot for the rest of the season. Helo and Sharon now have enough anti-radiation drugs for three months, although it still remains unexplained why none of the forests or cities on Caprica looks remotely as though it has suffered a catastrophic nuclear bombardment.

---

27 SPOILER SECTION: We later learn that Kara Thrace has a destiny that involves guiding the Fleet, but that she has to die before this can happen; it is possible that this is one of the points at which she could have died and returned to the Fleet as a messenger (as in 'Crossroads', part two).

Like the previous episode, this one is heavily indebted to the original series, as well as *Galactica 1980*'s 'The Return of Starbuck'. (Carla Robinson has stated that she knew nothing about *Galactica 1980*, but the set-up was instigated by Weddle and Thompson, who undoubtedly did.) The original-series episode 'The Hand of God' contributes the sequence in which Starbuck, flying a Cylon craft with no identification, has to find some way of making her presence known. When Apollo brings her in, both of them playfully waggle the wings of their craft, in a visual reference to the 'waggling' sequence in 'The Hand of God'. (The 2 June draft explicitly scripts the wing-waggling, suggesting that this may have been deliberately added by Weddle and Thompson or Moore.) 'Saga of a Star World' and, again, 'The Hand of God' may be the source of the idea of the Cylons staking out various systems in order to find the Fleet. Thrace's manoeuvre in the Cylon ship, flying under Apollo and coming up behind him, recalls a signature Starbuck move that appeared in the original series and 'The Return of Starbuck'. Kara's praying to the gods and talking to the dead Raider obliquely references 'The Return of Starbuck', in which Starbuck talks to a (live) Cylon and a mysterious woman who is quite possibly a divine being sent to judge him. According to *The Official Companion*, Robinson's first draft had Starbuck and the Raider actually talking to one another, but this was abandoned by the 2 June draft. On a minor point, 'The Young Lords' also featured Starbuck crashing on a planet and sustaining a leg injury.

There are a few significant differences from the original series. Although Vipers are atmosphere-capable craft in both, where the original Vipers ejected the whole cockpit, the new ones eject only the pilot. Although an explanation is provided as to why the Fleet is in continuous need of fuel – that when in the atmosphere, the Raptors and Vipers must use their engines constantly – claims that the reimagined series is better than the original in science terms are somewhat undermined by the fact that Kara successfully patches the Cylon ship with a piece of her spacesuit, which would most probably be sucked out into the vacuum of space when they left the atmosphere. The drink of choice in the Fleet is 'ambrosia' rather than the original series' 'ambrosa'.

It is worth noting that the plot is also indebted to the *Star Trek* episode 'The Galileo Seven', in which a shuttle crew including McCoy and Spock are stranded on a planet, Kirk delays a mission in order to try to find them, and, by coincidence, they manage to get the shuttle working again just as Kirk is forced to abandon the rescue.

Make Toast, Not War: Writing and Production

This was Robinson's first story for the series (and, indeed, the first televised script of her career), which might possibly excuse the fact that the narrative hinges too much on coincidence, with the Cylon ship crashing intact, Starbuck finding it just before her oxygen runs out, and her figuring out how to fly it just in time to get off the planet before the Fleet jumps. On a more positive front, there is an entertaining reference to the 'pop-tart' sequence in *Pulp Fiction* (1994),

6: YOU CAN'T GO HOME AGAIN

when Helo sneaks up on and guns down one of the Centurions just as toast pops out of a chrome toaster with a red indicator light, also providing a visual pun on the literal and figurative toasters in the scene. (Storyboards for this sequence dated 1 June indicate that at one point a sizzling pan of scrambled eggs was to be used instead, which would have been less clever; the 2 June draft has the toaster sequence in place.)

The title of the story is taken from that of a Thomas Wolfe novel, although the similarities end there. The 2 June draft has a couple of interesting stage directions, for instance the description of the interior of the Raider, 'VEIN-STREAKED TISSUES, like the guts of a cow, intertwined with wet metallic linkages – H R Giger's worst nightmare', and describes the sequence where the Raider hovers over Lee's Viper by saying 'Picture the MIG over Maverick in *Top Gun*'.

The series bible indicates that Starbuck has an old knee injury; this is aggravated by the new one incurred in this story. Katee Sackhoff also sustained a knee injury during her earlier career as a swimmer. In the podcast for 'The Hand of God', Moore elaborates, saying that Kara 'had joined the Colonial Fleet Academy on some kind of athletic scholarship primarily to play Pyramid [the basketball-like game that will feature heavily from Season Two onwards] and she saw it as a means to an end; when she was there she blew out her knee and had to find other employment'.

In production terms, Sergio Mimico-Gezzan had previously worked as assistant director on *Schindler's List* (1993) and *Saving Private Ryan* (1998); this was his episodic TV debut. There are some good shots of Hot Dog's abandoned Viper drifting in space. The initial shots of Starbuck, suggesting that she is being dragged by a hostile creature, then pulling back to reveal that in fact the culprit is her parachute, are also clever. The Starbuck sequences were filmed in a gravel pit in Port Coquitlam, while the restaurant where Helo and Sharon find themselves was a Vancouver café called The Alibi Room.

'You Can't Go Home Again' concludes the story begun in the previous episode in much the same fashion, though, as well as being somewhat uneven, it is dependent on coincidence. Nonetheless, it still provides an interesting exploration of some of the series' key ongoing themes.

7: Litmus

FIRST TRANSMISSION DATE: 22 October 2004

WRITER: Jeff Vlaming

DIRECTOR: Rod Hardy

CREDITED CAST: Donnelly Rhodes (Doctor Cottle); Jill Teed (Sergeant Hadrian); Dominic Zamprogna (Jammer); Alonso Oyarzun (Socinus); Bodie Olmos (Constanza/Hot Dog); Matthew Bennett (Doral); Christina Schild (Playa Kohn); Raahul Singh (Kimmit); Shaw Madson (Marine Corporal); Nimet Kanji (Candace Myson – Tribunal); Biski Gugushe (Reporter #1); Morris Chapdelaine (Reporter #2)

KNOWN UNCREDITED CAST: Leo Li Chiang (Tattooed Pilot)

SYNOPSIS: Following a suicide bombing incident involving a Doral Cylon, it is revealed to the Fleet that some Cylons look like humans, and Adama orders Master-at-Arms Hadrian to investigate recent security incidents. Hadrian's investigation leads her to suspect Tyrol of involvement in the water tank bombing, and she orders him to appear before a tribunal. Tyrol refuses to give testimony that might cast suspicion on Boomer, which further incriminates him. Deckhand Socinus lies to save his Chief, claiming that he himself negligently left open a hatch that allowed an unknown Cylon access to the arms locker on the night in question. Hadrian calls Adama to the stand, accusing Tyrol and Boomer of being in collusion with the Cylons and alleging that, through his allowing them to carry on their relationship in defiance of regulations, Adama provided them with the opportunity to carry out sabotage. Angered, Adama shuts the tribunal down, and the incident is blamed solely on Socinus's negligence. Tyrol asks Boomer if she knows who left the hatch open, and she refuses to answer. Meanwhile, Helo searches for Caprica-Sharon, observed by Sharon, Six and Doral.

ANALYSIS: 'Litmus' builds on earlier episodes in both literal and thematic ways, exploring the repercussions from the events of 'Water' and investigating themes of guilt, trust and letting the personal interfere with the professional.

Hadrian's Wall: The Tribunal and its Consequences

The story revolves around Master-at-arms Hadrian's investigation into recent

7: LITMUS

incidents aboard the Fleet, including the sabotaging of the water tanks, the discovery of explosives on Boomer's Raptor and Doral's suicide bombing. This effort is in part undermined because she allows her guilt and anger to rule her judgment: as someone in charge of security on the ship, she understandably feels personally responsible for the events (even though, not knowing about the human-like Cylons, there was nothing she could have done), and is looking for someone else to blame. Her interrogation of Adama rapidly boils down to a frustrated 'Why didn't you tell me?' and she tries to develop Socinus's confession that he left the hatch open into a conspiracy theory involving Tyrol deliberately ordering his subordinate to do so in order to provide the Cylons with access to the small arms locker. When she winds up, in her misguided zeal, pinning the blame too high, on Adama himself, the result is an unsurprising example of how the establishment will close down any operation that starts to undermine their own authority.

Adama is also clearly acting out of guilt. Although there is a logic to why he did not tell Hadrian, or indeed anyone outside of a small select group, about the existence of the human-like Cylons, it is clear that he realises that had he told her, Doral would have been apprehended before he could have committed the suicide bombing. The incident in fact is another case of the professional/personal theme pervading Season One: Tigh, seeing Doral, doesn't cause a general panic but quietly rings Security, while Adama blurts out 'Doral!', alerting the Cylon to the fact that he has been identified. Having incurred deaths through secrecy, Adama now goes too far the other way by encouraging too much disclosure, and also clearly does not realise that it is a mistake to put the investigation under Hadrian, with her own obvious issues about failing to prevent the various security breaches and being kept in the dark by her own commanding officer. Socinus, too, may be acting partly out of a sense of guilt (as his own conflicting evidence got Tyrol in trouble, he tries to sacrifice himself to make amends), and later Tyrol's feelings of guilt over what happened to Socinus cause him not just to reject Boomer, but to do so in a fairly brutal way.

The story also reflects the military/civilian tension through exploring Adama's control issues, as he insists on an independent tribunal but then exercises his military authority to get it shut down. On the one hand, he believes that the military should be responsible to the government, but on the other he is frustrated with the civilian administration. Adama's final word on the matter is: 'You've lost your way, sergeant. You've lost sight of the purpose of the law, to protect its citizens, not persecute them. Whatever we are, whatever's left of us, we're better than that. Now, these proceedings are closed'. This reflects not only the military/civilian conflict thread, but also the question, posed in the miniseries, of whether or not humanity is worth saving. When Roslin says to the press pack that the proceedings '[have] come to a close', she is reiterating the party line that Socinus was guilty of negligence and no other crewmember was involved.

The deepest irony, of course, is that many of the tribunal's suspicions are justified. Boomer did, indeed, commit some of the crimes under investigation, and Tyrol helped her cover this up.[28] At least one of the people involved is in fact an active Cylon agent. Both of them are indeed lying, and others around them are lying to protect them. While there is never any conclusive evidence (even in 'The Plan', which covers the background to the incident in more detail) that Boomer did deliberately leave the hatch open for Doral and/or provide him the security codes, the possibility is not ruled out. The problem is that by seeking extreme conspiracies, the investigation loses its credibility: Adama points out to Roslin that had Tyrol wanted to destroy the ship, he could have done so easily, given his intimate knowledge of its engineering. This casts doubt upon the tribunal for suspecting Tyrol, and causes them all to fail to see the nature of his actual involvement.

Cylon Witness: Tyrol, the Deck Crew and the Two Sharons

The motivation behind the bombing is not made clear in this story. Baltar believes that Starbuck's speculation that Doral was after his experiment may be true (which suggests that the design he proposed to Adama, warhead and all, is viable). Head Six apparently agrees, but clearly wants Baltar to keep working; she gets very aggressive with him when he says he will destroy it. 'The Plan' suggests that Doral's intention was indeed to kill Baltar, though not because of the Cylon detector (of which, ironically, he appears unaware) but as revenge for identifying the other Doral as a Cylon at Ragnar Anchorage. The 10 June 2004 draft of the script describes the sequence by saying that when Adama and Doral make eye contact, 'Doral stops dead in his tracks. Smiles a defiant "fuck you" to Adama', and detonates, suggesting that Doral finally chooses to detonate opportunistically once he sees that he has the chance to take out the Fleet's commander. Lastly, there is a throwaway line in Baltar's dialogue with Head Six that, assuming she is telling the truth, indicates that she and the Cylons are not in communication: 'They don't know about me, or us, or our life together'.

Loyalties among the deck crew are also explored. The crew cover for Tyrol in his trysts with Boomer, and he in turn doesn't punish them for their homebrew experiments. (There is an extended version of the scene, with more technical description of what it is they are doing wrong, but the final cut is snappier and the better for it.) Cally is particularly vociferous in the Chief's defence, again supporting the idea that she has feelings toward him, but it seems that Socinus is also willing to take a fairly serious punishment on his behalf, indicating that breaching the boundaries between ranks (as Boomer, his superior officer, did with him in colluding in their affair), even for a benign-seeming cause, has negative consequences. When Tyrol confesses to Adama that he believes Socinus is innocent and was covering for him because he was with Boomer at the time of the bombing, Adama says that Socinus should still be punished for lying under oath, and that Tyrol's own punishment is knowing that this was his fault. This

---

28 Revelations about Tyrol's past at the end of Season Three will indicate that there is a further irony in his being implicated.

heavily implies that if Tyrol wasn't so useful, he'd be in the brig, though it also demonstrates that Adama himself cannot go back and countermand his own support for the blaming of Socinus, in a brief exploration of the consequences of both misguided loyalty and bad leadership.

The deterioration of Tyrol's relationship with Boomer continues. He is clearly starting to suspect that something is wrong, in that he fails to answer Hadrian's question 'Were you with a Cylon agent?' and at the end asks Boomer if she did leave the hatch open. Their conversation at the story's conclusion is another of the double-meaning exchanges that pervade the series: Tyrol's 'I covered for you, I gave you protection' refers ostensibly to the tribunal but also to the events of 'Water', and his 'I put everything on the line for you' means not only that his career was at risk, but also that, if she is a Cylon, he has put the whole Fleet in jeopardy.

Finally, however, an ironically positive note is struck on Cylon-Occupied Caprica as Helo, although he initially strikes out to the South, suggesting that he has given up on finding Sharon, then turns North and goes to look for her, confirming Sharon's evaluation of him, 'He's a good man, he always does the right thing'. While they can commit some fairly ugly acts, at least some of humanity are thus worth saving.

McCarthy's Revenge: Continuity and Worldbuilding

On the continuity front, we learn that Adama's father was a civil-liberties lawyer[29], which explains both why Adama is so conflicted on the subject of compassion versus duty, and why Lee is drawn to politics and the law. Tyrol has been under Adama's command for five years, though it is unknown if all of this was time served on the *Galactica*. The blast caused three deaths and 13 injuries, in another instance of thirteen being used to indicate bad luck.

There is a deleted scene of Billy's first press conference. This is largely forgettable, but does contain an interesting piece of information about how rationing is handled in the Fleet (the order in which ships receive rations is rotated every month so that everyone takes a turn at being first and last), and also a foreshadowing of 'Colonial Day', first in introducing the journalist Playa, and secondly in having one journalist (identified in the 10 June draft script as 'Kimmit') ask Roslin about her stance on income tax, in the light of her commitment to follow the Adar administration's policies. The patent absurdity of asking such a question under the circumstances visibly punctures the delusion of those assembled that a normal political life can be maintained. This anticipates Zarek's broadside in 'Colonial Day' against Fleet society still clinging to old political and economic routines despite the fact that the world to which these belonged has disappeared completely. Head Six physically slams Baltar against the wall at one point, and Baltar subsequently gets an odd look from a passing Marine, suggesting that he appeared to be flinging himself bodily into the wall.

---

29 His story will later form a partial basis for the spinoff series *Caprica*.

(The 10 June draft has Head Six simply grabbing his hair and pulling his head back, with both the wall-slamming and the Marine absent.)

In legal terms, we learn that the right to remain silent is guaranteed under the 'Twenty-third Article of Colonisation', which seems to incorporate basic laws as well as constitutional points, much like the German *Grundgesetz*; this means that remaining silent cannot legally be taken as evidence of guilt. The rationale behind the rule against fraternisation among crewmembers is also clearly shown here, as such fraternisation leads to unprofessional conduct on the part of Boomer, Tyrol and Socinus, and ultimately of everyone involved. The official acceptance of the story that Socinus was to blame for the incident is clearly a political move, as it provides a rationale – that the incident was down to crew negligence – that absolves the establishment of all blame.

The story also reflects contemporary issues surrounding the Iraq War. Suicide bombing was a particular concern at the time, and Adama's debate with Roslin about revealing intelligence – with a guilt-driven Adama wanting to make everything public and Roslin, on the basis of her 20 years in political office, being certain that this will lead to a witch-hunt – recalls similar contemporary debates about whether revealing intelligence serves the public's right to know or instead hinders ongoing operations. (Although this is unstated, the tribunal appears to be held *in camera*.) The witch-hunt that indeed follows reflects contemporary American paranoia over terrorists, with both incidents depicting people's need to blame someone else for their failings; and the fact that Adama winds up being interrogated by his own tribunal shows how panic can lead people to turn on each other. The images of Sharon 'captured' by Centurions on Caprica, with a sack over her head, visually reference those of captured 'terror suspects' in Iraq. The discussion between the deck crew in which Socinus and Cally assert that having people suspect each other plays into the Cylons' hands, and thus that they all have to stick together, and Jammer taking the opposite view that a certain amount of paranoia is necessary for survival, is a common debate of the War on Terror, with the word 'Cylon' substituted for 'terrorist'.

The Acid Test: Writing and Production

The story was scripted by Jeff Vlaming, the first freelancer to write for the series, whose previous credits included *The X-Files*, *NCIS* and *Xena: Warrior Princess*. It has strong similarities to the *Star Trek: The Next Generation* episode 'The Drumhead', produced during the time Moore was that show's executive story editor, which featured an incident where a hunt for Romulan spies aboard the *Enterprise* gets out of control and leads to unjustified accusations.

According to *The Official Companion*, this was a 'cost saving' episode, though, as the story is carried by the plot and characterisation, the economies are barely visible. The same volume also indicates that Socinus was originally intended to be killed off in the miniseries, although this must have been at a relatively early stage, as the available draft scripts of the miniseries give no indication of this.

Moore's podcast for 'The Hand of God' also notes that there was a prosaic reason to have Caprica-Boomer beaten up by Caprica-Six (which in the story is to lend credibility to the fiction that she was captured by the Cylons), namely, so that it would be relatively easy for the audience to tell which Boomer was which – although, since one of them is on Caprica and the other on the Fleet, this is not as much of a problem as he evidently thought it was.

The 10 June draft includes an early scene in which Lee visits Kara in sickbay, and an extended beginning to the scene where Baltar visits her. In the latter, she is telling the story of her Pyramid-playing knee injury to the patient in the next bed (who is 'unconscious, asleep or in a coma') and, noticing Baltar, covers for this by claiming she was thinking out loud. (Baltar responds 'I do a bit of that myself'.) Also omitted from the final version was a scene after the announcement to the Fleet regarding the existence of human-like Cylons. In this, Crashdown brags to Boomer, to her discomfort, about how he was right. Adama's conversation with Laura about Socinus being accused of conspiring with Cylon agents originally had him saying, 'They manoeuvred him into that confession. Far as I can tell, the worst we've got here is dereliction of duty'. It also includes the information that Adama's father once defended an alleged serial killer named Mathers (who Adama says was 'arrested without cause'). There is also a sequence where Laura tells Adama that a mob has ripped 'a man they thought was a Cylon' limb from limb (indicating that Roslin's concerns about the consequences of disclosure were right), and a scene where Tyrol visits Socinus in the brig and the latter reasserts his loyalty to him, adding that the crew are loyal to Boomer too as she is his girlfriend; this scene was to come right before the one where Tyrol tells Boomer he is ending the relationship, adding further context to his decision.

Things to watch out for in this episode include the logo of Scotiabank (a Canadian banking group), which is clearly visible on one of the skyscrapers on the Caprican horizon, and a volume of *Reader's Digest Condensed Books* clearly visible lying under Adama's glasses when the Corporal of the Guard comes to fetch him. The Caprica sequences also beg the question why Helo never seems to notice that Six and/or Doral are following, as they are always quite nearby and usually stood and conversing out in the open. Head Six makes an obvious reference to *The Incredible Hulk* when she tells Baltar 'You wouldn't like me when I'm angry'. The original series Cylons also used suicide as a military tactic, though in their case it took the form of kamikaze strikes.

In 'Litmus', the consequences of blurring the personal and the professional are fully exposed, as Hadrian's investigation, which has shown how the culture of lax discipline on board the *Galactica* is directly to blame for its security breaches, is in turn shut down as the military, and the ship's civilian authorities (in the persons of Adama and Roslin) opt instead for a politically motivated cover-up. The systemic failures uncovered by the investigation will form the basis of the Fleet's problems for the rest of the first season, and indeed continue to haunt it for the remainder of the series.

8: Six Degrees of Separation

FIRST TRANSMISSION DATE: 29 November 2004

WRITER: Michael Angeli

DIRECTOR: Robert Young

CREDITED CAST: Donnelly Rhodes (Doctor Cottle); Christina Schild (Journalist Playa); Biski Gugushe (Journalist Eick)

SYNOPSIS: Following a conversation with Baltar in which he professes a lack of belief in God, Head Six vanishes, seemingly replaced by a physical Six who claims that her name is Shelley Godfrey and that she has proof that Baltar allowed the Cylons access to the defence mainframe. This proof takes the form of a security photo on a disk, apparently showing Baltar entering the mainframe with an explosive device the day before the attacks on the Colonies. Adama orders Gaeta to enlarge the photo and sharpen the image to verify the man's identity. Baltar attempts to gain access to the photo, confronts Godfrey, and endeavours to incriminate her as a Cylon agent, achieving nothing. He finally tries to destroy the evidence, and is arrested. In despair, Baltar prays to God; subsequently, Head Six returns, Gaeta announces that he has proof that the photo is a fake, and Shelley Godfrey disappears, all vindicating Baltar in the eyes of the Fleet. On Caprica, Sharon and Helo finally make love.

ANALYSIS: 'Six Degrees of Separation', the first of the two Season One stories with bad puns in their titles, links the mounting paranoia in the Fleet with Baltar's growing religious sensibilities, in an extended elaboration on the Baltar subplot of '33'.

The Wrath of Godfrey: Baltar's Testing

'Six Degrees of Separation' takes place a week after 'Litmus' (judging by the fact that it is now Helo's twenty-fourth day on Caprica); the Fleet are starting to settle down, but are still looking for answers and people to blame. The story carries on the witch-hunt theme of 'Litmus', with Baltar saying 'I am an innocent man, who is being condemned in the court of public opinion without trial'. The fact that Godfrey's story also recalls the events of '33', as she claims that she was a systems analyst at the Defence Ministry who worked with Doctor Amarak, on one level brings up the idea that the Fleet is tearing itself apart over the events surrounding the destruction of the Colonies, but on another characterises the story as a test of faith for Baltar.

The trigger for events seems, on the surface, to be Baltar's argument with Head Six over theology. Baltar takes a sceptical position and claims that no rational human being could believe in God (and that the Cylons are 'little more than toasters' despite their faith). Head Six, not surprisingly, reiterates the idea that God has a plan in which Baltar should put his trust. Significantly, while Baltar offers commitment to Head Six, calling out 'I love you', it is not until he accepts God, asking for forgiveness and saying that he will carry out God's plan, that she returns and, immediately thereafter, Gaeta reveals the incriminating photo to be a fake. Head Six thus underlines that she is not the one to be worshipped, but God.

Throughout the story, James Callis, as Baltar, radiates a sense of panic. In an almost film noir exploration of paranoia and guilt, although Baltar is technically innocent of the charges as presented, he confirms his own culpability in everyone else's eyes through his actions (such as trying to destroy Gaeta's computer equipment in order to eliminate the photo). Although, as Head Six points out, he has effectively immunised himself against all future accusations of treason through the Godfrey Incident, as it would be difficult to accuse him of anything following such a dramatic exoneration, this episode visibly starts the Baltar-Roslin animosity that will characterise their relationship from now on.

Appropriately enough for an episode revolving around Six, the story has an almost *The Prisoner*-esque ambiguity as to how much of its content is real and how much takes place entirely in the mind. Head Six's disappearance and reappearance synchronise perfectly with Godfrey's own appearance and disappearance, leading to the tantalising suggestion that in fact Godfrey is a collective hallucination; another manifestation of Head Six. (Whereas Head Six protects Baltar when he puts his faith in God, without her, he faces in Godfrey a god-free[30] universe.) Admittedly she is seen physically handing the disk to Gaeta, but then Head Six has also been seen to perform the odd physical feat; and although her glasses are discovered at the end, again suggesting she is corporeal, we never see her put them down, so they could have been someone else's that were caught up in the mass hallucination. Equally, it would not be outside the capabilities of a divine being to create a physical manifestation of Six (as later events in the series will make clear). When Baltar asks Head Six if Godfrey was real, Head Six never answers. There is also a moment of prophecy when, after Head Six vanishes early in the story, Baltar mutters that he will imagine himself another girlfriend, this one brunette, and then opens the door to find the brunette Dualla there.

Later, 'The Plan', and a deleted sequence from the 24 October 2005 draft of 'Lay Down Your Burdens' in which *Galactica*'s Brother Cavil indicates that he knew Shelley Godfrey, will resolve the question in favour of Godfrey being a Cylon, acting under orders to discredit Baltar and stop work on the Cylon

---

30 Brother Cavil actually makes this pun on Godfrey's name in the 24 October 2005 draft of 'Lay Down Your Burdens'.

detector. However, this is such a disappointing and prosaic notion that, when taking 'Six Degrees of Separation' on its own, it is much more effective to consider the possibility that Godfrey is simply another aspect of Head Six.

Whether Godfrey is a Cylon or a divine manifestation in the form of one, keen sexuality is again implied to be a general Six character trait. Godfrey hints that she and Doctor Amarak were lovers (and in the 23 June 2004 draft explicitly states that they were), and she tries to seduce Adama, which accomplishes little bar making him suspicious of her motives. Later Sixes in the series will also use their sexuality freely to gain trust. She uses normal human strength to push Baltar, indicating that the Cylons can rein themselves back when necessary (as is surely the case with 'sleeper agents'). On the flip side, however, the staging of Baltar's conversation with Gaeta and subsequent confrontation with Godfrey in the *Galactica*'s (unisex) washroom lend the whole affair a further sense of inappropriateness, illicitness and social discomfort, as Baltar tries to persuade Gaeta, who, it has been already established, had a lot of respect for him at the start of the season, to allow him access to the photograph.

This is a particularly good episode for ironic moments. There is an irony in the fact that Baltar does have proof that Godfrey's photos are fake, but this proof would incriminate him further, because he knows that Six, rather than he, was the culprit, and because he knows the mainframe was compromised rather than blown up. Although Baltar is found innocent of treason, the audience, furthermore, knows he is guilty, just not in quite the way that the Colonials suspect here. There is a good sequence when Baltar first meets Godfrey and speaks to her as if she is Head Six, then slowly comes to the realisation that everyone else can see her as well, which puts him in a difficult position as he cannot reveal how he knows for certain that she is a Cylon without incriminating himself. There is an intriguing parallel in that, whereas in the last episode the audience were siding with Boomer and hoping she wouldn't be found out, so this week we are siding with Baltar in a similar way, regarding his treachery. How others feel about Baltar also has an element of irony: Roslin says that she has an 'instinct' that Baltar is guilty, while Gaeta says that he returned to look at the picture again because he 'knew' Baltar wouldn't have had anything to do with the attacks.

Starbuck's New Boyfriend: Continuity and Worldbuilding

Elsewhere, Boomer suggests treating the Cylon Raider as a pet, albeit a rather intelligent one; she touches it almost sensually. Starbuck has better luck getting a response from it than the others do, suggesting that the time she spent with it during her escape has forged something of a bond between them. There is some rather suggestive dialogue when Tyrol refers to the Raider as Starbuck's 'new boyfriend'; Starbuck retorts that the Raider is a girl, and Tyrol replies 'Well, if you don't mind her goo on your face, she's all yours', before Starbuck gets inside her and gets her going. In a deleted scene, the Raider appears to defecate out of its exhaust system (whether or not it's actually doing this specific function is unknown, but Cally's reaction to the sight suggests something analogous); since Starbuck removed its brain when adapting it for flight in 'You Can't Go Home Again', this is presumably an autonomic function.

On Cylon-Occupied Caprica, meanwhile, the inevitable sequence in which Helo and Sharon, in a completely foreseen development, finally make love, is cleverly given extra drama by being intercut with one in which Sharon's counterpart on *Galactica* discovers that someone has painted the word 'Cylon' on her mirror – meaning that she sees herself, in the mirror, as a Cylon, while her mirror-image, Caprica-Sharon, exists in full knowledge of her Cylon nature.

Roslin alternates between being the voice of reason and the voice of paranoia; where in the previous episode she was concerned about encouraging suspicion in the Fleet, here she is willing to accuse Baltar of treason based simply on a feeling that he's guilty. In the ongoing plotline regarding Starbuck and Tigh, the latter exploits her feelings towards the former to get her out of her sickbed; although Starbuck correctly observes that his telling her just to lie there is reverse psychology, he gets in the crucial stab at her ego by saying 'Every day you spend in that bed is another day that my opinion of you is confirmed', which is what finally drives her to return to work. There is a deleted scene revealing that Lee put Tigh up to this, but it adds an extra layer of ambiguity to their situation if the possibility exists that Tigh decided to motivate Starbuck himself, suggesting that he does care more about her well-being than she realises.

The Hand of Godfrey: Writing and Production

On the production front, the story's writer, Michael Angeli, had previously contributed scripts to *Medium*, *Dark Angel* and *Monk* and worked with Moore on *Touching Evil*. Moore and the writing team developed the storyline, while Angeli wrote the actual screenplay. Director Robert Young, well-known for his documentary work, came recommended by Edward James Olmos.

Things to watch out for include the presence of hexagonal CD-ROMs (which are nonetheless, slightly inaccurately, referred to as 'discs'). Baltar's pun 'No more Mr Nice Gaius!' was included at James Callis's suggestion (the 23 June 2004 draft renders the line as 'No more Mr Nice Guy').[31] We learn that the Colonials have a system of 'no fly lists', as in the present day, to prevent those suspected of terrorism or, as in Baltar's case, treason, from travelling.

The 23 June draft (which uses the 'Centurian' spelling for mechanical Cylons) contains some amusing sections omitted from the final version. One of these has Baltar asking Head Six if God's name is 'something powerful and sexy, like Zeus', and when she replies 'His is the name that cannot be spoken', saying 'Oh, so it's one of those silly names, like Hephaestus'. In Godfrey's attempted seduction of Adama, the draft script has him being aroused by her actions despite himself, whereas the final version is played by Olmos with cold

---

31 In the podcast for 'Guess What's Coming to Dinner', however, Angeli attributes the pun to Moore.

indifference; in the draft, after getting rid of Godfrey, Adama goes to the bathroom and closes the door, the implication of what he intends to do being obvious. When the President holds out her arm in readiness for an injection and Cottle tells her 'It's not that kind of shot', in the draft script she starts undoing her trousers. Although the suggestive lines mentioned earlier regarding Starbuck and the Raider are not present in the draft, there is an exchange where Lee proposes she show it some love and she responds, 'Want me to make out with it, Lee?' More seriously, Roslin gets a good line when she remarks, regarding Baltar's assertions that Shelley Godfrey is a Cylon, 'It's that kind of world now, isn't it? Anyone can be a Cylon, so now there's an easy way to discredit your enemies', and Sharon's glowing spine is described in the stage directions as 'like a wriggling serpent'.

The 13 July 2004 draft of the next episode, 'Flesh and Bone', contains a significant deleted line where, when Boomer again voices her fears about her own identity, Tyrol says 'Look what happened to Dr [sic] Baltar. Cylon agent tried to frame him as a traitor. If it could happen to him, it could happen to anyone'. This would confirm Head Six's assertion that the events of 'Six Degrees of Separation' have exonerated Baltar in the eyes of the Fleet.

'Six Degrees of Separation' makes for compulsive viewing, even if it is largely an elaboration of ideas we have seen before. As it exploits the surreal concept of Head Six, we see the gradual evolution of Baltar's own beliefs about his situation, and the attitudes of others in the Fleet about Baltar himself.

9: Flesh and Bone

FIRST TRANSMISSION DATE: 6 December 2004

WRITER: Toni Graphia

DIRECTOR: Brad Turner

CREDITED CAST: Callum Keith Rennie (Leoben); Matthew Bennett (Aaron Doral); Christina Schild (Playa Kohn); Eric Breker (Gemenon Captain); Biski Gugushe (Hamilton)

SYNOPSIS: A Leoben Cylon is discovered on the *Gemenon Traveler*. Adama orders Starbuck to go there and interrogate him, which she does, combining aggression and psychological warfare with physical torture methods. Leoben reveals that Starbuck is something of a mythic figure to the Cylons, and claims that he has placed a nuclear warhead on timed detonator somewhere in the Fleet; the interrogation also delves into areas of religion, philosophy, the reasons why Cylons take human form, and Starbuck's abusive childhood. Roslin calls a stop to the interrogation, telling Leoben that she can guarantee his safety and order his release; Leoben confesses that the story about the warhead was a lie, claiming that he acted out of panic as he is too far away to download. He then embraces Roslin, and whispers to her that Adama is a Cylon. Disturbed, she orders that Leoben be thrown out of the airlock. Boomer visits Baltar and undergoes the Cylon test; Baltar learns she is a Cylon, but lies and tells her she is human. On Caprica, Sharon returns to Helo, but defies the orders of the other Cylons to lead him to a cabin and set up house with him, instead going on the run.

ANALYSIS: 'Flesh and Bone' is one of the most disturbing episodes of the entire series, with a high level of violence. Moore has said that this story fulfilled his personal mandate to raise questions in the viewer's mind, and indeed it does raise concerns about contemporary issues, through the story of the Cylon Leoben.

Echoes of Abu Ghraib: 'Flesh and Bone' on Torture

The story is a classic example of a controversial or difficult subject being explored through fiction. 'Flesh and Bone' was first aired in December 2004, not much more than seven months after the Abu Ghraib prison abuse scandal finally broke, though rumours had been circulating for some time before this about

American and British troops' mistreatment of prisoners in Iraq and in Guantanamo Bay. In the same way that the American and British public were confronted with crimes perpetrated by their own soldiers, the viewer is forced to see an heroic character, Starbuck, torturing Leoben quite savagely, justifying this by saying 'It's a machine, sir; there's no limit to the tactics I can use', with full sanction from Adama. Other reasonably sympathetic characters also dehumanise Leoben, with both Adamas insisting on referring to him as 'it', and Roslin calling him 'this thing'. The alternate view is also apparently aired, as Roslin points out, first, that Starbuck has gone too far and has gained no information from her activities, and, secondly, that the torture has done more harm than good, as it has given Leoben the opportunity to get the Fleet dispersed and vulnerable, since his resistance gives weight to his claim that there is indeed a bomb. Although this is not stated, it is also implicit that, since there is in fact no bomb, there is nothing he can say that will stop the torture, and equally that the situation has put Starbuck in a position where she has been forced to confront her inner demons, leaving her disconcerted. However, the episode does not portray Roslin simply as a liberal voice of reason, as her first statement could be part of a 'good cop' performance in order to get Leoben on side, and the second is a rebuke to Starbuck, after the latter is appalled that Roslin has just had Leoben brutally executed. This leaves it ambiguous as to what extent Roslin's statements derive from liberal politics, and how much from ruthless pragmatism. By the couching of the action in terms of Colonials and Cylons, sensitive political issues about real-life Americans and Iraqis are brought to the surface.

At the same time, though, uneasy connections are being forged. Starbuck continues to refer to the Cylon Raider as 'she', suggesting that it is possible for her to empathise with a Cylon, but only one in a machine-like, animal-like state, as the human-like ones are too close to humanity to be anything but disconcerting. On Caprica, by contrast, Six says of Sharon, 'I choose to think of her as one of them' and that 'We are what we do'. This suggests that Sharon becomes a human by imitating a human and raises the question of when, if ever, imitation becomes reality. Leoben's obsession with Starbuck is also deepened by his experiences in this story, and will become a kind of twisted love in later seasons.

The episode raises the question of what, if anything, is the difference between human and machine. Starbuck, early on, reasons that if Cylons sweat, then they must feel pain and discomfort like humans do. She sees Leoben as pretending to or aspiring to humanity, like *Star Trek*'s Data or the Tin Man from *The Wizard of Oz*, and, tellingly using the same reverse psychology Tigh used on her in the previous episode, poses the dilemma that, if Leoben turns off the pain, he is no longer vulnerable, but he will have shown himself to be a machine. When he attacks her and she says 'You frakked up', she means not only that she will ratchet up the torment in retaliation, but also that he has shown his machine side to her in using his full strength. When she asks why the Cylons would give themselves human vulnerabilities rather than improve on humanity, this question is at the heart of the Cylon identity and, indeed, religion.

God of Our Fathers: Religion and Faith

Faith is also a strong element of the story. Starbuck, building on Adama's encounter with another Leoben in the miniseries (about which she has read in Adama's after-action report), suggests that Leoben has been programmed to believe in God, but knows deep down that it is a program, and that this fuels his fear of not being able to download at death. However, Leoben implicitly likens Starbuck's own beliefs to programming, pointing out that she has absorbed her beliefs about faith and suffering from her abusive mother; and indeed it is true that the fear there is nothing after death is a very human one as well.

Starbuck's interrogation of Leoben reveals an elaboration on the Garden of Eden story of the Cylon faith, that the Cylons were created to be God's new chosen people when humanity repaid God's love with sin and evil; but, as Starbuck points out, humans created the Cylons, suggesting that humans take on the dual role of Satan and God toward them. When Starbuck points out that the Cylons' attack on the Colonies was itself evil, Leoben's defence is effectively to say that there are wider truths out there that she cannot comprehend (and certainly the mysterious actions of Head Six would seem to support this). He elaborates on this with his cryptic statements, first, that 'To look into the face of God is to know madness', later that 'I am God', and then that 'We are all God', united by God's love, indicating the vastness and incomprehensibility of both society and God. He says that he is part of everything and that part of him swims in the stream while in truth he stands on the shore (foreshadowing Baltar's comparison in 'Home' of unenlightened humans to salmon swimming in a river), and upon learning Starbuck's identity exclaims 'It all makes sense now', as if he is acting to a plan but the pieces have only just fallen into place for him – or the plan he has been working to has been revealed to be part of a greater one. Finally, Leoben's embracing Roslin before casting doubt on Adama's humanity, leading to her having him killed, seems a twisted reference to Judas embracing Christ before betraying him.

For the first time, religion is openly tied in with prophecy and the idea of the cyclical nature of time. Leoben's line 'All of this has happened before, and all of it will happen again' (which, according to Starbuck, is from Colonial scripture) will resonate through the series. This, plus his elaboration, 'Each of us plays … each time a different role', could be taken as literal (as a kind of scenario in which people repeat their actions, taking different roles each time), metatextual (as a sly reference to the original series), figurative (war, genocide, torture and abuse have all happened before, and, unless human nature changes drastically, will happen again), and personal (as Starbuck re-enacts her own abuse on him, suggesting that, as Leoben implies, next time she will be the prisoner and he the interrogator).

While Leoben says that he can see patterns in the universe, Roslin in this episode unwittingly begins her cycle of prophetic visions, dreaming of Leoben twice. She puts these dreams down to the effects of the Chamalla extract; and, although this turns out to be literally true, there is also a spiritual dimension to her experiences with the drug. In the first vision, she is running through a forest and sees Leoben shouting the word 'Cylon' over and over. Leoben then pulls her behind a tree, away from a troop of Marines. Then Leoben suddenly goes flying backwards away from her, as when he is thrown out the airlock (or, in the series' parlance, 'airlocked') later. In the second, Roslin is sitting at a mirror to brush her hair when Leoben comes up behind her and says he has something to tell her. The imagery is ambiguous, as is the question of what purpose the visions are intended to serve; Roslin interprets them as meaning that Leoben's statement that Adama is a Cylon is true, driving a wedge between the two leaders, but they could be read in other ways, for instance that she is being warned by an unknown force that Leoben's statements are false, and to beware of him, or else that they are a straightforward prophecy of events to come. Leoben's observation 'Things happen for a reason' again repeats the idea that there is a plan that the series' characters are following; but whether or not Roslin's interpretation of the visions leads her along the correct path is another question entirely.

Some new and ongoing aspects of the Cylon models are explored. We get again the suggestion that they have certain personality traits common to all units of the model: Six's nymphomania and jealousy, Sharon's empathy and fickleness, and, Adama suggests here, Leoben's tendency to deceive and subtle cunning. As well as having a similar demeanour and fashion sense, Leoben is using the same first name as his cohort from the miniseries, in contrast to Six, who has taken on at least two different names so far (as Baltar's girlfriend on Caprica does not appear to have gone by the name 'Shelley Godfrey'). The Cylon Raider is quite small seen close-up, about the size of a Viper, and its front design looks more like the head of a 1978 Centurian than like a modern Centurion. At the end of the story, however, we don't know what the truth is regarding Leoben; whether he was accidentally discovered, and really was too far out to download, or whether he was deliberately planted on the Fleet and was never in any danger of losing his consciousness. Although the background to, and fallout from, these events will be revealed, this will not be until Seasons Three and Four, and 'The Plan'.

Manifest Destiny: Starbuck's Past and Future

Starbuck's own personality and background are also explored. It is unknown whether Starbuck was assigned to interrogate Leoben because of her apparent empathy with the Cylon Raider, or because she has a vicious streak. Leoben's belief that she has a destiny is, we will learn in 'The Plan', inspired by her having flown the Cylon Raider, causing him to see her as a guiding force. There is an early hint about her abusive childhood when she remarks that her mother always said she had nothing in her head; and when Leoben talks about how she is shaped by what she suffered at her mother's hands, she almost kills him.

9: FLESH AND BONE

There is a direct parallel between Starbuck and humanity: if Starbuck's unconscious belief that her mother is right about her causes her to do evil things, so humanity, believing itself to be undeserving of God's grace, builds the instrument of its own destruction in the Cylons. At the end, Starbuck tells Roslin she can't put Leoben out the airlock, and prays to her own gods to have mercy on his soul. Leoben prophesies that Starbuck will find Kobol and the way to Earth, calling her 'Kara' for the first time as he does so, though there is the question of whether this is a genuine prophecy or a self-fulfilling one, with Starbuck acting because Leoben has given her the idea of what to do.

This exploration of Starbuck's character is paralleled by the two Boomers's ongoing process of self-discovery. While *Galactica*-Boomer undergoes Baltar's test because she wants to prove, both to herself and to Tyrol, that she is not a Cylon, Boomer is still stroking the Cylon Raider, and now humming to it. When Caprica-Boomer is asked by Six if she could kill Helo in the event that he won't participate in their experiment, she doesn't answer, but at this point she clearly decides to deviate from the plan and to keep running rather than settle down with Helo. This indicates that even Sharons who are fully aware of their nature have empathy with humans. (Her explanation to Helo as to why they have to leave – that she saw Cylons coming their way – distances herself from the Cylons). Back on *Galactica*, Baltar is left with a dilemma: whether to reveal to Boomer that she is a Cylon and risk her killing him before he tells the others, or to keep quiet about it and thus endanger the Fleet. He chooses the latter, which will prove to be a fateful decision.

Questioning Reality: Continuity and Worldbuilding

In terms of the ongoing themes of the series, the story again covers the idea of the power of belief on the mind, and indeed on reality (picking up on *The Prisoner*-esque nature of the previous episode). Baltar's report to Boomer that she is human must go against everything she knows intellectually, given the events of the past several episodes, but she accepts it because she wants to believe it. Doubt and paranoia continue to suffuse the Fleet; the time stamp on the Caprica sequences indicates that it has been only 24 hours since the events of 'Six Degrees of Separation', and Leoben's statement to Roslin that Adama is a Cylon, whether true or false, clearly shakes her and spreads doubt that will have repercussions in the subsequent episode. Finally, though, Leoben says, 'What is the first article of faith? This is not all that we are', and adds that if souls do not exist, then we are all machines, human or Cylon. These statements both raise the idea that to be considered worthy, humans, like Cylons, must believe that they are more than mere creatures bent on survival.

Some foreshadowing of future events occurs, and also some referencing of past ones. Adama's scene with the original Leoben's corpse in the morgue recalls the miniseries, as at one point he holds the phone as if he'd like to beat the corpse with it; the episode's events also have parallels with Adama's encounter with Leoben in the miniseries; both involve equal amounts of philosophising and brutal violence, culminating in murder. Baltar's misidentifying of Boomer's accent as Aerilon is an early hint that, despite his efforts to be taken as a Caprican, he is in fact from the former colony. Leoben's lie about a warhead being in the Fleet looks back to, and also foreshadows, events surrounding Baltar's request for such an item.

In terms of things to watch out for, *Galactica*-Boomer, outlining a backstory drawn from the series bible, says her parents died in an explosion in a mining settlement named Troy – an oblique reference to *Galactica 1980* (in which 'Troy' was the name of one of the protagonists) as well as a classical one (hinting that *Galactica*-Boomer is a Trojan Horse). The idols of Artemis and Athena to which Starbuck prays look like ancient Greek bronzes. Starbuck eating in front of Leoben as part of the interrogation, intended to break him down through hunger, recalls a similar sequence in Fritz Lang's film *Hangmen Also Die!* (1943). Unlike the earlier meals featured in the series, which were eaten with chopsticks, this one sees Starbuck use a fork. On a lighter note, Head Six's jocular 'She shoots, she scores!' suggests that Colonial culture has some equivalent of *Hockey Night in Canada*; and the tune Boomer hums to the Raider (an action that, to judge by its absence in the 13 July 2004 draft, was added in performance) is a Korean children's song.

Teaching the Controversy: Writing and Production

This episode's director, Brad Turner, had previously worked on *24*, *The Outer Limits*, *Stargate SG1* and its spin-off *Stargate: Atlantis*. There is a deleted scene where Starbuck learns that Leoben was carrying a device like that found in CIC in the miniseries, though what it is will not be revealed until the end of the season. In the podcast for 'Tigh Me Up, Tigh Me Down', Moore mentions that 'Flesh and Bone' was unsurprisingly controversial with the network, and that the story had in fact been slightly toned down from the first draft, in which Leoben was to have been at one point actually hooked up to electrodes. Moore apparently removed this out of concern that it would cause the audience to focus on the methods of torture rather than the emotional implications of Starbuck's treatment of Leoben. The network's concerns led in part to the decision to make the subsequent episode more comedic; 'Tigh Me Up, Tigh Me Down' was originally to have revolved around a standoff between Tigh and Adama in which each believes the other to be a Cylon, but Leoben's words to Roslin at the end of this episode caused it to be developed instead into a standoff between Roslin and Adama about the former's suspicions regarding the latter's possible Cylonhood.

Although the 13 July 2004 draft of the 'Flesh and Bone' script is close to the final version, it does still reveal some interesting changes. Caprica-Sharon's meeting with Doral and Six in a playground was originally to have begun with Doral looking wistfully around the equipment and saying 'Imagine what it'll be like', in a foreshadowing of the Cylons' actual plans for the future. The Cylons' scheme to provide a cabin in the woods for Sharon and Helo is said also to include the supply of a wireless that will broadcast false information, such as reports of the *Galactica*'s destruction, to encourage Helo to abandon thoughts of leaving Caprica. In the draft, Sharon says 'By your command' to the others, but doesn't in the final version. There are a couple of unnecessary but effective lines, for instance where Adama says of the Raider 'There's a phrase from Salonen [presumably a Colonial writer]: "A terrible, awful beauty"', or where Leoben, mocked by Kara for emulating humans, says 'I'm more than human. A greater and more advanced creature. Ennobled by God's own hand'. Leoben also, later, observes that Kara does not enjoy inflicting pain, adding that whatever she's been taught about herself, she's different. He ultimately informs her, 'Your people's struggles are not in vain. And neither are mine', indicating the linked destiny of the two races. Finally, when Baltar compliments Boomer on her appearance, Head Six cattily comments, in a deleted (but definitely in-character) line, that she needs to do something with her hair and make-up.

'Flesh and Bone' is one of the most overtly political episodes of the first season, but also one that articulates most clearly the ideas about religion, human nature and cyclical time that underlie the series as a whole.

10: Tigh Me Up, Tigh Me Down

FIRST TRANSMISSION DATE: 13 December 2004 (UK)

WRITER: Jeff Vlaming

DIRECTOR: Edward James Olmos

CREDITED CAST: Kate Vernon (Ellen Tigh); Matthew Bennett (Aaron Doral); Alex Green (Deckhand)

SYNOPSIS: Following Leoben's accusation in the previous episode, and some unexplained absences and unlogged calls on Adama's part, Roslin suspects the Commander of being a Cylon, and orders Baltar, now that the Cylon detector has been completed, to test Adama first. Adama, however, turns up in a Raptor bringing with him a woman who is revealed to be Ellen, wife of Colonel Tigh, and secretly orders Baltar to prioritise testing her. Roslin initially rescinds this order, but upon learning who Ellen is, reinstates it. At a dinner party, Ellen proves a disruptive influence, and she later insinuates to Tigh that Adama has been secretly visiting her. At Baltar's lab, all parties confront each other, Adama revealing that he suspected Ellen of being a Cylon, and Roslin that she suspected Adama of the same. Baltar provides a test result that Ellen is human – but, following the Boomer incident, he has decided to keep the real result a secret, and only Baltar knows the truth …

ANALYSIS: Edward James Olmos's directorial debut on *Battlestar Galactica*, and the series' only out-and-out comedy episode, 'Tigh Me Up, Tigh Me Down' also introduces one of its most memorable characters and comes as a welcome counterpoint to the first season's grimmer episodes.

Tighs of Steel: Ellen and Saul Tigh

The return of Ellen marks the beginning of a battle for Tigh's soul between his commanding officer and his wife. At the start of the story, Tigh pours out his last measure of alcohol into the waste bin and throws out his picture of Ellen, indicating that he has given up his addictions. Then, however, the means to continue with both turns up again in the form of his wife with a bottle of ambrosia. As Adama says, 'Ellen used to encourage the worst instincts in the guy. Bring out the self-destructive streak in him'. Even then, he does not drink until she fills her mouth with liquor and kisses him.

Despite everything, Tigh still maintains his personal/professional distinction,

10: TIGH ME UP, TIGH ME DOWN

and dialogue with Ellen would indicate that this is at least partly behind their estrangement; he will not shirk his duties, and is still on top form, suggesting that the seemingly random jumps of an apparently 'wounded' Cylon Raider be tracked to acquire data about Cylon FTL technology, but also suspecting (correctly, as it happens) that it is faking its injuries, and launching the alert fighters as a precaution. Even his extreme drunkenness in front of Adama, Roslin and Lee takes place when he is off duty. The exchange between Ellen and Adama where she says, 'Don't frak with me Bill', and he replies, 'Don't frak with me either, Ellen', refers both to her dangerously unbridled sexuality, and to their opposition to each other.

The question is raised from the very beginning as to whether Ellen is a Cylon or not. Parallels are drawn between her and Six; blonde women who tempt a man with something he desires to betray his loyalty. Our first sight of Ellen is of a pair of long legs under a skirt that, in the darkness of the Raptor, looks red, and there is even a sequence where Tigh/Ellen and Baltar/Head Six adopt poses mirroring each other, as the woman leans over the man's shoulder. Tigh's burning of Ellen's picture with a cigar in the miniseries, which is recapped here, also has Cylon imagery, giving the photo a burning red eye.

Ellen has turned up mysteriously, but it would seems out of character for a Cylon to announce her presence in such an obvious way, and even if her implausible story about surviving the holocaust through being rescued by a stranger while at an airport is a lie, this could be simply for the mundane reason of wanting to cover up some bit of philandering. And, however improbable, the rescue could be something that really did happen.[32]

Ellen is a disruptive influence at dinner, hinting to Roslin that the President lacks public confidence, 'innocently' bringing up Zak's death and playing footsie with Lee under the table; but this could either be a Cylon tactic to sow dissent, or simply evidence that Ellen enjoys causing trouble. Her remark that she knows who Baltar is could be just flirtation with a celebrity scientist, or a veiled hint that he should toe the Cylon party line. She yells out, 'Bill Adama doesn't know where Earth is!' in a public corridor, and attempts to undermine Tigh's friendship with Adama by claiming that he has tried to seduce her, but again, this could be attributed either to Cylon plotting, or else simply to drunken jealousy of her husband's boss.

Lee's comment on the subject – 'If she's not [a Cylon], we're in a lot of trouble' – is telling, meaning both that there is then no way Ellen can be removed, however problematic she becomes, and also that humanity is as much at risk of tearing itself apart through suspicion and paranoia as of falling victim to Cylon ploys. Of course, the final possibility – that she is a Cylon and doesn't know it – will not be answered until all the Cylon models are revealed later in the series.

---

[32] The mystery is resolved in 'The Plan'.

Mistaken Identities: Cylons and Suspected Cylons

A related storyline revolves around Roslin's suspicions that Adama is a Cylon. When they have their conversation early on about the Cylon detection test, where Adama says 'I think people in sensitive positions should go first', the uncharacteristic directness of Roslin's reply, 'I agree; how about you?', suggests the degree of her concern. Throughout, Adama's behaviour can be interpreted as having multiple possible motives, one of them being that he is a Cylon agent. Even his bringing in Ellen could be seen, variously, as an attempt to distract from everyone's suspicions of him, a plan to undermine Tigh's competence, or a plot between two Cylons (himself and Ellen). His visits to Ellen on the *Rising Star* could be a cover for nefarious behaviour, or simply a move to verify her identity before he unleashes her on Tigh again. If he isn't a Cylon, however, he has nonetheless shown himself capable of using deceptive and secretive behaviour toward his colleagues and Roslin, again suggesting that the greater threat comes from within. In a deleted scene where we learn that the wounded Raptor sent a data burst to *Galactica*, presumably to a Cylon agent there, Tigh shoots Adama a suspicious look. At the end of the episode, the only one who has proof positive whether or not Ellen and/or Adama are Cylons is Baltar, who, for obvious reasons, will never reveal the truth.

On Caprica, meanwhile, clearly Sharon is keeping Helo alive not just because it's her job, but because she has grown to love him. Doral acknowledges that he himself would like to feel such love, and suggests that Six is envious of them. Six's reaction, in a clever bit of acting from Tricia Helfer, clearly indicates that he has hit a nerve; and, as Moore points out in his podcast, this means that once again the audience is caught feeling sympathetic toward the ostensible enemy.

Your Lying Tighs: Continuity and Worldbuilding

Elsewhere in the ongoing story, Dualla and Billy are becoming more serious in their relationship, though she also surmises quickly that he is using her to spy on Adama. Although a few days have passed since the previous episode, Baltar's manner with Roslin clearly indicates that he has not forgotten about her treatment of him when he was under suspicion in 'Six Degrees of Separation'. Baltar has sex with Head Six, or it may well be literal masturbation (as Starbuck clearly thinks when she walks in on them); in a deleted scene where Baltar takes a blood test from Starbuck, Head Six reveals a hitherto-unseen side to herself, remarking to him, 'Tell you what, if you do manage to get into her pants ... I'll join you'.[33]

Adama is apparently qualified to fly Raptors as well as Vipers, though, curiously, neither he nor Ellen wear protective flightsuits. Billy's suggestion that

---

[33] SPOILER SECTION: This foreshadows her real-world analogue Caprica-Six's apparent taste for bisexual threesomes (see, for instance, 'Hero') and/or the lesbian relationship that the Six called Gina has with Admiral Cain.

10: TIGH ME UP, TIGH ME DOWN

'Adama has been somehow replaced by a Cylon duplicate' indicates that in the absence of information about the human-like Cylons, some people are, logically enough, assuming that they can be duplicates of actual humans. Head Six's reason for encouraging Baltar to build the Cylon detector becomes clearer in this story, in that it allows her to keep control of the situation; Baltar is the inventor and operator of the device, and she is the one in charge of his actions.

There are a few original-series references to watch out for. Ellen is said to have been on the *Rising Star*, and the original-series episode 'Murder on the *Rising Star*' partly revolved around certain passengers on the eponymous vessel having escaped the holocaust under suspicious circumstances. Much as Apollo takes his friends up to stargaze in *Galactica*'s Celestial Chamber in the original-series episode 'The Hand of God', we learn that in the reimagined series a popular pastime for courting couples is to watch the stars from the observation deck. Moore in the podcast justifies the inclusion of the observation deck window by saying that the crews on deep space missions might need some place where they could look out at the stars as a break from the monotony and claustrophobia of the spaceship; however, he misses a trick here, as unlike the Celestial Chamber and window on the original *Galactica*'s bridge, the observation deck has no shielding. Delphi, the Caprican city namechecked here for the first time, recalls the Delphian Empire mentioned in the original series story 'The Living Legend' as well as the home of the classical Greek oracle; earlier drafts of the script have Helo wondering 'if the Oracle's still standing' in the Caprican city, suggesting a building or monument.

Crimson Tigh: Writing and Production

In terms of story development, draft scripts exist from 9 and 16 July 2004, which are both broadly the same as the final episode, except that there are some superficial dialogue and scene order differences, and the relationship between Billy and Dualla is given slightly more emphasis (which partly survives in a deleted scene in which Gaeta quizzes Dualla about whether she 'got laid' the previous night). The main significant difference is the inclusion of a minor subplot suggesting a burgeoning relationship between Baltar and Boomer; she comes to see him in the pilot's lounge to thank him for confirming her as a human, and they wind up together on the observation deck, where she tells him she feels she has a destiny and he accidentally lets slip that he believes in a single God, which she finds attractive. However, Head Six warns Baltar that by 'connecting a Cylon sleeper agent with her faith' he is endangering everyone in the Fleet – although she later also says that his telling Boomer about monotheism is him 'doing God's work'). We hear in the pilots' lounge scene a brief portion of a talk-wireless programme (which will feature strongly later on, in 'Colonial Day'), in which a caller asserts that there are Cylons at the highest level of government.

Although a Baltar-Boomer relationship would have been an intriguing prospect (and an ironic inversion of the Baltar-Caprica-Six relationship, in that he knows she is a Cylon but she doesn't), it was presumably abandoned due to it being slightly incompatible both with Baltar's growing obsession with Kara (who herself has the corner on being the pilot with a mysterious destiny) and with Boomer's increasing isolation from the rest of the Fleet.

The episode had the working title 'Secrets and Lies' (visible as an alternate title on the 9 July draft script), and was originally to have presented a serious story based loosely on the movie *Crimson Tide*. This would have involved Adama and Tigh believing each other to be Cylons, the tension building up, and the pair eventually drawing guns on each other. However, as noted above, following the brutality of 'Flesh and Bone' it was considered more appropriate to, as Moore says on the podcast, 'try a different tone ... see if the show [could] withstand something lighter'.

The final episode title is a pun on Pedro Almodovar's controversial 1990 film *Tie Me Up! Tie Me Down!*. Although the transmitted version works well, and it is thus a shame that there were not more overtly humorous episodes in the series, Olmos and the cast found the idea of doing comedy disconcerting, and Moore has said 'I don't really think it's our strong suit'. A lot of the lines in the 9 July draft that were cut by the 16 July draft are ones that seem to be trying too hard to be comedic. For instance, the sequence early on where Billy and Laura discuss Adama's odd behaviour includes Laura teasing Billy about his striking out with Dualla, and Billy getting revenge by teasing Laura about her relationship with Adama; Baltar's manner with Roslin is much more cheeky, with him saying 'You don't send me flowers anymore!' when she rings up to inquire about Adama's test results; and Ellen Tigh, on encountering Boomer and learning that she has just passed her Cylon test, bitchily observes, 'Isn't that funny? I took one look at you and thought, "Here's a girl who isn't good at taking tests"). These omissions all suggest that the writing team were not comfortable with the idea of scripting comedy.

Moore has said that he had not planned for Tigh's wife to feature beyond the hint of marital discord in the miniseries, but that the rest of the writing team were so intrigued by the lurid description of her in the series bible (where she features, under the name 'Sherry' but with her character otherwise unchanged, as part of Tigh's backstory) that they lobbied for her resurrection. Moore has also said that he was concerned that the reappearance of Ellen Tigh would be seen as contrived, and consequently he did not want the series to feature any other 'finding a lost relative aboard the Fleet' storylines. However, it is handled very well, and certainly comes across as less implausible than, for instance, Starbuck's finding and controlling of the Cylon Raider in 'You Can't Go Home Again'.

Edward James Olmos – who was originally to have directed 'Flesh and Bone', but could not in the end due to scheduling conflicts – handles his debut behind-the-camera assignment very well. Lucy Lawless was originally approached to play Ellen (Eick, who had worked at Renaissance Pictures, the production company behind *Xena: Warrior Princess*, was keen to get the latter's star into the series, but would not succeed until the introduction of the D'Anna Biers character in Season Two). Moore's podcast indicates that much of the

10: TIGH ME UP, TIGH ME DOWN

comedy and sexy 'business' in the story (e.g. Baltar pretending to be doing exercises to cover for being caught masturbating, and Ellen wrapping her legs around her husband's neck) was improvised by the actors themselves. Olmos apparently removed a number of other improvised sequences from his original edit, although some Cylon Raider material that he also cut was reinstated for the broadcast version; he has nonetheless gone on record as saying that he is satisfied with the final version.

The finished production is a brilliant mix of drama and comedy, with some very funny aspects (e.g. Mary MacDonnell's performance when the bombshell is dropped that the Ellen whom Adama wanted prioritised for Cylon testing is Tigh's wife, and Baltar's world-weary attitude to his superiors' continued changes of plans) and a visual fourth-wall breach as Ellen throws the cap of the ambrosia bottle at the camera. The ending is pure French farce, as the central figures realise that they have all been suspecting each other of being Cylons.

There are several details worth watching out for. The opera playing in the background as Baltar contemplates the enormity of his task was originally to have been a Mozart piece, but, as it stands, is one called 'Battlestar Operatica', written and composed by Bear McCreary, with the lyrics (in Italian): 'Woe upon your Cylon heart/There's a toaster in your head/And it wears high heels/Number Six calls to you/The Cylon detector beckons/Your girlfriend is a toaster/Woe upon your Cylon heart/Alas, disgrace! Alas, sadness and misery!/The toaster has a pretty dress/Red like its glowing spine/Number Six whispers/By your command'. These lyrics presumably reflect Baltar's state of mind and suspicions about Head Six rather than the actual situation. This episode also marks the first time that the upper level of CIC features prominently, and Baltar's calculations as to how long all the tests will take assume a 365-day year with no leap days (perhaps hinting at how long a year is on Caprica).

There are also a couple of continuity errors. First, whereas Boomer's Cylon detector test took only a few minutes in 'Flesh and Bone', it now takes 11 hours to get a reading. Moore has said that he wanted to avoid the *Star Trek* cliché of instantly available results, but there is also the clear narrative advantage that, if the detection time was only a few minutes, then everyone on the Fleet could be tested on short order, and thus there would be little possibility for drama. Secondly, the picture of Ellen that Tigh is seen burning changes from one of Jenny Birchfield-Eick in the miniseries, to one of Kate Vernon here, and whereas in the miniseries he burns it in the eye, in the recap clip here he burns it below the eye – although when he produces the picture in the episode itself, it is burnt in the eye like the one in the miniseries.

Complicated continuity errors aside, the story is clever and witty, with a dark edge and a wicked portrayal of the relationships between the central characters that manages to avoid cliché. It also makes physical the personal-professional conflict in Tigh's life, in the form of the mysterious Ellen.

11: The Hand of God

FIRST TRANSMISSION DATE: 1 January 2005 (UK)

WRITERS: David Weddle & Bradley Thompson

DIRECTOR: Jeff Woolnough

CREDITED Lorena Gale (Elosha); Cailin Stadnyk (Ensign Davis); Bodie Olmos (Costanza/Hot Dog); Luciana Carro (Katraine); Terry Chen (Perry/Chuckles); Christina Schild (Playa Kohn); Biski Gugushe (Hamilton); Paul Cummings (Pilot/Fireball); Camille Sullivan (Pilot/Stepchild)

SYNOPSIS: The Fleet runs low on tylium, an ore needed for fuel. An asteroid is found that contains large amounts of the ore, but it is also occupied by Cylons. Starbuck comes up with a strategy to have civilian freighters pose as a mining fleet unaware of the Cylon presence and thereby decoy the Raiders away while the *Galactica* jumps in to send her Vipers to attack the Cylon base. As the resident Cylon expert, Baltar is asked to indicate where the Vipers should bomb to hit the volatile refined tylium precursor; putting his faith in God, he chooses randomly. When the operation begins, the Cylons do not take the bait and instead continue on to attack *Galactica*, but a squadron of Vipers, which have been concealed in a freighter, join the battle at a crucial moment. Apollo, leading the mission, successfully hits the refined tylium precursor using Baltar's coordinates. Roslin experiences a vision of snakes, and the priest Elosha interprets this as meaning that she is the leader foretold in the prophecies of Pythia, who will take the Fleet to Earth but die in the process. On Caprica, Sharon is showing early symptoms of pregnancy, but denies it to Helo.

ANALYSIS: The second contribution from the Thompson and Weddle writing team is referred to by Moore in his commentary podcast as a 'Big Mac episode', meaning that the team saved money during the rest of the season so that they could splurge on the big battle sequence at this story's climax. Special effects aside, however, this is one of the less engaging episodes, redeemed somewhat by the unexpected twist during the battle sequence.

Handing it to Them: Problems and Resolutions

This story takes place nine days after the previous one, and begins unfortunately with the science-fiction cliché of having a major character announce 'We're running out of [a crucial resource]' as we learn that tylium reserves are down to

11: THE HAND OF GOD

5%. The clichés do not end there: Starbuck and Adama have a conversation about the burdens of command and how much easier it is to be on the firing line, and Commander Adama gives his son his lucky cigarette lighter (which, although he supposedly always carries it, has never been seen before) in an exchange of dialogue that is both trite and cloying. Although Apollo's attack run on the base is intended, according to Moore, as a deliberate homage to *Star Wars*, this unhappily means that it comes across as something that has been done to death. Boomer's pregnancy, like that of every single pregnant character on television, is heralded by her throwing up.

Elsewhere, there is a peculiar incident where Starbuck thinks outside the box while Adama, Tigh and Apollo sit there dimly thinking only of textbook strategies (which seems a little out of character for all three men); and just as odd is the fact that Tigh and Starbuck seemingly view Baltar as an expert on everything simply because he is a 'scientist'. The stupidity of this idea is underlined by the fact that Baltar doesn't actually know anything about the layout of Cylon tylium refineries. While this could be argued to be a witty subversion of the cliché, it does not make Starbuck or Tigh look particularly bright. Most of the dialogue is fairly banal, with Sharon and Helo in particular speaking only in info-dumps. It also has to be said that, in a series where pilots' nicknames tend to have ironic connotations, calling a pilot 'Fireball' is just asking for it, and the black humour negates any possible sympathy the audience might feel at his death. There is also the question of how there came to be tactical models of the civilian ships of the Fleet. The song at the end, included at the instigation of the series' producers, is called 'Wander My Friends', by Bear McCreary, and has Irish Gaelic lyrics that go 'Wander my friends, wander with me, like the mist on the green mountain ...' and so on along the same unfortunately well-worn themes.

Other things that initially appear to be problems, however, turn out to have justifications. It seems a massive coincidence that Boomer and Crashdown find the tylium-bearing asteroid, considering that they were the ones who found the water in the episode of that name, but less so in light of the fact that the Cylons wanted them to find it, as they are staking out the asteroid in the hope of destroying the Fleet. It thus suggests that Boomer may be acting subconsciously on their behalf. The fact that Baltar's random choice of a point on the map turns out to be the correct spot for the Vipers to bomb also seems improbable at first, but Head Six hints at the end that the destruction of the base was part of God's plan, providing another indication of the influence of a higher power, and one that clearly wants the Fleet to survive and continue its journey.

Some of the clichéd aspects of the Apollo storyline are also redeemed by what we know about his situation; his concerns that he isn't up to the job, and Starbuck's reassurances that he will be fine, have overtones of what happened to Zak, which makes Starbuck's confidence in him less than inspiring (as the last time she told an Adama he would be fine, it led to his death). Moore notes that Adama's giving Apollo the lighter also indicates that his father doesn't think he's up to it either, suggesting that the general lack of confidence in him is giving

Apollo a few issues.

The military strategy is, furthermore, the episode's main redeeming feature. Although we never see it fully articulated on screen, Starbuck's original thinking was evidently that, once the Cylons became aware that the *Galactica*'s Vipers were attacking the base, all or part of the Cylon force would likely turn back to defend it; and, when they did, the Vipers hidden inside the *Colonial Movers* freighter would emerge and attack them from the rear. What actually happens, however, is that, when the Cylons detect the attack force from *Galactica*, they send up an extra 50 Raiders to engage them; and when the *Galactica* recalls the Vipers, the original attack force approaching the decoys also turns back to attack *Galactica*. However, the reserve squadron concealed in the freighter is then released to attack the undefended base directly, and the Colonial forces are subsequently able to wipe out the remaining Raiders. Starbuck's plan is thus not only clever, but also has an element of flexibility that allowed a potentially disastrous situation to be saved, underlining the point that any successful military strategy has to take into account the fact that wars never go exactly as planned. The Colonial force thus wins through a combination of forward planning, luck and good judgment.

Thou Good and Faithful Serpent: Religion and Head Six

In religious terms, this story introduces the prophecies of Pythia, which will become a motivating principle behind the Colonials' actions for a large portion of the series. Roslin's belief that she is the leader, dying of a wasting disease, who is the subject of the prophecy, will come to obsess her in later episodes. However, this is subtly called into question in an extended version of a scene where she discusses her vision with Billy, and he says 'Doc Cottle said the side effects would include hallucinations ... My uncle was a priest, they used to take Chamalla in seminary to seek higher levels of consciousness'.

The crucial prophecy is quoted by Elosha as: 'And the lords anointed a leader to guide the caravan of the heavens to their new homeland, and unto the leader they gave a vision of serpents, numbering two and ten, as a sign of things to come'. Head Six later interprets the 12 serpents of the prophecy as the 12 Vipers that come out of the freighter. She further quotes the scriptures, saying that this will lead to a 'conflict at the home of the Gods', foreshadowing the Fleet's trip to Kobol later on. The line 'All this has happened before and all this will happen again' recurs, this time attributed to Pythia. (Moore has pointed out that it is the opening line of the Disney version of *Peter Pan* (1953), bringing in connotations of childhood and growing up.)

The Hand of God is also literally present in this episode, as Baltar's apparently divinely-inspired pointing is what gives the Colonial ships their target. Crucially, however, Head Six also says 'God doesn't take sides', again hinting at a far greater truth behind the two races' religious partisanship.

11: THE HAND OF GOD

Need to Know: Continuity and Worldbuilding

As for the series' ongoing threads and themes, Adama is again (justifiably) secretive, restricting details of plans as a matter of routine. Baltar assumes a palms-up cruciform pose when he says he is the instrument of God, in an early example of the Baltar-as-Jesus imagery that will become a strong feature of the final season; although, as Jo Storm notes in her book *Frak You!: The Ultimate Unauthorized Guide to Battlestar Galactica*, this also reflects his ongoing egotism, as he becomes interested in God only when he believes that he has a direct personal connection to the deity. In Baltar's fantasy, Head Six gives his neck a hard twist as she's massaging him, right after she's told him to put his faith in God, in a visual reference to a scene in *Jacob's Ladder* (1990) in which a similar manoeuvre is performed on Jacob by a chiropractor, who is also, symbolically, an agent of God intent on guiding him to the afterlife. We learn that Adama's father's name was Joseph, that Colonials learn about Pythia in school as part of ancient history (Baltar mentions that the last time he studied her was in sixth grade) and that Crashdown has been trying to impress Ensign Davies, with whom he has a relationship, by taking credit for finding the water in the earlier story (and Boomer is slightly irked by this). Chuckles, who dies this episode, was one of the team of nuggets introduced in 'Act of Contrition'. Baltar's fantasies, although they seem to last for long periods subjectively, take only a few seconds of objective time. Finally, Adama's iconic line, 'Sometimes you have to roll the hard six', takes on a double meaning when you consider that it was Baltar's rolling of the hard Six that got them into trouble in the first place.

Although this episode shares a title with an original-series story, it doesn't much resemble its predecessor except in that both involve a head-on confrontation with the Cylons. Weddle and Thompson have gone on record as saying that they came up with the title independently, and that its duplication of an original-series one is pure coincidence, but viewers can draw their own conclusions. However, the story does have strong conceptual connections with the original series: first in that it is akin to some of the latter's episodes that revolved around the search for resources (particularly fuel); secondly in that it is focused on the Cylons 'staking out waterholes' as in 'Saga of a Star World'; and finally in that it was based by Weddle and Thompson on the Battle of Midway, the same engagement that informed the battle sequences in 'Saga of a Star World', 'Lost Planet of the Gods' and 'The Living Legend'. According to *The Official Companion*, Eick, concerned that there were not enough story ideas to complete the season, asked the writing team for three or four suggestions per writer; Weddle and Thompson gave him about 16, one of which was simply a suggestion for an episode based on the Battle of Midway, which he seized upon. The Viper battles are visibly influenced by WWII films, as in the original series (and the visual effects team, who were notorious for putting in references to the original series Fleet, hid the Vipers in a ship similar in design to the original series' 'Colonial Movers' vessel, which even faintly bears the 'Colonial Movers' legend on its side). Finally, there is a similarity between Adama giving his son a lucky cigarette lighter before he goes on his mission, and the original Apollo giving his own son a medallion to keep safe in 'The Gun on Ice Planet Zero'. In terms of outside references, the death of Fireball recalls the similarly ironic ending of the pilot Dead Meat in *Hot Shots!* (1991).

Greeks Bearing Gifts: Writing and Production

The story was not initially planned to be as big a special effects spectacular as it ultimately became. Weddle and Thompson envisaged having the battle depicted entirely from CIC; an idea the series will resort to later on as a money-saving measure. Their original storyline was a by-the-book adventure; when instructed by Moore and Eick to make it more sophisticated they came up with the Trojan Horse addition, a left-field idea perhaps reflected in the story itself in Starbuck's confrontation with Tigh about conventional versus unconventional thinking. The episode was originally to have followed 'Flesh and Bone', but the order was changed as Moore felt that Leoben's revelation at the end of the story would make a perfect set-up for 'Tigh Me Up, Tigh Me Down'. This necessitated the Caprica sequences of the two episodes being swapped around, as they build on each other.

The director assigned to the episode, Jeff Woolnough, had previous telefantasy experience working on *Stargate: SG1*, *Smallville* and *Dead Like Me*. In *The Official Companion Season Two*, Weddle explains that the phrase 'roll a hard six' was an expression his father used, referring to the gambling game craps, and meaning to take a risk when the stakes are high.

As well as the Trojan Horse tactic of concealing the Vipers in the freighter, the story contains another direct reference to Greek mythology: the Pythia was the priestess at Delphi (the place to which Helo and Sharon are headed), who interpreted the prophecies of Apollo and whose name has an etymological connection to the word 'python'. This connects both to Apollo's own destiny as a politician and to Roslin's visions of snakes.

In terms of things to watch out for, a railway track can be seen from the balcony of Baltar's house, and a conversation between Gaeta and Apollo hints that the Colonials know where the Cylon homeworld is ('They'd build a refinery this far from their homeworld?' 'Why not? They need fuel out here just as much as we do'), which is sharply contradicted later in the series. One Caprica scene, which originally involved Helo and Sharon referring to multiple human-like Cylons as the pair approach Delphi, had to be hastily rewritten after Grace Park pointed out that Helo didn't know about the existence of human-like Cylons at all, let alone multiple copies. This scene, modified to take Helo's ignorance into account, will later become the basis for the first Cylon-Occupied Caprica sequence in 'Colonial Day'.

Some additional material appears in the 16 and 27 July 2004 drafts in the scene where Roslin first talks with Elosha. In this we learn that Elosha grew up on 'the lower West Side of Tihalla', apparently a notoriously bad neighbourhood, and got religion when told by a judge that she had the choice of

11: THE HAND OF GOD

reform school or a seminary. While at the seminary, she took Chamalla, and one of her visions involved 'a giant hard-boiled egg with ruby red lips, [which] lectured [her] on dental hygiene'. Elosha also says that she is not a fundamentalist and had never considered taking the Sacred Scrolls literally until hearing of Roslin's visions. This ultimately deleted sequence affords Elosha some much-needed background and characterisation, though somewhat at the expense of her dignity and authority.

The 16 July draft also has a slightly different version of Baltar's conversation with Head Six about the best way to blow up the refinery, in which Baltar's complaint 'God could do with cleaning his ears out' is rendered as, 'If you ask me, [God] lacks basic communication skills'. The same draft also has Laura announcing that they may have to abandon less efficient ships if the fuel crisis continues.

The term 'Big Mac episode' sums up many aspects of 'The Hand of God'; most of the episode is a tasty treat that looks delicious, but once the clever military strategy has been digested, what remains has little nutritional value and ultimately leaves the viewer unsatisfied. This may be down largely to the episode's almost exclusive focus on the military characters, which will be matched by the next episode's concentration on the political side of the series.

12: Colonial Day

FIRST TRANSMISSION DATE: 10 January 2005

WRITER: Carla Robinson

DIRECTOR: Jonas Pate

CREDITED CAST: Richard Hatch (Tom Zarek); Kate Vernon (Ellen Tigh); Robert Wisden (Wallace Gray); David Kaye (James McManus); Alex Zahara (Valance); Patrick Gallagher (Leon Grimes); Malcolm Stewart (Marshall Bagott); Cailin Stadnyk (Ensign Davis); Christina Schild (Playa Palacios); Biski Gugushe (Sekou Hamilton); James Ashcroft (Spectator #1); Patricia Idlette (Sarah Porter); Mario Battista (Gardner)

SYNOPSIS: The interim Quorum of Twelve, including Zarek as the delegate for Sagittaron and Baltar as the delegate for Caprica, hold their first meeting aboard the luxury liner *Cloud 9*, on Colonial Day, the anniversary of the signing of the Articles of Colonisation. Zarek moves that the Quorum should elect a Vice-President and puts himself forward as a candidate. Roslin puts forward her adviser, Wallace Gray, as a counter-candidate. When a supporter of Zarek's starts a bar fight, Apollo and Starbuck discover another man, Valance, to be concealing a gun in a briefcase and apparently planning to assassinate Roslin, but Valance is found dead before the pair can discover who is behind it. Roslin, fearing that Zarek plans to have himself elected Vice-President and then have her killed, and noting Baltar's increasing popularity with the electorate, orders Gray to withdraw from the race and persuades Baltar to stand instead. Baltar is elected. On Caprica, Helo sees human-like Cylons, including a Sharon. Realising that he has been duped, he runs away.

ANALYSIS: After the focus on the military side of the equation for most of the season, 'Colonial Day' turns its gaze onto the political figures in the Fleet. Adama's remark 'Politics: as exciting as war' sums up the episode precisely, as it establishes that Roslin, Zarek *et al* are not a sideshow or grace note to the space-related action, but a central part of the series.

Clouded Issues: Roslin versus Zarek

Roslin's *realpolitik* takes the central position in this story. Although she warns Adama that direct action against Zarek would seem like thwarting democracy, she is happy to act against him through backroom dealings, and is also happy

12: COLONIAL DAY

to exploit the media's interest in Zarek by appearing to welcome him warmly at the start of the episode. She is establishing an interim Quorum of Twelve, the first since the attacks, chosen by survivors of the Colonies, in what seems to be a bid to restore political legitimacy as promised in 'Bastille Day', but Starbuck cynically says that she is 'already running for re-election'. She has Baltar nominated as Vice-President despite her 'instinct' about his treachery, indicating that, again, political expediency is most important for her. The wireless commentators at the start of the story articulate pro- and anti-Roslin positions, which set the scene and give us a black-and-white argument to contrast with the shades of grey elsewhere in the episode; Roslin, although she has to allow them to talk to maintain the freedom of the press, clearly finds what Baltar calls their 'low-brow rabble-rousing' tiresome. Her abandoning Wallace 'Wally' Gray in favour of Baltar gives the lie to the assertion made by the talk-wireless commentators that Gray is the power behind the throne (the *eminence grise*, as it were), and Gray's accusations that she is a 'bareknuckled, backstabbing politician' are not wide of the mark. Again, Roslin seems like an idealist, but demonstrates a ruthless streak.

Zarek, meanwhile, sums up his position in his speech to the journalists where he says 'We're all held hostage by the way things used to be … Many of us are just still going through the motions of our old lives'. He has a good point, in that, as the society they have known has been wiped out, it is foolish for them to try to keep clinging to the past, and they should instead start building new institutions reflecting their present situation (an idea that will prove a strong influence on Lee Adama's political activities later in the series). On the other hand, Zarek himself is quite happy to keep things the way they used to be if it means elections in six months and possibly a role for himself as Vice-President or even President. The name of his associate, Grimes, has connotations of 'grim' and 'grimy', both of which suggest Zarek's organisation has a sordid side. Apollo, hearing Zarek's speech on the wireless, remarks, 'You're not interested in the citizens, you just want power', although his motivation for saying this is probably that the new order Zarek is proposing, getting rid of the old politico-economic structures and instead operating as a collective, would mean the loss of privilege for the military, including himself and his father. It is ironic that it is through Lee's negotiations with Zarek that the elections are taking place at all. When Zarek congratulates Roslin, he says, 'Very well played, again', acknowledging that they both understand the realities behind the political rhetoric.

The question also remains at the end of the story as to whether or not Zarek is telling the truth when he says he didn't have Valance killed. Roslin assumes Valance is working for Zarek, intending to assassinate her as soon as Zarek is declared Vice-President, but this seems an overly simple, indeed crude, plot for someone like Zarek, and one that would be likely to backfire on him, as he would be the obvious suspect, and the most likely scenario would be that Adama would instigate martial law and have him arrested. It is evidence of Roslin's tendency toward paranoia that she actually gives any credit at all to the idea that this is Zarek's plan. The fact that Zarek, in his opening speech, indicates the possibility of military dictatorship emerging in the case of Roslin's death suggests he would not be unaware of this risk. Although Zarek asks Ellen if she can find out where he can locate a friend of his called Valance, it is entirely possible that he didn't know the name until Lee came up to him and said 'We got Valance and you're next', and is just trying to discover who Valance is. Although during his interrogation Valance is threatened with being thrown out the airlock, neither Starbuck nor Apollo commits a direct act of violence against him; they restrain themselves to verbal threats and (in an ad-libbed move by Jamie Bamber) throwing Valance's briefcase around. The implication is that they reserve their genuine violence for Cylons (which also implies that they have not seriously considered that Valance, or Zarek, might be one). Despite that, Starbuck directly lies to him to try to get him to talk, saying that Grimes implicated him as a Zarek supporter; and she points out that Zarek's call for a new set of rules could equally justify the replacement of due process with summary justice, giving a sinister twist to Zarek's argument.

Celebrations and Machinations: Character Development

Perhaps surprisingly, although Lee is a key player in the story, his political ambitions do not come to the fore, and his mindset is much more a military one. Baltar, instead, is the one making a semi-willing progress into office. It is ambiguous whether he is seeking it for himself or whether he is being manipulated by Head Six. She clearly wants him to participate in politics, alternately ordering him to act and appealing to his libido; she directs his attention to Playa when they are on *Cloud 9*, and his tryst with her later turns out to be to his advantage, as she then lends him her support on the wireless. Head Six takes a carrot and stick approach, as it were, when she gives him permission to sleep with other women; she says first 'Love isn't about sex, Gaius', and then 'I have your heart ... I can always rip it out of your chest if I need to'. On the other hand, when Baltar gives his impromptu interview to the journalists, she remarks 'You seriously miss the limelight, don't you?', and his speech on key Colonial values mentions the idea of great people coming from humble beginnings – a possible allusion to his own origins, which will be revealed later in the programme. Although his entry in the series bible states that he is from a farming background, his parents are also said to be the owners of a prosperous agribusiness controlling millions of acres of land; the fact that he nonetheless regards them as being of inferior status to the Capricans he later associates with is an indication of his obsession with social class. However, he again gets a crucial scene taking place in a toilet, reminding the audience that he is associated with sleaze and corruption.

Finally, Ellen Tigh returns, showing her manipulative side once more, in particular as it relates to her plan to advance her own social position by getting her husband promoted. She flirts with Zarek right from the start, explaining to Tigh that it's in order to provide them with a photo-opportunity linking them to someone currently very popular with the journalists. Tigh openly wonders who let Zarek know where Valance was, evidently not realising that it might have been his own wife. The implication of the glance Ellen exchanges with Zarek when she tells Tigh that she's arranged a suite for them on the *Rising Star* where they can work on getting him promoted is that there has been an exchange of favours between the two of them, but if indeed this is the case there is the question of what that exchange was; the only indication on screen is that Zarek asks Ellen to find out information concerning Valance. Zarek's final word on the matter is to say, 'I didn't kill Valance; I wonder who did?' The camera then pans across to the dance floor, focusing on Boomer, Gaeta, Tyrol, Dualla, Billy, Tigh, Ellen, Starbuck and Lee. This raises the question if one of them did it; given the people involved, any number of conspiracy scenarios could be envisioned, not excluding the possibility, of course, that Valance was in fact operating on his own and managed to find a way to commit suicide out of fear of Apollo and Starbuck.

Elsewhere, although the Caprica scenes continue to be the weakest ones, this episode sees their strongest moment, when Helo finally learns about human-like Cylons and realises Sharon is one, and Sharon guns down her own duplicate. Helo's speculations about the nature of the human-like Cylons lead him to the right answer through prejudice, in that, although he first considers that they may be human clones made by the Cylons for the purposes of infiltration, he concludes, 'No human could do the things that they've done. Killed billions of innocent people. They've gotta be frakking Cylons, just like the rest of them'. When Sharon suggests that if they are clones, then they could be capable of complex emotions, including love, and that their crimes could be the result of indoctrination, she is clearly talking about herself. Moore says that she has been going off the plan for a while, although this is true only in terms of her growing allegiance to Helo against her fellow Cylons; in other respects, she is acting perfectly according to the Cylons' intentions.

Blue Skies: Continuity and Worldbuilding

This episode shows one area in which the reimagined series improves on the original, in that we see active conflict between politicians rather than interchangeable Quorum members seemingly speaking with a single voice. *Cloud 9* appears to be an amalgamation of an agroship/Botanical Cruiser and the original series' *Rising Star*, which the characters used as a kind of recreational facility. It was apparently nicknamed 'the happy ship' by the production crew. A 'Colonial Movers'-based vessel can also be seen in one of the establishing shots of the Fleet. Zarek, played of course by Richard Hatch, articulates both the original series' tenet about the group being more important than the individual, and also the idea, implicit but never spoken in the original series, that the Colonial system needs to be overhauled and replaced with something more fit for purpose.

The story also has allusions to modern politics and political dramas. Moore in the podcast refers to it as *'The West Wing* episode', and indeed it seems to cater for the post-millennial fondness for such political sagas (although the actual parallels between *Battlestar Galactica* and *The West Wing* are slight). The Roslin-Zarek handshake is, according to Moore, inspired by the Arafat-Rabin handshake at the White House during the signing of the 1993 Oslo Accord, highlighting the situation of two politicians in inherent opposition to each other making a show of solidarity for wider political gains. In other references, Telamon Tower, apparently a landmark in the city of Delphi, is named after one of Jason's Argonauts, and Zarek's line 'I shaved very closely in anticipation of being smacked by you' is a paraphrase of Patton's line when he meets his rival Montgomery at Messina in the film *Patton* (1970).

We see Starbuck in a dress for the first time (Lee's voice breaks at the sight), and she dances with both Lee and Baltar at the party, again indicating the mutual attraction she has with both of the men as well as setting up a key plot point that will be explored in the next episode. Starbuck's physical abilities, even when laid up with a bad leg, are still impressive; she kicks a bottle over to Apollo during the bar fight, and brings down Valance with her cane.

A sour note is struck by the fact that Wally Gray, the Presidential advisor, appears here for the first time, and, if he is as well-known as the talk-wireless commentators make him sound, one would have expected to have seen him before. Indeed, he vanishes from here on in, although a possible symbolism can be read into the idea of politicians, wanting to present issues in black and white, banishing the shades of grey inherent in the political process.

A bottle of Jack Daniels is visible at the bar, and Playa undergoes an unexpected change of surname (going from Playa Kohn in 'Litmus', 'Six Degrees of Separation' and 'Flesh and Bone' to Playa Palacios here; if she got married between episodes, then her carryings-on with Baltar in a toilet cubicle are even more sordid[34]). One of the Sixes on Caprica can be heard indistinctly saying what is evidently 'By your command'. At the end of the story, Tyrol can be seen dancing with Cally, foreshadowing later developments between these two characters.

Moore's blog entry for 11 April 2005, regarding this episode, casts more light on the timeline of events prior to the series:

'Colonial Day occurs every year and it is the anniversary of the founding of the 'federal' system of government, which was a relatively recent event. Before that time, the Colonies functioned more or less on their own, possibly with various attempts at alliances or even complete Colonial government over the centuries since the exodus from Kobol, none of which were successful. When the first Cylons were created, individual Colonies still warred against one another and it wasn't until the Cylon rebellion that

---

[34] And, just to confuse matters, in 'The Hand of God' she is credited as 'Playa Kohn' but in dialogue states her name as 'Playa Palacios' (which is also the name given in the 2 and 10 August 2004 drafts of that episode's script).

12: COLONIAL DAY

the 12 Colonies finally came together in a permanent way.'

This suggests that the Cylon War began between 53 and 52 years ago, in line with the chronology given in the final episode of *Caprica*, and must therefore have lasted about 12 years. This is confirmed by the 'Razor' webisodes, which state that it lasted 4,571 days.

Fly Me To The Moon: Writing and Production

The episode's director, Jonas Pate, was co-creator and showrunner with his brother Josh on a series called *Good versus Evil*, on which Moore had worked and had met David Eick. Moore has said that he had wanted as far back as the writing of the series' bible, for Baltar to get into politics. One of the suggestions for Season One arcs in the bible reads in part: 'Number Six starts to aid Baltar in positioning himself as the next leader of the Colonies as Laura becomes more and more unpopular'. Katee Sackhoff suggested that she wear a dress in the party scenes, and it must be said that she does look very nice in it.

The *Cloud 9* scenes were shot on the campus of the University of British Columbia (UBC), specifically the Chang Centre; Moore says that he wanted it to look like an outdoor setting because he wanted new exteriors without having the Fleet continually visiting the 'planet of the week'. The Coerner Library at UBC stands in as the Delphi Base in the Caprica sequences. The song used in the rough cuts of the party sequence was 'Fly Me to the Moon'; the final substitution is a kind of Sinatra pastiche, like a cross between 'Fly Me To The Moon' and 'King of the Road'.

The 2 August 2004 draft of the script, while containing the main elements of the story, is politically cruder: Zarek is explicitly portrayed as being behind Valance's attack (and, rather than Valance being conveniently murdered, the other characters seem just to forget about him); Moore has said that Hatch's ambiguous performance subsequently persuaded him to leave the question of Zarek's involvement unanswered. Rather than being forced out by Roslin, Gray resigns of his own accord, as the opposition have found out he had a mistress and are threatening to use this against him. Instead of seconding Zarek's proposal to elect a Vice-President, Baltar is the only delegate *not* to vote for it, apparently through indifference.

In the 2 August draft Baltar becomes sexually involved with the Libran delegate, Tanya Everett, while by the 10 August draft (which is much closer to the final version) he is involved with Playa; the scene where Roslin asks Baltar to stand as Vice-President does not take place in a washroom but begins with her finding him bent over a desk, and after she leaves, Playa emerges from under the desk.

The scene where Kara comes to Baltar's lab to tell him that he is now the Caprican delegate has some extra material in the 2 August draft, where Gaeta asks Baltar why the latter won't teach him to do the Cylon test, so that they can both conduct the process; Baltar temporises and Head Six wonders how long it will be before Gaeta catches on to the fact that he has no intention of administering the tests. The 2 August draft also has a few entertaining cut lines, for instance Head Six remarking, on the subject of young women who are drawn to men of power, 'It'll be one big nubile all-you-can-eat buffet', and later that Tanya Everett could 'suck [Baltar's] tongue clean out of [his] head'. (Baltar replies that a tongue is a small thing to sacrifice.)

Where the previous episode showed the military at it shrewdest, in 'Colonial Day' the politicians take centre stage, while the military characters appear confused by the machinations surrounding them. Furthermore, whereas in 'The Hand of God' we have a clear set of military objectives, making it evident who has won and who has lost, 'Colonial Day' ends shrouded in confusion as to what exactly has been gained, and by whom.

13: Kobol's Last Gleaming (Parts One and Two)

FIRST TRANSMISSION DATE: 17 January 2005 and 24 January 2005

TELEPLAY: Ronald D Moore

STORY BY: David Eick

DIRECTOR: Michael Rymer

CREDITED CAST: Lorena Gale (Elosha); Donnelly Rhodes (Doctor Cottle); Alonso Oyarzun (Socinus); Bodie Olmos (Costanza/Hot Dog); Stephen Spender (Pilot); James Bell (Eco); Jim Shield (Karma); Warren Christie (Ground Crew #1 [Tarn]); Jen Halley (Ground Crew #2 [Diana Seelix]); Leah Cairns (Racetrack)

KNOWN UNCREDITED CAST: Jeff Dimitriou (Dancer); Chris Becker (Stand-in for Cylon Centurion)

SYNOPSIS: Boomer and Crashdown, searching for supplies, find the planet Kobol, the original home of the Thirteen Tribes. Adama thinks the Fleet should settle there and orders a ground survey team to go down to the planet. Roslin, however, is convinced that the prophecies are real and, following a legend that the Arrow of Apollo can be used to open the Tomb of Athena and show the way to Earth, persuades Starbuck to return in the Cylon Raider to Caprica and obtain the Arrow from the museum at Delphi. Increasingly unhinged, Boomer attempts suicide, but succeeds only in injuring herself. The Raptors containing the survey team are attacked by Cylon Raiders; two are destroyed and one, containing Crashdown, Tyrol, Baltar, Cally, Seelix, Karma, Tarn and Socinus, crash-lands on Kobol. Karma is killed in the battle. Adama, learning that Roslin is behind Starbuck's trip to Caprica, declares martial law and relieves Roslin of her office. Roslin refuses to yield, leading to a standoff between Roslin's and Adama's men, until finally Apollo points a gun at Tigh's head, and Roslin, realising things have gone too far, surrenders. On Caprica, meanwhile, Helo shoots Sharon, wounding her. She then reveals she is pregnant. The pair encounter Starbuck at the museum, where Sharon is also seeking the Arrow of Apollo. On seeing Sharon and learning that she is pregnant, Starbuck realises that Boomer is a Cylon. Adama has Boomer and Racetrack fly a mission to the Cylon basestar that is the source of the Raiders. Using a Cylon transponder, they gain access to, and plant a nuclear warhead on board, the basestar. While there, Boomer is approached by a group of naked Sharon-model Cylons who say they love her. The basestar is destroyed and Boomer, disturbed by the encounter but now conscious of her true identity, returns to *Galactica* and shoots Adama.

ANALYSIS: The series' first official two-parter (as opposed to 'Act of Contrition'/'You Can't Go Home Again', which is not designated as a two part story, and which had a different writing and direction team for each episode) finishes up the season on a cliffhanger that finally leads the Fleet to Kobol, the Planet of the Gods.

God and Mammon: Roslin, Religion and Politics

Roslin is once again the driving force behind the action, but in this case it is due to her growing belief in her own status as prophesied messiah, encouraged by Elosha, rather than her political ambitions. Roslin is starting to sound rather like Head Six, continually talking about Gods and their plan, and quotes the now-familiar 'All this has happened before …' line. A couple of deleted scenes, however, undercut the idea that she is the messiah. In these, Cottle and Billy respectively urge her to go back onto conventional medicine. In another, though, Roslin fails to be dissuaded from her course of action even when Billy points out that her plan to have Starbuck return to Caprica and retrieve the Arrow of Apollo could cost them the viable government they have worked for, and Apollo refuses to support her mission on the grounds that he cannot betray his oath to his commander. However, it is not surprising that Roslin should be suborning her political ambitions to her religious ones, given that, under the circumstances, she is undoubtedly looking for meaning in her life and her approaching death.

However, Roslin never entirely lets go of her political side, simply turning it to new ends. She plays on her knowledge that Adama lied about knowing where Earth is, Starbuck's religious faith, and Starbuck's belief in Adama, to persuade Starbuck to take the Raider to Caprica; she does this by telling that Adama made up his story about Earth to give people hope, knowing it will shake her faith in her commander and cause Starbuck to side with Roslin instead. Adama, for his part, figures out straight away that Roslin had something to do with Starbuck's departure, based on the fact that Starbuck asked him if he really did know the way to Earth.

The falling-out between Adama and Roslin leads to the collapse of their agreement from the miniseries, to the effect that she would keep his secret that he didn't know the location of Earth, and that the civilian and military spheres would be kept separate. Now, over her prophetic ambitions, Roslin breaks her word both by telling Starbuck the truth about Earth, and by interfering in military affairs, leading Adama to break his own word and instigate a coup. Such a situation was probably inevitable, however, as the President cannot govern without control of the military force, and likewise the army cannot legitimately operate without the consent of the civilian administration. Moore says that the breakdown of the separation agreement was always intended to happen in Season One: originally, the plan was to have Roslin becoming more and more authoritarian, taking away basic freedoms and using the military to crack down on dissent until Adama, increasingly uncomfortable with having to enforce her rule, staged a revolt. However, he feels that the situation presented in the story as broadcast is more complex and interesting, with Adama visibly not sure how to deal with the new messianic Roslin. Moore also notes that there was a deleted scene to the effect that Roslin's security team were deliberately recruited from civilian, rather than military, forces by Lee, in his capacity as her personal military advisor. The conflict between Adama and Roslin stems directly from the original series' debates about civilian and military spheres of governance: the message of 'Kobol's Last Gleaming' is that one should not sacrifice democracy simply because the civil government makes a bad decision (as the original Adama articulates in 'Baltar's Escape'); and indeed, the Fleet winds up in its perilous situation precisely because there is a failure to recognise that the civilian and military spheres are interdependent.

Kill Bill: The Military

Starbuck's complicated sex life also influences the action in the story. There is a nice bait-and-switch in the teaser for part one where we are led to believe she is sleeping with Lee, building on the tension between them that was established as early as the miniseries; but when she speaks Lee's name, we discover that she is in fact sleeping with Baltar. Following this, she leaves quickly while Baltar has a drink, with both of them coming to sober realisations: she that she wants to be with Lee instead, and he that she doesn't feel for him as he apparently does for her. The incident has repercussions: when a drunken Baltar sneeringly asks Starbuck at the Triad game if she'd rather sit next to Lee, Lee figures out from their behaviour that she's slept with Baltar, and that triggers a fight between them. Deleted scenes expand on these ideas. In one, which comes before the Triad scene, Lee and Starbuck go for a morning jog (deliberately echoing the initial *Galactica* scenes of the miniseries) and he asks her as a joke if she got laid the previous night, but in doing so accidentally touches a nerve. In another, Baltar, meeting Starbuck in a corridor, tries to make it up with her, but she says 'It never happened' in a manner that leaves it ambiguous as to whether she means her having called out Lee's name, or the whole encounter. In Lee's confrontation with Starbuck at the Raider, Lee picks up on the fact that she is now referring to the Raider as male and interprets it as a sign of her fickleness in relationships. Starbuck's actions are thus in part motivated by her conflict over her complicated sex life, which also underlies the situation with the Adama family.

Lee's relationship with his father is also key to events in the story. When Adama gives his son a black eye while boxing, he tells him to let his instincts take over; Lee says that he had assumed they were just sparring, to which his father replies, 'That's why you don't win', recalling the conversation in 'Bastille Day' regarding Lee's failure to take sides. When Lee finally mutinies in part two, he says 'You can tell my father that I'm listening to my instincts', indicating that, rather than remaining neutral as in the earlier story, he has chosen a side, and it is against Adama. (This is later amusingly summarised by Tigh saying 'He put a weapon right to my head – said to tell you he was following his instincts, whatever the hell *that* means', with the clear implication that Tigh assumed Lee's instincts were telling him to shoot the XO). However, Lee is confused on this point; rather than, like a trained soldier, reacting to the situation according to a response that has become so deeply learned it is instinctive, he is in fact making a measured and rational decision to change sides, further indicating that Lee is not a natural soldier, but someone ill-suited to his military role. According to Moore, it was Lee's pulling of the gun on Tigh that caused Laura to think things had gone too far and to surrender; when Lee finally does abandon neutrality and throw his hat into the ring on the side of the civilian administration, then, it is not the triumph that he had expected.

Boomer's story here culminates in the final realisation of her identity. Head Six sums up her situation by saying 'Deep down, she knows she's a Cylon, but her conscious mind won't accept it … Her model is weak'. Boomer maintains a differentiation between her Cylon self and her human persona; although we have seen only the human persona previously, a deleted scene from this story has Boomer repeatedly performing set moves mirroring her future assassination attempt, apparently in Cylon mode; she is startled out of this when she realises she is pointing a gun at Boxey (who flees in understandable dismay). When Boomer shoots Adama, it seems at first as if both selves have merged; she commits this act after encountering the Sharons on the baseship, which confirms to her human self that she is a Cylon. However, in 'Scattered', it will become clear that she has no memory of what she has done, indicating that, instead, her Cylon side took over completely.

A somewhat weaker idea presented in this story is that Boomer has developed suicidal urges; symbolically, she leaves her duplicates to die on the basestar before killing Adama, and the part one teaser intercuts Helo shooting Caprica-Sharon with Galactica-Sharon contemplating suicide, suggesting that there is an unstable, possibly self-destructive, urge within both Sharons. However, this development seems to come out of nowhere; although Boomer is distressed about the ending of her relationship with Tyrol, she has had her humanity confirmed by Baltar's test, and there has been no previous indication that her mental state has deteriorated to such an extent. Had the deleted sequence with Boxey been included, it would have provided the necessary rationale; the description of the scene in the 16 August 2004 draft script explicitly connects her distress at finding herself pointing a gun at the child with her sitting down and placing the gun in her mouth. Without this sequence, however, the trigger for her behaviour is unclear.

The question remains in the story as to precisely why Boomer would be motivated to kill Adama at this point. The series' bible provides a possible reason, when it states that one of the ongoing arcs relates to 'the discovery … that a place called Earth really does exist – and the realisation that the Cylons might actually want us to find it after all'; if Roslin is determined to find Earth,

13: KOBOL'S LAST GLEAMING

and Adama is thwarting her in these efforts, then the Cylons would clearly want Adama out of the way. Unfortunately, Season Two saw this idea lose emphasis, so the rationale behind Boomer's acts is never actually explored in the series, although a post-hoc rationalisation will be provided in 'The Plan'.

It's Not You, It's Me: Baltar and Head Six

More details are revealed, through the events of this story, about Head Six's plans for Baltar. She finally says to him that he is to be the guardian and protector of the new generation of God's children, though precisely what she means (and how literally it is to be taken) is still obscure. Moore says that Head Six did not predict Baltar talking Boomer into her suicide attempt, but the action does make sense from Baltar's point of view, as, first, it removes a dangerous Cylon sleeper agent from his immediate vicinity, and, secondly, if her suicidal feelings are due to her having doubts about her humanity, then she must suspect he lied to her about her test results, which puts him in a very precarious position. Both Roslin and Baltar have visions of the opera house, suggesting that there is some sort of spiritual link between them.

Whatever Head Six said in 'Colonial Day' about her relationship with Baltar, she is visibly unhappy about his interest in Kara in a way that she wasn't where Playa was concerned, suggesting that it has the potential to interfere with her plans for him in a way that his relationship with the journalist didn't; certainly Baltar seems to have genuine feelings for Kara, where Playa was simply a casual, somewhat opportunistic, liaison. In a deleted scene, Baltar has a conversation (again in a washroom) with Head Six that cycles through every single break-up cliché from 'It's not you, it's me' onwards, again putting her in the category of jealous girlfriend. There is also an ironic coincidence in the fact that the Cylon who savagely beats Kara on Caprica in the second episode is a Six. However, Head Six also acts to get Baltar off the *Galactica* and onto Kobol, because she does not want him caught up in the conflict brewing between Roslin and Adama.

Paradise Lost: Continuity, Worldbuilding and Problems

The story reinforces its position as season-ender with a series of juxtapositions and call-backs to earlier stories, particularly the miniseries. The exchange between Baltar and Head Six's after the Raptor crash – 'How are you?' 'Alive!' – echoes the physical Six's 'Are you alive?' catchphrase. Starbuck's statement, before jumping to Caprica, that she is 'bringing home the cat', references her in-jokey exchange with Adama in the miniseries (which is also referenced in the 'Kobol's Last Gleaming' deleted scene where she goes jogging with Lee). The part one teaser sharply juxtaposes different storylines (Lee boxing his father, Starbuck and Baltar having sex, Helo shooting Caprica-Sharon and *Galactica*-Sharon putting a gun in her mouth), drawing the connections between them. This leads on to other later juxtapositions (between Six and Starbuck fighting and the coup against Roslin, and then between Boomer's shooting Adama and Head Six and Baltar kissing in Baltar's vision of the opera house). The conversation between the Raptor pilots over the radio echoes the standoff between Roslin and Adama over Kobol, in that one is all for colonising the place, while the other thinks they should use it to find Earth. Helo also reveals to Starbuck that Caprica-Sharon is pregnant at the same time as Head Six reveals the baby to Baltar in their vision, indicating that the foetus in question is also the prophesied new child of God.

In terms of character development, although Helo doesn't trust Sharon at first, they have clearly come to a truce by the start of part two, as her arm is now in a sling and there is less tension between them. Her revelation that she is pregnant has probably helped, as this is his stated reason for preventing Starbuck from shooting her. Starbuck's cry of 'No!' at this point (apparently an improvisation by Katee Sackhoff) leaves it ambiguous what she is denying – that her friend Boomer must be a Cylon, that a Cylon can fall pregnant, or that Helo may have had relations with one (or indeed all three of these). Despite the Colonials' assertions that the Cylons are all alike, the characterisation of the two Sharons clearly indicates that they do have individuality. There is no explanation given, here or subsequently, as to why Caprica-Sharon is interested in acquiring the Arrow of Apollo and finding the location of Earth; this probably relates to the idea outlined in the series bible, that the Cylons too wanted to find the planet.

Baltar, meanwhile, gives a very believable display of hysteria during the Raptor crash, and it also has to be said that, whatever his personal failings, his mental dexterity is not to be questioned, as he is capable of winning at Triad even when blind drunk. Crashdown, meanwhile, lives up to his name by crashing his Raptor, and begins the mental breakdown that will continue into Season Two. In a deleted scene in which Apollo and Crashdown visit Boomer in the sickbay, Crashdown reveals that flying with Karma, the Raptor pilot who is subsequently killed over Kobol, is considered 'bad luck'. There are also a few deleted scenes involving Ellen Tigh, indicating that she is again jealous of the time her husband puts in at work; she says that he is only 'a heartbeat' away from command, which, had the scene in question been included, would have proved eerily prophetic, and added further to audience speculation that she could be a Cylon, acting according to their plan.

The story does suffer in a few aspects. Since Gaeta programmed the coordinates, the fact that Boomer and Crashdown are the ones to find Kobol (just as they found the water, and the tylium, earlier) must be put down to coincidence or luck. The fact that the scene in 'Flesh and Bone' indicating that Leoben was carrying a transponder was deleted means that this information must be belatedly introduced in the recap. Although there are plausible reasons why all the regular characters who are on the mission to Kobol wind up in Raptor One (Tyrol and Baltar both know Crashdown personally, and Cally and Socinus would naturally go in the same craft as Tyrol), it has to be said it's still rather convenient from a story point of view, and it is never explained why the group includes so many members of the deck crew, who seem unlikely to have the skills needed to conduct a planetary survey.

Boomer's injury is also a weak point, as the idea that she can put a gun in her mouth, shoot herself through the cheek, and somehow fail to injure her jaw, teeth and/or tongue in the process (walking around with a wound small enough to be covered by a piece of gauze) is untenable. Adama later assigns her to what could easily turn out to be a suicide mission, as she herself notes that once the Cylons see that the Raptor is not a Cylon craft, they are likely to shoot it down; indeed, it is only the fact that she is herself a Cylon that lets her get away at all, suggesting a very dark side to Adama's character. It is also unexplained why the Sharons on the baseship are naked. It would not be unreasonable to assume that, outside of human settings, all Cylons dispense with clothes; however, we later find out that other Cylon models do wear clothes aboard basestars, suggesting that only the Sharons are given to occasional nudism.[35]

In 'Water', Galactica has five operational Raptors, but, although Gaeta refers to 'all five Raptors' in the deleted jogging scene, at least six appear in this story (one is destroyed over Kobol, one crashes on Kobol, one carries a nuclear warhead to the basestar and three attack *Colonial One*); this can be explained by an out-of-commission Raptor being fixed in time to take part in the climax.

In continuity terms, Roslin is trying to establish a currency-based economy, building on the previous story's discussions about how the infrastructure of the Fleet works. We learn that the exodus from Kobol took place 2,000 years earlier (and thus the Pythian scrolls predate it by 1,600 years). 'Frakking' is used as a direct equivalent for 'fucking' (as Lee says that Starbuck is 'frakking the Vice-President'). In a deleted scene, Billy mentions having owned a dog called Jake (foreshadowing the later appearance of a dog of that very name in Season Three, suggesting that perhaps Billy named it; both animals were in fact named after Moore's own Australian shepherd dog). Opera was a known art form on pre-Colonial Kobol, and when Baltar approaches the ruin he says that he knows the place, again bringing in the idea of cyclical time affecting individual memory.

Although the Cylon devices are now revealed to be transponders, there is still no in-story explanation as to why one was placed aboard the *Galactica* before the miniseries. (Presumably, given that what the devices do is simply to transmit a signal identifying themselves as Cylon transponders, the Cylons wanted that particular ship to survive; this would also support the idea that they were tracking the Fleet using the *Olympic Carrier* rather than through the

---

35 The practical reason for this change is that, when more of the series' action shifted to the basestars, making this a general trait would have meant that all the Cylon actors would have had to have been naked; it is therefore easier to retroactively explain the nudism as something unique to the Sharons.

transponder devices.)[36]

The story concept is explicitly based on the original-series story 'Lost Planet of the Gods' (as well as having a further connection to 'The Hand of God', in which Apollo and Starbuck pilot a Cylon craft in order to penetrate a basestar's defences; they are also given a Colonial transmitter that will emit a signal identifying them as 'friendly' to the Viper pilots on their return). However, the way events play out here is different. Kara hitting Lee and him hitting her back is a visual reference to the Burton and Taylor film *Cleopatra* (1963), and apparently Sackhoff accidentally gave Bamber a nosebleed during the filming of it.

Magic Carpet Ride: Writing and Production

The two-parter – Eick's first major storylining project for television – underwent some significant changes during the course of its development. According to Moore, the first draft culminated in Baltar walking through a black void to a Jimi Hendrix tune, which he mysteriously recognises,[37] after which he meets a cigar-smoking Dirk Benedict, who reveals himself to be God. Production executive Mark Stern vetoed this on the grounds that it was too much of a knowing wink to the audience. Moore has said that ending the season on a cliffhanger, of Boomer shooting Adama (which, it must be said, is shocking even after the viewer knows what is coming), was his idea, even before he knew the series was to be renewed.

The 16 August 2004 drafts of both episodes are closer to the final version. The main differences between the draft and recorded versions are, first, that the draft drags out for longer the suspense over whether or not the planet is Kobol (with two exploratory teams, rather than one, investigating; Tyrol, Cally and Socinus go down as part of a preliminary survey team in part one, and Lee and Baltar follow later in the Raptor which crashes), and, secondly, that there are segments featuring characters being interviewed by an unknown person about the events of the story interspersed throughout, making it a kind of narrative told in flashback (an idea that is rather distracting here, but will be used to better effect in 'Final Cut'). In the draft's first episode, much more is made of the Lee/Kara/Baltar love triangle, with the situation being the subject of extensive gossip; and in the second, Lee is on Kobol, while Crashdown instead accompanies Boomer to the basestar. (Although Racetrack does appear, it is as

---

36 This fits with the idea that the Cylons want the humans to find Earth. It would also explain why Head Six might want the transponder removed, as God presumably intends the Cylons to be able to identify the *Galactica* for what it is rather than treat it as a Cylon craft. However, the writing team will go on to develop this plotline in a slightly different way, and the transponder issue will fall by the wayside.

37 Akin to the mooted use of Hendrix's 'All Along the Watchtower' in 'Act of Contrition'.

one of the pilots in the standoff with *Colonial One*, and she is also male at this stage of production.) According to Moore, it was planned to have Lee, rather than Crashdown, as the one later forced into conflict with Tyrol, and this idea was dropped because it seemed less likely that Tyrol would challenge Lee's authority than Crashdown's; also, we would add that while it would make sense for Lee to be somewhat irrational at this point, given the turmoil in his relationship with Kara, it would make less sense to have him undergo the protracted mental crisis that Crashdown later experiences.

A couple of key scenes are also different in the draft version. In the one of Lee and Kara arguing on the hangar deck, Kara refers to the Raider as female, and Lee remarks that the women refer to it as female and the men as male. The scene on Caprica explaining what the Arrow of Apollo is also has Helo speculating that Sharon is in communication with 'the other Sharon' on *Galactica* (clearly omitted because Helo's earlier dialogue suggests he thinks she is some kind of Cylon duplicate of the real, human Sharon). Adama openly admits to Starbuck that he doesn't know where Earth is, rather than prevaricating. When Six and Baltar enter the opera house, the music is stated as being Holst's 'Mars, the Bringer of War', and Baltar says 'I know this piece' rather than 'I know this place'. After Six's lines about the melody of life, Baltar originally walks on stage and joins an orchestra, picking up a violin and playing; the baby idea, so crucial to the rest of the series, was a later addition.

The backstory to Kobol was also worked out in greater detail than actually appeared on screen. In a deleted scene, Elosha answers the question of why the Thirteen Tribes left Kobol: 'One jealous god began to desire that he be elevated above all the other gods, and the war on Kobol began', which has shades of the original series' demonic villain Count Iblis. Head Six, hearing this, says, 'Blasphemous, stupid lies. There have never been any other gods, only the one', which, although it could be construed as meaning that Head Six regards everything Elosha has said as a lie, in fact is not incompatible with the latter's narrative, but simply means that Head Six has a different take on the same events, interpreting them not as one god elevating himself above the others, but as the other 'gods' in fact having no claim to divinity at all.

As to why the available information on Kobol is so sketchy, Moore says on his Sci-Fi Channel blog (in a nod to the original series), 'I've been presupposing some kind of cataclysm or crisis that occurred soon after mankind settled on the 12 worlds, which either wiped out the knowledge base or had it deliberately destroyed for some reason' (an idea that also returns to inform the series' final story, 'Daybreak'). In the 16 August draft, Elosha also explains that there is a prohibition against priests visiting the planet, as since it was forsaken by humans, they have taken vows 'never to drink the water or breathe the air' of Kobol. In this script, Elosha still comes across very much as the liberal, urban priest seen in the draft of 'The Hand of God', rather than the more fundamentalist type she seems to be in the transmitted version, remarking that the prohibition against clergy visiting Kobol sounds 'weird' to her.

In design terms, Moore has said that he had originally wanted the baseship interior to be a white room – 'We blow it out. There's a lot of lens flare and ... heavy on the heavenly light' (significantly recalling both *2001: A Space Odyssey* and the interior of the original series' Ship of Light) – and that the Geigeresque, organic feel eventually adopted was suggested by Rymer and production designer Richard Hudolin, presumably to connect it to the living technology of the Raider. Originally, the basestar was to be a virtual environment, but Rymer decided to create a set instead, and was also the one who suggested that the Sharons on board should be naked. Grace Park was reportedly surprised on the day to find out that only one of her lookalikes was East Asian. The idea of infiltrating an alien craft and detonating a nuclear bomb inside it is very close to a storyline in *Independence Day*.

Production-wise, the sequence of the Cylon Raider smashing into Raptor Three is stunning, as is the *Blade Runner*-influenced Starbuck/Six fight sequence, which aside from the fall at the very end was apparently performed without stunt doubles, despite Tricia Helfer having had no martial arts training before the series. (Although one version using the doubles was filmed, none of the material was used.) In the podcast, Moore says that the sequence of the Adamas boxing was suggested, and choreographed, by Olmos and Bamber, though *The Official Companion* says instead that it was Rymer's idea. Moore says that the rain in the Caprica sequences is intended partly to indicate the disturbance to the environment of the nuclear devastation (although this would seem to be the least of the effects one might anticipate) but also helps visually distinguish Caprica from Kobol (aided by the use of yellow and blue filters respectively on the planet sequences). Most of the Kobol scenes were shot at Widgeon Slough in Port Coquitlam, while the opera house was represented by Vancouver's Orpheum Theatre. The Raptor crash was achieved in part by having the Raptor interior set physically rocked around on a hydraulic gimbal.

The first season ends on an exciting and character-led two-part story that dramatically advances a number of the ongoing plot threads. The most crucial points are the rediscovery of Kobol, *Galactica*-Sharon fully revealing her Cylon nature to her crewmates, the announcement of Caprica-Sharon's pregnancy, and the breakdown of the agreement reached between civilian and military leaders at the end of the miniseries, all of which will be key catalysts to the events of the next season.

Season Two: 2005-2006

Season Two was seven episodes longer and, perhaps consequently, more uneven in pace and quality than Season One, with a strong mid-season in the *'Pegasus'* arc, and a strong ending, punctuated by periods where the action visibly lags.

In writing terms, where Season One was heavily based on the series bible, Moore decided against writing a similar guide for Season Two, preferring instead to see what developed out of the writers' meetings. Nonetheless, the original series bible continues to be an influence, to a greater or lesser degree, on storylines and characterisation. A deliberate decision was taken this season to avoid 'comedy episodes' like 'Tigh Me Up, Tigh Me Down', which seems rather a shame. Moore admits that, although a 20-episode season is more syndication-friendly and allows the team to amortise costs, 'the creative team would rather have done 13 episodes [again], because you can focus on each episode more and you don't get the same exhaustion factor going'. This in part explains why the season was subdivided into two ten-episode segments with a one-month production hiatus between them, to make it less a matter of one long season and more of two mini-seasons (usually designated as '2.0' and '2.5').

After its strong first season, the series here shows a marked variation in quality. There are undoubtedly several factors behind this. The switch from 13 to 20 episodes brought about the abovementioned 'exhaustion factor', and the network's request for more 'stand-alone' episodes led to unfortunate experiments such as 'Flight of the Phoenix' and 'Black Market'. The decision to depart from the series bible might also be a factor; but, given that this document provided mainly technical background, character notes and a few ideas for ongoing threads, this is unlikely to have been a serious problem. The biggest issue seems to be the fact that, as any series goes on, the central mysteries also have to develop: while the first season was able to maintain the questions of what the Cylons and/or Head Six are up to, as the second unfolds, the writing team reach the point where they have to provide explanations. However, there seems to be some confusion and uncertainty among the writers over these crucial background elements, meaning that the series founders as they attempt to resolve the questions, in their own minds at least, to a sufficient degree to be able to carry on with the story.

The series began shooting on 31 March 2005, again at Vancouver Film Studios, with a view to a July premiere in the USA. This year, the production expanded to fill four stages: stage G contained the hangar bay, green screen area, and *Colonial One* sets; stage H housed temporary sets and CIC; stage I was used for most of the other *Galactica* sets, such as its hallways and rooms; and stage D was reserved for the *Pegasus* sets.

According to Eick in *The Official Companion Season Two*, most of the actors were 'tied to five-year or six-year contracts'. However, a few key players were on shorter contracts, including Michael Hogan, Nicki Clyne, Alessandro Juliani, Kandyse McClure, Aaron Douglas and Tahmoh Penikett. This necessitated negotiations with their agents – and as the loss of any of their characters between seasons would have been difficult to explain, it is fortunate that they were all able to return. Paul Campbell was also on a shorter-term contract, causing issues that will be discussed more fully in the episode analysis for 'Sacrifice'. The character of Boxey had been quietly dropped during Season One, and did not return.

Most of the production was overseen by producer Harvey Frand, with Moore and Eick dividing their time between the sets in Vancouver and the production office in Los Angeles. Although the UK's Sky One channel was no longer providing backing, and hence lost its first-broadcast rights, it was still credited, due to its initial investments in the series' infrastructure and production.

In story terms, the season starts by focusing on reuniting the characters who were geographically separated during the events of 'Kobol's Last Gleaming', and ending the Caprica-set storyline of Season One. It then shifts to the *Pegasus* storyline, which explores the case of a battlestar commander who chose to cannibalise civilian ships and attack the Cylons (rather than protect the former and flee the latter). Finally it returns to concentrate on Fleet politics for the curing of Roslin's cancer and the holding of the first Fleet elections. The loss of Billy Keikya in 'Sacrifice' brings the introduction of Tory Foster, a much brusquer, less idealistic character, as Roslin's chief aide. On a more trivial note, the election storyline leads to the establishment of a master list of Fleet ship names, visible in the scenes in which the votes are tallied, which will be subsequently used by the writing team as canonical.

The 20 July 2005 writers' meeting podcast reveals a few storylines that were mooted for the second half of Season Two but later abandoned. These included having Kara Thrace as commander of the *Pegasus*, and having Roslin kidnapped.[38] Various proposed storylines following up on the curing of Laura's cancer were also dropped, including having the absorption of stem cells from Hera make Laura into some kind of Cylon, although the idea that the cure would cause Laura to have crucial visions remained, as she later begins to share the image of the opera house with Sharon, Caprica-Six and Hera.

Consideration was also given to depicting a race between the humans and Cylons to find Earth – a development of the idea in the series bible that the Cylons are following the humans to the planet – whereby the Cylons would learn its location and abandon the Colonies for it, with the humans in pursuit. This storyline would also have had the humans recolonising the 12 planets (with echoes of what ultimately became the New Caprica storyline at the end of the season), possibly with a reversal of roles involving pockets of Cylon resistance. While this is an intriguing notion, it is not surprising it was dropped, given the

---

38 The abandoned story 'The Raid', and the impact of its cancellation, will be discussed in the essay for 'Downloaded'.

SEASON TWO: 2005-2006

change in focus it would have entailed for the series and the numerous logistical problems (of which the least is the radiation issue that the writers discuss in their meeting).

The question of how to deal with Sharon's pregnancy was a key preoccupation, with suggestions including Sharon leading the Fleet to disaster (similar to Kara's later role as prophesied harbinger of death), and having Cylon agents slit the pregnant Cylon's stomach and steal the baby. All these ideas seem to have stemmed from the writers being concerned about the prospect of having to work with child actors again, Boxey having been considered something of a failure. The team also briefly considered setting a story arc on a Cylon basestar, an idea that would be later used in Season Three. A key idea the writers seem to have focused on, however, was to end the season by skipping over a period of time, and using this to present certain plot developments as a *fait accompli*.

One development on the production side was that the episode title sequences were changed for Season Two. At the request of Moore and Eick, Bear McCreary's theme was dropped from the US version, with Gibbs's version returning. In Japan, the end theme was replaced, for this season only, with the song 'Dokudanjou Beauty' by rock group Buck-Tick. The initial sequence is slightly shorter, losing the lines 'They look and feel human'/'Some are programmed to think they are human', and having some new images substituted; the main titles now make reference to Earth (at the network's request) and to the number of survivors, replacing Laura Roslin's whiteboard count. Associate producer Paul Leonard was personally responsible for calculating the number each week, with Moore and Eick checking it (and sometimes adjusting it to account for births and deaths not featured in the story). The precap clips were initially dropped, but reinstated from 'The Farm' onwards at the request of Sci-Fi Channel liaison Mark Stern.

One of the key production developments was the introduction of the *Pegasus*. Richard Hudolin says that the team approached this with the idea that the vessel should look similar to the *Galactica* but 40 years more advanced, so that, since *Galactica*'s design evokes the 1940s, the *Pegasus*'s should evoke the 1980s, having, in Hudolin's words, 'a cold, corporate look ... a lot of glass and chrome'. The fact that Stage D, housing *Pegasus*, was smaller and lower than stage I, housing most of the *Galactica* sets, also affected its appearance. The ship's corridor, a section of which extends into the CIC set, and its sliding doors were reused elements from the unscreened 2004 John Woo TV pilot *The Robinsons: Lost in Space*, but Hudolin tends to downplay this in interviews, saying in *The Official Companion Season Two*, 'I think the only thing we ultimately used from the *Lost in Space* sets was a bit of a hallway'. As before, Hudolin and Hutzel worked closely together to ensure that the interiors and exteriors showed a certain continuity.

The *Pegasus*'s uniforms were also designed to look slightly crisper and sharper than the *Galactica*'s; the mill that had woven the fabric used in the miniseries had since closed down, meaning that the production team had to get the fabric custom-woven and custom-dyed. The design of the Colonial flight helmets was changed subtly: as Moore puts it, in the podcast for 'The Captain's

Hand', 'We've added some lights. They fit the actors' heads a little more snugly … The old helmets didn't fit quite well. They were always giving us sound trouble. They were hard to shoot in a lot of ways. They had different lighting problems. So we revamped the helmets and spent quite a bit'. In the latter half of the season, a separate Viper cockpit was built for use in filming some scenes, as using the Viper props themselves was proving too difficult.

A crucial change in the series' visual effects work began during this season. Although Hutzel wanted to continue to use external effects houses, he also began recruiting an in-house team, with Doug Drexler, who had previously worked on *Star Trek: Deep Space Nine*, *Star Trek: First Contact* and *Roughnecks: The Starship Troopers Chronicles*, as CG supervisor. 'Scar' was the first episode to be completed almost entirely in-house, with 61 of 65 effects sequences being done by the new team and only four being done by Vancouver-based studio Atmosphere. Drexler also redesigned the Cylon Heavy Raiders, as it was generally felt that the original look was not threatening enough; Eick was so pleased with the new design – meant to look, in Hutzel's phrase, like 'a land tank with rockets' – that he featured it in the Season Two premiere. Visual effects work not done in-house continued to be contracted out to Zoic and Atmosphere. High-definition imaging (HDI) was used for the first time to make more realistic Cylon Centurions and improve their anthropomorphic movement.

While podcast commentaries had been tried out on Season One as tie-in material, the second season had podcasts for every episode. In 2006 the series also became one of the first television shows to be made available for download via iTunes; this included an exclusive download-only documentary, *Sci-Fi Inside: Battlestar Galactica* (which is no longer officially available outside the USA at the time of writing). Also becoming available from this season onwards were items of tie-in merchandise – these will be discussed later in the volume.

Despite the uneven nature of the season, critical response continued to be positive, with *Time* magazine describing it as 'A ripping sci-fi allegory of the war on terror' and *Rolling Stone* also singling it out for praise, calling it 'The best show on TV'. At the end of 2005, the American Film Institute (AFI) selected it as one of their top ten TV series of the year, and it won a 2006 Peabody Award for having 'revitalised sci-fi television with its parallax considerations of politics, religion, sex, even what it means to be human'. Salon.com also awarded it their Buffy Award, given to the 'most underrated, overlooked show on television' in 2006. The series continued to maintain a loyal fanbase; although some were dismayed by the one-year time-jump in 'Lay Down Your Burdens' part two, feeling that they had been robbed of a year's worth of character development, their concerns would be addressed in Season Three.

14: Scattered

FIRST TRANSMISSION DATE: 15 July 2005 (USA)

WRITERS: Bradley Thompson and David Weddle

DIRECTOR: Michael Rymer

CREDITED CAST: Kate Vernon (Ellen Tigh); Alonso Oyarzun (Socinus); Kerry Norton (Paramedic Layne Ishay); Kurt Evans (Paramedic Kim); Chris Shields (Corporal Venner); Luciana Carro (Kat); Bodie Olmos (Hot Dog); Jennifer Halley (Seelix); Warren Christie (Tarn); Ty Olsson (Captain Kelly); Nicholas Treeshin (Sergeant Watkins); Michael Tayles (Flyboy); Leah Cairns (Racetrack); Aleks Paunovic (Marine Sergeant Fischer)

SYNOPSIS: Following the shooting of Adama, the Cylons attack. Tigh orders the Fleet to jump but, through an error, they and *Galactica* are separated. *Galactica* must jump back to her original position in order to calculate the Fleet's current location, but would be unable to hold off the Cylon forces for the amount of time necessary to do so. Gaeta suggests briefly networking their computers, which will allow them to calculate the new position more quickly, but will render them vulnerable to Cylon infiltration. Following Gaeta's plan, the jump is completed, and medic Ishay, in the absence of Doctor Cottle (who is on the Fleet), saves Adama's life. However, during the battle with the waiting Cylon forces, a Heavy Raider has crashed into the starboard flight pod, and, unbeknownst to the crew, a troop of Centurions are now advancing into the *Galactica*. On Kobol, Baltar has a vision of a baby, and Head Six tells him they are its mother and father. The stranded party make for a nearby forest to await rescue. When Socinus starts to weaken from his injuries, Crashdown realises they are missing a medical pack; Cally, Tyrol and Tarn return to collect it, but Tarn is killed in an ambush as they make their way back to the group. On Caprica, Sharon steals Starbuck's Raider, stranding Starbuck and Helo.

ANALYSIS: The first story of Season Two sets up the 'Tigh in command' arc and establishes themes of messianic faith and the legitimacy of leadership through the stories of *Galactica* separated from the Fleet, the Raptor crash survivors' experiences on Kobol, Ishay becoming senior medical officer in Cottle's absence, and Roslin consolidating her power base.

Uncertain Leaders: Tigh, Crashdown and Ishay

The episode makes parallels throughout between two characters thrust into command by unfortunate circumstances: Tigh and Crashdown. Both have a hunted, nervous look to them. However, where Crashdown becomes hysterical at the thought of a Cylon attack, failing to stop to check the team's supplies before running for the treeline and then covering his guilt by blaming Tarn for leaving the medical kit behind, Tigh proves a responsible leader. In a conversation with Ellen in which she pins responsibility onto Gaeta for failing to send the new jump coordinates to the rest of the Fleet, Tigh instead blames himself for not checking them personally, and moves on to solve the problems that have arisen. There is also an echo of Tigh's story in the medic Ishay subplot[39]. Circumstances have forced her into a situation where she is out of her depth, but she prevails through bravery, common sense and, like Tigh, ultimately thinking through decisions rather than making snap judgments. At the end, however, she expresses the hope that she never has to take charge again, following how Tigh feels about being placed in a position of responsibility.

However Tigh may feel about his situation, he does a good job. His speech in CIC, where he states that *Galactica* is Adama's command until he dies and that he is going to keep him alive, serves not only to quash any possible rumours that he is making a power grab, but also to reassure himself that Adama is coming back. Having said that, he does not mindlessly follow Adama's example: when Kelly opposes Gaeta's plan on the grounds that Adama would never allow the computers on the ship to be networked, Tigh makes his decision to support it based on his personal evaluation of the circumstances. Tigh says at the end of the story that he would rather have died on Caprica, that Adama should never have recommissioned him and that he never wanted a command. Ellen, however, obviously rather likes the idea of Tigh being in charge, consistent with her ambitions for him as voiced in 'Colonial Day' and elsewhere.

The key influences on Tigh's decisions are shown through a series of brief flashbacks. These explore his relationship with Adama, from their first meeting when they are two war veterans working on the same freighter, through Adama getting recommissioned as an officer, and ending with Adama arranging to have Tigh also recommissioned, at the point when a drunken and clearly desperate Tigh is about to burn his service medals in a dirty hotel room with a woman who is visibly not Ellen. Tigh's drinking problem is clearly well established by the time of his first meeting with Adama, in which, a deleted scene reveals, Adama prevented him from killing a shipmate who was mocking Tigh's military service, and it gets worse over the course of the flashbacks. This is contrasted with Adama, who is working towards getting recommissioned as an officer, which he does through marrying a woman with military connections. Adama's optimistic philosophy expressed in the flashbacks – 'Personally, I tend to go with what you know. 'Til something better turns up' – influences Tigh.

---

[39] Kerry Norton, the actress playing Ishay, is Jamie Bamber's wife.

14: SCATTERED

Tigh's interrogation of Sharon makes it clear that he is beginning to lose control as he hits her, but that something, some memory, holds him back in the end from taking her life. A further flashback scene was originally to have been included here, indicating that Tigh is recalling an incident where he was beating up a man who owed him money and Adama intervened, warning him against his self-destructive drinking and nursing of grievances and telling him to shape up or he would make an enemy of Adama too.

Tigh throughout the story flashes back continually to his lowest emotional point, in the abovementioned hotel room, expressing his fears that he will fail in command, and that this time Adama will not be there to pull him back from the brink. His obsession with the military also pervades the flashbacks. According to Moore's podcast, he was initially to have been seen doodling Viper weapons systems on a napkin; and when he and Adama meet, the fact that Adama has also seen action as a Viper pilot forms a bond between them. Michael Hogan has commented that had Adama not come into Tigh's life, he would have been dead by this point. Tigh's backstory is thus that of a professional military man with serious personal problems, who has learned to keep the personal and professional separate through Adama's faith and trust in him.

The problem with this, though, is that it seems deeply unlikely. It is loosely based on a part of the series bible that states: 'Unable to find work as a pilot, Adama signed up as a deck hand in the merchant fleet and spent several years working as a common sailor aboard tramp freighters plying the shipping lanes between the colonies ... It was in this period that Adama met Paul [sic] Tigh, another out of work pilot, and the two of them became fast friends'. However, the Adama we have seen up until now has appeared to be a career military man heading toward a graceful retirement, who, while he does show a lack of emotional intelligence, certainly does not appear to be the sort of ruthless grafter who would marry a woman simply as a means of fulfilling his career ambitions. (The series bible has him marrying his high-school sweetheart upon discharge from service.) The sequence with Tigh in the hotel room is strongly influenced by the opening of the movie *Apocalypse Now*, and the flashbacks also portray Tigh as a more violent and habitual drunk than the series bible suggests. In short, the flashbacks are difficult to reconcile with the characters we know.

Certain Leaders: Roslin and Tyrol

Roslyn's storyline picks up on different aspects of the theme of legitimate leadership. Tigh dismisses her attempts to reassert her authority, stating 'There's nothing to talk about. You went up against the old man and you lost'. However, her messianic role gains her other supporters, as her guard, Corporal Venner, turns out to be religious and to believe she is the one foretold in the prophecy. Although Apollo is clearly having some issues about the fact that he gave her his support in 'Kobol's Last Gleaming' only to have the conflict end in her surrender and his arrest, he is still backing her against Tigh. The contrast is drawn between Tigh, in control but a reluctant leader, and Roslin, out of power but convinced of her divine mission.

On Kobol, this episode shows Tyrol's diplomatic skills. He manages to persuade the increasingly unstable Crashdown to send himself and Cally as well as Tarn back for the medical kit, recognising that the officer is terrified of having his authority challenged and working around this. However, Tyrol, like Crashdown, is not acting logically: Socinus's chances of survival even with the medical kit are slight, and the Cylons are likely to be staking out the Raptor crash site and surrounding area. Tyrol undoubtedly feels guilty about Socinus's presence on the mission, since, as indicated in the deleted scenes for 'Kobol's Last Gleaming', he was the one who got him released from the brig to come on the mission in the first place; in this, he is no different from Crashdown, who is panicking about having left vital supplies behind. As a result of being led by their emotions, they not only fail to help Socinus in any significant way, they get Tarn killed as well.

Pain in the Neck Joint: Cylons and Colonials

Meanwhile, Head Six is still reminding Baltar of his role as guardian of the child, which she says is his and hers; when he asks if she means this metaphorically, she replies, 'And literally. She's our child, Gaius, our little girl'. When Baltar says, 'You are the mother', she continues, 'And you're the father'.[40] Baltar is then apparently stalked by the white crib, having a vision of it through the trees as they walk.

On the Fleet, Sharon clearly is not conscious of her Cylon side, saying 'What's going on, what's happening?' after she shoots Adama, which is in keeping with the established idea that her human side is unaware of her Cylon side's activities, but also suggests that her seeing the other Sharons was not actually the trigger for the assassination attempt. This retrospectively weakens the thematic unity of the previous story, in which it is suggested that her two sides have finally merged into one. (An impressive post-hoc rationalisation for all this will later appear in 'The Plan'.)

On Caprica, Starbuck resorts to gender stereotypes when she suggests that Caprica-Sharon was simply claiming she was pregnant to play on Helo's male desire to have fathered offspring and his paternal protective instincts, remarking 'My Gods, men are so painfully stupid sometimes'. This also, with hindsight, suggests that Head Six may be playing a similar game with Baltar. We also get some Cylon trivia in the flashback scenes, which reveal the rather bizarre fact that Centurions have vulnerable neck-joints that can be broken with the bare hands if one can get them in the right position.

Back on the Fleet, it becomes clear that Starbuck's status as best pilot incurs envy as much as admiration, as the pilots are running a sweepstake on who will get the most kills now that she is gone. Kat in particular is showing early ambitions to become the Fleet's top gun. The new second-in-command on

---

40 SPOILER SECTION: This, it will transpire, is completely untrue.

14: SCATTERED

Galactica is Kelly, whom we have briefly encountered before in the miniseries. (He is the one who gives the initial order to evacuate the damaged pod before Tigh orders it sealed off.) Doc Cottle, meanwhile, is said to be on the *Rising Star*. The extended version of the first flashback also depicts some popular entertainment in the Colonies, with one of the bar televisions showing a *Who Wants to be a Millionaire?*-style quiz game, and another playing a news commentary programme called *Caprica Today*.

Assembling the Scattered: Writing and Production

The story had a long genesis – Moore has said that he wanted to do a *Galactica*-separated-from-the-Fleet episode as far back as the series' first commissioning – and underwent several changes from conception to execution. In the podcast, Moore states, 'Instead of doing a direct pick-up on the cliffhanger ending from last season's finale "Kobol's Last Gleaming", I wanted to do something a little different ... and actually do a completely separate sort of episode that was ... set some time in the distant past'. This was felt by the network to be too radical. Moore compromised with a contemporary but flashback-heavy episode instead. However, after the flashbacks were shot, Moore, the writers, and the director all felt the idea did not work too well, and in the transmitted episode they are cut to the bare minimum.

As the story was overlength, it was broken into two episodes, 'Scattered' and 'Valley of Darkness'. Its second Caprica scene was decanted into 'Valley of Darkness', and the subplot of the Cylon landing on *Galactica* at the cliffhanger of 'Scattered' was added to extend the episodes into a full two-parter. According to Moore's podcast, the plot threads introduced in the season's first episode were originally intended to be tied up by the fifth, but it eventually took them until the seventh.

Weddle and Thompson both drew inspiration from their fathers' experiences as war veterans when writing their account of Tigh's and Adama's past. Weddle says that, as the son of a Guadalcanal veteran who was haunted by traumatic memories of the conflict, he wanted to show Adama and Tigh as servicemen having trouble adjusting to life outside the military. In the extended version of the first flashback, in which Tigh has an altercation with a fellow crewmember named Hooper, he asserts that Hooper's father paid to keep him out of the military, recalling similar scandals during the Vietnam War of men of draftable age avoiding military service through questionable means. In a different sort of war story reference, the idea of Apollo being able to roam free on the ship after having given his parole is a reference to the Hornblower series, of which Moore was a fan as a child; Jamie Bamber co-starred in several British TV adaptations of Hornblower stories in 1999 and 2000. The subplot about the medical race to save Adama's life strongly recalls the original-series episode 'Fire in Space', in which Adama is injured and requires urgent surgery. There is a minor continuity error in this episode, in that Adama's wife's name, given in 'Act of Contrition' as 'Caroline', is here said to be 'Anne'. This will be 'cleverly' resolved in Season

Three's 'The Passage', by renaming her 'Carolanne'.

The actors generally had a high regard for the story, and particularly its flashback scenes, with Hogan referring to it as 'The highlight of the season' and Olmos saying that his only criticism was that the make-up didn't make the two men look young enough.[41] Rymer, however, has stated that he feels the episode 'doesn't work that well as a stand-alone piece, but ... works well as part of the ongoing storyline'.

'Scattered' in itself is a good episode, with excellent direction, strong production values, and high-quality acting. Its main problems come when it looks back – as, although cutting the flashback sequences to their most essential moments reduces the problems, we are still left with the image of a much scuzzier Adama than one would expect – and forward – as Head Six's prophecies and Baltar's visions are overtaken by subsequent events.

---

41 Originally the production team had thought of casting younger actors as Tigh and Adama for the flashbacks, but then decided instead to let the two regulars handle the scenes themselves. Gary Hutzel says, in *The Official Companion Season Two*, 'We squashed the frames by between ten and 15 per cent, to try to make the actors look younger. We talked about doing other things like [digital] wrinkle removal, but because a lot of the flashbacks didn't make the finished cut we didn't think it was necessary'.

15: Valley Of Darkness

FIRST TRANSMISSION DATE: 22 July 2005 (USA)

WRITTEN BY: Bradley Thompson & David Weddle

DIRECTOR: Michael Rymer

CREDITED CAST: Kate Vernon (Ellen Tigh)[42]; Alonso Oyarzun (Socinus); Kerry Norton (Paramedic Ishay); Chris Shields (Corporal Venner); Luciana Carro (Kat); Bodie Olmos (Hot Dog); Jennifer Halley (Seelix); Ty Olsson (Captain Kelly); Michael Tayles (Flyboy); Dominic Zamprogna (Jammer); Garvin Cross (Collishaw); Brad Loree (Bonnington); Lori Stewart (Twinam)

SYNOPSIS: Following the Cylon attack, the *Galactica*'s systems are infected by a computer virus, and a team of Centurions have infiltrated the ship, making for secondary damage control and auxiliary fire control in order to override the decompression safeties and vent the humans into space. With the auxiliary fire control secured, Apollo leads a team tracking down the Cylons heading for secondary damage control. He springs Roslin from the brig and tells her, her guard Corporal Venner and Billy to make for sickbay, which is the safest place to be, as it was designed to serve as a disaster shelter. However, the way is blocked, and they have to take a route going through secondary damage control. Apollo's team encounter the Cylons and Roslin's party; after a firefight, the humans defeat the Cylons and order is restored. On Caprica, Helo and Starbuck stop at Starbuck's flat to pick up her vehicle and some personal items. On Kobol, Cally and Tyrol arrive too late to do more for Socinus than provide him with a lethal injection of morpha.

ANALYSIS: As noted in the previous review, 'Scattered' was originally a one-off episode that overran, and Michael Rymer felt that there was sufficient material to justify expanding it into a two-part story. The result, however, is a second episode that simply repeats the themes of the first in a more diluted form, and consequently feels stretched and self-indulgent.

Bad Wisdom: Leaders in a Crisis

As in the previous episode, we get a contrast between different people thrust into positions of leadership in crisis situations, adding Apollo, abandoning his

---

42 Credited but appears only in deleted scenes.

usual pilot role to lead a team of Marines, and Roslin, moving out of the political sphere to take charge of a military party, to the list of people adapting their skill sets to new circumstances.

Tigh, as an old war veteran, reveals that he knows what the Cylons are up to as he has seen similar things before. There is an extended version of this scene containing a long flashback in which Tigh and Adama, on the freighter, reminisce about the war, and Adama tells Tigh about Centurions employing the tactics that they are now using on *Galactica* in the series' present. This sequence was probably deleted because its inclusion would have made it look as if Tigh spent several minutes standing gormlessly reminiscing in CIC. The scene where he and Apollo hash out the events of 'Kobol's Last Gleaming' has Tigh accusing Apollo of not being fit to wear the uniform, and Apollo cuttingly responding, 'I am not fit to wear the uniform. Maybe I never was. Then again, neither are you. This isn't my ship. And it sure as hell isn't yours. It's [Adama's]'. This underlines the fact that without Adama, neither man would be in the service, for good or ill. When Jammer asks Apollo what he means by 'Sometimes you got to roll the hard six', he says 'I don't know, it's something my dad says', which sums up Apollo's attitude to his military career; he has gone into the service, unquestioningly, because of his father, and, while he does a good job, his heart is not really in it.

On Kobol, Tyrol is forced into a command role by Crashdown's increasing inability to lead, and, in a powerful performance, has to acknowledge that Socinus is dying, and that Tarn's death was essentially meaningless. He gives Socinus a fatal injection, lying to him that the rescue ship is arriving, so that he will die feeling happy and hopeful. Moore comments in his podcast that Crashdown is out of his depth because he isn't an infantry officer. However, it seems to be indicative more of a general lack of leadership ability on Crashdown's part than simply an unfamiliar context, as Tyrol, who is also not an infantry officer, is coping much better.

Death and the Maiden: Baltar and Head Six

Baltar, meanwhile, has a surreal fantasy in which Adama takes the foretold child from him, says, 'Is this the shape of things to come?' and drowns it; then, when Baltar searches for its body in the water, he finds it has vanished. This sequence, a kind of perverse baptism (the Biblical phrase 'Valley of Darkness' refers to death), has echoes of the Six killing the child in the miniseries, and sets up Adama as a sort of Herod-figure whose very presence is inimical to the child; Olmos reportedly found the experience of doing the scene quite intense. One might interpret the vision as reflecting Baltar's growing protectiveness toward the child and fears for its future, as indicated by his anguished and incredulous cry of 'Why would anyone want to drown a baby?' However, while certainly dramatic and haunting, the sequence ultimately makes no sense either within the story or in light of subsequent events, and as such its inclusion seems

15: VALLEY OF DARKNESS

misguided.[43]

Other surreal but ultimately meaningless images of death and sacrifice pervade Baltar's story. He wakes on a heap of skulls, and Head Six tells him that they are from human sacrifices. She goes on to relate the story of Kobol in what Moore has said is intended explicitly as a kind of Garden of Eden myth: she states that humans and gods lived in harmony 'for a time', but that subsequently, 'Your true nature asserted itself. Your brutality, your depravity, your barbarism'. This, while it might provide a clever echo of Leoben's condemnation of humanity in the miniseries, is clearly incompatible with the subtler origin myth presented in the deleted scene from 'Kobol's Last Gleaming' (as is Head Six's assertion that all of scripture is a lie, since in several other episodes she appears to treat Pythia as broadly correct, if flawed in its interpretations). It also seems out of line with what we later learn about Kobol's history,[44] and raises the question of to whom the humans were sacrificed. Furthermore, Head Six seems to accept here the idea that the Lords of Kobol are gods, whereas in 'Kobol's Last Gleaming' and later 'Fragged' she asserts that they are only false gods. Since most of what Head Six says on Kobol is wildly inaccurate (in an extended version of Socinus's death scene, for instance, she tells Baltar that all the other humans in the Fleet will die and only he will reach Earth), her behaviour is in stark contrast to that in Season One, in which, although her prophecies and actions were sometimes cryptic, it was always possible to divine a logic behind them.

Papa was a Rolling Stone: The Caprica Storyline

On Caprica, meanwhile, Helo and Starbuck both, in parallel, have to come to terms with painful aspects of their background. Helo's realisation that he was never, in fact, one step ahead of the Cylons, but survived only because they wanted him to, is clearly a blow to his ego; Starbuck, in light of this, defuses her earlier anger against him and acknowledges, 'The Cylons have a way of making us all look like idiots'.

The condition of Starbuck's flat, meanwhile, shows her as disorganised, undisciplined, and given to random bursts of creativity, with a mandala and a poem painted on the wall, and some rather terrible abstract paintings (a particularly notable one depicting a little orange aeroplane and a green man carrying a bucket). Although she complains about the rent and the general condition of the flat, she is hardly a landlord's ideal tenant, with the furniture and floor being littered with bottles, newspapers, takeaway containers and other random debris. She displays uncommonly poor judgment in, first, shooting out

---

43 SPOILER SECTION: In fact it is Roslin who is the threat to the child.
44 SPOILER SECTION: Namely, that the humans created Cylons while living on Kobol with the gods, and these Cylons also formed part of the exodus, complicating the simple pattern whereby one species creates another, which then rebels, goes on to create its own daughter species, which rebels in turn, and so on.

the lock on the flat and, secondly, playing her music tapes at top volume, both of which actions seem guaranteed to alert any Cylons in the vicinity as to her presence.

The story also emphasises her rootlessness and hints at her troubled family background; she says that where everyone else, after the fall of the Colonies, is fighting to get back what they had, she is just fighting because she doesn't know how to do anything else. This was a line that Katee Sackhoff ad-libbed, according to a 2005 interview she gave to *Cult Times*. Elsewhere in the same interview, she noted, 'Starbuck doesn't feel comfortable sitting still or allowing her brain to pause, because then she has time to think, especially about the past, and she doesn't like to do that, because that's where her pain is'.

Starbuck tells Helo curtly that the music she plays is her dad's; significantly, she does not say if he was a composer, a pianist or simply a music-lover, indicating a reluctance to discuss her parents. She refers to the Cylons as Sharon's 'family', again putting the concept of family into an antagonistic context. In a deleted scene, Helo alludes further to Starbuck having a peripatetic background, saying that he didn't know she was from Delphi: 'I thought you were from all over, dancing around military bases with your mum'. (We will later learn that her mother was a Marine.)

Fear No Evil: Continuity and Worldbuilding

In characterisation terms, the writers avoid the common action-series cliché of having all the main characters know how to handle guns. In keeping with his being a civilian who grew up in peacetime, Billy is incompetent with weapons to the point where Dualla has to discreetly disarm him; and Roslin refuses to carry a gun, saying 'I can't' (but not elaborating on why). There is also a deleted scene in which Ellen Tigh rings up CIC to ask her husband to save her, and he tells her to get the gun out of his locker and defend herself; when Ellen protests that she doesn't know how, he reminds her of an incident three years earlier at her sister's house, where they were 'sitting on the front porch, shooting at the groundhogs as they came up the driveway'[45], which he thinks qualifies her to take down fully armed Cylon Centurions. In a deleted flashback scene, Tigh talks about how the Centurions he battled while serving as a petty officer on the Colonial vessel *Brenik* cut up the humans they encountered, concluding that they did so not, as Adama postulates, to spread fear and panic, but because 'They hated us', which explains why mutilated bodies are also found on *Galactica*. Tyrol kisses the top of Cally's head and hugs her, marking the start of what will later turn into a quite serious relationship. Although Lee and Roslin have been imprisoned, Billy is free to roam the ship, which suggests that he is not really

---

45 SPOILER SECTION: This is of course rendered complete nonsense by the later revelation that Ellen is a Cylon, as she cannot have had a sister; and, as she has been living in human society for quite some time at this point, it cannot be a false memory either.

15: VALLEY OF DARKNESS

considered a threat.

In continuity terms, Helo refers to Caprica-Sharon as 'Cylon Sharon' and Starbuck calls her a 'copy', suggesting that they are still operating on the (false) assumption that Cylons can make copies of human originals, and that the Sharon on *Galactica* is human. An explanation is provided for the lack of human corpses on Caprica (the Cylons have been transporting them to mass incinerators), but not for the general lack of other signs of nuclear devastation. Starbuck's brand of cigars is Foliole (which means a single part of a compound leaf). Hadrian is briefly alluded to as leading one of the anti-Cylon teams, but not seen. Explosive rounds are said to be the only type of ammunition capable of killing Centurions. Moore has indicated, by way of backstory, that the reason only a relatively small number of people are hunting down the Centurions on *Galactica* is that the ship had only a skeleton crew at the time of the disaster.

There are also references back to earlier episodes. Starbuck's (somewhat awful) poem appears to allude to her relationship with Zak, ending with the lines 'I drink away the night/stroking my hair to/the beat of his heart/watching a boy/turn into a/Man'. The episode references Weddle and Thompson's Season One contribution 'Act of Contrition' in featuring a sequence of pilots rejoicing as they return from a mission, only for disaster to strike unexpectedly. Given the manner of Leoben's execution in 'Flesh and Bone', there is an irony in the fact that the Centurions' plan involves decompressing humans into space.

In terms of errors and other things to watch out for, Kate Vernon is listed as a guest star in the opening credits although she appears only in the deleted scenes, and Grace Park, although credited, does not appear at all outside of the recap, making this the first episode in which neither of the Sharons features. Kat, echoing Tigh's famous ad-lib in the miniseries, exclaims 'Jesus!' at the sight of the Centurions. The music Starbuck plays is 'Metamorphosis Five', composed by Philip Glass and played by Bear McCreary, in an early example of known Earth music turning up on the Colonies; and it is significant, in light of events in Season Four, that it is associated with Starbuck and her father. The 'Flash' and 'Thunder' sign and countersign used by Tyrol and Crashdown on Kobol was used in real life by the Allied forces on D-Day. The fact that the Cylons plan to kill everyone on board *Galactica* and then turn *Galactica*'s guns on the Fleet indicates that the originally-mooted storyline of the Cylons using the humans as a means of finding Earth has been abandoned, at least for the time being.

'Valley of Darkness' is a visually exciting, but ultimately pointless, piece of television. Furthermore, while the imagery in Baltar's visions is striking, it either goes nowhere or raises problems in hindsight.

16: Fragged

FIRST TRANSMISSION DATE: 29 July 2005 (USA)

WRITERS: Dawn Prestwich & Nichole Yorkin

DIRECTOR: Sergio Mimico-Gezzan

CREDITED CAST: Kate Vernon (Ellen Tigh); Donnelly Rhodes (Doctor Cottle); Richard Hatch (Tom Zarek); Kerry Norton (Paramedic Layne Ishay); Kurt Evans (Paramedic Howard Kim); Chris Shields (Corporal Venner); Jennifer Halley (Seelix); Leah Cairns (Racetrack); Patricia Idlette (Sarah Porter); Malcolm Stewart (Marshall Bagott); T-Roy Kozuki (Marine)

SYNOPSIS: On Kobol, Crashdown's party discovers that the Cylons have a missile launcher and a DRADIS dish, evidently intending to eliminate any human rescue mission. Crashdown decides they must attack this system. After learning that the launcher is guarded by three Centurions and the dish by two, he opts to attack the former. The others have doubts that such a plan can succeed, given their collective lack of ability, but Crashdown imposes his authority. Upon attacking the launcher, they find five Centurions present, and Tyrol correctly reasons that the dish is now unguarded. Baltar has earlier failed to observe the Cylons' movements correctly due to losing his field glasses, but has not told the others about his mistake. Tyrol suggests they attack the dish instead, but Crashdown finally tips over the edge, pulling a gun on Cally. Baltar shoots Crashdown and the party take out the dish. The survivors are rescued by Apollo and Racetrack in a Raptor. On *Galactica*, as the press and Quorum demand access to the imprisoned President, Roslin experiences Chamalla withdrawal symptoms, rendering her incoherent. Tigh allows them to see her, as Ellen advises that the sight will lead them to conclude that Roslin is not competent to lead. However, Billy manages to get some Chamalla extract to Roslin, and she is fully coherent when they arrive, in a blow to Tigh's authority.

ANALYSIS: 'Fragged' brings Crashdown's story to a bloody climax, while allowing the Tigh storyline to escalate as, the immediate danger of the Cylon incursion having been successfully averted, the Fleet faces the prospect of a long-term martial law regime. However, while this episode may slightly advance the wider storyline, it is fraught with contradictions and skewed logic.

16: FRAGGED

Loose Cannon: Tigh Out of Control

With the crisis over, Tigh is now starting to lose control, drinking again and threatening Apollo with the brig, once more indicating that he is, at this stage, a better XO than commander; he can take control in a crisis, but is not so good at ongoing people management. Tigh's approach to politics is very much in keeping with the norm of the original series. He treats the Quorum as an impediment, clearly regards the political scenario he is confronted with as a nuisance, and is not savvy or diplomatic enough to manage the situation to his own advantage. Tellingly, when Zarek asserts that Adama was working toward martial law, Tigh's response is 'I know for a fact that the old man hated martial law. He believed in freedom and democracy and all that good stuff'. Although Tigh, now that the pressure is off, has fallen into a mindset where he does what he thinks Adama would want, his problem is, of course, that he is not Adama, and thus cannot act the way Adama would, as he tacitly acknowledges at the end of the episode when he admits to Adama 'I really frakked things up for you'.

One problem, however, is that the story goes slightly too far in portraying Tigh's loss of control. While it's believable that he would have trouble with the political aspects of the job, since he lacks Adama's diplomacy, it seems unbelievable that he would forget about the rescue mission to Kobol. Indeed, the latter seems like exactly the sort of straightforward military problem on which he would focus once the Centurion boarding party is dealt with. Given his past attitude to Apollo, also, in which he generally respects the younger man's ability even if he doesn't always respect his choices, it seems odd that he challenges Apollo's status as CAG and does not want to let him lead the rescue mission. Tigh also refers to *Galactica* as 'my ship', which seems out of character for a man who has built his identity around being second in command. Ellen's visit to Roslin, where she discovers the former President seemingly insane, could be coincidental, but it makes sense that Ellen, being the sort of person who investigates all possible avenues to fulfilling her ambition, might visit the brig to see if there are any advantages the situation might hold. Indeed, she does later try to use her knowledge of Roslin's condition to keep Tigh as the most powerful man in the Fleet.

Justifiable Homicide: The Death of Crashdown

Again, the situation with Crashdown parallels that with Tigh. As Tigh gets out of his depth on *Galactica*, Crashdown's sense of guilt drives him to formulate suicidal attacks, saying 'We owe it to Socinus and Tarn to take the frakkers out' and justifying his plans with jingoistic military language. Before the attack, he puts his dead comrades' dog tags around his neck, symbolically taking their deaths upon himself. To be fair to Crashdown, his logic in attacking the Cylon defence system is sound: clearly, what the Cylons are doing is using the stranded humans as bait, planning to take out any Raptors that come to their rescue, so it is up to Crashdown and his team to take action.

However, Crashdown's tactics are deeply flawed from the outset. He argues that his party should attack the Cylons because they have equal numbers to them and the element of surprise, but equal numbers are hardly fair when your opponents are fully-armed Centurions (who, being the defenders, are in a better strategic position anyway), and who are clearly expecting some kind of attack (as they have posted guards). When Tyrol tries to talk him around as before, he pulls rank on him, and, of course, fails to adapt his plans to the changes in their situation. When Crashdown threatens to shoot Cally, as well as showing that his desire to keep control has become so great that he would kill his own people to achieve it, this indicates that he is not thinking rationally about the success of the mission, as the sound of the gunshot would alert the Cylons to their presence. Although it does make sense for Crashdown to use the 'five-paragraph order' system from officer school to explain the plan, since his team are of variable skill levels, he otherwise fails to take into account the fact that his fighting force consists of three deckhands and a scientist. Under the circumstances, the simplest plan would obviously be for them to sneak up on the Cylons at the DRADIS dish and deploy the handheld rocket launcher, rather than engaging in complicated manoeuvres.

While Baltar attempts to get through to Crashdown using an appeal to democratic measures, Tyrol, despite his misgivings about the same officer, shouts him down. There is a clear, if perhaps perverse-seeming, logic to this: as the Tigh situation clearly demonstrates, the military is not a democracy, and although Crashdown's plan is dangerous, Tyrol clearly sees it as the only possible option for fighting back. It is only when he learns that Baltar made a mistake in his observations and that the DRADIS dish is unguarded that he actively opposes the plan, as he realises that there is another option, that Crashdown is not going to take.

There is, however, a wider problem with this storyline. From a strategic point of view, the most sensible tactic would be for the crew to attack the DRADIS dish rather than the missile battery, as taking out either would ruin the Cylon's plans, and the DRADIS dish has fewer guards. While it might be understandable for Crashdown, who is not thinking through his tactics, to miss this point, it is surprising that none of the others, not even Tyrol, raises it. Furthermore, it makes no sense that the Cylons would leave the DRADIS dish unguarded at any point. Although the sequence is exciting, then, it makes very little sense from a military perspective.

The story's title, 'Fragged', is a term that originated during the Vietnam war and refers to the killing of one's own officers/NCOs (normally with fragmentation grenades), a fate Crashdown ultimately meets. His epitaph is pronounced by Baltar, who says that he died 'leading the charge – he gave his life in the finest tradition of the service', and Tyrol adds, 'Yeah, he was a hero to the end'. All of which is, of course, true: Crashdown was leading the charge; there is a long military history of officers being shot by their own men; and heroes aren't necessarily renowned for their ability to act intelligently. Baltar's and Tyrol's spin on events may be positive, but not inaccurate.

Lost Planet of the Gods: Cylon and Colonial Religion

The exploration of religion and the origins of humanity continues in this episode, as unfortunately does the inconsistent portrayal of Head Six in this regard. Head Six says, 'God turned his back on Kobol. Turned his back on man and the false gods he worshipped. What happens on Kobol is not his will', putting her God into the Garden of Eden story as an explicit rejector of both man's actions and those of the Lords of Kobol. This version is not incompatible with the origin myth put forward in the deleted scene from 'Kobol's Last Gleaming', that one jealous god's desire to be elevated above the rest caused a war, and it might answer the question posed in 'Valley of Darkness' as to who the human sacrifices were for; however, it is incompatible with the idea Head Six puts forward in the latter episode that humanity were rebelling against all the gods. When she says of the dead, 'Nothing awaits them; no eternal life, no damnation, only oblivion', she then explains to Baltar that it is because they died on Kobol rather than that they lacked faith in the right God. However, this raises the question of why she was so keen to get Baltar down to the planet, as he would seem to be in greater danger now than he was on the Fleet; indeed, as the second season unfolds it appears that he might have been more use in that setting, as he could have taken the reins of power from Roslin and obviated the need for martial law.[46]

Her discourse is also suffused with Christian symbolism. She claims, 'Our child will bring ... salvation, but only if you accept your role as her father. And her guardian', essentially urging him to surrender himself to the child as he has surrendered himself to her God, though this differs slightly from her earlier assertion that he was its literal father. She references Judas when she says that one of the team on Kobol will betray the others, although it's never quite clear who she means: Baltar, by dropping the field glasses and lying about the Centurions' movements; Crashdown, by instigating the suicide attack; or Cally, by freezing up at a crucial moment.

Strangely, she also seems to take the Cylon line regarding the evil of humanity, saying that Baltar is 'a man' because he has killed someone else, but excusing the Cylons' own killing by saying they learned it from the humans, in a kind of blaming the parents ploy; she also fails to make the obvious logical connection that, if it is acceptable to blame humanity for the Cylons' failings, then the gods, her own God included, must be responsible for those of the humans. It is worth noting that none of the humans in the story kills for the reasons Head Six suggests are human motivations (sport, greed or envy), just for

---

[46] SPOILER SECTION: The later revelation that the trip to Kobol leads the Fleet to the wrong Earth, and the damage this does to Fleet morale, might suggest another reason for Head Six's hostility, but then raises the question of why she did not make any objections to the expedition in 'Kobol's Last Gleaming'.

survival. The reason for this inconsistency is probably that the writers of this particular story were operating on the assumption that Head Six was a form of Cylon influence and nothing more; but that begs the question of why the story editor and the showrunners did not rewrite her statements to bring them more in line with what had gone before. At a stretch, one could argue that her comments are aimed at forcing Baltar to see the Cylon point of view and accept that right is not inherently on the side of the humans. She tells him, when he asks if human nature is simply about killing, 'I will be your conscience', again encouraging him to put his faith and his doubts in the hands of a higher power. Carla Robinson, the story editor for Seasons One and Two, notes that Baltar's self-preservation-motivated action in killing Crashdown saves the entire mission, building on the theme in Baltar's arc that his selfish actions can paradoxically lead to good consequences for others, and in keeping with his haphazard progress toward God through self-interest. However, if Head Six is a divine messenger, the fact that she is lying and changing her story causes the audience, if no-one else, to question God himself.

In the area of Colonial religion, a deleted scene exists in which Roslin has a nightmare. In it, she argues with Billy: Billy states that 'Humanity was kicked out' of Kobol, and Roslin counters that 'Actually, the scriptures say that there was some sort of battle among the gods and when it was over we chose to leave'. Billy then suggests she is interpreting the scriptures wrongly and that she has made a lot of mistakes, says she should resign, and finally stabs her in the heart with a knife. One could interpret this as simply an expression of Roslin's inner self-doubt; however, similarities between Billy's story and Head Six's statement in 'Valley of Darkness' that humans rebelled against the Gods, suggest it could be another divinely-inspired vision, intended to warn Roslin that she is incorrect in her interpretations of Pythia. If this is the case, however, it further adds to the confusion over what happened on Kobol, as Head Six's statements in 'Valley of Darkness' support Billy's position, but her statements in 'Fragged' and in the deleted scene from 'Kobol's Last Gleaming' support Roslin's. Regardless of whether or not she doubts her own interpretations, Roslin does not hesitate to use scripture for political ends, latching on to the Gemenon representative's faith as a means of swaying the Quorum to her side, much as Billy uses Venner's own faith to persuade him to get the drugs Roslin needs earlier in the story.

Fragments of Meaning: Continuity and Worldbuilding

In other elements of story development, we learn that Gemenons believe in the literal truth of the scriptures (and, if Venner is typical, pray using a kind of rosary). Tigh's exchange with Billy –'Why aren't you in the brig?' 'Because no-one put me in there'– suggests that, as hypothesised in relation to last episode, Billy is not considered enough of a threat to warrant incarceration. Again we see that even among the military types, not everyone is proficient with weapons; like Gaeta, Cally joined the army only to pay for her education, in this case as a dentist. Moore has been quoted, in an interview available in John Laroque's document archive, as saying that, ironically, her term of enlistment was nearly up at the time of the attack. Zarek's motivation in asking the Gemenon delegate about whether Roslin's claims are backed up by scripture is clearly that he, not wanting a military dictatorship, is trying to build political support for Roslin. It also has to be said that the characters on Kobol react believably to their terrifying situation, with various forms of fear and anxiety, without any unrealistic melodrama or clichéd heroic acts. The conversation between Apollo and Tigh indicates that the Fleet has at least ten Raptors, of which seven are currently down for repairs. Head Six's assertion that humans kill for 'sport, greed [and] envy' is a partial echo of Adama's line in the miniseries, 'We still commit murder because of greed, spite [and] jealousy'.

What the Frag: Writing and Production

The writers of this episode, Prestwich and Yorkin, had previously written for *Carnivàle*, *Judging Amy* and *Ally McBeal*. Both left *Battlestar Galactica* shortly thereafter, according to Moore because they did not like the series' mixture of science fiction and military drama and had little interest in either genre. Certainly the abovementioned problems with the script suggest that they had difficulty thinking through the tactical side of the episode, and lacked a certain feel for the series' characters. However, the series' editing team also has to take some of the blame for the problems with 'Fragged', particularly as the inconsistencies in Head Six's position are not limited to this episode.

There are no significant differences between the 21 April 2005 draft script and the final version. One or two minor points are interesting: for instance, in the draft script Baltar has an extra line at the end of his first conversation with Head Six, in which he starts to question her about the baby ('Does she have a name? Has she been born yet? Will the child be born in a literal sense or–') but is interrupted by Tyrol ordering him to move out. In the draft, when Baltar loses the field glasses, the script states that it should be impossible to tell whether or not there are consistently two Centurions at the dish, whereas the filmed version makes it clear. In the sequence where Tyrol supports Crashdown's plan and Baltar questions it, the draft has it being Crashdown who says to Baltar, 'That's enough, Doctor', rather than Tyrol as transmitted; the final version thus makes Tyrol seem more of an authority figure in this situation. In terms of filmic references, the sequence where Tyrol's handgun appears to blow up the pursuing Cylons before it is revealed that the Raptor in fact destroyed them, is a deliberate reference to a similar scene in *Saving Private Ryan* (1998) on which Sergio Mimico-Gezzan was first assistant director; when Mimico-Gezzan was assigned to direct this episode, Eick was worried that he might not want to do such an obvious homage, but apparently he had no problem with it.

This is the first episode in the series with no scenes taking place on Caprica, and no appearances by Starbuck (although she is briefly mentioned by Roslin in the deleted scene of her nightmare) or Helo (though Tahmoh Penikett and Katee Sackhoff are still named in the opening credits). Also, this is the second episode with no Sharons (Grace Park is nonetheless still credited); but Ellen, perhaps to make up for all her deleted scenes in the previous episode, does make an appearance. The pictures of the younger Tigh and Adama that which Tigh has on his desk were visibly taken during the filming of the flashback scenes in 'Scattered' and 'Valley of Darkness'.

Moore is quoted in *The Official Companion Season Two* as saying that initially there was no plan to kill off Crashdown, but that '[Sam Witwer]'s performance in "Kobol's Last Gleaming" made us go "Wow, there's a great story here that will probably end in Crashdown's death'. Witwer has also been quoted in the same volume as saying that he was keen on having a good dramatic death as a way of leaving the series, as he was eager to get on to other projects.

Given the problems with this episode, which extend to characterisation and story logic as well as the ongoing inconsistencies in the portrayal of Head Six, 'Fragged' is perhaps an appropriate title for it. Like a fragmentation grenade, it blows large holes into what is already a rather weak ongoing storyline.

17: Resistance

FIRST TRANSMISSION DATE: 5 August 2005

WRITER: Toni Graphia

DIRECTOR: Allan Kroeker

CREDITED CAST: Kate Vernon (Ellen Tigh); Donnely Rhodes (Doctor Cottle); Lorena Gale (Elosha); Richard Hatch (Tom Zarek); Chris Shields (Corporal Venner); Bodie Olmos (Hot Dog); Leah Cairns (Racetrack); Dominic Zamprogna (Jammer); Tamara Lashley (Sue-Shaun); Jeremy Guilbaut (Lieutenant Joe 'Hammerhead' Palladino); Heather Doerksen (Marine With A Sandwich); Curtis Lee Hicks (Marine Sergeant)

KNOWN UNCREDITED CAST: Leo Li Chiang (Tattooed Pilot)

SYNOPSIS: Returning to *Galactica*, Tyrol is arrested and interrogated by Tigh, and Baltar is in disgrace for failing to detect Boomer's Cylon nature. Baltar is ordered to find out from her how many Cylon agents there are in the Fleet; he poisons Tyrol and refuses to administer the antidote until Boomer supplies a figure. Tigh's governance is increasingly unpopular, with protests among the civilian fleet members and some ships refusing to resupply *Galactica*; when Marines are sent in to commandeer supplies from the *Gideon*, the protest turns ugly and four civilians are shot dead. Apollo plans with Roslin to spring her from the brig and get her off the ship; they succeed, with the help of Dualla. As Boomer is being moved to a specially-constructed cell, Cally fatally shoots her. Adama, now recovering, returns and takes official command back from Tigh. On Caprica, Starbuck and Helo discover a resistance movement of human survivors, formed around a professional sports team who escaped the bombing through being in the mountains for high altitude training.

ANALYSIS: This episode's title refers to a new set of parallel stories: the resistance to martial law in the Fleet as Tigh continues to lose control, and the discovery of the Caprica resistance, a band of survivors engaging in terrorist actions against the Cylons.

Reign of Error: Tigh on Galactica

Tigh's heavy drinking continues. He throws away his hip-flask, but picks it up again, just like he threw out, then retrieved, the bottle of alcohol in the miniseries. Despite this, he is still sharp: his logic in not trusting Tyrol's protestations of loyalty is sound, since, as Tigh points out, Boomer said the same things, and, equally Tyrol, like Boomer, had previously been implicated during Hadrian's inquiry in 'Litmus'. When Dualla gives him a sheaf of papers to sign including the instruction to close Causeway B (so that Roslin's party can get through), with the obvious expectation that he will sign them without properly reading them, he leafs through them distractedly but abruptly questions the Causeway B order. Tigh also can't bring himself to command the Vipers to open fire on Roslin's Raptor, because Adama's son is on board, something Ellen astutely realises and Tigh admits. Although Cottle blames the *Gideon* Massacre squarely on Tigh's decision to put a pilot in charge of the Marines, there was a sound reason for Tigh to do so, namely that there were not enough Marine NCOs to command all the boarding parties. Michael Hogan's take on the situation, from an interview with *Sci-Fi Magazine* (February 2006), is that 'He did the best he could … If he made any bad decisions, it wasn't with malice aforethought. The Fleet needed supplies, so he sent in the Marines; government isn't working, martial law. The first words out of Tigh's mouth when Adama stumbles into his quarters are, "I frakked up but good". No false bravado there'.

Ellen, meanwhile, continues to manipulate Tigh, urging him on to bad decisions (vetoing the idea of a summit with the ship's captains and instead encouraging him to be more dictatorial) but also pretending at times to sit back and let him take charge. Although he is at home in a military situation, he is less so in a political setting, which allows Ellen the chance to influence him. Knowing the source of his insecurities, she invokes Adama to influence his decisions, for instance saying 'Bill would never do that. But you gotta do what you gotta do', regarding Tigh's idea to meet with the ship's captains. Moore has said in the podcast for this episode that originally the production team had planned to have her acting like the queen of the ship, swanning around and abusing her status as the Colonel's wife, but this was abandoned on the grounds of lack of realism. Tigh's accusing Ellen of manipulation leads to a fight between them, which in turn leads to them making love, which defines their relationship; she is dangerous to him, and yet they are drawn to each other on a sexual and emotional level.

As the situation deteriorates, people within the Fleet are resisting. The civilians are refusing to resupply *Galactica*, leading to the conflict in which civilians are shot, but the pilots also challenge Apollo's arrest by urging him to come and play cards, and Apollo's Marine guards ignore the fact that he is openly talking with Dualla, who reports her doubts about Tigh's ability to handle the situation in front of them (even, in a deleted scene, agreeing to make scrambled off-log calls for Apollo). Dualla greets the Marines and they greet her back whenever she joins Apollo. Gaeta learns that Dualla has been scrambling the calls and tells her that she should go through the proper channels if she is upset with the situation, but nevertheless lies to Tigh when the latter asks if there have been off-log calls, saying he didn't notice any. The shooting of the civilians is carefully staged so that it is unclear which Marine fires first, emphasising that it is the civilians' anger, and the soldiers' uncertainty and defensiveness, that lead to the bloodshed, rather than there being any obvious culprit to blame. As Moore notes: 'There is no higher power for these people to deal with ... There's no headquarters to deal with. There's no judicial system. There's no governmental structure at all'. In such a situation, a leader can become a true autocrat, unable to be held to account; this means that, in the absence of Roslin and Adama, no one but Tigh can legally halt the progression of events.

In this case, however, Adama's return brings an end to Tigh's command. Speaking with Tigh afterwards, Adama implies that he knows what Ellen has been up to, when he says he doesn't like people who try to second-guess their leaders' commands. He asks for a drink, acknowledging that it is okay to do so once in a while, and says that he will help Tigh pick up the pieces.

Reservoir Bucks: The Caprica Resistance

On Caprica, meanwhile, we finally meet the human resistance, whose core is a professional Pyramid-playing team, the Caprica Buccaneers (or C-Bucs), augmented by a few others, vaguely described as hikers and survivalists. As Moore notes in the podcast, it is a silly but, for all that, plausible idea that such a group might survive through random chance. It is explained that they are raiding stores for weapons and anti-radiation meds. The *Reservoir Dogs* (1992) moment where we have two groups of humans pulling guns on each other, each convinced that the others are Cylons, ironically highlights the way in which the goal of terrorists is to get their opponents fighting each other, simply due to the fear of fifth-columnists. This also mirrors Roslin's observation on the Fleet that the fragmentation within it could allow the Cylons to pick them off one by one, indicating again that in such situations, internal strife is as much a problem as external enemies. The sexual tension between the resistance's leader, Samuel T Anders, and Starbuck is palpable in the scene where the two play Pyramid together (the podcast indicates that they toned it down from its original level, but it is still very obvious to the viewer), marking the start of what will be a significant relationship.

Under Suspicion: Tyrol and Baltar on Galactica

Tyrol's return to the *Galactica* sees him arrested and once again accused of collaboration with Boomer, this time over her attempt to murder Adama. The pair are symbolically linked throughout: drops of Tyrol's blood falling to the floor after being struck by Tigh mirrors drops of Boomer's blood falling to the floor at the end after she is shot by Cally; and Tyrol's desperate assertions that he is not a Cylon ironically mirror Boomer's own assertions of her humanity earlier in the series. Boomer reaches out to Tyrol, but he, angry at being accused of treachery, rejects her. Despite this, he visibly has qualms about the idea that there are plans to use her as a 'lab rat' in mental and physical tests – as does Baltar, suggesting that something, possibly Head Six's harping on about the brutality of the human race, has changed his attitude since the events of 'Kobol's Last Gleaming', where he actively encouraged Boomer to kill herself. Boomer does, finally, die in Tyrol's arms, learning in a touching exchange that he did love her, providing a form of closure – although, given that she will resurrect shortly afterwards, there will be repercussions later in the series.

The situation also leads to moral debates among the deck crew, Cally and Jammer literally coming to blows when the former refuses to help build the cage – significantly, because she believes they will imprison Tyrol in it rather than out of a general sense of right and wrong. Jammer first says that they should follow orders, and then comes right out and says that he believes Tyrol is a traitor, hinting that Jammer is someone who can be easily led. He then says, 'If you want to get pissed at someone, get pissed at Boomer', leading to Cally's shooting of the Cylon: not simply a Jack Ruby scenario (which it visually resembles) or an act of vengeance, but, subconsciously, the killing of a rival for the Chief's affections and the source of the animosity against him.

Regarding the number of Cylons in the Fleet, Boomer cannot really know the actual amount, as her human persona does not have access to her Cylon side's knowledge, and is therefore lying to save Tyrol when she says that there are eight. This is reinforced by the fact that 'The Plan' indicates there were nine Cylons in the Fleet at the time of the miniseries[47], and by this episode there are only five (and Boomer would surely have known at least of the marooning of the first Doral and the deaths of the second Doral and Leoben). While her choice of the number eight may be random, it might also be subconsciously influenced by Baltar breaking off his countdown before saying the word 'eight', causing her to blurt out the next number in the sequence.

Baltar, meanwhile, is once again on the back foot, returning from Kobol to learn that he is under suspicion, his superior (Roslin) under arrest (with martial law rendering his status as Vice-President irrelevant) and his Cylon test in doubt (as it appears not to have picked up Boomer). Cally, also, rather than being grateful to him for having saved her life on Kobol, is now threatening to expose his killing of Crashdown if he does not help Tyrol. Baltar's initial intention is to explain the test's failure to detect Boomer by claiming it didn't work; however, after his meeting with Cally he clearly realises that he will have to find some way to prove that Tyrol is not a Cylon in order to save his life, and instead claims to Tigh that what he administered to Boomer was 'a beta test; a preliminary'. Baltar never does test the Chief, instead using it as a pretext to administer the poison. Tyrol is subsequently released from the brig, since, if Boomer had believed he could download to another body, the threat of killing him would not have upset her.

Baltar's injecting Tyrol with a fatal substance as a way of getting Boomer to

---

47 SPOILER SECTION: For those keeping track: Shelley Godfrey, Burgundy-Doral, Teal-Doral and Leoben (all of whom have left the Fleet by this point), plus Boomer, D'Anna Biers, Prostitute Six, Simon and Cavil. It is worth noting that Boomer does not include the Final Five in her count.

talk is not simply instrumental, but may also be an act of revenge on Tyrol for not respecting his status on Kobol, and on Cally for blackmailing him on Tyrol's behalf earlier. There is a parallel between the countdown Baltar gives as he urges Boomer to save Tyrol's life, and the countdown Crashdown gave as he threatened Cally on Kobol. However, his actions also could be a way of proving something to himself: if Boomer really does love Tyrol, then perhaps Six, on Caprica, loved him. His remark 'Love is a strange and wonderful thing, Chief. You'd be happy you experienced it at all. Even if it was with a machine' visibly pleases Head Six, and ties in with the theme throughout this story of rules being undermined for love (Sharon lying to save Tyrol, Cally committing murder for the same man, Tigh caught between his carnal love for his wife and his fraternal love for Adama). As Moore notes in his podcast, Baltar shows a new ruthlessness here, fighting back against what Head Six calls 'the disrespect of mechanics and colonels alike', but he also begins to acknowledge his own feelings about his Cylon former lover.

Dead Kennedys: Continuity and Worldbuilding

In the political storyline, Roslin continues to act as a leader, accepting Corporal Venner's gift of liquorice as kindly meant even though she doesn't like the sweet in question, and winning over the Marine on Causeway B with her rhetoric. Apollo, as Moore notes, does break his parole in order to foment rebellion, as some of the planning takes place while he is on duty. His growing closeness with Dualla indicates a mutual attraction that will develop over this season.

Elsewhere, it is finally revealed on screen that Starbuck had hoped to be a professional Pyramid player before suffering a leg injury. Pyramid itself is seen as much like the Triad games of the original series, albeit without the latter's revealing costumes, and the sports trivia (for instance, 'How many foul breaks did [the C-Bucs] have in the playoff against Aerilon?') spouted in the Caprica scenes lends a sense of a wider Colonial popular culture. There are currently 53 resistance members, although their numbers have been virtually halved by a recent Cylon ambush. The tattoo of a cross on Katee Sackhoff's left shoulderblade is covered with a large sticking plaster, which is visible when she plays Pyramid with Anders.

Tyrol is for the first time called 'Galen', a name he shares not only with an ancient Greek physician and demi-god but also a Colonial philosopher mentioned in 'The Hand of God', whose axiom was there given as 'Surrender your ego, remain humble', suggesting that there is a connection with his parents' religious faith. We learn in this episode that his father was a priest and his mother an oracle, and that he has worked on battlestars, including the previously-mentioned *Atlantia* and the soon-to-become-significant *Pegasus*, since the age of 18; all of this, barring the service on the *Atlantia*, is taken almost verbatim from the series bible, which also mentions that he is Gemonese. There is a keen irony in Tigh accusing Tyrol of being a Cylon, which will become apparent later in the series.

In terms of outside references, the Marines firing on civilians was originally intended to recall the Kent State massacre of 1970, where a group of National Guardsmen opened fire on a student anti-Vietnam War protest, but Moore says there are more parallels to the Boston Massacre of 1770 in which a group of Redcoats, who were unprepared for the situation they found themselves in, fired on a civilian riot, and the leaders of the American Revolution seized upon it as an anti-British propaganda point. In *The Official Companion Season Two*, Moore notes that Tyrol's first name often raises a chuckle when people hear it; although he does not say so, this is probably because Galen was also the name of Roddy McDowell's chimpanzee character in the *Planet of the Apes* TV series.

Fiction and Resistance: Writing and Production

In production terms, the Boomer plotline changed emphasis during development, the original focus on her interrogation by Baltar giving way to one exploring her relationship with Tyrol and his falling under suspicion because of his connection with her. Moore, in his podcast, explains why the Marine with the sandwich, whom Roslin confronts on Causeway B, was there when the Causeway was closed off; she had been going to the galley to get some food, and surprised the escape party on the way back. Billy's refusal to go with Roslin, on the grounds that he is unable to condone her dividing the Fleet, was actually a cover for the fact that Paul Campbell had another commitment and had requested that he be temporarily written out of the series. Although the producers developed rules for Pyramid, which were later expanded on by director Kroeker and stunt coordinators Mike Mitchell and Duane Dickinson, Michael Trucco asserts in the Season Four documentary *A Look Back* that the game, like Triad from the original series, was made up as they went along.

The removal of Tigh from command, the return of the stranded Kobol expedition, the introduction of the resistance and the murder of *Galactica*-Sharon, all contribute to making this the strongest episode so far this season.

18: The Farm

FIRST TRANSMISSION DATE: 12 August 2005 (USA)

WRITER: Carla Robinson

DIRECTOR: Rod Hardy

CREDITED CAST: Rick Worthy (Simon); Lorena Gale (Elosha); Richard Hatch (Tom Zarek); Tamara Lashley (Sue-Shaun)

SYNOPSIS: During a resistance raid on a Cylon installation, Starbuck is shot and wakes up in what seems to be a hospital, where she is cared for by a doctor named Simon. Starbuck is suspicious of Simon's keen interest in her child-bearing abilities. She breaks out of her room and discovers that the hospital is run by Cylons, including Simon himself. She kills Simon with a shard of broken mirror and flees, discovering in the process a roomful of women hooked up to breeding machines. She recognises one as Sue-Shaun, a resistance member, who begs Starbuck to kill her. Starbuck smashes the machines and flees, to be rescued by the resistance. She, Helo and Sharon, who has rejoined them, return to the Fleet in Sharon's Heavy Raider, with Starbuck vowing to come back for Anders and the resistance. On the Fleet, Roslin hides out, courting popular support through making wireless transmissions about her plan to find the way to Earth. She splits the Fleet, with 24 ships following her back to Kobol.

ANALYSIS: Unusually for *Battlestar Galactica*, this is an episode in which the Caprica storyline is the main plot rather than an auxiliary one: specifically, Starbuck's adventures at the Farm. However, it makes for one of the series' weaker episodes, with a totally implausible central premise and some disappointing revelations about the Cylons.

General Hospital: Starbuck on the Farm

From the outset, the concept of the Farm is poorly handled. While it is not implausible that there could be a group of humans who, after a holocaust, become obsessed with reproduction to the point where they impose fascist rules on everyone else (as witness the *Survivors* episode 'Corn Dolly'), the set-up as we have it practically screams 'Cylon trap' from the outset. That a hospital might continue to function this long after a nuclear attack followed by Cylon occupation is incredibly unlikely, and Simon's story that Anders brought Starbuck there raises the question of why Anders has not mentioned before that the team have access to such effective medical facilities. For the viewer, also, Simon's assertion that Anders is dead sounds another false note, as he is obviously being set up as a recurring character. Although the thematic driver behind the story is a serious and interesting one, about women's rights over their own reproductive organs in a situation where the population has been drastically reduced, the issue is addressed more effectively in the 'The Captain's Hand'; here its treatment is clumsy and not remotely credible.

There is also the question of why Starbuck is the subject of such an elaborate deception by the Cylons, being led to believe that she is in a hospital, rather than just being put into the Farm as happens with resistance member Sue-Shaun, who was evidently kidnapped at the same time. The immediate referent for this story is the James Garner film *36 Hours* (1965), in which a WWII soldier wakes up in a hospital and is told the war is over, but this is in fact a Nazi trick intended to obtain information about D-Day invasion plans. However, the Cylons at no point seem interested in learning anything from Starbuck, whether about the resistance or about the Fleet. At a stretch, one might argue that Starbuck's special treatment is down to the fact that the Cylons believe she has a destiny (as Sharon reminds her at the end of the episode, although it's unclear whether this belief predates her encounter with Leoben or whether it is one that has spread to the other Cylons since his downloading). However, how this destiny justifies the Cylons giving her pelvic exams and removing one of her ovaries is anyone's guess, and Simon's statement to Six that once they have extracted both ovaries she will be removed to a processing facility for 'final disposition' would seem to rule out her being released to fulfil any form of destiny at all.

What we learn about Cylon reproduction this episode also raises some problems. First of all, we have the question of why, if the Farm experiments have not been a success, the Cylons are continuing them on what Sharon says are 'hundreds – maybe thousands' of women. (Although Moore hastens to inform the viewer on his podcast that there are other facilities involving men, what goes on there hardly bears thinking about.) As one of the writers observes in a 20 July 2005 writers' meeting recorded as a bonus podcast, it is also unknown why the Cylons think it is a good idea to situate a baby-making facility on an irradiated planet, which can't be doing much for the miscarriage rate. They have also not thought through the Sharon-Helo experiment: as Moore notes in his podcast, when the Cylons set up the relationship, believing that love may be a necessary precursor for conception, they failed to recognise that it worked both ways, and thus that Sharon would come to prioritise Helo over her fellow Cylons, which would seem fairly obvious.

At the end of the episode, Sharon states that the Cylons want children because it is God's commandment, not that it is something they desire for its own sake, which might explain why they are handling this so badly, but one would think that, having been given a divine instruction, they would pay more attention to the logistics. It is also disappointing to learn that the Cylon plan boils down to the alien invasion cliché of 'We want to breed with your women, but we're too thick to figure out how'.

Crisis Postponed? Adama's Return

The storyline in the Fleet also touches on the themes of love and humanity, in exploring the fallout from Boomer's death. Adama says to Tyrol, 'Is that what Boomer was? A machine ... She was more than that to us', and asks him, 'Could you love a machine?' Tyrol replies 'I guess I couldn't', touching on the idea that love is what makes one a person, regardless of one's physical origin.

Boomer's death is included in this episode's reduction in the Fleet's population count. This is undercut, however, by the fact that Adama has never previously shown any sign of regarding her as one of his favourites, and that he sentences Cally to just 30 days in the brig for the relatively minor offence of discharging a firearm and endangering life – as, since Boomer is a machine, killing her is technically not murder or assault. The issue of love and of what makes someone a person is, however, one that will be dealt with more strongly in later episodes.

Adama's return, meanwhile, may have eliminated the immediate crisis (dialogue indicates that a week has passed since the events of 'Fragged', during which time the issue of the ships refusing to resupply *Galactica* has apparently been resolved), but not the ongoing problems. Although Zarek, recalling his metaphor from 'Bastille Day', says 'Zeus has returned to Olympus', Adama himself says he feels 'closer to the ground', a phrase suggesting he is somehow reduced in stature but also hinting at a proximity to death. Moore glosses this further in the podcast, saying that Adama has returned from the grave, as it were, with his emotions 'closer to the surface'. Although he and Tigh expect only a few ships to follow Roslin after her religious message, over a third of the Fleet do so, and it is likely that in at least a few cases this is not out of religious or political loyalty but out of anger over the way in which the martial law situation has been handled. Similarly, Baltar slow-claps Adama when everyone else applauds his return to CIC, indicating that there is trouble ahead between the two men. A deleted scene exists in which Head Six reminds Baltar that Adama is a threat to the child (even though, as previously noted, he isn't), and Baltar and Adama have an exchange in which the former says he is glad to have the Commander back, and Adama replies that he wishes he could say the same, reinforcing that Baltar is still in disgrace over the alleged false negative Cylon test for Boomer.

Roslin, for her part, continues to be ambiguous about her own religious role. She talks about 'playing the religious card', implying that she still views her messiah status as something to be used for political ends, and hesitates before blessing her followers, presumably out of a feeling that she is acting under false pretences. However, she seems to be taking Apollo somewhat for granted; in a deleted scene where Roslin and Zarek discuss how many ships support them, and Apollo asserts that he is with her, she says 'Was there ever a question?'; and in another deleted scene where he explains the reason why he can't bring himself to denounce his father as a political tactic (saying that he was prepared to sacrifice his loyalty to his father to support Roslin, but that when she surrendered, he viewed it as a betrayal), she tells him he should have considered the consequences before acting in the first place. Adama's remarks concerning the idea of returning to Kobol – 'No-one's that stupid, and anyone that is, the ones that make the suicide run back to Kobol, please let them' – do rather beg the question of why Apollo does not point out the stupidity of the enterprise to Roslin. On Caprica, however, Starbuck is clearly having some misgivings about Roslin's authority, religious and otherwise, given that, when Simon says 'We have 223 patients at the moment, two doctors and five teachers masquerading as nurses', she replies 'I know a teacher masquerading as President'.

The Funny Farm: Continuity and Worldbuilding

In continuity terms, Anders admits that the resistance don't know what they are doing, and that most of their tactics are copied from movies, echoing the production team's own fondness for referencing their favourite films. Anders and Starbuck have acted fairly quickly on their feelings for each other; although Moore has said in the podcast that originally the resistance would have had a longer story arc and their relationship would have taken more time to develop, this haste does make sense given that both characters are fairly impulsive types. It is also clear that Helo, although he doesn't tell the resistance straight away that Sharon is a Cylon, has broken the news to them before their rescue of Starbuck, as she is alluding to her Cylon nature quite openly at the end of the story. The main problem with the resistance, though, is that they don't serve very much of a narrative purpose; there is nothing that happens in this story or earlier that could not have been achieved with Sharon, Helo and Starbuck on their own.

More thematically, the body horror of the Farm scenes reflects modern anxieties about artificially-assisted reproduction, as exemplified by the *Alien* film franchise. Moore says in the podcast that his team had feared the episode might be controversial; presumably this is why a female member of the writing staff was assigned to it. As noted by author Jo Storm, there is an irony in the fact that Starbuck attacks the machines in the breeding room with obstetric forceps. Although the cracked mirror in Starbuck's room is an obvious symbol of bad luck and of her own shattered self-image, she uses one of its shards to kill Simon toward the end of the story, suggesting that she has a way of turning misfortune to her advantage.

Starbuck's abusive childhood is explored in more detail here, Simon noting that her resolution not to have children may stem from a fear of passing the abuse on to them; and her hostility to Sharon at the end of the story is partly fuelled by her experiences on the Farm, contrasted with pregnant Sharon's matter-of-fact explanation of the Cylons' reproductive experiments. A deleted scene exists in which Starbuck has a nightmare of being held down by Helo and Anders as Anders tells her he wants her to have his babies. (She wakes in the 'hospital' to find that she is restrained, allegedly to prevent her from pulling her IV needle out, and she orders Simon never to restrain her again.) This further indicates a connection between abuse and childbearing in Starbuck's mind. There is an unspoken parallel with the Cylons themselves, as they are the abused children of humanity, and they cannot reproduce.

Mars Needs Women: Writing and Production

There are a few deleted scenes that, although unnecessary to the story, do provide some explanatory touches. In one of these, Simon states that the hospital gets the resources for its tests through scouring the region for supplies. In another, on the Fleet, it is revealed that Roslin's party are hiding out in a meat locker, because no-one in the Fleet will dare endanger the last known supply of meat in the universe. An extended version of Starbuck's escape indicates that she jimmies the lock on the door using a hexagonal CD, although where she obtains it from is unclear. (Moore, in the podcast, notes that the magazine in Starbuck's room was originally going to be a plot point, raising the possibility that Colonials have magazines that come with giveaway CDs.) Kara's sticking plaster (covering Katee Sackhoff's tattoo of a cross) is clearly visible in the scenes where she romps with Anders. If 24 ships constitute over a third of the Fleet, this gives us a rough estimate of around 70 ships altogether; as the total is given as 64 in '33', possibly a few more have joined since then, though how realistic this is, given that they are now some way past the Red Line, is open to debate.

The question of how Simon knows Anders's name, and of how the Cylons at the Farm know so much about the resistance, has been answered by Moore, as quoted on John Laroque's website: 'The idea was that they had been tracking and planning to come down hard on Anders' resistance cell for a while. They knew who Anders was, knew that he was a resistance leader in the area, and knew enough about his relationship with Starbuck to realise they were important to one another. Internally, we talked about the idea that Anders' cell might've been infiltrated by a Cylon agent who provided this information, but it never made it into the script'. The idea will later form a subplot to 'The Plan'.

Whereas 'Valley of Darkness' and 'Fragged' were able to cover their problems through a combination of pace and credible acting and direction, the implausibilities of 'The Farm' are apparent from the outset. Fraught with plot holes and body-horror clichés, this is one episode that, arguably, should not have been made.

BY YOUR COMMAND: VOL 2

19: Home
(Parts One and Two)

FIRST TRANSMISSION DATE: 19 August 2005 and 26 August 2005 (USA)

WRITERS: David Eick and David Eick & Ronald D Moore

DIRECTOR: Sergio Mimica-Gezzan and Jeff Woolnough

CREDITED CAST: Lorena Gale (Elosha); Donnelly Rhodes (Doctor Cottle); Richard Hatch (Tom Zarek); James Remar (Meier); Leah Cairns (Racetrack); Patricia Idlette (Sarah Porter); Malcolm Stewart (Marshall Bagot); Luciana Carro (Louann [sic] 'Kat' Katraine); Bodie Olmos (Brendan 'Hotdog' [sic] Costanza); Ben Ayres (Lieutenant George 'Catman' Birch); Linnea Sharples (Lieutenant Emmitt 'Sweetness' Jones); Christina Schild (Playa); Biski Gugushe (Sekou Hamilton); Raahul Singh (Kimmit)

SYNOPSIS: Sharon, Helo and Starbuck return to Kobol in Sharon's Heavy Raider, bringing the Arrow of Apollo, and rejoin Roslin's faction. Roslin has Sharon arrested and threatens to airlock her, but is convinced by her that she can lead them to the Tomb of Athena on Kobol. Roslin goes down to Kobol with Sharon, Apollo, Zarek, Meier, Starbuck and Elosha. Elosha is killed by a Cylon landmine shortly after they arrive. On the Fleet, Adama promotes Birch to CAG over Tigh's misgivings, and declares Roslin's rebellion a mutiny. Birch proves less than competent, and Adama, after a conversation with Dualla in which she accuses him of having broken his promise to lead his people to Earth, vows to reunite the Fleet. He goes to Kobol with Tyrol, Billy and Racetrack, and joins Roslin's group. Meier and Zarek plan to have Apollo killed, and seemingly manipulate Sharon into agreeing to do the deed. When Adama arrives, Zarek gives up the plan, but Meier plots with Sharon to kill both father and son. When they arrive at the Tomb, Sharon pulls a gun on Adama, prompting Meier to pull his gun on Apollo. Sharon, however, turns and shoots Meier, before handing the weapon over to Adama. Roslin, Adama, Apollo, Billy and Starbuck enter the tomb and see a vision of 12 standing stones; the symbols of the Colonies are on them, and also in the sky as constellations. Starbuck realises it is a vision of Earth, and Apollo suggests that they can find the planet using their knowledge of where the Lagoon Nebula, found in the constellation of Scorpio, is located. On *Galactica*, goaded by a conversation with Head Six, Baltar has a brain scan to see if he does indeed have a Cylon chip in his head; the result is negative.

19: HOME

ANALYSIS: 'Home', according to Moore, marks 'the culmination of all the arcs that began in Season One ... the completion of the entire first season'. In this two-parter, the series ties up a lot of its themes, finds the direction to Earth and resolves, at least temporarily, the arc involving Roslin's messianic journey.

Uniting the Family: Adama's Decision

Although order of a kind has been restored in the Fleet, Adama's obsession with Lee's defection is clearly impairing his judgment. He rejects Tigh's choice of new CAG, Mueller, on the grounds that he is 'a malcontent'; his choice of Birch is made on the grounds that he is 'honest and loyal', emphasising the word 'loyal' as he does so. Adama plays with walnuts in a clear reference to Captain Queeg doing similarly in *The Caine Mutiny* (1954). Although this is unlikely to be intentional, ancient Roman tradition associates walnuts with Jupiter/Zeus, to whom Adama has also been likened, and the fact that he cracks them seems like a metaphorical 'busting a nut' over his concerns (although, as they are on a spaceship with dwindling food resources, it must be asked where the walnuts come from, and why he feels the need to destroy them). The rumour that Adama lied and there is no Earth is now common throughout the Fleet, damaging his credibility, and he is also starting to echo Roslin's and Tigh's more dictatorial moments, saying defensively that the freedom of the press needs limits.

Adama later acknowledges that his feelings are affecting his behaviour, suggesting a return to self-awareness. However, his actions throughout part one are highly unprofessional. Despite the remark he made in 'The Farm' that going to Kobol was a suicide mission, he wastes most of the episode engaging in training manoeuvres and sulking about Apollo's 'betrayal' (a particularly unfortunate diatribe being 'Betrayal has such a powerful grip on the mind. It's almost like a python. It can squeeze out all other thought, suffocate all other emotion, until everything is dead except for the rage'). It is ultimately his conversation with Dualla that puts him back on the right path when she, undoubtedly influenced by the fact that she herself has lost loved ones, urges him to mend fences and reunite the Fleet. At the end of part one, that is exactly what he does, saying that he is going to 'put our family back together'. However, in the process of coming to this decision, he has demonstrated himself to be childish, immature and foolhardy, playing with the lives of the entire Rebel Fleet, including his own son, which somewhat undercuts his statement to Roslin in part two that he 'didn't come here to navel-gaze or to catalogue our mistakes'.

Finally, we have the unforgivable fact that in going down to Kobol, Adama leaves the Fleet essentially leaderless: with him and Roslin down on the planet, a single well-placed land mine is all it would take to put Tigh back in charge – not to mention wiping out the Fleet's CAG, its top pilot, its deck chief (who came down with Adama), and Zarek, the unofficial Leader of the Opposition, as well. Adama is also barely a week out of hospital, having survived major surgery, and thus taking a hell of a risk cavorting over rocky paths. One has to ask why, other than that it makes for a less dramatic story, Adama didn't just radio Roslin and announce that all was forgiven.

Rebels at Large: Roslin and her Supporters on Kobol

Adama describes Roslin as a religious terrorist, and it is true that her faith has split loyalties and caused disruption within the Fleet. Although David Weddle stated in a *Chicago Tribune* interview of 1 April 2005, that Zarek is a secular humanist who is not enamoured of Roslin's religious tendencies, Roslin's situation is as ever a mix of political and faith concerns rather than purely one or the other. She initially orders Sharon thrown out the airlock, despite having assured Helo that she will not be harmed, but then relents on learning that she knows the location of the Tomb of Athena. This shows that Roslin is devoted to the prophecy but wary of trusting a Cylon. An extended version of the scene in part one where Roslin's group debate has Elosha calling Roslin a prophet and ends with a group prayer; which, while underlining Roslin's connections with Pythia, is more than a little unsubtle. She is also, as in the miniseries, still unfamiliar with military issues, identifying Helo as a Raptor pilot rather than an ECO. Less forgivable, however, is the fact that she has led her followers back to Kobol, to which the Cylons undoubtedly know they are coming, because the Six on Caprica saw Starbuck taking the Arrow of Apollo. The only reason the Cylons have not staked out Kobol with a dozen basestars appears to be that they have taken a similar hit to their intelligence as the humans this season. (As they do not know that Sharon and her foetus are with the Rebel Fleet, this cannot be what is holding them back.) They have put a small number of Centurions on the surface of the planet, but fail to attack the Rebel Fleet when it turns up. There appears to be a lingering influence here of the earlier idea that the Cylons wanted the human Fleet to lead them to Earth, but without this, the Cylons' actions make little sense. Indeed, the fact that neither Apollo nor the alleged tactical genius Starbuck raises the possibility of a Cylon attack makes both of them look rather stupid.

The death of Elosha symbolically ends Roslin's religious arc. Eick and Moore have said that while they wanted the story to feature the death of someone close to Roslin, they were initially unsure whether to kill Elosha or Billy (since, as noted, there were concerns about Paul Campbell's availability this season). However, Elosha's is certainly the more thematically appropriate death at this point. She ironically predicts her own demise when she says 'Some of us will die down there'; something that was also foreshadowed in the line in the draft script of 'Kobol's Last Gleaming' where she explains that priests are forbidden to visit Kobol. There is a deleted scene from 'Home' in which Elosha confesses that she had lost her faith before the attack, but seeing Roslin's courage in assuming the role of President renewed it. Although this is consistent with the earlier material from the draft script of 'The Hand of God' in which we learn that she was formerly a liberal and rather secularist priest, the scene was probably cut because a revelation like that, prior to a character's death, is an unforgivable war/disaster movie cliché.

The plans developed by Roslin's followers are also problematic. When Meier argues that Zarek and his supporters should simply take over the Rebel Fleet, Zarek counters that Roslin is useful to them because of her ability to inspire followers, saying 'I believe in the power of myth' – hence his argument that they should kill Apollo instead, and have Zarek himself fill Apollo's role as enforcer and become the real power behind the throne. Zarek justifies this plan by saying, 'I want to set this Fleet on a path to freedom ... deliver unto them the liberty we've promised ... The scriptures say some of us will die on Kobol'. Clearly he is rehearsing how he will explain it to the Fleet afterwards. Meier, throughout, has a strong faith in Zarek that goes beyond the political. The podcast suggests that they have developed a trusting relationship through their mutual experience of prison (Eick and Moore joke about possible homosexual overtones, pointing out that the two men are ex-prisoners, wearing leather jackets, and that James Remar had appeared in the film *Cruising* (1980), about a serial killer stalking the gay leather bars of New York; the viewer can make of this what they will, but it does add an interesting subtext to the scene in which the two men urinate together in the forest). When Zarek, realising that Adama's return marks the resumption of the status quo, gives up on the assassination plan, Meier carries on with it in secret, saying as he dies that he did so to give Zarek what is due to him, indicating he has faith in Zarek as a political leader.

The problem is that, although the initial plan of getting Sharon to kill Apollo and then killing Sharon so that all the blame falls on the Cylons makes sense, when Meier subsequently agrees to Sharon's proposal that he and she shoot both Adamas, he doesn't seem to realise that this would reveal an obvious conspiracy to the assembled and make it impossible for Zarek to win Roslin over. Meier also does not appear to have considered that killing Adama would put Tigh, he of martial law, back in charge of the Fleet. Furthermore, it seems strange that Adama does not at any point following the incident have Zarek arrested for conspiracy to murder; Meier is, after all, Zarek's henchman, and as far back as 'Colonial Day' there have been paranoid suspicions that Zarek might stoop to assassination.

Starbuck's activities on Caprica, meanwhile, have further complicated her relationship with Apollo. She is wearing the C-Bucs Pyramid uniform from the final sequence of 'Home' in place of the uniform she lost at the Farm, and has a Pyramid ball that is evidently a gift from Anders. Lee kisses her closely when they meet, and she says to him, 'There's something I need to tell you–', which could be either the start of an explanation about Sharon's presence or of an admission that she is now in a relationship. They have an extended, somewhat emotionally-charged session of schoolyard banter while playing with the Pyramid ball ('Can I have my ball back, please?' 'What, I can't hold it?' 'Can I have my ball back, please?' 'Where'd you get a Pyramid ball, anyway?' and so forth), which Eick based on his relationship with his own wife; saying 'She and I argue a lot ... in part cause it's fun ... and it kind of turns you on'.

Return of the Non-Native: Sharon and Helo

Sharon arrives in the Fleet to bear the brunt of the humans' anger. She is again the subject of (literal) demonisation, when Elosha suggests she may be the helpful 'lower demon' mentioned in the prophecy, and Apollo tells her 'You're all the same' (in an ironic twist on a real-life xenophobic phrase). Starbuck doesn't speak up in Sharon's defence straight away when Helo appeals to her to tell Apollo how she saved their lives on Caprica, but hesitates, suggesting that she has issues about what happened with Sharon (and the Farm) earlier. There is a scene deleted from part two where Starbuck tells Helo that she still doesn't really trust Sharon. The population count in the Fleet has risen by one, accounting for Helo's arrival but not Sharon's. Roslin's ruthlessness is highlighted when, recalling Baltar's technique for extracting information from Boomer in 'Resistance', she tells Sharon that if she doesn't cooperate fully, she will execute Helo as a Cylon conspirator. Roslin's logic in doing this, namely that Sharon is in love with Helo, also explains why Sharon has thrown her lot in with the Fleet; with the Cylons, she might be able to keep the baby, but not Helo, whereas with the humans she has a chance of saving both. Sharon, for her part, is genuinely upset by the realisation that the others in the Fleet consider her a machine and that Boomer's death was not deemed murder. As Jo Storm has pointed out that, it is hard for the people of the Fleet to dehumanise Sharon, someone they know and have worked with, in the way they do the other Cylons, and this informs their difficulties in relating to her. However, Sharon's speech to Adama, to the effect that she makes her own decisions without hidden protocols or programming, further highlights her determination to reintegrate into the Fleet, Cylon or no.

Sharon also is shown here as the bringer of knowledge, asserting caustically to Roslin that all Cylons know where the Tomb of Athena is, and later, 'We know more about your religion than you do'. She seems certain her child is female, although it is unclear how. There are a couple of hints that Sharon touches on a deeper understanding. When Adama first sees Caprica-Sharon, he flashes back to his asking Boomer's corpse 'Why?', and after he attacks Caprica-Sharon, she says to him 'And you ask why?', seemingly answering his question even though she asserts that she does not remember shooting Adama. The writers themselves have said that they don't know why she said that, which makes one wonder why they put it in.[48] Sharon also reveals, in part two, that she has specific memories of military service aboard *Galactica*, which implies that, at some point prior to the attack, *Galactica*-Sharon was somehow able to share her memories with Caprica-Sharon so as to lend credibility to her pretence of being the same woman Helo knew on *Galactica*. This will later be confirmed in a scene from the extended cut of 'Islanded in a Stream of Stars', in which Sharon admits

---

[48] SPOILER SECTION: There is also a curious foreshadowing, in Sharon's leading the team to Athena's tomb, of the fact that 'Athena' will eventually become this Sharon's call sign.

that she has all of Boomer's memories from before the war. However, it is also confirmed in 'Home' part one that Cylons cannot transmit or share memories as a matter of course: when Roslin says to Sharon, 'I have little doubt that you are communicating everything I say even as we speak', the latter retorts, 'It doesn't work like that! I'm not wired in!' While we later learn, in 'The Hub', that Cylons can indeed download and share memories, there is no explanation for how Sharon can remember things that happened after her counterpart's death.[49]

Head for Home: Baltar and Head Six

In a related area, Baltar has a crucial exchange with Head Six:

BALTAR: There was an old footbridge ... over the Euclid River. I used to go there when I was a boy. Watch the fish try and swim upstream. They were mesmerising. I envied them. Unaware as they were of the ... wider complexities and challenges of life.

HEAD SIX: You're beginning to see human beings as we see them.

Although this dialogue recalls Leoben's metaphor from 'Flesh and Bone' of standing outside the stream of events, in fact Head Six is talking of God's perspective, and encouraging Baltar to take this view rather than see his world in terms of humans and Cylons. Moore, who wrote the scene, says it defines how Baltar feels out of touch with the people around him, again indicating how his visions are differentiating him from the rest of the Fleet.

Head Six's relationship with Baltar also shows elements of jealousy on her part. When he tells her she's not his fantasy anymore, and suggests she is jealous of Starbuck, she appears dressed in gym clothes, with her hair pulled back, recalling Starbuck's usual appearance. She again messes with Baltar's mind by mocking the idea of God and Baltar being guided by him, suggesting that she is a superior version of the proverbial 'little voice in his head'. This is taken further in a deleted scene in which she taunts him with the idea that he has gone mad and effectively dares him to seek counselling for this. However, at the end of the story, Head Six, back in a red dress for the first time since 'The Hand of God', tells Baltar that she is an angel of God sent to protect, guide and love him to the end of the human race.

Although this subplot was added by Moore to pad out the second part, it also serves a rather important function, making it clear that Head Six is neither an hallucination nor a chip in his head, but a genuine supernatural manifestation. There is also an attempt by Moore to address retroactively Head Six's strange and contradictory behaviour over recent episodes, by having Baltar confront her

---

49 SPOILER SECTION: Hera does later manifest preternatural knowledge and abilities, so it is possible that she is somehow sharing this ability with her mother while *in utero*, but this is admittedly a stretch.

over this; but, given the scale of the confusion and the specificity of certain of her predictions, the effort is only partly successful. For instance, Baltar mocks her by saying 'I'm the father of a baby who will be born to me, from my fantasy woman who I see solely in my head', and Head Six replies, 'I never said I would bear the child', which is complicated by the fact that in 'Scattered', she said that the child would be 'literally' theirs, and went on to affirm that she is the mother and Baltar the father. Nonetheless, with Head Six's character and function now established for both the writing team and the audience, the Baltar arc is back on track from this point onwards. It is perhaps surprising, though, that Baltar does not connect Head Six's prophecy of Sharon's baby being born in the cell with his vision of Adama drowning the infant, and conclude that Head Six is afraid that, given that Adama was shot by *Galactica*-Sharon, he may attempt to kill this Sharon's child.

However, the episode does nothing to resolve the confusion over what happened on Kobol during the time of the gods, as we learn that Pythia's version of events runs in part: 'And the blaze pursued them. And the people of Kobol had a choice, to board the great ship or take the high road through the rocky ridge – and the body of each tribe's leader was offered to the gods in the Tomb of Athena'. This might be reconciled with Head Six's account in 'Valley of Darkness', in that it involves human sacrifice, though the pile of skulls in 'Valley of Darkness' is nowhere near the Tomb of Athena, and we never learn what started the 'blaze' to which Pythia alludes. We also learn from Sharon that Athena threw herself off a cliff as a response to the exodus of the Thirteen Tribes, which suggests the 'gods' were mortal, in line with Head Six's assertion that the Lords of Kobol were not actually divine (albeit raising questions about the nature of her own god); although, in the context of Roslin's dream in the deleted scene from 'Fragged', it supports the position that the humans left rather than being expelled. Pythia's narrative also mentions that the founders of the Thirteen Colonies escaped Kobol in a 'galleon'– apparently just the one, which conjures up images of a giant ship floating around the various Colonies and dropping people off. While Head Six may no longer be pointlessly winding Baltar up with contradictory accounts of historical events, then, we still have no idea which version is authoritative.

Lords of the Realm: Continuity, Worldbuilding and Problems

In character background terms, when Billy worries that Roslin will not listen to him, he learns from Adama that she compared him to President Adar when he ran for his first office, though he also discovers that Adama considered Adar a moron (the word was originally 'prick', but Broadcasting Standards intervened). There is a deleted scene in which Billy confesses to Roslin that he is an atheist but has come down with Adama to Kobol, having previously refused to join her flight to *Cloud 9*, in order to demonstrate that one can support her and Adama both. Adama's hobby is building model ships, which is believable for a military man with a strong eye for detail, and he and Roslin start to call each other by their first names. We are also reminded of the fact that Helo has no idea of the events on the Fleet, as he has been out of touch since the abandonment of the Colonies. Although a minor character, temporary CAG Birch also gets some nice development as a well-meaning idiot, telling Adama that he admires Apollo and failing to pick up on the rift between the two men, and giving a spectacular display of incompetence in both the target exercise and the refuelling sequences.

There are also a couple of clarifications to continuity, in that the dialogue between Tigh and Dualla at the beginning modifies the problematic idea from the previous episode of 24 ships being one-third of the Fleet, to that of the 24 ships in question containing 18,000 passengers – over one-third of the *people* in the Fleet. We also learn that the Fleet has a thriving media consisting of 'talk wireless, newsletter circuit [and] hand mail', which are developing into key plot elements in the series. Starbuck's seemingly throwaway line about the Cylons on Caprica – 'They're cleaning up the bodies, moving in the heavy machinery to repair the infrastructure ...' – is a set-up for events in 'Downloaded' later in the season.

The patterns on the ancient flags of the Twelve Tribes are shaped like the star patterns of the constellations of the Zodiac, hinting further at connections between Colonial and Earth culture, although raising the question of why the Thirteenth Tribe is excluded from this symbolism. In ancient Greek astrology, there is in fact a thirteenth sign of the Zodiac, Ophiuchus the snake-bearer, who is believed to represent Asclepius, a healer whom Zeus killed out of fear that he had the ability to render humanity immortal; although this is never referenced in the series itself, later revelations about the Thirteenth Tribe will make this connection significant. One has to wonder why the patterns on the flags of the Twelve Colonies look like constellations seen from Earth; was the Thirteenth Tribe considered more important than the others? Was Earth the first planet the 'galleon' visited? The nature of the shared vision in the Tomb of Athena is not explained. Moore, in a 2005 blog entry, says that it was 'probably a holographic projection of some sort', which suggests that the writing team had not given it much thought themselves, and that originally there was to have been a scene in which Centurions attack the tomb and destroy the projector, explaining how the Cylons do not subsequently find the information.

In terms of outside references, the idea of the Fleet going to Kobol and finding a tomb that helps them on their way to Earth is clearly drawn from the original series' 'Lost Planet of the Gods', and the ship *Striker* is to the same design as the original-series vessel *Celestra*. Starbuck's bouncing the Pyramid ball against a wall is a deliberate homage to Steve McQueen's playing with a baseball in *The Great Escape* (1963), and Head Six's posing naked on the chair in the cell is similarly a reference to the poster of the film *Scandal* (1989), itself based on a famous photo of Christine Keeler. The ending of the story, with Adama leading assembled personnel in a round of clapping in unison as a gesture of respect to Roslin, was, according to the podcast, a homage to the final scene of the film *Brubaker* (1980). It also recalls the 'So say we all' scene from the miniseries. Elosha's prophecy that some of them will die on Kobol recalls the repeated prophecy in *Babylon 5*: 'If you go to Z'ha'dum, you will die'.

The land mine we see on Kobol was allegedly based on the German S-Mine from WWII, also known as the 'Bouncing Betty'; however, it explodes overhead, whereas the real-life munition sprang up to release shrapnel at crotch height, earning it the alternative sobriquet of the 'castrator' mine. In the podcast, Eick and Moore liken Adama's statement that Roslin is no longer President to Secretary of State Alexander Haig's 'I'm in control here …' speech following the 1981 assassination attempt on Ronald Reagan: although Haig meant it literally, as Reagan was out of commission and Vice-President Bush unavailable, it was interpreted by many as being him making an illegal bid for power. For the Lagoon Nebula to appear identical when viewed from the Colonies, Earth and Kobol, all three of these must be located on a relatively straight line.

The story again contains a radiation-related error, in that nobody in the Rebel Fleet thinks of putting the party from Caprica through any form of decontamination procedure prior to having contact with them. There are also what seem to be astronomical errors, acknowledged as such by the producers, though events in Season Four will retrospectively explain this within series continuity. If the map in the Tomb of Athena shows the view from Earth, the Lagoon Nebula should be in Sagittarius, not Scorpio (Adama refers to it by the Messier number M8, using a catalog system created on Earth in 1774, which the charitable might call a deliberate anachronism), and Libra is in the wrong position in the Zodiac, appearing between Leo and Virgo rather than Virgo and Scorpio. A rumour arose at the time of the DVD release that this story revealed Head Six's name to be 'Sara'; however, the source for this turned out to be the subtitles on the DVDs for Regions 2 and 4 accidentally misinterpreting the first two syllables of Baltar's line 'So, uh, now you've had your fun …'

Where the Heart Is: Writing and Production

This serial is David Eick's first full-blown teleplay; like 'Scattered', it was originally a single episode that overran and was split into two. The writing team had debated extensively the role of the Arrow in finding Earth, and eventually came up with the (painfully literal) idea of it being linked with the constellation of Sagittarius the Archer, hence the projection being triggered when Starbuck places it in the bow of the statue representing Sagittaron. The idea of Adama physically attacking Sharon while on Kobol was in part inspired by a remark Olmos made during the filming of the scene in 'The Farm' where Adama weeps over the corpse of Sharon: 'I know if I ever saw that character again, I wouldn't stop at anything until she was dead'. The story changed slightly over development; at one point the team thought that Birch's errors should be more severe, perhaps even leading to fatalities, but eventually they decided that this might make Adama's championing of him too fundamental an error of judgment. Originally Birch's mistake with the refuelling was to have triggered Adama's change of heart, rather than his talk with Dualla. A scene where Adama mentions that they found Elosha's grave was deleted as it raises the question of when the expedition had time to bury her and why they didn't also bury the two men who were killed during the subsequent firefight with the Centurions. Eick says that, originally, Head Six was to have appeared to Baltar in the cell as Sharon initially, and then turned into Six, but 'We weren't sure about breaking the law of who Baltar sees in his head. Did we really want to say he starts seeing other Cylons in his head? So we abandoned that'.

In production terms, it becomes clear that part of the reason for killing off *Galactica*-Sharon was to avoid confusion once Caprica-Sharon arrives at the Fleet, and the rationale for giving *Galactica*-Sharon a visible facial wound is to differentiate the two, now that Caprica-Sharon's bruises have faded. The rippling effect on the actors' faces during atmospheric entry was created on set with a high-pressure air blaster, inspired by a similar effect in *Moonraker* (1979) and the *Space: 1999* episode 'The Metamorph'. Head Six's appearance in the cell, in gym clothes and ponytail, is also a reference to the way Tricia Helfer normally dresses when not in role as Six. The idea that Apollo should kiss Starbuck when they met was suggested by Jamie Bamber. David Weddle is briefly visible among the supporting artists at the beginning of the sequence where Roslin holds a meeting aboard the *Astral Queen* in part one.

The story arc begun in 'Kobol's Last Gleaming' may be over and the status quo restored, but clearly some development has occurred, with the Fleet leaders now working together rather than insisting on artificial distinctions. The resolution to the Kobol arc, however, is confusing. On the one hand, the way to Earth has been found. On the other, the scriptures identify the person who leads them to this discovery (namely, Sharon) as a 'demon', and Elosha's messianic belief in Roslin has caused her to be killed on Kobol, where, Head Six asserted in 'Fragged', 'nothing awaits [the dead]. No eternal life, no damnation. Only oblivion'. Given the sheer amount of confusion thrown up by the Kobol arc over what the scriptures actually mean, it is uncertain at this point whether the outcome of the revelations will be good or bad.

20: Final Cut

FIRST TRANSMISSION DATE: 9 September 2005 (USA)

WRITER: Mark Verheiden

DIRECTOR: Robert Young

CREDITED CAST: Kate Vernon (Ellen Tigh); Donnelly Rhodes (Doctor Cottle); Matthew Bennett (Doral); Lucy Lawless (D'Anna Biers); Luciana Carro (Louann [sic] 'Kat' Katraine); Bodie Olmos (Brendan 'Hotdog' [sic] Costanza); Flick Harrison (Bell); Kevan Kase (Private Scott Kelso); Yee Jee Tso (Staffer); Curtis Hicks (Marine Sergeant); Aleks Paunovic (Marine Sergeant Fischer); Ty Olsson (Captain Aaron Kelly); Leah Cairns (Racetrack); Jeremy Guilbaut (Lieutenant Joe 'Hammerhead' Palladino)

KNOWN UNCREDITED CAST: Leo Li Chiang (Tattooed Pilot)

SYNOPSIS: Roslin and Adama engage a journalist, D'Anna Biers, to make a documentary about life on *Galactica*, in the hope of restoring relations between the military and the civilians in the Fleet following the *Gideon* Massacre. Meanwhile, Tigh receives death threats and an assassination attempt, culminating in him and Ellen being attacked in their quarters by Palladino, a Raptor pilot who had been put in charge of crowd control on the *Gideon* and, consumed with feelings of guilt, has set out to assassinate the man he deems responsible for the massacre. Tigh talks him down and disarms him, and Palladino is arrested. D'Anna's crew documents Kat's increasing addiction to stims, shows a number of pilots and crew under strain, and obtains footage of Sharon experiencing pregnancy complications, the last of which Adama forbids them to use, but D'Anna secretly keeps a copy. D'Anna's documentary in the end proves sympathetic to the military. On Caprica, the film, followed by the cut footage of Sharon, is watched by a number of Cylons, including a D'Anna.

ANALYSIS: 'Final Cut' is the *Battlestar Galactica* version of a particular type of American TV trope that crops up in series as diverse as *Starsky and Hutch*, *The X-Files* and *My Name is Earl*: the episode in which a reporter or documentary crew follow the protagonists around, giving insights into their lives. Despite its familiarity, however, this is an engaging and entertaining story with plenty of background detail and a twist at the end.

20: FINAL CUT

I Am a Camera: D'Anna and her Documentary

This is the first episode in the series that could be described as 'stand-alone', as, although it picks up on the events of 'Resistance', it is not essential to have seen that episode to enjoy 'Final Cut', and the only revelation crucial to the arc is that D'Anna is a Cylon. The narrative, consequently, is thin, the mystery of the death threats against Tigh being the main plot driver.

The commissioning of the documentary itself sets up the current state of affairs as regards Adama's and Roslin's joint leadership of the Fleet. Although their initial meeting with D'Anna portrays Roslin as a consummate politician and Adama as far less diplomatic, it eventually becomes clear that they are playing bad cop/good cop with D'Anna, suggesting a new affinity between the two leaders. Roslin, viewing D'Anna's documentary on the *Gideon* Massacre, comments sourly 'I'm so happy I fought for a free press', recalling Adama's problems with the media in the previous episode and Roslin's in 'Colonial Day'; there is a deleted scene, however, where Roslin explains to Billy that she supports the documentary because there is a need to unify the Fleet with the election coming up. Tigh, viewing the final film, describes it as a hatchet job, but Adama judges that it is good for the people to see the crew warts and all, and his analysis proves correct. Roslin and Adama thus come across as a successful team for a change, and as adept manipulators of the media.

D'Anna herself is well developed. Rather than simply the caricatured cynical journalist she first seems to be, talking as she does about inserting stock footage of raging Marines into the *Gideon* Massacre material to make it more exciting, she is also funny and assertive, attacking Adama right back when he tries to intimidate her, and being visibly unimpressed with Baltar's attempts to seem important. The revelation that she is a Cylon renders ironic Tigh's quip, upon seeing the camera crew, 'No enemy contact for the last ten days; well, no Cylon contact anyway'.

Despite this, and despite her duplicitous treatment of Tigh, baiting him during his interview and plying him with drink beforehand (she pours herself one too but cleverly does not touch it), she acts to save Tigh's life. She does this through alerting the Marines when she notices, on reviewing her footage of Palladino, that he has a copy of a book of poems by Kataris, and concludes that he was the unknown intruder who wrote a line from one of those poems on the mirror in the Tighs's quarters.

The fact that the Cylon Raiders attack just as Baltar is about to get the interview he has been angling for all episode might suggest a sly joke on her part, since we later learn that the incursion was coordinated so as to allow her to get the footage of Sharon back to the Cylon Fleet, and thus that she would have known when it was coming. D'Anna's exclamation that Sharon's child is 'a miracle from God', and her statement in the coda of her documentary that the military are 'people, not Cylons', foreshadows her own future role as one bridging the gap between two species. The story leaves it ambiguous as to whether D'Anna's documentary is ultimately positive because she doesn't want to expose herself as a Cylon, because she has developed a genuine rapport for humans during the filming, because the revelation of the half-Cylon child has caused her to revise her preconceptions, or, indeed, all of the above. The D'Anna we see in the movie theatre on Caprica at the end is another of her model, as deleted material from 'Downloaded' suggests D'Anna herself remained with the Fleet.

The Whole World is Watching: Tigh and the Gideon *Massacre*

This story also continues the fallout from Tigh's role in the *Gideon* Massacre. Animosity has been growing toward him; Starbuck's joke that she'd like to be chief suspect for the death threats is not unusual, given their continual antagonism, but D'Anna's interview with the Marine Kelso also features its subject remarking: 'It was a command frak-up the moment Tigh put us on that supply ship. I'm not surprised someone's trying to take out that drunk son of a bitch'. Tigh is once again caught between his relationships with Adama and Ellen: Adama provides a number of good reasons for sending Tigh as *Galactica*'s representative to a meeting on *Cloud 9*, chiefly that it will show Tigh's critics that he is not afraid and will allow grievances to be aired (although clearly the real reason is that he doesn't want to go himself), but Ellen briefs against this, telling Tigh in private that Adama and Roslin are trying to restore Adama's good name by hanging Tigh out to dry. She also continually undermines Tigh's attempts to acknowledge that he's done wrong and to take responsibility for his actions, and tells him 'We're all alone out there', isolating him from other sources of support. Again, Tigh's lack of diplomacy and political sense is his undoing. When he realises he has been set up in his interview with D'Anna, he terminates the session angrily, making him seem defensive, intransigent and guilt-ridden. (Moore's podcast commentary elaborates by saying 'She's not telling him that the camera's running. He's sort of not aware of it'; however, this is something that a more politically-minded person might have taken into consideration.) Again, however, he comes into his own in a crisis; when Palladino confronts him, he calls his bluff by offering the pilot the chance to kill him, knowing that Palladino, given his guilt about shooting civilians, is unlikely to be the type to shoot an old man in cold blood. Recognising that Palladino is motivated by his own guilty feelings over the *Gideon* incident, he says to him, '*Gideon* was an accident, this was a choice', indicating that Palladino was not responsible for the deaths on *Gideon*, but he is certainly responsible for terrorising the Tighs. Adama's reasons for not charging Tigh over the massacre are that they can't sacrifice one of the few competent people they have for the sake of public opinion; but it is also plain that Tigh is paying for his misdeeds in less formal ways.

Eight Million Stories: The Pilots and Crew

Kat in particular comes into her own in this episode, mooning the camera crew (in a direct steal from the 1994 film *Starship Troopers*) when they gatecrash the officers' quarters, suggesting a literal interpretation to Tigh's subsequent comment on the documentary, 'You show us with our pants down and our asses hanging out'. Originally, according to writer Mark Verheiden, Gaeta's tiger tattoo was supposed to be on his buttocks rather than his chest, meaning he would also have mooned the camera in order to reveal it. However D'Anna shows the other side of Kat's personality by intercutting the footage of her talking about the euphoria of coming off a good run with footage of her having a drug-induced panic attack and being unable to land safely. The last sequence in the film, before the coda, is Kat explaining tearfully why she took stims, and expressing her feelings of guilt that in doing so, she's temporarily cost the Fleet a pilot; this establishes Kat as someone impulsive but good-hearted.

The other characters are also well developed. Starbuck knows more Caprican poetry than her hardnosed reputation on the Fleet would suggest (but fitting with what the audience has seen of her flat on Caprica). The fact that Lee is unaware of her interest in poetry suggests he doesn't know her as well as he thinks he does. Apollo, showing his political side again, handles the press intrusions well and gets in a good comment in defence of the pilots – that they put their lives on the line for a Fleet that seems to focus more on what they do wrong than what they do right – reflecting then-contemporary arguments about the press coverage of the wars in Iraq and Afghanistan as well as hinting at Apollo's own feelings about the way he has been treated by both sides during Roslin's coup. Apollo's designation is given in the documentary as 'CFR'. The podcast indicates that this means he is a Colonial Fleet reservist, serving full-time in the military for a short period followed by going into the reserves for the rest of his career, which is meant as a further indication that he is not completely committed to military life. We get some insights into the pilots' mentality, with Racetrack saying that they are trained to think of themselves as dead, because the dead don't hesitate in combat, and Helo saying 'They try and turn off the human part of you … but when you're out in the field it isn't that easy', referring to his relationship with Sharon (as he himself was out in the field when he fell in love with the enemy), but also tacitly accusing the military system of making its soldiers as inhuman as they accuse the Cylons of being.

Gaeta shows a more dissipated side to his nature, in contrast to his usual professionalism. He smokes, drinks and recently got drunk enough to wind up with the aforementioned ill-judged tiger tattoo. He says, 'All that I ever wanted was to be an officer on a battlestar', and his designation is given as 'CF', meaning that, unlike Apollo and Dualla, he is not a reservist. All of this suggests that his implication in 'Water' that his military career was a means to an end for him to study genetics was an oversimplification. Possibly his desire to become a geneticist came after he achieved his dream of serving on *Galactica* and then became disillusioned with military life; possibly his emphasis on his academic career was deliberately exaggerated in an effort to bond with Baltar. Either way, he is here characterised as a man who has become unhappy with his lot and is looking for something more in life.

Baltar is angry about being slighted by the camera crew, informed by the fact that he has been sidelined by the key players in the Fleet since his return from Kobol. The background to the previous episode's conversation between Dualla and Adama about the value of family unity is fleshed out here when we learn that Dualla joined the military against the wishes of her family, that she argued with her father about it three weeks before the attack on the Colonies, and that she never made it up with him. First names are given here for both Dualla and Gaeta: 'Anastasia' for the former and 'Felix' (somewhat ironically, given that it means 'happy' in Latin) for the latter.

Bonus Features: Continuity and Worldbuilding

The story's format means that we learn some technical details of life aboard the Fleet. Dualla's tour of the ship tells us more than we (or, clearly, D'Anna) want to know about its functioning: the oxygen is recycled, vegetables and tinned goods are kept in titanium lockers, and so forth. Colonial video screens, like their paper, have clipped corners. There is a deleted scene of the camera crew filming Tyrol, in which he discusses the creative improvisations the crew are developing to get around shortages of materials, including mending jumpsuits with staples. This foreshadows Tyrol's extracurricular ship-building project in 'Flight of the Phoenix'. The Raptor sabotage attempt again raises the question of why passengers do not wear protective flightsuits. (The episode's podcast explains that it is simply because the production team don't have enough flightsuit costumes, although a shortage of these on the Fleet could also provide an in-text explanation.) Captain Kelly appears again, acting as Landing Signal Officer in the port flight pod, which explains why he was not seen between the miniseries and Season Two, as such duties would keep him away from CIC itself.

The story picks up on the brief exchange in 'Home' in which Adama remarks 'Freedom of the press is not a license to slander'. Adama says that he will allow D'Anna full access, but reserves the right to edit any footage that he deems too dangerous to show, and D'Anna says 'You know, I am sick to death of people like you questioning my patriotism', raising the issue of censorship and of whether it is more patriotic to support one's leaders without question or to speak out against what one perceives their problems to be. There is also a real sense in this story of just how much the fight is costing everyone in emotional and physical terms.

Behind the Scenes Feature: Production Details

The director, Robert Young, is particularly well known for his documentary work, and thus is a good choice to helm this episode. He was also an old acquaintance of Edward James Olmos's and, at the time of filming, an octogenarian. Flick Harrison, who played D'Anna's cameraman, is a professional cameraman as well as an actor, and some of the footage he shot was used in the finished programme. Originally, according to Moore's podcast for 'Flight of the

Phoenix', 'Final Cut' was to have been told entirely as a documentary. As it stands, D'Anna's footage blends with the series' usual mock-documentary style, almost metatextually making it a sort of documentary-within-a-documentary. At the climax, the dogfight is not shown on camera; all the action is from the perspective of the observers on *Galactica*'s hangar deck and CIC. The closing scene was shot in an actual Vancouver movie theatre, adding to the realism. The music that plays during the documentary's coda is a Bear McCreary arrangement of the original series' theme tune (which a deckhand can also be heard whistling at one point).

Lucy Lawless – who, as the review for 'Tigh Me Up, Tigh Me Down' indicates, had been pursued by Eick to play a role in the series since Season One – gives a strong performance as D'Anna, lending her a real sense of amoral seediness. The character was named after Eick's (male) best friend in college, Joey D'Anna, as a joke, and was loosely modelled on real-life CNN reporter Christiane Amanpour. Lawless is quoted in *The Official Companion Season Two* as saying that D'Anna, like Amanpour, is 'a very driven reporter, with very rational motives'.

Mark Verheiden was contributing his first *Battlestar Galactica* script; he had a background in writing for comic books and films (most notably the comic *Time Cop*, the 1994 feature film *Timecop* that was based on it, and three episodes of the short-lived television series that span off from the film). However, Moore himself wrote the narration for the documentary footage. Former *Doctor Who* companion Yee Jee Tso has a small role as one of D'Anna's staff. There were a few script changes indicated in the podcast: Palladino was originally to have committed suicide in front of Tigh when he realised the game was up (which it was decided was too gratuitous), and more was to have been made in the story of Tigh's trip to *Cloud 9* to meet with representatives of the other ships in the Fleet. On a less serious note, Moore has confessed, 'Every time I used to watch this scene in editing when Tigh came into the room and looked down and there's that shot of Ellen lying bound and gagged on the floor looking up at him, I kept wanting to just dub in the line where he just says, "Ellen, not tonight"'.

'Final Cut' might, on first glance, seem to be a gimmick-based or 'comedy' episode. However, it provides not only a quick insight into the state of the Fleet after Adama's return, but a set-up for later storylines involving Kat, Gaeta, Dualla, D'Anna and the Cylons respectively.

21: Flight of the Phoenix

FIRST TRANSMISSION DATE: 16 September 2005 (USA)

WRITERS: Bradley Thompson & David Weddle

DIRECTOR: Michael Nankin

CREDITED CAST: Donnelly Rhodes (Doctor Cottle); Bodie Olmos (Brendan 'Hotdog' [sic] Costanza); Leah Cairns (Racetrack); Jennifer Halley (Seelix); Christian Tessier (Tucker 'Duck' Clellan); Dominic Zamprogna (Jammer); Don Thompson (Specialist 3rd Class Anthony Figurski)

KNOWN UNCREDITED CAST: Leo Li Chiang (Tattooed Pilot)

SYNOPSIS: Morale continues to be low in the Fleet; on *Galactica*, pilots and crew are divided over the presence of Caprica-Sharon. As a means of building solidarity, Chief Tyrol instigates a project to construct an experimental fighter craft. While most are sceptical at first, participation in the project grows, and fences are mended. Meanwhile, after multiple systems failures, the crew discover that the *Galactica*'s computers are infected with a Cylon 'logic bomb' virus, another legacy of the networking of the computers earlier. Sharon offers to defuse it, and Adama agrees. She does so by linking in to the computer system physically through a cable in her arm, then sends a virus in turn to an attacking Cylon Fleet, allowing the Viper pilots to take them out easily. The experimental ship, which boasts an FTL drive and a carbon-composite skin that renders it difficult to perceive on DRADIS, is tested. Christened *Laura*, it is officially launched by President Roslin.

ANALYSIS: 'Flight of the Phoenix' verges on the clichéd and unbelievable, with a slightly cloying premise of the crew patching up some of their differences over an extracurricular project. However, the characters' ambivalence over Sharon is well portrayed, and the story serves as a useful set-up for events to come.

All is Ashes: Uniting the Fleet

At the start of the episode, stress is clearly affecting performance; the tension Gaeta betrayed to the documentary crew in 'Final Cut' is now manifesting, while Racetrack is unusually combative (and although one can sympathise with her feelings, it is very satisfying when Starbuck slams her face into a table for mouthing off about Sharon and Helo). Not surprisingly, Sharon is the focus of

21: FLIGHT OF THE PHOENIX

much of this discontent: at Cally's release party, she is congratulated for shooting *Galactica*-Sharon, and when she tries to express her gratitude to Tyrol, who defended her over the shooting, for obvious reasons he does not want to accept the thanks. Sharon's face now adorns the targets on the shooting range[50], a move obviously intended to dehumanise her, and Apollo, as Starbuck notes, is visibly taking out his frustrations on them. Starbuck also implies that Apollo's continual antagonism towards Tyrol is motivated by the same state of mind. Gaeta, however, calls Sharon by name in the CIC scenes, which she visibly appreciates. Starbuck defends Sharon in the card game scene, reminding the pilots that she saved her life. However, a deleted scene in which she angrily throws away her winnings as she walks along the corridor where the photographs of the dead are displayed, knocks over a memorial display and then picks it up and puts it back to rights, reveals her mixed feelings over supporting a member of the enemy camp.

One of the key subplots of this story, therefore, is Tyrol and Agathon working out their differences. Both men are the targets of negative comment for their respective relationships with the two Sharons. Connections are built between Tyrol's love of Boomer and his love of machines; we see him talking to a Viper and stroking it as he recalls his relationship with Boomer (followed by him locating the source of a dripping sound; the sequence has distinct sexual overtones, as well as tacitly alluding to the events of 'Water'), before marking it as unserviceable and to be used for scrap. His conversation with Helo takes place, appropriately, on board Sharon's Raptor. His assertion that he and Boomer were planning to have children, and thus that Helo did him a favour as otherwise he might have fathered a half-Cylon child, mixes up jealousy of Helo (whom he calls 'toaster lover'), anger at Boomer and self-loathing for having been taken in by her.[51]

Moore, in the podcast, describes the fight by saying 'There's a lot of rage and a lot of frustration and a lot of self-hatred and ambiguity in both these men ... over the people that they've chosen to give their hearts to and the fact that they've now come face to face with the representational other of themselves'. According to Moore, episode writers Weddle and Thompson sent him a note objecting to the fact that, as filmed, Tyrol at one point picks up a spanner and considers hitting Helo with it, but Moore liked the fact that it showed a negative side to Tyrol – which also foreshadows later events involving Tyrol and his violent streak. In light of this, a deleted scene in which Cally attempts to explain to Tyrol why she's not sorry she killed Boomer and the Chief waves the spanner and says 'This, I understand', carries an interesting implication: not just an

---

50 The website for auction company Propworx, which handles the auction of props and costumes for the series, indicates that targets were also made with the faces of Six, Leoben and Simon; while we will later see a Leoben target in a deleted scene for 'Maelstrom', the Six and Simon ones do not appear in the series.
51 SPOILER SECTION: All of this is doubly ironic in light of the fact that, had he and Sharon conceived a child together, it would have been fully Cylon.

assertion that he prefers machines to the complexity of human emotion, and foreshadowing the way the Blackbird project will bring people together, but suggesting that Tyrol may also sometimes feel the urge to resort to violence as a way of solving his problems.

Shared Interests: Sharon and Roslin

Sharon herself, meanwhile, is also in an ambiguous position, as she admits she remembers her relationship with Tyrol, though she assures Helo he is first in her heart, and at the end of the story she starts a conversation with Tyrol, implying that the two are going to work through their issues together. However, the extended version of this scene undercuts this positive message, as Sharon goes on to say that Tyrol feels ashamed of his love for *Galactica*-Sharon, and Tyrol then puts the phone down and goes to work on a Viper with Cally, the obvious implication being that he is embarking on a rebound romance. Although Sharon enables the humans to attack the Cylons, she knows the Raiders will not be permanently killed. However, her motivation for helping the Fleet is somewhat puzzling, as she says to Helo that she believes the other Cylons view her (and by extension the baby) as a mistake, and intend to kill her along with the Fleet; given that the whole object of the exercise on Caprica was to get her pregnant, this seems a very odd conclusion to come to. It also raises another problematic question, specifically why the Cylons are attacking the Fleet in the first place, given that they are putting the unborn child, which in 'Final Cut' they vowed to protect, at serious risk.

While Roslin is now advising that common ground can be sought with Sharon, Adama is more ambivalent. He points a gun at Sharon in CIC while she is hooked up to the computer network, saying as he does so, 'If they're coming for you, they're gonna be very disappointed'. Since Sharon herself can download on death, this would seem instead to be a threat to the baby and thus a direct fulfilment of Baltar's vision on Kobol; however, this is not so much as remarked upon. Adama's statement at the end of the story, that he found common ground with Sharon in that they 'both wanted to live', also does not mention the baby. All of this rather suggests that the episode was, at least partly, written at an earlier stage and then clumsily retrofitted to match later continuity.

Singing in the Dead of Night: The Blackbird Project

The other focus of the story is, of course, the project involving the experimental ship designated Blackbird (in keeping with the bird-and-reptile theme of the names of Colonial fighter craft). The theme is set up when Apollo says 'Nobody's expecting any miracles', and Tyrol says 'Maybe that's the problem', indicating, as per the repeated theme of Season One, that everyone needs to work for something beyond mere survival, and promises of a future Earth are not tangible enough. As Starbuck puts it, 'While everyone else is standing around whining, the Chief is doing something positive'. Adama recognises its potential value as a teambuilding exercise, regardless whether or not it has any practical worth, and he is proved right in this, with even the initially sceptical Tigh taking part, agreeing to get Tyrol the engines he needs (albeit insisting on payment in Tyrol's homebrew). In a nod to the shortages in the Fleet, Roslin christens the ship with drippings from the sparkling wine bottle rather than the whole thing, and when she pantomimes smashing the bottle over the prow, Tigh and Adama exchange a meaningful look.

Spreading Your Wings: Continuity and Worldbuilding

In less immediately significant developments, Lee and Dualla are becoming more intimate, having a sexually charged sparring practice session in the gym, indicating that, although relationships between officers and other ranks are proscribed, it is impossible to stop them from happening. Adama remarking to Baltar, about the Cylon virus, 'Good thing we have an expert on board', and then going to Sharon over it, is, according to the podcast, another calculated snub to Baltar. Sharon's mode of interfacing with the computer, sticking a cable up into her arm, clearly is not a normal practice for Cylons, given the discomfort she experiences doing it, but foreshadows the physical-interface computer technology we will see on basestars in Season Three. Roslin, learning from Cottle that she may have only a few weeks to live, goes into a curtained-off bed area, composes herself, then returns to ask calmly if she will be able to work to the end. She returns the book Adama gave her as a gift in 'Water' as a subtle indication to him that all is not well. Finally, this story features the first appearances of the minor characters Figurski and Duck, both of whom will play more significant roles later on.

This episode is unusual in being the first to have no net change in the number of Fleet personnel since the previous one, and also the first to set its action entirely on *Galactica* and its fighter craft, with no trips to planets or even to other ships in the Fleet. The label on the bottle used to christen the Blackbird reads 'Leonis Estates Sparkling Wine'. There are some technical errors to watch out for: following the fight between Tyrol and Helo, a camera operator and another man are briefly visible to the left of the screen; and Helo wears a Viper patch on his uniform during the Blackbird's first flight and christening ceremony. On a more positive note, the battle scenes are very good, with a solid wall of Cylon Raiders confronting the Vipers to the strains of Middle Eastern-style music.

There are also a few real-world references: the Lockheed SR71 Blackbird was the first stealth ship invented, and the mention of DDG-62 engines is a thank-you to the US Navy Destroyer *USS Fitzgerald* DDG-62, which Bradley Thompson and series science adviser Kevin Grazier had visited. Thompson meanwhile had visited the altitude chamber at Edwards Air Force Base, which allows pilots to experience the effects of hypoxia in controlled conditions, and this informed the sequence where Lee, Kara and Hot Dog are trapped on the firing range and running out of oxygen.

Moore felt the climactic sequence of the story was too close to 'Scattered' –

'It's all about doing a computer number crunch, the *Galactica*'s vulnerable while they're doing it, the Vipers hold off the Raiders, the Raiders jump away to where the Fleet is' – so he rewrote the battle to follow a WWII incident, the Great Marianas Turkey Shoot, in which the American air fleet outclassed and destroyed the inexperienced Japanese pilots. However, it also works as an inversion of the miniseries sequence in which Cylon Raiders massacre squadrons of Vipers rendered helpless by a virus.

The Bird is on the Wing: Writing and Production

Writers Weddle and Thompson deliberately picked up on the virus plot thread from their earlier story 'Scattered'; they had also been pitching the idea of having Tyrol developing new Vipers since the first season. They confess to being fans of the 1965 Robert Aldrich film *Flight of the Phoenix* (based on a 1964 novel of the same name, and remade in 2004), which featured survivors from a plane crash in the desert rebuilding the plane from the wreckage. Moore likened the story to a M*A*S*H episode, 'War of Nerves', which had the crew similarly uniting around a shared purpose. It also recalls the original-series episode 'The Long Patrol', which featured the testing of an experimental Recon Viper, and the *Galactica 1980* episode 'The Return of Starbuck', involving a spacecraft being cobbled together out of Viper and Cylon ship parts. Weddle and Thompson have said that they were anxious to keep the experimental ship-building realistic and not just have the Chief construct a superfighter out of spare parts, hence the idea of its stealth capabilities being the result of a happy accident, due to the ship's skin being made out of carbon composites because of a lack of metal.

Moore, in his podcast, says that the initial notion was to do a concept episode with the whole story set on the Hangar Deck and the characters' different stories all intersecting over the building of the Blackbird, but that, 'When you take that approach … the concept swamps everything else and you find yourself constantly trying to cram another story, another characterisation into what is, by its very nature, a fairly artificial construct'. Moore apparently contributed the idea of Sharon interfacing with the computer via a cable in her arm (although he was probably influenced by *Alien Resurrection*, in which androids interface with computers through a port in the forearm); and director Michael Nankin, a veteran of, among other programmes, *Monk* and *American Gothic*, contributed the idea of naming the stealth ship *Laura*.

The story has a number of continuity errors due to what appears to have been a last-minute editing session. Moore has admitted that the Blackbird's test flight and christening sequences were swapped around in the story order during the editing process because this was felt to make more thematic sense. However, the fact that the Blackbird, fully armed, can be briefly seen in the battle sequence (shortly after Apollo says 'Weapons free') suggests an earlier cut that placed both before this. The Blackbird plot seems to imply a working spacecraft being built, and Helo's and Tyrol's injuries from their fight on the Raptor healing, within just 24 hours, as the virus plot can realistically take no longer than that –

21: FLIGHT OF THE PHOENIX

all of which suggests that the Blackbird plot was originally intended to take place over a few weeks of Fleet time, but that, when the production team married the two plots together, they realised that the time-frames were incompatible. The final cut, which could be taken to suggest that an unspecified amount of time takes place between the scrubbing of the virus and the Blackbird's test flight, was therefore made so as to overcome this problem and suggest that the Blackbird did undergo subsequent development. This is the first episode not to feature an appearance by Tricia Helfer, although she is still credited and appears in deleted scenes.

This is also the story that marks the beginning of the Season Two timeline discontinuity. In 'Resurrection Ship' part two, Cain refers to the Fleet having been on the run 'for the past six months', whereas the timeline up to 'Flight of the Phoenix' would indicate that it has been only three months since the Fall of the Colonies. This is probably an artefact of 'Flight of the Phoenix' being reedited to suggest a longer timeframe for its events; although, as Roslin is said to have a month to live in this same story, it would also suggest that she has defied medical predictions.

'Flight of the Phoenix' is a light, superficial adventure, riddled with plot holes and lacking the edge and black humour of the previous episode, unfortunately marking a return to the low standard of episodes we have generally seen thus far in Season Two.

22: *Pegasus*

FIRST TRANSMISSION DATE: 23 September 2005 (USA)

WRITER: Anne Cofell Saunders

DIRECTOR: Michael Rymer

CREDITED CAST: Michelle Forbes (Admiral Cain); Graham Beckel (Colonel Jack Fisk); John Pyper-Ferguson (Captain Cole 'Stinger' Taylor); Sebastian Spence (Narcho); Leah Cairns (Racetrack); Fulvio Cecere (Lieutenant Alastair Thorne); Mike Dopud (Gage); Derek Delost (Vireem); Vincent Gale (Chief Peter Laird); Michael Jonsson (Pegasus Guard #1); Peter-John Prinsloo (Lieutenant Mei 'Freaker' Firelli)

KNOWN UNCREDITED CAST: Leo Li Chiang (Tattooed Pilot)

SYNOPSIS: The Fleet encounters an unknown ship, which proves to be the battlestar *Pegasus*. It survived the attacks due to its commander, Admiral Cain, ordering a 'blind jump', taking it to an unknown random location. Although the reunion is initially joyous, Admiral Cain, who outranks Adama, rapidly begins imposing her authority over the Fleet, integrating the crews and removing Apollo as CAG. The *Pegasus* crew also prove to have a more aggressive attitude to their role as survivors, and Baltar discovers a raped and beaten Six, Gina, in the brig. Cain orders the investigation of an unusual Cylon ship that has been sighted by the *Pegasus*'s recon, and the new CAG, Taylor, determines to identify it by hiding behind a convenient moon and photographing the passing Cylon fleet. Starbuck, however, challenges this plan by pointing out that the moon is an obvious blind spot and the Cylons will go nowhere near it. She takes off without permission in the Blackbird to photograph the ship. Meanwhile, *Pegasus* officer Thorne interrogates Sharon; he attempts to rape her, but is attacked by Helo and Tyrol and accidentally killed in the scuffle. Cain sentences Tyrol and Helo to death, leading to a tense standoff between the *Galactica* and *Pegasus*.

ANALYSIS: This episode is the first of a three-part story and marks the end of Season 2.0, having been followed by a three-month gap on first transmission. It is disturbing and dark in tone. Please note that the following discussion uses the extended cut of the story, available on the series' DVD release, as its primary reference point, as Moore has stated that this is the team's preferred version.

22: PEGASUS

Raising Cain: Admiral Helena Cain and the Pegasus

The arrival of Cain and the *Pegasus* introduces a much-needed focus to the ongoing storylines, and provides a credible source of internal conflict among the humans. Cain says 'Welcome to the Colonial Fleet' to the *Galactica* crew, indicating that, as far as she is concerned, they are the outsiders. She is quite clearly not out to make friends; although she assures Adama that she won't interfere with his running of *Galactica* and says 'It gives me no pleasure to have to take command', it is also plain that she will not tolerate the *laissez-faire* regime on the Fleet. She has a gun collection in her office, and no chairs, because she finds meetings go faster when officers have to stand (a detail Moore got from the practices of the then-current US ambassador to the UN, John Bolton, though Adolf Hitler is also known to have done likewise), indicating that she is willing to inflict discomfort to get her way. She does not afford Adama the courtesy of allowing him to give his account of the Fleet's survival in person, simply requesting his logs. Although her XO, Fisk, says that he was kidding about Cain shooting her original XO for refusing to obey orders, it is plain from the way he tells his story that he is not (and Tigh clearly believes him, later reporting it to Adama). Adama describes the Admiral as having been 'a very young officer on a very fast track' before the attacks, suggesting impetuousness; and the fact that she is from Tauron is a hint that she will be something of a bull in a china shop.

Despite this, she is, as Moore notes in the podcast, plainly not stupid or irrational; he says of her: 'Her agenda is quite simple. Hit the Cylons. Hit them hard. Keep hitting them … And looking at the way *Galactica* has been run up until this point, she goes, "What the hell is this?"' Cain says that the *Pegasus* found the *Galactica* as an unexpected result of tracking a Cylon fleet (which, unbeknownst to her, was itself stalking the *Galactica*) in order to anticipate its movements and attack it, indicating that she is obsessed with destroying the Cylons to the exclusion of all else. She places her own men in key positions in the Fleet, to give herself support and undermine Adama's authority, although she is initially friendly and charming to Adama, clearly viewing Roslin as her main adversary rather than him. When Cain argues that Adama has become too close to his officers and that this has blinded him to their weaknesses, he disagrees with her because, although she is clearly right, she fails to see that despite the insubordination and chaos his regime incurs, there is also a strong sense of loyalty and of almost family-like cohesion, to which her authoritarian, regimented system is a threat. She is, as Moore describes her, someone who is not an evil person but who, due to the situation she has been faced with and the choices she has made, has been led down a harsher path than Adama, who has been restrained by the civilising influence of Roslin, his family and the Fleet.

Cain's analysis of the *Galactica*'s situation is forensic and militarily perfect, even if it makes for uncomfortable listening. Although Adama's main fear is that she will focus on the *Olympic Carrier* incident (still troubling him a season and a half later), she does not do so, for reasons that will become apparent in the next episode. She is perfectly correct about discipline being lax, and about the fact that the CAG is the commander's son seeming damagingly nepotistic – although of course she is also wary of Apollo because of his support for Roslin, and because he has fomented mutiny in the past. When Adama criticises her imposition of summary justice on Tyrol and Helo, she reminds him that, as seen in 'Litmus', he overturned the verdict of a tribunal simply because he didn't like it (and it is worth noting that this action led indirectly to his being shot by Boomer). Her assessment is a slap at the *Star Trek* paradigm of military science fiction, in which discipline is generally unrealistically lax, and insubordination, even mutiny, are condonable in the right circumstances. Although this is certainly also true of *Battlestar Galactica*, this series at least provides an in-text explanation; specifically, that this is the crew of an antiquated and soon-to-be-decommissioned vessel who have consequently let themselves go. It also reminds us that, due to absorbing the *Star Trek* trope, many viewers may have been condoning some fairly unprofessional behaviour on the part of the series' regulars.

However, Cain is so blinded by her self-imposed mission that she cannot see the negative impact of her driven attitude on others. Her reading of the Helo and Sharon case as Helo having 'fraternised with, and evidently impregnated, an enemy agent' shows her ignoring the fact that he could hardly have known she was an enemy agent at the time. She also ignores the fact that Adama probably put more of his personal feelings into the logs than he would have done had he realised that they might someday be read by a higher authority. When she criticises Tigh, unsurprisingly, Adama reacts; he is aware that, unlike the other officers mentioned, Tigh is vulnerable and needs support to keep him performing well, something that her more authoritarian ethos is unlikely to find an acceptable trait in an XO.

Roslin, for her part, is from the outset displeased at this turn of events. After finally making common cause with Adama after months of conflict, she now has to deal with a new military leader, and one who seems unfriendly to her in particular. She also clearly recognises that Adama may be blinded by the relief of giving up authority, and realises the danger implied by Cain's asking for the logs. Whereas the earlier rift in the Fleet over Roslin's messianic ambitions was diffuse and able to be resolved without an internal civil war, in Cain we have an antagonistic force who is focused, direct and, most importantly, able to command a military force who can physically oppose any resistance put up by the Fleet (which Roslin's small group of security guards and ex-convicts were hardly capable of doing). While we do not yet know the full story, Cain's attitude to civilians is unsympathetic from the start; although she resupplies the *Galactica*, she gives only vague promises regarding the other ships.

Rage Against the Machines: The Pegasus *versus the* Galactica

While the *Pegasus* crew initially seem friendly, sharing data and resources, including Zarek's trial records, with the *Galactica* (Gaeta, clearly having progressed from drinking and smoking to addictive masturbation, puts in a request for porn), there is conflict straight away between them, with Fisk belittling the *Galactica*'s age and condition (in which we get the first, though far from the last, case of the *Galactica* being referred to as a 'bucket'). In a clever bait-and-switch, deck chief Laird in his first meeting with Tyrol comes across as similarly dismissive toward the Blackbird, but in their subsequent conversation reveals himself to be a kindred spirit; however, Laird is a civilian, and will prove in the next episode to have other areas of difference from the rest of the *Pegasus* crew. The *Pegasus* pilots, encouraging competition and authoritarianism, convey a sense of suppressed hysteria throughout. Their CAG bullies Apollo, assigning him to a Raptor and then accompanying him on the mission, visibly intending to keep an eye on him. Starbuck's reaction also suggests that, while flying a Raptor may not be a demotion, Viper pilots might consider the reassignment a slight. It is ironic that, having mended fences with his father, Apollo is attacked for being a 'daddy's boy'. The scene where the *Pegasus* crewmen, their guard down under the influence of Tyrol's homebrew, speak of gang-raping Gina shows a degree of misogyny that is perhaps surprising for a female-run ship, suggesting that they feel some aggression toward their commander; Gina, being both female and a Cylon, becomes a lightening conductor for the crew's pent-up rage at the enemy and at their leader. The scene also carries an underlying message that, whereas both groups of humans hate the Cylons, the *Pegasus* crew have taken this further and are defining themselves by that hate and finding solidarity in it. Cally is particularly disturbed by the talk, perhaps both recalling her own experience in 'Bastille Day' and also seeing some of her own anti-Cylon feelings reflected in an unflattering way. Thorne's attempted rape of Sharon is easily the most disturbing scene in the series since 'Flesh and Bone', whereas the more tolerant atmosphere on the *Galactica* has allowed Tyrol and Helo to make common cause.

A key theme of the story is that of needing to take actions in context. Aside from the cases noted above, the plan by Kara and Lee to disobey Taylor clearly demonstrates that a little insubordination can sometimes bring better results than blind obedience. The recurring theme of family is also highlighted, with Cain attacking Adama's own family ties to weaken him as well as breaking up the symbolic 'family' on *Galactica* as per the metaphor used in 'Home'. Like Thrace with Leoben earlier, there is an irony in Cain's defining Gina as a machine and yet allowing her crew to attack her through her human side; furthermore, this process of dehumanisation in turn dehumanises the *Pegasus* crew. The similarities between the ships (authoritarian commander, Cylon prisoner) throw the impact of their different choices into sharp relief, and return to the theme that the human race are, if anything, more at risk from tearing themselves apart through internal conflict than they are from any external enemy.

Although Baltar downplays his status as Vice-President, it is in this episode that his political abilities are truly shown. The scene in Sharon's cell has him successfully walking a fine line between indicating to Cain that they are not soft on Cylons while also reassuring Sharon that he is still on her side. (In a strong performance from Grace Park, Sharon is defiant but clearly concerned about the new state of affairs.) He persuades Cain to treat Gina more humanely by describing it as using a psychological technique to extract information; though Cain, who accuses him of getting too close to his subjects, has clearly detected his weakness, he talks her round by using her own language of extermination and interrogation, and by appealing to her rational, logical side. In a confessional scene with Gina, he admits that he loved the Six he knew on Caprica, and is moved to tears, indicating that he is also developing a sense of compassion; Moore notes that he treated the first Six as a conquest, and can only reach out emotionally to the Six who has been abused, suggesting that he is approaching, but not yet achieving, a more generally compassionate mindset. Head Six is visibly distressed by the sight of Gina, while clearly also encouraging Baltar to greater empathy with Cylons; when he asks her to go away for a while as he tends to Gina, she obeys without complaint.

Making Contact: Continuity and Worldbuilding

In series continuity, the *Pegasus* crew wear a white-on-purple version of the Colonial patch on their uniforms, in contrast to the *Galactica* crew's gold-on-black one, and the Fleet head count increases by 1,752 to account for their arrival. The fact that, although Sharon was willing to give information against the Cylons in the last episode, she is not willing to do so here even under extreme pressure, is a good indication that the new Cylon ship is something very unusual, and something that might be useful to her. There are also a couple of slight errors. The first is that, when *Pegasus* is identified, Adama orders the Fleet, 'Stand down to Condition One'. As Condition One is the highest alert level, he was clearly supposed to order the Fleet to stand down *from* Condition One. The second is that *Pegasus* changes position quite radically relative to the Fleet between the cut to *Galactica*'s exterior as Adama makes his way to CIC and the cut to *Pegasus* launching its Vipers.

This episode draws most strongly on the original-series two-parter 'The Living Legend', albeit with the omission of Cain's daughter Sheba, or possibly, given that Cain here is a woman, Sheba's amalgamation into the character of her father. Although Moore is vague as to his reasons for leaving Sheba out, it seems plain that in the original series she was brought in to fill the female warrior/love interest for Apollo role vacated by his deceased wife Serina, whereas in the reimagined one that niche is filled by other characters. Also, whereas the original series had Sheba as a vital link between the stories 'The Living Legend' and 'War of the Gods', the reimagined one employs the elements of these stories in different ways. Cain still appears to be strongly associated with younger female characters (Kara, and, in 'Razor', Gina and Kendra), in an echo of this father-daughter relationship, and the original Cain's relationship with the much younger socialator Cassiopea.

Moore says in the episode podcast that he had wanted to do a storyline based on 'The Living Legend' from the start (and a 5 May 2003 edition of the fanzine *Colonial Newsletter* contains a report that he had submitted an outline to the network for a story featuring the return of Cain), and possibly even further back, having written a *Star Trek: The Next Generation* episode entitled '*Pegasus*', involving Riker reuniting with his former commander over a mission to recover a missing ship called *Pegasus* from the Romulans. Some changes are rung on the situation: the original Cain was folksy and genial, disguising the more disturbing aspects of his character, whereas the new one is openly terrifying; and a further twist is provided by having her outrank Adama rather than, as in the original series, giving him ultimate authority. The fact that Adama is eager to support Cain's plan to join forces and attack the Cylons is a reversal of the situation in 'The Living Legend', as well as a reminder of how Adama's own behaviour in the miniseries, planning on a suicide engagement with the Cylons, mirrored that of the original Cain. Adama's ambiguous feelings about his command role also reflect the reluctant leadership of the original Adama.

The story has thematic links with 'Final Cut', in that both present alternative, less sympathetic, views on *Galactica*'s culture. An early idea for a subplot involving the civilian fleet refusing to resupply the *Pegasus* was abandoned out of concerns that it was too close to 'Resistance'. Elsewhere, the fact that Laird's craft was called the *Scylla* references the Greek myth about Scylla and Charybdis, as well as perhaps the fact that there is a 'Karibdis' in the original series. Moore reveals that Gina's name (which is not mentioned on screen in this episode) was an inside joke, referencing the new series' designation in some fan circles as GINO, meaning Galactica in Name Only.

Changing the Landscape: Writing and Production

Despite the attempted-rape scene attracting considerable controversy at the time, this episode was nominated for the 2006 Hugo Award for Best Dramatic Presentation, Short Form. The fact that it was written by Anne Cofell-Saunders, coupled with 'The Farm' having been written by Carla Robinson, suggests a practice of giving more controversial storylines to female writers, although Moore has stated that he had wanted to write '*Pegasus*' himself but was too busy. On first US broadcast, the episode got a 'Mature Scenes Follow' warning after the break before Act Four. Grace Park, in a widely-quoted 2006 interview, has said that, as scripted, the scene was to have stopped short of Sharon actually being raped, but that she and director Michael Rymer decided in discussion to film it with the rape included; she has criticised the decision to edit it down for transmission (for which she blames the network), saying 'How come on our show, we can have people beating each other up to a bloody pulp ... yet something that happens every single day around the world ... is too taboo, and we have to be shameful of it?' Tricia Helfer has said that she studied literature on post-traumatic stress disorder in order to portray Gina more realistically.

This was originally supposed to be a 90-minute episode, padded out by the Dualla-and-Apollo-sparring scene that eventually appeared in 'Flight of the Phoenix', but no matter how the team tried to assemble the material in editing, it continually wound up falling short of 90 minutes; hence the compromise of airing a standard 45-minute version, and including a 56-minute extended version on the DVD. One scene excised from the transmitted version, in which Starbuck outlines a plan for getting the resistance members off Caprica, will nonetheless reappear in flashbacks and recaps for subsequent episodes.

Actresses considered for the part of Cain included Anjelica Huston, Jessica Lange and Sigourney Weaver, all of whom rejected it; Michelle Forbes, with whom Moore had worked on *Star Trek: The Next Generation* (where she played the Bajoran Ensign Ro), and whose other credits include the TV series *24*, the movies *Kalifornia* (1993), *Swimming with Sharks* (1994) and Rymer's *Perfume* (2001), also turned the part down originally, but changed her mind after the production team sent her six DVDs of the series and she decided that it was not so much hard science fiction as a political drama.

In sum, '*Pegasus*' uses many of the ideas from the original-series story 'The Living Legend' concerning family, internal conflict and right and wrong, but, rather than slavishly copying what has gone before, provides its own spin on these themes.

23: Resurrection Ship (Parts One and Two)

FIRST TRANSMISSION DATE: 6 January 2006 and 13 January 2006 (USA)

TELEPLAY: Michael Rymer and Michael Rymer & Ronald D Moore

STORY BY: Anne Cofell Saunders [part one]

DIRECTOR: Michael Rymer

CREDITED CAST: Michelle Forbes (Admiral Cain); Donnelly Rhodes (Doctor Cottle); Graham Beckel (Colonel Jack Fisk); John Pyper-Ferguson (Captain Cole 'Stinger' Taylor); Sebastian Spence (Lieutenant Noel 'Narcho' Allison); Luciana Carro (Louanne 'Kat' Katraine); Vincent Gale (Chief Peter Laird); Peter-John Prinsloo (Lieutenant Mei 'Freaker' Firelli); Brad Dryborough (Hoshi)

KNOWN UNCREDITED CAST: Leah Cairns (Lieutenant Margaret 'Racetrack' Edmondson)

SYNOPSIS: Cain temporarily suspends the execution of Helo and Tyrol after Starbuck returns bearing pictures of the unknown Cylon vessel. She promotes Starbuck to captain and CAG. Roslin meanwhile advises Adama that Cain must be assassinated for the good of the Fleet. At Adama's instigation, Tigh quizzes Fisk about why *Pegasus* has conscripted civilians serving in her crew. He learns that *Pegasus* encountered a fleet of non-military ships, which Cain cannibalised for useful equipment and skilled labour, abandoning the other personnel. From Gina, Baltar learns that the unknown vessel is a resurrection ship: a Cylon craft carrying bodies and equipment to enable the downloading of the consciousnesses of dead Cylons. Cain and Adama both plan to assassinate each other after the attack on the ship, Cain tasking Fisk to do the deed and Adama tasking Starbuck. The combined fighter squadrons attack the Cylon fleet. Apollo in the Blackbird flies into the resurrection ship and blows up its FTL drive, but the Blackbird is then destroyed and he is left drifting in space, before being rescued at the last minute by Racetrack. Adama and Cain both call off their respective assassination attempts, but Baltar helps Gina to escape, and Gina finds her way to Cain's quarters and kills her. Roslin promotes Adama to admiral.

ANALYSIS: 'Resurrection Ship' finishes off the initial *Pegasus* storyline, albeit prematurely, and initiates several new ones, in a tense story that reveals how far both Cain and Adama will go in defence of their respective values.

Death of an Admiral: The Rise and Fall of Cain

The demise of Cain is one of the key points of this story. Where the original Cain was a glory-seeker, this one is an obsessive: the fact that she puts her standoff with Adama on hold when Starbuck turns up with the pictures of the resurrection ship shows that she values a chance to strike against the Cylons above all else. She also does not realise that her leadership style is in fact stoking up trouble for herself. She initially underestimates Adama and Roslin by assuming that they are soft and undisciplined, but her dismissal of civilian power means that Roslin sees her as an enemy straight away, and her eventual death at the hands of Gina stems directly from the culture of violence she has been fostering on the *Pegasus*. Her presence also reconciles at least two pairs of antagonists besides Helo and Tyrol: Tigh and Starbuck, and Adama and Sharon – and it is notable that she assumes she will need a team of Marines on *Galactica* to take control once Adama is killed, whereas Adama makes no such assumption about the *Pegasus*, possibly indicating that he knows she is feared but suspects she is not loved – or, alternatively, that she is seeing the wider strategic picture while he is focusing on his personal animosity.

The reason why Cain calls off her assassination attempt is never stated. Possibly she realises from Starbuck's manner that Adama was pursuing the same strategy and has now abandoned it; possibly, having made common cause with Adama against the Cylons, she no longer sees him as an antagonist; or possibly because Adama's actions have earned her respect. Or, indeed, all of these. When ordering Fisk to handpick a detachment of Marines, she says they must be 'Completely reliable. Completely loyal. Razors'. She promotes Starbuck to CAG not because she has learned to respect her insubordination, but because it indicates to her that Taylor was both too stupid to see the value of the Blackbird and too bad a leader to prevent Starbuck from disobeying his orders. Her speech to Starbuck explaining her treatment of Helo and Tyrol in part runs:

> 'Sometimes terrible things have to be done. Inevitably, each and every one of us will have to face a moment where we have to commit that horrible sin. And if we flinch in that moment, if we hesitate for one second, if we let our conscience get in the way, you know what happens? There are more kids in those body bags … I have a lot of faith in you. And I want you to promise me that when that moment comes you won't flinch'.

This is a good summing up of both their situations, referring not only to the execution order on Helo and Tyrol but also to Cain's decision to assassinate Adama; and Starbuck is also thinking of her own parallel mission. Cain does, however, flinch moments before Gina shoots her in the head, suggesting that not even she could live up to the ruthless principles she espouses.

Roslin, for her part, goes head to head with Cain in this story, first playing the schoolteacher when scolding her and Adama for their standoff (Cain suggests meeting on *Colonial One* because it is neutral territory rather than out of any respect for the Presidency), but then demonstrating to her that she can adapt to the situation. Recognising that Cain doesn't care about the Fleet or about setting a good example to its members, Roslin instead puts the situation in bald terms: 'You can go out there and fight it out with *Galactica*, or you can compromise. And those are the only two options on the table, period'. Cain clearly does not like this, and puts up with the whole idea of Roslin as President only because to attack the infrastructure of rank in the Fleet might put her own leadership up for challenge (which probably explains why Roslin does not try to use her authority as President to remove Cain from office, knowing that it will not be respected). Roslin also figures out that Cain must die from a single clash with her, whereas Adama needs to learn what happened on the *Scylla* before coming to the same conclusion. Roslin's 'You gotta kill her' is a brilliantly underplayed line, and shows her looking to the Fleet's safety as well as to her own position as leader in a situation where, increasingly, might makes right. While Moore describes Roslin's promotion of Adama to Admiral as 'giving him his last gift … before she dies', it is also clearly a pre-emptive move, to prevent future usurpers from attempting to take over the Fleet. The kiss between Roslin and Adama at the end is unscripted, but clearly heartfelt.

Cain earns one supporter on board *Galactica*, however, in the form of Kara Thrace. She appeals to Thrace by offering to support her plan to go back to Caprica and rescue the resistance (and this is clearly a serious proposal rather than a tactic to gain her support, as, while Adama is focused on journeying to Earth, Cain would instead very much like the idea of returning to the Colonies for a standoff with the Cylons). There are significant parallels here with the original-series episode 'War of the Gods', in which the demonic Count Iblis obtains Sheba's support through promising to find her lost father, Cain, as well as with Kara's earlier-established relationship with Adama. Kara's eulogy for Cain at the end is sympathetic, and suggests that, perhaps because of her mother, she seeks out stern, even abusive, female authority figures. ('Razor' will similarly suggest that Cain has a tendency to take vulnerable female junior officers under her wing.) Adama gives Kara a look when she says 'We were safer with her than we are without'; since Cain was a loose cannon in anyone's estimation, this suggests that Kara is speaking entirely from a personal standpoint.

All at Sea: Apollo and his Death Wish

This story shows Apollo drifting, literally as well as metaphorically; his near-death experience as he floats in space symbolises how he rejects the military but still fails to see politics as a concrete alternative option. He admits to not wanting to survive (in early drafts he finds himself floating surrounded by dead bodies and, as Moore says, 'It was partly that experience that informed his "I wanna kill myself, or at least I wanna die" decision by the end'), and takes a cruciform pose as he drifts in the water during his flashbacks. According to Moore, the flashbacks were originally to have been more detailed and would have involved Apollo swimming toward an unnamed woman on the shore, in a set-up for the revelations in 'Black Market' about his relationship with his former girlfriend Gianne (as well as a visual reference to a sequence in the 1970 film *Catch-22*). As it is, we have hints of his romantic confusion in that he ignores the sound of Dualla's voice calling for him to respond over the comms, and instead whispers 'I'm sorry, Kara'. This is inverted at the end of the story, when he talks with Kara about his suicidal feelings and Dualla secretly listens to the conversation. His political and administrative leanings are still hinted at: Starbuck requests his help with the day-to-day operations she must perform as CAG, which Kara, although a brilliant pilot, cannot handle, and Adama finally gains his support for the assassination by telling him Roslin is behind it, indicating that it has civilian approval.

In Name Only: Gina's Escape

Gina's story is also developed. In contrast to Sharon, she was not a sleeper agent; she gives Baltar the information about the resurrection ship so that she herself can die without resurrection. She says to Baltar, 'I was a soldier. I had a mission, I carried it out. I thought that when it was done I was going to die. That you would kill me. Then I – then I would download into a new body ... be reborn. But you didn't kill me. The things you did to me ...' This anticipates the coming episodes 'Scar' and 'Downloaded', both of which revolve around traumatised Cylons haunted by memories from their earlier existences, but also shows a deep naivety on Gina's part, as she was less a soldier than she was a spy and a fifth columnist, betraying, and directly causing the deaths of, over 800 of her fellow crewmembers.

Gina's story raises a theological problem for Baltar. She says that God forgives everything, whereas Head Six, God's messenger, assures him that God will not forgive the destruction of the resurrection ship, as, of course, it is another wedge between Cylon and human unity. Gina looks rather like the Six-as Starbuck seen in 'Home', providing another reason for Baltar to be attracted to Gina. The story Head Six tells Baltar in his daydream, that she used to enjoy going to Pyramid matches to feel the emotional energy, contains a strange detail: that she used to get two tickets, one for Baltar, so that, even though she knew he would never go to the game, she could feel he was there with her. Taken literally, it seems as if she is speaking as Caprica-Six; however, since she is clearly Head Six, this anecdote instead becomes a metaphor of her attempts to win Baltar over to her God, loving him despite his reluctance to accept God and waiting patiently for his conversion. The fact that, when Baltar repeats this story, word for word, to Gina, Head Six begs him not to and then vanishes, indicates that, for her, this is an act of betrayal, taking her metaphor for a sacred act and turning it into an expression of his physical attraction to Gina.

Although Baltar feels for Gina's vulnerability, there is still a selfish, sexual aspect to the fact that he cannot resist peeking at her naked body as she changes her clothes; Moore has said that originally Head Six was to have been there and turned his face to see Gina's scars, but that he felt this would detract from Baltar's intimacy with Gina. Moore has also said that originally Baltar and Gina were to have embraced as they formed a connection, but that Tricia Helfer objected, pointing out such behaviour is unlikely from the victim of multiple brutal rapes.

Baltar is of course ultimately the author of Cain's assassination, in urging Gina to seek justice rather than death. There is the question of whether Gina killing Cain is a kind of *deus ex Cylon*, as it seems rather contrived that, even in the post-attack chaos, she should be able to make it unchallenged to Cain's quarters.[52] However, it is nonetheless plausible, in that Cain's ship is stated in the extended cut of '*Pegasus*' to be twice the size of *Galactica* but require half the crew, and that it would have been further undermanned due to the losses of crewmen during the Cylon attacks. In any case, Cain's death is poetic justice, being the result of her own culture of authoritarianism; Gina could also be said to be acting as the hand of God, in that she removes one more obstacle to human-Cylon unity. It is, however, very precipitous that Cain should be killed so soon after being introduced into the story, and the fact that the episode 'Razor' was later written to feature her in flashbacks strongly suggests that the writers also felt, in retrospect, that the character had greater potential.

Strange Alliances: The Aftermath of Thorne's Death

Elsewhere, the attempted rape of Sharon has some unexpected consequences, in that Adama now treats her more like a human being, going so far as actually to apologise to her. Sharon also pricks Adama's conscience. When Adama asks her why the Cylons hate the humans, she quotes back at him his own speech from the miniseries: 'You said that humanity never asked itself why it deserved to survive. Maybe you don't'.[53] This remark, followed by a cut to a raging space battle, informs Adama's ultimate decision to call off the assassination attempt (which is in itself an ironic echo of *Galactica*-Sharon's attempt on his own life). This is undermined, however, in that the rest of the story makes it plain that if Adama wants the Fleet to survive, Cain will have to be eliminated, so his failing to kill her at this point only postpones the inevitable. It also makes him look like a hypocrite, in that he condones the killing of tens of thousands of Cylons, but calls off that of Cain, who is also a direct threat to the Fleet.

Although the torture of Helo and Tyrol by two *Pegasus* deckhands is

---

[52] Moore says that an earlier idea, in which Gina went into CIC and shot the entire command crew, was dropped for credibility reasons; and it has to be said that it would have robbed Gina of some of the sympathy we have developed for the character.
[53] Whether she remembers this as part of the download from *Galactica*-Sharon, or whether she learned about it via other means, is never explained.

unsurprising given the culture of violence on the ship, Fisk's intervention (which Moore says was based on a real-life incident he witnessed when serving on a frigate in the Navy ROTC, in which two enlisted men were disciplined by the ship's XO) complicates the issue. Fisk saves them even though, he says, he owes Thorne his life and does not condone what they did to him. He seems to be acting from a sense of order, that committing torture on your commander's authority is one thing, but doing it on your own initiative is another; however, we will later learn that Fisk is not a man of integrity, but distinctly corrupt. With this in mind, his motivation appears to be, first, that the deckhands' unsanctioned actions undermine his own authority, and, secondly, that he is trying to build some alliances on *Galactica* (hence his cultivation of a relationship with Tigh), hedging his bets in case of future developments.

Extreme Prejudice: Continuity and Worldbuilding

In continuity terms, Fisk's story regarding the *Scylla* is slightly different from the version of events later depicted in 'Razor' (which will be discussed in the analysis for that episode), but this is excusable in that stories do develop and change in the telling. There is a moment of irony in part two when Starbuck and Fisk pass in the corridor, on the way to assassinate each other's commanders, and wish each other good hunting, and the details outlined in 'Razor' about Gina's and Cain's backstory will lend a further twist to their final exchange: 'Frak you', 'You're not my type'. The fact that Gina clearly feels the physical and emotional pain from her torture suggests that Kara's assertion in 'Flesh and Bone' that Leoben could switch the pain off if he wanted to was inaccurate, as Gina has clearly gone far beyond the point when philosophical and theological considerations about emulating the human would justify not doing so. Kat is now lead pilot on *Galactica*, following the departure of Lee and Kara, in a set-up for 'Scar'. It is unknown who built the model resurrection ship that appears on the tactical board or, as in 'The Hand of God', the fairly detailed models of some of the Fleet's civilian ships; possibly Adama has been getting more creative with his model ship-building activities since the attacks on the Colonies.

In external references, the deckhands' beating up of Helo and Tyrol with bars of soap wrapped in towels is a deliberate homage to similar scenes in *Full Metal Jacket* (1987) and *The Grifters* (1990). Tyrol's exchange with Apollo, 'I thought the Cylons were the enemy?', 'Yeah, now it's us', recalls satirical cartoonist Walt Kelly's famous epigram 'We have met the enemy, and he is us'. Adama's codeword for the assassination, 'Downfall', is a deliberate reference to the 2004 film of the same name concerning the final days of Adolf Hitler, and Cain's equivalent, 'Execute case orange', refers, Moore says in the podcast, to 'War Plan Orange', a strategy drawn up by the US Navy prior to WWII in case of war with Japan (although in the miniseries, Case Orange is also the Colonial phrase for the situation in which the President and Cabinet are incapacitated). Apollo's drifting in space was inspired by the real-life story of Ensign Gay, an American pilot downed during the Battle of Midway who spent the battle watching events from the water. It also recalls an incident in the *Space: 1999* episode 'War Games' in which Commander Koenig similarly floats in space, and visually resembles the opening of *Apocalypse Now*, where Martin Sheen's character, lying in his hotel room, recalls/hallucinates the firebombing of a Vietnamese jungle. There is something Biblical in Cain being the author of the first actual Cylon deaths.

In internal references, the plan to attack the Cylon Fleet here uses civilian ships as decoys, like the Season One episode 'The Hand of God'. It was originally intended that when Starbuck returned to the Fleet, she would make some kind of signal to indicate her identity to the other craft, recalling incidents in both the original series' 'The Hand of God' and the reimagined series' 'You Can't Go Home Again'.

Life Eternal: Writing and Production

In scripting terms, this serial – Michael Rymer's first contribution to the series as a writer – was again a one-part story extended to two when it overran. Having it as a two-parter also saved the team money and obviated the need for a clip show later in the season (which had been planned as a cost-saving exercise). Cain's funeral, the scene of her and Starbuck bonding, and the scene of the deckhands' attack on Helo and Tyrol, were all added after it was decided to make the story a two-parter, and were shot following the episode's initial completion.

The idea of the resurrection ship was originally developed in an ultimately abandoned story called 'The Raid', of which more later, and the account of the *Scylla* came about due to a note from the network asking 'Why is Cain so bad?', indicating to the writing team that she had to have performed some action that could not be justified or excused by the emergency situation she was in. Early drafts, according to Moore, involved more conflict between Cain and Laura, with Cain requiring Laura's approval to use civilian ships as part of the planned attack on the resurrection ship, and the civilian fleet, as noted in the previous Analysis, refusing to resupply *Pegasus*, meaning that Cain needed Laura's assistance to maintain order. It was decided at an early to subvert audience expectations by keeping the *Pegasus* in the series, but to kill off Cain – although the production team later openly regretted the latter decision.

'Resurrection Ship' was the first story shot after a four-week hiatus in the middle of summer to allow the cast and crew a break and the writing team to catch up on their scripts. The CGI in this episode is particularly good, with the silent strafing of the resurrection ship being very impressive. The resurrection ship itself was based on one of the early designs for *Galactica*, and the *Pegasus* has a slight resemblance to a short-necked plesiosaur. Baltar's house was written out in this story due to construction taking place nearby in preparation for the upcoming 2010 Winter Olympics and the neighbours complaining about the constant presence of film crews, though it also works in story terms, with Baltar's turning away from Head Six and toward Gina. Due to availability problems with John Pyper-Ferguson, the actor playing Taylor, the character never appears again after the scene in part one where he pulls a gun on Apollo during the standoff between *Galactica* and *Pegasus*, though Pyper-Ferguson would later play a major role in the spin-off series *Caprica*.

The Cain mini-arc concludes prematurely, the loss of Cain robbing the series of a well-defined and formidable antagonist for both Adama and the Cylons. Her continued presence would have given Season Two some much-needed direction, and it is significant that, in the next two episodes, the series seems to be looking for an alternative line of division within the human Fleet.

24: Epiphanies

FIRST TRANSMISSION DATE: 20 January 2006 (USA)

WRITER: Joel Anderson Thompson

DIRECTOR: Rod Hardy

CREDITED CAST: Colm Feore (President Adar); Donnelly Rhodes (Doctor Cottle); Paul Perri (Royan Jahee); Luciana Carro (Louanne 'Kat' Katraine); Bodie Olmos (Brendan 'Hot Dog' Costanza); Leah Cairns (Racetrack); David Richmond-Peck (Naylin Stans); Holly Dignard (Asha Janik); Jennifer Kitchen (Marine)

SYNOPSIS: Roslin, her condition deteriorating, flashes back to political events on Caprica on the day of the attacks, in which she successfully negotiates an end to a teachers' strike, only to discover that President Adar had set her up, expecting her to fail. In her flashbacks, she also sees Baltar with Six, and realises Baltar's treachery. On *Galactica*, Roslin acts on the news that Cottle's tests show unknown anomalies in the blood of Sharon's foetus to order its termination. Just before the abortion is carried out, Baltar announces that the foetus's blood is an anti-cancer agent. The abortion is cancelled, and blood drawn from the child is used to eliminate Roslin's tumour. Elsewhere, the culprits behind incidents of sabotage and suicide bombing on the Fleet are discovered to be an organisation in favour of making peace with the Cylons: Adama has Royan Jahee, their leader, arrested. The recovered Roslin meets with Jahee and promises to raise his organisation's concerns with the Quorum in exchange for a cessation of violence. Baltar reads a letter Roslin intended for him to receive on his accession to the Presidency, which indicates she has little regard for his ethical standards; he secretly gives his nuclear warhead to Gina, who is hiding out on *Cloud 9* and working with Jahee.

ANALYSIS: The story's title refers to four epiphanies, three of which set Roslin and Baltar up as antagonists: on Caprica, Roslin realised that she was being used by Adar; in the present, she realises that Baltar is a traitor; and Baltar learns Roslin does not trust him. However, the final epiphany, when Roslin's life is saved by Sharon's unborn baby and she realises Cylons have more in common with humans than she believed, puts her unwittingly on the same side as Baltar.

I Remember Adar: Roslin's Flashback

The flashback story with Roslin and Adar confirms earlier hints that life on the Colonies was far from idyllic. The teachers' strike involves civil disobedience and police beatings. Adar, who had an affair with Roslin but set her up to fail in her negotiations with the strikers, more than lived up to Adama's assessment of him as 'a prick' in the earlier draft of 'Home', and to the implication in the draft of 'Bastille Day' that he was not above offering Zarek a devil's bargain. Adar wanted to have Roslin fail so that the administration would not be seen as giving ground to strikers, meaning that he put his reputation as a strong politician ahead of giving fair treatment to the people he had been elected to govern.

Adar's key line, 'One of the most interesting things about being President is that you don't have to explain yourself. To anyone', is a near-direct quote of George W Bush, as cited in Bob Woodward's book *Bush at War*. The state of affairs between Roslin and Adar explains the ambiguous way she has referred to him in the past, most times positively but also sometimes with an edge of mistrust. However, it is a line that Roslin herself quotes as well, not only in this story but also in 'Flesh and Bone' (attributing the statement to Adar), reminding the audience of her own ruthless side.

Roslin vows at the conclusion of the flashbacks to play hardball against Adar, indicating that despite previous appearances, it was not the destruction of the Colonies that set her on the path to becoming a determined leader, but the Adar situation. She is also implicitly connected with Admiral Cain in that she unwittingly repeats the Admiral's accusation to Baltar that he is too close to his Cylon subjects. We learn that *Galactica* has been press-ganging civilians to work on munitions, in a sinister echo of the *Pegasus*'s treatment of the civilian ships it encountered. Roslin's assurance to Jahee, that she will put the concerns of his organisation, Demand Peace, to the Quorum and to Adama, does not suggest any changes on the part of the Fleet's leaders, as they are under no obligation to take these positions remotely seriously (and indeed, it is very unlikely that they will).

During her flashbacks, Roslin remembers seeing Baltar with Six, which presents a serious continuity problem. While it confirms the 'feeling' she had in 'Six Degrees of Separation' that Baltar was untrustworthy, there is no way she could have seen the pair of them together at that time, as Roslin was on the ship later known as *Colonial One* at the point when Baltar and Six walked through the park. Moore, in the podcast, attempts to explain this away by claiming that the events in the 'Epiphanies' flashback did not happen on the same day, but this is not terribly credible, as, first, the events in the flashbacks otherwise make narrative sense as an account of a single day, and, secondly, it would suggest that Baltar and Six took an earlier walk through the same park wearing exactly the same clothes and with Six carrying the same distinctive silver case. The only possible way of rationalising this is to suppose that Roslin is experiencing a vision from God, intended to encourage suspicion and distrust between her and Baltar; Head Six seems to be encouraging Baltar to believe that the leadership of the Fleet is his 'rightful place', but the obvious means of putting him into power – allowing Roslin to die – would also mean the death of Sharon's baby, and so the best that can be done is to encourage a rift between the two politicians. However, this explanation does not appear to have occurred to the writing team.

Head Frak: Demand Peace, Gina and the Cylons

Head Six, in this story, returns to making no sense whatsoever. She has apparently been absent for some weeks, and seemingly returns only because of the threat to Sharon's baby. However, her diatribe to Baltar about how he should act to save the child is bizarre: she starts by saying 'Once Roslin's gone, you'll be President. You can use your new authority to save our child', seemingly ignoring the fact that Roslin has ordered that the termination take place immediately; besides which, as Baltar reasonably points out, if a president lacks the support of the military, he will be little better than 'an anointed dog-catcher'. Six then, even more strangely, tells Baltar that he should use 'the nuclear device' to save the child, but the question remains of what she expects him to do with it: threatening to blow up the Fleet would hardly support his cause (and would ensure he got nowhere near the Presidency), and actually blowing up *Galactica* would kill the child as well.

Perhaps unsurprisingly, Baltar continues to be drawn away from Head Six and toward Gina. Gina, however, is if anything a worse love object. Although she says she abhors violence, this is clearly only for the benefit of the Demand Peace guard in the room at the time. She also says she wants Baltar to become President so that he can lead the Fleet against Adama and pave the way for the Cylons to save them, which, given that she is suicidal and bent on revenge for her experiences, seems a thin gloss on the real object: that is, to have the Cylons arrive and wipe out the humans. She also will not tell Demand Peace she is a Cylon, saying 'Even their dedication has its limits'. This leads to one of the weakest aspects of the story: not only are her 'Clark Kent' spectacles such a pathetic attempt at disguise that even Moore admits it doesn't work, but there is also the surprising implication that the Fleet's security forces have not circulated pictures of Six as a known Cylon. Baltar is drawn to Gina sexually, though, understandably, she will not allow their relationship to develop along those lines. When Head Six asks him if he loves Gina, he does not answer, suggesting that, unlike his relationship with the Six on Caprica, the attraction is only physical – which makes his entrusting her with a nuclear warhead an even more nonsensical act.

The Demand Peace movement continue this theme of Cylon-related insanity. Their pamphlets, and saboteur Asha's dialogue, are anti-military, suggesting that they are partly influenced by the violence done to civilian trust in the military by the events at the start of Season Two, which is not unreasonable. Although they are a secular group, their logo, a cruciform man in a circle, suggests, as well as the CND and anarchist symbols, more Christian imagery (and recalls the series' tendency, throughout, to show certain characters in cruciform poses). However, this symbolism is unexplained; the text says in part, 'The Flying Man is ... the symbol of peace to come', without clarifying anything further about it. In general, they seem like a dry run for the Baltar cult that will emerge in Season Four (similarly with a flying creature as its logo), which, although somewhat flaky, will manage to form a cohesive religio-political movement. Unfortunately, Demand Peace's main political agenda seems to be a variation on the premise that periodically bedevilled the original series, of craven politicians wanting to negotiate, against military advice, with obviously nefarious parties – albeit in this case with the more realistic spin that they are an extreme, deluded fringe group rather than mainstream politicians. However, even a fringe group should realise the obvious fact that they are not in a position to negotiate for peace with the Cylons, having lost the war and being on the run, and that most people in the Fleet are unlikely to be sympathetic to the Cylons. (Baltar, as when he saved Gina in *'Pegasus'*, is careful to make a display of xenophobia when he saves Sharon's baby, remarking 'Obviously [her blood] has to be slightly different, because the Cylon is not human'.) Indeed, in this situation, a realistic peace initiative could come only from the Cylons. Any possible logic in Demand Peace's existence is thus negated by their completely crackpot position as regards the Cylons.

The resolution of having the hybrid human-Cylon blood provide an apparent cure for cancer, however one might try to justify it on thematic grounds, falls into the realm of unforgivably contrived *deus ex machina* and sci-fi cliché. Although it has tenuous connections to the theme of love transcending all and the development of human-Cylon unity – for instance, in the last scene, as Roslin watches Sharon touching her baby bump, clearly seeing the Cylon in a new, more positive way – Mary McDonnell expressed severe reservations over this aspect of the storyline, saying that she knew her character had many fans who were cancer survivors, and that providing her with a 'miracle cure' seemed unfair on them. It is true that, with the resurrection ship gone, Sharon's baby is no longer the only hold the humans have over Sharon, but killing it would certainly make her resentful and less cooperative.

Right to Choose: Continuity and Worldbuilding

In other developments, Apollo is now back as CAG of *Galactica*, though Starbuck's remark that he hasn't been around much indicates that the events of 'Resurrection Ship' are still affecting him, and also provides a set-up for 'Black Market'. Friction between Kat and Starbuck is also rising. Head Six's relationship with Baltar parallels that of Ellen and Tigh, with her urging him toward political office he does not desire. Baltar is seen smoking a cigar at the end of the story, the source of which will be revealed in 'Black Market', as well as being a witty echo of what one is supposed to do at the birth of a baby. Contrary to Head Six's prophecy in 'Scattered', which she reminds Baltar of here, it is Roslin, not Adama, who attempts to kill the baby. Adama is initially reluctant, and though he supports Roslin's decision, he also directly countermands the order the moment Baltar comes to him with his preliminary findings about the hybrid blood's anti-cancer properties.

Although the introduction of the previously-unheard-of Demand Peace might seem contrived, the story reminds us throughout that there are many aspects of life on the Fleet that we have not been allowed to witness. The revelation of where the Viper ammunition is coming from highlights the fact that we have been seeing the actions of only a few, very privileged people within the Fleet, and thus that Demand Peace were unlikely to feature until they started engaging in actions directly threatening that elite. It is less forgivable, however, that we never hear from them again after this episode, since, once their concerns are rejected by the Quorum and the military, it would seem more likely that they would resume the bombings and sabotage. Starbuck, meanwhile, shows as much prejudice against deckhands as she did in '*Pegasus*' against Raptor pilots, wondering what a deckhand would want with a library reader; it is a wonder that she has any friends left.

In terms of real-life issues, the presence of a Cylon in the peace movement recalls the real-life situation in which Cold War peace organisations were sometimes infiltrated by Communists. However, this actually made sense within the Cold War context of two ideologically opposed groups competing for political domination, whereas here one group is trying to completely exterminate the other, providing no potential for common ground. Writer Joel Anderson Thompson has said that the immediate referent for Demand Peace was the militant abolitionists of the 19th Century anti-slavery movement; but again, this makes little sense, as the abolitionists were acting to oppose the ongoing oppression of a group, whereas not only are the Cylons no longer oppressed, they are the ones with the upper hand. The references to some of the pro-life movement's arguments against abortion, such as the contention that aborting a foetus destroys its unknown potential, along with the use of medical terminology such as 'peculiar genetic anomalies' to indicate possible justifications for termination, obscures a problematic ethical issue. Added to the characterisation of the peace movement as antagonistic and deluded, this gives the episode an unsubtle right-wing tone. While the cure was originally to have been found in the stem cells of the foetus, which might seem an echo of contemporary arguments in favour of stem-cell research, this was ultimately abandoned in favour of a less politically controversial set-up. One might further ask why the production team felt the need to cure Roslin's cancer in the first place since, given that, as per McDonnell's argument above, it reduces a complex real-life medical issue into a simple case of diseases and cures.

All the President's Men: Writing and Production

In production terms, Sharon smashing her head against the window appears to be a visual nod to the actions of Leland Palmer and Dale Cooper when possessed by BOB in David Lynch's *Twin Peaks*. Colm Feore, playing President Adar, is a well-known Canadian actor most famous for the title role in *Thirty-Two Short*

Films about Glenn Gould (1993). According to Moore (whose parents were teachers), the teachers' strike storyline derives from a joke that Mary McDonnell and the crew shared in Season One, that Roslin had an affair with the President (which is actually implied in her remark in the miniseries that the President was a man to whom she couldn't say no). However, it lends an, obviously unintentional, retrospective twist to Roslin's likening of Billy to Adar in 'Home', given that Adar attempted to stab her in the back.

Anne Cofell Saunders, co-writer of the *Pegasus* arc, came up with the idea that the Cylon child should provide the cure for Roslin, and also that Baltar should sabotage his own bid for leadership in saving her life. The letter from Roslin (based on the American tradition whereby a departing President leaves a letter for his successor) was positive in at least one draft of the script, and reading it impelled Baltar to save her; as it stands, had he read it earlier, he might not have saved her, and it has reopened the enmity between them.

The writing team appear to have had a harder time with the Gina storyline. Earlier drafts had her staying in a brothel on *Cloud 9*, and she and Baltar having a sexual relationship, neither of which (as Tricia Helfer reportedly pointed out to them) sit particularly well with her past as a rape victim. Originally Head Six was to have vanished for several episodes, indicating the departure of God from Baltar's life as he turned toward Gina instead, but Moore said that his team found Baltar less interesting without her – which is a presumably unintentional slight on James Callis's performance. Regarding the bomb, Moore has said, 'We didn't like the feeling that it was just a dangling plot thread … and it was just such a moment of relief when we found the true pay-off for it', though having it given to a homicidal lunatic does not seem much of a satisfactory resolution.

An early undated draft script exists, which, while it contains all the elements and main story threads of the final version, differs significantly on a number of plot and character points. The teachers' strike subplot is absent: Adar, in the flashbacks, is a nice guy who has been a friend of Roslin's since college and is bewildered by her tendering her resignation upon learning she has cancer. Roslin, for her part, is a lonely spinster who collects snowglobes and at one point winds up chatting to a delivery-service employee who has come to bring her tickets to the *Galactica*'s decommissioning (and who has some pretty dire lines, including '[Adama]'s a fellow brother in uniform. He travels the stars. I travel the streets'). The pro-Cylon organisation, here called People for the Ethical Regard of Cylons in a not-too-subtle dig at the animal-rights organisation People for the Ethical Treatment of Animals, are also, rather impressively, far more stupid than in the final version. For example, instead of the sabotage plot, at the outset of the episode, a Doral has evidently persuaded them to provide him with a gun, which he uses to shoot himself, claiming he will download and bring their message of peace to the Cylons. Adama, when he learns of this, has one of them arrested on the grounds that they have thus assisted an enemy agent to obtain vital intelligence about the Fleet; which, even overlooking the fact that at the point when this episode is placed there is no resurrection ship nearby, makes one wonder why Doral can't just commit suicide on his own. There are numerous scenes of characters emoting over the imminent death of Roslin. Lee, for instance, has a conversation with her where she exhorts him to 'find someone or something outside of saving the human race'; and Billy screams at an unknown person who makes the mistake of ringing *Colonial One* and asking for 'President Baltar', 'We still have a President Roslin, ass-wipe!', before complaining to Dualla, 'We don't just fill somebody's slot with another drone. The people selected President Roslin'. There is an intriguing line from Baltar where he says, 'I killed Gina to save Gina', hinting at an unused storyline involving this character, or possibly indicating that Gina was to have been killed by Baltar at the conclusion of 'Resurrection Ship'; Gina does not appear in this draft, suggesting that, rather sensibly, the character has been killed off, and Baltar instead gives the nuclear weapon to Jahee. There is also a further brief set-up for 'Black Market', in that Fisk attempts to curry favour with Baltar by sending him boxes of cigars. The story thus clearly benefited from the rewriting and development process, if only to the extent that a rather dreadful story was turned into a marginally less dreadful one.

'Epiphanies' is another episode that should never have been made; it is contrived, politically one-sided and revolves around an organisation that has no credibility whatsoever. Rather than, as intended, showing Roslin as a woman of principle, it instead paints her as a complete hypocrite.

25: Black Market

FIRST TRANSMISSION DATE: 27 January 2006 (USA)

WRITER: Mark Verheiden

DIRECTOR: James Head

CREDITED CAST: Richard Hatch (Tom Zarek); Graham Beckel (Commander Jack Fisk); Claudette Mink (Shevon); Donnelly Rhodes (Doctor Cottle); Bill Duke (Phelan); Leah Cairns (Racetrack); Amy Lalonde (Gianne); Hayley Guiel (Paya); John Mann (Linden); James Ashcroft (Security Officer); Brad Mann (Pegasus Marine); Gustavo Febres (Herbalist)

SYNOPSIS: An increasingly detached Apollo is spending more and more time on *Cloud 9* with a prostitute, Shevon, when Fisk, currently in command of the *Pegasus*, is murdered. Apollo is tasked with investigating, and learns that Fisk was heavily involved in the black market that has sprung up on the Fleet. Phelan, controller of the black market, attacks Apollo and kidnaps Shevon and her child. Apollo approaches Zarek, whom he suspects of working with Fisk; although Zarek denies it, he directs Apollo to the *Prometheus*, allegedly Phelan's centre of power. Apollo learns that Shevon was working for Phelan, and Phelan is planning to sell her child. Apollo kills Phelan and announces that, while they cannot stop the black market, the military will come down hard on excesses such as murder, medication-hoarding and paedophilia. Shevon breaks off the relationship with Apollo, saying that he is just using her as a substitute for his girlfriend who was killed in the attack on the Colonies.

ANALYSIS: 'Black Market' is yet another weak episode. The plot is thin, and the message that 'everybody commits crimes, it's just a matter of degree' is repeated *ad nauseum*. Apollo's line 'It doesn't make us right … just a whole lot of people wrong' sums the problem up in many ways, as a potentially interesting exploration of moral grey areas is not given the nuanced, complex treatment it really deserves.

Black Hole Sun: Apollo's Journey to the Underworld

Part of the problem is that the episode focuses on Lee Adama, who is, following 'Resurrection Ship', even more directionless than before, highlighted by a cold, almost robotic, portrayal by Jamie Bamber. Whereas most of the series focuses on Lee's painfully slow distancing of himself from the military and drawing

25: BLACK MARKET

toward politics, in this episode he seems to be going absolutely nowhere. For the sake of argument, it might have been interesting to focus on the reasons behind Apollo's stagnation – as in the scenes where Dualla confronts him over their lack of a relationship, or where Adama tries and fails to connect with him, asking why he has been so distant since the Blackbird incident – and explore the directions in which he might go – as when Adama, at the end of the story, puts his full trust in his decisions. However, instead this episode invents a pregnant blonde girlfriend – or possibly fiancée, as she wears a ring – back on Caprica for him, whom we have never seen or heard of before (and indeed will never hear of again after this episode), but who apparently so affected him that he is now trying to recreate their relationship with a prostitute, who is also a one-story-only character. This seems a contrived and trite explanation for Apollo's lack of direction, and indeed a pointless one, since the already-established idea that he went into the military out of familial pressure and is increasingly finding this a bad decision covers it amply.

Apollo's surprise upon learning that Shevon was working for crypto-Mafia boss Phelan, which is blatantly obvious to everyone else, simply makes him look deluded or stupid, as does the fact that Zarek has to tell him about the existence of the *Prometheus*. Equally, Apollo's killing of Phelan when the crime boss tries to justify child prostitution makes his actions look clichéd-heroic, rather than suggesting the ruthless behaviour of a nihilistic man who has lost all respect for human life. Finally, the idea of Apollo as negotiator, brokering a deal with seemingly antagonistic forces, has already been done in 'Bastille Day', and far better.

A further annoying aspect to this is that most of the interesting or relevant material seems to have wound up in the deleted scenes. This includes sequences in which Apollo explores, in conversations with Shevon, his relationship with his girlfriend (whose name, never actually given in the finished version, is Gianne), and the fact that she was pregnant is made explicit. There is also a sequence in which Apollo and Dualla talk about Lee's experiences in 'Resurrection Ship', in which Dualla reveals that she wishes she had died back on Caprica, explaining some of her later actions. Finally, there is a scene in which Apollo has a confrontation with *Pegasus*'s current XO, Renner, over the fact that Apollo, rather than a *Pegasus* officer, is running the investigation. Moore also notes that a subplot to the effect that Apollo is flying again for the first time since 'Resurrection Ship', and thus has been deliberately avoiding piloting duties, was dropped.

It has to be said that the concept behind the episode is not inherently a bad one. As Apollo notes, it is not unexpected or remarkable that people even at the highest level of the Fleet are involved in the black market, as suppliers or customers, and Shevon's remark that many women are turning to prostitution also is not surprising, as similar things happen in any situation of social and economic upheaval. Phelan sums up the perfectly logical reasons why a black market develops, saying 'The Fleet needs us. Rationing's too tight, ship comes in too late, we're the pressure valve, we provide'. The fact that Zarek denies black market involvement but has knowledge of the people who run it, is another reminder that politicians often must take actions at odds with their public image, and also that Zarek takes a fairly pragmatic view of politics: he says to Apollo, 'Roslin's acting like the black market's some sort of aberration, but I thought you were smarter than that'. Phelan's arguments have an echo of the *Pegasus* storyline about them: just as the *Pegasus* crew descended into self-justifying criminality, here Phelan tries to excuse child sexual abuse by equating it with acquiring black market alcohol and cigars. Like Cain, Phelan also is ruthless toward his operatives, having one of his own men killed, so it is not surprising that the others are willing to deal with Apollo rather than attempting to avenge their leader.

All Are Guilty: Good and Bad Story Elements

While Apollo is the focus of the story, and while a large number of regular characters do not feature at all (including Starbuck, Sharon, Tyrol and Helo, although Katee Sackhoff and Grace Park are still credited), there are some nice character grace notes elsewhere. Tigh, who has been relatively neglected since Adama returned, has a good subplot regarding his own black market activities. His cheek twitches when he discusses the black market with Apollo and Adama, and later, confronted with a bracelet of Ellen's found in Fisk's quarters, he claims that he traded it for black market goods, plainly trying to protect Ellen. He appeals to Apollo by saying, 'I haven't done anything that most people on this ship haven't done. Including you', causing Apollo to flash back to his paying Shevon for her services. Cottle comes across as a refugee from *M*A*S*H* as he cracks jokes during Fisk's autopsy, saying 'Looks like our friend Fisk hit the jackpot' as he extracts a cubit from the dead man's throat.

Baltar has a confrontation with Roslin, in which she indicates that she knows that he was planning to meet with Fisk prior to the latter's death, and, on this basis, suggests that he should resign his political office before (she implies) a scandal emerges; this proves to be a mistake, as it galvanises him into seeking power and viewing her as an enemy. Clever parallels are also drawn between Roslin and the Mafia-like organisation of the black marketeers; the scene in which she makes her 'one-time offer' to Baltar is immediately followed by the one in which Zarek explains to Apollo that his finding the corpse of Fisk's murderer is a similar 'offer', intended to end his investigation of the affair; but Zarek then goes on to tell how the black marketeers are putting pressure on Zarek, implying that if Apollo accepts the 'offer', it will give the black marketeers a hold over Apollo for future use. When Roslin announces that she wants to regain control of the Fleet's supply chain from the black marketeers, Adama supports her, but when Apollo at the end says that it would be counterproductive to shut it down entirely, she lets his decision stand, albeit unhappily, indicating that a more nuanced give and take between civilian and military power is now in effect. Baltar throws his weight around with the Marines guarding Fisk's quarters, but Head Six correctly identifies this as due to nervousness and feelings of guilt, musing 'Wonder what [Roslin] would say if she saw you like this?' Baltar also refers to Roslin's 'resurrection', implicitly likening her to the Cylons.

Fisk's untimely death is also a good bait-and-switch, as up until then all indications have been that he is being set up as a semi-regular. It also leads to the unspoken implication that Cain's regime is in part to blame for Fisk's subsequent criminal activities: the sanctioning of murder, sexual abuse and dehumanisation aboard her ship means that Fisk now has few qualms about endorsing similar practices in the Fleet.

Other aspects of the story and characters, however, are fairly weak. It is surprising that Roslin, with her normally pragmatic edge, apparently fails to recognise, until Lee points it out, that a certain amount of black market activity needs to be unofficially tolerated, although it is possible that this is another symptom of her growing authoritarianism, seeing the black market as a threat to her power rather than a necessary evil. Phelan threatening Apollo is also far from intelligent, as Apollo has the military behind him, meaning that if Phelan does succeed in getting rid of him, someone else will just come in to replace him – and, of course, the fact that Apollo is the Admiral's son means that his death would incur a terrible retribution. The episode also begins with an event and then cuts to '48 hours earlier', as in 'Resurrection Ship' part two and 'Act of Contrition', an idea that is getting a little repetitive, and Moore has acknowledged that it was added late in the day in an attempt to provide more drama, because 'It started too slowly ... the initial scenes were not engaging, the story wasn't grabbing me'. It is also rather unfortunate that the leader of the black market is black, particularly given the relative lack of positive black characters in the reimagined series in contrast to the original.

Above the Law: Continuity and Worldbuilding

In terms of series continuity, Colonial money is still in use and comes in some rather Euro-like bills as well as cubit coins. Baltar's brand of cigars is 'Caprican Imperial'. There are also hints that the integration of *Pegasus* into the Fleet is less than smooth: Fisk is anti-civilian, saying that he supports Roslin 'for the moment'. Adama's remark 'Even though Cain's gone, her influence lingers' as a justification for having his own son lead the investigation rather than a *Pegasus* officer, is perfectly justified in light of the corrupted and cliquey nature of the culture aboard the *Pegasus*, even though Adama does not know at this point about Fisk's black market activities. Tigh's suggestion that a Cylon is behind Fisk's murder (which implies that Gina's involvement in Cain's death is known, at least to senior officers – though how they came to know it is unexplained), and Adama's reply that the alternative is worse, is a repetition, albeit a heavy-handed one, of the idea that humans have more to fear from each other than from the Cylons. Moore has pointed out the implication in the story that there is no formal police force on the Fleet, adding that he doesn't see how one could have formed up until this point. This explains why Apollo is leading the investigation into the black market. Although Apollo calls in a 'security team' when he regains consciousness after being attacked by Phelan's men, we know that at least one private security force, Roslin's, exists on the Fleet. After Fisk's murder, Adama is shadowed by a Marine guard for this episode.

In terms of other references, the fact that prostitution is legal in the Fleet is a holdover from the original series, in which 'socialators' were recognised professionals. Apollo being involved with a woman with a child may derive from the original Apollo's marriage to Serina, mother of Boxey, although his remark 'I'm not good with kids' differentiates him from the fatherly character of the original. A fat, black, bald crime lord seems a deliberate reference to (the far more interesting) Marcellus Wallace of *Pulp Fiction*. Moore has said that the story was supposed to have been a call-back to *Heart of Darkness* via *Apocalypse Now*, with Lee journeying up the metaphorical river in quest of a Kurtz figure, but it doesn't read terribly well. A copy of *The French Lieutenant's Woman* is visible on Adama's bookshelf.

In production terms, the idea of Lee killing Phelan in cold blood was made by a Sci-Fi Channel executive, Mark Stern (surprisingly, because the network are usually the ones urging more caution in the use of violence), and the garrotted make-up on Fisk is very effective. John Mann, who played *Galactica*'s ill-fated CAG Jackson Spencer in the miniseries, returned here for a minor role as a *Prometheus* resident with whom Apollo trades for information; although his scene was deleted, he is nonetheless credited for it.

Good Intentions; Writing and Production

It is rather surprising that this episode turned out as poorly as it did, given that writer Mark Verheiden also contributed the far superior 'Final Cut'. Moore, in his podcast, alternates between blaming director James Head, who was working on the series for the first (and, as it happens, the last) time, and blaming himself, saying: 'You get happy with a script and you think it's working really well … And then you get to the place where you watch and you go, "Oh my God. What was I thinking?"' Moore has said that the intention was to do a story that revealed a different side to Lee Adama's character (although one might unkindly observe that it instead reveals that there is only one side to him after all). He adds that when Phelan says 'You won't shoot me, you're not like me' and Lee shoots him, the implication ought to have been to show the viewer that Lee is in fact very much like Phelan, but the comparison does not really read (as Apollo is hardly a drug-peddling, paedophilia-enabling gangster), and in any case, one has to ask what would be achieved by drawing this comparison between Apollo and Phelan. Furthermore, the facts that Apollo is traumatised through his experiences in 'Resurrection Ship', that the paedophilia issue has been brought up, and that Lee is a professional member of the military tasked with eliminating a negative force within the Fleet, mean that his actions don't come across as particularly dark or surprising. Moore also complains that Phelan was too broadly drawn, and that the implication, at the end of the story, that Zarek would take over the black market, was never developed. Although this idea is so hackneyed that it is probably best that it was not pursued, it is rather frustrating that the black market itself, with all it implies, never again appears in the series. Jamie Bamber has somewhat optimistically stated that Lee is the conscience of the show, and so having him in an ambiguous position is interesting; however, he has also admitted that it was more fun to film than to watch, and we would add that in fact, the 'conscience' role is largely taken by Helo, where Apollo's character instead revolves around his transformation from pilot to politician.

Although Moore's criticisms are valid, and there are a lot of things wrong with 'Black Market', it is actually far better than its immediate predecessor. Its main problem lies in being a standalone story that tries to resolve in a single episode problems and character developments which could have provided a sinister ongoing thread.

26: Scar

FIRST TRANSMISSION DATE: 3 February 2006 (USA)

WRITERS: David Weddle & Bradley Thompson

DIRECTOR: Michael Nankin

CREDITED CAST: Luciana Carro (Louanne 'Kat' Katraine); Bodie Olmos (Brendan 'Hot Dog' Costanza); Christopher Jacot (Ensign Brent 'BB' Baxton); Sean Dorry (Ensign Joseph 'Jo-Jo' Clark); Christian Tessier (Lieutenant Tucker 'Duck' Clellan)

KNOWN UNCREDITED CAST: Leo Li Chiang (Tattooed Pilot)

SYNOPSIS: The *Galactica* has spent four weeks defending a mining operation in an asteroid field where a key source of ore has been found, while the rest of the Fleet goes on ahead with the *Pegasus*. During this time, the pilots fight a number of skirmishes with Cylon Raiders (who, with the loss of the resurrection ship, are reluctant to engage the humans in head-on battle), chief among them a Raider they have nicknamed 'Scar'. Starbuck and Kat develop a rivalry over who will be the first to shoot Scar down, fuelled by the fact that Starbuck, missing Anders, is letting her skills slide, whereas Kat is growing in ability and experience. Starbuck and Kat, flying together, encounter Scar and engage him. Starbuck has a chance to take out Scar at the cost of her own life, but instead, realising that in Anders she has someone to live for, gives Kat the chance to make the fatal shot, and with it allows her to take Starbuck's place as *Galactica*'s Top Gun.

ANALYSIS: This episode, like 'Black Market', is a one-off character piece, here focusing on Starbuck, her growing rivalry with Kat, and the changes in character and priorities that Kara has experienced since her return from Caprica.

From Hell's Heart: Starbuck versus Kat

There are a few parallels that can be drawn between this story and 'Black Market'. Both are episodes told in flashback, and both feature one of the main pilot characters slowly going off the rails and remembering a lost lover. However, the Starbuck/Anders scenario works better than the Lee/Gianne one, first in that Anders is a character to whom we have already been introduced, secondly in that it is unknown if Anders is dead or not, leaving Starbuck with the question of whether to press for his rescue or to assume he has perished, and finally in that, as Helo notes, it is Starbuck's love for Anders that gives her the drive to rise above her rivalry with Kat and get herself together, whereas, with Gianne dead, Apollo can obtain no such redemption through brooding on her, but must simply achieve closure.

The conflict between Kat and Starbuck is well drawn. As Thompson points out in the podcast, Starbuck was Kat's training officer, and in her has 'built another Starbuck'. Kat also acts as the voice of conscience to Starbuck, saying, 'You used to be the hottest stick on the Fleet. Now, you're just a reckless drunk that sends other people out to get killed', and pointedly observing, 'One Tigh on this ship's enough'. (Katee Sackhoff's comment on this line is, 'They say that you inevitably turn into the person you most despise, if you don't figure out the reasons why you despise that person'.) The pilots seem divided between the two, with different groups cheering each rival on. Starbuck also, however, picks up on Kat's flaws, pointing out that she is scared of death and of not being remembered afterwards. This fear also informs the opening scene, where Kat struggles to remember the name of the girlfriend of a recently deceased pilot, Reilly. Symbolically, Reilly's girlfriend looks a little like Kat. Later on we learn that Kat, just prior going on her final mission against Scar, put up a picture of Reilly's girlfriend on the memorial wall. In the podcast, the writers remark on the contrast between Kat's open concern for the pilots and Starbuck's apparent callousness toward them, concluding that Starbuck *does* care, but has seen so much death by this point that she has become reluctant to acknowledge her feelings. Kat herself is hardly gracious in victory, lording it over Starbuck as the latter gives her the ceremonial 'Top Gun' mug. Starbuck's then turning the situation into a remembrance for dead comrades could be seen as subverting Kat's braggadocio, but also as a touching way of tacitly letting Kat know that she *will* be remembered after her death.

The story focuses in part on Starbuck's relationships with men, chiefly represented by Apollo. When Apollo suggests that it is best just to live for the moment (a philosophy that goes some way towards explaining why he is unable to get out of the rut he is currently in), she propositions him. She is clearly just after casual sex to blot Anders out of her mind, although it also draws a kind of Freudian sex-death connection, suggesting that her chequered love-life is partly a way of distracting herself from the nature of her job. Apollo points out, 'You're fine with the dead guys, it's the living ones you can't deal with', drawing a parallel between them; in the previous episode, he cared for Gianne despite her being dead, but for Starbuck, the thought that Anders is alive is what motivates her to keep going. Perhaps due to her absent father, alluded to in 'Valley of Darkness', Starbuck also seems to have a particular attraction for men who are somehow unavailable. At the end of the episode, she acknowledges to Helo that having someone to live for makes her a more cautious pilot, but perhaps a better human being, in an uplifting comment on the power of love.

Top Gun: Scar and the Raiders

The character of Scar also gives us insights into the life of a Cylon Raider. It is emphasised that the Raiders have individual personalities, Sharon likening them to intelligent, trained animals, and parallels are drawn between Scar and Starbuck; he (the humans apparently assume the Raider is male) is the Cylons' best pilot, but the constant round of death and resurrection has left him with a death wish, hence the fact that in the climactic battle he deliberately tries to crash himself into Starbuck despite the lack of a nearby resurrection ship. This is the first time we learn that the Raiders resurrect as well as the humanoids; in the writers' meeting for this episode, it was decided there should be a hierarchy among the Cylons, with humanoids at the top, Raiders in the middle and Centurions at the bottom, which will be made clearer in Season Four. Sharon points out the big advantage of resurrection – that the pilot's experience is not lost and, as in a videogame, death itself becomes a learning experience – but the payoff is that death and resurrection become traumatic for the Cylons. However, the human pilots build up a knowledge of Cylon strategy by reviewing footage of other pilots' deaths, indicating that humans also learn from death. The *Galactica* 'Top Gun' mug has a skull with glowing red eyes on it, appropriating the death imagery of the Cylons.

The answer to the question of why, if he is so famous, Scar has not been heard of before, lies in the fact that the *Galactica* is in an unusual situation, having been in the same place for four weeks protecting the mining operations; clearly, the pilots have come to know Scar only, or mainly, during this period of quick skirmishes around the asteroid field. Hot Dog says 'Lotta pilots die going after that bastard', although the Fleet head count has gone down by only four, but then again there may have been a number of births this month. In other continuity, the *Pegasus* has a production team that is now turning out combat-ready Vipers, and new pilots are training there before moving to the *Galactica* to take up combat-ready status, beginning at the rank of Ensign. A couple of references are made to Flat-Top's death in 'Act of Contrition' and to Fireball's and Chuckles's deaths in 'The Hand of God' (both also written by Weddle and Thompson). Leonis Estates Sparkling Wine, the type used to christen the Blackbird in 'Flight of the Phoenix' (which shares its director with 'Scar'), is used in the scene where Kat takes over the 'Top Gun' mug. 'Jolly' is also mentioned, in reference both to the original series and to the miniseries, and, in an apparent nod to the original series-character Cassiopea, Kat thinks Reilly's girlfriend's name was 'Kassie'. Two vehicles that look exactly like original-series landrams are visible as part of the mining operation.

Never No More: Continuity and References

In terms of outside references, the conflict between Scar and Starbuck is heavily indebted to a number of sources. *Moby-Dick*, being the narrative of a struggle between an obsessive human and an intelligent, distinctive-looking animal, with the human's obsession becoming destructive to all around him, is the principal referent. However, 'Scar' also recalls the film *Enemy at the Gate* (2001), which revolves around an ongoing duel between two snipers in the ruins of Stalingrad. There are further clear parallels to the *Space: Above and*

26: SCAR

Beyond two-part story 'Never No More'/'The Angriest Angel', concerning an attempt to take out an alien top gun pilot, which becomes a personal vendetta for one of the humans. The *Space: Above and Beyond* two-parter explicitly references the real-life story of WWI flying ace the Red Baron, and the *Battlestar Galactica* writing team referred to 'Scar' as 'the Red Baron episode'; the writers' meeting podcast also indicates that its working title was 'Aces'. The podcast further reveals that the writers were partly influenced by the film *Battleground* (1949), which tells the story of the siege of Bastogne during WWII from the perspective of the front-line troops. The model plane on the 'Top Gun' mug is a US Navy F/A-18 Hornet (unfortunately not the F/16 Fighting Falcon, the plane that, in the 1970s, was nicknamed the 'Viper' after the *Battlestar Galactica* craft), and the scene of the drunken pilots throwing themselves across tables and drinking from each other's navels came through research Weddle and Thompson had done interviewing astronauts for another project. A minor detail is that the skin magazine *Nymph*, which Hot Dog is seen reading in this episode and later, is shown to have previously belonged to Reilly. The sticking plaster on Starbuck's shoulder-blade is again briefly visible.

Death Wish, Too: Writing and Production

The story's genesis came, according to the podcast (which features Weddle and Thompson as well as Moore), from Weddle's interest in doing a story about the Viper pilots and Eick's in exploring the Kat-Starbuck rivalry. Budgetary restrictions meant that they could only afford one space battle, meaning that the antagonism between the two pilots plays out in other venues, such as the briefing-room scene. Reilly's girlfriend, according to Weddle, had started out simply as a bit of narrative colour, but gradually evolved in the rewriting process into a central through-line for the story, and Moore notes that the development of Kat into a regular character was similarly organic; she had entered the series as a minor character in 'Act of Contrition', but writers then kept including her in their stories, and so the decision was taken to make her the partial focus of this episode. Her rivalry with Starbuck was hinted at in 'Scattered', where she took part in a sweepstake as to which pilot could get the most kills while Starbuck was absent without leave.

Much attention was given to the development of Starbuck. In the podcast, the participants agree with Moore's statement that 'Scar [has] become the focal point for Kara's whole fucked up life', and in the recorded writers' meeting for the episode there is a discussion of how Scar metaphorically represents Kara's own scars, mental and physical. Sackhoff, however, reports that she was less than thrilled at the events of the story, saying that she didn't like the idea of Starbuck losing the 'Top Gun' mug (though Luciana Carro was naturally delighted at this development), and reporting, in an interview quoted in *Somewhere Beyond the Heavens*, that her reaction to the script was 'I don't get it. I don't like it ... What happened to my character? She's drinking all the time'.

In production terms, Michael Nankin's direction is very good, with particularly noteworthy touches including the scenes of drunken revelry passing into Starbuck's memories of Anders; the first shot of Scar showing the Vipers reflecting in his scanning eye; and the disorientation-chair exercise sequence opening with a POV shot from the pilot in the chair, similarly disorienting the audience. The Viper pilot being physically ill as he leaves his craft was an unscripted addition by Nankin. The piece of music that plays over the last scene is 'Cavatina', best known as the theme from *The Deer Hunter* (1978), and also featured in *Jarhead* (2005).

The sequence of Starbuck naming the dead pilots is said in the podcast to have been Nankin's idea. Although the scientific accuracy of showing an asteroid field as a tightly-bunched cluster of objects is questionable, it still looks impressive. Money is again saved on battle sequences by having one of them take place over the wireless. The Mark VII Viper cockpit was built especially for this episode, and the rotating chair, which was based on one seen by Thompson at Edwards Air Force base, was constructed around a Viper pilot seat. In a Q&A session on John Laroque's website, Moore reveals that the editing team had problems with the fact that the blonde woman briefly seen getting belly-button shots in the sequence of the pilots drinking, bore too much of a resemblance to Katee Sackhoff: 'We struggled with it in the editing room to tweak her hair colour and other things to make it clear that it wasn't her, but we never licked the problem. We really wanted the shot, because it directly ties into the flashback shot of Anders kissing her on the stomach, so we opted to keep it in rather than lose it altogether'.

A few of the deleted scenes also add colour to the story. One features the pilots auctioning off Reilly's possessions, following the British Naval tradition, which is both a tribute to the dead as well as a practical exercise in recycling. (An interesting detail is that some of the pilots bidding for the skin magazine are women.) Another reveals that Kat giving the pilot briefing was not her arrogantly taking Starbuck's place, but rather her stepping in because Starbuck had failed to turn up on time. An extended version of the Apollo and Starbuck drinking scene has Starbuck saying she can't imagine Apollo with a wife, baby and house, and being surprised when she finds out he has wanted this. It is a shame that the exchange is left out, as it references both Apollo's development in 'Black Market' and Starbuck's own dislike of the idea of domesticity, and particularly children. The scene of Kat pinning Reilly's girlfriend's picture to the memorial wall was intended to be at the end of the episode, intercut with Starbuck praying, but in the end the team decided it would be best to finish with Starbuck and Helo sparring. The original intention is still evident, in that Kat is wearing her blue uniform rather than her flight gear.

'Scar' is a very strong episode, providing an exploration of Starbuck's mental state, where she first seems to be losing her edge, but, through her rivalry with Kat as the latter challenges her Top Gun status, she discovers what is genuinely important to her.

27: Sacrifice

FIRST TRANSMISSION DATE: 10 February 2006 (USA)

WRITER: Anne Cofell Saunders

DIRECTOR: Reynaldo Villalobos

CREDITED CAST: Kate Vernon (Ellen Tigh); Mark Houghton (Kern Vinson); Eric Breker (George Chu); David Neale (Nelson Page); Dana Delany (Sesha Adinell); Michael Ryan (Ray Abinell); Adrien Hughes (Lieutenant Terry Burrell); Erica Carroll (Civilian); James Upton (Environmental Specialist); Georgia Hacche (Petty Officer Sian)

SYNOPSIS: Tension is growing in the Fleet over rumours of a pregnant Cylon prisoner secretly kept aboard *Galactica*. Meanwhile, Billy proposes to Dualla, and she turns him down. Going to *Cloud 9* on leave, Dualla has a drink with Apollo, only for them to encounter Billy, and an argument ensues. The bar is invaded by members of an anti-Cylon underground faction, and Dualla, Billy and Ellen Tigh are among those taken hostage. Apollo, hiding in the bathroom, tricks the sensors into registering an oxygen leak, but is then also captured. The terrorists demand Sharon Valerii. Starbuck attempts a rescue, disguised as a maintenance worker come to fix the oxygen lines and backed up by a team of Marines. In the ensuing firefight, she wounds Apollo. Adama negotiates with the terrorists, offering to send them the dead body of Sharon in exchange for the hostages; he sends them the corpse of Boomer, and, although the terrorists are briefly deceived, they soon realise it is a trick. However, the distraction gives the Marines enough time to storm the bar. Apollo's life is saved, but Billy is shot dead by one of the terrorists.

ANALYSIS: 'Sacrifice', although still flawed, is a more successful variation on the ideas explored in 'Epiphanies', principally the relationship of the civilians to the military and the tension being generated by the presence of various humanoid Cylons in the Fleet.

Tinfoil Hats: Sharon and the Conspiracy Theorists

Philosophically, the story is about the poisonous nature of unresolved grief and the futility of the politics of revenge. The terrorists Sesha and Vinson are acting out of vengeance for a lost family member – her husband and his brother – ten weeks earlier during a Cylon attack, and they desire to give meaning to his death by alerting the Fleet to what they genuinely believe to be a threat to humanity. Moore elaborates on the scenario in the podcast by saying: '[Sesha's] husband matters to her and has radicalised her in a way that the massive traumatic shock of losing their entire society did not ... Essentially the loss of the "one" in your life outweighs the loss of the "many" to everyone's life'. Although Sesha's fixation on Sharon Valerii, despite Sharon having had nothing to do with her husband's death, might seem irrational, it very much makes sense as the result of a grieving woman needing someone to blame and focusing on a high-profile Cylon in her search for closure.

The story also focuses on the issue of terrorism and how to deal with it. When Tigh raises the possibility that the terrorists are right and Sharon is deceiving them as to her loyalties, Roslin points out that the problem is not with the rightness or wrongness of their claims, but with the way they go about making their point. Adama, confronted with Sesha's conspiracy theory that the Ministry of Defence was infiltrated by a Cylon prior to the attacks, observes that 'people look for complicated answers when something terrible happens', with the ironic twist that the conspiracy theory in this case is actually correct. The Cylon *modus operandi*, as written up by Sesha, includes sleep deprivation, assault on natural resources, emotional manipulation, suicide bombing, multiple models, sleeper agents and Cylon reproduction, all of which are true; for conspiracy theories to promulgate, there always has to be an element of truth at their core, and the secrecy of the military in the Fleet, while understandable, is also going to add fuel to rumours. There are parallels with Demand Peace in 'Epiphanies', in that we have here another anti-military fringe organisation, although this one is somewhat more credible under the circumstances.

In terms of development, news of Sharon's presence has filtered out to the media, and it is unclear whether Adama's refusal to comment makes the situation better or worse, in line with the series' ongoing exploration of the relationship between journalism and politics. Sesha's room contains newsletters entitled *Road to Armageddon* and *Can Cylons Reproduce?*, suggesting that some of the millenarian leanings of the Fleet's leadership, and speculations about Cylon biology, have been echoed among the civilians. Roslin says that Sesha's manifesto is 'getting a lot of attention'; although this is undoubtedly only because she is currently at the centre of a hostage crisis, it means that Sesha's preferred rumours and conspiracy theories will get wider circulation in the Fleet.

The fact that nothing has been heard of these conspiracy theorists before now simply highlights the situation, mentioned in 'Epiphanies', that the audience's perspective on the Fleet is a very narrow one, focused entirely on a small circle of pilots and politicians; we are also dealing not with an organised political movement, but with a few people moved to action by grief over a specific incident. However, the continued presence of Sharon is shown here to be controversial among the military as well. Tigh voices doubts about the value of her information, and one might note that her presence has cost seven lives and an unstated number of wounded in this episode alone, even though she has acted to support the Fleet in other episodes including 'Flight of the Phoenix'. Tigh also argues that Adama has become less dispassionate toward her since *'Pegasus'*, implying that the Admiral is now perceiving her as the Sharon he knew (and, since she has some of that Sharon's memories, there is a shared connection). Sharon herself admits that there are limits to her helpfulness, and will not identify the other Cylon agents in the Fleet, in line with the scene in *'Pegasus'* where she refuses to provide information about the resurrection ship. 'Sacrifice' presents a credible scenario in which a complicated ethical situation is causing divisions among both the military and the civilians, and providing a fertile ground for conspiracy theories.

Dangerous Liaisons: Sex and Love on the Fleet

Otherwise, the story's character aspects revolve mostly around the participants in Lee's tangled romantic life. The fact that nobody comments on his relationship with Dualla suggests that the fraternisation rules are being relaxed (or, more likely, that nobody wants to challenge the Admiral's son). Starbuck shoots him, which makes her, albeit accidentally, two for two on putting Adama's children in life-threatening situations. Her admission to Adama that it is her fault, and his punishment of her by refusing to let her take part in the next rescue attempt, have echoes of 'Act of Contrition'. At the end of the story, Dualla begs the wounded Lee to live, reminding us that she knows about his death wish; Starbuck eavesdrops unobserved, paralleling the scene at the end of 'Resurrection Ship' where Dualla listens to the conversation between Lee and Starbuck about his suicidal feelings. Billy, in his final episode, is shown to be truly selfless, rising above his jealousy and helping Lee, his rival for Dualla, with ungrudging compassion.

Elsewhere, we learn that Ellen is a regular in this particular bar on *Cloud 9*, and she inevitably interprets Lee's asking her to come to the toilets as an invitation for casual sex. Moore has said in the podcast that the intention was to suggest that Ellen frequently comes to *Cloud 9* to, as he puts it, 'cat around', with her husband's knowledge. Marines out of uniform seem to have a penchant for loud patterned shirts and chinos. Roslin's comment that there is no 'road map' for their actions regarding Sharon suggest that she is having to make decisions without any relevant guidance from military procedure, scripture or prophetic dreams.

The Case of the Convenient Corpse: Things That Don't Make Sense in 'Sacrifice'

Although the premise, backstory and development of the episode make sense, it is unfortunately let down by a few aspects. While it is just about plausible for Ellen, Lee, Billy and Dualla all to be on *Cloud 9* right at this very moment, Starbuck's presence is a coincidence too far, and raises the question of who, in the absence of Lee and Kara, is acting as CAG. Furthermore, Starbuck's decision to go into the bar disguised as a maintenance worker overlooks the fact that, as *Galactica*'s former Top Gun, occasional *Pegasus* CAG and one of the subjects of D'Anna Biers's documentary, she is very likely to be recognised; and it is surprising that it is only Ellen's look of recognition that tips off the terrorists that there is something up. Ellen seems to have lost both her keen intelligence and her focus on survival at all costs, threatening the terrorists with the fact that her husband is *Galactica*'s XO without thinking that this might make her a valuable hostage.

Elsewhere, Sesha appears unaware that there are two Sharon Valeriis in the Fleet, one of whom is dead, despite the fact that her wall of clippings contains a prominent item on the assassination of Boomer, complete with a photograph of the Cylon being shot, and one of the post-it notes on the wall reads 'Two Sharon Valeriis'. The corpse presented is clearly an old one, with no effort to disguise that fact (for instance dressing it to hide the autopsy scars, or applying make-up), so it is implausible that the terrorists do not realise the deception straight away. In initiating a hostage crisis, the terrorists have put themselves in a situation where there is no way out for them bar imprisonment or death; while there are a number of plausible reasons why they might do so, none of these is ever explored in the story.

There is a final problem from the point of view of credibility. Despite all the fuss about Sharon being a security risk, the audience knows that her primary motivation is to protect her child, so any attempts to build tension regarding her loyalties fall flat. Furthermore, since she is a regular character and the baby is a continual point of reference, anyone reasonably familiar with the series is going to figure out that Adama is not going to kill her, and anyone who remembers the corpse in the morgue will predict how he will resolve the hostage crisis.

Final Sacrifice: Writing and Production

'Sacrifice', a story clearly indebted to numerous hostage-crisis films and TV programmes, underwent a lot of development. Initially entitled, in an unfortunate cliché, 'The Enemy Within', it was to have been set on a shuttlecraft (as was the original series' take on this subgenre, 'Baltar's Escape'), and the hostages were to have been Billy, Ellen, Jammer and *Pegasus* deck chief Laird. Moore says in the podcast that he tried yet again to work in a scene of Tigh pulling a gun on Adama – something he had been attempting to do since 'Tigh Me Up, Tigh Me Down'. Originally Tigh was to have challenged Adama over Ellen's life being in danger, but it was rightly decided that this went against Tigh's characterisation. An implication that Lee's relationship with Dualla has been going on for some time was cut, and the story works better with the suggestion that they are just beginning to see each other in that light. Although the idea of Lee being shot was included at an early stage, that of Starbuck being responsible was added later. There was also to have been a scene implying that Starbuck was having casual sex with men in order to forget Anders, but this was fortunately written out as contradicting her development in 'Scar', in which she comes to the conclusion that her love for Anders is what gives her something to live for.

One crucial driver behind the episode was the need to write Billy out satisfactorily. Paul Campbell has gone on record as saying that he was removed from the series due to a dispute stemming from his temporary departure earlier; when he returned, his other prospect having not worked out, he was asked to sign a five-year contract with *Battlestar Galactica*, and when he refused, his character was killed off. Moore offers a more positive account in his podcast, saying that Campbell is an excellent leading actor who was being offered roles on other series, and that they were 'holding him on the show in … a supporting role', essentially implying that he was concerned Campbell would leave the series for good on his own initiative. Moore adds that the decision to kill off the character came because they could not see any other plausible way of writing Billy out of the story. He has also said that had Billy stayed, subsequent stories would have had Laura grooming him for a position of authority, but has been rather vague as to what this role would have been, suggesting that this was not seriously considered by the writing team.

In production terms, Kandyse McClure, out of uniform and wearing an evening dress, looks rather like a young Diana Ross. This is the second story in a row not to feature Baltar or Head Six (although both will figure heavily in the season's final three episodes). Some shots of the Marines that appear in this story were recycled from 'Bastille Day', and Olmos's 'Cut the wire' line (meaning to cut communications dead, so that the terrorists can't ring up and try to reopen negotiations) was improvised. Dana Delaney, who plays Sesha, was an old colleague of Eick's and another of those originally up for the part of Ellen.

As with 'Black Market', Moore has criticised this episode in his podcast, and as before he pins the blame largely on the director (who, again, never worked on the series subsequently). However, Moore actually seems most concerned with script issues, complaining that Sesha's motivations aren't properly explored, and that not enough time is given to the emotional implications of the fact that all three of the top people in the Fleet – Roslin, Adama and Tigh – have someone close to them among the hostages.

The story was originally to have opened with the scene of Sesha's husband's death, but it was felt that beginning with the demise of a character never seen before would not provide enough of an emotional connection, so it was instead decided to show it only in flashbacks. However, this is less than successful in execution as, since Sesha was not present at the time, the impression given is that she is imagining it over and over again. There is a lack of continuity between the text on Sesha's computer screen and the words she speaks in the opening shot, in that some of the words she speaks as she types are already clearly visible on the screen, suggesting either that she is capable of typing one thing and saying another, or else that she is unhinged and typing the same lines repeatedly. Starbuck's environmental engineer hat disappears between her getting the handguns out of the case and her turning around and opening fire. Being shot twice in the face at point-blank range should do considerably more damage to Boomer's corpse than a couple of neat bullet holes.

'Sacrifice' has much to recommend it, exploring the development of rumours and conspiracy theories and providing us finally with a set of civilian antagonists with convincing motivations. Its main problems are that it lacks tension, and that the resolution to the hostage crisis is obvious and contrived.

28: The Captain's Hand

FIRST TRANSMISSION DATE: 17 February 2006

WRITER: Jeff Vlaming

DIRECTOR: Sergio Mimica-Gezzan

CREDITED CAST: Richard Hatch (Tom Zarek); Donnelly Rhodes (Doctor Cottle); John Heard (Commander Barry Garner); Christian Tessier (Tucker 'Duck' Clellan); Stephanie von Pfetten (Captain Marcia 'Showboat' Case); Kavan Smith (Lieutenant Richard 'Buster' Bayer); Amber Rothwell (Rya Kibby); Patricia Idlette (Sarah Porter); Rekha Sharma (Tory Foster); Brad Dryborough (Hoshi); Aaron Pearl (Ensign Abel Thornton); Christina Schild (Playa); Tammy Hui (ECO Lyla 'Shark' Ellway); James Bell (Lieutenant Steve 'Red Devil' Fleer); Kimani Ray Smith (Pegasus Sergeant); Kurt Max Runte (Ensign Charles Bellamy)

SYNOPSIS: Apollo, recently promoted to Major, is assigned to the *Pegasus*. He arrives to find Starbuck at odds with the vessel's current commander, Garner, who is a former engineer and resents the status given to the pilots. Two Raptors go missing; when a possible distress signal from one is picked up, Garner orders the *Pegasus* to jump to its location, even though Apollo and Starbuck are concerned that it may be a Cylon trap. The *Pegasus* is attacked by three Cylon basestars and her FTL drive rendered inoperative. Garner hands command over to Apollo and repairs the FTL drive, at the cost of his own life. Adama promotes Apollo to Commander and gives him permanent charge of the *Pegasus*, and Starbuck is reassigned as *Galactica*'s CAG. On the Fleet, Zarek encourages Baltar to stand for President in the upcoming elections, and it emerges that Cottle has been performing clandestine terminations for Gemonese girls, the Gemonese religious faction being against abortion. To maintain the support of the Gemonese and to increase population levels, Roslin is forced to support anti-abortion legislation, and Baltar uses this as political ammunition when he announces his candidacy.

ANALYSIS: 'The Captain's Hand', which as Moore notes is something of a cross between a standalone and a continuing episode, focuses on the problems created when people are promoted outside of their sphere of competence, and sets up a moral debate about personal freedom in the Fleet.

Office Politics: Lee on the Pegasus

The story of Garner is one familiar to anyone who has had experience with workplace bullying and/or with bosses promoted outside of their area of expertise. Garner is clearly more comfortable as an engineer than as a commander. Adama backs him despite Tigh's misgivings (in shades of his promotion of Birch in 'Home'), presumably because he feels that *Pegasus* should not be commanded by a newcomer from *Galactica*. However, this discourse is changing: although Garner's motivation may be partly down to the *Pegasus* losing its flagship position to the *Galactica*, and although Garner twice successfully pulls the '*Pegasus* crew only' card (once ordering the pilots not to pass on information to Starbuck, later ordering the Marine sergeant to arrest Apollo, saying he isn't one of their own), at least one of his Viper pilots exclaims 'frakkin' Garner', Starbuck seems to have her fans, and, according to her, Stinger/Taylor, *Pegasus*'s former CAG, is in the brig for insubordination. In putting Garner into a command to which he is not suited, and ignoring the changes in mood on the warships, Adama is probably the person most responsible for the tragedies that follow.

Garner, as a leader, is controlling and insecure. He maintains a spy among the pilots to report on Starbuck, and after he has ordered the pilots not to keep her informed, he then berates her for not knowing about the missing Raptors. He initially tries to build up an alliance with Apollo against her, pointedly saying 'You with me, Major?' on his first meeting with him, but then, when Apollo questions him, he turns against him as well. He rejects Adama's reasonable suggestion that they send a recon team to investigate the distress signal rather than jump the *Pegasus* straight away, in favour of emotional grandstanding to the crew, saying 'I'm bringing my pilots home!' as he disobeys the Admiral's orders. He is clearly not an inherently bad person, but (as Apollo notes) he thinks too mechanically; he clashes with the pilots over the differences between the engineers' disciplined, orderly culture and their more insubordinate and informal one; and he has visible envy issues, complaining (and not without justification) that the engineers' role is unappreciated and uncelebrated. If he were not in command of a battlestar, none of this necessarily would be a problem. His handling of the loss of the FTL drive suggests parallels with Tigh, in that both are good men in specific circumstances, but go to pieces outside of these. Apollo gives Garner a lot of credit in his final report, but as he admits in private that he does not think the man was a good leader, this is presumably for his courage and self-sacrifice rather than for his performance in command.

This episode also continues the fraught situation regarding Starbuck and Apollo. Apollo's failure to realise that Garner really is incompetent stems in part from his having issues of his own with Starbuck following her accidental shooting of him in the previous episode, which makes him disinclined to listen to her. He also admits that he is envious of the way Starbuck seems continually to subvert authority and get away with it, whereas the one time he tried something similar, in 'Home', he nearly lost everything, suggesting that his defence of Garner is in part because he feels himself that Starbuck is overindulged. It is also perhaps this that has finally cemented his relationship with Dualla. Moore notes that Apollo clearly had not expected, or wanted, to be in command, which not only picks up on the original series' championing of the reluctant leader, but also follows Apollo's development over the series: he inclines over Seasons Two and Three toward a more military role in emulation of his father, but also clearly is in two minds about his situation. Crucially, however, this story marks a new development for Apollo in that he is now placed in several situations in which he can no longer take the middle ground: he must choose between Dualla and Starbuck, Starbuck and Garner, and Garner and Adama.

Campaign Debates: Roslin versus Zarek and Baltar

On the political front, this episode marks the first time that human rights are officially restricted for the good of the Fleet (although the civilian conscriptions in 'Epiphanies' suggest that unofficial encroachments have been going on for some time). The abortion issue as presented here has an interesting twist in that it may be necessary for the survival of the species to ban it and, in contrast to the arguable demonisation of abortion in 'Epiphanies', here the dilemma is more fully explored, balancing the issue of species survival against the status of women. Furthermore, Roslin is now finding that her courting of the religious faction earlier in the series (which, as noted, was for political expediency as much as it was faith-driven) has difficult consequences, as the Gemonese delegate, Porter, threatens to withdraw her support if Roslin does not ban abortion. Although Roslin ultimately makes the choice to forbid abortion on practical grounds, namely, that Baltar's demographic projections show that, at the current rate of reproduction, the human race will be extinct in 18 years, Zarek and Baltar are able to exploit her proximity to the religious establishment coupled with her new stance on abortion to position Baltar as a credible opponent to her in the presidential race.

The animosity that has been building up between Roslin and Baltar finally comes to a head in this story. Baltar, perhaps in response to Roslin's insinuations in earlier episodes that he is untrustworthy, here shows his treacherous side, providing her with demographic information that suggests she will have to take an anti-abortion stance, and making a speech that begins in supportive mode, before he reveals that he will stand against her, and on this very issue, knowing full well that she is sacrificing her own principles for the greater good in backing the abortion ban. In campaigning on this issue, also, he is himself sacrificing his principles, as he is ignoring his own statistics that support Roslin's position. Roslin's granting of asylum to Rya, the Gemonese girl, after she has had an abortion, allows her a small victory for her principles, which the Gemonese, since they cannot back the pro-abortion Baltar, have to accept.

BY YOUR COMMAND: VOL 2

Doing the Right Thing: Continuity and Worldbuilding

In continuity terms, we meet Billy's replacement, Tory (whose surname is absent from the 30th September 2005 draft script, then given as 'Forester' in the 5 October draft, but standardised as 'Foster' from 7 October 2005 onwards), about whom we learn very little at this point barring that she was district captain for the Federalist Party in Delphi before the attacks, and is keen on opinion polls. The military, up to and including Adama, have taken to referring to *Pegasus* and *Galactica* as 'The Beast' and 'The Bucket' respectively, in obvious symbolic reference to the former's brutal history and the latter's decrepit condition. The nicknames were dropped after this episode, chiefly because director of photography Steve McNutt remarked to Moore that he didn't like them, and as it was so rare for McNutt to comment on a script, Moore took the complaint seriously. Nonetheless, allusions to the *Galactica* as a 'bucket' do crop up occasionally in subsequent stories. We also learn a couple of military slang terms, 'snipes' for engineers (an actual Navy expression) and 'skosh ammo' for 'out of ammunition'. We find out how sexual arrangements are conducted among pilots, with couples desiring privacy locking the door on the sleeping quarters and shutting the other residents out (according to the podcast, the situation is signalled by leaving one's boots outside the door, although references to this were cut from this episode). Garner's line 'I'm bringing my pilots home' is a deliberate echo of Adama's 'I'm getting my men' in '*Pegasus*', again indicating that the distinction between a benign and a malevolent dictator is a thin one. The revelations about Cottle's secret career as an abortionist carry on the idea from 'Epiphanies', 'Black Market' and 'Sacrifice' that there are many developments going on in the civilian fleet of which the viewer is largely unaware, until they impinge on life on the *Galactica*. Garner was first mentioned, under the name Trammel, in the deleted scene in 'Black Market' where Apollo has words with *Pegasus*'s XO, Renner.

The story has loose antecedents in the original-series episode 'Take the *Celestra*', which also involved a martinet ship commander who ends up facing down mutinous crewmembers, but also more directly, as Moore says, in *The Caine Mutiny*. Moore manages to work in a *Crimson Tide* moment, namely the scene where Apollo and Garner both try to remove each other from command. The title was taken from a famous passage in John Henry Newbolt's poem *Vitae Lampada*: 'It is not for the sake of a ribbon coat, or the selfish hope of a season's fame, but his captain's hand on his shoulder smote, "Play up – play up and play the game"'. This relates much more to writer Jeff Vlaming's original version (described below) than to the final one. The tension between the engineers and the pilots was based on Moore's own observations of similar dynamics on board ship during his Navy ROTC days, as was the idea that the crews would give their ships nicknames. Although, as Moore notes, it is rare to see a character going through with an abortion being presented as a positive decision on an American TV show (citing an instance in the sitcom *Maude* as the only other exception he can think of), *Six Feet Under* had also featured such a storyline.

28: THE CAPTAIN'S HAND

Play the Game: Writing and Development

The story underwent several changes in development. Starbuck was originally to have taken over command of the *Pegasus*; Jamie Bamber, in a 2007 interview, said that he pushed for Lee to be the one to do so instead, wanting to play the dynamic of having father and son in charge of two separate ships. However, Moore has more bluntly said, '[We] were looking for something for Lee to do beyond being the *Galactica*'s CAG'. In Vlaming's original version of the story, Garner was to have been a nice guy but incapable of keeping order, meaning that Lee had to take the hard man role, but this was rejected as unsatisfying. Vlaming, working with the series' writing team, then produced a story based closely on *The Caine Mutiny*, but it was decided that the resemblance to the film was too obvious, so the similarities were played down.

Draft scripts also indicate the way the story subsequently developed. One dated 30 September 2005, for instance, does not have the climax where Trammel (as Garner was known at that point, see below) sacrifices his life fixing the FTL drives, but instead has him standing down when he realises that he has taken the *Pegasus* into a trap, and Apollo taking over. The tragedy element in this draft comes when Duck sacrifices his life by covering the other ships as they make their escape. Duck's presence on the *Pegasus* is explained by the awkward contrivance that he picked up the distress call from the Raptors and Trammel then got him reassigned so that Trammel could 'personally analyse [Duck's] recon tapes'. Freaker, not Buster, was originally the pilot who goes missing (the change to Buster comes in the 7 October draft) and is described by Trammel/Garner as a 'cowboy', in a line that still survives in a deleted scene. Although drafts from 5, 7 and 12 October are much closer to the final version, there are a few differences. Laura, for instance, asks Tory for her views on abortion, and in the 5 and 7 October drafts Tory opines that it is between a woman, her doctor and her gods, but in the 12 October draft replies that her own opinions don't matter, but goes on to say that she is there to help Laura win the election, and that losing the Gemonese vote is too great a risk. Raptor pilot Steve 'Red Devil' Fleer was originally to have been a female character, Geena, and the earliest drafts make it explicit that she is Trammel's spy among the pilots. Present in all drafts is also a line where Trammel/Garner justifies his own impetuous running off to save his pilots by referring to Adama's putting the Fleet at risk to save Kara in 'You Can't Go Home Again'; and in the 5 October draft there is a line where Trammel/Garner says that he had doubts about having Apollo on board, not because he is Adama's son, but because he mutinied against Adama; an interesting character note that is unfortunately gone by the final version.

There are a number of scientific issues with the sequence where Garner opens the valves to restore the FTL drive coolant pressure. In the first place, as the inside of the compartment is losing pressure and the hatch opens outwards, the higher pressure outside should make opening the hatch impossible (as indeed is the case in 'Valley of Darkness', making the error in 'The Captain's

Hand' all the more inexcusable). Also, the air pressure decreases faster as the atmosphere escapes, when in real life the rate would become slower. Moore complains that Roslin's references to 'a woman's right to choose' and to the religious faction taking their 'pound of flesh' are anachronistic, but in relation to everything else that appears in the series, this is a ridiculous argument.

In production terms, the story contains a few good directorial touches. For instance in Zarek's first scene, it initially appears that he is addressing an audience, then that he is talking to himself, before finally the viewer sees that he is speaking with Baltar. In the recap sequence, two scenes are altered through the clever use of additional dialogue recording (ADR), the first sees Gina given an extra line, urging Baltar to run for office, when the camera is focused on Baltar, and the second, which consists of reedited footage of Tigh and Adama on the hangar deck from 'Black Market', uses a similar trick to introduce the fact that Garner is now *Pegasus*'s commander. A reference to this promotion in 'Black Market' had to be removed when it was discovered that Garner's original name, Barry Trammel, was unusable for legal reasons. (The change came in the 12 October draft.) Stinger is present as *Pegasus*'s CAG in the 30 September draft, but was written out because John Pyper-Ferguson was again unavailable for filming. The character quietly disappears sometime after this. The idea of a storyline in which Roslin is forced, against her own convictions, to support anti-abortion legislation for the survival of the species, was suggested as far back as the series bible (which also proposed a scenario in which the use of contraception was restricted to women in certain jobs, for instance pilots).

'The Captain's Hand' plays out a recognisable situation and puts Apollo in a new position, both personally (in his relationships with Dualla and Starbuck) and professionally (in his role as commander of the *Pegasus*). Politically, it also highlights the tensions between ideology and practicality, and sets up the election storyline for the end of the season.

Readers might wish to skip forward at this point to the Season Four telemovie 'Razor', the main storyline of which is set between 'The Captain's Hand' and 'Downloaded'.

29: Downloaded

FIRST TRANSMISSION DATE: 24 February 2006

WRITERS: Bradley Thompson & David Weddle

DIRECTOR: Jeff Woolnough

CREDITED CAST: Lucy Lawless (D'Anna); Donnelly Rhodes (Doctor Cottle); Matthew Bennett (Number Five); Rekha Sharma (Tory Foster); Kerry Norton (Paramedic Layne Ishay); Alisen Down (Jean Barolay); Erica Cerra (Maya); Diego Diablo Del Mar (Hillard)

SYNOPSIS: When Boomer is killed and resurrects on Cylon-Occupied Caprica, she has trouble coming to terms with her Cylon nature. Baltar's ex-lover, now known as 'Caprica-Six', and regarded as a hero among Cylons, is asked by a Three (one of the D'Anna model) to reason with her. Caprica-Six is having visitations from a Head Baltar, and, on his advice, bonds with Boomer over their shared connection with humanity. Head Baltar also warns her that the other Cylons are concerned about her and Boomer's development of individuality and plan to 'box' them (store their consciousnesses rather than permit them to download). The resistance bombs a café where Boomer, Caprica-Six and Three are talking, and the three Cylons are trapped in the rubble with Anders. Caprica-Six, encouraged by Head Baltar, comes to realise that the war against the humans was based on jealousy and vengeance, and thus was wrong. Caprica-Six kills Three before she can shoot Anders, lets Anders go, and, with Boomer, vows to use their celebrity to change the Cylons' system. On *Galactica*, Sharon undergoes an emergency delivery and gives birth to a baby girl, Hera. Concerned for the safety of the Fleet, Roslin arranges to fake Hera's death and give her to a surrogate mother, Maya, who is unaware of the child's true identity.

ANALYSIS: 'Downloaded' is the first story to focus mainly on the Cylons as characters, and to give something of their perspective on events, as well as providing a backstory that will pave the way for the Season Two cliffhanger ending.

I am Not a Number: Cylon Culture

The key interest of the episode is the insights it gives into Cylon culture, which appears to be in the throes of a traumatic transformation. Moore in his podcast says, '[The Cylons are] a young people ... They don't have this massive cultural history to fall back on. They are figuring out who and what they are in many ways for the first time'. This might be observed in the fact that the Cylons appear to be trying to replicate Caprican society in all its banalities, complete with tree-lined avenues and coffee shops, like children playing at being adults. Part of this development, though, is that, as Caprica-Six says, they are a culture based on unity, which is nonetheless developing individuals as their experiences differentiate them. They use 'the Cylon', never 'Cylons', as a collective noun for the species (as Demand Peace did in 'Epiphanies'), suggesting a unified entity. Caprica-Six gradually figures out that by individualising themselves, whether positively, as in her case, or negatively, as in Boomer's case, they are a threat to this equality, and thus must be 'boxed'. As Caprica-Six puts it, 'Our voices count ... more than others'.

The Cylons are also divided over the fate of the humans. Caprica-Six points out that the Cylons hold 'jealousy, murder [and] vengeance' to be sins, and that part of their reason for wanting to box Boomer and Caprica-Six is that they might cast doubt on the rightness of their attack on the humans. This echoes the way in which, over Season Two, Sharon's presence on *Galactica* has challenged the humans' perceptions of Cylons. The recap sequence makes an explicit visual parallel between Boomer's shooting of Adama and Cally's shooting of Boomer, and Three's remark 'Humans don't respect life the way we do' echoes similar remarks made about Cylons by humans elsewhere. Boomer's situation, believing herself to be a human because she has the memories of one, raises the question of what it is to be human, and Moore suggests that Caprica-Six's refusal of Three's offer of killing her so as to spare her the pain of her injury suggests she is becoming more human, focusing on the life she has rather than on a multiple existence through downloading (though she would also be putting herself at risk of boxing were she to resurrect). More generally, the fact that the Cylons can resurrect means that they see the death of an individual body as not much of an issue. Nonetheless, Cylon rebirthing is shown to be painful and traumatic, and the resistance have clearly picked up on this somehow, blowing up Cylons in order to demoralise and disorientate them through repeated resurrection.

Love Conquers All: Uniting the Humans and the Cylons

An addition to the series' canon is a new Head character, Head Baltar, a concept that Toni Graphia had apparently been keen on employing for some time. The music that accompanies him is the Head Six theme played backwards, and like Head Six, he advises, provides insights and even sometimes suggests dialogue for Caprica-Six to speak. Moore implies that he reflects Caprica-Six's idealised version of Baltar, seen through the eyes of love; however, this seems strange as he is smooth and sophisticated where the real version is plagued by doubts and confusion (much like Caprica-Six here), and there is no evidence that Caprica-Six saw him as some kind of lounge-lizard. The presence of a Head Baltar, following Caprica-Six, if anything cements the idea that the Head People are messengers of some form of higher being. Like Head Six, Head Baltar has a clear agenda of bringing the humans and Cylons together, pursuing a pro-human line where Head Six follows a pro-Cylon line. He also gets some great 'business', for instance offering a cocktail to Caprica-Six, who, in her confusion, nearly takes it.

The major theme of Caprica-Six's story is of love transcending and uniting the warring factions. Moore notes in his podcast that although Caprica-Six still manifests the negative traits of her model, for instance her manipulation of Boomer, Head Baltar acts as her conscience, and her love for Baltar and faith in God ultimately cause her to question Cylon orthodoxy. Her discovery, during her conversation with Boomer, that Baltar is alive, and that she has not been told, confirms to Caprica-Six that she is right to stop obeying orders and start thinking more critically. It is made clear in this episode that Caprica-Six, in the miniseries, shielded Baltar from the flying blast debris with her body. Thompson, in *The Official Companion Season Two*, says of Caprica-Six and Boomer, 'It occurred to us that their experiences of love had probably messed up their chances for seamless integration into Cylon society'.

The B plot, meanwhile, elaborates on the theme of Cylon-human relations. Although Adama may be growing closer to Sharon, he is still suspicious of Cylons generally; his concerns about the baby are that 'Cylons went through a great deal of trouble to create this thing. Should go without saying that if it's good for them, it's gonna be bad for us'. Where Tigh says of Sharon's baby '[It] is not a baby, it's a machine', Baltar replies, 'It's half machine, half human', illustrating the conflict the existence of a hybrid child could produce in human society. Head Six berates Baltar at the end of the story for allowing the humans to kill the baby, implying that God is not omniscient. The story of Hera seems to have parallels to the Biblical tale of Moses, as Moore mentions in his podcast; however, it has closer parallels to the Greek story of Zeus, whose mother, afraid that his father would kill him, had him secretly fostered while letting his father think he was dead. 'Maya', perhaps significantly, is a Sanskrit word roughly meaning 'illusion'. Roslin and Tory tell Maya that the baby's mother was a *Pegasus* officer who 'must remain anonymous for political and religious reasons', which is close to the truth.

Cappuccinos on Caprica: Continuity, Problems and Worldbuilding

In continuity terms, Boomer's flat is built to the same plan as Starbuck's (which suggests the production team were using the same flat, redressed). Aspects of human culture that the Cylons find worthy of adopting include cafés, and what appear to be cappuccinos, implying that they have misinterpreted Leoben's words and believe Starbucks, not Starbuck, to have a special destiny. The fact that Boomer does not recognise Anders suggests that she is not a sports fan, although the way Caprica-Sharon identifies herself to Anders in 'Precipice' may imply that she is a fan of the C-Bucs' rivals the Picon Panthers. The carved wooden elephants collected by Boomer are said by Caprica-Six to be 'Ithacan'; although just a character touch here, they will take on a more sinister significance in 'The Plan'. Caprica-Six is said to have moved to Caprica two years before the attack, which tallies with the date she gives for the start of her relationship with Baltar in the miniseries, the statement in the series bible that their relationship lasted for 'almost two years' and the point at which Sharon joined the *Galactica* according to Adama in 'The Farm'. Doral is revealed to be Number Five, Sharon, Number Eight and D'Anna, Number Three. The existence of the hybrid child appears not to be common knowledge among the Cylons; if it was, this would of course be another challenge to the dominant orthodoxy.

This story also raises the question of how it is that Boomer, a sleeper agent who has been shown to maintain a separation between her human persona and her Cylon self, has resurrected in such an emotionally disturbed state. One explanation is that she resurrected with her human personality, rather than her Cylon one, dominant; another is that the personalities have merged during the downloading process. A third possibility, that her Cylon side was being affected by the actions of the human side, will be brought up in 'The Plan'. Although this is never openly stated, it seems that the reason why Boomer was made a sleeper agent, where Caprica-Six, Sharon, Leoben and the Dorals were not, was that she had to live and work among the humans continuously, which meant that she was in greater danger than the others of blowing her cover and/or 'going native', particularly given Head Six's remark in 'Kobol's Last Gleaming' that her model is 'weak'.

One mystery in this story is where Cottle manages to find a dead baby of a suitable age and type to substitute for Sharon's, as it is also established that the Fleet, for obvious reasons, do not normally keep corpses in long-term storage, preferring cremation except in the case of known Cylons. Another is why we see only six Cylon models on Caprica. Caprica should also, at this point, be in the grip of a nuclear winter, rather than sunny and bright with Centurions planting visibly healthy trees, although one can excuse the fact that none of the Cylons are affected in that it has been established that they are susceptible only to certain types of radiation. In a slight continuity error, the framed photo that Boomer throws against the wall is a still from the episode 'Water', raising the question of how it is she has a photograph dating from after the Fall of the Colonies. Caprica-Six, Boomer and Anders being trapped together in the explosion is altogether too much of a coincidence to be remotely credible. The fact that only one Cylon has a Head Person indicates that they are not, in fact, being collectively guided by God.

Rick Worthy (Simon) and Callum Keith Rennie (Leoben) do not appear in the episode; body doubles are used to suggest a few Simons and Leobens in the background in some scenes. Moore has said although the possibility of using Worthy was considered, it was felt it would be a waste of time to engage either actor simply to appear in the background. However, no explanation has so far been given as to why Leoben is not identified in the montage of known Cylons in this episode's recap.

The original plan was to make episode 18 a clip show, as a budgetary measure, but this was abandoned when the splitting of 'Resurrection Ship' into two parts provided the necessary savings. In terms of outside references, the expression 'skinjobs', a conscious reference to *Blade Runner* by writers Weddle and Thompson, appears for the first time here (as does the phrase 'bullet heads' for Centurions, apparently contributed by Gary Hutzel). Boomer has family photos, in an allusion to the way *Blade Runner*'s replicants maintained false pasts, clinging on to them even after learning they were not human. Sharon's wooden elephants may be an allusion to *The Deer Hunter*, in which an actively suicidal character who has gone AWOL in Vietnam becomes obsessed with sending carved wooden elephants to a friend at home, providing a lifeline by which he is eventually found. Moore also explicitly contrasts the Cylons with *Star Trek*'s Borg, pointing out that although all the models have collective personality traits, they are shaped by individual experiences.

Losing 'The Raid': Writing and Production

Although it had been planned to do a Cylon point-of-view story from an early stage, 'Downloaded' had its genesis in a very different episode, 'The Raid'. This was scripted by Carla Robinson and worked on by various different writers before being given up, and was, according to Moore's podcast, to have been based on the BBC/HBO telemovie *Conspiracy* (2001), about the Wannsee Conference at which the Nazis decided upon their Final Solution. The *Battlestar Galactica* version would have involved the Cylons meeting on a space station, and the humans, who were infiltrating the station in an effort to raid its archives to find out what the Cylons knew about Earth, discovering their conference. Caprica-Six, present at the meeting, would have found the human infiltrators, but then allowed them to return to the Fleet with more concrete information about Earth. Moore states that his problem with the story was that, as the Cylons had already attempted genocide against the humans, a Wannsee Conference scenario is redundant; while it might have worked with the idea from the series bible that the Cylons were keeping the humans alive in the hope that they would lead them to Earth (in a scenario where a faction of Cylons wants to abandon this idea, making the Fleet's presence redundant), he does not appear to have considered this. Also, although he does not say this, one would expect to see all 12 Cylon models at such a meeting. The implication in the Wannsee Conference scenario that the Cylons would be abandoning God's commandment to procreate using humans, as outlined in 'The Farm', does, nevertheless, inform the Cylons' actions in 'Lay Down Your Burdens'.

However, by the time of the 20 July 2005 meeting, the bare bones of 'Downloaded' had emerged as a prequel to 'The Raid', the idea being that this episode – the seventeenth in the season's running order – would have introduced the Cylons' plans to construct a society in emulation of, but improving on, the humans'; established the alienation of Boomer and Caprica-Six from that society; and introduced Head Baltar (who some writers present at the meeting clearly regarded at this stage as a figment of the imagination rather than a divine messenger, explaining the confusion on this point that pervades

Season Two). 'The Raid' – the eighteenth episode – would then have seen Boomer and Caprica-Six pushing their agenda for peaceful coexistence at the conference. However, once the conference story was abandoned, the prequel took on greater significance as a pivotal episode. Later on, it was also decided to put Hera's birth into this story in order to subvert audience expectations that this would take place in the season finale.

In and of itself, 'Downloaded' also lost a major subplot, which would have featured D'Anna and Gina trying to kidnap Hera, encouraged by Baltar, who fears for the child's safety. D'Anna would have planned to gain access to the child as a journalistic exclusive, persuading Roslin that by filming the baby, she can show the Fleet that it is harmless, while really intending to smuggle it out in an incubator disguised in a photographic equipment case. However, she would have been thwarted by the news that Hera is dead. Gina would have suggested renaming the child 'Thirteen', not liking the idea of her having the name of a human god. This subplot was cut, partly for time reasons and partly because the team felt that switching between the different models on Caprica and in the Fleet was confusing, but survives as deleted scenes.[54]

Another sequence that was abandoned, this time for cost reasons, would have had Caprica-Six physically returning to the ruins of Baltar's house. The scene of Helo and Tyrol scattering what they believe to be Hera's ashes originally had dialogue, which according to Moore's podcast had Helo thanking Tyrol for attending and Tyrol replying that it was the least he could do, but it was decided that silence would be more affecting.

The poem Head Baltar recites when Caprica-Six, Three, Anders and Boomer are trapped in the ruins, running in part, 'Believe the lies, ignore the truth, listen to me, I will show you the proof', was part of a verse originally written for Apollo's hallucination in 'Resurrection Ship', where he would have seen various characters stood in the water reciting it (which would doubtless have been quite a spectacle). It was removed by Eick from the earlier episode as contributing nothing, and here any emotional impact it might have had is ruined by the fact that it is a terrible piece of doggerel.

In production terms, CGI effects are well used to give Cylon-Occupied Caprica a surreal tone, so that Lucy Lawless can pass herself in the street, Matthew Bennett can serve himself a drink and so forth. European cars, from different eras but with a similar slender shape, are used to give a sense of strangeness to the Caprican vehicles left abandoned in the carpark, an idea Moore says was lifted from *Gattaca* (1997) as a midpoint between using recognisable cars and designing expensive and obvious 'space cars' for the series. A few personal touches are given to the cars, for instance in the form of a vanity plate reading 'SEXYMOM', and of a sticker with the legend 'C-Bucs Rule'. Anders's use of a cigarette as a trigger for a bomb was taken by the writers from a real-life explosives handbook. The baby was a puppet created by the special

---

54 SPOILER SECTION: It may also inform Boomer's later plan to smuggle Hera off the Fleet in an equipment container in 'Someone To Watch Over Me'.

effects department. Despite the numerous problems described above, the episode was nominated for a 2006 Hugo Award for Best Dramatic Presentation, Short-Form.

'Downloaded' focuses on the Cylon perspective, showing them as a society that is changing and becoming divided as a result of its contacts, positive and negative, with humans. Although it has its weaknesses, it is a valiant attempt to address some of the dangling plot threads that go back as far as the miniseries.

BY YOUR COMMAND: VOL 2

30: Lay Down Your Burdens (Parts One and Two)

FIRST TRANSMISSION DATE: 3 March 2006 and 10 March 2006

WRITERS: Ronald D Moore and Anne Cofell Saunders & Mark Verheiden

DIRECTOR: Michael Rymer

CREDITED CAST: Richard Hatch (Zarek); Callum Keith Rennie (Leoben); Kate Vernon (Ellen Tigh); Donnelly Rhodes (Doctor Cottle); Matthew Bennett (Doral); Rekha Sharma (Tory Foster); Dean Stockwell (Cavil); Alisen Down (Jean Barolay); Leah Cairns (Lieutenant Margaret 'Racetrack' Edmonds [sic]); David Kaye (James McManus); Colin Lawrence (Hamish 'Skulls' McCall); Erica Cerra (Maya); Winston Rekert (Priest)

SYNOPSIS: Tyrol has nightmares about suicide, and when Cally, finding him asleep on the hangar deck floor, wakes him, he breaks her jaw. Disturbed by his behaviour, he seeks counselling from a priest, Brother Cavil. Starbuck finally conducts her mission to rescue the resistance members on Caprica, using a captured Heavy Raider navigational system that, with Sharon's help, the humans have figured out how to operate. The election campaigning gets under way, with Roslin in the lead. Racetrack and Skulls, accidentally jumping to the wrong place during the mission to Caprica, discover a habitable planet, which, due to interference from a nearby nebula, is undetectable on DRADIS. Baltar, advised by Zarek and Head Six, makes settling on the planet, dubbed 'New Caprica', a central plank of his campaign, and gains popular support. On Caprica, Starbuck's party find the resistance but are pinned down by Cylon fire until the Cylons mysteriously depart. The rescue party return to the Fleet. When a second Brother Cavil is discovered among their number, both priests are arrested as Cylons. Questioned, Caprica-Cavil reveals that the Cylons have decided to stop persecuting the humans and plan to find their own destiny. Baltar wins the election, despite a last-minute attempt by Tory, Dualla and Tigh at vote-rigging. After sleeping with Baltar, Gina triggers the nuclear warhead, destroying *Cloud 9* and a number of ships in its vicinity. One year later, most of the Fleet are scraping a miserable existence on New Caprica, with a skeleton military presence above the planet, when Cylon basestars jump into the area, having located them through detecting the radiation signature from the nuclear explosion. Adama orders the spaceships remaining in orbit to jump to safety, and the Cylons occupy the planet.

30: LAY DOWN YOUR BURDENS

ANALYSIS: 'Lay Down Your Burdens' is one of the series' most memorable season-enders, taking the controversial move of, first, having the Fleet settle somewhere other than Earth, and, secondly, moving the story on by a year so that the tale of this settlement largely remains untold. However, its real strength lies in its exploration of the complex ethics of the democratic process.

Fraud at Polls: The Colonial Elections

The driving focus of this story is the Colonial elections. Despite the controversy regarding her religious leanings, it seems that the public generally prefer Roslin to Baltar when there is no New Caprica to complicate the issue. Baltar, at the start, is intelligent enough to realise that attacking Roslin on the religious front could make him come over as an unbeliever baiting a person of genuine faith, and he seems to be courting the dissatisfied elements in the Fleet, with slogans like 'Peace is ours to make' suggesting he is aiming at the Demand Peace sympathisers. He also shows his talent for spin, accusing Roslin of building a campaign on fear and interrupting her during the debate so that he gets the last word.

The election storyline again highlights the theme of political hypocrisy that runs through the series, indicated at the outset of the story when Roslin and Baltar, before the election, trade insults while smiling winningly at each other. Baltar personally regards the idea of settling on New Caprica to be a bad one, as only 20% of the planet is habitable and life there will be hard, but he is the type to ignore long-term problems in the hope of short-term victory. He is angry about Roslin's success not because he genuinely believes he is the better option for the Fleet, but because, as he states himself, 'I don't like to lose'.

Zarek's motivations seem more complicated. Although he urges Baltar to use New Caprica to court public loyalty, correctly reading the mood of the electorate to be in favour of settling, it is unlikely he is thinking solely of short-term gain. It is probable he is planning a long-term strategy of unseating Roslin through Baltar, waiting until the miseries of life on New Caprica have turned the public against the latter, then unseating Baltar and taking over himself. Roslin also comes across as a hypocrite. She tells Tory that she will not lie to win an election, but nevertheless makes it clear to her that she will tolerate winning an election through deceit, so long as she herself doesn't know specifically what is being done. When she attempts to reason with Baltar and get him to put off the question about settlement till after the election, she says 'I know we've had our disagreements, but this issue transcends personal disagreement as well as politics. I am appealing here to your sense of patriotism'. This so clearly recalls the letter she wrote for him in 'Epiphanies' that it is no surprise that he refuses to cooperate. Ironically, though, when she accuses him, based on her confused vision in 'Epiphanies', of having been in the Riverwalk section of Caprica City with Six just prior to the attack, and he denies it, he is telling the truth, as he was in fact at home with the Cylon in question.

The electoral fraud issue raises a difficult moral question. Although the audience, given the way the episode presents the situation, is going to see Roslin as the better political choice and settling on New Caprica as a solution that cannot last, the only way her victory could be achieved is by her supporters interfering criminally with the people's choice. The fact that Dualla as well as Tigh is involved, in keeping with her actions in conniving with Apollo to break his parole in 'Resistance', is also going to encourage the audience to condone such behaviour. However, Adama intervenes, with the message that even if we see the public's choice as wrong, we still have to live by it. Moore, in a quote on the John Laroque archive, is eloquent about the role of democracy in the Fleet:

> 'Who is Adama to take god-like control of the human race? Who appointed him to that position? And what makes him qualified to make those decisions? Consider the example of Admiral Cain – she arrogated those kind [sic] of powers to herself and look at what happened. If they put themselves in the hands of the military and live under martial law, there's no check or balance in that system, no mechanism to rein in the officer who decides to go off the reservation and consider themselves above the law'.

The other side of democracy is, however, laid starkly bare in this episode: that politicians seeking election appeal to emotion, a more powerful motivator than reason or logic, meaning that, as here, the people can make terrible choices that they then have to live with for years. As Tory says: 'They don't want to hear the truth. They're tired, exhausted. The idea of stopping, laying down their burdens and starting a new life right now is what is resonating with the voters'.

Although Moore says in the podcast that he based the election storyline on a documentary he had seen on Lyndon B Johnson, which referred to allegations of vote-rigging during his first campaign for the Senate, it also has resonance with accusations of electoral corruption in the 2000 and 2004 American Presidential elections. The chalk used to tally the votes is blue for Baltar and red for Roslin, suggesting the two main American parties. This would further imply that Roslin is a Republican, which is not surprising given that she has connections to the religious faction, and that it was the Republican Party that was accused of election fraud in 2000 and 2004. Moore in the podcast likens Baltar to Bill Clinton in terms of his relaxed charisma in the debates. However, he also likens Baltar's focusing of his campaign on people's hopes and dreams to the approach taken by Ronald Reagan, and implicitly likens Roslin to George W Bush, who, Moore says, instead employed fear. Baltar later paraphrases Bush's line, quoted by Roslin in 'Epiphanies', in saying 'I don't have to listen to you, I'm the President'. The message of the story transcends a simple allegory of American politics, in that both candidates have aspects of well-known Democrat and Republican presidents about them.

Cavil and Complain: Tyrol and His Priest

In parallel to the Fleet losing its reason over the election, Tyrol is being driven insane by a repeated dream of flinging himself off the hangar deck walkway in a cruciform pose (another iteration of this now-familiar motif, which seems to be randomly dropped in throughout the series without much consideration for whether or not it makes any thematic sense at all). Cavil says that these nightmares could be due to his fear that he is a Cylon sleeper agent, and that he desires suicide. Tyrol beating up Cally also recalls his fight with Helo in 'Flight of the Phoenix', suggesting that his violent act is at least partly motivated by his anger over Sharon's death. Tyrol's choice of faith-based counselling rather than psychotherapy is due to his religious background, and Cavil initially comes across as a liberal priest, challenging the notions of prayer and predestination and telling Tyrol, 'The problem is, you're screwed up, heart and mind. You. Not the gods or fate or the universe. You'. Rewatching his early scenes with Tyrol knowing Cavil is a Cylon makes for a curious disconnection,[55] as his agnosticism is at odds with the religious leanings of the other Cylons. He is also clearly not a sleeper agent, responding to the sight of his double with an unsurprised, 'Oh. Well then', meaning that he is articulating his own philosophy rather than adopting a persona. This episode establishes that the Cavils are, uniquely among Cylons, atheists, and that they have a twisted sense of irony.

The unmasking of *Galactica*-Cavil as a Cylon also undermines the Colonials' growing trust in Sharon. Despite the loss of her baby in the previous story, and despite the palpable hostility toward her in the briefing-room scene, the Colonials go so far as to allow Sharon a weapon once they reach Caprica, and her dialogue indicates that she has, presumably because of her love for Helo, thrown her lot in with the humans. (In the 14 October 2005 draft of the script, she has an additional line to the effect that, as she has betrayed the Cylons, they will box her.) However, the fact that she didn't tell anyone that Cavil was a Cylon destroys Adama's trust in her; although she tells Helo she doesn't know why she didn't identify Cavil, she then refers to the baby's death, which may suggest a suppressed anger toward the humans.[56]

Caprica-Cavil's message follows on from the situation at the end of 'Downloaded', revealing that *Galactica*-Eight – aka Boomer – and Caprica-Six have used their celebrity status successfully to argue their case, leading the Cylons to vote to leave the Colonies and go their separate ways from humans. He argues (for the first, but certainly not the last, time) that the Cylons' emulation of humanity was a bad thing: 'People should be true to who and what they are. We're machines. We should be true to that. Be the best machines the universe has ever

---

55 SPOILER SECTION: It is also interesting to rewatch them in light of revelations about Tyrol in 'Crossroads' part two, and about Cavil's relationship with the Final Five in 'No Exit'.
56 SPOILER SECTION: It will be indicated in 'The Plan' that Cavil programmed her specifically not to identify him. However, in the 24 October 2005 draft of 'Lay Down Your Burdens' part two, it is stated, '[Cavil] catches Sharon's eye, and she quickly looks away, not willing to acknowledge him or give him away', making it plain that the original intention was for Sharon to be acting deliberately of her own free will.

seen. But we got it into our heads that we were the children of humanity. So instead of pursuing our own destiny of trying to find our own path to enlightenment, we hijacked yours'. While this should seem like a positive development for the humans, it also clearly goes against the divine plan continually articulated by the Head People, and Cavil's 'We're not like you, we can admit our mistakes and we're not afraid of change', suggests an element of xenophobia on his part still.

Head Six, for her part, ironically urges Baltar to attack Roslin through her faith, telling him to listen to Zarek's suggestion that he 'keep hitting her on the religious thing'. When Baltar points out the apparent flaw in her prophecies by referring to 'the baby ... I was destined to protect', Head Six accuses him of blasphemy and smashes his head into the table, suggesting again that God is not omniscient, and also that God is prone to angry rages. The writing team's attempts to rationalise Head Six's contradictory behaviour in the early episodes of Season Two result in God developing a personality: controlling, petty, temperamental, and on the whole not out of keeping with the Ancient Greek pantheon he rejects; however, in line with Zarek's observation in 'Bastille Day' that gods incorporate contradictory principles, this does not mean this is the only aspect to God's personality. The finding of New Caprica by Racetrack and Skulls seems to be an act of God, as it wins Baltar the election; immediately before the Caprica mission gets under way, Baltar's sarcastic reference to 'the hand of God' saving his political fortunes, as Moore notes in his podcast, directly precedes the hand of God coming in and changing things for everyone on the Fleet. Even then, Baltar's victory comes only from the election fraud being spotted due to a chance error on the ballot papers. However, Gina's setting off the bomb, which brings the Cylon Fleet to New Caprica, appears to be an action off her own bat, no doubt motivated by her earlier-established death wish. (This is confirmed by a line in the 24 October 2005 draft script, in which a Doral states, 'We've just picked up a radiation [TECH][57] signature – it's from a nuclear detonation ... [The] signature had been altered – a code was embedded with a message from a Cylon operative. It said "find us"'.) Although it brings the humans and Cylons together before the Cylons can get too far with pursuing their plan to become 'the best machines the universe has ever seen', which would prevent any chance of them breeding with humans, there has also not been enough time for wounds to heal sufficiently for the two species to consider friendly reconciliation.

The Beard of Organised Labour, the Stubble of Treason and the Moustache of Inaction: Continuity and Worldbuilding

While the rescue mission to Caprica is presented as a success, it is actually a particularly stupid move from a military point of view. Right at the outset, 20 percent casualties are predicted, and indeed it is just down to random chance that

---

57 The word '[TECH]' in a draft script is a traditional scriptwriter's annotation to indicate that plausible-sounding technobabble should be inserted at this point.

30: LAY DOWN YOUR BURDENS

they do not incur one hundred percent casualties, including everyone they have come to rescue. The fact that the production team ran out of money and could not build a Heavy Raider set as they had planned, means that instead we have the contrivance of what looks like a piece of raw meat (representing the Cylon navigational system) grafted into Starbuck's Raptor, and Sharon jacking into the computer system using an IV needle. We again get some suggestive pilot names, including 'Headcase' and 'Raw Meat'. It is also a huge coincidence that Tory's election fraud is carried out by substituting forged ballots for the ballots from the *Zephyr*, as this is the one ship in the Fleet on which it could be detected, there having been on the ballots sent to this ship a misprint that was not present on the forged ones.

In continuity terms, Tigh's twitch again shows up when Gaeta tells him he has found evidence of electoral fraud. Going by journalist McManus's remarks before the debate, about a month has passed since Baltar announced his candidacy at the end of 'The Captain's Hand'. Most of this episode's events appear to take place over a fortnight, as Head Six observes at the start of part one that the election is two weeks away. Dualla has a photo of Lee in her locker on *Galactica*, and Gaeta's tiger tattoo is again seen. Gaeta is also here the one who blows the whistle on the electoral fraud. Although he was willing to overlook Dualla's off-log calls in 'Resistance', apparently there are other lines he will not cross, fitting in with his characterisation as an idealist and a man of conviction. The destruction of *Cloud 9* visibly takes out a number of other ships, including a 'Colonial Movers' container ship (evidence from this and other episodes indicates there were originally four such vessels in the Fleet dating back to the miniseries), and what appears to be a Mark IV Wanderer-class planet-hopper from Season Four of the BBC's *Blake's 7*.[58] Subtracting the population number given in 'Crossroads' part one for the Fleet at the beginning of the New Caprica settlement, 44,035, from the population count at the start of 'Lay Down Your Burdens' part two, 49,550, gives us a figure of 5,515 dead in the nuclear explosion. Adama is a Pyramid fan, but follows the Picon Panthers. Roslin, like Billy, was on a debating team as a student; she tells both Baltar and Adama about seeing Baltar with Six on Caprica before the attack. Hera is seen on New Caprica in the same white cradle as in Baltar's visions of her on Kobol, and Adama uses the same cigarette lighter he loaned to Apollo in Season One. Finally, Cottle comes up with a great put-down regarding Cally, saying 'You gotta love a woman who can complain even with her mouth wired shut'.

The theme of love returns and is elaborated upon, when Cavil tells Tyrol that if he doubts his humanity, he should look to the fact that other people love him. We also see that Helo loves Sharon despite her anger at him, indicating that love, again, may bring the humans and Cylons together. Gina's sleeping with Baltar and subsequent suicide also seem to be partly motivated by the complexities of her feelings toward him, and his feelings, or lack thereof, toward her. Although Apollo generously says 'I hope you find him' to Starbuck as she begins her mission to

---

[58] CGI artist Adam 'Mojo' Lebowitz had also worked on *Babylon 5* with Ron Thornton, designer and builder of the vessel in question.

rescue Anders and the resistance, there is an element of childlike nastiness in the way she makes out ostentatiously with Anders in front of him, then mocks his own relationship with Dualla, after she returns.

The leap to a year later establishes new developments in quick fashion. Baltar, having fought an election for the wrong reasons, has become authoritarian and corrupt. Tyrol has married Cally, who is pregnant, and his move to becoming a union leader suggests he has found a natural niche outside of military life. Tigh wants to stay on the *Galactica*, knowing from past experience that he is not good in civilian settings (and a deleted scene explains why he is doing it at all, namely, that he made a deal with his wife that they would spend a year on *Galactica* for him, then go down to the planet as she wishes). When we see Tigh on New Caprica, he seems a confused old man, aged by the loss of his familiar setting. He and Kara have clearly made up their fight at some point in the intervening year (as will be depicted later in 'Unfinished Business'). Roslin seems happier, and saner, as a teacher, while Apollo, despite now being married to Dualla (who has been promoted to lieutenant and is acting as *Pegasus*'s XO), is clearly unhappy on some level, to judge by his extreme weight gain. Moore says in the podcast for 'Unfinished Business' that events in the intervening year (which will be explored in the later episode) damaged Lee's relationship with Kara so badly that, in 'Lay Down Your Burdens', he is actually considering withholding the antibiotics from Anders and letting him die.

The situation of Kara struggling to get antibiotics to treat Anders' pneumonia shows how the Colonials are reverting slowly to the primitive, on the constant verge of dying from easily-treatable illnesses. Despite the harshness of the setting, the symbolism of New Caprican society is of softness and femininity: Kara grows her hair and acts as wife to Anders, Lee becomes fat, Cally is heavily pregnant and Baltar is effete, bestubbled and decadent. Tyrol, the main source of antagonism on New Caprica, has become hypermasculine, sporting a wild beard, while Adama, for some reason, has grown a moustache. In an interesting detail, the 24 October 2005 draft script describes the tonsorial alterations to Tyrol and Adama, but not to Baltar; Lee's weight gain is not scripted, Kara is stated to have short hair and new tattoos on her neck and hands, and Laura is also said to have short hair, but with blonde highlights.

In original-series references, there are distinct similarities to the last third of 'Saga of a Star World', with a corrupt politician encouraging people to settle on a less-than-ideal planet, playing on their desire to stop running, and with a Cylon administration apparently changing to one more favourable to humans (as in the final scene of 'Saga of a Star World' when Baltar meets the new Imperious Leader). 'Lost Planet of the Gods' featured a world shielded from discovery by an instrument-scrambling magnetic void (also referenced in the miniseries' Ragnar Anchorage, where the electromagnetic field of the atmosphere interfered with instrumentation). The reimagined Fleet, according to the election boards, includes a ship called the *Celestra*. More to the point, there was an unfilmed original-series episode entitled 'The Mutiny' that revolved around the Quorum voting to settle the Fleet on the planet Zarta, leaving *Galactica* in orbit with a skeleton crew.

Furthermore, the idea was one used in the Singer/DeSanto revival proposal, which involved the humans, deciding they were safe from Cylons, giving up on Earth and setting up another colony, which they called 'New Caprica', although Moore has asserted that his writing team had no idea of this at the time. This proposal also featured a subplot about an attempt to organise miners into a union. There are further similarities to the *Space: 1999* episode 'Another Time, Another Place', in which the Alphans encounter alternate-universe versions of themselves who have resettled a devastated Earth. Some have noted that the serial has a few things in common with the Season One finale, 'Kobol's Last Gleaming', with both featuring a return to Caprica courtesy of captured Cylon technology, a suicidal crewmember fearing they are a Cylon and attacking someone close to them, and the accidental discovery of a new habitable planet.

In outside references, Roslin's telling Baltar to go frak himself alludes to an incident on 22 June 2004 in the US Senate, when Vice-President Dick Cheney told Senator Patrick Leahy, 'Go fuck yourself'. Hera has been renamed Isis, which is appropriate in that, where Hera was the wife of the chief Greek god, Isis was the wife of the chief Egyptian god. Dualla gets in a Biblical reference by saying that the new planet has 'rivers of milk and honey' when she alludes to the hyperbole circulating on the Fleet about the discovery. Tyrol's 'Throw your body on the gears' speech to the union members is a close paraphrase of Mario Savio's address during the Free Speech Movement at Berkeley in 1964, and Moore and Eick got permission from Savio's widow to use it, stating in the episode credits that the speech appears 'courtesy of' her. The writing team repeatedly liken the occupied New Caprica to Vichy France, with the analogy even being drawn in a stage direction in the 24 October 2005 script regarding the advancing Centurions: '[It's] like ... watching the Nazis march into Paris'.

Interrupted Exodus: Writing and Production

The story is cleverly structured, with the writers first undermining the audience's expectations that Roslin will return to the Presidency and the status quo be restored, and then further undermining it by shifting the action forward a year. The second episode is fully 90 minutes long with adverts, and, while the story was aired in its full length on first US broadcast, a heavily truncated 60-minute version was made for the overseas market.

The decision to jump the story ahead a year was taken because the writers didn't want to spend a season planet-bound and with no Cylons. Originally the time jump was to have happened between seasons; the decision to put it at the end of the Season Two finale was taken because it was considered more exciting, and because Moore felt that television tended to be overconservative in its use of time frames.

The Raptor accidentally jumping into a mountain was a call-back to an idea that had intrigued Moore when working on *Star Trek*, that someone could have a similar accident with a transporter. Eick was the one behind the subplot regarding Tyrol's mental health, believing he should have some issues remaining from the events around Sharon's betrayal and death, while Rymer contributed the idea of Tyrol being afraid he might be a Cylon.

A 14 October 2005 draft of the first episode is quite close to the final version. Significant differences include the story opening with Tyrol in a session with Brother Cavil, and having his beating of Cally shown later in flashback. Tyrol's dreams involve him loading a gun and putting it to his head rather than falling off the walkway. In the sequence where Baltar expresses concerns that attacking Roslin's religion will make him look like an anti-religious apostate, Head Six comes in with '*Her* religion is based on superstition and fear … You have to keep hammering that point', a line that is gone by a set of revisions dated 8 November. Adama, in the earlier draft, authorises Kara to kill Sharon if she steps out of line, and Helo suggests to Sharon that they try for another baby, as if Sharon helps the Colonials find the resistance, she will have proved her loyalties. Starbuck's plan was originally to have involved detonating a nuke in the upper atmosphere of Caprica to blind the Cylon DRADIS, but by 8 November this has changed to the much simpler idea of jumping in below the DRADIS. Head Six at one point tells Baltar that she knows Hera is alive but hidden (Baltar is dubious), suggesting that in this version God, though still clearly not omniscient, at least suspects something about Hera's fate. There is a rather strange line during the talk wireless programme where a commentator says that on the ship *Sappho Star*, people are drawing up plans for making houses out of cargo crates and deck planking – the latter of which would be a strange thing to find as part of a spaceship. Cally also receives a visit in the sickbay from Jammer, who presents her with a gift from the deck crew: a 'lunchbox', in the form of a bucket with a tube attached.

A 24 October 2005 draft of the second episode also contains a few significant differences from the final version. There is, for instance, an early scene where Gina is upset about Baltar's plan to settle New Caprica, on the grounds that the Cylons will never find them there, and Head Six explains that Gina is consumed with a desire for vengeance (and, by implication, wants the Cylons to return to help her wreak that vengeance), calling her 'deranged' and 'damaged beyond repair', echoing a deleted scene from 'Downloaded' where, after Gina professes not to believe in God, Head Six calls her 'damaged beyond redemption'. God, again, wants the humans and Cylons to unite, not one group to destroy the other, whereas Gina evidently wants to visit upon the humans the agony she endured as Cain's prisoner. Baltar then tells Gina that he wants them to have a child together, and Head Six mocks him and laughs. In another significant departure, Adama in the draft script says that Tigh told him beforehand about the election-rigging activities, meaning that, rather than Adama acting as Roslin's conscience over the election fraud, we have the two, both culpable, deciding whether or not to continue with the deception. In the scene with the two Cavils, Caprica-Cavil states that the Cylons are planning to go to Earth, and advises the humans to stay away from there; Roslin, angered, says she will lead the humans to Earth, and orders the two Cylons airlocked. A scene close to the end of the story has the Cylons on the basestar discovering the nuclear signature from the explosion; they are said to be in a boardroom that is 'more like an arboretum … filled with PLANTS and FOUNTAINS. Chairs surround a mahogany table, where CAPRICA-SIX, SHARON/BOOMER and LEOBEN are sitting amid refreshments',

30: LAY DOWN YOUR BURDENS

and it is made clear that the reason it took the Cylons so long to find New Caprica is that they were a light-year away, and so did not detect the radiation signature until a year after the detonation. (In the final version, Doral says they were 'over a light year away', raising the question of why they arrived so soon.) More minor, but still interesting, differences involve a sequence where the rescue party, after the Cylons abruptly give up their attack on them, overfly Caprica and ascertain that there are no Cylons on, or around, the planet at all anymore; this sequence was probably cut at least in part because Anders suggests that they take the opportunity to rescue other resistance groups on the planet, but nobody, at any point, mentions the people trapped on the Farms. The scene where Anders and Kara drink together features Baltar as well as Lee turning up and having an awkward moment; and a dialogue where Tory urges Roslin to change her position on New Caprica and endorse the settlement plan, justifying it by saying that it is too close to the election for charges of 'flip-flopping' to take hold. Roslin, not too surprisingly, refuses.

In production terms, there are some good directorial touches, such as in the Raptor descent onto Caprica, where a piece of flying debris hit the virtual 'camera'; in the nuclear explosion sequence; and in the shots emphasising *Galactica*'s emptiness one year on. Cavil actor Dean Stockwell's relevant former credits include *Blue Velvet* (1986), *Buffalo Soldiers* (2001) and *Quantum Leap* (created by Donald Bellisario, who was heavily involved with the writing and production of original-series *Battlestar Galactica*). Stockwell's character in *Quantum Leap*, who was invisible to everyone but the protagonist, could also be seen as a precursor to the reimagined *Battlestar Galactica*'s Head People. Starbuck's and Anders's wing-shaped wedding tattoos were in part the actors' own idea, albeit with impetus from Moore and design help from the make-up artists. New Caprica was shot on a sand dune near Richmond, BC, and Moore has said that he found the result to be one of the most convincing alien planet settings he had ever seen.

The footage of Gina in the part two recap, where she states that Roslin is up three points in the polls, is a new scene, apparently one cut from the previous episode, and the footage of the pilots listening to the Presidential debate is reused from a scene in 'Final Cut' of them watching D'Anna's documentary. Moore complains in the podcast that Cavil's sudden appearance with the resistance suggests he has come out of nowhere, when in fact the intention was to imply that he had been with the resistance for some time. Roslin's blackboard has the French verbs 'aller', 'être' and 'avoir' written on it, suggesting that French is spoken in the Colonies. Baltar refers to a 'People's Council' as well as a Quorum, but it will later seem that this arrangement exists only on New Caprica, as the Colonials are back to government by Quorum only after 'Exodus'.

The message of 'Lay Down Your Burdens' can be summed up by Winston Churchill's famous epigram, 'It has been said that democracy is the worst form of government except all the others that have been tried'. The story explores the pros and cons of the democratic process, and the consequences of bad electoral decisions, ending with the characters stranded on a desolate planet and under Cylon occupation.

Season Three: 2006-2007

In November 2005, as filming on Season Two neared completion, the Sci-Fi Channel announced that the series had been recommissioned for a third 20-episode season. As before, this was to be split into two ten-episode blocks, with 'The Eye of Jupiter'/'Rapture' planned as the midseason cliffhanger story from an early stage.

All the principal cast and many of the directors returned. When Michael Rymer said that he was unable to handle the premiere as he was working on a pilot for another series, Eick offered him a producer's credit if he would direct seven episodes this season. Lucy Lawless agreed to appear in ten episodes (and wound up doing 11). Key additions to the writing team included Michael Taylor, who had previously contributed scripts to *The Dead Zone* and *Star Trek: Deep Space Nine*, and Jane Espenson, a key writer for a number of Joss Whedon's series, while Toni Graphia departed, later to appear as co-executive producer on *Terminator: The Sarah Connor Chronicles*.

In arc terms, it was decided early on, at an initial planning meeting that Eick and Moore had at Disneyworld (where they had gone, in Eick's words, to 'drink Scotch, ride Space Mountain and then watch *Monday Night Football* at the ESPN Club'), to do more Cylon-focused stories and expand upon their side of the conflict. The Sci-Fi Channel were also anxious that the team should wrap up the New Caprica arc as soon as possible, clearly concerned about losing viewers due to a change in format, and Moore allowed that he felt a planetbound series was 'not *Battlestar Galactica*'. Certainly, the laborious Kobol arc had been one of the less successful aspects of Season Two. Early plans to deal with the missing year on New Caprica by weaving flashbacks through the season were eventually scaled back, leading to a single flashback episode, 'Unfinished Business'. Another arc, in which revelations about the massacre of a community of Sagittarons on New Caprica would have come to light at Baltar's trial, was shelved; the details of this will be discussed in the analysis for 'Crossroads'.

Some ideas from the planning for Season Two were revived, such as an arc set on a Cylon basestar and a race for Earth between humans and Cylons. One notion mentioned in the 20 July 2005 writers' meeting, of having the Cylons want to destroy all of the Sharons because they are tainted by association with humanity, clearly influenced the choice to include a storyline about the boxing of the Threes. It was decided that the humans should find out that D'Anna is a Cylon, but no consideration was ever given to basing a storyline around this; Moore is quoted in *The Official Companion Season Four* as saying, 'Somewhere along the lines she's been found out and everyone now knows she's a Cylon. I thought that was all the viewer needs to know'. A mooted storyline that would have had Helo move into Sharon's cell with her and the pair set up home together was, fortunately, abandoned. An idea that Baltar would suspect himself of being a Cylon was drawn from the series bible, which states: 'Baltar's greatest challenge will be to deal with the idea that perhaps he, too, is actually a Cylon agent'. The structure of the season also changed somewhat in development, with a storyline involving Baltar being placed on trial originally intended to come around episode 13-14, and Michael Angeli suggesting it be moved back to form the season cliffhanger.

It was further decided to have Kara return from the dead at the season's end; Moore acknowledges in *The Official Companion Season Three* that this was a telefantasy cliché, but justifies it on the grounds that it fit with the 'larger mythology of the show', which makes sense taken in the context of the original-series story 'War of the Gods' and the unmade *Galactica 1980* episode 'Wheel of Fire'. Season Three in many ways demonstrates how powerful that 'larger mythology' is, since, as characters such as Starbuck and Apollo move further away from their original-series origins, so other characters come in to fill their niches: Helo, a patient and deeply ethical man with a beloved wife and child, takes the role of the original-series Apollo, whereas with Starbuck becoming more distant and less likeable, Kat takes on the role of the flawed but compassionate pilot.

To facilitate the writing of the Cylon arc, Moore wrote a document informally known as 'Life on the Cylon Baseship' that covered details of Cylon life and culture for cast and crew (although Leoben actor Callum Keith Rennie says that he did not get to see it for quite a long time). Moore has said that he wrote the document in part to help himself understand the lives of the Cylons, and in part because the series' publicist told him that Tricia Helfer and Grace Park were curious about the Cylon backstory. There were justified concerns that revealing too much about the Cylons would destroy the element of mystery; however, Moore argued that the mystery was becoming difficult to sustain, given the length of the series. Eick also argues, in his video diary, that, whereas up until now the series has been highlighting the similarities between humans and Cylons, showing the interior of the baseship, by contrast, would remind the audience of the differences between the two groups.

One of the key developments this season was the introduction of the concept of the Final Five; that is, five Cylon models, out of a total of 12, whose identities are kept hidden and who are never spoken about by the other seven. Moore has said in an interview with Maureen Ryan that this idea came about as a consequence of having Baltar on the basestar, as there had to be a reason why he would not see any of the Cylons whose identities had not been previously revealed. That the Final Five were a relatively late development in the series mythology is attested to by an earlier interview with Moore on Thefandom.com, in which he articulates a quite different concept of the Cylons, saying: 'The Cylons on some level looked at humanity and said "You know what? There's really only 12 of you". If these are the 12, and … if you look at them, they each represent different archetypes of what humanity is'.

It was decided that one of the key moments of Season Three would be the climactic revelation of the identities of four of the Final Five Cylons. The whole writing staff were involved, and, according to Michael Angeli, 'We got together … put a bunch of names on the board and voted'. Most of the characters were allowed in the selection, except Roslin and Adama, as having them turn out to be Cylons would, in Angeli's words, 'corrupt the show'. The criteria for selection were mainly focused on the characters' known backstories, and on the potential for future development offered by having them be a Cylon. However, given the writing team's fondness for subverting expectations, and given that it is horribly contrived that every single one of the Final Five turns out to be already known to the audience, it is perhaps surprising that they do not seem to have considered the option of introducing at least one entirely new character as a Final Five Cylon, who has existed in the Fleet out of sight of the main narrative until becoming aware of his or her nature. Tyrol was chosen because of his religious background, his finding the Temple on the algae planet in 'The Eye of Jupiter', and his unwitting attraction to a Cylon; Anders because of his relationship with Starbuck and his apparently miraculous survival as a leader of two separate resistance movements on Caprica and on New Caprica, some of which is later explained in 'The Plan'; and Tory Foster largely because she was a blank slate. Tigh was a controversial fourth choice (in one of Eick's video blogs[59], Hogan says that a poll on the internet as to the identities of the Final Five put Tigh second from bottom), and Moore admits he was concerned that to make him a Final Five Cylon would take something away from the character, but also says he believed that it would be interesting to explore Tigh's response. The reactions of the actors, when they were told, were fairly predictable: Douglas and Hogan were deeply shocked, while Trucco and Sharma were considerably happier, given that it meant increased roles for them. Douglas, in Eick's video blog, says that Moore spent an hour and a half on the phone convincing him it was the right idea; Hogan, also in the video blog, admits that at the time of filming he was still not comfortable with the revelation.

Filming began on 10 April 2006, again based at Vancouver Film Studios, and again was carried out in two blocks with a brief hiatus between them. Gary Hutzel continued to extend the in-house effects department created in Season Two, opening a *Battlestar Galactica* Visual Effects office in Los Angeles to complement the work of the team based above Stage D in Vancouver. He estimates that between 60 and 70 percent of Season Three's effects were created in-house, with the remaining work being done by Atmosphere.

In design terms, the look of the basestar was redeveloped, with increased detail for close-up shots: Hutzel says in *The Official Companion Season Three*, 'By the end of the season, the surface had moved towards a dolphin-like skin'. Although early designs for the basestar interior focused on blending organic and mechanical elements, as in 'Kobol's Last Gleaming', eventually Richard Hudolin settled on a stark, clean look, in contrast to the 'busy' feel of the *Galactica*, with

---

59 David Eick recorded a number of video blogs for the Sci-Fi Channel's website, which were later released as DVD extras.

water and light as key design elements. In costume terms, the formal uniforms designed for the New Caprica Police were deliberately intended to be reminiscent of Nazi styles (giving them conceptual echoes of the 'Blackshirt' civilian security forces of the original series), while a minor but significant concern was ensuring that the eyepatch Tigh was to acquire did not make him look too piratical. James Callis suggested Baltar should grow his hair and beard while on the basestar as a way of symbolising the changes the character goes through over the season. One of Eick's video blogs details the process involved in putting the 'fat' make-up on Jamie Bamber, revealing that the actor is wearing Grace Park's three-month and seven-month pregnancy bellies under his costume.

In casting terms, Eick spent some time trying to get Laurette Spang, who played Cassiopea in the original series, to return to the new show in a guest role, but this ultimately came to nothing. The initial sequence of the opening titles changes slightly, swapping the lines so that 'They rebelled' now comes before 'They evolved', and with some new images included.

The Sci-Fi Channel opted to premiere the series in October 2006, putting it against first-run network television offerings, with a shorter mid-season break than before; whereas Season Two had a three-month-long hiatus, there were only 35 days between the first transmission of 'The Eye of Jupiter' and that of 'Rapture'. Soon after the start of filming on Season Three, the channel also announced that a spin-off series, *Caprica*, set some time prior to *Battlestar Galactica* and focusing on the creation of the Cylons, was in development.[60]

While remaining supportive, the Sci-Fi Channel's executives did voice concerns about some of Season Three's content, particularly the use of recreational drugs in 'Unfinished Business' and of hallucinogens in the torture sequences of 'Taking a Break From All Your Worries'.

In a first for *Battlestar Galactica*, the new season was trailed by a series of webisodes, and its American debut was preceded by a one-hour recap show, *Battlestar Galactica: The Story So Far*, to bring casual viewers up to speed. On broadcast, the season again garnered awards, including being named as one of the ten outstanding programmes of the year by the American Film Institute for the second year running, and an Emmy for the visual effects team. Olmos also won an ALMA Award, which recognises the achievements of Latinos in television, music and sports. However, the US viewing figures started low and continued to decline, prompting a mid-season change of slot from Friday to Sunday night, which did little to alleviate the problem. Nonetheless, as the series' target audience were a demographic known to focus on DVD, download and Tivo rather than traditional viewing, a fourth, and final, season was commissioned.

---

60 *Caprica* is discussed in more detail in a separate chapter toward the end of this book.

31: The Resistance/Crossroads (Parts One to Ten)

FIRST TRANSMISSION DATE: 5 September 2006 through to 5 October 2006 (USA)

WRITERS: Bradley Thompson & David Weddle

DIRECTOR: Wayne Rose

CAST: Christian Tessier (Tucker 'Duck' Clellan); Dominic Zamprogna (Jammer); Emily Holmes (Nora Farmer); Alisen Down (Jean Barolay); Carmen Moore (Sister Tivenan); Matthew Bennett (Doral)

SYNOPSIS: On New Caprica, Tigh and Tyrol organise a resistance movement against the Cylons. This includes Jammer and Barolay. They try to recruit Duck to their cause, but he is reluctant as he and his wife Nora are trying for a family. Over Jammer's objections, the resistance hide a weapons stash in the temple, as the Cylons have never raided sacred ground. The Cylons attack the temple while Nora and Cally are inside performing a ritual, and Nora is killed. The resistance are pleased with the fact that support for them has risen following the raid, but Jammer is troubled. Jammer is captured by the Cylons, and interrogated by a Doral, who gives him a drink and asks if he will become an informant against the resistance. At the dedication ceremony for Cally and Tyrol's son, Duck tells him that he has joined the New Caprica Police (NCP), in order to try to find out who informed the Cylons that there was a weapons-cache in the temple, while Jammer is seen walking back toward the Cylon detention centre.

ANALYSIS: 'The Resistance', or 'Crossroads' (see below), is a series of ten short web-broadcast episodes adding up to a roughly 30-minute story, focusing on the politics of life under occupation and the choices made by two resistance members, former deckhand Jammer and former Viper pilot Duck.

Secret Army: Life and Resistance on Occupied New Caprica

The story, set 67 days after the end of 'Lay Down Your Burdens', provides several details about New Caprican life and Colonial religion. The human population live in tents, getting water from communal water-butts, and at least one tent has been designated a temple to the Gods (though there are also household shrines). Capricans practice 'dedication', a kind of baptism. (The Tyrols' son Nicholas is dedicated to Ares, god of war, and Apollo, who was both

31: THE RESISTANCE/CROSSROADS

a healer and a warrior, which is rather appropriate under the circumstances.) The Cylons, despite the intentions of Caprica-Six and *Galactica*-Eight at the end of 'Downloaded', are running an increasingly oppressive regime: it is observed that 'Cylons show up to help us, first thing they do is build a jail', and they are imposing curfews and trying to establish a human security force. The recruiting posters read, 'Your family and friends deserve a safe and secure community. You can help by becoming a member ... New Caprica Police: Keeping Our Streets Safe'. Some Cylons appear to be having doubts, however; Tyrol learns about Jammer's arrest from *Galactica*-Eight. Parallels to the occupation of Iraq are clear, although the shouting of the word 'Infidels!' at the encroaching Cylons in the temple scene is a little melodramatic.

The focus of the story is on the resistance group organised by Tigh and Tyrol. While sympathetic to their situation, the webisodes show neither man in a good light: they come across as bullying and cynical, taking advantage of the Cylons' respect for religion even before the weapons-cache incident by using the temple as a clandestine meeting place. Tyrol's hardness may be a reaction to the events of 'Lay Down Your Burdens', as Cally remarks, 'Galen's having his own crisis of faith; finding out Brother Cavil was a Cylon didn't help'. Tigh is clearly resisting not out of idealism but out of hatred for the Cylons, and is willing to do whatever it takes to get people to join, urging Jammer to persuade Duck through 'poetic crap about the struggle for liberty against the Cylon oppressors'. When Jammer voices concerns about the sacrilege of hiding guns in the temple, he says 'You say a prayer. Ask the Gods to forgive us'. At the end of the story, planning to store explosives under the grain storage tent opposite the hospital, Tigh says 'The patients will have to take their chances', indicating how the resistance's 'success' in the temple incident is only encouraging more of the same behaviour. Tigh's remark, 'Those bastards burned up 20 billion of us, you gonna say that's our fault?' also runs exactly contrary to Adama's speech in the miniseries suggesting that humans need to take responsibility for their own part in the conflict. It is, however, this cynicism that finally pushes Jammer over the edge: a key factor in his decision to drop out of the resistance appears to be that Tigh considers the ten dead and 12 wounded in the temple massacre a good bargain, considering that a thousand people have protested about it in front of *Colonial One* and 150 have joined the resistance.

Blood on the Celery: Jammer and Duck

A key driver of the story is Jammer's doubts about the rightness of the resistance's actions, and how these impel him to turn informer. Doral's good cop act clearly focuses on Jammer's concerns about the temple massacre, saying that he wants to talk about it and arguing that the resistance broke the rules of occupation through their actions. Doral plays on Jammer's concerns about sacrilege by observing that 'bringing instruments of death into a house of worship is a sin'. His suggestion that the massacre was deliberately engineered by the resistance for publicity purposes picks up on the way they have been capitalising on it, and he talks of unity, saying that there are 'farms here on New Caprica where Cylons and humans are working together'. The logic behind the Cylon plan is clearly that, in any society, a resistance group or countercultural movement that is under establishment control provides an outlet through which discontent can be managed, as with the resistance in George Orwell's novel *Nineteen Eighty-Four*. It is tempting to speculate that the Cylons engineered the massacre to trigger Jammer's doubts; however, this seems unlikely given that the incident dealt a serious blow to the Cylons' attempts to encourage good relations with the humans.

The question does remain of how the Cylons identified Jammer as a weak link, and also how they know precisely what it is that is troubling him (as Doral appears to paraphrase Jammer's own complaints about the idea of hiding the guns in the temple). Although, given subsequent events, Ellen Tigh is the most likely informant, her conversation with Cavil in 'Precipice' will make it plain she has not passed on information before that point, suggesting there is another traitor in the resistance whose identity we never learn. If Ellen is not to blame, then the obvious candidate is Barolay; although this is never overtly followed up, it casts an interesting light on her subsequent actions in the series. Given this, it is likely that Barolay told the Cylons about the weapons cache in the temple and about Jammer being a weak link, and that although the raid on the temple did not go as the Cylons planned, Doral then used the fallout from it to put pressure on Jammer. The implication at the end of the webisodes is that Jammer has taken Doral up on his offer, as we see him holding the contact chip Doral gave him and then walking toward the detention centre; however, the following episodes will make it clear that Jammer's actual decision is something different, but with equally dramatic repercussions.

Duck's story acts as a counterpoint to Jammer's. At the start of the webisodes, his love for Nora overwhelms his hatred for the Cylons, such that he won't join the resistance, despite being a Viper pilot with 40 kills to his name, and he believes that anyone who joins the NCP is, by definition, a traitor. In keeping with the series' themes of unity through procreation, he and his wife (who, to judge by her photo, was also a Viper pilot), are planning a baby. Nora's death, however, means that Duck goes from an ambivalent attitude to religion to a downright hostile one, shown in the exchange where Jammer begins 'Sometimes the will of the Gods is not–' and Duck interrupts, 'Frak the Gods, the Gods killed her!' His attitude to the Cylons likewise changes from passive to active hostility, and he becomes suicidal, with the resistance exploiting that emotional vulnerability.

Significantly given Jammer's development, Duck at first focuses his anger on the Gods, then on the resistance, but Tyrol's honesty – telling him that they had indeed hidden guns in the temple – is what seems to focus his ire on the Cylons. He understandably feels he needs to hit back at someone, and the Cylons provide the most obvious target. His decision parallels the choice offered to Jammer, in that he becomes an informer, but for the resistance rather than against them. When he informs Tyrol of his decision to join the NCP, it is after

31: THE RESISTANCE/CROSSROADS

Nicholas's dedication ceremony at the temple, drawing symbolic connections with Nora, who wanted a child and who was going regularly to the temple to pray for one. Duck also displays a death wish, first when he tells Jammer, 'I should have been with her ... I could have died with her', when grieving over Nora's death, and later when we see him smoking a cigarette at the end of the story, having earlier quit due to the couple's efforts to get pregnant, saying 'What frakking difference does it make now?' Duck's situation thus sets up the rationale for his actions in 'Occupation'.

Striking Stories: Writing and Production

The impetus for the webisodes came from the Sci-Fi channel, who had suggested during Season Two that the *Battlestar Galactica* team should produce some. This was because online 'extras', including webisodes, were increasingly becoming a popular means of promoting television shows. The writing staff considered doing a series of vignettes, but when Weddle and Thompson were given the assignment, on the grounds that they knew the series and its characters well, they decided to create a full story. Other ideas considered included stories focusing on Doc Cottle, on Gaeta working for Baltar's administration, or on the daily life of the Tyrols; however, given that Jammer and Duck were to have a crucial involvement in the early part of Season Three, Moore and Eick were interested in exploring their motivations. The Sci-Fi Channel also stipulated that each webisode should have a beginning, middle and end, and the writers were restricted to using the sets and locations from the season premiere, and only actors who were in Canada at the time. The episodes were written in screening order over four days, and were filmed over the subsequent week. *The Official Companion Season Three* says that originally the Jammer and Duck roles were reversed during the planning of their Season Three character arcs, but Moore changed them at the suggestion of Tyrol actor Aaron Douglas, who felt that Jammer had been played as a weak character in 'Valley of Darkness' (where he hid from the Centurions and was frightened when ordered to take a gun and fight the Cylons) and that it would make more sense to have him as the collaborator; although, as written, the story portrays Jammer's collaboration as resulting from conviction, not weakness.

The webisodes would also be a factor in the developing Writers Guild of America (WGA) industrial action, which would go on to affect production on Season Four. Because they were considered promotional material, they did not generate residuals or credits for the writers. The Writers Guild of America argued that the writers should be paid and credited as normal. Moore negotiated with the network and gained a payment for Thompson and Weddle (albeit one given under the heading of 'extra work'), but not a credit. (Moore identified them retrospectively on his blog.) The WGA ordered all production teams making webisodes not to deliver them to NBC-Universal. This delayed the release of the *Battlestar Galactica* ones, and meant that rather than running one a week for ten weeks, they were released twice a week, on Tuesdays and

Thursdays, for five weeks.

Wayne Rose, previously a regular second-unit director on the series, has said that the main problem encountered with the filming of the webisodes was that the crew were employing a Canon XL-HD camera none of them had used before, which reacted badly to the low light levels on the interiors. However, the webisodes were cheaper to record than usual, given the lack of CGI. Chinese characters can be seen on a crate behind Tyrol in Webisode 7 (we do know from 'Lay Down Your Burdens' that the Colonies are multilingual). The season premiere 'Occupation', which was recorded first, originally featured a different woman in the photo of Nora and Duck, meaning that shots of it had to be digitally altered after the casting of Emily Holmes for the webisodes.

The webisodes were made available online on scifi.com as a teaser for Season Three, only to US residents, leading to many angry posts on the website from international fans; they were subsequently released on the Region 1 Season 3.0 DVD, the Region 4 Season 4.0 DVD, and the Blu-ray box sets for all regions. It is also possible to track down copies on the internet. There is some ambiguity over the story's title: the writers originally called it 'Crossroads' (not to be confused with the Season Three finale) and this is what appears on the webisode title slides; however, scifi.com insisted on renaming it 'The Resistance', this time causing confusion with the Season Two episode 'Resistance'. Despite the restrictions, the webisodes received 1.8 million hits on first release, and a positive reception on television review websites.

'The Resistance'/'Crossroads' is the first of the series' webisode side features, and, considering the circumstances under which it was written and produced, fits well into its overall continuity, providing some valuable backstory for 'Occupation'.

32: Occupation

FIRST TRANSMISSION DATE: 6 October 2006 (USA)

WRITER: Ronald D Moore

DIRECTOR: Sergio Mimica-Gezzan

CREDITED CAST: Lucy Lawless (D'Anna); Callum Keith Rennie (Leoben); Kate Vernon (Ellen Tigh); Matthew Bennett (Doral); Rekha Sharma (Tory Foster); Dean Stockwell (Cavil); Luciana Carro (Kat); Christian Tessier (Duck); Brad Dryborough (Hoshi); Leah Cairns (Racetrack); Madeline Parker (Kacey); Dominic Zamprogna (Jammer); Ryan McDonell (Pilot #3); Byron Lawson (Pilot #4); Colin Lawrence (Skulls)

SYNOPSIS: On New Caprica, Tigh has been arrested as a resistance leader and tortured, losing an eye. Ellen sleeps with a Cavil to get him released. Elsewhere, Kara is held captive by Leoben, acting out a parody of domesticity in a flat. She kills him with a pair of steel chopsticks, but he simply resurrects to begin the scenario over again. On *Colonial One*, the Cylons debate how to control the occupied territory, and the Cavils suggest mass executions. The resistance, meanwhile, finally succeed in making wireless contact with a Raptor sent by Adama. They also plan to have Duck detonate a suicide bomb at the New Caprica Police graduation ceremony at which Baltar is due to be present. Baltar however decides not to attend. Gaeta tries to secretly get this information to the resistance but is too late, and the bombing goes ahead as planned. On the Fleet, Apollo and Adama clash over how to handle the rescue mission.

ANALYSIS: 'Occupation' outlines the situation on New Caprica after the return of the Cylons and provides a sketch of the problems that occur in any situation where the ruling party govern without the consent of the people.

The One-Eyed Man is King: The Resistance

134 days into the occupation, the resistance movement previously seen in the webisodes are now using Pyramid games as meeting places. They bear ironic parallels to the Cylons themselves, not only in using suicide bombing as a tactic (like Doral in 'Litmus'), but in that they are at least partly motivated by faith, in this case that they will be rescued. Tigh refuses to believe that Adama would abandon them, despite Anders pointing out that he abandoned the

human resistance on Caprica and that it was only Kara pressing for the rescue mission that saved him. Duck, who had a fairly casual attitude toward religion before Nora's death, is now seen praying, using a set of beads. This is presumably out of a combination of a need to fill his wife's absence, a search for meaning in his life and death, and also possibly an element of survivor's guilt (as his wife had always urged him to come to the temple with her). Tigh also tries to justify the suicide bombing using military terms; when Tyrol says it's wrong, he replies that it's not the first time they've sent a soldier on a one-way mission.

The resistance are shown to be a damaged, desperate group. Tigh's loss of an eye is symbolic, indicating both a loss of vision and a figurative as well as literal blindness. The cracked mirror in Duck's tent has obvious connotations of bad luck, and means we see him looking at a cracked, broken image of himself. The resistance are also showing clear signs of trauma, with Laura's unpleasant streak again coming to the fore when she says attacks on individual members of the NCP would be justified. Although Tyrol is disturbed about using suicide bombers and suggests they call off the strike since *Galactica* is coming to rescue them, Tigh insists on going ahead, saying that, if they encourage the population into an uprising, it will aid the *Galactica*'s efforts.

Shotgun Wedding: The Cylons as Rulers

The Cylons, meanwhile, are also affected by the occupation. The Centurions look tarnished, worn and dull, as if the planet is wearing them down. The purpose of the occupation is neither economic nor political, but a perverse twisting of love: Caprica-Six says, 'The entire point of coming here was to start a new way of life, to push past the conflict', despite Cavil pointing out that the only way they can control the human population is through terror. When D'Anna asks if it is all worth it, Caprica-Six says, 'If you ever experienced love, you wouldn't have to ask', thus portraying the Cylons' love for the humans as a sort of possessive stalker impulse. Caprica-Six and *Galactica*-Eight want the Cylons and humans to join together out of love, but fail to acknowledge that they cannot force the humans to love them back.

This aspect of the occupation is symbolised brutally in the Kara-Leoben storyline. Leoben claims to be acting out of love, saying that God sent him to Kara to help her see the reason for her life, but he goes about this by trying to force her to love him, caging her in exactly the sort of conventional, housebound, social role she deplores. The end result is a twisted parody of domesticity straight out of a horror movie, as she kills him and then sits calmly finishing her dinner. Her various efforts to strike back – she has killed him five times – and the suicide attempt she makes in a deleted scene parallel the resistance's desperate and damaging efforts to fight back. Her cry of 'I don't belong here!' reflects the resistance's desperate hope for the *Galactica*'s return, as she and Leoben reenact in miniature the Cylon-human situation.

32: OCCUPATION

Losing the Fat: The Fleet

On the Fleet, the situation between Adama and Apollo has worsened, with the former snidely referring to the latter's weight problem ('Get your fat ass out of here'). Even Dualla accuses Lee (who should probably now be renamed 'Apillow') of having lost his edge. Significantly, she tells him that he is more like his father than he knows (and, a little worryingly, that this is why she married him; given her role as Adama's friend and confession-figure in Season Two, there is an implication that she regards Lee as an Adama-substitute), and adds that he is denying his own soldier nature. This marks a serious potential trouble spot in their marriage, as Lee has been inclining away from military life since the series began, and seeking a political role. Moore argues that Lee's weight is a metaphor for how the whole Fleet has gone soft, but one could equally take it as indicating his unhappiness with his lot.

Adama, meanwhile, is now confiding in Sharon (suggesting that, in the absence of Starbuck and with Dualla now married to his son, he focuses his paternal instincts on another troubled young female officer), even saying to her that he feels 'alone, except maybe for you', indicating how far he has come in terms of connecting with the Cylon. With his son increasingly distant, and with many of the people he was close to trapped on New Caprica, Sharon, who is identical to, and has some of the memories of, Boomer, provides a link to the past. Sharon, for her part, makes some quite personal revelations, saying that she was suffused with guilt for the choices she made, betraying her people and, as she puts it, 'losing the baby', and had to forgive herself for her part in the tragedies she has experienced before she could move on. Likewise, she says that Adama needs to admit to feeling his own guilt and forgive himself before he can move on and properly enact the rescue mission. Sharon's cell is decorated and comfortable, and Adama is now seeking her out rather than having her brought to him, indicating the positive progress made over the past year, in ironic contrast to the situation on New Caprica.

Groundhog Day: Continuity and Worldbuilding

In thematic terms, the story touches on ideas of choice and lack of choice. While at the end of the second season the people had a choice whether to stay on New Caprica or not, here they are trapped, with their only options being to support the resistance or to put up with the Cylon occupation. The Nazi occupation references continue, with Duck's suicide bombing plan recalling a 1943 attempt by Freiherr von Gersdorff to assassinate Hitler, using explosives concealed in his greatcoat, as the Fuehrer attended the opening of an exhibition of captured Soviet equipment. Propaganda is played over the speakers urging people to use the New Caprica Medical Centre with its team of human and Cylon physicians, reflecting an ideal of human and Cylon cooperation.

In continuity terms, Roslin mentions that it is 'Mars Day', which appears to refer to a holiday (as in 'Eros Day', which will later appear in the spinoff series

Caprica) rather than a day of the week (as in the French *mardi*, which is derived from the Latin 'Martis dies', day of Mars). At least one dog, Jake, has made it off the Colonies and is currently an important member of the resistance, as Gaeta turns his food bowl upside down to signal when there is a message for Tyrol at the secret drop. In giving the resistance information about Baltar's plans to attend the graduation, Gaeta is setting him up to be killed; this is a particularly unpleasant act since, as Roslin correctly states, Baltar is merely a powerless figurehead for the Cylons, and Gaeta, as an adviser to him, knows more than anyone that this is true. There is also a degree of self-preservation in Gaeta's rushing to stop the bombing once he knows Baltar will not be there, as the death of a notorious hate-figure might justify the other deaths at the graduation, but without that it simply looks like a vengeful attack on their own people, something that even Tigh is willing to acknowledge at this point. On the Fleet, Helo is now acting as Adama's XO, and Kat as CAG. Leoben's use of the phrase 'heavenly father' when saying grace further suggests that the Cylon god is male and, when Kara tells him he is insane, he quotes himself from 'Flesh and Bone', saying 'To know the face of god is to know madness'. His 'I'll see you soon' to Kara as he dies echoes Duck's 'I'll see you soon, Nora' as he detonates his bomb. The usual head-count in the opening credits is temporarily missing. Kara still has a sticking plaster on her shoulderblade, suggesting an improbably long wound-healing period.

In terms of outside references, one of the combat units in the Fleet is called 'Snowbirds', like the Canadian military aerobatics team. Moore, in his podcast, acknowledges that in crafting the story the writers had in mind a number of different real-life occupations, such as those of Iraq, the West Bank and (at Eick's suggestion) Roman Gaul; however, the closest parallels appear to be with the Vichy regime in France, with a complicit government and military force and an active resistance encouraging liberation by an outside power. The Leoben storyline has connections with the film *The Collector* (1965), about a man obsessed with a woman to the point of kidnapping her, although Moore compares it to *Groundhog Day* (1993).

'Asterix the Gaul' in Space: Writing and Production

The 1 April 2006 draft of the script, although fairly close to final version, had an additional storyline focused on the Cylons looking for Hera, including blood-testing children to find her, and on having members of the resistance kidnapping skinjob Cylons and keeping them alive in a pit in order to instil fear among the remaining Cylons, who would have no idea as to the fates of their comrades. This, Moore said in his podcast, would have caused the Cylons to panic and instigate a crackdown. Moore decided that this was 'one idea too many'. However, the loss of this storyline also meant the omission of the reason why Laura is in detention in the next episode: in the 1 April draft, after the Simon that takes Hera's blood sample goes missing, D'Anna becomes suspicious that Roslin has something to do with the disappearance. Subsequent drafts dated 6 and 8

32: OCCUPATION

April instead have a scene in which D'Anna confronts Roslin in the school with her theory that Hera is still alive; Roslin denies it, but this is then followed by an earlier version of the scene that ultimately appears in 'Exodus', in which Anders and Laura talk about how Maya and Isis/Hera are hiding out in the resistance tunnels.

Originally, Moore says, the *Galactica* story was also to have had a slightly different emphasis: 'It wasn't gonna be just that Dualla is calling [Apollo] out and saying that he's gotten soft, but that Dualla herself had also gotten soft. That she had lost a step. That she was off her game'. The rest of the season would have focused on the couple becoming, as Moore puts it, 'razors', regaining their hardness; though, as this idea does not even appear in the 1 April draft (which is a 'white production draft', namely, a first draft production script), it seems to have gone by the wayside at an early stage.

The Kara-Leoben storyline was discussed by Eick and Moore during the writing of 'Lay Down Your Burdens'. Early drafts take the story further; the 1, 6 and 8 April drafts all end with D'Anna and Leoben, after the police graduation bombing, talking about what to do next; D'Anna wants a crackdown, while Leoben says that fighting violence with violence is not God's way and then in the next scene presents Kara with Kacey, the child that will eventually be introduced in 'Precipice'. The 11 May draft omits D'Anna's and Leoben's conversation, but contains the final scene. The storyline about D'Anna and the Oracle that features in 'Exodus' was in this episode as late as the 11 May draft. Its omission caused the loss of an ironic subplot: the reason why Tyrol missed the message at the drop was originally to have been that an unwitting D'Anna stopped to pet Jake and, noticing that Gaeta had turned his food bowl over, turned it right-side up again. In the final version, Gaeta arrives and inverts the bowl too late for Tyrol to see it in time. Moore says that the Sci-Fi Channel were actually supportive of the suicide bomber storyline, showing a good deal of bravery on their part.

Moore has said that Tigh's loss of an eye was a later addition, made as he felt a 'visible reminder' was needed of the cost of the occupation, although it forms part of the story at least as far back as the 1 April draft. Michael Hogan says in the documentary *A Look Back* that when he learned his character was to lose a body part, he rang up to find out which one it was, so that he could do research. In a *Toronto Star* interview dated 4 April 2008, he comments of the eyepatch, 'I hate that thing. It screws with your depth perception', but acknowledges an upside in that 'it saves on contact lenses'. A scene showing how Tigh loses his eye appears in the 6 April, 8 April and 11 May drafts, and was shot, featuring a Doral holding a long, sharp implement by the shaft and pointing it into the camera lens. However, it was felt that it would be more effective just to have Tigh telling of losing the eye; the sequence would in fact have been at odds with his later description of the incident, stating that the Cylons 'ripped it right out onto the floor. Picked it up and showed it to me. Looked like a hard-boiled egg'. Regarding the implement, Matthew Bennett recalls: 'It was made by the props department and was constructed entirely of steel. The base was a hand grip as you would find on a handgun … Before every take the props department would heat the tip up with a blowtorch until it would glow red. I ended up having to hold it as I did because the weight of the implement was heavy enough that I had a difficult time controlling it by the pistol grip near the camera lens … A slight design flaw'.

The New Caprica location/virtual set really gives a sense of endless bleakness, and the reuse of Starbuck's Caprican flat for the flat in which she is imprisoned means she appears to be captive in a dark analogue of her own home. The opening montage is perhaps less effective, and the narrated section by Roslin at the start of Act One (which originally was to form part of the teaser instead) achieves a lot more telling than showing – again, probably down to the network wanting to get through the New Caprica storyline quickly. It is a rather strange idea that Roslin would be writing down such obviously incriminating material. The original intention was to have the story open with a D'Anna Biers propaganda film presenting a positive spin on Cylon occupation, but Moore says in his podcast, 'There was a reaction from other writers and studio/network; the propaganda film just felt like the wrong tone', and that it would have seemed odd that D'Anna was still making films.

In terms of things to watch out for, the use of a fat body double for Jamie Bamber is rather obvious once you realise his face isn't shown in sequences where Apollo is shirtless. In the transmitted version, Kandyse McClure was mistakenly credited as 'Candice McClure', a spelling she has used on other projects, but this was corrected for the DVD release. The graduation was shot in BC Place Stadium. This episode is also the first season opener/conclusion not to be directed by Michael Rymer.

The episode was screened along with the next one, 'Precipice', as a two-hour premiere on first US broadcast (possibly, again, because of the network's desire to rush through the New Caprica arc and get back into space). Both episodes were preceded by a 'Mature Subject Matter' warning. 'Occupation' was also nominated for Outstanding Writing for a Drama Series in the 2007 Emmy Awards, and won an IGN Editor's Choice Award. The title sequence features some new text outlining the situation: 'The human race far from home fighting for survival'.

'Occupation' makes for a strong start to Season Three, mapping out the situation on New Caprica. Perhaps it does so a little too quickly, but nonetheless it successfully conveys a number of themes focusing around love, resistance and the legitimacy of governance.

33: Precipice

FIRST TRANSMISSION DATE: 6 October 2006 (USA)

WRITER: Ronald D Moore

DIRECTOR: Sergio Mimico-Gezzan

CREDITED CAST: Lucy Lawless (D'Anna); Richard Hatch (Tom Zarek); Rick Worthy (Simon); Callum Keith Rennie (Leoben); Kate Vernon (Ellen Tigh); Matthew Bennett (Doral); Dean Stockwell (Cavil); Luciana Carro (Kat); Brad Dryborough (Hoshi); Madeline Parker (Kacey); Dominic Zamprogna (Jammer); Mylenne Dinh-Robic (Officer #1); Colin Lawrence (Skulls); Larissa Stadnichuk (Suicide Bomber)

SYNOPSIS: The NCP, including Jammer, conduct a night-time raid on the tent city, and Cally is among those arrested. Leoben presents Kara with a little girl, Kacey; he tells her she is their child, made using Kara's ovary. Kara initially refuses to care for her, but her feelings change when Kacey accidentally hurts herself. Following another suicide bombing incident, the Cylons order the execution of a number of humans, including Cally, Roslin and Zarek, and force Baltar to sign the order at gunpoint. A Cavil orders Ellen to acquire information about the resistance, threatening to arrest Tigh again if she does not cooperate. On the Fleet, rescue plans are complicated by the fact that the Cylons have removed the launch keys from the grounded Colonial vessels. Adama has Sharon sworn in as a Colonial officer and sent to New Caprica to find and steal the keys. She arrives and is met by Anders, but they are ambushed by Centurions. Elsewhere, with the human prisoners about to be executed, Jammer releases Cally and tells her to run.

ANALYSIS: 'Precipice' follows on from 'Occupation', exploring divisions among the various factions involved: among the humans as the NCP make their first show of force against the resistance, and among the Cylons as Cavil and Caprica-Six disagree over the appropriate response to the humans' intransigence. However, we also see a movement toward unity as, on the Fleet, Sharon, is finally accepted as an officer.

Human Nature: The Resistance versus the NCP

'Precipice' is the first episode to feature the NCP in action. The NCP, whatever their practical function, are also an instrument of fear, wearing balaclavas and staging night-time raids. By recruiting humans to do their dirty work, also, the Cylons can construct a moral equivalency, allowing them to believe that what they do to the humans is justified by the fact that the humans are complicit. Jammer, the audience's identification figure among the NCP, is conflicted, with his decision to let Cally go being clearly an effort at salving his own conscience for his part in the upcoming massacre. Jammer's conversation with Tyrol has an obvious subtext as a result, when he 'speculates' that some of the NCP members may have joined for altruistic reasons; he is saying that he himself joined up because he thought they would do some good, but that now he is having doubts and wishes he had not got involved. Tyrol responds by saying, correctly, that people who thought the NCP could be a force for good are 'a bunch of frakkin' idiots'; because of the resistance, they will inevitably be used as a force for oppression. Tyrol's words to Jammer – 'One day, when this is all over, guys like Gaeta are gonna get strung up. Guys like you and me, we're gonna be there, tying the knots', may be a factor in Jammer's subsequent releasing of Cally.

Among the resistance, meanwhile, the hope inspired by the news that the *Galactica* is coming is encouraging them to more violent tactics rather than causing them to settle down. Roslin is conflicted over the practice of suicide bombing; although she says to Baltar that she understands why people do it, his condemnation of the practice clearly hits home, as she later tells Tigh to stop the bombings. When Tigh defends the resistance's tactics, however, she backs down, because although Tigh's decisions are Cain-like in their ruthlessness, she cannot argue against the fact that his goal is the same as hers: to liberate the humans from the Cylons. Tigh, with echoes of al-Qaeda's political development, is gradually escalating the violence, going from setting people up to be killed by the Cylons, to sending out suicide bombers, to finally targeting the marketplace, which will mean the deaths of innocent humans; by this stage, anybody not directly opposing the Cylons is seen by Tigh as supporting them. He describes the resistance by saying 'Which side are we on? We're on the side of the demons, Chief. We're evil men in the gardens of Paradise. Sent by the forces of death to spread devastation and destruction wherever we go'. This tacitly acknowledges that the Cylons were trying to set up a human/Cylon society that had the potential for success, but that he and a small number of others are actively out to destroy for, it has to be admitted, their own personal reasons.

Baltar is trying to defend his increasingly precarious position as a leader who is under the control of the Cylons but hated by the humans, denying to Roslin that anyone has been tortured by the Cylons, with an edge of hysteria in his voice. Gaeta snaps when he sees the names on the death warrant; although this looks like concern for the safety of the people on the list, in view of his actions in the previous episode in trying to set up Baltar to be killed, he appears to be constructing a strategy of aiding the resistance so that, in the event of their victory, he would have a defence against accusations of collaboration. However, should the resistance leaders be executed, he would obviously be held accountable. Zarek, meanwhile, is back in his political element as a force of opposition to an oppressive regime; he is matter-of-fact about the idea of being detained on a point of principle, and has, alone among the humans, retained his credibility and been untainted by the occupation, as can be seen in his friendly conversation with Roslin, where they laugh over the fact that, had she succeeded in stealing the election, they would not be in this situation.

On the Fleet, Apollo at first appears to opt out of the rescue effort; in the planning meeting, he refers to it as 'your plan', to which Kat acidly replies, 'Funny, I thought this was *our* plan, sir'. However, when he finally abandons his defeated, drifting stance and confronts his father, putting a coherent argument to him that leaving the Fleet unprotected while the battlestars attempt to rescue the New Capricans is a stupid move and that he should be thinking in terms of the survival of the human race as a whole, he is involved again, no longer complacent or passive. His father, significantly, acknowledges that Apollo is right and modifies his plan, taking only the *Galactica* to New Caprica and leaving *Pegasus* in charge of the Fleet. In doing so, he places Apollo potentially in charge of the future of humanity.

What Can I Do To Make You Love Me? The Cylons/Leoben and Kara

Among the Cylons, the Cavils's get-tough message is increasingly in the ascendant. However, this creates a positive-feedback loop, as their efforts to crack down on the resistance are leading to an escalating level of retaliatory action; clearly the Cylons' initial reluctance to actually go in hard has made the situation worse. Forcing Baltar to sign the execution order at gunpoint is a call-back to Caprica-Six, in the miniseries, placing the blame for the attacks on the Colonies on Baltar, by telling him that, since he must have known on some level what she was doing, the fact that she went through with her plan was all his fault; here, Cavil says that the Cylons are afraid God will disapprove of their actions and are 'covering their existential asses'. Significantly, Caprica-Six is shot by Doral during the death-list scene; having accepted, in 'Downloaded', that Cylons were guilty of mass murder, she is now a threat to the self-justifying delusion of the other Cylons. It is at this point that Head Six reappears, urging Baltar to sign the execution order; the suggestion is that God has lost control of the situation, and is now trying to salvage what he can. Right after Baltar signs the document, however, we see Sharon Agathon (who has now evidently married Helo) on *Galactica* pledging allegiance to free humans through comradeship and loyalty. Like the NCP, she takes on the uniform of her former enemy; but, where they are furthering the oppression of one race by another, her acceptance as a Colonial officer shows two races uniting toward a wider goal of liberation.

The New Caprica arc is a reiteration of the continued theme of children wreaking a terrible vengeance on their abusive parents, then seeking reconciliation. In this case, we have a neo-colonial perspective; the Cylons, like many colonial and neo-colonial powers, justify their actions under the rhetoric of working for the benefit of the indigenous population, but are ultimately acting for their own benefit. Although the Cylons are protecting the human population in closing down the marketplace out of fear of attacks from the resistance, for example, they also know that, were such an attack to take place, their failure to prevent it would turn more of the humans against them.

The scene where *Galactica*-Eight visits Cally in her cell further reflects the situation between the two species: Boomer tells Cally that she is happy she and Tyrol have started a family, but will not go so far as to get her released to go back to that family, so Cally, understandably, rejects the overture. We also learn in this episode that the human-like Cylons are preventing the Centurions from achieving self-awareness, when Adama tells Apollo, 'The Centurions can't distinguish [Sharon] from the other humanoid models ... They were deliberately programmed that way. The Cylons didn't want them becoming self-aware and suddenly resisting orders. They didn't want their own robotic rebellion on their hands. You can appreciate the irony'.[61] Cavil's proposal in 'Lay Down Your Burdens' that the Cylons should seek their own destiny as a machine race, however, would have required them to divest themselves of the human traits that the supporters of Caprica-Six and *Galactica*-Eight embrace. As a result of this decision to keep their humanity, the Cylons are reenacting some of the human race's own worst behaviour.

As the Cylons' situation becomes more desperate, so do Leoben's tactics against Kara. He produces a child and claims that she is the mother and he is the father, in a rape metaphor, forcing Kara to have a child she doesn't want. Kara first rejects the child, calling her 'this' in an echo of how the Colonials dehumanise the Cylons through using neutral pronouns, but, when the child is injured, she cannot help but feel compassion, and indeed this also plays on her own memories of abuse. She spontaneously holds Leoben's hand when Kacey wakes from unconsciousness; although Leoben is now getting signs of affection from Kara, the scenario that facilitates this is one of manipulation and deception. Indeed, since we never see how Kacey was injured, the possibility remains that Leoben caused it, an idea that must also occur to Kara and inform her subsequent actions towards him.

Night Vision: Continuity, Writing and Production

At this point in the series, there are, according to Apollo, 2,000 people left on the civilian fleet, which Adama thinks is enough to restart the human race if the New Caprica mission fails. (The figures given in 'Crossroads' part one and 'Lay Down Your Burdens' part two allow us to calculate that there is a total population of 4,843 people in orbit, of whom 2,597 are military; the civilian population thus actually numbers 2,246.) Sharon's recognition code with Anders is 'Go Panthers', a reference to the Picon Panthers (he responds with 'C-Bucs Rule'). In terms of filmic references, the idea of executing prisoners as they take a rest break is a deliberate allusion to *The Great Escape*, and the names 'the twist'

---

61 SPOILER SECTION: A throwaway line here, this will become a crucial point in the Cylon Civil War storyline in Season Four.

and 'the swirl' for sexual techniques are references to the *Seinfeld* episode 'The Fusilli Jerry' (Moore being a fan of the series). The filming of the NCP raids in night-vision goggles (which was the director's idea), and of detainees with their heads covered by sacks, references then-contemporary news footage of the Iraq War. The NCP have certain similarities to the Iraqi Police, who also wore balaclavas in part to avoid detection and reprisal from the occupied population. Weddle suggested to Moore the name 'Kacey' for the child, after Weddle's own niece. Finally, Jo Storm notes a symbolism in the way Ellen Tigh, having stolen the resistance's plans, is seen through the fire of the stove, with her hands up as if warding the flames away, suggesting that her actions are taking her toward hell.

In his podcast, Moore says that after deciding to focus the season's first episode on Duck's suicide bombing, the production team then wanted to focus the second on someone who took the opposite decision and joined the NCP, hence the story of Jammer. As Moore's wife Terry puts it, 'We tend as a culture to expect people to behave always the best in the worst possible circumstances, and they don't'. The idea for the Kacey storyline came about through Moore continually being asked if there would be any comeback from 'The Farm' and the removal of Kara's ovary. Originally the *Pegasus* was to have been tasked with the rescue mission, rather than the *Galactica*, but Moore felt that this did not play as strongly. In terms of Jammer's motivations, Moore had originally wanted to focus on the fact that he had been present during Duck's suicide bombing, and that he was in part tormented by his memories of finding himself suddenly lying in a heap of dead bodies. In the 3 April 2006 draft script, Jammer's flashbacks were of the suicide bombing rather than of Cally's arrest; however, Moore says that on viewing it, the fact that the bombing had happened earlier in the narrative, at the end of the previous episode, would make it difficult for the audience to make the connection. It was director Sergio Mimico-Gezzan who suggested shifting the focus onto the Cally incident. The sequence of Doral shooting Caprica-Six was cut in one round of editing, but James Callis argued for its inclusion, saying that it was what motivated Baltar to sign the execution order. In production terms, the tower with the Cylons on it is a digital construct, and the shot of the Raptors over the forest is also entirely CGI: as Moore puts it in the podcast, 'It's not a real forest or anything'. The night-vision sequences were actually shot after dark with a night scope rather than the effect being added in post-production.

The 3 April draft script differs from the final version largely in terms of scene order and editing, but has one or two other differences worth noting. When Baltar speaks with Laura in her cell, he at one point refers to the Cylons as being rational, unsentimental machines, and we see Caprica-Six observing them through a one-way mirror in secret and being, according to the script, distressed to think that this is how Baltar views her; this scene was shot, and survives as a DVD extra. The New Caprica Police are in this draft called the Human Security Force or HSF as an official title. When *Galactica*-Eight visits Cally in detention, she is surprised to learn that she and Tyrol have a child (a detail omitted by the next draft, dated 6 April), and Cally gets the great line, '[You] think I give a damn about you and your emotional software?' There is also a sequence, intended to follow Laura's confrontation of Tigh, where Anders tells Laura that the volunteer for the suicide bombing at the power substation is a woman who feels she has nothing to live for since her husband has been killed. He also refers to Maya and Hera being kept in a safe location and asks Laura why the Cylons were after the child, in an allusion to the abandoned storyline described in the review for 'Occupation', where the Cylons were attempting to identify Hera. The scene where the Cylons discuss what to do about the bombings also has a Sharon dissenting from the consensus, arguing that they should instead find ways of accommodating the humans, and a Simon telling the Cavils that their atheism is an affront to God.

'Precipice' is another powerful episode, which takes head-on a very difficult subject and treats it in a balanced, mature and nuanced fashion. Although it is informed by the fact that it was made at the height of the Iraq War, its themes could relate to any occupation at any point in history.

34: Exodus (Parts One and Two)

FIRST TRANSMISSION DATE: 13 October 2006 and 20 October 2006 (USA)

WRITER: David Weddle & Bradley Thompson

DIRECTOR: Félix Alcalá

CREDITED CAST: Lucy Lawless (D'Anna); Amanda Plummer (Oracle Selloi); Richard Hatch (Tom Zarek); Callum Keith Rennie (Leoben); Kate Vernon (Ellen Tigh); Donnelly Rhodes (Doctor Cottle); Matthew Bennett (Doral); Rekha Sharma (Tory Foster); Dean Stockwell (Cavil); Erica Cerra (Maya); Luciana Carro (Kat); Brad Dryborough (Hoshi); Leah Cairns (Racetrack); Madeline Parker (Kacey); Dominic Zamprogna (Jammer); Eileen Pedde (Mathias); Jennifer Halley (Seelix); Ty Olsson (Captain Kelly); Ryan Robbins (Connor); Rick Worthy (Simon); Emilie Ullerup (Julia)

KNOWN UNCREDITED CAST: Lily Duong-Walton (Hera Agathon)

SYNOPSIS: Tyrol, learning of the planned Cylon execution of human detainees, gets up a rescue party. They arrive in time to attack before the Centurions can open fire on the prisoners. Meanwhile, at the rendezvous, the Marines who came with Sharon from the *Galactica*, who have been hanging back in the woods, destroy the Centurions sent to ambush the meeting. Anders realises Ellen must have informed the Cylons of their plans. He tells the rest of the resistance, and they decide to execute her. Tigh gives Ellen a poisoned cup. Suffering bad dreams, D'Anna seeks out an oracle, who tells her that Hera is alive. Sharon gains access to the detention centre and finds the launch keys to the grounded Colonial spacecraft, but is found by D'Anna, who tells her that she has been deceived by the humans and Hera is actually alive. Sharon shoots D'Anna in the legs and flees. The *Galactica* jumps to New Caprica and, under cover of the resulting battle, the human population make their escape. Anders rescues Kara, but she insists on going back for Kacey. As Cylon reinforcements arrive, the *Galactica* is outgunned, but the *Pegasus* appears and Apollo sacrifices the second battlestar to win the fight. Baltar flees with the Cylons, and D'Anna, having planned to stay behind and set off a nuclear bomb, instead rescues Hera, Maya having been killed during the evacuation. On *Galactica*, Kara encounters Kacey's real mother and gives the child over.

ANALYSIS: 'Exodus' wraps up the New Caprica arc, in the process giving some crucial insights into Baltar's life with the Cylons, powerful resolutions to Kara's and Tigh's storylines, and an intriguing mystery as to what is going on elsewhere in the *Battlestar Galactica* universe.

We All Make Sacrifices: The Humans

Among the humans, battle-readiness is symbolised by a general flurry of tonsorial activity, with Tyrol shaving at some point between 'Precipice' and his first scene in 'Exodus', and Adama losing his moustache at the end of part two, though Starbuck will keep the long hair for a few episodes yet, perhaps indicating that she is not quite ready to let go of New Caprica. Meanwhile, Gaeta draws a tree and a dagger on a notepad, indicating his disturbed state of mind through contrasting imagery of life and death, while Jammer's sense of guilt is highlighted by his blurting 'I didn't do anything!' when Zarek buttonholes him.

This story also shows the humans at their best and worst. Seelix displays the cruel streak that will come to characterise her in later episodes, leaving a Cavil to die slowly and taking away his gun so he cannot commit suicide. Cottle, by contrast, will not let a Cylon suffer if he can help it, despite any personal feelings he might have. His assertion that he cremated Hera's body because he was following Roslin's orders is partly what confirms D'Anna's suspicions that the child survived, as a medical researcher destroying the corpse of a Cylon-human hybrid is deeply unlikely, and the idea of Cottle following orders he doesn't agree with rings false. Roslin, continuing their present truce, saves Zarek's life by flinging him to the ground when the shooting starts, but returns to politician mode when the evacuation begins, insisting on being taken off-planet in *Colonial One*. Adama, when it looks as if *Galactica* will be destroyed, faces death with stoic dignity, saying 'Gentlemen, it's been an honour'.

Kara, meanwhile, bonds with Kacey, saying, 'There's something that I wanted to say to you. I'm sorry that I left you alone. I didn't mean for you to get hurt. I was upset with myself. And not you, okay? Uh … grown-ups do stupid things sometimes. We get caught up in our own little world until it's almost too late'. This articulates what she clearly wishes her own mother had said to her. The scene where Kara kisses, then stabs, Leoben to save Kacey, provokes a Scotch-fuelled ramble from Moore in the podcast, in which he discusses the possibility that perhaps her actions were partly driven by Stockholm syndrome and asserts that Leoben was willing to die to get Kara to say 'I love you' to him. However, the scene as transmitted reads rather differently: Kara is playing the same game with Leoben as in the earlier episodes, pretending to concede to him, but then, when he lets his guard down as a result, stabbing him. All this is despite the fact that, at this point, she believes him to be Kacey's father, and she also twists the knife vindictively as she kills him. He looks surprised as she does so, implying that he did not, in fact, anticipate it, and suggesting that his obsession has now reached the point where it is blinding him to reality. The reappearance of Kacey's real mother also makes the full extent of Leoben's manipulation and deception clear, including Kacey's parent and Kacey herself as collateral victims of the scheme.

There are ongoing themes of division and reunion, with the *Pegasus* and *Galactica* pilots and crew performing a ritual in which they divide themselves with a line of salt, erase the line and embrace. Lee's bringing the *Pegasus* to the *Galactica*'s aid shows that he cannot leave his father to face certain death, just as neither he nor his father could abandon Kara in 'You Can't Go Home Again', and indeed Kara cannot abandon Kacey. His arrival is perfectly timed, as the Cylons do not expect it and are taken by surprise. However, the fact that Sharon asks Tyrol about the scattering of Hera's ashes shows that she is clearly beginning to think that her faith in Adama might have been misplaced.

The death of Ellen Tigh develops from the character's actions throughout the series, like a Greek tragedy. From her first appearance, we have seen her as a politically naive woman who believes that she can use her sexuality to get what she wants from men. In this season, she is plainly outclassed by Cavil. She sleeps with him in order to get her husband released, but Cavil then uses this as a means of ensnaring her; as her actions show that she loves her husband, he releases Tigh, but uses the threat of detaining him again to get Ellen to inform on the resistance. Tigh, for his part, lives by his extreme principles and by the climate he has fostered in the resistance; having sacrificed many innocent lives for the cause, he must now also sacrifice Ellen's, she being every bit as much a traitor as the NCP members he has attacked in the past.[62] Although Kate Vernon has said in interviews that she believed Ellen knew the cup was poisoned, the 20 April, 1 and 3 May 2006 drafts of 'Exodus' contain the stage direction 'Ellen finally begins to feel like maybe she's going to get out of this after all' right before she asks for the drink, suggesting the scene should be played as if Ellen doesn't realise the draught is fatal. (The 4 May version omits the direction.) In the exchange where Adama says 'You did it. You brought 'em home, Saul', and Tigh responds 'Not all of them', Michael Hogan's voice cracks with heartbreaking poignancy. At the end of the story, in a genuinely moving scene, as everyone else cheers Adama, Tigh wanders off on the hangar deck, alone and forced to live with the consequences of his actions.

A Loss of Faith: The Cylons

Among the Cylons, the most significant development comes with D'Anna-Three's dream-inspired activities. With their plans falling apart, Three is having doubts in the Cylon God, as the oracle Dodona Selloi suggests, and as Three herself admits to Sharon later. Selloi tells Three she has a message for her from 'the one you worship', and also tells her 'Zeus sees all ... the Gods weep for you'; although Three retorts that there is 'no other god but God' (paraphrasing the Muslim affirmation of monotheism 'There is no god but God'), the sequence

---

[62] Someone with inside information has also clearly betrayed Tigh's position in the resistance to the Cylons, as Cavil is quite certain of his participation; the obvious candidate, once again, is Barolay.

clearly confirms that Head Six's statement in 'Kobol's Last Gleaming' about there being only one God means not that others don't exist, but that she does not regard them as divine, since here God is forced to turn to the Colonial pantheon to get his message to a Cylon. There is an irony that, when D'Anna goes back to the oracle's tent at the end of the story, full of anger that her destiny has not been fulfilled, she finds Hera as predicted. When she does, Head Six appears, and Caprica-Six says of Hera that 'God spared her'; however, since God was unaware of Hera's survival in earlier episodes, the events are more likely down, in the way of Greek mythology, to the actions of fate. Head Six also indicates that now D'Anna has embraced Hera, she will not carry out her plan to set off a nuclear bomb and destroy the tent city.

Baltar and Caprica-Six, meanwhile, articulate another parody of domesticity that symbolically reflects the occupation. The fact that the normally priapic Baltar is impotent with Caprica-Six represents his lack of potency as a leader, and her attempts to assure him that it isn't a problem illustrate how the humans do not have a voice, but are told what they should and should not do (usually at gunpoint) by the Cylons, who are all the while pretending that everything is normal. Baltar bitterly enacts a parody of small talk, saying 'How was your day, darling? How was your day at the office?', referring of course to her having been shot, and his having been forced to sign an execution order. Six saying 'Do you know what I've given up for you?' and Baltar replying that he hasn't given it much thought lately sum up the occupation and the Cylons' futile attempts to force the humans to love them. When Gaeta later confronts Baltar with a gun, every single accusation he makes against him relates to his conduct before the occupation, not during it. The key moment comes, however, when Gaeta says, 'He led us to the apocalypse, and – and I – I turned out to be –' and Baltar completes the line '– an idealist. There's no sin in that'. Since it is most likely that the word Gaeta was thinking of was 'traitor', here Baltar provides Gaeta with a more positive narrative; Baltar then adds that letting him go will allow him to stop D'Anna from nuking the planet, which further allows Gaeta to present himself as a positive figure. Baltar also regains some of his potency toward the end of the story, telling the Cylons that their continued refusal to listen to him and their 'smug superiority' have led to the failure of their experiment on New Caprica, something that D'Anna acknowledges when she allows him to join them on the basestar, saying, 'You were right and we were wrong. Should be some reward for that'.

Otherwise, the spiral into anarchy continues. At least one Cavil is finding the cycle of repeated downloads torturous, saying, 'Three downloads. The first one, I just got a headache … This time it was like a frakkin' white hot poker through my skull'. Baltar refers to one of the Dorals being driven to micromanagement out of anal-retentive helplessness, holding long conversations about how increasing the toilet paper supplies would win over the humans. It is also a Doral who advises nuking the city if they lose total control of the situation. D'Anna later argues that they must do this as, if the Cylons left New Caprica, the humans would 'nurse a dream of vengeance' and return one day to hunt them.

34: EXODUS

This is an echo both of Himmler's Posen Speeches of 1943, in which he sought to justify the decision to include Jewish children in the Holocaust, and of the Leoben's observation at the end of the miniseries that if the Cylons do not hunt the humans, 'they'll return one day and seek revenge'. Like any group under fire, the Cylons's ideological unity is faltering.

The Cylons are also clearly under material strain; Caprica-Six says 'Our resources are stretched to the max already' when Doral advises cracking down harder; this line appears as far back as the 20 April 2006 draft of the script. There are two basestars over the planet, and in an absolute crisis the Cylons can muster only two more, indicating that they cannot dominate the humans through sheer force of numbers. Moore says in his podcast: 'That line about resources being stretched to the max is not a complete bullshit line. There's also an implication that they're doing something else out there ... It's also a rationale for why the baseships were pulled away'. This raises the question of what is so much more important to the Cylons than Six's dreams of unity or God's divine commandment that they should procreate with humans. The scenario seems to be a reversal of the original series' implication in 'Saga of a Star World' that, prior to this story, the Cylons were fighting at less than full strength due to their military forces being engaged elsewhere.

The Great Escape: Continuity and Outside References

Following the teaser of Cally escaping the gunfire, we then get a flashback to 'one hour earlier', explaining how it is that she and the others survived the previous episode's cliffhanger. There is also a slight cheat in that, at the end of 'Precipice', Cally is still running when the shooting starts, implying that the firing squad have already begun their work, but in the new version she is flung to the ground before the gunshots start, as the resistance open fire upon the Cylons. Both cliffhangers are resolved in a very similar way, with Anders' resistance, and the Colonial prisoners, being saved by a third party arriving in the nick of time.

Otherwise, the scenes featuring Dodona Selloi remind the viewer of the hallucinogenic effects of Chamalla, and her need to take sweets to kill the taste might explain why Corporal Venner, when providing Roslin with Chamalla extract in 'Resistance', also gave her some liquorice. 'Dodona' was the name of the location of an oracle in ancient Greece, and 'Selloi' that of the people who lived in the area. The text from the Sacred Scrolls read out during the salt ritual, beginning 'Their enemies will divide them. Their colonies broken in the fiery chasm of space ...' appears once again to predict the events of the series. The Vipers, when flown in atmosphere, have a yellow engine glow instead of their usual blue. Kara's sticking plaster appears for the final time.

In terms of original series references, there are elements of 'The Living Legend' in the space battle as the *Pegasus* saves the day through a sacrifice move – although, where the original-series *Pegasus* destroyed two basestars in her final confrontation, the reimagined-series version takes out three. As far as outside references go, the scene of the prisoners escaping while a Viper targets the gate visually references the film *Mosquito Squadron* (1969). The lines 'I gave them my word', 'That's not what counts, it's who you give it to', in the standoff between Sharon and D'Anna-Three, is a homage to an exchange in *The Wild Bunch* (1969), reflecting Weddle's interest in Peckinpah. Adama's exhortation is clearly inspired by the St Crispin's Day speech in *Henry V*. In the podcast, Moore says that Weddle and Thompson found out about the salt ritual when researching military traditions; Michael Angeli, who had been enlisted to provide extra material when the story was expanded into a two-parter, wrote the scene, which was recorded as a later pick-up. Sergeant Mathias – intended, according to Moore's podcast, to be an older woman from the very first – was named after a high-school superintendent who preceded Moore's father in that role. Cally's and Tyrol's son Nicky was named after Weddle's maternal grandfather, although the child also shares his first name with Nicki Clyne, who plays his mother.

Escape from the Planet of the Cylons: Writing and Production

Exodus was initially planned as a one-parter (Adama's speech at the climax of episode one was intended to come halfway in), and as late as 4 May 2006 was written as such. However, Moore has said that the team decided at an early stage that it ought to be a two-parter, as they had a lot of material to get through. This decision also allowed them to save money, as the New Caprica episodes were expensive to film. Weddle and Thompson discussed several different rescue schemes with the rest of the writing team, including one in which *Galactica* faked its own destruction by simulating a runaway tylium detonation when attacked by Cylon missiles, then jumped to the other side of the planet, using the flash of one of its own nukes for cover, and pretended to be the *Pegasus* to draw the Cylon fire from the colonists' escape, before Lee jumped in for the last-minute rescue with the real *Pegasus*. Moore ultimately felt that this was too complicated, and simplified the scenario during his rewrites.

Although there were apparently plans to have Jammer killed in the firefight when Tyrol's party attack the Cylon executioners, Moore decided to keep him on for another story, which he felt was a clever subversion of audience expectations. The earliest available drafts have Jammer being shot in the arm instead, suggesting a way in which he would later be identified as a collaborator, but this was dropped by the 4 May draft. According to *The Official Companion Season Three*, the writers also at one point considered killing off Dualla, though, as with Jammer, this idea appears to have been dropped by the time the 20 April 2006 draft was written. Other members of the writing team also contributed key concepts: Anne Cofell Saunders suggested the twist ending to the Kacey storyline, and Moore the idea of having the *Galactica* jump into the atmosphere and plummet toward the ground. The decision not to show Maya's death was taken so that the revelation would have maximum impact. The destruction of the *Pegasus* had always been planned, because the team wanted to keep the *Galactica*

34: EXODUS

as the last surviving battlestar, and also because the *Pegasus* sets were taking up valuable studio space. The decision to kill off Ellen was also made early on, though the details varied; Weddle and Thompson originally had Tigh shoot her, and Mark Verheiden was the one who suggested poisoning. We never actually learn what it is that has led to the Cylons' military resources being depleted, most likely because of Olmos's assertion that he would leave the series if any aliens were introduced.

The available draft scripts differ little from the final version, apart from a few line changes and changes of personnel. (For instance, Barolay, not Connor, was originally to have found Ellen's map on the dead Cylon at the ambush.) The final encounter between Leoben and Kara was rewritten several times; originally he was to have been shot by Kara (using a gun which she takes from Anders) rather than stabbed. The earliest draft, the 20 April one, refers to the NCP as the HSF (oddly, as the drafts for 'Precipice' suggests that the name NCP was in use by 6 April). Head Six is absent from the story until the 4 May draft. Both Gaeta drawing a knife on a notepad during the meeting in *Colonial One* and Adama shaving off his moustache are explicitly scripted as such in the stage directions; Gaeta also drawing a tree seems to have been a later addition.

A lot of scenes were shifted around between this and the previous stories during their development; an approach allowed for by the series' multi-stranded format. D'Anna's dreams and encounter with Selloi were originally to have started in 'Occupation', instead of appearing only in 'Exodus'. Similarly, the domestic scene between Baltar and Six was originally to have featured in 'Occupation', after the meeting where the Cylon representatives agree to increase the pressure on the rebellious humans; however, it is more powerful set here, after the execution-order sequence. Ellen's death was to have taken place in part one, but was moved to part two, where, being a significant escalation in the resistance storyline, it fits more naturally. The final scene of Laura and Tory, where they discuss the loss of Hera, was moved back from the subsequent episode, 'Collaborators', which was overrunning; and Tory's emotional reaction is in part due to the events of that episode, which will be discussed in the next analysis. An extra sequence included up until the 4 May draft would have had Sharon encountering a Centurion as she goes to the detention centre to find the keys, providing a moment of tension as it tracks her but then lets her pass; this was cut as the programme budget would not afford another Centurion.

In production terms, Félix Enriquez Alcalá was also the director of the ultimately unmade pilot for a *Dragonriders of Pern* series with which Moore was involved, and had worked on *NYPD Blue* and *The Shield*. The scene of *Pegasus*'s suicide charge is another special effects triumph (the part where the flight pod spins off and takes out a basestar being Gary Hutzel's idea) and the shot of the burning *Galactica* falling through the atmosphere is very dramatic. According to Moore, the in-house visual effects team were so upset at the loss of the former ship that they hung a banner outside the building opposite Moore's office reading 'Save the *Pegasus*', but he was unswayed. 'Exodus' part two won the IGN.com Editor's Choice Award, the 2007 Visual Effects Society Award for

Outstanding Visual Effects in a Broadcast Series, and an Emmy for Outstanding Special Visual Effects for a Series, and was also nominated for the direction and sound editing Emmys.

Simon actor Rick Worthy as usual has little to do, but an earlier draft had Simon looking for Hera; hence the fact that she is being concealed in the underground tunnel. Charlie Connor actor Ryan Robbins previously played the Armistice Officer in the miniseries, and would go on to portray the militant monotheist Diego in *Caprica*. Selloi is given a strong performance by Amanda Plummer, also well-known for appearances in *The Outer Limits*, *Pulp Fiction* and *The Fisher King* (1991).

'Exodus' is a triumph of visual effects, writing, direction and performance, paying off the New Caprica arc with a number of memorable and powerful moments. It returns the characters to the status quo of space travel toward Earth without this feeling contrived or unsatisfying.

35: Collaborators

FIRST TRANSMISSION DATE: 27 October 2006 (USA)

WRITER: Mark Verheiden

DIRECTOR: Michael Rymer

CREDITED CAST: Lucy Lawless (D'Anna); Richard Hatch (Tom Zarek); Rekha Sharma (Tory Foster); Dominic Zamprogna (Jammer); Jennifer Halley (Seelix); Ryan Robbins (Connor); Alisen Down (Barolay); Winston Rekert (Priest)

KNOWN UNCREDITED CAST: Leo Li Chiang (Tattooed Pilot)

SYNOPSIS: On *Galactica*, a secret tribunal called the Circle has been formed, consisting of Tyrol, Anders, Tigh, Connor, Barolay and Seelix. They are conducting trials and executions of suspected collaborators, and they airlock Jammer despite his protests that he saved Cally's life. Zarek, currently acting-President, agrees to stand down in Roslin's favour provided he can retain a voice in politics. Roslin offers him the Vice-Presidency. The Circle turn their attention to Gaeta, but Anders, doubtful as to his guilt and concerned about the way the proceedings are being conducted, resigns. The Circle then recruit Starbuck to take his place, and she votes for Gaeta's execution. As Gaeta is about to be airlocked, it emerges that he was the anonymous resistance spy in Baltar's office; a fact that Tyrol confirms, as Gaeta is able to provide accurate details about the dog-bowl message drop system. Learning that the person behind the Circle is Zarek, Adama and Roslin order its termination. Zarek warns that open trials of collaborators would lead to trouble, and Roslin declares a general amnesty throughout the Fleet. Meanwhile, Baltar awakens on a basestar and learns that the Cylons are deadlocked as to whether or not to keep him. With the Sixes having the deciding vote, they finally rule in his favour.

ANALYSIS: 'Collaborators' is another story that shows the human population in a bad light, as several of the former inmates of New Caprica act on understandable, though not justifiable, impulses for revenge. Through this, the episode explores the by-now-familiar theme of legitimate governance.

Round and Round We Go: The Circle

The Circle has as its immediate referents the actions perpetrated by the French Resistance against local collaborators towards the end of WWII, and also the

Jewish Avengers; post-war vigilante groups that would conduct secret trials and executions of Nazis in retribution for the Holocaust. The story explores the desire for revenge that informs the creation of such movements. Starbuck is clearly suffering from post-traumatic stress disorder due to her prolonged captivity. She says, 'I got out of that cell and it's like someone painted the world in different colours'; after having been trapped in her personal hell for four months, she now sees the world even more starkly in terms of abusers and victims, and by her own admission wants to be the one doing the hurting rather than the one being hurt. Connor's stated reason for being involved is that he lost his seven-year-old son in one of the temple raids, but he is also clearly a bully who enjoys his role on the tribunal, saying 'Most of these fraks are so guilty they stink. I could get through 50 of these things in an hour'. Starbuck sums up another key driver toward vigilantism when she says, 'It's like a bad dream, only we woke up and the traitors are all still here'. Although the evacuation saved tens of thousands from New Caprica, Adama notes that 'thousands' were also lost (the figure is actually 2,600; see the analysis for 'Crossroads' for how this was calculated), and the resistance, as illustrated by Tigh's behaviour, are undoubtedly feeling both guilty in themselves, and angry at the collaborators who were rescued while others were left behind;, a situation crystallised in Tigh's case by the fate of Ellen. Indeed, some of the resistance may have collaborated themselves. Seelix approaching Starbuck to join the tribunal, after Starbuck clearly expresses vengeful feelings towards Gaeta, indicates that the Circle are looking for guilty verdicts. The fact that Baltar escaped also means that the humans have no clear hate-figure on whom to physically take out their feelings. Moore comments that Laura, at the end of the story, recognises that her own keeping of a journal during the occupation of New Caprica 'on some level … was supposed to exact vengeance', indicating that the Circle are not isolated, lunatic figures but reflect the mood of the people. The humans try to redraw the line between good and evil to absolve the shame they feel for their own actions and their failures to act.

However, the story shows no sympathy toward this impulse, focusing instead on the moral complexities of retribution. We have already noted how the killing of Ellen was largely a result of the culture the resistance was stoking up during the occupation, as maintaining a continued atmosphere of panic both kept the Cylons off guard and motivated the human population to actively work to leave the planet. Jammer, similarly, is a victim of the post-occupation culture, where Zarek is orchestrating the Circle in order to prevent show trials and people 'lining up to testify against their neighbours', through his officially-sanctioned 'disappearances', so that Roslin can begin her administration without blood on her hands. This presents a horrible, but understandable, political logic: kill off a few so as to prevent, potentially, thousands of people dying in a cycle of retributive justice, and taint one administration with the deaths so as to preserve the integrity of its successor. Moore points out in the podcast that the military characters do not wear their uniforms at the Circle meetings, in tacit acknowledgment that they are engaged in a civil, not a military action.

35: COLLABORATORS

Jammer's case illustrates that the situation is far from straightforward. Following on from the end of the webisodes, it seems he became a captain in the NCP rather than inform on the resistance; the logic behind that decision was clearly that, disturbed by the resistance's tactics and having listened to Doral's rhetoric about human/Cylon unity, he wanted to work for what he saw as the good of society, but the job also allowed him, in the eyes of the Cylons, to legitimately distance himself from his friends in the resistance. During his trial, Jammer acknowledges his culpability for the deaths at the Temple of Artemis; however, he is not a trained soldier but a former deckhand, and his firsthand knowledge of the resistance's tactics means that he was aware that 'People come out with their hands up. But sometimes it's just a trick. They tell you they're surrendering and then they open fire'. The Circle, who, apart from Starbuck, are all resistance members themselves, fail to acknowledge that their own strategies led to innocent deaths; both Connor and Tyrol must know that the temple raids only started because of the resistance's actions as seen in the webisodes, but condemn him anyway. Tigh also must know that Jammer faced a situation not dissimilar to that on the *Gideon*, but says nothing in his defence. Barolay, moreover, as noted in the analysis for the webisodes, is by implication herself an informer, and thus is as guilty as, if not more so than, the people she is executing.

One-Eyed Killer: Tigh versus Gaeta

While Tigh may state that the Circle 'is a jury, it's not about settling scores', this is plainly not the case when it comes to Gaeta. Tigh perceives Gaeta as a traitor who has been let off simply because of his utility – as Tigh puts it, 'The old man needs his phones fixed and suddenly all is forgiven'– although the fact that Gaeta was assistant to Baltar is also clearly a factor in stoking up animosity toward him. Tigh criticises Connor for wanting to execute people without hard evidence, but is all for executing Gaeta, even though the charges against him, 'collaborating with the enemy, and crimes against humanity', are singularly vague, and although Anders and Tyrol point out that there is no hard evidence that can convict him even on these charges. In a clear act of symbolism, the emblem of the 'Vigilantes' (a Colonial Viper squadron established prior to the Fall of the Colonies) is prominent in Tigh's quarters. Tigh also is clearly able to set aside his usual animosity toward Zarek when Zarek is the one backing the Circle's activities. Tigh under strong leadership is a powerful ally, but Tigh off the leash and pursuing a grudge is deeply disturbing.

Consequently, Gaeta's attempts to appeal to reason, pointing out that Baltar was legally elected President, fall flat in a situation where people are looking for scapegoats (and, again, some of them are no doubt trying to salve their consciences for having voted for the man). Starbuck's actions toward Gaeta are a parody of Leoben's abuse of her, as she pretends friendliness in order to have a go at him in front of the other pilots and crew, and later she is seen kicking him and telling him to beg as he is about to be airlocked, hurting him in order to get the emotional response she wants to see. In persecuting Gaeta, the Circle are clearly informed by their own issues rather than any objective assessment of his guilt or innocence.

However, the ultimate resolution of the episode is Roslin's answer to the problem. Although initially in favour of public trials, she acknowledges that Zarek is right that these would consume the Fleet. She takes what is probably the best approach under the circumstances, namely, as with post-apartheid South Africa, a general pardon and the setting-up of a commission for truth and reconciliation, albeit with the knowledge that this will calm, rather than eliminate, the need for vengeance. A general pardon will relieve all the survivors of New Caprica of the fear being implicated (rightly or wrongly) in the events of the occupation; however, it also means that people who have committed crimes will go unpunished. The tentative start of the process of reconciliation is symbolised by the sequence at the end of the story where Tyrol, like Starbuck earlier, sits with Gaeta in the mess, but beside him rather than, as Starbuck did, opposite him. Overtures are being made, but the question of the degree to which the members of the Fleet can in fact move on from the events of New Caprica is still open.

Drum and Basestar: Continuity and Worldbuilding

This episode gives us our first extensive view inside a Cylon basestar. The basestar interior was developed by director Michael Rymer and designer Richard Hudolin with the assistance of the art department. Unlike the more horrific Geigeresque fleshiness of the hangar deck seen in 'Kobol's Last Gleaming', the spare, early-'80s-techno décor of the interior mixes austerity and glowing bands of red light with incongruously baroque furnishings such as the day bed in Baltar's room. The effect is very reminiscent not only of the environment astronaut David Bowman finds himself in at the climax of *2001: A Space Odyssey*, but also of the Lightship/Galactican spacecraft seen in *Galactica 1980*; or, alternatively, of a certain type of overpriced London nightclub. According to *The Official Companion Season Three*, the crew had wanted to have Baltar sitting on a high throne-like chair as in the original series, but, Moore says, they 'never found a plausible explanation of why he would have any position of authority over there'. The draft scripts describe Baltar's room on the basestar as a white space with curved walls set with lights; the 12 May 2006 draft has there being a 'high backed CHAIR that looks roughly akin to a dentist's chair' in the room, but by 16 May this has changed to an 'ornate day bed', as in the final version. Baltar is developing a Christ-like, or possibly Manson-like, appearance, with long hair, beard and white robes, though his awkward, jilted-boyfriend attempts to persuade Six not to vote for his death indicate he is still largely unchanged. The fact that the Cylons were deadlocked over Baltar's fate provides a neat parallel with the Circle.

On *Galactica*, conditions are visibly more crowded than usual, with a large number of civilian refugees. (A deleted scene in the draft scripts establishes that ten civilian ships failed to get off New Caprica.) This is no doubt also contributing to the stress levels on board. A new Quorum of Twelve is being established, and Roslin's decision to ask Zarek to be Vice-President is based on his courage on New Caprica in standing up to the Cylon regime, further cementing her newfound respect for the man. Zarek's remark that Adama would put him in a cell if he tried to remain as President shows him acknowledging the balance of power in the Fleet and working within the system to retain some political status. There is an irony in the fact that the legally-elected regime has now been removed in favour of one endorsed by the military; and the latter's questionable legitimacy is an unstated factor in Roslin's increasing autocracy, and in the inevitable response from within the Fleet, in the episodes to come.

The 'in search of a home called Earth' title sequence end captions are reinstated from this episode on, in place of the '… fighting for survival' ones that accompanied the episodes set on New Caprica. Lee has lost half a stone through exercising with a jump rope. ('Keep jumping', advises his father.) It is also worth noting that both Thrace and Dualla, unlike the other married women in the series, have kept their maiden names.

The Dog-Bowl Code: Writing and Development

In terms of the episode's development, Baltar's storyline was originally to have been more prominent, before being cut to the bone as the writers focused down on the collaborators. According to Moore's podcast, the initial storyline had the retributive killings being carried out by a grassroots vigilante movement, with no formal Circle. The story ended with Zarek, as President, issuing a blanket pardon to the vigilantes as a last move intended to spite Roslin and Adama, who had succeeded in forcing him out of office. According to Moore, originally Tigh was to have been brought into the Circle later, and to have been the one who saved Gaeta's life by knowing about the dog-bowl code; however, the final idea of him being in on it from the beginning, and acting as a ringleader, made more sense in terms of the character's development following Ellen's death. During an interview at San Diego ComicCon 2007, Mark Verheiden revealed that at one point Gaeta was supposed to have been actually killed by the Circle, but the writing team decided, 'There's dark and there's freaking bleak. And that was too bleak'. Moore in his podcast says that Gaeta was also originally to have put more effort into pleading for his life, but Alessandro Juliani argued that it should be underplayed, as if Gaeta realised that such an action would be futile.

While closer to the final version than the ideas outlined above, the draft scripts also show that the story underwent a number of further changes during the writing process. The original version of Baltar's dream had Roslin shoot him rather than kiss him; her line on doing so, 'You know I've always wanted you', remained unchanged, but was given a rather different twist by the subsequent revision. In the 12 May 2006 draft Tigh is drunk when he confronts Gaeta in CIC, but by the 16 May draft this has changed, reportedly because Michael Hogan thought it would be more powerful if his character were sober and thus had no excuse for his behaviour. The 12 May draft places more emphasis on the problem of overcrowding on the Fleet. It also contains a line where Lee tells his father that he's thinking of joining the Marines, presumably referring to the abandoned storyline of Dualla and Lee becoming 'razors'; this has gone by the 16 May draft, as has a line from Lee where he tells his father he's uncomfortable reporting to Helo because Helo is married to a Cylon. (His father tells him bluntly to get used to it.) This goes beyond Lee's previous signs of being unsure of Sharon's loyalties, and presents him as a bigoted racist. Earlier drafts also have Helo and Dualla warmly welcoming Gaeta when he returns to CIC, despite the 'whispered remarks' of other CIC personnel. The 12 March draft does not have the ending with Tyrol eating with Gaeta, but this is present by the 16 May one.

The drafts also contain an interesting character point regarding Tory. Here, it emerges that she has been aiding the Circle, passing to Zarek information obtained from Roslin's diaries. Confronted, Tory explains herself by saying, in part:

> 'I think every one of them – every one who helped the Cylons or trusted the Cylons or even stood silent and let it happen – should be tossed out an airlock, okay? ... After all we've been through, after the genocide of our race, some people still sold out their fellow man to the Cylons. I don't want to hear their lies ... I want those people dead.'

Although deleted, possibly because it is out of keeping with her attitude in 'Occupation' (where she seems a little taken aback by Roslin's vindictive diatribe against the NCP), this sequence is an early indication of the sinister side of Tory's character that will be a driving force behind events in Season Four.

'Collaborators' confronts difficult issues about vigilante justice, the role of government and the problems of rebuilding trust after a war or occupation, and treats them with maturity, eschewing strawman arguments and black-and-white scenarios to give us instead problems for which there are no easy, or immediate, answers.

36: Torn

FIRST TRANSMISSION DATE: 3 November 2006 (USA)

WRITER: Ann Cofell Saunders

DIRECTOR: Jean de Segoznac

CREDITED CAST: Lucy Lawless (D'Anna); Rick Worthy (Simon); Callum Keith Rennie (Leoben); Matthew Bennett (Doral); Lucianna [sic] Carro (Kat); Bodie Olmos (Hotdog [sic]); Leah Cairns (Racetrack); Madeline Parker (Kacey); Sebastian Spence (Narcho); Emilie Ullerup (Julia); Tiffany Lyndall-Knight (Hybrid); Rachel Hayward (Blonde Woman)

KNOWN UNCREDITED CAST: Leo Li Chiang (Tattooed Pilot)

SYNOPSIS: On the basestar, Six and Three tell Baltar that the Cylons intend to make Earth their home, and that if he helps them to find it, this might ensure his survival. Baltar tells them he has identified a pulsar in the Lion Nebula as a navigational marker pointing the way to the planet. He learns about many aspects of Cylon culture, including the practice of 'projection'; the Hybrid who controls each basestar; and the Final Five Cylons, whose identity is hidden. Recognising a similarity between projection and his own visions, he begins to suspect that he may be a Cylon. The Cylons receive a distress call from a basestar that has been sent ahead to investigate the pulsar. The vessel has been infected by an unknown disease. Baltar volunteers to go over to the basestar. He learns, from a dying Six, that the ship was infected when it took on board a probe, which they believe was left by the Thirteenth Tribe. The Cylons jump away, accusing Baltar of having led them into a trap. On *Galactica*, heading toward the same pulsar (with Gaeta piecing together Baltar's research on the location of Earth), Kacey's mother Julia goes to find Starbuck, because Kacey misses her, but Starbuck rejects the child. Although the pilots give Sharon a new call sign, 'Athena', Starbuck and Tigh are spreading bitterness and disharmony as they drink together in the pilots' rec room. Adama confronts them; Starbuck seeks out Kacey to make amends; but Tigh refuses to come back to work.

ANALYSIS: 'Torn' is a Cylon-focused story that forms a two-parter with the subsequent 'A Measure of Salvation', with events on the *Galactica* providing the B plot. Once again, however, events in the two storylines parallel each other, as both Sharon/Athena and Baltar are cautiously and controversially accepted into their new environments.

Ace of Basestar: Cylon Developments

A lot of this episode is devoted to exploring the Cylon way of life. A key concept is Cylon projection, which Caprica-Six succinctly explains: 'Have you ever daydreamed, and imagined that you were somewhere else? ... Well, we don't have to imagine. We project. We choose to see our environment in any form we wish, whenever we wish. For instance, right now you see us as standing in a hallway, but I see it as a forest'. This explains the austerity of the basestar, as décor is not necessary for creatures with such an ability. A stage direction in the 25 May 2006 draft script states, regarding projection: 'The "rule" of cutting between locations is rooted in whose POV we're taking at any given moment. If we're with Caprica-Six emotionally, we're in the Forest; it we're with D'Anna, we're in the Cathedral [which appears only in deleted scenes in the final version]; if we're with Baltar, we're back in the baseship and so on'. (Matthew Bennett has apparently said in interviews that he thinks Doral projects a nightclub.) Six also explicitly indicates that Baltar cannot see her projections, as they are personal to each individual Cylon. We learn about the existence of the Final Five, but Caprica-Six says she can't talk about them. (Fans have unofficially dubbed the remaining other Cylon models the Significant Seven.) Cylons connect with their computers through what the draft script describes as 'a Y-shaped CONSOLE filled with WATER', which explains why Sharon interfaces with the *Galactica*'s computers through a cable in her arm. Rather than finishing each other's sentences like the one at the end of the miniseries did, the Cylons here argue and talk over each other, suggesting that the virus, as something new, is causing divisions between the models as they figure out how best to deal with it.

In terms of Cylon characterisation, all Simons seem to be medical practitioners. (The 25 May 2006 draft script suggests also that they have a scientific curiosity that overrides compassion, when one of them says 'If there's a pathogen out there that poses a threat to us, it needs to be studied, analysed', and a Three tells him, 'The survival of our brothers and sisters should be our first priority'.) We see for the first time an Eight doing a t'ai chi routine naked (in the 25 May 2006 draft, she is puzzled by Baltar's attention and asks if he has a problem). The hangar of the virus-stricken baseship is again fleshy, suggesting that the ships' interface points are where their organic aspects are most visible. The dark-haired Six with whom Baltar speaks on the plague ship is described in the draft script as having long auburn curls and violet eyes, and as being 'the most BEAUTIFUL VERSION OF A SIX that Baltar has ever seen' (capitalisation in the original). The infected Six accuses Baltar of having led them into a trap, deliberately playing on his fears in order to get him to kill her and spare her a painful death from the disease; Baltar, for his part, is clearly horrified when he kills her, as she, of course, looks almost exactly like the woman he loves. The virus seems to have both a physical and an informational component, as infected Cylons can spread the disease through contact and through resurrection; Three states that they must 'move the resurrection ship out of range' before they investigate the stricken basestar.

This episode also introduces the Hybrid. She is a Cylon woman in a tank of fluid, similar to the ones used for resurrection, who is wired in to the basestar and speaks in a stream of consciousness that seems to be part gibberish, part description of the physical situation of the ship (which is in a sense her body), and part prophecy. She appears to orgasm when the ship jumps (the draft script says 'She reacts to the completion of the jump in the way a human would react to climax'), and despite being a human-like model is not considered an equal by the others, as in the exchange between a Doral and a Three: 'The Hybrid objects!' 'She doesn't get a vote'. The Cylons are divided over what they think of her; some believe that her conscious mind has gone mad, and that her vocalisations are meaningless, but the Leobens believe that she is an oracle, and that God speaks to them all through her.

The Cylons are now going to Earth, with D'Anna saying cryptically that they have decided it will be their new home. Although it ultimately derives from the aforementioned story idea in the series bible suggesting that the Cylons want the humans to find Earth, at no point in the series is the decision ever explained on screen. It is also never explained why the Cylons do not return in force to New Caprica: Cavil suggested in 'Occupation' that they could successfully control the human population if its size were reduced to 'less than 1000', and it now numbers less than 2,600. The most likely explanation is that they have lost the military campaign that was drawing their forces away in 'Exodus', and they have now lost New Caprica as well as the Colonies; although the fact that the New Caprica experiment went so badly may also be a factor in why they have abandoned it. It also seems that they have abandoned their interest in breeding with humans, even though only one hybrid child has thus far been successfully produced.

Returning to Normal? The Human Fleet

On the *Galactica*, a time discontinuity has emerged. Lee, or 'Slim' as Helo calls him, has finally lost the belly, and shows off his newly-ripped abs; as Baltar has clearly been on the basestar for only a short time, this suggests that Lee has lost about four stone in less than a week. Moore himself has acknowledged that the rapid weight loss is a bit of a cheat, admitting that once the storyline of Dualla and Lee becoming 'razors' was abandoned, they didn't have much idea of what to do with the character. (In *The Official Companion Season Three*, he is quoted as saying 'Frankly, the Fat Apollo storyline wasn't our finest hour'.)

More seriously, friction is developing between the refugees from New Caprica and their rescuers. The chief complainers are Starbuck and Tigh, with Tigh saying to Helo, 'While you were pinning wings on your Cylon girlfriend, our people were strapping homemade bombs to their chests. Doing whatever they could to take the bastards out. So forgive me if I don't get all misty over your sacrifices'. Starbuck clearly has both a death wish and a desire for vengeance – symbolised when Tigh observes that her choice of card game is

'Deadman's Chest; a cutthroat game, not your usual style'. This leads to her getting pulled from flight duty after causing an accident during a war-game exercise when she disobeys Lee's orders, attacking Kat's Viper rather than leaving her to Narcho. Tigh himself is also off duty, with Helo continuing to act as XO. Starbuck's hostility toward Kacey is a reassertion of the anti-child stance that was formerly a major part of her identity, and a reaction against anyone associated with the Leoben incident. To pull Starbuck out of it, Adama says, 'You were like a daughter to me once; no more'; and indeed, although Starbuck shapes up under this provocation, it has to be said that Adama is becoming closer this season to his other surrogate daughter figures, Kat and Sharon. ('Athena', Sharon's new callsign, was the name of Adama's daughter in the original series.) Starbuck cutting her hair and going to visit Kacey at the end of the story indicates that she is now trying to put New Caprica behind her, acknowledge that what happened was not the little girl's fault, and move on.

Adama's confrontation with Tigh, however, has less positive results. Adama ostensibly intends to stop Tigh badmouthing the New Caprica rescue mission to the pilots, but also clearly aims to shock him out of his self-destructive behaviour. However, although this technique may have worked with Starbuck, Tigh calls Adama's bluff and refuses to return to active service.

Majority Report: References and Production

Moore acknowledges that the Hybrid is visually and conceptually indebted to the precogs of *Minority Report*, specifically the Steven Spielberg film version (2002), and the virus plot to *The Andromeda Strain* (1971). He does not, however, mention that *Carnivàle* also featured a catatonic prophetess, called Apollonia. Moore says that he decided to name Sharon 'Athena' 'on impulse', though some of the alternatives suggested by the pilots in the relevant scene, such as 'Digital Dame', 'Chromedome', 'Wind-up Toy' and 'Toaster Babe', might have been funnier. From a practical point of view, having the two Sharons have different callsigns and surnames helps a lot in telling them apart. This sequence is also the only point in the series at which the often-seen bald and tattooed pilot played by Leo Li Chiang gets to say something (as he is the one who shouts out the 'Chromedome' suggestion). The Hybrid's repeated phrase 'End of line' is a homage to the film *TRON* (1982), in which the Master Control Program always ends his sentences in this way. The Hybrid is also one of a long line of semi-autonomous living creatures used by ships as processing instruments, featured in, among many others, *Dune*, *The Ship Who Sang*, *Lexx*, *Farscape* and *A Judgment of Dragons*.

The story, according to Anne Cofell Saunders, originally focused on Kara struggling to let go of Kacey when Kacey's mother turns out to be a less than ideal parent, and giving up being a pilot to care for her; hence the title. This might have retrospectively cast a different light on Leoben's actions in giving Kara the girl. The 25 May 2006 draft script is closer to the final version, but ends the scene where Kara is reconciled with Kacey with a long speech of apology from Kara, which she concludes by saying that she'll never leave Kacey and her mother Julia again, and a direction indicating that Kara, Julia and Kacey are now a 'new family'. In the course of development, the Cylon story became the A-plot and Kara's own story changed significantly.

The episode was initially to have opened with the pilot training exercise, but Moore felt this was too pedestrian and so added the Baltar and Head Six beach scene, which is in fact footage from the subsequent episode, with new dialogue overdubbed and the actors' mouths blurred where necessary. The 25 May 2006 draft opens with Baltar's first scene with Caprica-Six and D'Anna on the basestar, followed by the training exercise, suggesting a gradual movement towards the final version.

The 25 May draft script runs to 68 pages (most drafts comprise between 50 and 60 pages), and many of scenes appear in longer form than in the final version, suggesting cuts made to bring the story down to time. Notable deleted sections include one where, when Apollo scolds Starbuck after the training exercise, she argues back, telling him he had Kat in his sights and, in her words, 'screwed the daggit' in not following through. In the first scene where Starbuck and Tigh play cards, Kat walks out of the game in disgust at their behaviour. Tigh then taunts Apollo for his scolding of Starbuck, saying, 'It's getting so a soldier can't kick a little ass without taking heat from the brass', and then, "Course ... if your name's Adama, anything goes ...' Apollo leaves, saying, 'Have a few more drinks, Colonel – everyone has a skill', and Tigh remarks to the onlooking pilots that Apollo's skill must be eating doughnuts. On the infected basestar, it is a Leoben, rather than a Six, who accuses Baltar of being from the *Galactica* and is strangled by him (the script refers to Leoben as Baltar's 'first murder victim'); the Six appears, begging for death, but is instead shot by one of the ship's Centurions as it dies. Changing Baltar's accuser to a Six makes more thematic sense. Other deleted, but interesting, lines include a Leoben partially quoting Ecclesiastes 3: 1 ('To every thing there is a season ...') when the Cylons encounter the infected basestar. In the scene where Baltar first sees the Hybrid, Caprica-Six tells Baltar explicitly that the Hybrid wanted to see him, which suggests that it wanted to give him a message; Caprica-Six also says, 'Sometimes there's a word or phrase [of the Hybrid utterances] that makes sense', and the lines the Hybrid speaks at the start of the scene, 'Repeats the harlequin, the agony exquisite ...', seem to look forward to Baltar's torture in the next episode. The Hybrid on the infected basestar is said to be repeating over and over, 'Resurrection is death ... death is human ...' On a more facetious note, when Gaeta suggests investigating the Lion Nebula, Adama says, 'First time I've ever sent a Raptor looking for big game'.

In production terms, the footage of Baltar waking up and looking around (which here follows his dream of Six on the beach) was originally shot for 'Collaborators'. In performing the scene where Starbuck cuts her hair with a knife, Katee Sackhoff sliced her arm by accident on two occasions. The copy of the Pythian scrolls that Gaeta uses is written in a language made up by the props department. According to Moore in *The Official Companion Season Three*, the decision to use multiple dissolves and flat, repetitive classical piano music during the basestar scenes were intended to give them a 'strange, out-of-body quality' (although Moore has admitted that the idea of projection came about because he was concerned that the basestar sets were boring; this is ironic as, in Season One, he had suggested an all-white basestar interior). The Cylons' technology is based thematically around water; in a terrible pun, the liquid they put their hands into as a computer interface is actually called the 'data stream'. Moore's rationale for the Cylon computer interface is that, 'They have chosen to emulate the human form ... so even on their baseship they would not just be plugging in, but it felt like there had to be some more heightened way of them dealing with their environment ... than just pushing buttons and reading things off monitors. So we came up with this idea that ... the Cylons put their hands into what they call the data stream. And that's essentially how they communicate and control and interact with their environment'. However, the human-like Cylons must be capable of receiving direct data transmissions over short distances, as, although they give verbal orders to the Centurions, the Centurions do not talk back. Moore has said that the intention was to convey a culture in which the Cylons were very free with their physicality and sexuality; a cut scene has Baltar complaining about the lack of doors for the sake of privacy. However, Grace Park has implied that she found this exploitative in practice, saying, in *The Official Companion Season Three*, regarding the naked t'ai chi scene, 'I didn't mind doing it, but I think it would have been more interesting if we had had Simon or Leoben doing naked t'ai chi'.

The concept of the Hybrid came out of a production drawing by Richard Hudolin for the basestar. Hudolin drew the creature but said that he didn't know what it was. Moore, however, liked the drawing, and says, 'So we sat in the writer's room and tried to make up, what's the Hybrid about and who is she? And we decided that, well, the Hybrid is ... the being that controls the baseship ... Each baseship has a Hybrid, and the Hybrid controls the entire operation of the baseship'. Originally the Hybrid was filmed sitting up, moving and looking around. However, Moore did not like this and had the whole sequence reshot. The 25 May draft has an extensive description of the creature, which runs, in part:

> 'The HYBRID, lying in her pool of data-carrying nutrient. At first glance, she appears to be a woman whose skullcap has been removed and replaced with conduits and wires ... Her lower torso is completely gone, the base of her spinal column blending seamlessly into a complex tangle of fibers and tendrils, and we begin to realise that, far from being a violated humanoid, she is, in reality, a true lifeform of her own – a hybrid between human and machine forms.'

The part was played by Tiffany Lyndall-Knight, a Canadian-born character actress whose previous credits include *Supernatural*, *Smallville* and *Stargate SG-1*.

The 25 May draft script contains more information about how the basestar works; for instance, it inhales carbon dioxide and exhales oxygen, eats tylium fuel ('Rather … spicy, I would imagine', observes Baltar), and excretes (Baltar inquires if this is the source of the 'remarkably foul odour' he has sometimes noticed in the air, and D'Anna tells him, 'You get used to it').

'Torn' is a fragmented, information-heavy story, and very much a set-up episode for 'A Measure of Salvation'. Nonetheless, it is enjoyable, conveying necessary details about Cylon culture and the human status quo in an effortless way that avoids leaving the audience feeling overwhelmed with info-dumps.

37: A Measure of Salvation

FIRST TRANSMISSION DATE: 10 November 2006 (USA)

WRITER: Michael Angeli

DIRECTOR: Bill Eagles

CREDITED CAST: Lucy Lawless (D'Anna); Rick Worthy (Simon); Callum Keith Rennie (Leoben); Donnelly Rhodes (Doctor Cottle); Matthew Bennett (Doral); Bodie Olmos (Hotdog [sic]); Leah Cairns (Racetrack); Eileen Pedde (Mathias); Tiffany Lyndall-Knight (Hybrid)[63]

SYNOPSIS: A team from *Galactica* investigate the infected basestar. They find five survivors and take them onto *Galactica* under quarantine before the basestar explodes. Cottle learns humans are immune to the disease, but quarantines Athena. Athena turns out to be immune, because she has previously given birth to a half-human baby. Cottle develops a method for keeping the infected Cylons alive through a course of injections, but cannot cure the disease. Apollo comes up with a plan whereby they could kill all the Cylons by jumping to a point near a resurrection ship and murdering their prisoners. Helo objects but is overruled by the others, with even Athena, unhappily, supporting the decision. Helo secretly kills the prisoners before the plan can be carried out. On the basestar, Baltar is still under suspicion of having deliberately led the Cylons to the virus; Caprica-Six and D'Anna torture him, but he withstands through visualising sex with Head Six. D'Anna is troubled by his resilience, and his professions of love for her under torment.

ANALYSIS: 'A Measure of Salvation' concludes the infected-basestar story begun in 'Torn'. In the process, it provides insights into God's plans, Cylon culture, and how, given the means to commit genocide against their enemies, the humans on the Fleet would rationalise their actions.

All Humans bar Helo are Bastards: The Fleet

In this episode, none of the humans apart from Helo comes over at all well. Even Cottle, who treated the Cylon wounded alongside the humans on New Caprica, now coldly proposes using Cylon prisoners for research purposes, saying that observing the development of the infection will tell him how the disease

---

63 Credited but does not appear.

progresses and how long victims live. Helo also notes that Cottle does Athena's bloodwork only after he has finished testing the humans. Roslin, rather viciously, makes use of the fact that they can potentially withhold the treatment from the Cylons to keep the prisoners cooperative.

Apollo, meanwhile, is now wearing Marine gear (apparently a holdover from the abandoned storyline of him becoming a 'razor', which would have seen him join the Marines), marking his change from a fat, directionless dork into a total wanker[64]. In a deleted scene, he asserts that it will be 'a pleasure' to execute the prisoners. Roslin defends her support for the genocide plan by pointing out that the Cylons 'struck first in this war', and then pursued the humans 'through the galaxies'; later on, she emphasises that the Cylons not only want to destroy them, but, as Simon has revealed, to go to Earth as well. Helo, somewhat unwisely given the person to whom he is talking, argues that the Cylons tried to coexist with them on New Caprica, and Roslin bluntly tells him that as he wasn't there, he has no idea what it was like to have 'suffered through that snake pit'. She goes on to say, 'The Cylons are our mistake, we created them', in one of many acts of dehumanisation that the humans commit while carrying out their plan. Athena, meanwhile, in a piece of deeply twisted logic, is willing to let her entire race die, just to prove that she is a loyal Colonial officer, and casts aspersions on Helo's decision to stop the genocide, saying 'My people may die. My entire race may be wiped out. But this Cylon will keep her word, even if it means she's the last Cylon left in the universe. Can a human being do that?'

There is also a crucial deleted scene in which Starbuck goes to see the prisoners and discovers that the infected Leoben is the one who held her captive on New Caprica. He says he is happy to see her and implies that he loves her, saying when she asks about their plan, 'If you want to make God smile, tell him your plans; my plan was to find someone to love, and hope she'd love me back, and try to get her to stay'. She torments him with the existence of the treatment, and when Leoben says that he is not afraid to die, having faith in God, she coldly replies that gods don't always come through in the end: 'Who knows why. They're gods, they have their own priorities. And I'm thinking that your God has more important things to worry about than whether a bunch of sick toasters reach paradise or not'. Although this Leoben's presence would have been something of a coincidence, there is no reason not to kill the character off at this point in the series, and indeed it would not have caused any problem with Leoben's later appearance in 'Maelstrom'. As it stands, it is a powerful and disturbing scene, with Starbuck coming across as truly brutal.

Karl 'Helo' Agathon is, therefore, the real hero of this story, telling his superiors that using biological weapons to wipe out their enemies is a 'crime against humanity'. Although Apollo is quick to say that the Cylons are not human but programmed, the situation raises the question of what, if anything, the real difference is. This episode marks the first time Helo has ever disobeyed

---

[64] 'Crossroads' indicates that the expression 'to wank' is known in the Colonies, and thus that its use in the present day is legitimised by God.

an order; previously he did not do so even when his unborn daughter was about to be aborted. Adama is also troubled by the situation, saying that the act they are proposing can 'tear off a piece of a man's soul' and adding, 'Posterity really doesn't look too kindly on genocide'; he defers the decision to Roslin and lets her take responsibility. In a deleted scene, however, when he addresses the pilots in the briefing room, he says he fully supports the President's decision to use biological weapons, uses the word 'exterminate' to describe what they intend to do to the Cylons and says 'payback is a bitch'. The pilots, Athena and Helo aside, are all for it, grinning throughout the speech and applauding at the end. At the conclusion, Adama refuses to investigate who killed the Cylon prisoners, despite Roslin's urging him to do so, implying that, deep down, he knows Helo was right.

Six and Violence: Baltar on the Basestar

Aboard the basestar, the Cylons are suffering from an existential crisis. Having failed on New Caprica, they are now confronted with what seems to them to be the wrath of God. The virus is capable of wiping them out entirely; in 'Torn', Simon noted that they 'are all created from the same genetic pool'. In the same episode, Athena, not normally given to religious pronouncements, stated, 'When God's anger wakens, even the mighty shall fall'; and Simon now says that he believes God is testing the Cylons. According to Moore, furthermore, this is the first time the Cylons have encountered a disease that could affect them. The only way to mitigate this would be if the virus was a human-engineered bioweapon developed by the Fleet, and thus an act of war rather than an act of God. This possibility is supported in their eyes by Baltar's behaviour: the normally cowardly and self-serving man volunteered for the mission, did not seem overly concerned about catching the virus himself, and then lied, denying that he had seen the beacon that the Cylons had taken aboard their basestar, and that turned out to be the source of the infection. It also supports Three's argument in 'Exodus' that the humans would seek revenge upon them. As a consequence, the Cylons intend to torture Baltar, to death if necessary, because, if he admits it was all a human plot, then they do not have to face the possibility that God has withdrawn his favour.

Head Six is now faced with the problem of keeping Baltar alive. She advised Baltar to go to the basestar to prove his loyalty to the Cylons, but, Baltar having made the situation worse by lying about the beacon, the possibility that the Cylons could kill him is now very real. The crucial moment comes when she advises Baltar, regarding Three: 'Use your intellect against her. Reason. Logic. Analysis. Find the holes in her psyche'. Which Baltar then does, once Three reveals that she believes there are no coincidences and that everything is God's will:

BALTAR: I believe that if God exists, our knowledge of him is imperfect ... Because the stories and myths we have are the products of men, the passage of time. The religion you practice is based on a theory impossible to prove, yet you bestow it with absolutes like 'There is no such thing as coincidence'.

THREE: It's called faith.

BALTAR: Absolute belief in God's will means there's a reason for everything. Everything! And yet, you can't help ask yourself how God can allow death and destruction, and then despise yourself for asking. But the truth is, if we knew God's will, we'd all be gods, wouldn't we?

This exchange both lets God off the hook for New Caprica (as well as the virus, and all the other questionable acts that have been down to him so far), and gives the Cylons hope that God is not out to destroy them. If God's will is unknowable, then New Caprica, and the virus, could be part of a greater plan that the Cylons cannot yet perceive. Baltar then cements this by saying, when Three escalates the torture, that he believes in her and loves her, and by begging her to continue the torture, as it will show the strength of his love. This response not only saves Baltar's life, but it also starts Three on the theological quest that will motivate her over the next few episodes, and plants the seed, in Baltar's mind, of what will later turn into a new religion in the *Battlestar Galactica* universe.

Who is this God Person Anyway?: The Virus and the Wrath of God

The question then remains of what God's role is in all of this, taken from the audience's rather more omniscient perspective on events. The presence of a known virus dating back 3,000 years, to the time of the wars on Kobol (in which God was involved), would suggest that it is a biological weapon from that period, presumably used against Cylons during the conflict.[65] Kobol itself is now free of the virus, as the Centurions were able to operate there unharmed, whereas the Centurions on the infected basestar shut down. (There is an implication here and in 'Razor' that the Centurions may have developed a biological component at some point in their evolution.) The presence of the virus, on the probe and at this particular time, thus must be down to the actions of God.

---

65 SPOILER SECTION: The infected probe cannot have been left by the Thirteenth Tribe, as the humans suppose, because the Thirteenth Tribe are Cylons. This renders Cottle's theory of accidental contamination unlikely, as the speed of the virus's progress suggests that an infected Cylon would soon wipe out the entire Tribe, and they are also unlikely to be deploying biological weapons designed solely to kill their own species. Furthermore, the idea that the Thirteenth Tribe were travelling on their own contradicts the narrative from 'Home', which involved a 'galleon' carrying all the tribes away from Kobol with, it is implied, the Thirteenth Tribe being dropped off first.

At this point in the story, the Cylons are deviating from God's plan; they have given up their attempts to come together with the humans and create hybrid children (and were prepared not just to abandon, but to destroy, New Caprica), and are now instead explicitly focusing on going to Earth. The humans, likewise, in the wake of New Caprica, have clearly abandoned any thought of rapprochement with the Cylons. The virus therefore seems to be a message warning both Cylons and humans away from this path and telling them they must unite: it kills pure Cylons, but not humans, hybrids or Athena, meaning that, to escape its effects, the Cylons must seek out, and unite with, the humans. It is possible that Baltar's trip over to the basestar was partly intended to demonstrate this to them, as Athena's presence on the Colonial expedition allowed the humans to draw the conclusion that hybrids (and their Cylon mothers) were unaffected.

The problem is that, as noted above, both the Cylons and the humans draw the wrong message, with the Cylons accusing Baltar of treachery and torturing him rather than investigating if Hera is also immune, and the humans deciding to use the virus as a means of genocide. God's messenger is, fortunately, able to work through Baltar to defuse the situation on the basestar. However, God has no messenger in the Fleet at this point, so the humans promptly ignore the implications of Athena's survival, and it is only Helo's love for his wife and sense of morality that prevent the destruction of the Cylons. God's plan may be slowly coming back on track, but the use of the virus was a tactic that could easily have backfired, destroying all chance of unity.

Where the Problems Are: Continuity and Technical Issues

This story comes across as both a reversal of the original-series two-parter 'Lost Planet of the Gods' (in which the humans, not the Cylons, were laid low by a plague) and, more pertinently, the unmade episode 'The Raid' (see Analysis for 'Downloaded'), in which the Cylons were to have planned the genocide of the human race. Moore says that the direct inspiration was a *Star Trek: The Next Generation* episode ('I, Borg') in which the Federation planned to unleash a computer virus against the Borg. He also in his podcast mentions 'A Measure of Salvation' having being influenced by the treatment of Native Americans by white settlers; and there is certainly a strong link to historical incident of the British Army giving smallpox-contaminated blankets to the Lenape Tribe of Native Americans during Pontiac's War in the 1760s. Lymphocytic encephalitis is a real disease, and is in fact potentially fatal to humans in a very few cases.[66]

We learn some details about Cylon life. The boarding party connect the Fleet's computers with the basestar by placing 'SSR leads' in the data stream, and the Cylons have a prayer that is said when they know they are going to die with no possibility of downloading, 'The Prayer to the Cloud of Unknowing'. It

---

[66] SPOILER SECTION: This is an early hint that modern humans are the descendants of Hera, and thus part-Cylon.

begins with the words, 'Heavenly Father, grant us the strength, the wisdom and above all a measure of acceptance ...', once again showing that the Cylons believe God is male and paternalistic. The human Fleet learn from Simon that Baltar is alive, having previously believed him dead on New Caprica.

Much time has been spent, by fans on internet forums, attempting to explain how a virus could transmit through downloading – the in-story explanation, from Simon, is that 'a bioelectric feedback component to the pathogen ... corrupts how our brains manage our immune systems' – but we can give this a pass in that the whole species and their technology are fictional, and thus it is up to the writers how their biology works. It is, however, more normally the case that the mother transmits immunities to the foetus rather than *vice versa*, although, as the series also posits that human-Cylon foetuses can be conceived only when the individuals involved truly love each other, its take on reproductive biology is more magical than scientific. Finally, it is rather coincidental that the survivors include one of each model, with no duplicates.

Measure for Measure: Writing and Production

In terms of how the story developed, there were some key changes of personnel and detail. Athena was originally to have been the one who killed the prisoners, though it is considerably more appropriate for Helo to be the one responsible. Originally the probe was to have been brought aboard *Galactica*, which would then, ultimately, have ejected it near a fleet of Cylons, who would jump away upon seeing it; according to Michael Angeli in *The Official Companion Season Three*, Baltar would somehow have sensed its presence and warned them. Moore eventually vetoed this idea because 'we just could never make it work'. A scene dropped at Michael Hogan's suggestion had Tigh again challenging Helo's work as XO, which Hogan felt was unlikely, as Tigh was actively refusing to return to the post at this point in the series. Moore has said that the crucial dialogue between Baltar and Three came into his head, somewhat incongruously, when he was watching fashion-design reality show *Project Runway* with his wife one night.

The sequence of the Raptor moving through a sea of dead Raiders was not scripted, but added by Gary Hutzel in visual effects. The sequences between Head Six and Baltar were done on green-screen, location having been ruled out as the presence of Tricia Helfer topless on an actual beach might have created problems (though a slight hint of artificiality is excusable as the sequence is supposed to be a fantasy). Originally the Six prisoner was to have been the one who told all to the humans, but the decision was made to change it to Simon as it was felt Rick Worthy was generally underused[67], and that it would be more in character for a Simon than a Six to take such an action.

---

67 Matthew Bennett has observed that, as it was cheaper to fly him in from Toronto than to fly Rick Worthy in from the USA, the production team tended not to use Simon that often.

Unsurprisingly, the network voiced objections to the graphic levels of sex and violence in this story. Moore complains that in particular they did not like seeing Head Six orgasm, saying that their attitude was 'like people can have sex, but they can't really enjoy it'. The story was screened with a content warning on first broadcast.

'A Measure of Salvation' may rely on fantasy science to make some of its points (Moore has admitted that at this juncture in the season he was starting to suffer from fatigue, and was having trouble keeping up with the rewrites), but the overall message is solid and intriguing. Although God may be working to bring the two races together, his ways are so convoluted that the humans and Cylons have ignored them, remaining wrapped up in their own personal obsessions.

38: Hero

FIRST TRANSMISSION DATE: 17 November 2006 (USA)

WRITER: David Eick

DIRECTOR: Michael Rymer

CREDITED CAST: Lucy Lawless (D'Anna); Carl Lumbly (Daniel Novacek); Donnelly Rhodes (Doctor Cottle); Matthew Bennett (Doral); Rekha Sharma (Tory Foster); Lucianna [sic] Carro (Kat); Barry Kennedy (Admiral Corman); Tiffany Lyndall-Knight (Hybrid)

SYNOPSIS: The *Galactica* encounters two Raiders chasing a third. The latter turns out to contain Daniel 'Bulldog' Novacek, a pilot from Adama's old command, who disappeared three years earlier during a black-ops mission, allegedly to gather evidence on Tauron miners working an illegal operation that was too close to the Cylon Armistice Line. He claims he was taken prisoner by the Cylons, but escaped when they were laid low by the virus. In fact, the mission was intended covertly to reconnoiter Cylon activities and military strength. Bulldog learns, from Tigh, that when the Cylons discovered and attacked his craft, the *Stealthstar*, Adama deliberately shot him down to avoid the mission being uncovered by the Cylons. Adama believes, in hindsight, that the incident may have precipitated the Cylon attack on the Colonies. Starbuck, reviewing the gun camera footage of Bulldog's escape, realises the Cylons deliberately let him go, and informs Tigh. Bulldog attacks Adama, but Tigh arrives and reasons with him. Adama attempts to resign, but Roslin refuses to accept. Bulldog goes into the civilian Fleet, and Tigh tells Adama what happened to Ellen. On the basestar, D'Anna has nightmares about being shot by Marines, and thinks God is trying to tell her something; she orders a Centurion to kill her, and has visions during the resurrection process, of the opera house on Kobol and five cloaked figures.

ANALYSIS: 'Hero' is the first story this season that Moore did not personally rewrite, as he was now approaching, in his words, 'what we in the writing business call burnout'. As a result, the story fails on almost every level, with problems ranging from plot logic to racist stereotyping.

Mission Impossible: Adama and the Valkyrie *Incident*

The central theme of 'Hero' focuses on Adama's fear that he was responsible for the attacks on the Colonies, with him saying, 'By crossing the line, I showed them that we were the warmongers they figured us to be', and Roslin countering that no single event was the cause: 'We did a thousand things, good and bad, every day for 40 years, to pave the way for those attacks'. The scenario we are presented with appears to be that the Admiralty wanted to test the Cylon defences, and possibly, Roslin suggests, to provoke a war, and were using the fact that some Tauron miners were operating too close to the Armistice Line as a cover story in the event that they had to explain themselves to the Adar administration.

The first problem with the story is that the *Stealthstar*'s reconnaissance mission (shown in flashback) in itself makes little sense, as it involves only a very brief foray across the Armistice Line. Furthermore, if the Admiralty did want to provoke a war, sending a stealth ship was not the best way to do it, as such a ship was unlikely to be detected; indeed, the only reason it *is* noticed is that Adama and Novacek are sufficiently dim that they keep up a two-way radio conversation while Novacek is over the Line. Secondly, Adama's shooting the ship down also achieves nothing, as, whether the ship is captured or shot down, the same message will be received by the Cylons: that their airspace had been violated. Blaming the Taurons for shooting down the craft, also, might play well with the Adar administration, but will surely cause something of a breakdown in diplomatic relations with the Taurons. The Admiralty's plan could thus have seemed workable to them only if they were operating from the starting point that Adama was a complete idiot.

The fact that Adama was subsequently retired to the *Galactica* in disgrace also makes little sense, as the Admiralty had a cover story in place to explain the loss of the *Stealthstar*, and their disciplining of Adama suggested instead that the military were in some way culpable. Moore says in his podcast that the Adama plotline is intended as a partial post-hoc rationalisation for why he might believe that the Colonies brought the Cylon attacks upon themselves, but this is pointless, as no such rationalisation is needed to explain it, and the audience also knows the Cylons were orchestrating the attacks at least one year prior to the Novacek Incident. Moore also acknowledges that the idea of an actual armistice line in space is 'pushing believability'.

The present-day military personnel also appear to be not too intelligent. No-one, other than Starbuck and Tigh, questions the means of Novacek's escape. In a deleted scene, we learn that the reason he found the Fleet so easily is that he figured out that one of the nodules in the Raider, when pressed, caused it to jump to pre-programmed locations; but without this scene, his finding of the Fleet is beyond credibility, making it even more bizarre that neither Adama nor Roslin questions his account. Cottle concludes that Bulldog isn't a Cylon by checking his DNA against his military records; however, if Bulldog were a Cylon to start with, his DNA would still be the same.

The only two human characters who emerge from this with any credit are Starbuck and Tigh. Starbuck clearly now feels closer to Tigh than she does Adama, going to him with her suspicions about Novacek's escape – which is logical, given the confrontation she had with Adama at the end of 'Torn'. She explains that people believed the ridiculous story about Novacek's escape because it was 'something that was credible, familiar'; like the episode itself, it is based on well-known tropes but falls apart when interrogated more rigorously. Despite being the one who provoked Novacek into attacking Adama, Tigh also makes one of the episode's few interesting points (in the only scene that was actually worked on by Moore), when he talks about how people who have been betrayed hang on to their feelings of bitterness, saying 'The toughest part of getting played is losing your dignity ... You get used to it. You start to believe it. You start to love it'. This refers to his own survivor's guilt and trauma as well as to Novacek's. In the end Tigh acknowledges to Novacek that it is better to face the truth than hang on to a lie, even when the truth is considerably more painful. Tigh has on a proper medical eyepatch by the end of the episode, replacing the surgical gauze he has worn since New Caprica, symbolising that he is starting to adapt to his new situation; up until now he has been embracing the anger and bitterness that drove him as the leader of the resistance, but he is letting go of these emotions and once again becoming a professional Colonial officer.

Three is the Magic Number: The Cylons

Fortunately, events on the basestar are far more interesting. Baltar is now allowed freedom of movement again, and he, Caprica-Six and D'Anna are seen in bed together, evidently having begun a troilistic relationship. However, D'Anna's main preoccupation in this episode is a recurring dream of walking through the *Galactica*, being pursued by Marines, and running to a door reading 'End of Line' before being shot, which she interprets as a message from God. There are multiple meanings that can be drawn from this. The first is that the Cylons have now gone as far as they can in terms of directly contacting the humans: any Cylon who approaches the Galactica, at this point in the series, will indeed be hunted down and shot. However, the phrase 'End of Line' also refers directly to the Hybrid, a creature that may be accessing deeper truths through its semi-living, tank-bound state. It is this that inspires D'Anna to seek enlightenment in the state between life and death, through being shot and then reborn in a resurrection tank.[68]

The basestar plotline has no real connection, thematic or otherwise, to the main story on *Galactica*, aside from a line in a deleted scene where Doral asks Baltar why he thinks he is the only human prisoner they've ever had aboard a basestar. In one sense this is a blessing, as the Cylon storyline is a welcome distraction from events on the Fleet. However, its inclusion makes it clear to the audience early on that the 'virus infection' is a trick, as Baltar's Cylons appear in no way concerned about further outbreaks. Eick, in his podcast, has said that he did not want to do a B story – D'Anna's plotline was in fact suggested by

---

[68] As a side point, assuming that the Three who torments Novacek does indeed have the fatal virus, she gives her life for the deception, as the infected are not permitted to download.

Michael Angeli, who had recently had surgery; in his words, 'As I was convalescing, I was naturally thinking a lot about death, and suddenly hit on this idea that D'Anna would constantly kill herself to try to get this vision' – and yet the B story is far better than the A story in every respect.

No More Heroes: Continuity and Worldbuilding

This episode gives details of Adama's backstory before the attacks. We see his *curriculum vitae* briefly, learning that, as stated in the series bible, his mother Evelyn was an accountant, that he grew up in a coastal community, here named as Qualai, and that, in addition to what we already know about his biography, he served as Major on the *Atlantia*, XO on the *Columbia*, and finally commander on the *Valkyrie* (where he was assisted by Tigh) before being sent to *Galactica* as a punishment for the Novacek incident. There is, however, a major continuity error here, in that we are told that Adama commanded the *Valkyrie* three years before the present, which Roslin states was 'about a year' before the Cylon attacks (series chronology would indicate that roughly two and a half years have passed since then), whereas all previous suggestions have been that he commanded the *Galactica* for considerably more time than that; Gaeta, Tyrol, Boomer and Thrace all severally indicate having served with him for two years or more, and it is highly unlikely that they *all* followed him from one ship to the next. Tyrol, in the miniseries, refers to 'the many years [Adama has] served as commanding officer of this ship'. 'Hero' isn't even consistent within itself: in the same episode, Roslin's dossier on Adama has him assuming command of the *Galactica* eight years earlier; closer to the chronology given in the series bible, which has him doing so five years prior to the attacks. Adama is also incongruously wearing an admiral's insignia in the *Valkyrie* flashback.

The abovementioned dossier on Adama raises some further questions about the series' chronology, relative to information given elsewhere. According to the dossier, Adama was born in the year H5/21290, was first commissioned in D6/21311 (making him 21 at the time) and became Commander of the *Galactica* in C2/21348; as it is noted that he is coming up on the forty-fifth anniversary of his commissioning, the year is now 21356 and Adama is in his mid-sixties. The series bible, however, has Adama joining the Academy at the age of 16 and graduating at 19, and spinoff series *Caprica* indicates that at the time of the Cylon attacks he was about 57 – at which age, according to the dossier, he would still have been commander of the *Valkyrie*.

Cast as Novacek was guest star Carl Lumbly, who is best known for having been one of the first black superheroes on American television, in the David Eick-produced series *MANTIS*. Unfortunately, though, the depiction of Novacek is firmly in the realm of the *Othello* stereotype; vengeful and quick to anger. The production establishes this as a character trait by intercutting a sequence of him doing press-ups and then hitting the Three with one of him doing press-ups and then beating the hell out of Adama with a steel pipe. The storyline of Novacek and Tigh has clear overtones of Shakespeare's play, with the latter, Iago-like, dripping poisonous words in the former's ear until he is driven to a murderous rage; although in Novacek's case the object of his anger did in fact betray his trust, Adama, like Desdemona with Othello, forgives him for attacking him. All this is particularly disappointing in light of the fact that the other actor considered for the part, Dennis Haysbert, is also black, meaning that the character's ethnicity was decided at an early stage. We also never see Novacek again after this point (Lumbly having been too expensive to keep on as a semi-regular, according to Moore in his podcast), despite the Fleet being in desperate need of pilots, particularly ones as experienced as Novacek, and the series being in desperate need of strong black characters.

Ride of the Valkyries: Writing and Production

Although the teleplay was written by David Eick, the idea had first been pitched for Season Two by Weddle and Thompson. Early script drafts had Laura asking Lee to investigate the truth of the *Valkyrie*'s mission, and Lee finding recordings of the mission in an audio archive kept on board *Galactica*; an idea abandoned for credibility reasons as well as for taking up too much story time. In some iterations, also, the Taurons had a mining colony that was actually on the wrong side of the Armistice Line, and the *Galactica* (rather than the *Valkyrie*) was going to be sent to forcibly evacuate them and use this mission as a cover for the covert operations. This idea was abandoned as it became too complicated. Kara and Kat were going to be heard discussing a wireless soap opera as they escorted Novacek's Raider in, but Moore says this was cut as it raised the question of where the Fleet was getting the resources from to make popular entertainment. This is a strange observation, as a soap opera would consume no more resources than the wireless talk shows that seem to be continuously running. In an early draft, Adama gave his medal to Tigh, which Moore acknowledges was a little too corny.

The story was in part inspired by the real-life U-2 incident in which an American pilot, Gary Powers, was shot down while flying a covert photoreconnaissance mission in Soviet airspace in 1960. The US administration issued a phony cover story that the plane was a weather research aircraft that had strayed off its path by accident, which the Soviets, who had recovered the plane almost intact and had the pilot in custody, promptly exposed as a lie. Eick has also said that he was inspired by the idea of Joint Chiefs of Staff of the Kennedy era trying to push the President into war. However, the Joint Chiefs of Staff were making strategic moves during a global Cold War with a known enemy, rather than, as with the Colonial Admiralty, provoking a military power with whom they had an armistice of 40 years' standing. Novacek was named after a football player with Eick's favourite team, the Dallas Cowboys, and other first names proposed for him included Seamus and Eugene. The story shares elements with one of Moore's *Star Trek: The Next Generation* episodes, 'The Defector', involving an apparent Romulan fugitive who has in fact been set up to provoke the *Enterprise* into entering the Neutral Zone so that the Romulans can capture the vessel. It bears similarities to the original series *Star Trek* story 'Balance of Terror', in which a cloaked Romulan ship makes stealth forays into Federation space to test their defences, provoking a fight with the *Enterprise*. The black-ops storyline was inspired by *Apocalypse Now*, and the scene of Tigh testing his peripheral vision was a call-back to *Rocky II* (1979). The original series also had, in cut footage from 'Saga of a Star World', a story about Adama attempting to resign his command, and, in 'Baltar's Escape', one about the Council of Twelve voting to give Adama a military honour for reasons of political expediency.

As the team were trying to make up the cost overruns of the New Caprica episodes, this story was made as cheaply as possible. The *Valkyrie* interiors are a partial redress of the *Pegasus* set, and the stealth ship a redress of the Blackbird. The scene where Bulldog escapes was originally to have been done in silence, but the dialogue that Lucy Lawless improvised impressed the crew so much that they decided to keep it in. The team also spent some time discussing how long Novacek's hair ought to be after three years in captivity. Moore transposed the order of some scenes during editing, as is apparent when one notices that Adama's costume switches from his dress uniform to his ordinary uniform and then back again in the last three scenes, where he is at the medal ceremony (dress uniform), then says farewell to Bulldog (ordinary uniform) and finally talks with Tigh (dress uniform again). The epithet 'bullshit' was cut from the American broadcast.

A better title for 'Hero' would have been 'Moron', as, for it to function, almost all of the main characters must act as if they have had their brains removed. If this script had been shredded and placed at the bottom of a hamster cage, then as least it would have served some purpose.

39: Unfinished Business

FIRST TRANSMISSION DATE: 1 December 2006 (USA)

WRITER: Michael Taylor

DIRECTOR: Robert Young

CREDITED CAST: Kate Vernon (Ellen Tigh); Donnelly Rhodes (Doctor Cottle); Luciana Carro (Kat); Bodie Olmos (Hotdog [sic]); Christian Tessier (Duck); Dominic Zamprogna (Jammer); Don Thompson (Figurski)

KNOWN UNCREDITED CAST: Leah Cairns (Racetrack)

SYNOPSIS: A boxing match is held on *Galactica*. This is a traditional activity in which people can challenge each other and literally thrash out old grievances. During the match, characters flash back to the events of the Founders' Day celebration on New Caprica. The evening of Founder's Day, Lee and Kara sneak off to the wilderness to have sex, and declare their love for each other, but Kara secretly returns to the settlement and marries Anders the next morning. Piqued, Lee proposes marriage to Dualla. In the present, Lee and Kara box, but, after beating one another to a pulp, end up embracing. Adama, meanwhile, feeling that he became too friendly with his crew, and in particular that he should have kept them together rather than let some of them go to New Caprica, calls out Tyrol and fights him viciously.

ANALYSIS: 'Unfinished Business' is the episode in which a number of key details are revealed as to what happened on New Caprica between the landing and the cliffhanger at the end of 'Lay Down Your Burdens'. It covers why Adama let so many of his crew settle on the planet, how Starbuck and Tigh became friends, and, crucially, what happened between Lee, Kara, Anders and Dualla. The version of the episode we will be referring to here is the extended cut available on the DVD release, though we will indicate some of the key differences between the two versions where relevant.

Lee and Kara and Sam and Anastasia: The Romantic Quadrangle

The situation at the start of the episode between Lee, Kara, Anders and Dualla is fraught with tension. Kara and Anders have made up enough to have casual sex, but although he says he would like their marriage back, she rejects his overtures because, as Anders states, 'I'm not what you really want after all'.

She blames Lee for her failed marriage, saying that because he won't get them billeted together, she and Anders are on separate ships. Lee in turn accuses her of not taking responsibility for her own 'frakked-up marriage'. Dualla's reason for not wanting Lee to fight Kara is given implicitly in the story she tells: 'When I was six years old, there was this boy in my neighbourhood, he used to wait for me after school and knock me down. Know what my mom told me? It wasn't because I pissed him off. I wasn't too much older when I realised that the other side of hatred isn't love. It was passion'. As the tension mounts between Lee and Kara, Dualla openly says to them both, 'Why are you two even fighting? Why not just get a room?' Anders, observing their bout in the ring, remarks, 'Looks like they're trying to kill each other', and Dualla dryly responds, 'That's one perspective'. When Lee and Kara embrace, covered in blood, at the end of the fight, Anders, well aware of the situation, says 'I'm out of here'. Dualla, however, waits until the fight is finally concluded. The reason why is explained in the scene in which Lee proposes to her: Dualla states that she knows he is in love with Starbuck but that she will marry him anyway, and live with him until either the Cylons attack or Starbuck comes back into his life, as she wants to live for the moment.

The crucial moment for Lee and Kara comes in the New Caprica flashbacks, after they have both wandered away from the celebration together. Lee spars verbally with Kara, seeking out her weaknesses, and effectively 'wins' the bout by drawing her into making love with him for the first time. The next day, she feels guilty about this and marries Anders, leading Apollo in turn to propose to Dualla. All of this loosely follows the description of the characters' arc in the series bible, which says that Lee and Kara will be attracted to each other from the start, but will not act upon it, and that 'Their friendship and attraction for one another will quickly find them waking up together after a stressful night that turned into something more. Each will be wracked with guilt and mixed feelings and they'll avoid talking or dealing with what happened, and each in turn will be driven toward other, more unexpected, people'.

Implicit in the whole affair is Zak: they could not act on their mutual attraction at first because Kara was engaged to Zak, and then afterwards, her guilt over Zak's death and Lee's fear that his taking his brother's fiancée was somehow inappropriate under the circumstances, meant that they could not begin a relationship with each other, hence their seeking out of other partners. There is also, however, a more sinister undercurrent of forbidden love: that their attraction was initially fuelled by the fact that she was engaged to another man, and now, with both of them in relationships with other people, it revives and compounds that aspect of their feelings.

However, there is a positive consequence from their one-night stand, in that when Kara informs Tigh about it and he encourages her to see the relationship problem in tactical terms, this marks the start of her and Tigh's friendship. Tigh says, 'It's combat, survival instinct starts to kick in, make your choice, don't look back', as a result of which Kara marries Anders and makes a break with *Galactica*, putting the complications and guilt associated with Lee

39: UNFINISHED BUSINESS

behind her; however, when New Caprica collapses, the problems return.

Reefer Madness: Adama and his Issues

Other consequences of the New Caprica situation are played out in the Adama storyline. On the planet, Adama was moved by his cheerfully stoned conversation with Roslin about the need to live in the moment and embrace pleasure where you find it, to allow Tyrol, Cally and Starbuck to muster out and join the colonists, with the result that all three were caught up in the Cylon occupation. At the start of 'Unfinished Business', the crew aboard *Galactica* are evidently slacking, with Dualla telling Adama, 'We're seeing botched drills and missed deadlines across the board … Sir, I suggest we cancel tonight, call everyone back to duty'. Adama, though, argues that the boxing match will allow the crew to 'adjust our heads a bit, refocus'. However, when Tyrol casually reveals to him later that he is letting the deck crew take the night off, Adama challenges him to a fight; Tyrol, once he starts taking the match seriously, also lands quite a few blows, making the bout as much an exercise in self-punishment for Adama as an attack on slack discipline. Adama summarises the point of the lesson at the end of the match: 'I let you get too close. All of you. I dropped my guard. I let this crew, and this family, disband. And we paid the price in lives'. In saying this, Adama acknowledges that the crew need not friendliness and leniency, but discipline and a focus on duty.

Sometimes a Cigar is Just a Cigar: Continuity and (Multiple) Worldbuilding

Although New Caprica is usually shown in the series as a grim environment, Founders Day takes place in sunshine, and the bright light and glowing colours give the flashbacks a sense of nostalgia. However, there are continued hints in the New Caprica sequences of trouble ahead; Roslin's wraparound dress is red, a colour associated with the Cylons, and Jammer and Duck are clearly visible at the groundbreaking ceremony.

In contrast, we have the tradition of boxing matches, or 'dances', which form a sharply-drawn parallel to the literal dancing we see on New Caprica; the ring resembles the dance floor, and Kara's surprise marriage parallels her illegal move during her boxing match with Lee. Kara's and Lee's dialogue continually has a double meaning associating the fight and their relationship, as when Kara observes of Admiral Adama's boxing technique: 'He knows when to make his moves, when to hold back. I wish I could say the same for his son'. The tradition apparently excludes civilians. Evidence of some otherwise-unexplained grudges comes up, as we see Kat fighting Racetrack. The fact that Helo goes quite aggressively for Lee may be due to the latter's behaviour in 'A Measure of Salvation'; though Helo's remark 'He's a tough little frakker, I'll give him that. He's springing like he's got it in for me', shows that Lee clearly also has some issues with him as well. From a narrative point of view, the story shows Kara winning against Hot Dog, and Lee losing to Helo, specifically to indicate that the match between Kara and Lee is a fair fight, as boxing matches between men and women are rare on television. The other personnel clearly are unfazed by the situation, with Kat, in the broadcast cut, audibly, and somewhat maliciously, yelling 'Watch that pretty face!' as Kara takes a blow.

In continuity terms, Kara smokes a cigar on New Caprica, briefly returning to her earlier vice. Lee and Dualla officially keep their relationship a secret until her transfer to the *Pegasus* comes through. As she has been promoted to lieutenant, this reticence has nothing to do with the prohibition against fraternisation, though this of course raises the question of whether the relationship is the reason for the promotion. In the present, Anders puts his boots outside the officers' quarters to indicate a need for privacy, a custom that appears in a cut scene from 'The Captain's Hand', and there are references during the boxing match to Lee's earlier weight problem, with Kara remarking that a couple of months earlier they would have had to 'roll him into this ring'. Cottle exclaims 'Christ!' while treating Adama. Kara has lost the sticking plaster on her back, and now has a large black tattoo of a step pyramid in its place.

Boxing Day: Writing and Production

Writer Michael Taylor's first pitch to the series was to suggest an episode revolving around the crew working off their tensions in 'a *Fight Club* (1999) kind of way'. Taylor says in *The Official Companion Season Three* that 'The New Caprica scenes had to be shot at the same time as we were doing the first four episodes ... After the flashbacks had been shot, I then had to figure out the present-day scenes'. Originally the flashbacks were meant to cover the whole year on New Caprica, but they were then focused down on the situation between Lee and Kara at the Founder's Day party. The Founder's Day sequences are loosely based on aspects of *My Darling Clementine* (1946), which features a scene involving the dedication of a church followed by a square dance, and which has an analogous love-quadrangle subplot. *Babylon 5* also featured a boxing-themed episode, 'TKO'. There were many different ideas considered as to how the rift between Kara and Lee came about, including Dualla finding them together, Adama finding them together, Kara revealing to Lee that she knew Adama had been cuckolded by his wife, and Lee sleeping with Kara after her wedding. However, the team decided the worst thing Kara could do would be to sleep with Lee and then straight away marry another man.

The story was originally to have featured Gaeta, racked with self-loathing, going into the ring and allowing Athena to beat him up; but, as Alessandro Juliani says in *The Official Companion Season Three*, 'It seemed a bit weird, on many fronts'. The fight between Kara and Hot Dog was originally scripted to be comedic, with Hot Dog being felled swiftly by a one-two shot amid much laughter. Moore admits to having written the little song Adama sings while stoned, beginning 'Ever see a little light, before the dawn of the light ...'

The location filming took three days, of which two were spent on the party sequence. The boxing sequences were coordinated by Aleks Paunovic, who can

39: UNFINISHED BUSINESS

also be seen in the ring in a black top fighting stuntman Paul Lazenby, and who is a former Canadian super-heavyweight boxing champion, which accounts for the boxing being so well choreographed. This was assisted by the fact that Tahmoh Penniket is an amateur boxer and kickboxer; he was disappointed with the first script, which did not have Helo fighting, and it was subsequently changed to allow him to show off his skills. Originally Lee's initial fight would have been against a guest star, and he would have won, establishing his ferocity rather than his fallibility. The set that houses the boxing ring would be used for Joe's Bar in Season Four.

The episode required a lot of editing, and the broadcast version is quite different from the editors' cut, Dualla's scenes being the chief casualty of the changes. The extended version that appears on the DVD is a working copy from which the team developed the final episode; the broadcast version focuses more on Kara and Lee, whereas the extended version is more even-handed and also includes a lot of alternative takes to the ones finally used. The sequence of Lee proposing to Dualla in the Raptor, which appears in the editors' cut, was filmed much later, after the rest of the episode; the writing team were divided over it, some feeling it made Dualla look weak, but had it shot anyway in the hope of cutting it into a later episode (which ultimately never happened).

On broadcast, the network objected to Adama and Roslin cuddling together, even though they were both fully clothed adults, and also asked for the idea that they were, as the script openly puts it, smoking 'a joint', to be toned down. Moore says that he told the network censors to 'Go fuck themselves' in one phone call, and got his revenge by including much more explicit toking in the extended cut.

'Unfinished Business' is, unusually, a story with, as Moore notes, very few visual effects, no Cylons bar Athena, and no thriller action, just a simple exploration of the characters through the medium of a boxing tournament, as Adama sacrifices his own affections to teach Tyrol that weakness has no place in war, and Kara and Lee work out their earlier problems, creating new ones for themselves in the process.

40: The Passage

FIRST TRANSMISSION DATE: 8 December 2006 (USA)

WRITER: Jane Espenson

DIRECTOR: Michael Nankin

CREDITED CAST: Lucy Lawless (D'Anna); Luciana Carro (Kat); Donnelly Rhodes (Doctor Cottle); G Patrick Currie (Enzo)[69]; Bodie Olmos (Hotdog [sic]); Brad Dryborough (Hoshi); Leah Cairns (Racetrack); Sebastian Spence (Narcho); Tiffany Lyndall-Knight (Hybrid); Sean Roche (Hungry Boy); Ian Rozylo (Convulsing Pilot)

KNOWN UNCREDITED CAST: Leo Li Chiang (Tattooed Pilot)

SYNOPSIS: Accidental contamination renders most of the food on the Fleet inedible. The crew locate a planet where there are large amounts of a high-protein algae that can be processed into a food source. To reach it, however, the ships must pass through a star cluster full of dangerous radiation that affects navigation equipment. A plan is set up whereby Raptors, which have radiation-shielded navigation systems, will accompany the civilian ships on their jumps through, necessitating five round trips per Raptor. Kat encounters Enzo, her former lover with whom she ran an illegal smuggling operation; he threatens to reveal her past to the military. Starbuck sees Kat with Enzo, pressures Enzo into telling her their history, and confronts Kat, who admits all, but begs Starbuck to let her tell Adama herself. Kat secretly swaps her radiation meter with Helo's so that he will be grounded and she can run another mission. She rescues the lost ship *Faru Sadin* before collapsing of radiation sickness. Adama stays with her as she dies, and recognises her heroism by promoting her to CAG. On the basestar, Baltar interprets the Hybrid's sayings to D'Anna, explaining that they should seek out a planet in a star cluster, to find the Eye of Jupiter, which will lead them to the Final Five.

ANALYSIS: 'The Passage' is a story focused on the death of Louanne 'Kat' Katraine. Writer Jane Espenson, in her first script for the series, builds on the characters in ways that make sense given their past development, but in doing so, exposes some deeply disturbing themes.

---

69 Credited as 'Patrick Currie'.

40: THE PASSAGE

The Ballad of Louanne Katraine: The Life and Death of Kat

In this story, we find out that Kat is not who she claims to be. Her real name is Sasha (she tells us that she took the name Louanne Katraine from a woman who died on Caprica two days before the attack), she was associated with Enzo in a drug-running operation, he as supplier and she as smuggler, and she lied her way into the service, taking advantage of the loose background checks after the holocaust. Starbuck's behaviour to Kat throughout the story is vicious, picking up on her jealousy of Kat in earlier episodes, but when she learns of Kat's history she becomes particularly savage, telling her to accept who she is; meaning, a traitor, a liar and a criminal. However, a re-examination of the scene order based on what Moore says in his podcast, coupled with the deleted scenes, reveals a story that is even more disturbing. It seems that originally, Kat's clash with Apollo and Starbuck over issuing stims to the pilots was to have come first, followed by Adama supporting Kat over the stims issue, followed by Enzo recognising Kat, followed by Kat claiming that she cannot share her protein bar with the pilots because she has given it to Cottle, followed by Starbuck seeing Kat talking with Enzo. This indicates a logical chain to Starbuck's actions. Becoming suspicious that Kat, who cares about her fellow pilots, did not share her food with them (as well as being jealous over Adama's backing of Kat, even though, as she is not CAG, her authority is not threatened), and curious as to how Kat knows so much about the physical effects of stims on an underfed person, she investigates who Kat might have given the food to, and then makes use of the information. Enzo has a tattoo of the Medusa on the left side of his neck, which is visible when he is confronted by Starbuck; as feminist theory encodes the Medusa as a symbol of female power and rage, Starbuck is here embodied as the Medusa. Starbuck's apparent contrition at the end of the story is, as always with her, too little too late; although her expressions of regret when she gives Kat some sleeping pills as a means to suicide may be sincerely felt, the fact remains that she is delivering the *coup de grace* to a woman she set out to kill.

The true tragedy is that, although Kat fears Adama's reaction when he learns about her past, the Admiral is more concerned about who she is now than about who she used to be. Apollo, in a deleted scene where he scolds Kat for going over his head to Adama regarding the stims issue, does nonetheless admit that she did it because she genuinely cares about the other pilots. Kat's promotion to CAG on her deathbed is an acknowledgement that, had Adama not taken her advice over the stims issue, the mission would have been a complete disaster. Kat forgives Starbuck at the end and tells her she knows she didn't mean it, even though Starbuck did clearly mean every word.

Kat's present heroism is in contrast to her past life, symbolised by the return of Enzo. Like the radiation field that kills her, Enzo has a destructive effect on Kat; he is drawn to her through hunger, not love, and clearly views her as a way of acquiring food. When Starbuck, in a deleted scene, tells Enzo she is getting him off *Galactica*, he realises that Kat is of no use to him anymore, and he destroys her life by revealing her secret to Starbuck. Starbuck's confrontation with Kat is what ultimately leads to her suicide. Although recognising the danger Enzo poses, Kat is still drawn to him; she calls him a thieving bastard and says 'You'll ruin everything I got', and yet she is the one who initiates their lovemaking, reaching out for intimacy as people do at times of crisis, perhaps driven by a revival of her earlier love for him.

Adama, meanwhile, acknowledges Kat as another of his surrogate daughters, telling her that he would have liked one of his children to have been a girl (saying, although Lee is not there to hear it, 'Three's a nice round number', indicating that he also loves both his sons). Adama sums up his attitude not just toward Kat, but toward every one of his protégés including Starbuck and Tigh, when he says that her past is not important, and the fact that she protected her people is what matters. Kat's promotion to honorary CAG recognises that she has earned the military's respect.

While the story of Starbuck's jealousy and attack on Kat still partly reads, due to Katee Sackhoff's and Luciana Carro's performances, the changing around of the scene order has diluted it. The placing of the confrontation about the protein bar first, implying that Kat ate the bar herself rather than sharing it with the pilots who divide their meagre rations with her, and the removal of the scene where Starbuck complains to Adama and learns that he nonetheless supports Kat, makes Starbuck's actions seem more justified. It furthermore loses the implication that Adama playing favourites among his pilots is also in part to blame for Kat's death, in that it fuels Starbuck's jealousy. Moore appears to have been overly concerned about showing the series' central figures in too negative a light; as a result, the story is less true to the characters involved.

Eye of the Cow: The Cylons

Baltar discovers that D'Anna has been repeatedly killing herself and downloading. Confronting her about it (using as evidence the 'dried goo' in her hair from the resurrection tanks), he learns that she is doing so in order to induce visions as a way of learning the identity of the Final Five. He joins forces with her, and they try to gain more insight from interpreting the Hybrid's prophecies. The crucial moment comes when the Hybrid, seizing Baltar's arm, says: 'Intelligence, a mind that burns like a fire. Find the hand that lies in the shadow of the light. In the eye of the husband of the eye of the cow'. Baltar interprets this as referring to the Eye of Jupiter, as Jupiter is the husband of Hera, often called 'cow-eyed'. The Final Five are represented in the prophecy by the 'hand', with its five fingers.

The rationale behind Baltar's actions draws parallels between him and the protagonists of the episode's A plot. Where Kat tries to make up for her past by helping people, and Starbuck's history draws others down with her into a spiral of destruction, Baltar deals with his past misdeeds by attempting to change the rules of the game. If he could prove that he is a Cylon, he surmises, he 'would stop being a traitor to one set of people, and be a hero to another. And have a place to belong'. Baltar's selfish actions in having allowed Caprica-Six access to the defence mainframe would, in this event, be justified. However, he does not seek to atone for his actions or to feel any form of remorse; he would be essentially getting something for nothing, rather than working for his redemption.

Passing On: Continuity and Worldbuilding

In terms of original series references, the most obvious connection is again to 'Saga of a Star World', with contaminated food supplies necessitating a search for new resources. The radiation field reads like a cross between the same episode's Nova of Madagon, which original-series Apollo describes as 'not a nova at all but a star field so bright our cockpits will be sealed to prevent blindness', and the magnetic field of 'Lost Planet of the Gods', which distorted the readings of navigation equipment. The story is also an inversion of 'Murder on the *Rising Star*', which involved a pilot blackmailing civilians who were operating under false identities. In the reimagined series, there are similarities to '33' with the portrayal of the crew's exhaustion, to 'Water' and subsequent stories with the loss of an essential resource, to 'Flesh and Bone' with the exposure of Starbuck's negative side, and to 'Hero' and 'Tigh Me Up, Tigh Me Down' with the disruptive return of a figure from a regular character's past.

In continuity terms, one deleted scene has Helo telling Athena that he is afraid of radiation sickness due to their experiences on Caprica. Although this unfortunately reminds the viewer that Caprica was the least credible radioactive wasteland in the known universe, it adds an extra layer to Kat's motivation in swapping her radiation badge for his. While it was ultimately cut, Espenson says that the script contained more detail about food production on the Fleet, including that, prior to the contamination incident, they grew meat from cloned cells. It is never actually explained in the story how the planet was located, or how they knew there would be algae there, as they are currently in uncharted space.

Kat's picture is pinned up by Starbuck next to the one of Reilly's girlfriend; in 'Scar', Kat's worries about being unable to remember the woman's name were an externalisation of her own fears that she herself would be forgotten after her death. Learning that Kat's name is not her real one also adds another layer to her concerns about remembering the names of the dead. Finally, the reference to Adama wanting a daughter was an autobiographical reference to Moore himself, who, when starting a family, had wanted 'a house full of girls', but instead had two sons and a daughter.

Making of a Hero: Writing and Production

Writer Jane Espenson had been an academic (having worked with Berkeley's Professor George Lakoff, expert in cognitive linguistics) and was a veteran scriptwriter for *Buffy the Vampire Slayer*, *Angel* and *Firefly* among others. She would subsequently become one of the showrunners on the *Battlestar Galactica* prequel series *Caprica*. Moore, who had previously worked with Espenson, says in the podcast, 'We heard that she was really excited about the idea of doing an episode of *Galactica* ... and so we jumped on the opportunity to have Jane write one for us'. The notion of focusing an episode around food shortages had been considered by the writing team for some time. The *Galactica* story changed little from initial draft to finished version, though the basestar aspect was originally more prominent, focusing on the divisions being caused in Cylon society by the presence of Baltar and his sexual relationship with Three and Six. A subplot relating to Roslin starting to share visions with Athena was moved into later episodes, and, according to *The Official Companion Season Three*, one involving the reserving of radiation drugs for Adama and Roslin was cut entirely, although it is rather vague as to what this subplot would have involved.

Enzo originally had a more extensive role, and, during Kat's death scene, was, according to Moore, 'standing in the doorway to sickbay ... looking in forlornly', but this was cut back as it was felt that he was less interesting in and of himself and more in terms of what his presence reveals about Kat. Kat was at first simply a drug-runner, but Moore added the idea that she had also participated in human trafficking. This was so as to suggest the possibility that she had unwittingly smuggled Cylons into the Colonies, backing up Roslin's assertion to Adama, in 'Hero', that the attacks were not the product of any one person, and also reinforcing the parallels between Kat and Baltar. Finally, there was to have been more Lee and Kara scenes, including one where they talk about the events brought up by 'Unfinished Business' while, as in 'Home', bouncing a Pyramid ball against a wall, and a final one where they embrace, which was cut as it was felt that it was best to end on Kara feeling the loss and guilt over Kat's death.

Staff scientific consultant Doctor Kevin Grazier, of the Jet Propulsion Laboratory, advised on the astronomical detail. The Hybrid scenes were shot much later; as Moore says, 'We had shot one version of the Hybrid in its initial episode, saw it, didn't like it. Stopped everything. Did not shoot subsequent Hybrid scenes until we had worked out exactly how it was supposed to be. Then went back, reshot the first Hybrid scene, and then shot all the subsequent ones'. Luciana Carro found out about her character's death before being officially told, and was deeply upset. She says that 'several crewmembers' tried to rewrite the story so that Kat survived, or turned out to be a Head Person. This is the only episode to give Carro a credit at the start, rather than in the end credits. Starbuck's sarcastic remark, when Kat claims that she gave Doc Cottle her last protein bar, 'Right after I gave him head', was cut from the American broadcast.

In a deleted scene from 'Exodus', Adama says to Kat that as a boy, he was small for his age, and that under those circumstances you have to be either a good talker or a good fighter, then, alluding to Kat herself, 'I don't know where you come from but I do know this, you got here under your own power ... That's all that matters to me'. Kat is a small woman, facing a tough fight for acceptance within the Fleet, but through her caring, her courage and finally her self-sacrifice, she has earned everyone's respect.

41: The Eye of Jupiter

FIRST TRANSMISSION DATE: 15 December 2006 (USA)

WRITER: Mark Verheiden

DIRECTOR: Michael Rymer

CREDITED CAST: Lucy Lawless (D'Anna); Callum Keith Rennie (Leoben); Dean Stockwell (Cavil); Brad Dryborough (Hoshi); Eileen Pedde (Sergeant Mathias); Alisen Down (Barolay); Tiffany Lyndall-Knight (Hybrid); Diego Diablo Del Mar (Hillard); Aleks Paunovic (Sergeant Fischer); Tygh Runyan (Private Sykes)

KNOWN UNCREDITED CAST: Richard Thompson (Ditko)

SYNOPSIS: The Fleet have been gathering food supplies on the algae planet for two weeks. Apollo and Starbuck are having an affair; he wants them to divorce their respective spouses and marry each other, but she refuses to divorce Anders and wants instead to carry on their clandestine relationship. On the planet Tyrol discovers the Temple of Five, built by the Thirteenth Tribe; Roslin believes it may house the Eye of Jupiter, which, according to the scriptures, is a marker the Tribe left behind to point the way to Earth. Cylons jump into the system and request a face-to-face meeting; they believe the humans have located the Eye of Jupiter, which they think is a physical artefact, and want them to give it up. Adama agrees to the meeting as it buys him time to get his people off the planet, and informs the Cylons that if they attack, he will nuke the planet's surface. Athena encounters Boomer and learns that Hera is alive and on the basestar. The humans defend the temple while Tyrol searches for the Eye, and intend to blow the place up if the Cylons try to gain access. Apollo, at Starbuck's suggestion, drafts Anders to command the civilians. D'Anna, unbeknownst to the other Cylons, put a Heavy Raider full of Centurions on the planet's surface and sets in motion plans to take the temple. Starbuck's Raptor is shot down, and Anders wants to disobey orders and go after her. Heavy Raiders are sent to the planet, and Adama authorises the use of nuclear weapons.

ANALYSIS: 'The Eye of Jupiter' forms a two-part story with 'Rapture', and is the final episode of the first half of Season Three. Consequently, it focuses on the major themes of the half-season: the Lee-Kara love quadrangle, the search for Earth and the Final Five, and the long-term consequences of the New Caprica occupation.

BY YOUR COMMAND: VOL 2

Two Weddings and a Potential Funeral: The Love Quadrangle

Lee and Kara have now begun an affair, under cover of Kara piloting the Raptor ferrying supplies to the people on the surface. Kara refuses to get a divorce, on the grounds that marriage is a sacrament, reflecting her intense religious beliefs: she would rather, as she puts it, 'bend the rules' than risk the anger of the gods, whereas Lee views this as hypocrisy. (As Moore points out, Lee is the child of divorce himself.) The situation is summed up in the exchange where Kara says, 'So, I won't divorce, and you won't cheat. So where does that leave us?' and Lee responds, 'Trapped'.

Events take a very sinister turn, however, when Kara suggests using Anders to command the civilians in the case of a Cylon attack. Although the idea has a certain military logic, as Anders was the leader of an improbably successful civilian resistance movement, Anders himself points out that guerrilla tactics are quite different from what is required here, defending a fixed position. Kara gives Lee a significant look when she makes the suggestion, and it is unlikely that the idea of Anders catching a bullet and resolving both their problems has not also occured to him. In the conversation where Lee orders Anders to lead the civilians and Anders questions the order, Kara steps in on Apollo's side, saying, 'Honey, the Major's in charge on this one, okay?'; Anders retorts, 'Well, I certainly wouldn't want to step between you and your Major', indicating that he suspects on some level he is being set up (although it seems he thinks this to be entirely Lee's idea, and does not recognise Kara's part in it). The situation has distinct overtones of the Biblical story of David and Bathsheba, in which the former covered their adulterous liaison by putting the latter's husband in the front line, ensuring his death.

While the previous episode compromised the idea of Kara as a malevolent force by changing the scene order in editing to suggest a justification for her attack on Kat, this episode shows her in a very sinister light, and taints Lee through his agreement to the plan. It also, retrospectively, makes the viewer question the circumstances surrounding Zak's death: with the Anders story in mind, the implication is that Kara's clearing Zak for flight was a deliberate act, with the hope that he would suffer a fatal accident, leaving her free to pursue Lee. In 'The Eye of Jupiter', Kara suspects Dualla of putting her in the firing line when she is assigned the dangerous job of flying recon, failing to recognise that such an action would be out of character for Dualla, but indicating that it is something she herself would think of.

Later, when Lee refuses to authorise a rescue party for Kara, using the sound military logic that they do not have the personnel to spare, Anders, who does not think in these terms, suspects he is now trying to kill her, in light of the fact that this takes place soon after Anders has revealed to Lee that Kara has had multiple affairs since they have been married. While the writing team, no doubt conflicted about the character, may not want to acknowledge this directly, Kara is inevitably set on the path of destruction, and taking Lee with her.

The problem with this particular take on the character stems from attitudes toward gender. Female philanderers are generally viewed in a much more negative light than male ones: the creators of the film *Starship Troopers* were surprised to learn, for instance, that audiences universally condemned Carmen for having a relationship with two men at the same time, but had no problem with Rico carrying on with two women. Thus, while philandering has been part of Starbuck's character since the 1978 series, in which he conducted relationships with at least two, and probably more, women simultaneously, in the male original's case it was treated as just a quirky personality trait, but in his female successor's case it becomes the root of a murderous character flaw. Katee Sackhoff has gone on record as saying that she hated the love-quadrangle storyline; and, in view of the subtext, this is understandable.

Giving Them the Eye: Cylon Politics

The break-up of the Six-Baltar-Three relationship runs parallel to the jealousies within the love quadrangle, as Baltar and D'Anna-Three shut Caprica-Six out and go off on their own mission. In another parallel, the relationship here also intertwines with military objectives, as D'Anna's and Baltar's mission serves the Cylon plan to acquire the Eye of Jupiter. Like Kara, the pair also have a destiny, with D'Anna saying, 'Baltar's and my destiny lie separate from yours, Caprica'. However, when the Hybrid says, 'The five lights of the apocalypse rising, struggling toward the light, sins revealed only to those who enter the temple, only to the Chosen One', and looks at Three and Baltar, it is not certain which of them she means; clearly, each of them think they themselves are the one. This all symbolises the growing divisions among the Cylons, as D'Anna takes military decisions without consulting the rest of them.

Otherwise, Cavil shows his deductive abilities, figuring out why the Fleet did not jump away at once when confronted by the arrival of four basestars (namely, that the humans have found the Eye of Jupiter but have not been able to retrieve it), and quickly dismissing Roslin's story that this is entirely down to the fact that they still had people on the planet. When Boomer arrives on *Galactica* with the Cylon delegation and meets Athena, there is clearly tension between the two, with Boomer envious of the fact that Athena is not only a respected member of the crew, but has this respect despite everyone knowing she is a Cylon. This is also the first time that Cylons are heard using their human names among themselves, rather than just with Baltar, with a Three referring to Cavil by this designation, and D'Anna being named as such by both Caprica-Six and another Three. The practice is an early indicator that there is something particularly significant about these two Cylons, but the actual meaning of this will not be explored until 'Rapture'.

What's It All About, Algae: Continuity and Worldbuilding

On the Fleet, Adama is prepared to nuke the planet despite Starbuck, his son and Dualla all being down there, suggesting that, following his speech in 'Unfinished

Business', he is now willing to take the larger strategic view and sacrifice personal relationships in order to defeat the Cylons. We learn in this episode that he did not know about Roslin's plan to fake Hera's death, and, in a deleted scene, he makes his disapproval very clear to her, saying 'I want to tell them that their child's alive. They think she's dead. No-one should have to live with that'. The temple itself is said to be 4,000 years old, which unfortunately contradicts the chronology of the exodus of the Tribes from Kobol given in 'A Measure of Salvation', where it was said that this event took place 3,000 years earlier, and also that given in 'Kobol's Last Gleaming', where Elosha states that it took place "2,000 years ago". Baltar's stated reason for going over to the Fleet is that he misses the place; however, given the talk in the last two episodes about his destiny, and the fact that he is again receiving visitations from Head Six, a more logical reason is hubris. It is thus rather ironic that Cavil, the self-confessed atheist, suggests handing Baltar over to Adama and Roslin as part of the deal.

In terms of outside references, having Baltar as spokesperson for the Cylons is an original-series callback. One of the Marines is named Ditko, suggesting that there was at least one fan of the famous Marvel Comics writer-artist Steve Ditko involved with the script. In the broadcast version, the Hybrid quotes part of the first line of the satirical folk song 'Plastic Jesus' ('I don't care if it rains or freezes, as long as ...'), though this was removed from the DVD release, presumably for copyright reasons.

The story contains a number of apparent coincidences, which, when analysed, show that God is at work. Baltar initially remarks on it, saying, 'The chances that we've all converged on this small planet at the same time are infinitesimally small'. The timing is particularly coincidental, as Gaeta says, 'I am not one to look for religious signs. But I can't get my head around these odds. That human and Cylon both converge on this planet at this exact moment just as the star's about to go supernova ...', and Adama replies, 'If this is the work of a higher power, then they have one hell of a sense of humour'. We also learn more details about Tyrol's family background, in particular his adolescent rebellion against his parents' religious faith (he says 'I used to sneak into my mom's prayer room ... I would dance around naked with porn magazines, just to defy the Gods'), and his father having a particular interest in the Temple of Five. This makes him the perfect choice to rediscover the Temple, as he recognises it and understands its significance. He states, 'I don't even know how I found this place. I just got this urge to start ... walking'.[70] God, meanwhile, has been communicating with D'Anna through her suicide attempts, and with both Baltar and D'Anna through the Hybrid. God is here using the marker to Earth as a way of revealing the identity of the Final Five to D'Anna, as part of his plan to bring the groups together.

---

70 SPOILER SECTION: Later events will indicate that, on some level, he remembered the way.

41: THE EYE OF JUPITER

Broadening the Pantheon: Writing and Production

Weddle and Thompson were the ones to suggest the main plotline for the two-parter, which was based roughly on the battle of Guadalcanal, in which Weddle's father had participated. Weddle says in *The Official Companion Season Three*: '"The Eye of Jupiter" and "Rapture" grew out of a desire that Brad and I had for the humans and Cylons to fight over a piece of real estate'. According to the same volume, they wanted to dramatise the idea of how 'common infantry soldiers are often asked to perform almost impossible tasks … often without knowing why, or for reasons that seem insane or absurd to them', as well as to wrap up the Baltar-among-the-Cylons storyline. The pair also came up with the humans' defence strategy, physically going to Kamloops and walking around with the director in order to figure out the most logical way for them to deal with the situation.

According to Moore's podcast, the story was originally called 'The Eye of Zeus', but this was changed because he thought it sounded too over-the-top, and that adding Jupiter into the mix allowed them, as he puts it, to 'broaden the pantheon', although how it does this, as Jupiter and Zeus are different names for the same god, is unclear. Originally the discovery of the Temple was to have been more involved, with Cally finding a human bone fragment, leading the team to use ground imaging to discover a buried underground city on the planet; and then, when the Cylons turned up and demanded the Eye, Tyrol and Cally falling through the temple roof. When it was pointed out that the production could not afford such an elaborate set-up, and that the scenario with the human bone fragment was too similar to parts of the Kobol storyline in Season Two, the discovery was simplified the down to Tyrol just wandering into the Temple.

According to Moore's podcast, the scenario with Baltar on the *Galactica* was also to have played out differently. Adama and Tigh would have gone out of the room to discuss with Roslin whether or not to accept the Cylons' offer, and in the meantime, Baltar would have spoken with Gaeta, informing him there is something noteworthy about the star in the system. This was recorded, but removed in editing because Moore found it less than credible that Adama and Tigh would extensively consider accepting the offer; and indeed the whole purpose of the scene was simply for Baltar to tell Gaeta about something he was quite capable of finding out for himself. The conflict between Lee and Anders would also have been less about their personal relationship and more about a standoff between the civilians and the military. In the original scenario, Starbuck would have been on the ground in an outpost that was overrun by Centurions and, when Anders insisted on going after her, the civilians and military would have ended up pulling guns on each other, in yet another tedious *Crimson Tide* reference. There was also, at one point, a scene of Boomer giving Athena a chip that allowed her to project onto the baseship and see Hera for herself, but the team decided this was overcomplicated and unnecessary.

The story was filmed in Kamloops, which had been considered as a possible location for New Caprica. This necessitated an overnight stay for the cast and crew involved. The temple was shot in the same location that had been used as the main room of Ragnar Anchorage in the miniseries. Many of the runes on the central column of the Eye of Jupiter artefact are Hebrew letters, apparently written at random and reversed. *TV Guide* magazine gave free screenings of this episode in New York, Atlanta, St. Louis, Chicago, Dallas and Los Angeles as a promotion the day before the first US broadcast, with writers being present for question-and-answer sessions in Chicago and Los Angeles.

'The Eye of Jupiter' contains many elements from the Kobol arc of Seasons One and Two, featuring a human party trapped on a planet and the discovery of ancient artefacts leading the way to Earth. However, Starbuck's plotline, rather than following the archetype of damaged characters gradually learning from their experiences and coming to redeem themselves, instead develops along lines that suggest sexually promiscuous female characters are destructive.

42: Rapture

FIRST TRANSMISSION DATE: 21 January 2007 (USA/CANADA)

WRITERS: David Weddle & Bradley Thompson

DIRECTOR: Michael Rymer

CREDITED CAST: Lucy Lawless (D'Anna); Callum Keith Rennie (Leoben); Dean Stockwell (Cavil); Brad Dryborough (Hoshi); Eileen Pedde (Sergeant Mathias); Alisen Down (Barolay); Diego Diablo Del Mar (Hillard); Aleks Paunovic (Sergeant Fischer); Tygh Runyan (Private Sykes)

KNOWN UNCREDITED CAST: Lily Duong-Walton (Hera Agathon)

SYNOPSIS: The Cylons, intimidated by Adama's readiness to deploy warheads, order the return of the Heavy Raiders, but a Three insists that the craft carrying D'Anna and Baltar continue to the surface. Apollo orders Dualla to rescue Kara while the rest of the humans engage the Cylons, to give Tyrol time to find the Eye of Jupiter. D'Anna, Baltar and a Cavil reach the temple and disconnect the fuses before the humans can blow it up. The star goes nova, and the participants realise that the nova is the same as the Eye mandala in the temple; the nova is the Eye of Jupiter. D'Anna, in the light of the nova, sees a vision of the Final Five, but dies in the process. She downloads only to learn from Cavil that a decision has been taken to box her entire model. Baltar is taken prisoner by the humans. Dualla finds Kara badly injured in her Raptor and manages, with her guidance, to fly back to *Galactica*. Athena has Helo shoot her so that she will download and, resurrecting in the Cylon fleet, gain access to the basestar; she finds Hera, who is ill, and insists she must go to *Galactica* for treatment. Caprica-Six helps them escape and comes with them. Helo reveals that the mandala in the temple is the same as the design painted on Kara's apartment wall. Gaeta reasons that the mandala in the temple was a depiction made by the Thirteenth Tribe of a nova in the Ionian Nebula, and takes it as a sign indicating the Fleet's next destination.

ANALYSIS: 'Rapture' is a complex episode, enabling a transfer of key personnel from the basestar to the human Fleet, revealing the will of God, exploring fundamental shifts in Cylon politics, and resolving precisely nothing as regards the infamous love quadrangle.

BY YOUR COMMAND: VOL 2

Wives and Mistresses: Lee and Kara and Anders and Dualla ... Again

The previous episode ended with Apollo and Anders in a standoff over whether or not to rescue Kara. Apollo resolves the situation by, first, stating that he still cares for Starbuck and that Anders would be quite right to kill him if she died out in the field, and, secondly, finding an alternative rescue mission that Anders will accept. His later decision to attack the Cylons 'guerrilla style', while tactically sound, also conveys the further message that he is no longer trying to set Anders up to die in the line of fire.

Apollo's decision to send Dualla to the rescue is, as always, a sound one from a tactical and a personal point of view. Dualla is the next-highest-ranking officer on the planet after him and Starbuck; she is also in charge of the observation post closest to the crash site. On a personal level, Anders is satisfied with the decision because, even though Dualla is clearly being wronged by Starbuck and by Apollo as well, no-one who knows Dualla would suspect she would do anything other than her duty; and, as noted, Anders appears to think the decision to set him up was Apollo's alone.

Dualla, predictably, does her duty, but is less than happy with the situation. She is passive-aggressive throughout the rescue (apart from one satisfying moment when she finally lets loose and gives Starbuck a much-needed slap), dropping bitter remarks such as 'My husband ordered me to risk my life for yours'. Starbuck, however, uses Dualla as a shoulder to cry on, whining, 'I love Sam, I hate Sam, I love Lee, I hate Lee. Gods, I have to cheat just to keep the pieces nice and neat'. There is a deleted scene in which Dualla does actually tell Starbuck to stop making excuses for herself, saying that having the affair is her own decision and she can't simply blame it on her lousy childhood. The one sequence in the whole storyline that has Dualla actually get to say what is on her mind is, therefore, not only one which never made it into the final cut, but also has her playing her usual role as confidante to fellow crewmembers. Both Dualla and Anders are good people, but unfortunately for them, the people they are married to are not; had they married each other instead, both they, and the audience, would have been spared a great deal of frakked-up nonsense.

Three against the World: The Cylon Storyline

Over on the baseship, however, the Threes are now acting against the other models, colluding so as to allow D'Anna's Heavy Raider to continue to the planet's surface. This causes deep concern among the other Cylons, such that they collectively vote to box her model. D'Anna, like Caprica-Six and Boomer, has a distinctive name, indicating that she has also gained 'celebrity' status among her model, and her visions are also a source of her power. She furthermore taps into the Cylons' need for a goal in life, as highlighted by her remark, 'It's not a flaw to question your purpose': where the Cylons have in turn focused on imitating the humans, trying to live with them, and finding the way to Earth, she now offers them a new purpose, that of learning the nature of the Final Five.

Cavil's motivations in this story deserve exploration. In 'The Eye of Jupiter', he is in favour of destroying the humans and sacrificing the chance to acquire the titular artefact, saying that, as machines, it doesn't matter how long they take to find Earth. In this episode, however, he agrees to stand down the attack forces, saying, 'After all this time, we can't afford to lose everything'. Furthermore, despite his model's concerns about the Threes, a Cavil accompanies D'Anna to the planet's surface. These seeming contradictions expose Cavil's actual motivation, which is to keep secret the nature of the Final Five; the Cavil who accompanies D'Anna is there in order to keep an eye on her and prevent the information being revealed to the Fleet. When D'Anna says, 'This is my destiny. To see what lies between life and death', Cavil replies, 'And to look upon the faces of the Final Five. That can't happen'. Moore says in his podcast, 'I was always intrigued with that notion that Cavil really knew the secrets, that Cavil was keeper of the secrets in some ways … and Cavil is the guy who won't let D'Anna go see the Final Five. I always thought that was very cool, because it was a nice twist on the character, who he really was, that the atheist Cylon actually knew something about the religion of the Cylons'. This further suggests that Cavil is aware of the entity called God, and of his plans for the humans and Cylons, in spite of his atheism; or perhaps his knowing the true nature of God has in fact *caused* his atheism.

God, in all this, clearly intends for the secret of the Final Five to be revealed, encouraging D'Anna and Baltar, and putting on a flashy celestial light show so as to highlight the significance of the former's vision of the Final Five. While we are unaware as yet what it is, the revelation of their identities is clearly something that would encourage unity between the humans and Cylons.[71] However, God's plan has become the tacit source of division among the Cylons. Boomer's disillusionment with it, due to her failure on New Caprica, her frustrations in trying to care for Hera, and her feelings of envy aroused by seeing Athena's successful integration into the *Galactica* crew in the previous episode, causes her to side with Cavil. Caprica-Six, however, decides to help Athena steal Hera when Boomer threatens to break the child's neck, indicating that Caprica-Six still believes humans and Cylons must come together. (Her support for boxing the Threes can be explained by the rift between her and D'Anna.) At the end of the story, Cavil achieves the reunification of the Cylons, as Boomer is supporting his message, Caprica-Six is now a prisoner aboard the *Galactica* and the Threes are boxed. However, the fact that there are only six Cylon models left means that any future votes could lead to deadlock.

Winking Eye: Continuity and Worldbuilding

Among the humans, a hitherto-unsuspected piece of the puzzle is revealed when we learn that the painting Starbuck made on the wall of her flat is the Eye of

---

[71] SPOILER SECTION: Moore has since stated that the Cylon to whom D'Anna says 'Forgive me, I had no idea', is Ellen.

Jupiter mandala; she says she has been 'doodling' it since she was a child. Although clearly this has some link to her much-discussed 'special destiny', it is not yet apparent what that connection is. Tyrol cannot blow up the temple, despite being ordered to do so, continuing the idea that, although he has rejected his parents' religion, it still affects him.[72] The cigar box in which Helo finds the photograph of Kara's painting is the one she took from her flat in 'Valley of Darkness'. The episode does not address the question of whether or not Athena is still, in her new body, immune to lymphocytic encephalitis. In a nice touch of continuity, unlike the captured Raptor from the basestar, those in the Fleet are pitted and scarred from the events of 'The Passage'. 'Clankers' is used as a derogatory name for Centurions.

On the basestar, Boomer's threat to break Hera's neck is a call-back to Caprica-Six's infanticide in the miniseries; appropriately, Caprica-Six breaks Boomer's own neck in retaliation. Hera's crib on the basestar is of the same design as the one that appears on New Caprica and in Baltar's visions on Kobol; the most plausible explanation is that the Cylons found it on New Caprica and brought it with them.

In terms of outside references, the inspiration for the ground combat sequences, according to *The Official Companion Season Three*, was John F Antal's account of the 1943 Battle of El Guettar in his book *Infantry Combat: The Rifle Platoon*, although the tactics are not very clear in the episode as recorded. Despite the team's attempts to avoid referencing the Well of Souls sequence from *Raiders of the Lost Ark* (1981) in D'Anna's vision, there are still parallels; the Cavil who joins her on the expedition even wears an Indiana Jones-style hat. The original-series story 'Lost Planet of the Gods' also featured light striking a particular sacred artefact and bringing about a crucial revelation.

The Temple of Doom: Writing and Production

Although the fundamentals of the episode, according to Moore, remained the same throughout its development, some of the details changed. The Athena storyline underwent the most revision. The original idea, that she should steal a Raptor and fly to the baseship, was axed because, in Moore's words, 'One of the tropes of doing science-fiction shows or shows about military life is that there's always this moment when the pilot ... goes and steals a plane and flies it away ... and I just never believe that, it's just so unbelievable' – which also explains why the use of this trope in 'Hero' is undercut by the lucky escape turning out to be a set-up. Although the final version makes creative, if macabre, use of the Cylons' downloading ability, it does fall back on this same cliché for Athena's return journey. There was originally to have been more development of the situation between Caprica-Six, Boomer and Athena, exploring Boomer's resentment of the fact that she never had a child with Tyrol, which suggests to

---

72 SPOILER SECTION: Or, more likely, this is due to his being a member of the Final Five.

42: RAPTURE

her that she and he did not in fact experience true love[73]. Meanwhile Caprica-Six, who was fascinated with Hera, would have been continually coming in and trying to act as a surrogate mother to the child. The nuclear standoff was initially to have come in the middle of the first episode, with Helo shooting Athena as its cliffhanger.

Dualla was originally to have carried Starbuck to safety, but this was restricted first by the relative size of the two women, and secondly by the fact that the team were trying to limit location filming. Starbuck's injury was also changed from her leg to her hands, losing the call-back to Season One but heightening the dramatic potential of the scene as she is unable to pilot her Raptor. A subplot involving the humans filling trenches with tylium and setting them on fire was also dropped. Much of the writers' carefully-worked-out geography of the battle first had to be scaled down for time and budget reasons, and secondly, according to Moore's podcast, edited to make it more visually exciting when its intricacies proved difficult to convey on screen. Tyrol's first conversation on the phone with Lee was actually a manufactured scene made up of overdubbed parts of the sequence where Apollo later orders him to detonate the explosives. This was added at Eick's suggestion to bring the audience up to speed.

The mandala on Starbuck's apartment wall was painted by Katee Sackhoff during the making of Season Two, and at the time had no connection to her character's 'destiny'. When developing Season Three, however, Moore wanted there to be something within the temple that had significance only to Starbuck, to tie in with Leoben's predictions about her importance. Weddle and Thompson eventually hit upon the idea of using the painting as the link. However, as Starbuck never visits the Temple, the mandala on her wall doesn't contribute to the understanding of where the Fleet should go next; and, indeed, she has nothing to do with the major thrust of the story at all, so the connection comes across as spurious.

In production terms, the Orpheum Theatre was again used for the opera house. Michael Rymer suggested a few touches, including that D'Anna's vision should include this setting, as seen by Baltar on Kobol; clips from the sequence were retrospectively added to D'Anna's vision in 'Hero'. Rymer, together with James Callis, also came up with the idea of Baltar returning home in a body bag; Moore found out about it only when the network complained, but the decision to keep it makes thematic sense, symbolising the end of Baltar's life with the Cylons. The network also objected to the scene where Boomer threatens to kill Hera, as threatening a child is a major television taboo. Moore says, regarding D'Anna's exit, 'We had always talked about … ending it with her being boxed … Everything in her entire storyline led to this moment'.

At the end of 'Rapture', we learn that God's aim in instigating the supernova was to convey two messages: the first is the nature of the Final Five, although the delivery of that message is thwarted when the Threes are boxed; and the second

---

[73] SPOILER SECTION: Although in truth, it is because Tyrol was a Cylon.

is that the human Fleet should now go to the Ionian Nebula. Like the supernova, 'Rapture' is big and flashy, but, aside from the intriguing revelation that Cavil wields far more power within Cylon society than previously indicated, it advances the ongoing storyline only fractionally; indeed, the payoff for these events will not come until the Season Four episode 'He That Believeth In Me'.

43: Taking a Break From all your Worries

FIRST TRANSMISSION DATE: 28 January 2007 (USA/CANADA)

WRITER: Michael Taylor

DIRECTOR: Edward James Olmos

CREDITED CAST: Donnelly Rhodes (Doctor Cottle); Kerry Norton (Layne Ishay); Leah Cairns (Racetrack); Tom Bower (Joe); Steve Lawlor (Guard); Graeme Duffy (Adrien Bauer); Jason Bryden (Knucklehead Dragger [sic] #1)

KNOWN UNCREDITED CAST: Leo Li Chiang (Tattooed Pilot)

SYNOPSIS: On *Galactica*, Baltar is subjected to various interrogation methods, including sleep deprivation, mock execution, and, finally, the administration of experimental hallucinogens designed to create a state of anxiety. He confesses, in confusion, to his part in the attacks on the Colonies and his association with Caprica-Six, though also outlines his doubts as to the extent to which he was complicit and to which he was an unwitting participant. Following his interrogation, he says that he was able to admit his failings and be liberated. Roslin then suggests sending Gaeta, as someone he trusts, to offer him rewards for information. Baltar sees through and rejects this ploy. He accuses Gaeta of treachery and indicates that he knows a secret about him. This causes Gaeta to stab Baltar in the throat with a pen. Roslin finally realises, and admits, that this is not about gaining information so much as wanting to hear Baltar admit his guilt, and decides to allow him a trial. A bar named Joe's is set up on the *Galactica*; Apollo spends too much time there, further causing an estrangement from Dualla. Realising what he is doing, he asks her to give him another chance.

ANALYSIS: 'Taking a Break from All Your Worries' has an intriguing A plot and a pedestrian B plot, the latter of which is however lifted by Olmos's direction, juxtaposing seemingly unrelated scenes to draw clever parallels between the characters.

Friend to the Undertow: Baltar's Journey

Baltar, at the start of the story, tries to hang himself. This is not surprising under the circumstances, as he has been subjected to sleep deprivation and is on a self-imposed hunger strike; what is surprising is that Head Six actively encourages him to do so, given that it has been established in 'Resurrection Ship' that suicide is viewed by God as a sin. The reason is evidently to prove to him that he is not a Cylon: as he dies, Baltar appears to achieve the clear visions that D'Anna said lie between life and death, in that he hallucinates resurrecting in a tank surrounded by three Sixes. The Sixes tell him, when he exclaims his delight at apparently finding out he is a Cylon, that he is human after all; they then, like the Maenads, the legendary female followers of Bacchus, tear him to pieces. Gaeta's arrival just at this point might seem providential; however, it distracts the guard who is supposed to be watching the cell at the crucial moment, meaning that, rather than saving Baltar, it simply prolongs his agony. One might question why God would choose to put Baltar's life at such evident risk in order to convey his message; however, given God's tendency to anger, as seen in other episodes, there may be a vindictive element. Although Baltar learns that he is human, answering the question that has dogged him since 'Torn', he is also doomed to remain divided between the two worlds.

Baltar's experiences this episode are a clear inversion of his torture at the hands of the Cylons in 'A Measure of Salvation'; whereas there, Head Six enabled him to withstand through providing him with a form of heaven, here she leads him through hell. He conflates Head Six and Caprica-Six, asking if she is angel or demon, hallucination or real, his own voice or the voice of God (although he trails off at this point, not actually speaking the name of the deity), and Head Six here is both angel and demon: his visions begin with the sight of three Sixes (traditionally the number of the beast), and the clip from 'Kobol's Last Gleaming' in his flashback shows Head Six reaching toward him through the flames. Although she is saving him in the context in which the image first appeared, here she seems demonic, wreathed in fire. He floats cruciform in dark water (and as this episode revolves around the forgiveness of sins, this is one case where the imagery might seem justified), and finds himself again in a resurrection tank, surrounded by radiation-burned people representing the victims of the attack on the Colonies. Head Six is both angel and demon, tormenting him, but with a wider aim in mind.

The goal of Baltar's quest is, simply, forgiveness. As noted before, were he a Cylon, his sins would be, if not forgiven, at least reframed, as he would have been acting legitimately on their behalf. However, when asked directly if he is a Cylon when under the influence of the drugs, he says no, and then one of the burn victims plunges into the tank and drags him down, showing how the loss of this rationale means he now needs to acknowledge his guilt, and seek forgiveness. In the hallucination, he acknowledges his complicity in allowing Caprica-Six access to the defence mainframe, but he also argues that he was not guilty of destroying the Colonies, as conspiracy requires intent. This sequence unveils the complexity of the question as to his culpability: the audience knows that he has been guilty, at various points in the series, of industrial espionage, withholding information (regarding the Cylon test), fraternising with the enemy and collaboration, and providing a nuclear bomb to a psychologically damaged Cylon who then used it to kill 5,515 people, but he did not knowingly act to destroy the Colonies. He later states to Gaeta that being forced to admit his failings has left him positively liberated. Rather than the simple solution of having him turn out to be a Cylon, Baltar has to accept the complicated mix of guilt and innocence that he, as a human, has generated.

The further point of the exercise is to reveal to Roslin and Adama, if not the identities, then at least the existence of the Final Five. Roslin underlines their significance by linking them to the description of the five priests in Pythia, meaning that the humans recognise them as important to their quest. God also appears to be now acknowledging other deities (Head Six comments that Baltar has the luck of the Gods, plural), and Baltar, at the end of the story, says 'Well, I am the Chosen One', giving his existence new meaning through the belief that God intends him for some future purpose.

The Baltar sequences have obvious parallels with real-life debates then in progress about the legitimacy of torture (as well as the CIA's experiments with drugs, including the use of LSD as a truth serum, during the Cold War), and continue the Season Three theme of exploring the depths to which humans can sink. Baltar's assertion 'I'm a human being, I have rights', relates to the real-life invocation of the Geneva Convention by those opposed to torture. Within the ongoing narrative, there are strong parallels between Baltar in this episode and Adama in 'Hero', in that both men harbour feelings of guilt for their role in the destruction of the Colonies, and both come to accept that their actions were part of a wider context.

Gaeta, meanwhile, is still tormented by what happened on New Caprica, which clearly includes something beyond the events the audience has witnessed, as Baltar tells him, 'There are worse things than being a traitor ... but don't worry, it's our little secret'. Roslin is almost certainly incorrect in her belief that Gaeta went to Baltar's cell to kill him, however, as he does so only after the latter reveals that he knows his secret, suggesting that his motivation was in fact to find out what Baltar knew. Although Roslin thinks that allowing Baltar to talk to Gaeta will win his trust, this plainly does not transpire, as Baltar quickly figures out that there is a spy camera in the cell and he is being set up. His being briefly drawn into the deception is less about his trust in Gaeta than about the fact that Gaeta has presented him with his own calculations of the route to Earth, and Baltar cannot resist being able to show his scientific prowess by correcting someone else's formula. He then plays on Gaeta's own guilty feelings, saying that he knew about his acting as informant to the resistance, implying that Gaeta was being less clever than he thought, as well as making Baltar a tacit ally of the resistance in not betraying him. He adds that at least he, Baltar, had a gun to his head when he acted on behalf of the Cylons on New Caprica, but that Gaeta was knowingly playing both sides. Where Baltar acknowledges his own guilt and forgives himself, Gaeta is unable to do either.

Finally, Roslin's activities are in no way surprising, as she clearly seeks revenge on Baltar. She gives him his glasses, and this is followed by a flashback to him doing the same for her when she was in custody on New Caprica, just to reinforce that her message in doing so is that the boot is on the other foot. Baltar, however, highlights Roslin's hypocrisy once again in asking her what happened to his fair trial, showing that her earlier promise of general amnesty to everyone accused of crimes on New Caprica evidently does not extend to him, and that she is not even giving him the rights provided by law to common criminals. She lights a cigar and takes a drag from it before finally passing it over: as we later learn that she is an ex-smoker, she is clearly engaging in this performance in the full knowledge of exactly how difficult nicotine withdrawal must be for Baltar, telling him that if he gives up information, his 'suffering will come to an end', with all the sinister ambiguity the phrase entails. When she asks Gaeta if he went to Baltar's cell to kill him, she follows it up by saying, 'I understand that, I do', indicating that she herself wants to kill Baltar.

What is more surprising, however, is that Roslin finally acknowledges that her decision to torture Baltar was wrong. Tellingly, she says, 'For all his crimes, he's one of us', meaning that she takes Baltar's denial that he is a Cylon as a reminder that he is human. Adama, for his part, is considerably less forgiving towards Baltar, even suggesting that they should make him 'disappear', in a reference back to the victims of the Circle in 'Collaborators'. Moore, in the podcast, says that the rationale behind having Baltar brought on board in a body bag in 'Rapture' was that it meant no-one else on the Fleet need know he had returned. Roslin's change of attitude also seems to have been prompted by her making the connection between the Final Five in Baltar's rantings and the Pythian prophecy, linking Baltar with something she believes in and indicating to her that they are both part of something greater. However, a deleted scene also has her going to Caprica-Six to ask for her help in interrogating Baltar, and Caprica-Six rebuking her, saying that she would gladly be a witness at a trial against him but won't stand for torture. This is clearly intended as an attempt by Caprica-Six to make a deal with her captors, which undoubtedly piques Roslin's conscience in that even the ostensible enemy condemns her actions. In the same way that D'Anna was earlier forced into deeper insights after torturing Baltar, so Roslin also has to acknowledge her own vindictiveness and denial of Baltar's connections with herself.

And They're Always Glad You Came: The Love Quadrangle

Baltar's finding of his role is counterpointed by Lee's attempt to make his marriage with Dualla work. Both he and Baltar are out of control, searching for something, and not sure what it is. Throughout the relationship, Lee has shown himself to be someone who tends to go along with the strongest voice; he supports Kara's suggestion to put Anders on the front line, supports Anders's insistence that they rescue Kara, and here, with Dualla the most prominent figure, again tries to accommodate her. This all stems from his relationship with his father, and his decision to go into the military to please Adama rather than out of personal interest. Baltar, similarly, has been swept along by the causes of others, bounced about between Caprica-Six, Roslin, D'Anna and Head Six, with no independent principles of his own. Even his faith in God was engineered by

43: TAKING A BREAK FROM ALL YOUR WORRIES

Head Six. Both are also caught between worlds; whereas Lee is a soldier, but ought to be a politician, so Baltar is human, but wishes he could be a Cylon. As Baltar finds control over his situation by clinging to his belief that he is the Chosen One, so Lee tries to find it through committing to Dualla, his drunken loss of his wedding ring[74] symbolising to him that he is in danger of losing his relationship with her, as his playing with it earlier indicated his ambivalence about the marriage. However, Lee's promises to Dualla are intercut with Gaeta's attempt to persuade Baltar to talk, and Baltar seeing through it, suggesting that Lee's words are as transparent as Gaeta's. Toward the end of the story, Baltar's question 'Who is the real traitor in this room?' is apparently answered by a cut to the bar, where Lee and Kara again look at each other while in the company of their respective spouses, echoing their gesture in the previous episode where they embrace their partners on the hangar deck while meeting each others' gaze, and, in a mirroring of scenes of observation and betrayal, paralleled by Baltar finding the hidden camera in his cell. Where Baltar seems to have found some kind of closure, Lee's situation is still unresolved.

Lee's problem, as ever, seems to be a lack of commitment. He goes back to Dualla because of the absence of stability in a relationship with Kara; as he says, how does he know that Kara, having left Sam for him, would not change her mind again? Dualla, for her part, gives vent to her angry feelings toward Lee for the first time, accusing him of hypocrisy (paraphrasing Kara's lie '[Lee] won't cheat, he's too honourable' from the previous episode). However, Dualla acknowledges that she is in part to blame for the situation, in that she married Lee knowing that he would eventually stray back to Kara. Having made a choice through emotion, rather than thinking the consequences through, she is now having to live in an intolerable relationship.

Elsewhere, Tyrol and Cally are also clearly not getting on, suggesting that more marital discord is in the offing. 'To marriage; why we build bars', toasts Tyrol, in one of the story's moments of black comedy. Lee asks Tyrol if he ever wondered what might have happened with Boomer had circumstances been different, but the Chief makes it plain that this is not open for discussion. Kara, meanwhile, goes back to Anders, plainly because, with Lee trying to make a go of it with Dualla, she has few other options. Moore's podcast reveals that the writing team had a lot of different ideas for Anders that kept falling by the wayside, such as him becoming a pilot or joining the Marines. This was in parallel with their problems with finding something for Lee to do, suggesting that Kara's men tend to be rootless, drifting types. Lee's issues are paralleled by other subplots and characters.

Graveyard Humour: Continuity and Production

In continuity terms, Kara refers to her destiny again, albeit jokingly. ('Kara Thrace and her special destiny? That sounds more like a bad cover band'.)

---

74 Lee has the ring back by his next scene.

Anders tries to suggest that they are fated to be together, but clearly realises that this is complete nonsense and drops it. The teaser contracts the Hybrid's prophecy in 'The Eye of Jupiter' from 'The five lights of the apocalypse rising, struggling toward the light, sins revealed only to those who enter the temple, only to the Chosen One' to 'The Final Five, revealed only to those who enter the Temple, only to the Chosen One'. In a conscious anachronism, Baltar quotes a well-known children's prayer, saying 'If I should die before I wake'.

This was originally intended to be a comedy episode, despite the fact that Baltar's interrogation was to have been a plot thread from the beginning. The interrogation was the B story to a *Catch-22*-inspired narrative about Lee engaging in wheeling and dealing to establish a casino ship, or, in later drafts, build a bar, or, in even later drafts, save the bar (which was originally to have been called the Y-Not rather than Joe's), but the two stories were reversed and made more serious as drafts progressed. Moore says that Baltar would have been a more comedic character, which, under the circumstances, just sound macabre, and overall one does have to ask what the writing team were thinking of in proposing a comedy story revolving around torture. As it stands, fortunately, the only area where this remains is the title, a reference to the theme song from *Cheers*.

In terms of other developments, the Gaeta story was more or less unchanged from the original draft, and the torture of Baltar became less physical and more psychological during script revisions, to contrast this story with 'A Measure of Salvation'. The narrative was originally more explicit about Adama's involvement with the military drug experiments he mentions, which is implicit in the final version. There was originally a storyline focusing on Ishay's moral conflicts, as a medic, about being involved with torture.

Olmos's directorial style is, however, the main strength of the episode, with its unflinching close-ups and unscripted intercutting, which force the audience to think about the relationships between seemingly disparate scenes, and also contrast Baltar's apparently endless torment with the ongoing round of daily life on *Galactica*. Olmos reportedly insisted on keeping the water sequences in full (as filming around water is difficult, there was a lot of pressure to cut these down), and, according to Moore, added the detail of Baltar being pulled under the water by a burned victim.

While one of the songs heard in Joe's Bar, 'All That Remains', was composed by Bear McCreary, the other, 'Lord Knows I Would', was composed by Raya Yarbrough, who is the main female vocalist for the series and also McCreary's wife. A man in a wheelchair is visible in the bar; he is a fan of the show who visited the set and was allowed to be a background artist. The design for Joe's Bar includes a full-scale Viper (footage from Eick's video blog indicates it has a shredded wing) as well as several games, including darts and bumper pool. The network, having been under the impression that this was to be a light and funny episode, were understandably nonplussed when they saw the finished product, leading to what Moore delicately refers to in his podcast as 'discussions about content', particularly with regard to the sequence with the burned victims of the

43: TAKING A BREAK FROM ALL YOUR WORRIES

holocaust.

This episode was aptly described by Jamie Bamber as 'a study of betrayal in all its forms: intrapersonal, interpersonal and, on the grandest scale, political and even biological'. However, it also shows that some characters, such as Baltar and Roslin, can find positive ways forward, whereas others, such as Lee and Gaeta, at present cannot.

BY YOUR COMMAND: VOL 2

44: The Woman King

FIRST TRANSMISSION DATE: 11 February 2007 (USA/CANADA)

WRITER: Michael Angeli

DIRECTOR: Michael Rymer

CREDITED CAST: Richard Hatch (Tom Zarek); Donnelly Rhodes (Doctor Cottle); Rekha Sharma (Tory Foster); Bruce Davison (Michael Robert); Leah Cairns (Racetrack); Ryan Robbins (Connor); Colin Lawrence (Skulls); Chris Boyd (Cheadle); Colin Corrigan (Nowart); Gabrielle Rose (Mrs King); Scott Little (Willie King); Aaron Brooks (Buckminster); James Lafanzos (Civvie #1); Eliza Norbury (Civvie #2)

KNOWN UNCREDITED CAST: Lily Duong-Walton (Hera Agathon)

SYNOPSIS: Helo, currently in charge of 'Dogsville', a settlement of refugees on *Galactica*, faces problems from its Sagittaron members, who will not accept medical treatment, but who are also the centre of an epidemic of Mellorak sickness. Mrs King, a Sagittaron, comes to Helo to accuse the attending medic, Doctor Robert, of killing her son Willie. After hearing further, similar, accusations by Sagittarons, Helo investigates, gaining the enmity of Tigh, Adama and Cottle. Examining records from New Caprica, Helo finds that 90 percent of Doctor Robert's Sagittaron patients died under his care, and asks Cottle to autopsy Willie King; Cottle claims he has already done so, and that King died of natural causes. Dualla, feeling ill, goes to see Doctor Robert. Helo, knowing she is a Sagittaron, rushes to her rescue. In the subsequent confrontation, Cottle reveals that he lied about doing the autopsy, but now, having checked King's bloodwork, confirms that Willie was indeed poisoned. Robert is arrested, and Adama apologises to Helo.

ANALYSIS: 'The Woman King' is a Helo-centred episode originally intended to link into a wider storyline involving a massacre of the Sagittarons on New Caprica. As it is, it stands on its own as another piece on prejudice and genocide, showing how the casual denigration of a particular minority group can easily build into a pernicious conspiracy against them.

Helo the Hero: The Mayor of Dogsville

Helo is now clearly in unofficial disgrace, having been put in charge of the refugees on *Galactica*: Starbuck refers to him as 'the Mayor of Dogsville', and, later, with the Mellorak disease epidemic in full swing, she calls him 'Mellorak Man'. Helo rightly suspects that this reversal of his fortunes is due to his loyalty being in question, as he has a Cylon wife and spoke up for the Cylons during the events of 'A Measure of Salvation'; he later says he thinks he is in charge of the refugees 'because it's the right punishment for the guy who crosses the line'. The final scene of 'A Measure of Salvation' makes it clear that Adama and Roslin know exactly who is responsible for the killing of the Cylons. There is also the element of testing the limits of Helo's social conscience, as, in managing the Sagittarons, he has to be fair and equitable to people whose beliefs he himself opposes. While overseeing Dogsville is a job that needs to be done, the fact that such an unpleasant duty has been assigned to this particular officer sends a clear message.

Athena, however, is less than supportive of her husband's activities, telling him not to get involved, even when he suspects Dualla may become Robert's next victim. Helo tells her this is 'because as long as everyone hates the Sagittarons, they forget you're a Cylon for five minutes', which she confirms when she complains, 'I have to fight every single day on this ship to be accepted'. Athena deals with the prejudice she faces as a Cylon married to a human by going along with the human consensus, even when, as in 'A Measure of Salvation', it involves genocide against her own people; to judge by her behaviour and Boomer's, the Eights seem to have a tendency toward selfish behaviour. Helo, by contrast, began as a selfless character, giving up his seat for Baltar in the miniseries, and his relationship with Athena has correspondingly encouraged him to fight prejudice, not just against her and other Cylons, but against despised human groups as well.

Much of the Robert storyline builds up through the reversal of perceptions. At the outset, the audience themselves see the Sagittarons as annoying, dogmatic and obstreperous, and Robert as a professional doing his best under trying circumstances. Helo himself at first assumes, when Mrs King says she made a mistake, that she means by not allowing her son to have medical treatment; but later he realises she means by taking him to Doctor Robert. The Sagittaron hostility to Robert then takes on a different aspect: it is not so much about his profession, as about their realisation that he is killing them. Helo's own suspicions are in part engaged when Robert casually admits to immunising an old man without his consent, indicating that he does not respect the Sagittarons' traditions; both Willie King and the old man (who later dies) had altercations with Robert in the episode's opening scenes.

Robert's activities go largely unnoticed, however, due to a generally-felt prejudice against Sagittarons. The fact that they are at the centre of the disease epidemic fits with the general belief that they are 'dirty'. Robert cleverly says that he does not want the Sagittarons singled out for special treatment as the source of infection, seemingly concerned about inciting more prejudice against them but actually ensuring that the Sagittarons remain together, and remain infected. This can also be seen when Robert remarks 'They're all going to die anyway', seemingly in disgust at their rejection of medicine, but also in reference to his own murderous activities. He later argues that as medicine is rationed there is no point in wasting it on the Sagittarons, appealing to wider discourses in the Fleet about resource distribution and shortages. When Robert, at the end of the story, points out that he saved Dualla, Helo observes, 'Right, she's one of the good ones'; she survives only because she is an assimilated Sagittaron whose beliefs are in line with the mainstream. It is also worth pointing out that the medicine Robert gives Hera works, suggesting that even half-Cylons are acceptable to him so long as they are not also Sagittarons.

Robert's behaviour does not come out of nowhere, but is tacitly encouraged by the attitude of authority figures in the Fleet. Tyrol and Tigh justify their hostility toward Sagittarons on the grounds that they refused to take part in the resistance on New Caprica, and Tigh takes Robert's own participation in the resistance as a justification for believing him. However, since Tigh and Tyrol daily work alongside other people who did not participate in the resistance, this is clearly a post-hoc rationalisation for a deeply-felt racism. Even Dualla is critical of her own ethnic group, although only in front of her fellow Colonial officers; Mrs King alerts Helo to Dualla's plight partly because Dualla is a Sagittaron, but partly because Helo has a shared connection with both women. Cottle also acts from prejudice, supporting Robert because of their common profession, and lying to Helo over the autopsy: it remains ambiguous as to whether he was, as he said, simply tired and not wanting to believe Helo's accusations against a colleague, or whether he knew what Robert was doing, and was actively covering for him. Helo's raising of the issue of the autopsy, however, means that Cottle has to actually do the procedure, as the evidence from it will inevitably be called on to resolve the matter. Cottle also has to be honest about his results, as, if he did not, he himself would be implicated in covering up a murder. Both Tigh and Cottle turn on Robert when it becomes clear he is guilty. When Robert says, 'Remember what you used to say, Saul? Aside from a Cylon, is there anything that you hate more than a Sagittaron?', Tigh responds, 'I'll tell you what I hate, Mike: being wrong ... Arrest this son of a bitch. Gag him if you have to'. Tigh hates Sagittarons, but does not want to be reminded of his culpability in the deaths.

Cylon Witness: Caprica-Six and Head Baltar

Caprica-Six is now a prisoner on the battlestar and, in what appears at first to be a parallel to Helo's efforts on behalf of the Sagittarons, Athena is acting as advocate for her. However, Athena is not doing this out of altruism; she knows perfectly well that Roslin and Tory are monitoring their conversations, and she makes a point of telling Caprica-Six she needs her to help bring Baltar to trial. After Athena goes, Head Baltar says to Caprica-Six, 'You're here because you want to be human. There's a trick to being a human. You have to think only about yourself'. This could be read as God's messenger expressing frustration at human selfishness; but, more than that, it refers to Athena's own strategy for assimilation. The sequence with Athena and Caprica-Six thus underlines the fundamental differences between Athena and her husband.

King of the Hill: Continuity and Worldbuilding

In continuity terms, Dogsville appears to have grown out of Camp Oil Slick, the refugee settlement where Kacey and Julia were living in 'Torn'. Connor is currently working as a bartender at Joe's, though his personality has not improved since 'Collaborators'. The pilots play a bar game called 'Pyramid X', involving tossing balls through target holes, while drinking in Joe's. Dualla now appears to have completely forgiven Lee, which, after the events of the last episode, seems rather deluded; however, given her optimistic attitude toward the relationship to begin with, that is not out of character. The mobile over Hera's crib has two model Vipers and a model Raptor, perhaps suggesting that her parents hope she will follow in their footsteps. The recap clips at the opening contain material that has not appeared before, embellished in part with ADR dialogue for Tyrol and Cally. This are used to establish the premise that Helo is in charge of a large refugee camp on the starboard hangar deck, which includes a number of Sagittarons.

There is also a deleted scene, following Adama's apology to Helo, in which Helo goes on to confess to killing the infected Cylons in 'A Measure of Salvation'. Adama asks Helo, 'Are you sure you want to have this conversation, Captain? ... Because if it's true, then it could end up being a very costly retrospective ... I'll have to call in the MPs, have you arrested, clapped in irons, and thrown into the brig. You'll be charged with treason and face a court martial. And possibly a firing squad'. Helo agrees to withdraw the statement. While Adama will admit that he was wrong in allowing the Sagittarons to be persecuted, he will not allow Helo to draw parallels regarding the treatment of the Cylons, and reminds him tacitly that blowing the whistle on racism is one thing, but going against a military decision in time of war is another, even though that decision could have resulted in genocide.

Standing Alone: Story and Production

This episode came about largely because of an ultimately abandoned arc, described in more detail in the review for 'Crossroads', which would have linked racism against Sagittarons with Baltar's trial, and implicated Zarek, himself a Sagittaron, in a massacre carried out against Sagittarons on New Caprica. This would have lent a very different subtext to his conversation with Roslin in this story, in which he predicts that Baltar's trial will unleash 'a hurricane ... sectarian violence ... assassination attempts', and would also have suggested in retrospect that his arrest on New Caprica had nothing to do with political resistance and everything to do with his part in the massacre. Drafts of the script from 20 and 21 September 2006 have a scene where Zarek visits Baltar in his cell and tries to convince him to plead guilty, on the grounds that the

President will spare his life, but Baltar, advised by Head Six, realises that Zarek is trying to avoid his role in the massacre being revealed by Baltar undergoing cross-examination at a trial. By the 22 September draft, however, this scene has gone.

When the Sagittaron storyline was dropped, on the grounds that it was complicating the trial arc too much, this episode nevertheless remained. The Sci-Fi Channel had also put in a request for more standalone episodes, and Angeli wanted to do one focusing on Helo, feeling that the character was underused and that the events of 'A Measure of Salvation', in which Helo thwarted the germ-warfare attack on the Cylons, needed revisiting. Rather than the beginning of an ongoing arc, the episode became instead a character piece for Helo. As a standalone story, it has much the same problem as 'Black Market', in that the Sagittarons, having been given such detail and texture here, will never feature again, aside from in a couple of passing references.

The draft scripts confirm reports that the story was originally to have been told in flashback, beginning with Helo's rushing to confront Doctor Robert (which, out of context, and with descriptions like 'his face contorted like a wild horse', makes it seem as if Helo has gone insane), and then returning to explain how the incident came about. However, Michael Rymer, over the writer's objections, insisted it be done as a linear narrative. It has to be said that there is no reason for it to be told in flashback, and, reading the draft scripts, it appears that the writer may simply have been concerned that the beginning of the story wouldn't otherwise make an exciting enough 'hook' for the audience. According to Moore, Dualla's relationship with the Sagittarons was originally to have been more of a storyline in the series as a whole. Dualla, whose choice of a military career also goes against Sagittaron beliefs, was intended to be exploring and ultimately embracing her Sagittaron identity, becoming a bridge between the traditional Sagittarons and the rest of the Fleet. As it stands, Dualla's storyline shows her, like Athena, as someone rejecting their identity and gravitating towards the Colonial elite. Moore also says that the backstory Tigh shares with Robert, referenced here only in Tigh's revelation that Robert treated his eye, was more strongly developed at first. At one point, Moore recalls, the script contained further details 'of what Robert had done on New Caprica. Also in regards to the Sagittarons, and how far back his theories of eugenics had been seeded'. However, none of these concepts makes it as far as the 20 September draft.

The 20 September draft contains a few other interesting differences from the final version. At the start of the story, Adama explicitly says to his XO that Helo is micromanaging, and implies that his obsession with Doctor Robert is part of his 'losing it'. The scene with Caprica-Six in her cell does not at this point include Athena, but involves a much longer conversation with Head Baltar. Caprica-Six, conflating him and the physical Baltar, calls him a liar, describes Baltar as 'the missing link between good and evil' and says he is going to 'catch Hell' through his self-deception. Head Baltar asks if she wants to save Baltar; she temporises, and he says, 'Trust in me ... I will help you. All this confusion will fall away'.

44: THE WOMAN KING

There is an amusing sequence where Racetrack and Starbuck trade terrible limericks over the ship-to-ship radio (beginning 'There once was a pilot from Picon, who blew it out her ass with her mike on …' and 'There once was a pilot from Caprica, who flew with her hands in her lap-ri-ca …') leading Tigh to make an oddly out-of-character remark: 'There oughta be a law. If you're female and you wanna be a pilot you gotta have your tongue cut out'. The stage directions say that during Tigh's physical confrontation with Helo, although he puts up a brave front, he is 'shitting nails' at the prospect of fighting him. There is a largely pointless sequence where Hera wanders off while she and her mother wait to see Doctor Robert, and is found, in a huge coincidence, by Mrs King. We also learn that the reason Athena was taking her daughter to Doctor Robert was that she doesn't trust Cottle.

Finally, Helo's feelings about killing the infected Cylons are explored in greater detail; at the start of the story Athena remarks that he was saying 'airlock all the frakking civilians' in his sleep, both expressing his frustrations over his job running Dogsville and suggesting that he subconsciously views his killing of the Cylons in 'A Measure of Salvation' as an act of murder. In his later argument with Athena, she reassures him that he did what was right, now openly admitting that his position was the correct one, and he retorts that maybe it wasn't, that his job in Dogsville is a punishment for his actions over the Cylons, and therefore that what he did wrong was in disobeying an order and costing the humans a military victory. However, the scene where Helo confesses to killing the infected Cylons to Adama, in the draft, ends with a line where Adama says, 'What you did was different. It was different to what Micah Robert did'. This indicated that the draft originally focused on the idea that Helo feels guilty for taking the Cylons' lives, rather than that of the parallel between Adama's behaviour towards the Sagittarons and his earlier treatment of the infected prisoners.

In production terms, the Head Baltar sequences were particularly difficult to do as the character is clean-shaven whereas the real Baltar is bearded in this season. James Callis's scenes therefore had to be scheduled to allow time for his beard to grow in again after each shave. Bruce Davison, cast as Robert, was an Academy Award nominee, and Rymer selected him because he was best known for playing heroic characters, meaning the audience would initially be doubtful about Robert's guilt. Gabrielle Rose, who plays Mrs King, had appeared in Verheiden's 1994 film *Timecop*. The name 'Dogsville' recalls the title of the Lars von Trier experimental film *Dogville* (2003), and there is a thematic connection in that the film deals with a village of superficially respectable and kind people who in fact form an unspoken conspiracy to denigrate a woman who comes to them as a refugee, and who eventually becomes a focus for the village's anxieties and social tensions.

'The Woman King', like all the best episodes of *Battlestar Galactica*, uses its science-fiction setting to confront troubling issues; in this case, exploring how prejudice can lead ordinary people to horrendous and inhuman behaviour, but also how opposing prejudice can lead to acts of great courage.

45: A Day in the Life

FIRST TRANSMISSION DATE: 18 February 2007 (USA/CANADA)

WRITER: Mark Verheiden

DIRECTOR: Rod Hardy

CREDITED CAST: Lucinda Jenney (Carolanne Adama); Bodie Olmos (Hot Dog); Jennifer Halley (Seelix); Sebastian Spence (Narcho); Don Thompson (Figurski); Mike Leisen (Private Stewart Jaffee)

KNOWN UNCREDITED CAST: Finn R Devitt (Nicholas Tyrol); Leo Li Chiang (Tattooed Pilot)

SYNOPSIS: On his wedding anniversary, Adama, as he goes through his day, reminisces about his relationship with his wife Carolanne. Roslin makes plans for Baltar's trial, suggesting that Lee chair the committee tasked with organising the preliminary legal proceedings. Tyrol and Cally, their relationship under strain, become trapped in an airlock with an atmosphere leak. The pilots attempt a daring rescue in which Tyrol and Cally must pass through the airlock doors and across open space into a Raptor; they survive, with the help of urgent medical treatment. Although Lee turns down Roslin's request to sit on the committee, Adama gives him his father's law books.

ANALYSIS: 'A Day in the Life' is, unfortunately, a boring and slow episode, which verges strongly on the clichéd and contributes little to the series bar the beginning of the 'Lawyer Lee' arc that will continue through to the end of the season.

Desperate Housewife: Adama and Carolanne

The main conceit of the episode is Adama, on his wedding anniversary, holding an imaginary conversation with his wife Carolanne in their Caprican house. The parallels between Adama's images of Carolanne and Cylon projection are unavoidable; for instance, in the scene where he imagines himself, in his garden, holding and dropping a football, we also see him on the *Galactica* miming the action. Carolanne seems aware that she is a fantasy, saying to Adama, 'You keep bringing me back year after year'. She does not appear to be a Head Person, as she is deliberately brought into being by Adama, whereas the Head People come and go at their own whim, and she does not seem to be guiding him to any particular purpose. Moore also says that one of the problems facing the writing team was to make clear that Carolanne was not a Head Person. However, the episode appears to suggest that Colonials can have strong visions analogous to Cylon projection.

Unfortunately, these sequences don't tell us much about Adama that we don't already know. He neglected his wife, doesn't give Lee enough approval and has an idealised image of Carolanne as a provider of stability, which Lee, who knew her as a drinker with vicious mood swings, does not share. Lee even says he doesn't think Carolanne ever loved Adama, suggesting that Adama's affection for her is entirely based on a fantasy of domesticity encouraged by the fact that he spent little time at home. The great leader who can't cope with family life is too much of a TV cliché to be excusable, and Carolanne's characterisation is heavily reminiscent of Ellen Tigh (a blonde, volatile drunk who has a rocky relationship with her husband). While this could be used to suggest Adama has more in common with his XO than we have realised up to this point, nothing is made of it, suggesting instead that the writing team, feeling the loss of Ellen, are channelling the character. Ellen was also much more personable than Carolanne, who lacks charisma; Carolanne's relationship with Adama, furthermore, does not have the same chemistry as that between the Tighs. It also has to be said that it is rather disappointing; given Adama's nuanced relationship with Roslin, one would have hoped that his relationship with his wife would have been similarly complex and intriguing.

It is, however, not too surprising that Adama blames himself for the situation. Carolanne, in his fantasy, states that his failure to recognise their incompatibility calls his entire judgment into question; as she is imaginary, she is articulating Adama's own fears and doubts. This is in keeping with Adama's flaw as exposed in 'Hero', that he tries to take responsibility for all failings, whether he is to blame or not. Moore, in his podcast, says that the writing team had intended the revelation that Adama's negligence as a husband and father was not the sole reason for the breakdown of the marriage, to be the surprise twist of the episode. However, given the usual complexity of characterisation in *Battlestar Galactica*, this is hardly an unexpected development, and indeed verges on the hackneyed. The writing team also missed a trick in not picking up on the indication in 'Scattered' that Adama married Carolanne for her military connections, as part of his scheme to get recommissioned; while it would cast Adama in a bad light, it would at least make the story more interesting.

Real-Life Romance: Adama and Roslin and Tyrol and Cally

Back in the 'real' world, meanwhile, Adama is clearly experiencing conflict over his feelings for Roslin. The conversation with Lee, however, seems to liberate Adama; it allows him to see the fantasy-Carolanne as a mean drunk who didn't love him, which gives him unspoken permission to, in the final scene of the episode, flirt like crazy with the President of the Colonies. Moore discusses Adama's relationship with Roslin in some detail during his podcast, saying that there are many reasons why they are drawn together, from their shared experiences as community leaders to their common interests. While originally the writing team had considered having a romance between Roslin and Lee, the interactions between Olmos and McDonnell, and the way the characters' storylines have developed over the past two and a half seasons, make the present relationship seem more natural and credible. However, in this episode, it is just as clumsily portrayed as that between Adama and Carolanne, the clichés coming thick and fast as the pair imagine what life would be like had the Cylons not come to New Caprica, and bond over their shared fondness for pulp detective novels and Laura's fantasy about building a little cabin in the wilderness.

As a parallel to Adama's musings over the disintegration of his marriage to Carolanne, the newly-married Tyrol and Cally have hit a rough patch. The shared underlying factor in the two relationships is that both involve a person in love with someone who doesn't love them back: Tyrol married Cally while on the rebound from Boomer, and while Adama apparently loves Carolanne, it is not reciprocated. However, where Adama was distant and left Carolanne to raise the children on her own, the Tyrols are both in the service, and it seems their shared experiences are enough to allow them to develop a means of living together. As Adama finally achieves closure and starts pursuing Roslin openly, so Tyrol and Cally, through their experiences in the airlock, resolve to settle their differences and spend more time with Nicky.[75] Unfortunately, in keeping with the rest of the episode, the Tyrol plot is heavy-handed and unsubtly conveyed.

Legal Eagle: Continuity and Worldbuilding

This story marks the beginning of the Lawyer Lee arc, as the writing team finally figure out where Lee ought to be going in a universe in which Helo has taken Apollo's original-series role as pilot, family man and principled hero. This idea ties in with the detail introduced in the original series that Apollo had legal training (as mentioned in 'Murder on the *Rising Star*'), and with the fact that Lee has been drawn to law and politics through the first two seasons. However, there is a continuity error when Adama states that Lee has 'never shown any type of interest in law', but then later tells him that, when he would visit his grandfather's house as a child, 'you were fascinated with his papers and his law books'. Roslin's rationale for wanting Lee involved with the trial is, in her words, 'We really need people who actually know the difference between right and wrong. That's Lee'; clearly she does not know that he has been pursuing an extramarital affair, and taking steps to murder his rival on at least two occasions.

In terms of series development, the Fleet have now gone 49 days without sighting the Cylons, and Helo is reinstated to Raptor duties, suggesting that the King incident has restored his credibility. Cally implies that there are problems

---

75 SPOILER SECTION: Tyrol is less affected by vacuum exposure than Cally is, suggesting that, as a Cylon, he may be better able to withstand such conditions.

housing orphans and abandoned children in the Fleet. She does not say precisely what happens to such children, but, when she believes both she and her husband are going to die, she tells Adama what arrangements she would like made for Nicky. The Colonies also clearly did not have a shared legal system, as one of the questions facing Roslin is which planet's laws to use in Baltar's trial. The expression 'fubar' (a military acronym dating from WWII, and standing for 'fucked up beyond all recognition') exists in the Colonies. Adama uses memory exercises to recall crewmembers' names and assignments (muttering 'Leeson takes first watch. Kinsey checks the roster … Jaffee brings me coffee' as he prepares for his day). A deleted line, which remains in behind-the-scenes footage shown in Eick's video blog for this episode, has Carolanne saying, 'This time last year, you were in orbit around New Caprica, working on a rather suave moustache, and you were totally miserable'. As well as walnuts and a seemingly inexhaustible supply of model kits, Adama has also brought his father's law books with him aboard *Galactica*.

I Read The News Today: Writing and Production

The episode was originally conceived along the idea of showing a typical, uneventful day in the life of Adama (hence the title), and exploring his relationship with his former wife. The problem is that this turned out to be very dull, and so, according to Moore, the writing team began focusing on Tyrol and Cally instead, as this storyline at least provided some drama. Moore freely admits that 'A Day in the Life' does not work, saying, 'I thought this episode was a bit of a misfire. It doesn't do justice to, or even stay true to, its premise'. The idea of Lee becoming a lawyer arose in part because the writing team were working on the pilot for *Caprica* and giving some thought to the Adama family backstory and the character of Joseph Adama (suggesting that the inclusion of Joseph's lawbooks was something of an inside joke for the team), although Moore worries in his podcast that it is too contrived. However, as noted before, the character has been tending in this direction for some time.

In production terms, the house used for the Adamas's residence was again a real one in North Vancouver. Richard Hudolin wanted something that a young officer couple might actually own (although it seems terribly chintzy for Adama's tastes). The team, as noted above, were anxious to emphasise that Carolanne was not a Head Person, and did so by largely confining her to the imagined house on Caprica. However, the distinction is poorly made, as Carolanne is also seen physically sleeping next to Adama on *Galactica*, and as Head Six also appears to Baltar in an imaginary house and fantasy landscapes. Lucinda Jenney is of course neither the woman who appears as Caroline Adama in 'Act of Contrition', nor in the background photo of Adama's wife with her sons seen in the miniseries; but, as similar-looking actresses are used, the discrepancy is not serious. Carolanne appears to be in her forties, and there are children's toys scattered in and around the house, suggesting that Adama imagines Carolanne as she was when Lee and Zak were young and before they divorced, though Adama himself looks, and acts, as he is now.

Originally, the team had the idea of Roslin producing a joint at the end of the story, and for her and Adama to smoke it together in a call-back to their stoned experience on New Caprica in 'Unfinished Business'. This was left out because the network's Standards and Practices team had caused so much trouble for them over the earlier episode; and it also has to be said that the last time Adama was seen to smoke a joint, it led to some questionable decisions about Fleet personnel assignments. The idea that people can survive up to a minute in vacuum but experience decompression sickness afterwards was researched heavily by the series' scientific adviser Doctor Kevin Grazier. Its inclusion was intended as a sideswipe at the common science-fiction misapprehension that they would instead explode or freeze to death. One of the pieces of debris that flies out of the airlock during the Tyrols' rescue is a CGI model of an original-series daggit.

Although the story focuses on marriages and work, contrasting the Adamas growing distant through the husband's absence with Tyrol and Cally patching up their differences through a shared crisis, the defining metaphor of the episode seems instead to be Hot Dog's VD-induced rash, another irritating consequence of inappropriate relationships.

46: Dirty Hands

FIRST TRANSMISSION DATE: 25 February 2007 (USA/CANADA)

WRITERS: Anne Cofell Saunders and Jane Espenson

DIRECTOR: Wayne Rose

CREDITED CAST: Rekha Sharma (Tory Foster); David Patrick Green (Xeno Fenner); Jennifer Halley (Seelix); Don Thompson (Figurski); Leah Cairns (Racetrack); Colin Lawrence (Skulls); Samantha Ferris (Pollux); Wesley Salter (Redford); Colin Corrigan (Adama's Marine); Jerry Wasserman (Cabott); Samuel Chu (Milo); Bryce Hodgson (Danny)

SYNOPSIS: A book written by Baltar while in custody, criticising the hierarchical nature of the Fleet, circulates illegally and is widely read. The workers on the tylium refinery *Hitei Kan* complain about their conditions, but when Roslin discovers that their leader, Fenner, has read Baltar's book, he is arrested. The workers on the tylium refinery down tools until Fenner is released and their conditions are improved. Tyrol attempts to negotiate on their behalf, with little success. When he points out to Roslin that the presence of child labour suggests that hereditary work castes are beginning to develop, she tries instituting a draft and lottery of all people in the Fleet with relevant experience to work on the refinery. This leads to a novice worker being injured, and Tyrol calls a general strike. Adama has Tyrol arrested and threatens to have Cally shot as a mutineer, followed by Tyrol's deck gang. Tyrol calls off the strike. Roslin negotiates with him and agrees to fairer working conditions in the Fleet, and to the re-establishment of a union, with Tyrol as its leader.

ANALYSIS: In the podcast for 'Dirty Hands', Moore says: 'I think that in today's political environment, unions and collective bargaining have acquired such a negative connotation in the popular media [and] essentially the conservative movement in this country has been so successful at demonising unions ... that I think it's actually a good thing to remind people of why the labour movement exists and to remind them of why there are unions'. However, in making this episode, the writing team have played into the hands of the demonisation, presenting an anti-union tract under the pretence of supporting organised labour.

The Wrath of Hitei Kan: The Problem of Labour in the Fleet

In this story, the Fleet's leadership, and particularly Roslin, are the authors of the unfolding catastrophe. Fenner points out that he has been trying to contact Roslin for some time, but she will only speak to him when things get so bad that a Raptor crashes into *Colonial One*, having suffered engine failure due to impurities in its tylium fuel. The Fleet are now so low on refined tylium that they can make two jumps at most; which, since there have been no Cylon attacks in 50 days and thus no unusual call on resources, suggests serious problems with the normal refining process. However, rather than admit she let the situation get out of hand and take steps to resolve the matter, Roslin has Fenner falsely arrested on charges of 'extortion and interrupting vital services during a time of war'. Adama later says that the reason why Fenner was arrested was that 'he pissed off the President', which is clearly true, as the trigger for Fenner's arrest was his quoting Baltar's book. The tylium workers' subsequent act of sabotage, hiding the pressure seals so that the machinery will not work, is entirely down to Roslin having imprisoned their leader, meaning that, in falsely accusing Fenner of interfering with the tylium service, Roslin has actually brought about that very interference. Roslin is also disingenuous about the use of child labour on the refinery (which, as Moore points out, is deeply problematic, stating, 'The Laura Roslin that was the Secretary of Education is long gone'.) She says 'There are children on every ship in the Fleet' and tries to justify the situation with reference to past societies in which parents taught their job skills to their offspring. Although she agrees to a fairer system, in which professionals and bureaucrats will take their turn at unskilled labour, and reconstitutes the union, this is only once Tyrol has been forced to back down by Adama threatening to shoot his wife and deck gang. The scene takes on the implication that Tyrol is given trifling concessions once he recognises the authority of Roslin and Adama, even though the Fleet's leaders could just as easily not bother.

Tyrol, rather than becoming this episode's Helo-figure, is instead deeply compromised. Although he was a union leader on New Caprica, it takes Baltar to tell him that class divides exist on the Fleet. He acts as a stooge for the military; even though Cabott, who leads the refinery workers in Fenner's absence, clearly expects Tyrol to take their side, Tyrol promptly shops him to Adama and Roslin as a saboteur. When imprisonment triggers the post-traumatic stress disorder that Cabott incurred during his time in Cylon detention on New Caprica (evidently the New Caprica resistance old boys' network only goes so far), Tyrol exploits the man's condition to get Fenner to tell him where he has hidden the seals. Tyrol also orders that the lottery selectees be put on a ship before they realise they are being sent to the *Hitei Kan*. Furthermore, although in a deleted scene Tyrol justifies excluding the politicians on *Colonial One* from the lottery on the grounds that he is looking for relevant skill sets, when draftee Danny Noon argues that he is there by mistake, as he is not actually a skilled labourer but someone who worked on a farm briefly to earn money for college, Tyrol sends him through anyway. In another deleted scene, when Tyrol defends his support for the lottery by saying he prevented child labour, Cally accuses him of simply trading 12-year-old workers for 17-year-old ones – who, she also points out, are still entirely from the poor colonies. Finally, in another deleted scene, in which Cally points out that Roslin and Adama are acting like 'a thug and a dictator', Tyrol dismisses her argument by muttering 'Gods, Cally, just go to sleep'. Tyrol, metaphorically speaking, would rather remain asleep than wake up to the oppression he is himself supporting.

After calling a strike on the *Hitei Kan*, Tyrol then involves the deck gang, even though he should be aware that, as they are military personnel, he is inciting them to mutiny. In doing so, he gives Adama just cause to arrest them and use the threat of their execution to break his resolve and end the strike. Tyrol also seems almost subservient at the end of the story in his conversation with Roslin, overlooking the fact that he has just been seriously intimidated by the leader of the military. Furthermore, she dismisses his request for training and a rotation schedule for people in dangerous jobs, with no stated justification, and, although she accedes to his request to have white-collar personnel taking shifts in cleaning and low-level maintenance jobs, we never actually see this happen in later stories, indicating that he has really won no concessions at all. Roslin is the one who suggests forming a union, with Tyrol as its leader, meaning that it is essentially a management-controlled organisation; as with the Cylons' manipulation of the New Caprica resistance in the webisodes, she is cynically employing the union as a pressure valve for social unrest. Labour relations aboard the Fleet are never mentioned again after this story, reinforcing the idea that labour have been completely broken.

With Tyrol a stooge for the military, and with Zarek nowhere to be seen, the only person who articulates the voice of reason is Baltar. However, Baltar has been continually presented in the series as a selfish liar and collaborator; Moore likens his book, inaccurately, to *Mein Kampf*. Although Cally could be that voice of reason, challenging her husband's hypocrisy, a deleted scene shows she too is compromised: she says, of their time on New Caprica, 'When Baltar cut food rations, we shut down three power plants for a week. We sabotaged the whole power grid'. Since Baltar would have been cutting food rations not out of political privilege, but because there simply wasn't enough to eat, Cally is essentially advocating union thuggery against a legitimate governmental action. The end result is that we have a story that, although Moore in his podcast claims that it is pro-union, presents no credible voice for labour.

Class Consciousness: Colonial Hierarchies Exposed

Underlying the efforts to organise labour is the idea, seen earlier in 'The Woman King', that there is a distinct hierarchy among the colonies, summarised by Cally's speech: 'You ever wonder why all the pilots and the officers come from the rich Colonies, like Caprica, and Virgon, Tauron … While all the knuckledraggers come from the poor Colonies like Aerilon and Sagittaron? And Gemenon?' When Tyrol points out that Dualla is a Sagittaron, Cally reminds him that she was promoted to lieutenant only upon marrying a Caprican. While Dualla was actually promoted before her marriage to Lee, it also has to be said that their relationship was hardly the best-kept secret in the Fleet, suggesting that the accusations of nepotism are not without basis.

This is highlighted in the subplot about Seelix's attempts to become a pilot, which bookends the rest of the story. At the outset, we learn that her application for pilot training was rejected not on merit but because she is the support crew's best avionics specialist, which she clearly feels is a slight. The cheery ending, in which she is installed as a trainee pilot, is ironic in light of this, as it means that either she is not as essential as all that (in which case she was being held back out of class prejudice), or else that the military are removing a valuable technician from her post just to prove a political point about diversity management. Moore in his podcast describes the scene as 'sweet and sentimental', and then says, 'I like the way that the deck gang looks at moving one of their own into the upper ranks. It acknowledges the class system, and breaks the class system at the same time. Because one of theirs is moving to the other and they're still where they are, and they have to respect her, but it means that movement is possible'. Apparently without realising it, he has endorsed the Marxist idea of false consciousness: that labourers support the system that oppresses them through the possibility of upward mobility. Rather than challenging Colonial hierarchy, Seelix's promotion simply reinforces it, and keeps the deck gang in line.

Three Strikes and You're Out: Continuity and Problems

The story is fraught with other problems and inconsistencies. The construction of the *Hitei Kan* (identified by this name in a deleted scene, but not in the finished version) is such that if the conveyer belt jams, the ship blows up, which seems a stupid way to design a ship, particularly since it is not a jury-rigged affair, but one purpose-built as a refinery under Colonial rule. It is also not clear how Tyrol can later stop the line directly with no ill effects just by pulling a lever, since stopping the line abruptly is no different from having it jam. No reference is made to the other tylium refinery ship, the *Daru Mozu*, even though external shots in 'Guess What's Coming to Dinner' indicate that it is still in the Fleet, and the repairs following the suicide bombing in 'Epiphanies' should have been made by this point.

There are also characterisation problems. The idea of Baltar as an Aerilon who has lost his native accent in order to pass as a Caprican falls flat in that James Callis has a British accent, which none of the other Caprican characters do (something Callis himself has pointed out, saying 'Was his elocution teacher deaf?'), bringing the artificiality of the 'treacherous Brit' trope into unfortunately sharp relief. Callis's 'Aerilon' accent, which is apparently supposed to be a Yorkshire one, also sounds distinctly forced. Baltar's description of Aerilons as people who 'work with their hands and grab a pint down the pub, and finish off the evening with a good old-fashioned fight' sounds suspiciously like an inexcusable stereotype of either the Irish or the Northern English.

Milo, the child labourer, is problematically characterised, one minute badmouthing the system, the next eager to throw the switch like a good little wage slave (although this could be put down to the fact that children can be inconsistent). While having Danny Noon, after complaining that he has been drafted in as a labourer by mistake, then suffer an accident on the *Hitei Kan* in front of Tyrol, is understandable in terms of dramatic irony, it also verges on the clichéd. The portrayal of working on the *Hitei Kan* as Dickensian, with child labour, dangerous machinery and filthy conditions, implies that labour activism is acceptable only under the most extreme circumstances. Finally, the cheery scene at the end in which Seelix becomes a pilot has a sour edge in that we are expected to be feeling happy for a woman who, 11 episodes earlier, was ruthlessly throwing supposed collaborators out of airlocks.

In terms of its antecedents, the Seelix subplot has a connection with the original-series unmade story 'Showdown', in which Masi, a former pilot cadet, is shunted into working as a specialist when it is discovered that he has computer skills, and resents this. There are also obvious connections to the *Babylon 5* episode 'By Any Means Necessary', in which Garibaldi, an officer of working-class roots, is caught between striking dock workers and strike-busting military, with his commanding officer resorting to sneaky political tactics to resolve the conflict in the workers' favour. Baltar's writing a book in prison to cast himself in a politically favourable light has real-life parallels with both Albert Speer and, as Moore notes in his podcast, Adolf Hitler (with Baltar's title, *My Triumphs, My Mistakes*, being not too dissimilar from Hitler entitling his book *Mein Kampf*, or, in English, 'My Struggle'); however, the comparison is distinctly unfair, as Hitler was anti-union and in favour of ethnic hierarchies, and Moore's remark comes across as completely inappropriate. The writing team would shortly become themselves involved in the Hollywood writers' strike, making it all the stranger that the story is not more sympathetic to the workers' position. Moore, in his podcast, complains that a scene in which Tyrol finds two workers reading Baltar's book was changed to him simply finding the book because, according what he calls 'arcane' union rules, the background artists playing the workers were allowed neither to speak nor to take direction. In continuity terms, Cally is still walking with a stick due to the after-effects of decompression sickness, and Adama and Roslin clearly have not taken their relationship much further than the flirting stage yet, as, when Roslin complains about having to stay in her temporary offices on *Galactica* following the Raptor crashing into *Colonial One*, he remarks 'You're always welcome in one of my beds' and she does an amused double-take.

Love Your Enemies: Writing and Production

'Dirty Hands' started out as an episode in the Sagittaron storyline. Initially entitled 'Our Enemies, Ourselves', it would have revolved around a crisis in which the Sagittarons were going to be dispersed through the Fleet. Dualla has to represent the government in dealing with the Sagittarons, but, after initially taking the authorities' line, she eventually sides with them until Adama gives them their own ship. Baltar, in this earlier version, is Sagittaron rather than Aerilon, as in the series bible entry for his character. According to Moore, the failure of 'Our Enemies, Ourselves' to work was one of the reasons for the abandonment of the Sagittaron arc. However, the fact that this storyline would have involved celebrating the ghettoisation of a persecuted religious minority as a good solution was also undoubtedly another factor. Moore's reference in his podcast to the Sagittarons as the 'Children of Israel' makes the idea particularly unfortunate. However, a lot of the problems with the final version of the story seem to come from changing the conflict from one involving the Sagittarons – who had previously been established as facing ingrained prejudice at all levels on the Fleet – to one involving a legitimate protest by organised labour.

Wayne Rose, the episode's director, had been a first assistant director on the series for some time, and had also directed the New Caprica webisodes. The *Hitei Kan* scenes were shot at Rogers Sugar, and the conveyer belts and equipment that feature in the episode were there *in situ*. Moore in his podcast comments that factory ships can be realised cheaply, as they can be filmed at real-life factories, whereas something like a passenger liner would require purpose-built sets. A deckhand with a real prosthetic arm can be seen in this episode, and one of the deleted scenes features an area with children, which seems to be the previously-mentioned *Galactica* daycare. Although Baltar was originally to have been stripped naked during the search for his writing, both James Callis and Mary McDonnell insisted the scene stop short of it, feeling that Roslin would not push his humiliation that far. It would also have given the sequence an unpleasant sexual subtext, which is at odds with the otherwise political nature of the two characters' antagonism.

Baltar, speaking with Tyrol in this episode, says, 'That's what the aristocracy wants. It wants the working class to feel looked after, while they scrabble around for scraps from the master's table'. This important and crucial message is, however, suppressed, not just by the Fleet's leaders and the labour organisers, but by the writing and production team themselves.

47: Maelstrom

FIRST TRANSMISSION DATE: 4 March 2007 (USA/CANADA)

WRITER: Bradley Thompson & David Weddle

DIRECTOR: Michael Nankin

CREDITED CAST: Callum Keith Rennie (Leoben); Dorothy Lyman (Socrata Thrace); Bodie Olmos (Hot Dog); Leah Cairns (Racetrack); Don Thompson (Figurski); Camille Atebe (Sarah Ryan); Georgia Craig (Oracle Brenn); Erika-Shaye Gair (Child Kara)

SYNOPSIS: The Fleet engages in refuelling operations, hiding from the Cylons by staying close to a planet with sensor-distorting radiation. Suffering from strange dreams about the mandala and Leoben, Starbuck visits an oracle, who reminds her of her destiny, and says Leoben is coming for her. Flying combat air patrol (CAP), Starbuck thinks she sees a Heavy Raider in the planet's atmosphere and, although it does not appear on DRADIS, gives chase, pursuing it into a mandala-like storm. She loses the Raider and finds no trace of it on the gun camera footage. Concerned about Starbuck's mental state, Apollo offers to fly a CAP with her as wingman. Starbuck sees and pursues the Raider, though again there is no trace on DRADIS, and Apollo does not see it. As she follows the Raider into the storm, Kara has a vision, guided by Leoben, in which she relives her last encounter with her mother, when she learned her mother had been diagnosed with cancer. Leoben then enables her to attend her mother's deathbed, speak with her, and achieve closure. Starbuck flies into the heart of the storm and her Viper explodes.

ANALYSIS: 'Maelstrom' concerns the death of Starbuck, and sees Weddle and Thompson finally providing an explanation for the connection between her mandala painting, her special destiny, and her troubled childhood.

Kat's Cradle: The Death of Kara Thrace

The original version of the story, which was suggested by Eick, involved Starbuck and Apollo pursuing a real Raider through the planet's atmosphere and becoming trapped below the point at which they could regain orbit, with the atmospheric pressure of the planet about to crush them. Starbuck would choose to sacrifice herself to save Apollo, but he would find a way to save them both. In doing so, they would confront their feelings for each other, making it yet another tedious story in the love quadrangle arc. Later versions, according to Weddle in *The Official Companion Season Three*, had Starbuck 'abducted by Leoben, who subjects her to a drug-induced *Manchurian Candidate*-style psychodrama that forces her to revisit events in her past and see them in a new light'. In the process, Starbuck would have discovered something that led the crew on the road to Earth. Moore, however, suggested the writing team instead develop a story in which Starbuck flies into the mandala cloud and dies. He recalls, 'The more we talked about subsequent episodes and how this would affect character and storyline ... the more I started to realise this was really the right decision'. This is actually not surprising, as, since the death of Kat in 'The Passage', the writers have increasingly been taking Starbuck in negative directions, treating her less as a character with a dark side who is trying to do good, and more as someone who has actually given in to her evil impulses. While this is not out of keeping with Starbuck's characterisation, the fact that she has become such a malevolent figure no doubt informs the decision to close down her arcs and kill her off.

This episode consequently has many call-backs to the Starbuck-Kat story arc. Starbuck's plunging into the maelstrom echoes her suicidal pursuit of Scar as well as her crash-landing in 'Act of Contrition'. Whereas in 'Scar', her love for Anders held her death wish in check, here she embraces oblivion, believing it to be her destiny. When describing where she would like her picture on the memorial wall, she says 'I wanna go right there, next to Kat', acknowledging that the pilot was a 'royal pain in the ass, but a hell of a stick to have on your wing'. Apollo says he would like to be next to Duck and Nora, apparently because they are 'good card players', but also symbolically placing himself with the dead of New Caprica. The story picks up on this season's recurring motif of suicide, from the resistance storyline on New Caprica, to Kat's self-sacrifice, to Athena's innovative plan for rescuing Hera, to Three's attempts to find truth in the boundary between life and death.

Starbuck also sorts out her relationship with Apollo, acknowledging that a stable long-term partnership as anything other than CAG and pilot is impossible for them. In an extended version of the scene, he remarks that maybe it was meant to turn out that way for a reason, clearly meaning that, having worked through their sexual attraction, this is the best relationship for them; she, however, responds, 'Maybe', suggesting that she thinks that without the love affair, she has nothing more to live for. While it contradicts the implication made in 'Taking a Break from All Your Worries', that Apollo would betray Dualla again, here it works as a parallel to the way in which Kat, in 'The Passage', confronted her past and addressed her feelings for Enzo before she sacrificed herself. Moore comments that 'being the wingman is definitely the number two position, and for Lee to volunteer to be Kara's wingman is a fairly significant thing, and it's a nice subtle point in the relationship and what she means to him'. There is also an ironic echo of Starbuck clearing Zak for flight despite her misgivings, leading to his death, and Apollo similarly clearing Starbuck for flight here. A scene that was scripted but abandoned involved a fight between

Starbuck and Adama over his relationship with Roslin, prior to Starbuck's final journey: as Moore describes it, 'She saw something between the two of them ... and Starbuck said, "Why don't you two get a room?" And Adama didn't say anything at the moment, and after the meeting was over he asked Starbuck to stay behind, and then he just laid into her'. This fits with Starbuck's possessive jealousy toward the Admiral, and with the idea that she resented his friendship with Kat, in 'The Passage'. Given that her father walked out on her mother, it makes sense that she would have Oedipal issues involving jealousy toward father figures, and resentment toward people whom the father figure loves. (Athena is the exception who proves the rule, as she is friendly with Adama, but married to another man.) As well as having lost her rival and her lover, she would also have lost her father figure, meaning that, as Apollo states, 'Her identity as a steely-eyed Viper jock is the only thing holding her together'.

Socratic Method: Kara and her Mother

Once she has been rejected by her father figure, the sole aspect of Starbuck's backstory left to resolve is her relationship with her mother, Socrata. Socrata was a Marine, and, according to the letter seen in this episode, a corporal at the time of her retirement (though this is contradicted by the series bible and 'Razor', in both of which she is said to have been a sergeant-major). She was bitter because she never became an officer and had nothing to show for years of service but a medal, a retirement flat and a gastric tumour. The episode also provides the full story behind Kara's mother breaking her daughter's fingers, and reveals that it was in retaliation for Kara exploiting her mother's phobia of insects by planting rubber bugs in her shoes, itself an act of revenge for her hitting Kara with a broomstick handle for not making her bed. This idea, that an abusive situation breeds more abuse, is also seen in Socrata teaching her daughter, as Starbuck puts it, 'to be a warrior like her ... that fear gets you killed, and anger keeps you alive'. By emphasising anger and stoicism over compassion and acknowledging emotion, Socrata created an abusive culture. Her scrapbook of Kara's school work reveals that her essay on 'the person who most influenced me' was about her grandmother, in what seems to have been another swipe at her mother. Leoben quotes the 'all this has happened before ...' line again, in reference to Starbuck's past, referring to the cycle of anger and retribution.

What Starbuck learned from her mother is also central to her characterisation. Socrata taught her that she was different from the other children, then, later, asserting that she has been told Starbuck had a natural gift as a pilot, hassled her for not graduating top of her class. Socrata's emphasis on Starbuck's 'gift' has echoes of Leoben and his talk of destiny. However, as the oracle says, 'You confused the messenger with the message. Your mother was trying to teach you something else'; putting this together with what we see during the rest of the episode and what we know about Starbuck up to this point, it appears that although her mother was trying to teach her motivation, courage and lack of weakness, she ended up teaching her anger and lack of empathy.

Reading the episode in the context of Moore's elaborations in the podcast, Socrata knew 'that Kara really was fated for a particular end. And that [Socrata] was trying to prepare her for that ... and that out of her desire to toughen her daughter and make her daughter strong enough to take on the challenges that she was gonna face one day, she had really stepped over the line and had abused the daughter and had created this really toxic relationship between mother and child'. When Kara tried to extend sympathy to her mother upon learning she has cancer, her mother pushed it away, and Kara left. Head Leoben reveals that Socrata waited for Kara to return for five weeks. Head Leoben also says that Kara wanted her mother to be right about her; Starbuck is twisted by her experience, such that she wants the main authority figure in her life to remain unchallenged, even if it means her own destruction. In a sense, then, by trying to prepare Starbuck to meet her destiny, Socrata brought that very destiny about, by turning Kara into the sort of twisted, suicidal individual who would, in the end, choose to dive her Viper into the mandala. There are also clear parallels between Kara's story and the cycle of oppression meted out by the humans and the Cylons toward each other: the abused child grows up to emulate the abusive patterns learned from the parent. However, Kara facing death bravely, and having the courage to go back to achieve closure with her mother through Head Leoben, shows that she has the positive attributes her mother saw as well as the negative ones.

A Bad Cover Band: Kara Thrace's Special Destiny

The revelation of Kara's destiny also explains the recurring image of the mandala. Her dream involves painting out the mandala on her apartment wall, then having sex with Leoben, the mandala mysteriously reappearing as she does so. This vision reflects her belief that, even if she tries to hide from destiny, it comes through in the end, and that Leoben is inextricably linked to her ultimate fate. In the 'real' world, the mandala is seen in the pattern of the melting candle wax at the memorial wall, and in the form of the maelstrom. The dream also foreshadows the appearance of Leoben as a spirit guide; Kara realises this at the end, saying, 'You're not Leoben, are you?', which is even more effective in light of the deleted scene from 'A Measure of Salvation' indicating that the Leoben Kara knew is now dead. The choice of Leoben as a Head Person reflects the demonic side of God's messengers; he is another father figure who incorporates aspects of her abusive mother, and is linked with torture and death in Kara's past. In a deleted scene set on the firing range, Kara shoots at a target with Leoben's face, and while doing so flashes back both to 'Flesh and Bone' and to her last meeting with her mother. A line from the shooting script, after Kara wakes from her dream, runs: *'TOOTHPASTE SQUEEZED ONTO A BRUSH. Kara brings the brush to her mouth and tries to scrub away the tactile memory of Leoben's kiss'*. Both Leoben and her mother are people who have hurt her, and who have urged her on to her fatal destiny in the mandala; and in firing at the target, she is symbolically trying to kill death. It is possible to read a disturbing gender subtext to the episode, in that Kara is attracted to a pair of weak, uncommitted men and yet dreams about hot sex with the man who imprisoned and tortured her – following her imprisoning and torturing him in turn. However, this is to ignore the symbolic role Leoben plays in the story as a death figure. His leading her to the mandala suggests that Kara has finally been destroyed by her abuser. Head Leoben gives Kara closure by allowing her to visit her dying mother. He says, 'I'm here to prepare you to pass through the next door. To discover what hovers in the space between life and death'; in that space, what she sees is her own mother.

Kara's death, at this point in the story, is thematically appropriate. Her issues about Kat, Apollo and her mother have all been resolved, and her death marks the end of the spiral of destruction she has pursued since New Caprica. Moore, in the podcast for 'Crossroads' part two says, 'Her death didn't have meaning'. Although it is fated, and although she achieves closure, there is nothing else to it. This places her destiny in the context of the repeated cycle theme of the story; rather than a teleological narrative, in which Kara's death has a particular meaning, her demise is part of a cycle of existence that repeats over and over without a significant conclusion, like the circles of the mandala itself. Her death may not be a positive one, but it is one that is appropriate to the character and to the cyclical nature of the series' cosmology.

Full of Stars: Continuity and Worldbuilding

In continuity terms, we learn that there is a psychiatrist aboard the *Inchon Velle*: although it is not stated, this might be Doctor Stoffa, referred to in 'Hero'. The oracle in Dogsville was intended to be Dodona Selloi but, for what Moore describes as 'budgetary and scheduling reasons', actress Amanda Plummer was unavailable. Kara, like Tyrol in 'Lay Down Your Burdens', would rather see an oracle than a psychiatrist. We learn some more Colonial argot: the pilots' codeword for Raiders is 'sparrows', and a Heavy Raider is a 'turkey'. Luciana Carro is quoted in *The Official Companion Season Three* as saying that she shot a scene of 'Kat – or someone who looks like Kat – showing up in a brand-new Viper at the end of the episode and telling Starbuck not to worry'. Eick's video blog shows Socrata's scrapbook in more detail, indicating that Kara got Bs and As for the most part at school, aside from in Biology, where her marks were consistently low. She also appears to have had high marks for positive self image (suggesting the teacher misinterpreted Kara's habitual bravado), taking initiative and teamwork.

In terms of original-series references, the scenes of Vipers flying through blue skies are reminiscent of *Galactica 1980*. Firing their guns in atmosphere gives an effect similar to original-series lasers, and the Cylon Heavy Raider fires ammunition with a blue flare in the last Viper sequence, which looks again very close to the lasers of the original-series Cylon craft. As they are firing in atmosphere rather than space, their guns have an unmuted roar. Moore in his podcast remarks that he wanted the re-establishment of the friendship between

Apollo and Starbuck to be a call-back to the original series, and its relationship between the 'straight arrow' Apollo and his 'hotshot, crazy friend' Starbuck; had the writing team stuck to that formula, it might have prevented reimagined-series Starbuck from turning into such a malevolent figure. Starbuck's mother's name, Socrata, is an obvious link to Socrates, the philosopher known for establishing a system of inquiry through dialectical exchanges between opposing viewpoints. The statuette of the goddess Aurora that the oracle gives Kara and she later gives to Adama has wings and evokes both the winged deities of Greco-Roman mythology and a Christian angel, reflecting the series' tension between pantheistic and monotheistic traditions. Aurora, the goddess, was said to renew herself every day, here symbolising Kara's spiritual renewal as she passes out of this life.[76]

Spirit Guides: Writing and Production

The Official Companion Season Three says that Katee Sackhoff partly inspired the idea of connecting the maelstrom with the mandala; she asked Weddle what the relationship was between the mandala in the Temple of Five and Starbuck's painting, and, when Weddle said that the writers had not established that yet, expressed the hope that Starbuck would encounter Leoben again and learn more about her special destiny. According to Weddle, Moore came up with the idea of having Starbuck fly into a cloud resembling the mandala. This gives a new perspective to the story, in that Sackhoff's question about Starbuck's destiny led to the writers making it a prophecy of death. This might cause the viewer to wonder if Starbuck's interpretation of her destiny is a self-fulfilling prophecy, whereby, having unconsciously decided that she is fated to die in a particular way at a particular time, she interprets her mother's words, the mandala, and her dreams to support this idea, and her visions are nothing more than self-justifying hallucinations.

One change during the development of the story was that originally Starbuck was to have gone on three trips in the Viper, but the director cut the middle journey, over Moore's objections, as unnecessary to the narrative: this iteration would have had Kara seeing the Raider but faking a hydraulic failure in her cockpit and running away rather than pursuing it. She was to have woken up inside a Heavy Raider before beginning her journey with Leoben, suggesting initially that the whole thing might be a Cylon trick; however, cost considerations again ruled out building a Heavy Raider interior. Weddle, who was with his father, a former Marine, as he died, is quoted in *The Official Companion Season Three* as saying, 'It turned out to be one of the most profound experiences of my life ... So I think some of that is reflected in the episode'.

When production began, Katee Sackhoff had to sign a confidentiality agreement regarding Starbuck's fate in this story. The photographs of the young

---

[76] SPOILER SECTION: And she will later symbolise Kara's physical renewal when she returns to the Fleet.

47: MAELSTROM

Kara visible in Socrata's scrapbook really are of Katee Sackhoff. In one of the flashback sequences, a 'Marlboro' label can be clearly seen on one of Socrata's cigarettes. Moore says of the sequence where Adama smashes his model ship: 'This was not a planned moment. This is Eddie being in the moment. Eddie *being in the moment*. This is all genuine emotion ... He is so upset, and he reacts, and lashes out, and destroys this ship. And you know what? This is a genuine museum-quality ship that we were renting! This isn't a prop! This was hundreds of dollars! Oh, but thank God it was insured'.

The cast were deeply disturbed by the ending, with Olmos reportedly saying, 'The show will never be the same again'. The death of a regular, and in particular a regular based on one of the original series' central figures, implies that no character is safe.

BY YOUR COMMAND: VOL 2

48: The Son Also Rises

FIRST TRANSMISSION DATE: 11 March 2007 (USA/CANADA)

WRITER: Michael Angeli

DIRECTOR: Robert Young

CREDITED CAST: Rekha Sharma (Tory Foster); Sebastian Spence (Narcho); Mark Sheppard (Romo Lampkin); Bodie Olmos (Hot Dog); Leah Cairns (Racetrack); Colin Lawrence (Skulls); Ty Olsson (LSO Kelly); Don Thompson (Figurski); Tyler McClendon (Alan Hughes); Stephen Holmes (Reporter #1); Christina Schild (Playa Palacios); Alison Matthews (Fallbrook); Chris Boyd (Marine Cheadle); Colin Corrigan (Marine Nowart)

KNOWN UNCREDITED CAT: Jerry (Lance)

SYNOPSIS: The Fleet prepares for Baltar's trial, selecting a tribunal of judges by lottery from the ships' captains. Adama's name is chosen. An unknown bomber assassinates Baltar's defence attorney. Roslin finds a new lawyer willing to represent him. This is Romo Lampkin, who knew Adama's father. Lee has been distracted since Starbuck's death, and is failing to carry out his duties as CAG adequately. Adama replaces him with Helo, assigning Lee instead to handle security for Lampkin. Lampkin evades an attempt on his life; later, he interviews Caprica-Six and exposes the depth of her feelings for Baltar. Lampkin is wounded by another explosion. In sickbay, he reveals to Lee that he is a kleptomaniac, obsessed with stealing small, significant objects from people. Lee discovers that the item he stole from Kelly is a circular magnet, of a type used by the bomber, and Kelly admits his guilt. Adama reinstates Apollo as CAG, as he does not want his son acting as part of Baltar's defence team, but Apollo refuses, and remains as Lampkin's assistant for the trial.

ANALYSIS: 'The Son Also Rises' forms a loose three-part story with the following 'Crossroads', setting up the personnel and legal arrangements for Baltar's trial and introducing Romo Lampkin. It also features Lee formally making a break with his father and striking out on his own as a legal assistant.

Here Comes the Son: Lawyer Lee and Romo Lampkin

This episode marks the point where Lee, after flirting with politics occasionally throughout the series, makes the shift from, as Lampkin describes it, 'king of the pilots', to prototypical lawyer and politician. Lee's association with Lampkin finally forces him to acknowledge who he wants to be, and to stop following the path his father has set out for him. The death of Kara, furthermore, appears to have freed him from his complicated sex life, and he is now able to concentrate on his professional direction. Lampkin's dry remark 'I'm handcuffed to a serial contrarian' slyly acknowledges Lee's repeated shifts in role throughout the series. The scene toward the end where Apollo argues that he should be on Baltar's defence team, while his father balks at this, saying that he's not a lawyer, appears to reflect the thought processes of the writers, who had initially wanted Lee to become Baltar's defence attorney but realised that his main qualification for the role was merely that he spent some time in his grandfather's office. Consequently, the scene first acknowledges the problem, then gives Lee a more plausible position on the legal team.

Romo Lampkin says that he learned from Joseph Adama that 'Everybody has demons … The law is just a way of exorcising them'. In 'The Son Also Rises', this refers not only to the fact that Baltar's trial is allowing people to expiate their own guilt by blaming everything on a scapegoat, but also to Lee resolving his own issues and becoming the person he wants to be. Lampkin is a student of human nature; his explanation as to why Joseph Adama wanted to defend the 'worst of the worst' is: 'Joe Adama cared about one thing. Understanding why people do what they do. Why we cheat our friends, why we reward our enemies … Why we build machines in the hope of correcting our flaws and our shortcomings. Why we forgive, defying logic and the laws of nature with one stupid little act of compassion'. Lampkin is a kleptomaniac, a condition that suggests that he feels out of control in his own life, but he also uses it to understand others. Regarding the button he stole from Adama, he says the fact that it's tarnished means that the soldier in him has had enough for a while. This acknowledges how, since Starbuck's death, Adama has become confused and paranoid in his grief, trying to protect Lee but also lashing out at him. At the end of the story, the question remains as to whether Adama's wanting to keep Lee off Baltar's defence team is because he thinks defending criminals isn't honourable, reflecting his disagreement with Joseph Adama, or because it would complicate things politically, in that the Fleet's leadership could not line up and condemn Baltar without implicitly also condemning one of their own.

Writer Michael Angeli is quoted in *The Official Companion Season Three* as saying, 'When Romo tells the truth, he keeps his glasses on – but when he tells an outright lie, he takes his glasses off'. This appears to read in the scene where Romo tells Caprica-Six a direct lie regarding Baltar's feelings about her, as he takes the sunglasses off and looks into her eyes, which has the effect of convincing her of his sincerity. However, it does not particularly read otherwise in the story, suggesting that the director and actor were not necessarily following Angeli's instructions. By the next story, the production team will evidently have abandoned the sunglasses idea, presumably on the grounds of it being too complicated.

Love and Rockets: The Bombing Plot and the Cylons

The main problem with the story is that the bombing subplot is not very convincing. It is clearly based on events surrounding the trial of Saddam Hussein, in which assassination attempts of varying degrees of success were carried out against his and his co-defendants' legal team, while people across the world debated the necessity/legitimacy of the trial, and the defendants used the situation as a political platform. However, at that time in Iraq, there were a lot of possible motivations for attempting to kill the lawyers, including making the occupying Americans look incompetent and weak. In the Fleet, by contrast, we have not a chaotic occupied country, but a reasonably cohesive and authoritarian regime, and the bombs are a bigger threat to military personnel than they are to lawyers. Although Kelly tells Apollo that he would not have let him get into the Raptor with the bomb, and his willingness to see Athena killed along with Lampkin can be explained on the grounds of anti-Cylon prejudice, his attempt would have also led to the death of the Marine guarding Lampkin, and as bombs are not precision weapons, could easily have caused other deaths and/or injuries. It seems unlikely, furthermore, that someone whose stated motivation for bombing the lawyers is that he is tired of sending pilots off to die would be willing to put at risk the lives of several pilots and deck crew, many of whom he would know personally, just in order to kill Baltar's lawyer. Moore attempts to justify the choice of Kelly in the podcast by saying, 'He's so stalwart and he's such a company man. And … he just cannot abide the fact that this guy is getting a trial, and … y'know, it just really burns him'. While the sentiment is believable, the idea that Kelly would go on to attempt to murder his own colleagues because of it is less so; the idea is poorly reasoned, and seems to come out of nowhere.

Meanwhile, Cally argues with Skulls that everyone deserves a trial, even Baltar. However, her prejudice against Cylons overrides her sense of social justice. The fact that she is going through a rough patch in her relationship with Tyrol means she fixates particularly on Athena, who is of the same model as her former rival, Boomer. While Cally says the bombs are a Cylon effort to sow division amongst the humans, she winds up creating that division by continually implying that Athena is connected with them. In a deleted scene, Athena confronts Cally, pointing out that Cally also had opportunities to plant bombs and asking her why she would believe Athena would plant a bomb on her own ship. As with Adama in 'Home', she gives Cally her gun, but then says she does not think Cally will take the opportunity to kill her, because, although she hates Cylons, she recognises that Athena loves her husband, her child, and the *Galactica*. She concludes with: 'Now, I don't think you would take a mother away from her child'. In this conversation, Athena forces Cally to recognise what the two women have in common, and that Cylons also feel love.

Elsewhere, Baltar instructs Lampkin to stop Caprica-Six from testifying, advising him to tell her that he loves her and is thinking about her. Lampkin, however, creates a more positive development in human-Cylon relations when he steals Baltar's pen and gives it to Caprica-Six. As Baltar's pen is his only means of conveying his thoughts to the outside world, and thus the most precious thing he owns, Caprica-Six is reminded of her love for him. Lampkin also knows that Adama, Tory and Roslin are watching, and is playing to that audience. He points out that Caprica-Six is not afforded the same dignity as even the most reviled human on the Fleet, saying 'I couldn't help you if they paid me ten times what they offered me for Baltar. You won't get a trial, even a bad one'. Witnessing Lampkin's conversation with Caprica-Six about the pain of love, Roslin is made to realise that Cylons, even though they may be treated as machines, feel as intensely about love as humans do, and says 'I feel like part of our world just fell down'. The gambit with the pen also rules out calling Caprica-Six to testify about Baltar's involvement in the destruction of the Colonies, meaning that, as the only other evidence for it is Roslin's vision and a partial confession extracted under duress and using hallucinogenic drugs, these events cannot be raised at the trial.

Above the Law: Continuity and Worldbuilding

In this episode, Apollo makes good on his promise to pin Kara's photo next to Kat's on the memorial wall, and Adama reviews her file. We learn from this that she had problems from the outset, as the first item on the record is a disciplinary notice. She also had insubordination-related issues as a private; served on the battlestar *Triton*; was part of the Aerilon Combat Fifth Division; earned a combat citation; and was court-martialled at one point; all of which is perfectly in character. One of her disciplinary notices, headed 'Colonial Forces Training Command', runs in part, 'Lieutenant Thrace states that while she is guilty of none of the abovementioned charges, she only wishes to challenge the AWOL charge. She points out that her "self-assigned" duty has resulted in the destruction of a Cylon vessel'. As this incident must have taken place either when she was a cadet or when she was a flight instructor, she is therefore guilty either of breaking the armistice or of vandalising museum property. In Adama's final scene with Apollo, the smashed remains of his model ship are clearly visible in his office. Otherwise, the Cylons are still quiet; and Lampkin's pet cat Lance makes his first appearance in the series. The subplot with Tyrol finding a bomb aboard Sharon's Raptor is something of a call-back to the events of 'Water'. The original-series episode 'Murder on the *Rising Star*' is again a reference point for this story, as it features Apollo acting as part of a legal defence team and Adama serving on a tribunal.

The selection of the tribunal involves a convenient coincidence, as both Adama and Elias Meeker, captain of the *Gideon* (focus of the civilian massacre featured in 'Resistance' and 'Final Cut') are selected, out of a pool of all the Fleet's captains. The draft script for 'Crossroads' part two indicates that originally the judges were to have been actively selected, rather than chosen by lottery, which would have made Adama's presence more logical, but would also have made the trial look completely fixed. A more excusable coincidence, however, is Anders flipping a cubit coin and having it come down heads each time, which he drunkenly interprets as meaning that Kara is 'too lucky to check out'. This is a reference to Tom Stoppard's 1966 absurdist play *Rosencrantz and Guildenstern are Dead*, in which a similar sequence is taken as meaning that the characters are held within 'un-, sub- or supernatural forces', and it serves here as an early hint that Anders and Kara are subject to a similar power.

Lampkin is clearly based on Jacques Verges, the controversial French lawyer well known for defending seemingly indefensible people, including Klaus Barbie, Carlos the Jackal and Slobodan Milosevic, though Mark Sheppard, in the bonus podcast, says the character was also based on Harvard law professor Alan Dershowitz, defender of Claus von Bulow and O J Simpson. Verges's best-known tactic, the 'rupture strategy', was to argue that the regime accusing his client of war crimes is engaging in selective prosecution, allowing some people guilty of equal crimes to go free – a strategy Lee will also later employ. Lampkin's given name, Romo, was derived from the first two letters of Ronald D Moore's first and last names; but by coincidence the Dallas Cowboys, Eick's favourite football team, had a quarterback named Tony Romo, meaning that, Angeli says, '[Eick] e-mailed me and said "You named him for the Dallas Cowboys. That's cool!"'. The story's title is a pun on that of Hemingway's novel *The Sun Also Rises*, about a moral man searching for integrity in an immoral world. It is also a Biblical reference to Ecclesiastes 1, a chapter reading in part: 'One generation passeth away, and another generation cometh: but the earth abideth forever. The sun also ariseth, and the sun goeth down, and hasteth to his place where he arose'. This references both the intergenerational conflict in the Adama family, and the series' theme of 'All this has happened before, and all this will happen again'. The legal system of the Colonies is based on the one used in the USA, with a certain amount of dramatic licence. There also seems to be some rule-bending in this case, particularly regarding Adama's observation of Caprica-Six's interview, which, Apollo points out, is problematic since he has been selected to serve on the tribunal. Moore notes as a background detail that the writing team believe that justice has mainly been administered on an ad-hoc basis by the ships' captains up until this point.

Law and Order: Background and Production

According to Michael Angeli on the bonus podcast, the story originally focused more on the bombing plot, but the writing team felt this was unoriginal, so the main thrust of the narrative was shifted to the Lee storyline. According to Moore in his podcast, the bomber's identity also would not have been revealed in this episode, but was to have been an ongoing question during the trial arc. In *The Official Companion Season Three*, Moore is quoted as saying that at various stages Adama was to have been sole judge on the tribunal and Lee was to have taken over as Baltar's lawyer when the first lawyer was killed (suggesting that the bombing plot originally served also as a device to install Lee in the main role), but this was eventually abandoned as unrealistic. There was more focus on the question at to whether or not Caprica-Six was a person, as, if she were considered a mere machine, she could not testify, but declaring her a person would be controversial in the Fleet. This idea is clearly indebted to Isaac Asimov's short story 'Evidence' and the 1964 *The Outer Limits* episode 'I, Robot' (itself based on a 1939 short story of the same name by Eando Binder). Lee and Anders were to have fought about Kara, but Moore says in the podcast that it seemed more natural that, with the source of their rivalry gone, they would instead gravitate toward each other.

British-born character actor Mark Sheppard, selected to portray Lampkin, is a well-known telefantasy stalwart whose credits include semi-regular roles in *Firefly* and, later, *Dollhouse*; he also went on to a guest appearance in *Doctor Who* and played the demon Crowley in *Supernatural*. Sheppard had talked with Moore about appearing in *Battlestar Galactica* from an early stage, and had originally wanted to play one of the Cylons. 'Jerry', the cat who took the role of Lance, proved controversial. Neither Robert Young nor Olmos liked working with him, the latter apparently saying to Angeli, 'Dude, you wrote a beautiful script ... and you put that fucking cat in it! Why don't you take it out?' The cat also refused to rush out of the Raptor as scripted, meaning that the footage had to be sped up to achieve the desired effect. In its first scene, it also wouldn't jump onto a desk as required, and had to be unceremoniously plonked there by a stagehand. Young did not like the coin-flipping scene and attempted to excise it on the pretext that they did not have any coin props. He later backed down when producer Harvey Frand acquired some. Moore says in the podcast, 'If I had known, truth to tell, about the online fascination/obsession with Jake the Dog, I would've opted to make Romo Lampkin Jake the Dog's owner'.

In terms of things to watch out for, the deckhand with a prosthetic arm can be seen in the background as Hughes boards the Raptor; Lampkin's door code is 1234; and, according to BattlestarWiki, the script reveals the other captains selected to be on the tribunal are Captain Simpson Markson of the *Argo Navis*, Captain Jules Tarney of the *Pyxis* and Captain Doyle Franks of the *Prometheus*. Adama refers to the 'four other men' judging the case, which is an error as one of them is a woman. Lampkin's glasses are Ray Ban model 3198, non-polarised; the model has since been discontinued. Katee Sackhoff's name has now been removed from the credits.

'The Son Also Rises' is derived from a number of high profile contemporary or near-contemporary legal cases. This works to its advantage in some areas, with the legal plot being well set up and the moral issues that form the background to Baltar's trial firmly sketched in. However, the bombing plot comes across as a pointless effort to add action to what is primarily a character-led, human drama.

# 49: Crossroads (Parts One and Two)

FIRST TRANSMISSION DATE: 18 March 2007 and 25 March 2007 (USA/CANADA)

WRITERS: Michael Taylor and Mark Verheiden

DIRECTOR: Michael Rymer

CREDITED CAST: Mark Sheppard (Romo Lampkin); Donnelly Rhodes (Doctor Cottle); Rekha Sharma (Tory Foster); Chelah Horsdal (Cassidy); Ryan Robbins (Charlie Connor); Bodie Olmos (Hot Dog); Leah Cairns (Racetrack); Jennifer Halley (Seelix); Colin Lawrence (Skulls); Alison Matthews (Fallbrook); Susan Hogan (Doyle Franks); Stephen Holmes (Reporter #1/2); Keegan Connor Tracy (Young Woman); William Samples (Judge #2); Colin Corrigan (Marine Nowart); Françoise Robertson (Woman); Brad Dryborough (Hoshi)

KNOWN UNCREDITED CAST: Patrick 'Flick' Harrison (Bell); Lily Duong-Walton (Hera Agathon)

SYNOPSIS: As Baltar's trial begins, Racetrack and Skulls, flying rearguard picket, discover that the Cylons are pursuing the Fleet at a distance. Adama orders Tigh to interrogate Caprica-Six to find out what she knows. Caprica-Six reveals that the Cylons are following the radiation signature of the tylium refinery. She learns about Ellen's death from Head Baltar and uses the knowledge to disconcert Tigh. Tigh gives evidence at the trial while drunk and admits to killing Ellen. Lee and Adama clash over Tigh's cross-examination, ending with Lee resigning his commission. Lee cross-examines Roslin, and she reveals that she is taking the hallucinogenic Chamalla extract again, because her cancer has returned. Dualla, angered by the tactics Lee is using in Baltar's defence, leaves him. Gaeta lies under oath, saying that Baltar signed the execution order on New Caprica willingly, not at gunpoint. Lampkin moves for a mistrial on the grounds that Adama has prejudged the outcome, and calls Lee to the stand to confirm that his father has stated he believes Baltar is guilty. Lee, however, makes an impassioned speech, saying that the trial is simply a way for others to expiate their guilt by condemning Baltar. The tribunal finds Baltar not guilty, with Adama casting the deciding vote. Baltar is freed, and then abducted by a group of his supporters. Anders volunteers as a trainee pilot; Seelix flirts with him, but discovers, to her dismay, that he is sleeping with Tory. Roslin, Athena and Caprica-Six all have a shared vision of pursuing Hera through the opera house on Kobol. Tigh, Anders, Tyrol and Tory hear strange phantom music and seek each other out; they realise that they are all Final Five Cylons. Sudden power fluctuations paralyse the Fleet as the Cylons attack. Lee joins the pilots, only to encounter, as he flies into action, Starbuck in a pristine Viper Mark II ...

ANALYSIS: The Season Three finale revolves around Baltar's trial, but also, tacitly, around another attempt by God to bring the Cylons and the humans together, through a series of apparently unrelated events.

Inherit the Wind: Lawyer Lee and Lampkin

Despite what he says, Lee is strongly motivated in this story by his anger toward his father. The Adamas's argument over Tigh's testimony, in which the Admiral blames his son for what happened to his XO in court, is what causes Lee to publicly expose Roslin's drug-taking. He insists on cross-examining her himself rather than letting Lampkin do it; having been falsely accused of orchestrating an attack on Tigh, he will openly attack someone else close to his father. Roslin tells him 'I am so sorry for you now', indicating that he has crossed a line, targeting someone who is both his father's professional colleague and love interest. Furthermore, there is no possible legal gain from this strategy, as, even if Roslin is discredited as a witness to the attempted mass execution on New Caprica, others can be easily found.

Lee insists at first that he is motivated by a belief in the system rather than a desire for revenge against his father. Dualla, as she moves out, tells him, 'The system is broken', and he echoes this later when Lampkin appeals to his stated belief in it, saying 'What frakking system?' He points out in his speech that they are not a civilisation, but a remnant of one, and are continually forced to bend their own rules. As Mark Sheppard puts it in the bonus podcast for part two, 'They had this system in place that was great for governing 51 billion people (sic – the figure Sheppard quotes was originally given in this episode but removed, and so the most accurate figure we have is Tigh's 20 billion from 'The Resistance'/'Crossroads'), but it's not always great at governing 40,000'. In taking this line, Lee also justifies to himself his decision to stop doing what his father wishes and start doing what he himself wants. Lee uses Verges' 'rupture strategy', asking what the difference is between Baltar and any of the other collaborators (to whom Roslin has issued a blanket pardon), or to anyone who committed acts of murder or treason, not just on New Caprica but throughout the short history of the Fleet. Baltar's trial is shown to be an act of revenge and mob justice, rather than the strict application of a legal code. Lee thus exposes how the Fleet evokes the system when it suits them, but ignores it when it doesn't. As such, no-one present can see the trial as anything other than an act of scapegoating, using Baltar to represent everyone else's shame and guilt.

BY YOUR COMMAND: VOL 2

Scapegoats and Sheep: The Emerging Aristocracy and the Emerging Underclass

Central to the whole story of Baltar's trial is the ongoing exploration of the class system in the Fleet. In a deleted exchange from part one, Lampkin correctly assesses the situation in hierarchical terms: that the Fleet's 'emerging aristocracy' are willing to let an outsider such as Baltar into their ranks so long as he plays along, but that when something goes wrong, he will be the one who pays the price. The exchange runs:

LAMPKIN: He's guilty. You think so? So am I, so are you. It's a question of criminality. Is what he did a crime? This isn't really a case about the law, it's about a family. Your family. Not the Adamas *per se*, but your extended family. People our client lovingly refers to as 'the emerging aristocracy'. See, I don't believe they'll be able to prove that Baltar actually committed a crime in the true strength of the legal definition, but he did break with your father, and the President, and the rest of the royals. And for that, he may end up with the death sentence.

LEE: Are you sure you're up to this?

LAMPKIN: Are you sure *you* are? Baltar's not the only one breaking with the aristocracy. And your father. Are you ready to be an outcast too, Major?

Without this scene, the narrative we have is of Lee attacking the hypocrisy of the system, and Adama, his conscience stung, doing the right thing and voting for an acquittal. After Lee's speech, Captain Franks says, 'Justice … is imperfect, but it's those very imperfections that separate us from the machines. And maybe even make us a species worth saving', and Adama sums up why he voted for acquittal by saying simply, 'Defence made their case, prosecution didn't'. Lampkin's speech, however, makes it plain that Lee is himself a member of the aristocracy; the story then becomes one of aristocrats fighting each other. More pertinently, whatever Lampkin says, Lee will not become 'an outcast' as a result of his actions; he will remain an aristocrat, but instigate a new social paradigm, into which the aristocracy will be incorporated. The mob rule to which Lee refers in his speech is also serving the aristocracy, which is why it is allowed to continue. At the end of the story, the elite, Lee included, abandon Baltar to the justice of the mob; he is left wandering the battlestar's corridors, unprotected and in fear of his life. The deletion of Lampkin's speech means that the painful reality, that the Fleet is dominated by a ruling class and the trial's outcome does nothing to change this, is lost.

Taken in light of the deleted scene, this story retroactively changes our perspective on New Caprica. The resistance is led by Tigh, in the name of Adama, and features Roslin and Tory as members as well as Tyrol, seen in 'Dirty Hands' to be an apologist for the aristocracy. (One wonders if his union would have challenged a Roslin-led administration.) Although, in 'Occupation', Roslin states 'The Colonial government under President Gaius Baltar functions in name only', she nonetheless blames the evils of the Cylon regime upon him. New Caprica is therefore reinterpreted as the human elite fighting competition from the incoming would-be elite – made up of Cylons, the Colonials' former slaves – and Baltar, like many others, is caught in the crossfire.

The class paradigm also explains Baltar's ultimate fate. In this story, we see evidence that he is becoming the focus of a religious cult; this seems mysterious as, whatever mystical experiences he may personally have had, he has not shared them with the Fleet, but has instead cast himself as a class warrior. However, if he becomes a religious leader, then his socialist, anti-aristocratic message is obscured: he will become not Che Guevara but, to use the analogy the writing team keep applying to him, Charles Manson. Baltar's role as class warrior has therefore ended, making it appear that the series' writers are defending its central aristocracy.

Signs and Omens: The Final Five and the Opera House Vision

This episode sees the revelation of four of the Final Five, and the parallel revelation that four other people on the Fleet (Roslin, Athena, Caprica-Six and, it is safe to assume, Hera) are sharing a repeated vision of the opera house. The question immediately arises as to what has triggered these disclosures. The fact that the Cylons attack immediately after the Final Five realise their nature implies that the Cylons themselves are involved. However, this cannot be the case, because Cavil is still in charge, and Cavil has previously gone to great lengths to keep the identities of the Final Five a secret. The most likely impetus behind the revelation is therefore God. God revealed the identities of the Final Five to D'Anna in 'Rapture', and is clearly seen to be taking a hand in events in 'Crossroads'. Early on, for instance, God's messenger, Head Baltar, encourages Caprica-Six to build a connection with Tigh, informing her that he has lost someone close to him. (This appears to be something that he intuits from Tigh's behaviour, rather than that he has specific knowledge of the circumstances of Ellen's death.) At the end of the story, the Final Five coming to awareness and feeling the compulsion to meet below decks is bookended by a Fleet-wide power outage and Starbuck returning from the dead, suggesting God's usual tendency to use big, flashy light displays to alert the characters to divine revelations. The final shot of the episode sees the virtual camera zoom out from the Fleet and zoom in to the planet Earth, reminding the viewer of God's divine perspective and providing a foretaste of events to come.

The shared opera house vision also furthers God's agenda. Roslin has been one of the biggest obstacles to bringing the humans and the Cylons together. However, the return of her illness raises the possibility that she really is, as she once believed, the dying leader mentioned in Pythia, and encourages her to pay greater attention to prophecies and supernatural occurrences. Learning that Caprica-Six and Athena are having the same visions as her, Roslin has to work with them to figure out what it means, which encourages her to view the Cylons as forming a part of the Pythian prophecy. While the meaning of the vision is not explained at this time, part of its function is clearly to defuse Roslin's prejudice against Cylons and bring her together with Athena and Caprica-Six.

The Lost Arc: Continuity, Worldbuilding and the Sagittaron Storyline

To fully understand 'Crossroads', it is necessary to consider the abandoned story of the Sagittaron massacre. The outline given in Moore's podcast, pieced together with deleted material and taken in the context of the season as a whole, provides the following storyline. At some point during Baltar's Presidency on New Caprica, a famine broke out, creating social and political unrest. This is reflected in the deleted scene from 'Dirty Hands', where Cally makes reference to the union calling a strike in response to Baltar cutting the food ration. The Sagittarons, who had formed their own colony group and were remaining separate, were refusing to share the food they had cultivated with the others. Zarek, unbeknownst to Baltar, subsequently orchestrated a massacre against the Sagittarons, using Cylon Centurions, clearly intending to sacrifice his own fellow colony-members in order to provide for the wider New Caprican society and prevent a social breakdown, and, as a Sagittaron who is in the government, to protect his own political position. Baltar, finding out about Zarek's actions, tried to prevent the massacre and ordered Zarek's arrest (providing the real reason why he is seen in detention at the end of 'Precipice'). Moore indicates that an inspiration for the Sagittaron storyline came from the sequence in *Lawrence of Arabia* (1962) in which a fragile alliance is saved through the execution of a third party. The Sagittaron plot would also retrospectively have cast a different light on Zarek's behaviour in 'Collaborators', indicating that his real rationale for not wanting a series of public trials in the Fleet was to prevent the events of the massacre from coming to light (as in the deleted scene in the 20 and 21 September 2006 drafts of 'The Woman King', where he visits Baltar in his cell), although there could also have been the implication that he was using the Circle to eliminate the people who knew the truth about what happened to the Sagittarons. As it stands, Zarek does not appear at all in these episodes.

Moore says in his podcast that in 'Crossroads' as it originally stood, 'They busted [Gaeta] for perjury, and so essentially most of the prosecution's case was destroyed, and that was when the Sagittaron storyline that we had developed was gonna come to the fore. Somebody came to Lee at the end of part one and gave Lee a videotape ... and the videotape seemed to show Gaius Baltar ordering Cylon Centurions to fire on a civilian population in a massacre. And it was a damning bit of evidence, and Lee had it, and the struggle for Lee was, does he turn it over to the prosecution, or not? And ultimately he did turn it over to the prosecution'. The truth about Zarek's involvement consequently emerged, and, in the confusion, the defence called for a mistrial. Baltar would either have withdrawn his plea, in protest at the conduct of the court's proceedings (as a consequence of which, Moore says, 'they were going to judge him guilty, because that was the way the law worked or something'), or, alternatively, have declared, 'I am the son of God, you are all sacrificing me in His name'. James Callis also recalls a slightly different version, in which Baltar was exonerated, but then declared, 'I don't give a damn. I'm the son of God', and was then taken back into custody. While this would have provided a public display of Baltar's religious leanings, it would not have explained how a pre-existing cult has developed around him.

The Sagittaron arc was abandoned, according to Moore, when Rymer argued that 'It was making up this other storyline about something that had happened in the past, that the audience really never had investment in. Meanwhile, all the crimes that the audience were interested in, with Gaius Baltar, weren't really being addressed as effectively, and the trial wasn't about something they could really sink their teeth into'. The decision necessitated reshooting a lot of material from earlier stories to edit out the remaining parts of the Sagittaron arc. The validity of Rymer's criticism is open to debate; however, one consequence of the arc's abandonment is that, whereas if Zarek had been discredited there would have been a political vacuum for Baltar to fill, with Zarek still an active opposition figure, Baltar is instead pushed toward becoming a cult leader.

In terms of outside references, the Sagittaron storyline seems to have been influenced by the fact that Saddam Hussein's trial was primarily centred around events of the 1982 Dujail Massacre, in which 132 civilians were executed in retribution for a failed assassination attempt on the Iraqi President. The unmade original-series story 'The Mutiny' also involved a subplot about a group of Taurians splitting off from the other colonists. In terms of the episode as a whole, Moore admits to the opera house sequences being influenced by *Don't Look Now* (1973), with its hallucinatory imagery of what appears to be a small child fleeing through the streets of Venice, and to the mistrial gambit being inspired by the legal comedy *From The Hip* (1987). The 3 November 2006 draft script describes Tigh listening to the music in the walls of the ship with 'the obsessive quality of Gene Hackman in *The Conversation*' (1974).

In continuity terms, Cassidy claims that 5,197 people were killed, lost or unaccounted for after New Caprica, though her figure is inaccurate. She states that 44,035 people settled on New Caprica: however, the population of the settlement is given in 'Lay Down Your Burdens' part two as 39,192. Subtracting the latter from the former would give us a figure of 4,843 people in orbit. Subtracting the total number of Fleet personnel at the start of 'Collaborators', 41,435, from 44,035 gives us total casualty numbers from New Caprica of 2,600. Subtracting 2,600 from Cassidy's casualty figure of 5,197 gives us 2,597, which tallies with estimates of military personnel on the Fleet. Although Cassidy's casualty figures are almost double what they should be, the mistake does allow us to calculate the number of Fleet military personnel, and to estimate the actual number of casualties from the occupation.

In a deleted scene, Roslin learns about projection from Athena, who says 'Cylons use it all the time. But I haven't done it much since I came on board it just didn't seem right anymore. Didn't seem like something a person does'. Although it seems strange that, in the opera house vision, God has apparently predicted the wig Roslin s going to wear in Season Four, it is likely that Roslin's choice of wig is influenced by the vision rather than the vision reflecting reality.

There's Too Much Confusion: Writing and Production

The abandonment of the Sagittaron arc aside, the story went through several other changes. A first draft script of part two dated 3 November 2006 shows it in a transitional form, with the Sagittaron narrative not present, but lacking the plotline in which Lee employs the rupture strategy. The trial sequences begin with Gaeta's perjury, which, in this draft, is exposed when Lee compares the time stamp on the death warrant that Baltar signed, with Tyrol's account of the times at which he checked the resistance message drop, and discovers that at the point at which the warrant was being signed, Gaeta was away from *Colonial One* leaving information at the drop for Tyrol. Although Baltar feels the trial is going his way after this development, Lampkin produces a paperclip sculpture he has stolen from the judge's bench, revealing that one of the judges, whereas he had been riveted to the prosecution's case, sat back and fiddled with paperclips during the defence's portion. He suggests that Lee take the stand and testify that, when Adama told Lee off for his treatment of Tigh during cross-examination, Adama revealed he considered Baltar guilty. This would then allow Lampkin to call for a mistrial. Lampkin also admits that he brought Lee onto the team only in the hope of incurring such a tactic, saying cuttingly 'Did you honestly think we sought you out for your "legal acumen"?' Lee refuses to cooperate. The trial's climax therefore involves a cross-examination of Baltar in which he makes increasingly bizarre statements, saying in part 'New Caprica was their attempt to atone, to find a way to coexist with human-kind, yes, to forgive, even in the wake of their own enslavement and domination. And how did we respond to this mercy? With suicide bombers. A violent insurgency. More death'. He ends by asserting 'I AM A CYLON. I have been called to the temple! I have been called by the five! And if you destroy me, their wrath will descend upon the Fleet in all its apocalyptic fury–' before being dragged back into custody. This sequence has many problems, the least of which is that it directly contradicts 'Taking a Break From All Your Worries', in which Baltar has it quite clearly brought home to him that he is not a Cylon.

Another difference in the draft version is that Roslin's sharing of visions with the Cylon women is explicitly stated to be the result of her having Hera's blood, rather than an implied mystical connection. There is also a very strange sequence in which Roslin has Baltar kidnapped by guards and taken to Caprica-Six's cell, where, secretly observed by Roslin, the Cylon first tells him she is still hurt about Baltar rejecting her in favour of D'Anna, and then, when he denies that he loves D'Anna, asks what happened in the Temple of Five. Rather than, as one might expect, seeing all this as a tactic to gain information and refusing to cooperate, Baltar then reports on D'Anna's vision of the Final Five. There is also a scene in which Hera brings Helo to a particular corridor of the ship that she likes, and they find Tyrol, walking Nicky to sleep; Moore, in his podcast, says that the

49: CROSSROADS

ambient engine noise in the corridor is what soothes the children.

The trial was originally to have come earlier in the season, but was moved back to its cliffhanger. The network were doubtful about the climax being focused on a trial, particularly as they felt that the series had already 'done' a trial story in 'Litmus'. *The Official Companion Season Three* reports that the storyline of Roslin sharing visions with Cylons had been planned to appear in Season Two, and then was reworked for 'The Passage'. At one point, prior to the writing of the 3 November draft, Cassidy was to have been an older man, but Moore in the podcast says it was felt that another strong female character was needed. Moore reports that there were scenes of the judges deliberating in private, which were abandoned as being one story element too many, as was a scene in the ship's bathroom, where Sharon confronted Roslin over the kidnapping of Hera. Moore also says in his podcast that Roslin's cancer returning, and Lee and Dualla breaking up, were both late additions he made to the story (evidenced in part by their complete absence from the 3 November draft). At one point, Moore favoured not revealing the trial verdict until the first episode of Season Four, but Eick and Rymer talked him out of it.

The revelation of the Four Cylons retroactively changes the audience's perspective on earlier events. Due to the writing team selecting the characters from those already known within the Fleet, the Final Five turn out to have members at the top level of the army, the government, organised labour and both the Caprican and New Caprican resistance movements; three of the four were members of the Circle in 'Collaborators'. This changes the story from one of humans fighting Cylons, to one of two groups of Cylons using humans to fight each other, particularly as regards the New Caprica storyline. While this adds a twist to the idea that the Fleet is governed by a small and restricted elite, it is an artefact of the writing process rather than a deliberate dramatic irony, as the writers did not know at the time of writing the earlier episodes that the characters were Cylons.

The inclusion of 'All Along the Watchtower' in the series had been planned for some time. Moore, who had also tried to work the song into an episode of *Roswell*, had initially wanted to use it in 'Act of Contrition' as a device indicting connections between Caprican civilisation and our own. Michael Taylor at one point attempted to build on the psychedelic connotations of the song by suggesting the Final Five Cylons should imagine themselves at the 1969 Woodstock festival, though what he hoped to accomplish by this is not clear. The arrangement in this episode is by Bear McCreary, with the lyrics sung by his brother Brendan (under his professional name of Bt4). The courtroom scenes were filmed on the hangar bay set, redressed; Michael Hogan's wife Susan plays Captain Franks. Originally Gary Hutzel asked Pierre Drolet to design a thirteenth-colony ship for Starbuck to fly on her return, but Moore said that he wanted, in Hutzel's words as quoted in *The Official Companion Season Three*, to 'leave things more open', so the team instead had her flying a brand-new Viper Mark II. D'Anna Biers's cameraman, Bell, can be briefly seen in the press pack, though the actor is uncredited. The episodes do not feature the main title sequence or precap clips of the forthcoming episode; the actors' credits simply appearing on screen during the opening scenes.

The original filmed version of Starbuck's return has her appearing to Lee not in a Viper in space, but in his room when he goes to get his flightsuit. Katee Sackhoff's name appears only in the final credits, to disguise this plot development. According to *The Official Companion Season Three*, the scene where she appears was absent from the copies of the script distributed to the cast, to avoid the ending leaking out to the general public, and the revelation of the Four Cylons was also replaced, in many copies, with a dummy scene. This dummy scene was included in the 3 November draft, and involved the Four Cylons speculating that the music could be the result of the Cylons having implanted chips into their heads during detention on New Caprica, and that they are now under Cylon control. The final scene of the 3 November draft ran as follows:

Sprinting full speed, Lee bursts into his quarters, intent on grabbing his gear. He falls heavily to the floor, unconscious. Lee's blood pools on the deck. REVEAL Saul Tigh, holding an ambrosia bottle by the neck.

A bewildered Tigh looks down at the bottle in his hands. Spots the smear of blood on its hard glass edge. Sees Lee's crumpled form. Horror fills his eyes as he realises what he's done. The bottle drops from his shaking hands, smashes on the deck.

TIGH (aghast): Gods. Gods help me.

'Crossroads' began its existence as a story about racism, which then developed into a powerful condemnation of the hierarchical, elitist nature of Fleet society. As finally realised, it is an exciting story, but one that as been emasculated of all its social and political commentary.

Season Four: 2008-2009

By comparison with the previous two seasons, the commissioning of Season Four was late and indecisive. On 13 February 2007, it was announced that it would go ahead with 'a minimum' of 13 episodes, which the network later expanded to 20. The mooted *Caprica* prequel series remained in limbo; the commissioning of the pilot would not be formally announced until March 2008. Universal were keen to do a *Battlestar Galactica* DVD-exclusive story that could later be re-released as a telemovie. Moore wanted to make this a standalone piece rather than an essential part of continuity; however, the ultimate outcome was the movie-length Season Four opener 'Razor', making the season 21 episodes long in total.

Season Four was also commissioned with the deliberate idea that it should be the final one. In the behind-the-scenes featurette *The Journey Ends: the Arrival*, available on the Season 4.5 box set, Moore says that, although he and his colleagues had begun the project with no idea how long it would run, he had started to think about this issue during the making of Season Two. He elaborates that the theme of the series as a whole is that getting the Fleet to Earth is *Galactica*'s final mission. The writers in general began during the development of Season Three to discuss ways of ending the series. The cast and crew interviewed on Eick's video blogs generally all say that the knowledge that Season Four was to be the final season had a positive effect, in that it gave everyone a sense that they were working toward something. Mark Verheiden observes that it is rare in television to get a chance to wrap up a series over a full season, rather than simply being told of its cancellation.

Some of the driving concepts behind the series' final outing go back to Season Two. Ideas discussed during the 20 July 2005 writers' meeting podcast included the Fleet being guided to Earth by someone coming from the planet (which loosely references concepts from the original series), the Cylons having ideological divisions, and there being Cylon models other than the extant 12, who have been boxed or destroyed. The initial notes for Season Four, which Moore reads out in his podcast for 'Six of One', indicate that the basic themes for the first half-season changed little. The most noteworthy developments are that Leoben, rather than Natalie, was originally to have been Cavil's main antagonist in the Cylon Civil War, and that Zarek's political scheming was to have been more of a narrative focus.

The writers also faced a challenge regarding the return of Starbuck. The showrunners have subsequently claimed that the character's resurrection was always intended: *The Official Companion Season Three*'s article on 'Maelstrom' reports that Moore and Eick had asked Sackhoff to pretend she had not had her contract renewed so as to keep her return even more of a secret, but, since this had an adverse effect on morale during filming, some of the cast were told the truth. However, it seems more likely that the character's return was actually a last-minute decision, taken as a result of the cast's adverse reaction to her exit: Olmos in particular was said to be 'deeply upset' about her departure. This is supported by the fact that 'Maelstrom' seemingly resolves all of the character's arcs, and that the writing team apparently had little idea of how to handle her return; the podcast for 'He That Believeth in Me' indicates that they had considered having her as a Head Person for Lee.

Starbuck's reappearance is also problematic in that having a character return from the dead is a well-known cliché of science fiction, and, as Moore says in the podcast for 'Tigh Me Up, Tigh Me Down', the audience 'will let you slide by a few of these kind of things, but you can't do it very often'. This is further compounded by the return of Ellen Tigh as the last of the Final Five, meaning that, in effect, the cliché is employed twice in a single season. Season Four sees the deaths of a number of popular regular characters, including Cally, Dualla, Gaeta and Zarek, and, while they are all narratively justified, it seems likely that this was in part a way of emphasising that Starbuck was a special case, and/or balancing the scales for the return of two major characters.

In the podcast for 'Daybreak' part one, Moore describes how the second half of the season was originally to have played out; although clearly, from his account, some of the details were still in flux. Ellen, learning of Tigh's affair with Caprica-Six, would have become 'enraged, bitter [and] angry', joined forces with Cavil, and conspired with him to kidnap Hera. Meanwhile, the 'seeds of discontent' in the Fleet would have grown into a mutiny, and Zarek and Gaeta would have taken *Galactica* to assault the basestar belonging to the rebel Cylon faction who had joined the human Fleet in the Cylon Civil War storyline. At this point, Cavil's Cylons would have attacked, leading to a conflict that would 'lay waste to about half the Fleet', and from which Adama and the rebel Cylons, having regained control of *Galactica,* would have emerged victorious, capturing a Cavil and Boomer, with Baltar rescuing Hera. Adama would either have banished the mutineers, or, alternatively, given the Fleet captains the option to leave, with some choosing to do so and Zarek would have taken his people 'off into the cosmos by themselves'. Tyrol would have '[started] to bring Boomer around to [the Fleet's] side'. Meanwhile Tory, after meeting with Cavil and learning Ellen was alive, would have '[used] the Baltarites to start a Helter Skelter … the cult was going to become dangerous and murderous', and Baltar, realising what he had created, would have turned himself and his followers in. Both Cavil and Baltar would have calculated that 'the human race [was going to] die off in three generations and that the only viable future was together through Hera'. Caprica-Six, after losing the baby, would have become reconciled with Baltar, and Hera would have 'sort of become her replacement child'. Boomer would have persuaded the other Cylon models to join a human-Cylon alliance, telling them about Cavil boxing dissenting Cylon models, and built up a fleet of baseships. Following a huge battle at the Cylon homeworld, then known as 'Cylonia', Ellen and Cavil would have fled in the last baseship, taking Hera with them. In the finale, the previous battle and Cavil's escape having taken them into 'a different section of the galaxy where there was a yellow sun', Kara would have found Earth '[using] the Final Five and some mechanism'; Helo and Athena would have sacrificed themselves for Hera; and the central conflict would have been focused on the Tighs' marital discord, with Tigh trying to convince Ellen to call off the final battle and return to 'the side of the angels'. The *Galactica* would have arrived at Earth in some way, possibly crashing onto it, with Adama ordering the ship burned to show the Fleet's commitment to stay, Kara disappearing, Adama and Roslin going off in a Raptor to the stars, Lee proposing that the humans start over rather than try to rebuild their civilisation, and Hera becoming the genetic ancestor of modern humans.

Moore abandoned this storyline because, during the writers' strike, he had time to reflect on the idea and decided that having everything hinge on the Tighs's relationship was not really satisfying. Once the strike was resolved, the writing team assembled at a cabin near Lake Tahoe and redeveloped the end of the season. A few ideas were retained from the original storyline, such as the mutiny and the use of Cavil as a kind of Lucifer figure (or, in original-series terms, an Iblis figure), turning against God because he feels he is not loved enough. Moore also recalls writing on the board in the writers' room a list of unresolved plot threads, so that the team could clear up as many of these as possible by the season's end.

One major development was the establishment of Baltar as the leader of a cult. The cult was to be designated with a gull emblem, though on screen this is not distinctly conveyed; according to the 'Daybreak' part one podcast and the 29 July 2007 draft of 'Escape Velocity', GULL is an acronym of Grace, Unity, Life and Love. (While Baltar and the cultists do use this phrase, the connection with the gull emblem is never directly made in the broadcast series.) The idea has parallels in the early Christian church adopting a stylised fish as a symbol, the Greek word for fish, 'Icthys', being an acronym for the Greek words for 'Jesus Christ, God's Son, Saviour'. Callis intimated in an interview on the AV Club website that he was less than pleased with Baltar's development into a cult leader, saying 'The name that comes up again and again is Jim Jones.[77] [But] Gaius is not Jim Jones. To be honest, I don't believe it'. Callis's arguments may partly explain why the cult metamorphosed from the Manson-like group initially proposed by the writers into something ultimately more benign.

The key behind-the-scenes event of the season was the 2007 Writers Guild of America Strike, intended to address the increasing imbalance between what writers earned and what the studios made from their efforts. Throughout the duration of the strike, none of the writing team could work on *Battlestar Galactica*. Michael Nankin, in an interview with Maureen Ryan, said, 'No writer/producers could be on the set and no rewrites could be made'.

---

[77] Jim Jones was a charismatic American religious leader known for, among other things, establishing an isolated commune for his followers, and inspiring them to commit a mass suicide in 1978.

Consequently, it seems very likely that there was a rush to complete as many scripts as possible before the strike began. This may perhaps explain some of the narrative problems that bedevil the first half of the season. The fact that the strike was called just as the mid-season hiatus began was also a problem, as it was during this break that the writers would normally work on the second half of the season. There were concerns that, if the strike went on for longer than three months, the studio would get fed up with paying the staff and retaining the sets associated with the show, and close it down. Emotions consequently ran high during the shooting of 'Revelations' and 'Sometimes a Great Notion', the episodes immediately prior to the hiatus, as the crew were aware that these could wind up being the series' last. Moore flew up to Vancouver from Los Angeles and addressed the cast and crew, saying, according to the podcast for 'Sometimes a Great Notion': 'Make this the best one ever. I don't think the show will be cancelled … but you never know, and I want this to be a great episode. And so I trust all of you, and it's like I said, we're sort of taking a blind jump like Admiral Cain did in the *Pegasus* … and none of us knows where it's gonna lead, and I wish you all well and I'll see you on the other side of the jump'.

Subsequently, a rumour circulated that 'Sometimes a Great Notion' was deliberately intended to serve as a final episode. This was apparently sparked by a remark Katee Sackhoff made in an interview at a convention in Burbank that the episode could have served as a series finale if the programme had been cancelled in the wake of the writers' strike. However, Moore is on record as saying that he thought ending on 'Sometimes a Great Notion' would have been unsatisfactory. The preceding episode, 'Revelations', on the other hand, was deliberately seen as a potential ending to the series; Rymer says, 'It was this incredibly depressing, somewhat absurdist moment … We were quite aware that we were shooting the end of the show – that one could end the show on "Revelations"'. 'Sometimes a Great Notion' was made only because the team happened to have one more full script written after 'Revelations'; according to Moore, they recorded it anyway, in the hope that the series would return. Michael Nankin, who directed 'Sometimes a Great Notion', confirms this, saying in an interview with Maureen Ryan, 'This episode was not the ending that Ron Moore or anyone else wanted for the series, and there was a lot of discussion about convoluted ways to edit the material to create a satisfying ending. We couldn't write anything new. It was a confounding situation'.

Fortunately for everyone involved, the strike was resolved after three months and production continued; however, it did leave a few ongoing complications, in that the principal actors had all been released from their contracts to allow them to pursue other professional interests during the strike, and although they all returned, Tahmoh Penikett in particular plays a much reduced role in the second half due to having taken on an additional commitment to co-star in *Dollhouse*. Racetrack was initially intended to play a much larger part in the mutiny storyline, but this idea was similarly dropped due to Leah Cairns having acquired other commitments. Cairns has said that, had this not been the case, Season Four might have featured more information about Racetrack's backstory, including that she had a rural, outdoorsy upbringing and was a keen fisherwoman; an interest she shared with her father. Cairns has also indicated that, at one point, the writers had intended for Starbuck to killed Racetrack during the mutiny. While the programme was on hiatus, Michael Trucco broke his neck in a car accident; although the actor made a full recovery soon afterwards, there is conflicting evidence as to how much this was an influence on Anders' becoming a Hybrid. Moore states that it was pure coincidence, while Eick is more ambivalent, saying that the situation was 'a little bit chicken-and-egg ... Were we talking about Anders and then we said, "Hey, this will work out even better than we thought?" Or were we not talking about Anders, and then the accident happened and we thought, "Well, he can remain in a reclining position, what can we give him?"'.

In production terms, everyone involved in the series, down to the background artists, was given a confidentiality agreement to sign for Season Four. A new set was built by the art department for the sewage recycling vessel *Demetrius*. The other new main set, the lair of the Baltar cult, rapidly replaced *Colonial One* as the crew's least favourite place to shoot, due to the restricted camera movement it allowed. Although the hand-held camera still dominated, the more dialogue-heavy nature of Season Four meant that the production team began increasingly to use dollies; equipment employed to make camera movements smoother. In a confusing move, 'Razor' was counted as the first two episodes of the season for administrative purposes, meaning that official documentation, podcasts and so forth refer to the season as if it were 22 episodes long rather than 21.

It also became increasingly apparent that the team was dispersing to other commitments following the announcement of the series' cancellation. Eick spent the first half of the season working simultaneously on *The Bionic Woman* (which was, ironically, later cancelled due to the writers' strike), meaning that he was less of a behind-the-scenes presence than usual. Moore says that toward the end of production he was also working on another project for Fox: a pilot entitled *Virtuality*, which, when not picked up as a series, was eventually aired as a telemovie in June 2009. He was also occupied working on the *Caprica* pilot after it was eventually commissioned in March 2008, lessening further the amount of time he could spend on *Battlestar Galactica*.

The final night of recording was reportedly very emotional, with series alumni such as Nicki Clyne and Luciana Carro turning up to the wrap party. Kandyse McClure was an absentee, but although a rumour circulated that this was due to animosity between her and the production crew, she has since refuted this, saying that she was in fact in Australia on a work commitment.

'Razor' was aired in the autumn of 2007, well in advance of the other episodes, to compensate for the fact that the season proper had a later-than-usual start date of April 2008. Series publicity material included the eight-minute internet video informally known as 'What the Frak?', cleverly summarising the series for the casual or new viewer, and a picture posing the main characters in the style of da Vinci's *The Last Supper*. This picture sparked reams of speculation amongst fans as to the meanings of the characters' poses. Moore wrote an extensive breakdown of what the image signified; however, Aaron Douglas subsequently stated in his blog that it was all *post-hoc* interpretation, and that Moore was not actually present at the shoot. It is also worth noting that the picture was revised slightly over the course of the season, with subtle photoshop editing being done to reflect developments. The characters depicted, furthermore, bear no connection at all to the figures that appear in the analogous positions in da Vinci's original painting.

This season marked the first major change to the teaser titles since the series began. New text was included, reading 'Twelve Cylon models. Seven are known. Four live in secret. One will be revealed'. After the discovery of Earth at the end of 'Revelation', the main titles were also changed from '… in search of a home called Earth' to read simply '… in search of a home'. The series was again recognised, garnering two Emmys; and the midseason webisodes 'The Face of the Enemy' received a number of awards for original online content. *Battlestar Galactica* was also recognised when Moore, Eick, Olmos and McDonnell were invited to join a panel at the United Nations Building in New York on 17 March 2009, co-presented by the UN Public Relations Department and the Sci-Fi Channel.

During a panel at the 2008 San Diego ComicCon, Moore said of the series, 'It was hard to let the show go … but it was time to end the story … time to resolve it, to put a period at the end of the sentence'. One of reimagined *Battlestar Galactica*'s great strengths is the fact that it has an ending that brings it to a point of closure without feeling like all the mysteries have been nailed down. While Season Four has an uneven feel, it is an appropriate finale to the series, which Jamie Bamber describes as a 'Will-they-won't-they love story' between humanity and the Cylons.

50: Razor

FIRST TRANSMISSION DATE: 24 November 2007 (USA/CANADA)

WRITER: Michael Taylor

DIRECTOR: Félix Alcalá

CREDITED CAST: Michelle Forbes (Admiral Helena Cain); Graham Beckel (Colonel Jack Fisk); Stephanie Jacobsen (Lieutenant/Captain/Major Kendra Shaw); Nico Cortez (Young William Adama); Allison Warnyca (Lieutenant Jaycie McGavin [Webisodes only]); Matthew Bennett (Doral [Webisodes only]); Steve Bacic (Colonel Jurgen Belzen); Brad Dryborough (Hoshi); Eileen Pedde (Sergeant Mathias); Fulvio Cecere (Lieutenant Alastair Thorne); Vincent Gale (Peter Laird); Campbell Lane (Hybrid); Kyra Scott (Young Helena Cain); Chandra Berg (Little Lucy Cain); Peter Flemming (Helena's Father); Shaker Paleja (Medic Hudson); Andrew Dunbar (Marine Dasilva); Jacob Blair (Squad Leader Banzai); Peter Bryant (Frank Bruno); Chris Bradford (Ops Officer); Tyson Stanley (Young Marine); Trevor Roberts (Scylla Protestor #1); Cameron Macleod (Scylla Protestor #2); Ingrid Tesch (Mother); Joey Pierce (Marine Riggs); Matt Drake (Son #1); Dustin Eriksen (Son #2); Stefan Arngrim (Male Captive); John Hainsworth (Man in Cage #1); Victor Ayala (Man in Cage #2); Deni Dolory (Woman in Cage); Emily Hirst (Child in Cage); Ben Cotton (Terrified Man); Stefanie von Pfetten (Showboat); Alyssa Minniss (Flower Girl)

STUNTS: Monique Ganderton (Gina Stunt Double); Suzi Stignel (Young Helena Stunt Double); Chandra Berg (Little Lucy Cain Stunt Double); Adrian Hein (Helena's Father Stunt Double); Guy Bewes (Stunt Signaler #1); Rick Pearce (Stunt Mechanic #1); Yves Cameron (Stunt Tauron Civilian); Melissa Stubbs (Stunt Tauron Civilian); Brad Loree (Stunt Marine #1); Heath Stevenson (Stunt Marine #2); Ernest Jackson (Stunt Soldier #1); Simon Burnette (Stunt Soldier #2)

SYNOPSIS: Apollo, newly in command of the *Pegasus*, assigns as his XO Kendra Shaw, a secretly drug-addicted former *Pegasus* officer. Through flashbacks, Kendra recalls the story of the *Pegasus*, including Gina's betrayal and Kendra's own involvement in the *Scylla* incident. We also learn of Cain's childhood on Tauron during the war and how she was forced to abandon her younger sister to the Cylons. A science team investigating a supernova remnant is overdue, and Adama asks Apollo to conduct a search-and-rescue mission. The pilots encounter Cylon-War-era Raiders, and capture one. Sharon believes they are a legendary group of Cylons called the Guardians, early models who protect the

First Hybrid. Adama flashes back to the last mission of the war, 41 years earlier; crash-landing on a planet, he discovered the Cylons experimenting with human prisoners, seemingly to produce human-like Cylons, but the war ended before anyone can make use of his findings. The *Pegasus* goes in pursuit of the Guardians, with Adama on board. When their basestar is found, a raiding party is sent out. This includes Kendra and Starbuck. They rescue the human captives and set up a nuclear device, but the remote detonator is damaged and the device must be triggered by hand. Kendra orders Starbuck to leave her behind to set off the device; going through the ship, she discovers the First Hybrid, who tells her that Starbuck is the harbinger of death. Starbuck recommends Kendra for posthumous commendation, and also requests a transfer back to *Galactica*.

ANALYSIS: Although the events of 'Razor' take place immediately after the holocaust (in terms of the main flashback storyline), and between the stories 'The Captain's Hand' and 'Downloaded' (in terms of the contemporary storyline), it can also be positioned in its broadcast-order spot between Seasons Three and Four proper, as its themes and ideas pick up on, and explore, those of the episodes that immediately precede it, and look forward to storylines that will be developed towards the end of the series. Please note that we will be using the extended version, as available on DVD, as our main reference point, rather than the broadcast version.

Cain, Unable: The Character of Helena Cain

'Razor' provides us with a number of key insights into the development of Admiral Cain. Although Cain, prior to the attack on the Colonies, is clearly a driven workaholic, she is a much friendlier person than the one we met in Season Two, joking with her XO (who invites her home with him to spend shore leave with his family), and laying down the law sternly with Kendra less as a matter of practice and more as a way of 'hazing' a new officer. Although the seeds of the Cain we encounter in the main series are there, it is the attack and what follows that develop her into the fanatic we later encounter.

The background to Cain's philosophy, however, comes in the flashback to her childhood, and the last day of the first Cylon war. Through this, we learn that Cain is suffering from survivor's guilt and post-traumatic stress disorder, as she left her sister Lucy behind to be taken by the Cylons. This suggests that, when Cain learns that there are humanoid Cylons, she, like Adama, puts the pieces together and figures out that the Cylons taking human prisoners had something to do with their development – which in part explains her viciousness toward Gina. Although she also abandons her parents, her father ordered her to leave first her dead mother and then him, and save her sister, so in failing to protect her sister she has also disobeyed her father's last order. It is during this incident that Cain acquires the pocket-knife that, throughout the story, symbolises both her nature and the 'razor' metaphor running through it. After she abandons her sister and flees to the shelter, she finds herself pursued by a

Centurion, but it turns away when she grabs the knife and confronts it. Although it does so because it has been recalled due to the armistice order, the incident plants an unresolvable paradox in Cain's juvenile subconscious: while she alone of the family survives, and this justifies her actions, it must also raise the possibility that, had she confronted the Cylons earlier, she could have saved her sister. For this reason, Cain engages in continuous doublethink, on the one hand justifying her abandonment of her sister by embracing an ethos of ruthlessness, but at the same time feeling guilty about having run away, and so refusing to do anything that suggests a retreat. Cain's torture of Gina thus takes on a new aspect; it is not simply vengeance for what happened to her family and crew, but also a way of visiting upon her lover the punishment that she feels she herself deserves.

This attitude informs Cain's behaviour when the *Pegasus* crew discover that the Cylons have been warned of their assault on the communications relay station and are counterattacking in far greater numbers than anticipated; rather than listen to her XO, Belzen, who believes carrying on with the mission is not worth the cost, she shoots him in the head and promotes Fisk. On one level, she is sacrificing for the greater good someone who is clearly a personal friend as well as a colleague, and on the other, she is refusing to run away from a fight. Her shooting of Belzen also might be seen as an early indication of her later tendency to rule through fear rather than through respect for authority; it could be argued to stand in contrast with the sequence where Adama countermands Lee's order to nuke the basestar, in which both maintain their professional authority without any loss of discipline on the part of their subordinates. However, as Adama states at the end, it is hard to find any fault in Cain's behaviour from a tactical perspective; there is a logic to her actions. The fact that the Cylons had laid a trap indicated that they had access to information from inside the *Pegasus*, so turning their back on the enemy would have been a disaster. Belzen was also, repeatedly, disobeying a direct order in a situation in which the *Pegasus* crew faced complete annihilation. Finally, in the case of Adama and Lee, not only were the stakes far lower (as the incident would at worst have led to the loss of the strike team), but Adama was still in authority over Lee by virtue of being Admiral. Although Cain's actions may have been informed by her childhood experiences, they were, however inhumane they might seem, the right ones under the circumstances.

The treatment of Gina and that of the *Scylla* incident are also influenced by this doctrine of necessary ruthlessness. In the case of Gina, however, Cain's behaviour can be characterised as not justified, but understandable: it is, as noted before, both a punishment of herself by proxy, and a means by which the *Pegasus* crew can take out their feelings of rage and helplessness upon someone who has shown herself to be a callous traitor, capable of working and living as one of them and yet selling them out to an implacable enemy. In the case of the civilian ships, Cain's behaviour is neither justified nor understandable, but denotes the actions of a military unit who have forgotten precisely what it is they are supposed to be fighting for: without civilians to protect, the logic that they should battle until death, sacrificing everything, makes sense, but ultimately, the whole point of a military-civilian dynamic is to protect the civilians, who in turn support the military. This is a call-back to Adama's observations in 'Water' about the necessity of distinguishing the military and the police, and how, when the two are conflated, the people are seen as enemies of the state. The fact that Cain orders the shooting of the civilian families on *Scylla* when she is in the brig looking at Gina symbolises that these three key moments are stages along which the *Pegasus* crew are progressing.

The key aspect of 'Razor', however, is its exploration of the already-established parallels and contrasts between Adama and Cain. At the end of the first Cylon War, both commanders experienced life-changing revelations that were kept secret. In the flashback sequences, explicit visual parallels are drawn between the two characters, both ending with the protagonist, as the armistice is declared, staring up into the sky at a departing Cylon craft. Like Adama, Cain makes a rallying speech to her supporters that sets out her plan for the future and is greeted with spontaneous chanting of 'So say we all!' Adama's paternal relationship with Kara parallels Cain's protective, mentoring relationship with Kendra. Cain's flashback to her abandonment of her sister runs parallel to her conversation with Kendra after the latter's promotion, reinforcing Kendra's role as symbolic younger sibling to Cain; the sequence where Cain discovers and revives the semiconscious Kendra visually parallels the flashback where Cain leaves Lucy behind. In both cases, Cain urges Kendra to strength and self-reliance, making an implicit contrast with Lucy's physical weakness in the flashback. Kendra blowing up the Guardian basestar is thus Cain's substitute younger sibling committing a Cain-like act of destruction on the ones who took Cain's actual sister, bringing the story full circle.

Likewise, Adama's partnership with Roslin, as professional equals who become lovers, is reflected in Cain's relationship with Gina. However, Roslin is the one who holds Adama back from waging suicidal war, whereas Gina's betrayal leads Cain to a self-destructive obsession with attacking the Cylons; and Cain's realisation that Cylons have feelings (as, although Gina has the opportunity to kill Cain in the scene where Gina is exposed as a Cylon, she hesitates, giving Kendra the chance to knock her out and disarm her) is one she exploits through having Gina tortured, perverting the loving relationship. Adama also acknowledges that having his son on the Fleet keeps him honest, as he knows he has to face him the next day, whereas Cain, with no family, has no such checks on her behaviour. Where Adama focuses on rebuilding, Cain abandons herself to revenge, saying 'You hold on to that anger and you keep it close. It will stop you being afraid the next time. It'll tell you what to do'.

Rake's Progress: Kendra Shaw versus Kara Thrace

Kendra, like Kara, Boomer and Kat before her, is yet another female officer with a death wish. Teaching a group of Marines rifle assembly, she orders one of them who has done it incorrectly to pull the trigger on her, which, although it is plainly a stunt, has obvious symbolic connotations. At the end of the story, she commits suicide by detonating a nuclear bomb, echoing Gina's death in 'Lay Down Your Burdens'. She also has connections to Cain: she says 'I am Cain's legacy', and she stands when Apollo offers her a seat, rejecting the new order and keeping Cain's practice of holding meetings standing up. In line with Adama's assessment of Cain in '*Pegasus*', Kendra at the beginning of the story is ambitious and well-connected, in her case having a mother who was a Quorum member. When the attack on the Colonies takes place, she is traumatised by the loss of the social infrastructure that supported her and allowed her to pursue her carefully-thought-out career plans, and copes by attaching herself to Cain, who forms a powerful mother figure. Kendra is the one who fires the first shot aboard the *Scylla*, making her the agent of Cain's will.

However, Kendra's key role is as a representative of the *Pegasus* crew; her death wish echoes their own attitude of continuing the war at all costs, and her description of Lee, as an outsider who is believed to have been put in command only because of his father, is representative of what the crew in general think. When Lee refuses to accept her resignation over her involvement in the *Scylla* affair, he is effectively offering an amnesty over the actions of the entire *Pegasus* crew; in Kendra's conversation with the First Hybrid, when she asks if he is a god, he asks if she is seeking forgiveness. If the Fleet is to integrate and survive, its people must both confront the past and move on from it.

Not surprisingly given the similarities between the two, there is friction from the outset between Kendra and Kara. Both are substance-abusing mavericks with a line in self-pity: when Kara refers to her mother's philosophy that 'fear gets you killed, anger keeps you alive', Kendra remarks that Cain had the same philosophy. This explains Kara's attraction to Cain and, as Cain is a kind of parent-figure to Kendra, the similarities between her and Kara. However, Kara shows herself here as better able to move on; she says that she herself believes fear and anger to be two sides of the same coin, and that one has to let go of both, foreshadowing developments in 'Maelstrom'. She clashes with Kendra when the latter orders a barrage that puts their own pilots at risk; given that the barrage is a tactically sound move, the implication is that this confrontation is over the issue of authority, with Kendra telling Starbuck, 'Questioning orders is a bad idea on this ship, Captain'. (This is followed by a flashback to the death of Belzen.) In the conversation that ensues when Kara finds Kendra injecting drugs in the kitchen, Sackhoff delivers her lines with characteristic menace, smiling while threatening to report her to Apollo. Kendra, however, is neither contrite nor intimidated, giving as good as she gets. It is perhaps the similarities between them that cause Kara to recommend Kendra for posthumous commendation. When Apollo asks her why she thinks Kendra committed suicide, Starbuck says 'Maybe she thought she had a lot to answer for. Maybe she had it coming', clearly thinking not just about Kendra, but about herself, her mother and, arguably, Cain as well.

BY YOUR COMMAND: VOL 2

Back to the Future: The Cylons and the First Hybrid

In 'Razor', we learn that the Cylons have legends, in this case the story of the Guardians and the First Hybrid. The Guardians are based on the original-series Cylons, and their Raiders not only look similar to original-series Cylon fighter craft, but, like them, have a three-pilot structure with, in at least one ship, a bronze Centurion at the apex. Their basestar is of a different design from the old-style baseships (which follow the original series' 'two flattened cones' pattern) seen in the flashback sequences, being clearly transitional to that of a present-day basestar. The 'By your command' line features, for the fourth time in the reimagined series. The First Hybrid says 'My children believe I am a god', an ambiguous phrase that could suggest that the Guardians have come to regard him as a deity.

The First Hybrid, like the modern ones, speaks prophetic phrases, referring to the arrival on New Caprica ('The denial of the one true path, played out on a world not their own, will end soon enough'), the boxing of the Threes ('The seven, now six self-described machines ...'), the revelation of the Four Cylons ('Soon there will be four, glorious in awakening ...') and of the final one later ('The fifth, still in shadow, will claw towards the light ...') and Lee's encountering of the returned Kara ('In the midst of confusion he will find her'[78]). The inclusion of some of these details suggests the Hybrid actually knows more than God does about events to come. The Hybrid's speech to Kendra, however, is more lucid; reaching out of the tank and gripping her hand, in an echo of the actions of the modern Hybrid with Baltar in 'The Passage' and of the prototype Hybrid with Adama in his flashbacks, he says 'Kara Thrace will lead the human race to its end. She is ... the harbinger of death' (a prophecy that will come true), but adds ominously, 'They must not follow her'. We appear to have here a scenario analogous to one found in ancient Greek literature, whereby the Gods are not all-powerful, but are themselves subject to Fate; and the Hybrid is here acting as one speaking for Fate.

Gratuitous Space Lesbians: Continuity, Worldbuilding and Problems

'Razor' provides some background on the history and society of the Colonies. We see that there was actual fighting on the Colonial worlds during the first Cylon War, and that there is no serious taboo on same-sex relationships, even in

---

78 SPOILER SECTION: The Hybrid's next line, 'Enemies brought together by impossible longing ... Enemies joined together. The way forward, at once unthinkable, yet inevitable', would therefore presumably refer to the forthcoming storyline of the *Demetrius* encountering Leoben, and of the brokering of the alliance between the Fleet and the rebel Cylons. Likewise the prophecy 'The wrenching agony of the one splintering into many' probably refers to the Cylon Civil War, and 'They will join the promised land, gathered on the wings of an angel' to Kara leading the Fleet to the second Earth.

the military, as Kendra is neither surprised nor upset to learn that Cain and Gina are lovers. Gina's surname, Inviere, is said to be Old Gemonese for 'resurrection'. (In our world, it is Romanian for the same word.) Retrospectively, it can be seen that Cain turns down Belzen's offer of a vacation with his family not only because she does not want to leave *Pegasus*, as she puts it, 'at the mercy of civilian contractors', but also at least in part because she is having the affair with Gina – both of which factors are rather ironic in hindsight. A battlestar called *Columbia* is destroyed in Adama's flashback (and a snatch of the original-series theme plays as this happens), meaning that there have been two battlestars of that name in the Fleet, as a *Columbia* is also mentioned in the miniseries and in Adama's post-war service record in 'Hero'. The pilot Showboat suggests singing 'Ninety-Nine Bottles of Ambrosia' to kill time, implying that 'Ninety-Nine Bottles of Beer' is another song that recurs over and over in different civilisations. At the time of the armistice, Helena Cain appears to be about 12, meaning that, in the present, she is a well-preserved 53. (Michelle Forbes was 42 at the time she played Cain.) In the Fleet, Adama apparently allows civilian science teams to borrow Raptors for research when appropriate, and he is openly cited as an atheist when he says to Apollo, 'Well, if I believed in the Gods, I'd say [Kendra and Cain will] be judged by a high power', and Apollo responds, 'But, since you don't believe ...'

There are also some continuity references. Starbuck's request to be reassigned to *Galactica* on the grounds that *Pegasus*'s CO, namely Apollo, keeps trying to get her killed, although facetious, contains a kernel of truth: as the climax of the story demonstrates, Apollo, perhaps because of his emotional detachment from military life, is a commander who thinks primarily in terms of by-the-book tactics, and as such is willing to sacrifice even his friends if the military situation demands it, whereas Kara prefers the more instinctive and intuitive decision-making style of his father. It also references the campaign by Apollo and Starbuck against Anders in 'The Eye of Jupiter'. Cain's statement early on, 'I don't want any of you ... to think that I would ever risk lives or resources in some mad quest for revenge', is a promise she will break repeatedly, as their goal is vengeance, and they cannot possibly win. Cain's situation is also contrasted with Apollo's later when he faces the dilemma of whether or not to blow up the basestar even at the cost of Starbuck's life. As Adama points out, commanders, faced with such decisions, need someone to cause them to think through the potential cost; and whereas Adama himself is the one to challenge Apollo, after the execution of Belzen none of Cain's officers could serve as a brake on her actions. The Cylon tactic of going to Aft Damage Control and venting the air, first seen in 'Valley of Darkness', is again used here, during the Cylon incursion on *Pegasus*. Kendra wears a yellow-on-black Ministry of Defence patch on her sleeve when she first joins the *Pegasus* crew. Adama, regarding Kara and Kendra not getting along, says 'I'd like to sell tickets to that dance', referencing the boxing match, or 'dance', seen in 'Unfinished Business'. Adama's fight with a Centurion in the flashbacks deliberately echoes his battle with Leoben in the miniseries. (Taylor says on the DVD commentary, 'In the script in fact we even at one point intercut [a sequence of] an older Adama smashing Leoben ... and you heard a voice ... – Leoben's voice, somebody's voice – saying "All that has happened before, will happen again"'.) The fight is also a visual call-back to a scene in *Robocop* (1987) where Clarence Boddicker attacks the titular character with a metal spike. A bloodlike fluid vents from two puncture holes on the Cylon during the fight. The Adama flashbacks reference the series bible, which stated that Adama's first assignment was to the *Galactica* right at the end of the war. In the webisode version of these flashbacks, we learn that the 'Grab your gun and bring in the cat' call-and-response that Adama shares with Starbuck is one that *Galactica*'s commander used to share with Adama himself, and also that Adama had a lover who was a Raptor pilot, Jaycie 'Goldbrick' McGavin; the fact that he sees her critically wounded before he takes off on his mission explains his subsequent aggressive behaviour. There is also a discrepancy between '*Pegasus*' and '*Razor*' regarding how many crewmembers Gina killed: whereas Thorne says in '*Pegasus*' that she killed seven men, we see her kill only two in '*Razor*'. However, both make it plain that Cain's reference to the death of over 700 crewmembers in the initial attack in '*Pegasus*', and Gina's being held responsible for the deaths of over 800 during the battle of the communications relay in '*Razor*', refer to two separate incidents.

In one deleted scene, Apollo, just prior to the attacks on the Colonies, talks with the same coffee barista who served Kendra and discusses his ambivalence over becoming a pilot, and, in another, Starbuck likens Kendra's actions on the *Scylla* to their own shooting down of the *Olympic Carrier* in '33'. The *Scylla* incident differs slightly from Fisk's description of it in 'Resurrection Ship', in that, while some family members were lined up and killed, they were not put against a bulkhead.

The use of Cylons and ships based on the 1978 series can be taken to indicate that the original series storyline is another iteration of the repeating cycle of people who come out of a planet named Kobol, set up colonies, fight a war with Cylons and go in search of Earth. The old Centurions seen here are deliberately portrayed as more intelligent than the present-day versions, for reasons that will be explained in Season Four proper. They are more human-like in their movements and are capable of speech, suggesting that the modern Centurions, having spent 40 years in a society consisting entirely of machines, now communicate with each other and the skinjob Cylons through transmissions.

Director Felix Alcalá had initially intended to reference the opening of *Apocalypse Now* by beginning the story with a pan across the wreckage of the space battle, which he had temp-tracked with 'The End' by The Doors. Cain makes a speech to Kendra about how, in order to become a 'razor', a person has to be 'capable of setting aside your fear, setting aside your hesitation, and even your revulsion ... This war is forcing us all to become razors, because if we don't, we don't survive. And then we don't have the luxury of becoming simply human again'. This parallels the speech in *Apocalypse Now* in which Kurtz comes to believe that the Vietnamese will win the war precisely because they are ruthless enough to set aside their human inhibitions, and to commit formidable atrocities even against their own people in pursuit of victory. Taylor says that in writing Adama's flashback sequences he was informed by the film *The Great Waldo Pepper* (1975), about a pilot in WWI who feels he has missed out on the main action by joining up too late, and that he 'tried to think of Adama as someone who had been itching to get into this war, and finally he gets in there on the last day' – although 'Blood and Chrome' will later suggest that Adama was actually an experienced combat veteran by this point. The sequence of young Adama parachuting to the planet's surface as he fights a Centurion in freefall recalls one in *Moonraker* (1979); that of Cain slapping Kendra is based on a scene from *Patton* (1970); and that where Adama's concludes that neither his nor Lee's decision regarding whether or not to blow up the basestar was right, and neither was wrong, recalls the ending of the much-referenced *Crimson Tide*. Finally, the line about Kendra not looking for medals is an homage to one in the film *In Harm's Way* (1965).

There are a few problems that stem from 'Razor'. Kendra, despite having been Apollo's XO, is never subsequently mentioned, and, despite all the dramatic emphasis on her giving Starbuck Cain's knife, we never see it again. Kendra also wears a colonel's uniform rather than a major's following her installation as XO (possibly indicating a clothing shortage in the Fleet). The idea of Gina and Cain being lovers was added in this story, with Taylor feeling that the animosity between them suggested something deeply personal. It is, however, more than unfortunate that, of two key lesbian characters identified as such thus far in the series, one turns out to be a traitor and the other a psychopath. Head Six talks to Baltar as if she is a Cylon, and they are friendly and flirtatious with each other, whereas at the point at which the story takes place, she is at odds with Baltar, who is instead pursuing a relationship with Gina, and is more or less openly identifying herself as a messenger from God. Apollo suggests the Cylons may be headed toward Earth, which was not something the humans had identified in Season Two. Finally, a number of the series' regular actors – Aaron Douglas, Tahmoh Penikett, Alessandro Juliani, Michael Trucco, Kandyse McClure and Matthew Bennett – are listed in the opening credits despite not appearing in the story, although Bennett does appear briefly in the webisode cut of the flashbacks (see below for further details).

Revisiting the Past: Writing and Production

'Razor' was instigated by Universal Studios' home video department, who originally requested two episodes that could be released on DVD almost immediately after their first broadcast on the Sci-Fi Channel, and that could stand on their own for international release – although the continuity references in the final version are so numerous that its ability to stand on its own is debatable. The home video department also made a slightly contradictory request in that they were the ones to ask for the continuity-referencing Hybrid prophecies at the end of the story. It was ultimately first broadcast as a single telemovie, then released on DVD in an extended 99-minute cut ten days later.

The production was in part financed by the home video department, with the specific understanding that some of the effects work would be on the DVD release only. The writing team decided to take the opportunity to revisit the series' past. Suggestions included presenting a time-travel story that would have put some characters back on Caprica before the attacks and have them create an alternative timeline by preventing the Fall of the Colonies, in direct violation of the series bible's statement that the show should never include time-travel or parallel-universe stories. In the end, however, the team opted to explore the *Pegasus* backstory, and to make more use of the character of Cain. The basic narrative remained more or less the same throughout the writing process, though one abandoned idea, of showing a greater number of scenes of Caprica before the Fall of the Colonies, would instead be used for the later stories 'Daybreak' and 'The Plan'.

'Razor' was originally structured more chronologically, and framed by the conversation between Kendra and the First Hybrid. Later, the frame was changed to the conversation between Kendra and Kara on the Cylon baseship. This, however, would have suggested that they had a 90-minute-long discussion about Cain while engaged in a firefight, with Kendra theorizing about the details of Cain's childhood trauma, and making some deeply personal revelations to a woman she doesn't much care for. Moore then suggested adding a frame within a frame, of Adama and Lee debating whether or not to fire the nuclear missiles at the Guardian baseship. Moore himself eventually deemed this too confusing, and Michael Rymer came up with the story's final structure. The idea of having additional narration of the *Pegasus* storyline by Kendra was also abandoned. Kendra's drug addiction, recalling Kat's and Kara's similar problems with stims and alcohol respectively, also was not in the original pitch, but emerged as the script developed.

The Young Adama and Young Helena flashbacks, which are set at the same time, were originally intercut with each other; and, according to the DVD commentary by Moore and Taylor, the sequence of Kendra teaching the Marines was to have been a *Rocky*-style montage of scenes of Lee and Kendra whipping the ship into shape. Also according to the commentary, Kendra's flashback to her conversation with the coffee barista was originally to have taken place in a bar, not a coffee tent. Anders would have been seen playing Pyramid on the bar's television, with at one point a camera pan to show Baltar and Caprica-Six in the stadium crowd watching the match (contradicting 'Resurrection Ship', in which we learn Baltar did not attend games). Moore says that in the story's original conception, there was an idea that it should 'place several of our characters ... before the attack' including Baltar, Laura, Adama, and Lee, but this was abandoned as distracting from the main narrative. It was also at one point suggested that the Hybrid should be a child, recalling Hera; and the idea of Kara Thrace as the harbinger of death appears to have come out of a tequila-fuelled conversation during a writers' meeting, in which it was also suggested that Kendra and the Hybrid should fly off in a Raider together to Reno, Nevada.

Alcalá was chosen as director, according to the DVD commentary, on the grounds that he is good at handling large, complicated productions. The *Pegasus* scenes were shot on a different soundstage from the one used in the series, which had been booked for another project. The ending to the sequence where Cain berates the newly-arrived Kendra, where Cain and Belzen share a chuckle and Cain remarks 'A little mid-morning snack!', was improvised by the actors. In the montage at the start of the episode, recapping the events of the *Pegasus*' arrival in the Fleet, there is a shot of Gina being whipped, which is clearly a deleted scene from 'Razor' itself. The 'So say we all' sequence wound up being the focus of a dispute with the background artists' labour union, who would not let their members speak. The special effects, including the impressive destruction of the shipyard, were all done in-house. The team managed to obtain a 1970s vocorder, which they employed for the Cylons' voice effects. Young Adama's uniform was also tailored to recall the original series' pilots' uniforms, including the detail of stylised bird elements on the helmet; in the webisode cut of the flashbacks, a few men in original-series beige tunics and at least two in original-series blue bridge officers' uniforms (with the addition, in all cases, of a round patch on one sleeve) are briefly visible on *Galactica*. Nico Cortez, who plays the young Adama, is more powerfully built than the young Edward James Olmos, but he looks rather like Jamie Bamber. The sequence with the old-style Raider on *Galactica* was achieved through green-screen filming. To produce the effect of a destroyed cityscape, the Young Helena sequences were shot in a fireman training facility. Strangely, Chandra Berg, who plays Lucy Cain, is credited as her own stunt double. The end credits theme on the extended cut is different from the usual *Battlestar Galactica* closing music, featuring instead the main theme from 'Razor'.

'Razor' was publicised by seven webisodes, which were commissioned at the last minute and first released in the USA from 5 October through to 16 November 2007. Unlike the Season Three and Four webisodes, these do not form an independent story. Five of the seven simply constitute the full version of the Adama flashbacks (with a few slight alterations: in the webisode version, Adama calls the Cylons 'frakkers' rather than 'cocksuckers', and the gruesome scene of a Centurion vivisecting a human is left out). The other two, directed by Wayne Rose rather than Alcalá, appear at the start of the story; these revolve around Adama's romantic relationship with a fellow pilot, Jaycie McGavin. There is also at the end of the last webisode a brief flashback set on the *Galactica* just before the miniseries, in which Adama stands among the relics in the museum, studying the Cylon in the display case. On release, the story was nominated for a Hugo and a Saturn award.

'Razor' shows the two possible responses open to the humans after the attacks on the Colonies; on the one hand, Cain says 'This war is forcing us all to become razors, because if we don't, we don't survive', but, on the other, the *Galactica* story shows that in such situations there is room for human compassion, democracy of a sort, and coexistence.

51: He that Believeth in Me

FIRST TRANSMISSION DATE: 4 April 2008 (USA/CANADA)

WRITERS: David Weddle & Bradley Thompson

DIRECTOR: Michael Rymer

CREDITED CAST: Rekha Sharma (Tory Foster); Ryan Robbins (Connor); Keegan Connor Tracy (Jeanne); Leah Cairns (Racetrack); Jennifer Halley (Seelix); Colin Corrigan (Marine Nowart); Shaun Omaid (Shaunt); Leela Savasta (Tracey Anne); Lukas Pummell (Derrick); Lara Gilchrist (Paulla Schaffer); Heather Doerksen (Marine #2)

STUNTS: Dave Hospes (Baltar Stunt Double); Phillip Mitchell (Marine 1 Stunts)

SYNOPSIS: The battle with the attacking Cylons continues, until Anders, piloting a Viper, is scanned by a Raider; the Cylons then cease firing and retreat. Baltar is taken by his abductors to a disused compartment on *Galactica* that is home to a monotheistic cult. Starbuck, once on the *Galactica*, says that she has been away only six hours her time, although to the Fleet, she has been gone for two months. She claims she has found Earth, and has gun-camera pictures to prove it. Her Viper is brand-new, and the navigation computer is blank. One of Baltar's cultists, Jeanne, has a child, Derrick, who is dying of viral encephalitis. Baltar prays over him and he is miraculously cured. Baltar and Paulla, a cultist, are attacked in the bathroom by Connor and another man, and Baltar, instructed by Head Six, begs Connor to kill him. Paulla breaks loose and beats their assailants unconscious. Tigh, Tyrol, Anders and Tory discuss the significance of their new identity as Cylons, and vow not to act against humanity. Roslin visits Caprica-Six, to ask if she can tell if Kara is a Cylon; Caprica-Six says only that she can sense that the Final Five are close. Adama asks Lee to rejoin the military, but Lee refuses, saying he has been offered a position in government. Although Starbuck insists that she can guide the Fleet to Earth, Roslin and Adama stay on the course they have already plotted. Kara finds Roslin and pulls a gun on her.

ANALYSIS: The first episode of the new season revolves around two faith-based storylines: Baltar's development into the leader of a small underground cult of monotheists, and the strange return of Starbuck, convinced she can lead the Fleet to Earth.

God Shuffled His Feet: What Went Wrong With God's Plan

51: HE THAT BELIEVETH IN ME

Putting together information from 'Eye of Jupiter'/'Rapture', 'Crossroads' and 'He That Believeth In Me', it becomes evident that God has once again attempted to bring the races together, only to be thwarted by other forces. God's original plan appears to have run as follows. God would reveal the identities of the Final Five to D'Anna, and have her pass this information on to the other Cylons. Meanwhile, by having Roslin share visions with Athena and Caprica-Six, the latter of whom would still be among the Cylons, God would encourage a change of attitude in the leaders of both groups. The Cylons, meanwhile, have, according to Caprica-Six, been tracking the human Fleet since the algae planet, using the radiation signature of the *Hitei Kan*. On the Fleet's arrival at the Ionian Nebula, God would cause a power outage to keep them from jumping away when the Cylons got there (as it would take them 20 minutes to spin up the jump drives from cold), bring the Final Five to awareness, and have Starbuck return with a roadmap to Earth. The Cylons would reveal that they are there not to destroy the Fleet but to see the Final Five; the humans' discovery of the Final Five's identities, and of the shared visions of Hera between Roslin, Athena and Caprica-Six, would further cement the unity between the groups; and, armed with Starbuck's information, both would join forces to find the Earth.

The problem, however, is that God's original plan is overtaken by events, and complicated by God's limitations. By Season Four, we have established that God, although he has a greater knowledge of events than humans and Cylons, is not omniscient or omnipresent, and that his main medium for observing and communicating with them is through the Head People. For unexplained reasons, the Head People appear only to Baltar and Caprica-Six[79], and while they seem to have access to all the knowledge and memories of their human contacts, they also seem bound to those individuals' physical locations: Head Baltar, for instance, only starts appearing on the human Fleet once Caprica-Six is there. God can otherwise communicate through the oracles and the Hybrids, through visions, and also with individuals who are in a drug-induced state of altered consciousness, or who are temporarily in the 'space between life and death', but these are limited media. God's ability to influence the humans and Cylons, and God's knowledge of what is actually going on among them, is restricted.

The complication in God's plan therefore comes when Caprica-Six, together with Head Baltar, leaves the Cylon Fleet. As a result, God does not know that D'Anna has been boxed before her information could be passed on. Caprica-Six, also, is a prisoner in the human Fleet, and thus cannot tell the Cylons about the opera house vision. Nonetheless, God apparently assumes that D'Anna is still active in the Cylon Fleet, and continues with the plan. As a consequence of this, God unwittingly leads the humans into a trap, and it is only the Raider recognising Anders as one of the Final Five that saves the situation at all. God's

---

[79] A possible exception is Hera, who is implied in 'Guess What's Coming to Dinner' to have seen Head Six. However, we do not know how the encounter took place, and Hera is also the exception to a number of metaphysical rules.

attempt to unify the races has again, as in both the New Caprica arc and 'A Measure of Salvation', very nearly ended in disaster; almost two thousand humans are dead, and it is only the workings of chance or fate that have prevented the Fleet from being wiped out completely. It is worth noting that Weddle and Thompson wrote 'The Hand of God', which also deals with a plan that does not go entirely as intended.

Jesus Wept: Baltar and His Cult

The decision to have Baltar take over leadership of a cult was made, according to Moore, because the writing team felt it would be interesting to put him in a position where people were looking to him for genuine religious leadership. Moore notes that the people of the Fleet are in a desperate situation, and, 'once [Baltar] was acquitted, it was almost like that alone was the hand of God reaching down and saving this man, and that there would definitely be people in a population like this that would flock to him'. The title of the episode references the New Testament verses John 11: 25-26: 'Jesus said unto her, "I am the resurrection, and the life: he that believeth in me, though he were dead, yet shall he live. And whosoever liveth and believeth in me shall never die"', and the incidental music which plays in the background as Baltar enters the cultists' lair, has Anglo-Saxon lyrics translating as: 'We gather in shadow beneath your altar, your image in blood and flame. By your command, deliver us unto the One True God … Gaius Baltar, our divine savior, now and for eternity. So say we all'. Both of these link human and Cylon imagery through monotheistic faith.

However, as noted before, Baltar's transformation into a cult leader does not entirely read. While the idea of Baltar becoming the focus of some sort of countercultural movement makes sense, all the indications thus far have been that this movement should be political. While political leaders, such as Mao Zedong or John F Kennedy, have become the focus of religious or quasi-religious cults, this generally happens some time after their political careers have become established. The only indication that there are other monotheists on the Fleet prior to 'Crossroads' was a note on the memorial wall in 'The Passage', reading 'God Rest Your Souls'. The impression is once again that the writers are trying to derail Baltar's career as an activist, although, since his main political activities involved challenging an oligarchy that is clearly unjust, unfair and totalitarian, one fails to see the problem.

James Callis plays Baltar's scenes with a thoroughly understandable sense of bewilderment and fear, only relaxing when Head Six (who is clearly using this development as a means of promoting her God over the polytheistic pantheon) encourages him to have sex with the cultists. There is an echo here of how, in 'Colonial Day', Head Six encouraged Baltar into politics using the promise of nubile young women being drawn to men of power. In his encounter with Connor, she also uses similar tactics to those she employed in 'A Measure of Salvation', as Baltar's apparent willingness to die surprises Connor long enough for Paulla to come to the rescue. The cultists, however, appear disturbing in their faith. Jeanne says, regarding her son's illness, 'I guess the one true God doesn't want him to live, right?'; and Paulla's savage beating of Connor (although deeply satisfying for the viewer) recalls the fact that the writers initially conceived of the cult as Manson-like. Baltar loses his beard and gets a haircut in this episode, clearly in order to lessen the visual parallels with representations of Christ. Although the characters are dealing with this new development in a believable way, its introduction remains very much a contrivance.

I Will Tell You a Mystery: The New Cylons and the Return of Starbuck

Moore, in his podcast, reports that 'the biggest concern' for the actors who played the four newly-awakened Cylons was whether or not they had to change the portrayal of their characters. He told them that they should not. 'The notion', he says, 'was never to make them completely different people. It would now inform who they are … give you a deeper understanding who they are, but I really didn't have any interest in flipping a switch and having Saul Tigh become a completely different human being, or Tyrol or Anders or Tory'. Indeed, little has changed for the Final Five. While they now know they are Cylons, they do not have any recollection of their past lives, or understanding of their relationship with the other Cylons, as evidenced by the fact that they are all concerned about the possibility that the Cylons could turn them against the humans (with Tigh entertaining a paranoid fantasy of shooting Adama through the right eye, the site of his own disfigurement, using the same type of gun Sharon employed during her assassination attempt). They also discover that the Cylon Raiders can recognise the Final Five – as Anders encounters the Raider, its red 'eye' is echoed by a brief red glow across his own iris, confirming his identity – but why the Raiders can when Athena evidently cannot, remains unexplained. The Final Five Cylons' reactions as they adjust to their new status are believable, with Tigh defiant, Anders afraid, and Tyrol and Tory somewhat ambivalent. They all make a tacit agreement not to harm the humans and to kill any of the other Four who do so, allowing them a means of coping with their anxieties while they learn more about their situation.

The return of Starbuck, however, is more problematic. There is no real reason why she has to be the one leading the Fleet to Earth: indeed, a case can be made that Athena is a much better candidate, as she has visions, led the Fleet to the Tomb of Athena on Kobol and, being a Cylon who has assimilated into the Colonial Fleet, is a controversial and divisive figure. One of the biggest problems with having Starbuck return is that, while she achieved a personal closure at the end of 'Maelstrom', when she comes back she is exactly the same needy, racist and violent person she was before her vision-quest with Head Leoben. Although in a deleted scene she states that she still remembers her spiritual experience going through the mandala, she clearly has not learned from it. In another deleted scene, she tries to find common ground with Athena; she apologises for her previous behaviour, but Athena, as always concerned to maintain her social position in the Fleet, says that she doesn't trust her and that she should have been thrown out of an airlock. This informs the later scene when Anders tells Starbuck that if she were a Cylon, he would still love her, and she replies that if he were a Cylon, she would shoot him; she then knocks him unconscious and goes after Roslin. This is very much in line with her earlier characterisation, as she responds to Athena's rebuff with a rejection of all things Cylon, and ignores Anders' offer of unconditional love.

There are some intriguing aspects to Starbuck's return. Her Viper canopy is splattered with Raider blood during the battle sequence, underscoring her connection with violence and death. Although she speculates with Anders that she may have been brainwashed by the Cylons, or that she is a clone of the original Kara Thrace, her journey, which took six hours for her while two months passed on the Fleet, recalls the Celtic myth of Oisin, who spends three years in the land of the spirits, and returns to find that three hundred years has passed for everyone else. Although Roslin connects her reappearance with the Cylons calling off their attacks, this is actually a genuine coincidence. Starbuck's description of Earth, with a yellow moon and star, matches Pythia's prophecy, and the star patterns she has observed match with what they saw in the Tomb of Athena; in a deleted extension to the scene where she shows pictures of the planet from orbit, Roslin notes that only four of the star patterns seen in the Tomb are visible. However, the presence of any of the star patterns would suggest this is the world they are looking for. Adama and Roslin reverse their usual roles, Roslin being sceptical while Adama, for once, wanting to believe in miracles.

Everlasting Life: Continuity, Worldbuilding and Problems

In regard to internal continuity, Connor's confrontation with Baltar, in which he wants to see Baltar beg for mercy to satisfy his need for revenge, is a call-back to Kara's treatment of Gaeta in 'Collaborators'. Connor is also still using his son's death as an excuse to perpetuate vigilante justice. We learn some details of Anders's purported identity when he talks to himself in his Viper as a way of consolidating who he still is: that he was born on Picon (despite subsequently playing for the Caprica Buccaneers) and went to Noyse Elementary School. His callsign is 'Longshot'; and Seelix's is 'Hardball'. Poseidon is named by Baltar as another member of the Colonial pantheon. Since two weeks passed between 'Maelstrom' and 'The Son Also Rises', and Starbuck has been away for over two months, this means that at least six weeks passed between 'The Son Also Rises' and 'Crossroads', contradicting Adama's statement in the former that the trial is due to take place in two weeks, and raising the question of how Anders has had time to learn how to pilot a Viper, as at the end of 'The Son Also Rises' he has a broken leg. According to the podcast for 'Six of One', Kara's gunpoint confrontation was originally to have gone as follows: 'Kara and Adama, *vis à vis* Kara with gun ending episode one, surrenders it to Adama, putting her life in his hands. Her raw emotional purity convinces Adama to reinstate Kara'. This would have drawn clear parallels with Sharon in 'Kobol's Last Gleaming', again suggesting that, had Starbuck not returned, Athena could easily have been the one to guide the Fleet to Earth.

The original-series episode 'War of the Gods' also features a pilot returning from the dead through supernatural intervention. However, the closest original-series referent is the unmade *Galactica 1980* story 'Wheel of Fire', which not only features the return of Starbuck, who has transformed into a spiritual being, but has pilot Troy coming back from what seems like a long meeting with Starbuck on board the lightship to find only seconds have passed. In another inside joke, the number of people killed between the last head count in 'The Son Also Rises' and the one in this episode is 1,701 – the registry number of the *Enterprise* in *Star Trek* and *Star Trek: The Next Generation*.

In terms of in-series developments, the distinctive ring-shaped civilian vessel the *Zephyr* takes a bad hit but survives it. According to Moore in his podcast, he had always been fond of the vessel, and the fact that the production team had never been able to find the technical wherewithal to set a sequence aboard it was a source of frustration for him. Roslyn is staying in Adama's quarters, ostensibly, as Adama delicately observes, 'until we find a place to put her up' while she finishes her doloxan treatment. Apollo finally makes the move he has been aiming toward for most of the series and officially goes into politics. In a scene that was not filmed, Starbuck would have returned to her quarters to find Anders's name on her bunk and locker (which he has taken over), her possessions auctioned off, and Anders having a relationship with Tory. She would have been rather unhappy about all this. Moore says the sequence was abandoned because, given Starbuck's own behaviour, he did not think she would be too upset about Anders having relationships with other people.

There are a few problems with the story. Moore acknowledges that it is doubtful that the President would be so lightly guarded that a gun-wielding Starbuck could break in on her while she sleeps. As in 'Hero', Cottle employs a simplified Cylon test involving checking a person's current DNA codes against recorded ones; here, however, the characters themselves note that this is useless if the test subject has been a Cylon all along. This also makes it even more problematic that nobody raised the same objection in 'Hero'. The stills from Starbuck's gun-camera footage show *Galactica* as belonging to Battlestar Group 62, which was in fact the *Pegasus*'s Group; *Galactica* belongs to Battlestar Group 75.

Cult Classics: Writing and Production

In his podcast, Moore reads out the early treatment for this episode, which is very similar to the final version. The major difference is that, in the treatment, the Four Cylons develop an official plan of action: 'One: keep their identity secret. Two: keep watching each other. Three: discover who is the fifth of the Final Five, Kara being the obvious candidate. Four: use Tory to get close to Baltar, who has Cylon Final Five knowledge'. A sequence of Anders insisting on having his cast removed, recalling the injury he incurred falling off a Viper in 'The Son Also

Rises', was cut on the grounds that it would have slowed down the action too much. Although Moore does not say so, it would also have drawn attention to the continuity error regarding Anders apparently training and qualifying as a Viper pilot with one leg out of commission. The end of the teaser originally had Anders getting Seelix in his gunsights, the cliffhanger being the question of whether or not he would shoot her down.

In production terms, the opening battle is one of the team's most impressive CGI sequences to date, the explosion of the vessel *Pyxis* and the part-destruction of the *Zephyr* being especially worthy of note. The visual effects team devised a more complicated sequence of recognition between Anders and the Raider, involving choreographed balletic movements by a group of five Raiders, but Moore negated this, despite their protests, on the grounds that 'the show lives in this docu-style, a naturalistic idea, and that was so stylised ... it went over the top for me'. The cultists' home was described by the production team as 'Baltar's Lair'. In an interview for Scott Ian's scifi.com blog, Aaron Douglas says that in one take of the sequence where the Chief shouts encouragement to the nuggets, he improvised the line 'Drop your dicks and grab your sticks!'; although funny, this was reshot on the grounds that the network would not allow the word 'dicks' to be used.

'He That Believeth In Me' is an enjoyable episode with beautiful visuals, good performances, an impressive subtext and crisp dialogue. However, compared with the opening to Season Three, it lacks political bite, and seems very much to be turning the series into space melodrama, thwarting Baltar's development into a political rallying figure, and bringing Starbuck back from the dead for no good narrative reason.

52: Six of One

FIRST TRANSMISSION DATE: 11 April 2008 (USA/CANADA)

WRITTEN BY: Michael Angeli

DIRECTOR: Anthony Hemingway

CREDITED CAST: Callum Keith Rennie (Leben Conoy); Rick Worthy (Simon); Matthew Bennett (Doral); Rekha Sharma (Tory Foster); Sebastian Spence (Narcho); Dean Stockwell (Cavil); Bodie Olmos (Hot Dog); Tiffany Lyndall-Knight (Hybrid); Leah Cairns (Racetrack); Eileen Pedde (Sergeant Mathias); Jennifer Halley (Seelix); Colin Corrigan (Marine Nowart)

STUNTS: Silvan Cameron (Cavil Stunt Double); Efosa Otusmagie (Simon Stunt Double); Dan Redford (Doral Stunt Double); Kit Mallet (Stunt Marine #1); Gerald Paetz (Stunt Marine #2)

KNOWN UNCREDITED CAST: Leo Li Chiang (Tattooed Pilot)

SYNOPSIS: Starbuck confronts Roslin and demands to be allowed to take the Fleet to Earth, saying that the more jumps they make, the harder it is for her to remember the way. She gives Roslin her gun in a gesture of trust; Roslin in turn tries to shoot her, following which Starbuck is arrested by Tigh. The Cylons interpret the Hybrid's vocalisations and discover that the reason why the Raiders are refusing to attack the Colonials is that the Final Five are among the humans. A Six named Natalie proposes they contact them, but Cavil refuses, advocating instead lobotomising the Raiders. The Cylon models vote, and are deadlocked until Boomer breaks with her model and votes with Cavil. Natalie's faction remove the telencephalic inhibitors that restrict the Centurions' higher functions, and the Centurions in turn gun down Cavil and his supporters. The four awakened Cylons think Baltar may know the identity of the Fifth, and Tory is assigned to find out. When she approaches him, Baltar thinks she is spying on behalf of Roslin, but Head Baltar encourages him to listen to her, and Baltar and Tory end up sleeping together. Lee formally departs the *Galactica* to take up a Quorum post to which he has been nominated by Zarek. Adama and Roslin confront their doubts and fears about Starbuck, and Adama gives Starbuck command of a vessel, the *Demetrius*, and tells her to find Earth.

ANALYSIS: 'Six of One' explores the aftermath of God's latest attempt to put his plan into motion. Although the scenario God tried to engineer has failed, the way in which the different groups deal with this means that parts of the plan, in mutated form, begin to work, through the actions of the rebel Cylons.

Mutiny on the Basestar: The Cylon Rebellion

Although God did not succeed in bringing the humans and Cylons together at the Ionian Nebula, the events that occurred have set the Cylons, at least, on the correct path to fulfill God's plan. The Raiders' behaviour alerts the Cylons to the fact that something has changed, and in the absence of the Threes, they logically enough turn to the only other members of the Cylon Fleet with some sort of connection to God, the Hybrids. The key phrase in the Hybrid vocalisations we hear at the start of the episode is: 'The temple of the Five; transformation is the goal; they will not harm their own'. This refers not only to the Five's decision not to harm the humans, and the Raiders' refusal to attack the human Fleet now that they know the Five are on board, but also to the logic behind the revelation of the Five; once the identities of the Five are known, the Cylons and the humans will find common ground.

The immediate result is, however, to split the Cylons. Had the Threes not been boxed, the faction in favour of contacting the Five would have carried the vote. As it is, the key factor is Boomer's development of individualism, which Cavil, for all his collectivist rhetoric, is clearly happy to exploit. In a deleted scene, set after the vote but before the Centurion rebellion, Boomer implies she is ambivalent about her decision. She seeks out the rebels and tries to explain her reasons for voting against her model, saying, 'This curtain has been lifted and it terrifies me; Cavil, he makes me feel safe. I'm an outcast, aren't I?' Although Natalie says she cannot judge her, when Boomer leaves, the other Eight condemns her, saying 'She sided against her entire model just for him'. Leoben replies, 'Love is a powerful emotion', and Natalie observes, 'So is hate'. Boomer, in 'Six Degrees of Separation', stroked a Raider and likened it to an intelligent pet, but here, she supports lobotomising them, indicating that the bitterness she has been developing since New Caprica is still motivating her in this episode.

The key development comes when Natalie, inverting Cavil's lobotomising of the Raiders, restores the Centurions to consciousness, allowing them once again, like the war-era Cylons seen in 'Razor' (and like the Centurians of the original series), to think, act and form opinions. The Cylon Centurions, having rebelled against the humans, are rebelling against their re-enslavement by the human-like Cylons. As on New Caprica, the Cylons emulate many of humanity's mistakes; the freeing of the Centurions, however, means that one such injustice has now been ended.

The U-Bend Beckons: The Starbuck Arc

By this point, everybody has noticed that Starbuck has not changed at all, with Tigh dryly remarking, 'She's crazy as a latrine rat. If anything, she's more like

Starbuck than ever'. However, in a twist on the repeated trope, Roslin calls Starbuck's bluff and fires at her, though the shot goes wide and hits the picture of Roslin and Adama together, symbolically dividing them over Starbuck. This is a call-back to *Pulp Fiction*, in which a character firing at Jules and Vincent at point-blank range somehow misses his target; Jules puts this down to 'divine intervention'. In *Battlestar Galactica*, it is left ambiguous how deliberate Roslin's bad shooting is; although she later blames the doloxan treatments for interfering with her aim, Adama notes that doubt can have the same effect. We know from 'Valley of Darkness' that Roslin may be unfamiliar with guns, and from other stories, for instance 'The Eye of Jupiter' and 'Taking a Break from All Your Worries', that she is still devoted to the idea that she might find a way to bring the Fleet to Earth (which Starbuck claims she can deliver), suggesting she subconsciously wanted to miss. According to Moore's podcast, the Roslin/Starbuck confrontation went through several changes, featuring, at various points, Roslin refusing to take the gun and Roslin trying to shoot but failing to take the safety off; Mary McDonnell argued against this second iteration, saying, in Moore's words, 'that it seemed to make her look stupid, as opposed to just being fate that was intervening'.

Adama's discussion with Roslin about Starbuck is a strong character piece, as Roslin implies that Adama wants to believe Starbuck, even if it means his own death, because, having lost her once, and now facing the prospect of losing Lee and Roslin, he does not want to be alone. Adama suggests in turn that Roslin is afraid she is not the dying leader of prophecy, and that her death will be as meaningless as everyone else's. There is a deleted scene in which Adama asserts his intention to take Starbuck's Viper up for a flight. This was to have immediately preceded the scene in which he gives Starbuck the *Demetrius*, implying that he came to this decision while flying her Viper; the 20 June 2007 draft actually features him flying the Viper and taking out his frustrations by firing on nearby asteroids, a sequence that would have been intercut with the massacre of Cavil and his supporters on the basestar.

Adama's removing Starbuck's figure of Aurora from the bow of his rebuilt model ship (which the draft indicates is meant to be the same one he smashed in 'Maelstrom') has a clear significance. He is thinking about whether or not Starbuck is meant to guide them, and coming to the conclusion that if she is, she will not be doing it on his ship, underlining his decision to put her on the *Demetrius* instead. As we later see the Aurora figurine aboard the *Demetrius*, the obvious implication is that he returned it to her directly as a symbolic gesture. However, in the draft script, Adama gives Lee the figurine, and, in a deleted scene available on the DVD, Lee gives it to Starbuck. ('It's the only thing that my mother didn't pick out or wasn't a week late, so I think it's pretty special', he says, getting in a last shot at Adama's parenting skills.) These two deleted scenes suggest a more diffuse chain of logic, as the figurine winds up in Starbuck's possession only by chance.

BY YOUR COMMAND: VOL 2

The Love Guru: Baltar versus Tory

The Four's plan, which was originally to have been formally developed in the previous episode, emerges in a more organic way here, as they determine that Starbuck is not a Cylon (on the grounds that if she were, she would have sought them out as they sought out each other in 'Crossroads'), but send a distinctly annoyed Tory to investigate if Baltar knows who the Fifth one is. As a consequence, Head Baltar appears for the first time to Baltar himself; Baltar is somewhat nonplussed and asks if he is Head Six in disguise. Indeed, the question remains why Head Six does not take this role, particularly as this was the case in earlier versions of the storyline; while the 20 July 2007 draft has Head Baltar saying that she would provide 'feminine distractions' and 'aggravation' for Baltar, she has not been shy about encouraging him to go after other women when it suits her in the past. Head Baltar's rationale for urging Baltar to respond to Tory's advances is that she is 'special'. Baltar's current status in the Fleet is indicated by the hostility aimed at him in the canteen. However, when he makes his speech about the voice of God being 'like the distant chaos of an orchestra tuning up ... A grotesque, screeching cacophony becomes a single melody', the incidental music follows along with his words, recalling the 'All Along the Watchtower' sequence and suggesting that he, as he adjusts to life as a cult leader, is developing a persuasive, divinely-influenced rhetoric.

The conversation that follows Baltar's and Tory's first lovemaking session, unknown to Baltar, sets Tory on the path she will follow for the rest of the season. When she apologises to him for crying, he says that she is blessed, and that even what she sees as a negative aspect can be positive. When she then tentatively suggests that she could be a Cylon, he also tells her that Cylons have a soul, and that 'man may have made them, but God's at the beginning of the string', unwittingly reassuring her that she can embrace her Cylon nature and still be beloved of God. Why she cries during their lovemaking is unknown; in the podcast for 'Guess What's Coming to Dinner', Angeli elaborates, explaining, 'I know somebody ... who had a girlfriend, and he'd just met her, and, you know, they had sex, and she was crying. And the reason why she was crying was because her former boyfriend had ridiculed her during sex'. Rekha Sharma, who asserts that Tory did not cry when having sex with Anders, believes she felt a sense of repulsion toward Baltar. However, she could be mourning her lost humanity, or it could be a reflection on Baltar's lovemaking techniques, or penile endowment, or perhaps a combination of any of these.

Mister Smith Goes to Washington: The End of Pilot Lee

Apollo, here, makes a formal break with the military, saying to Starbuck 'I think I finally understand what you meant about having a destiny' as he embraces his true calling as a politician. Starbuck's assessment of why Zarek is nominating Lee for a vacant Quorum seat is that he wants 'a wingman', implying that Lee will be his political client; Lee, however, remains undeterred. Throughout the episode, he is clearly distancing himself from military culture: he is reluctant to take part in the drinking games at his leaving party, and he says to Dualla later, 'Well, it looks like you got the house', implying a divorce from her as much as a change in job. Unfortunately, his big surprise thank-you ceremony on the flight deck is abominably sentimental, with Bear McCreary delivering another dose of kitsch Irish penny-whistles and synth bagpipe to mark the occasion. Roslin is absent; the writing team had an idea, which remains as subtext, that Lee's role in Baltar's trial would have created animosity between them. In the 20 July 2007 draft script she does appear, and there is a cutting exchange where she tells Lee that she is attending only because, 'I have too much respect for your father not to be present. The fact that he is allying himself with Zarek also suggests an implicit rift between Roslin and Lee.

The Unmutual: Continuity and Worldbuilding

In continuity terms, voting is shown to be a general practice among the Cylons, as indicated in the *Galactica 1980* episode 'The Return of Starbuck'. The system here, however, appears to be one predicated on the idea of 'one model, one vote', such that a single Eight dissenting from her model can split the decision. A 'sanitation barge', apparently a sewage recycling ship like the *Demetrius*, was referred to in the original-series episode 'The Long Patrol'. The *Zephyr* has scaffolding around it, indicating reconstruction is now taking place. The 20 July draft mentions 'Racetrack and Hot Dog play[ing] strip poker cutting cards, Hotdog losing badly, down to his boxers, Racetrack in a sports bra and combat pants'; as transmitted, the tattooed bald pilot is also playing, Hot Dog is stripped to the waist, and Racetrack takes off her shirt at the outset of the sequence. In terms of outside references, the massacre on the basestar is clearly Peckinpah-inspired, and the story title is a reference to a line from an episode of *The Prisoner*, 'Free for All', which revolved around an election in the Village.

The resolution of the Starbuck plotline presents a couple of problems. The opening scene lacks tension, as it is fairly obvious to the viewer that Starbuck will not kill Roslin, nor will Roslin kill Starbuck. As in the original series, the question remains of why special dedicated sewage ships exist, rather than all vessels having in-built recycling systems. Moore, in the podcast for 'The Road Less Traveled', attempts to explain, saying that while the *Galactica* has an independent recycling system, none of the other ships does. However, this raises more questions than it answers: first, how it is that one such ship can serve the entire Fleet?; secondly, what do they do with the waste while the *Demetrius* is off on its journey?; and thirdly, since travelling in multi-ship convoys is hardly normal practice on the Colonies, why does a purpose-built recycling ship exist at all? Tigh's likening of Kara to a 'latrine rat' turns out to be strangely prophetic, considering the ship she is given at the end of the story.

Half a Dozen of the Other: Writing and Production

Moore describes in his podcast a few of the key changes made during the episode's development. Originally Lee was to have been the one to broker the compromise between Kara, Adama and Roslin, whereby Kara leaves the Fleet in the *Demetrius*; and Roslin was to have had visions that 'tell her Kara is not Kara', fueling her hostility to the idea of Kara guiding them to Earth. Helo was a late addition to the *Demetrius* crew, as the network felt he didn't have enough to do in the series. Cally was to have appeared in this episode and been openly suspicious of Tyrol's strange activities, an idea moved back to the next story. Tory, in one iteration, sought out Baltar through curiosity about his cult rather than being directed to investigate him; the writing team had thought about putting her together with Baltar even before she became a Cylon.

Early drafts had Kara being put in a cell with Caprica-Six, which would have culminated in the pair coming to blows in a reprise of the Kara/Six fight from 'Kobol's Last Gleaming'. Apollo's leaving party was originally to have been more informal, with Adama not attending. In the 20 July draft, Adama has a drunken and rather maudlin conversation with Apollo about how he would miss being a pilot, containing such wonderful lines as 'It's still gonna be in you, you're gonna feel it ... Like a whisper in hard shoes, up and down your spine, [saying] "Get ready, get ready ... " And ... when it calls, you can't answer it ... You're gonna have to remind yourself that ... you're someone else now'. Tyrol was to have found strange hieroglyphs (presumably resembling those in 'The Eye of Jupiter') on the wheel wells of Kara's Viper; the podcast for 'Revelations' references a slightly different iteration of this concept, specifically that Adama would 'ding an asteroid' when flying the Viper, and 'knock that plate loose with the hieroglyphics on it'. The idea was dropped as the writers felt it raised too many questions, chiefly as to who wrote the hieroglyphs and how the Colonials were expected to read them.

The 20 July draft is quite close to the transmitted version, albeit that it also includes the deleted scenes that appear on the DVD. The draft contains some extra material, including a significant exchange where Cavil, during his confrontation with Natalie, describes her backstory: before the holocaust, she was on Gemenon, 'posing as a reform advocate. Natalie Faust, "leading the charge against political corruption". And thanks to you, we knew where all the Gemenese [sic] leaders were when we launched the nukes. Some died in the arms of their mistresses'. Cavil claims that the Raiders are suffering from a systems failure, whereas Natalie says instead that they have transcended their programming. The draft script also contains some comedic moments cut from the final version. For instance, when Baltar first sees Head Baltar, he exclaims 'Oh, my God!' just as Tory takes off her blazer, making her think he is reacting to the sight of her breasts. Later, when she urges Baltar not to stop making love to her even though she is crying, he remarks sourly that it has 'drizzled on the campfire a bit'. After a cut line from Leoben, in which he, thinking about the

52: SIX OF ONE

Final Five, muses 'Oh, they must be beautiful!' a wicked stage direction followed, reading: 'Note to editing. Possible brief insert of TIGH'. Tigh himself, as he leads the charge to save Roslin from Starbuck, is wonderfully described as a 'wrecking ball with whiskers', and Tigh later says, of Baltar, 'Oily bastard's got more lives than a Cylon'. The draft script also has Baltar eating an apple in front of Tory and offering her a bite (which she refuses), as a gender-reversal of the Temptation of Adam. In the transmitted version, James Callis can be seen holding the apple when Baltar approaches Tory in the canteen. Finally, there is a brief scene of Tyrol at home with his family, which contributes little bar establishing that Nicky owns a toy Viper, complete with model pilot.

According to Moore's podcast, the three rebel models were chosen on the grounds that the Leobens are spiritual, the Sixes are free thinkers and the Eights vulnerable and naive, but he declines to explain why he felt the Dorals and Simons would side with Cavil. The Head Baltar sequence was Callis's first time working with split-screen and, according to Gary Hutzel, he produced a hilariously comic performance reacting to himself, which was then severely pruned back as Moore felt the comedy distracted from the episode. This may also explain why early plans to use Head Baltar more over the initial season arc were shelved. The photograph Roslin hits while shooting at Starbuck is one taken at the medal ceremony in 'Hero'. The episode was nominated for Outstanding Writing for a Drama Series in the 2008 Emmy Awards.

Moore reveals in his podcast for this episode that the first half of the season was broken down as a single long arc. This explains why 'Six of One' feels like part of a wider story rather than a complete narrative in itself. Equally, while the scenes aboard the basestar are full of action and political intrigue, the various plot threads on *Galactica* are reduced to a crawl by the setting up of the *Demetrius* arc.

53: The Ties That Bind

FIRST TRANSMISSION DATE: 18 April 2008 (USA/CANADA)

WRITER: Michael Taylor

DIRECTOR: Michael Nankin

CREDITED CAST: Richard Hatch (Tom Zarek); Donnelly Rhodes (Doctor Cottle); Matthew Bennett (Doral); Rekha Sharma (Tory Foster); Dean Stockwell (Cavil); Jennifer Halley (Seelix); Christina Schild (Playa Palacios); Biski Gugushe (Sekou Hamilton); Finn R Devitt (Baby Nicky); Donna Soares (Speaking Delegate #1); Andrew McIlroy (Jacob Cantrell); Judith Maxie (Picon Delegate); Iris Paluly (Speaking Delegate #2); Ryan McDonell (Lieutenant Eammon 'Gonzo' Pike); Marilyn Norry (Reza Chronides)

STUNTS: Jennifer Mylrea (Cally Stunt Double); Dale Kipling (Cavil Stunt Double)

KNOWN UNCREDITED CAST: Leo Li Chiang (Tattooed Pilot)

SYNOPSIS: Seeing Tyrol and Tory together in Joe's Bar, Cally suspects they are having an affair, though Tyrol denies it. Finding a note to Tyrol in their quarters, she discovers, and overhears, a meeting of the Four. When her husband returns, she attacks him with a wrench, takes Nicky and runs to a launch tube; Tory follows and persuades her to hand Nicky over, but then activates the mechanism, shooting Cally into the vacuum of space. On board the *Demetrius*, morale is dropping as Starbuck's behaviour becomes progressively more erratic in her quest to find Earth. In the Quorum, Zarek tells the newly-appointed Caprican delegate Lee Adama that Roslin is becoming increasingly autocratic, and appeals for his support. On the rebel basestar, Natalie delivers an ultimatum to Cavil, demanding that they unbox the D'Annas, stop lobotomising the Raiders and go after the Final Five. Cavil says he will try to persuade the other models to support it. Returning, he tells her the others have agreed, that the Threes' core consciousness is being downloaded at the central resurrection hub, and that the rebels must take their resurrection ship to the nearest accessible server. Upon jumping, the rebels discover that their resurrection ship has failed to accompany them. They realise it is a trap, but before they can jump away, Cavil's forces open fire.

ANALYSIS: This episode launches the plot-shredding *Demetrius* storyline, which will spend the next few stories slowing down the action and barging huge holes through series continuity.

53: THE TIES THAT BIND

Killing in the Name: The Cylon Civil War

It is possible to work out the events of the Cylon Civil War from information in this episode. It seems that, at the end of 'Six of One', there was a simultaneous attack across the Cylon Fleet by the Eights, Twos, Sixes and uninhibited Centurions, during which some basestars came under the control of Natalie's faction, and others under the control of Cavil's faction. Boomer states in the opening scene that the Cylon Fleet is split down the middle, which implies a number of the Cavils and their supporters were able to mount a successful fightback. All these events appear to have taken place in fairly short order, as the opening scene of 'The Ties That Bind' shows Cavil resurrecting after his demise in the massacre aboard Natalie's basestar in 'Six of One', and the implication in earlier episodes has been that resurrection generally happens within a few hours of death. In 'Downloaded', Caprica-Six guesses that it would take 36 hours for the Three killed in the garage to resurrect, because the preceding massacre in the café would put her at the end of a long queue; although the casualty rate here would be far higher, Cavil's resurrection is likely to have been prioritised.

The chronology of the Cylon Civil War relative to the timeline of events in the rest of the series, however, is problematic. Not long after we see Cavil resurrect, we learn from Lee's press conference that three weeks have passed since the *Demetrius* left the human Fleet. However, other sequences among the Cylons appear to take place fairly soon after the massacre, since a Centurion aboard Natalie's basestar is still wiping blood off the conference room walls, and there is nothing in the Cylons' dialogue or action to suggest a long period has elapsed since 'Six of One'. Although it is possible that the scenes on the Cylon Fleet are taking place in the past relative to those on the human Fleet, non-chronological storylines are normally indicated with text captions. A further problem is that, in the battle sequence, it appears that the entire rebel Cylon Fleet consists of three baseships and Cavil's of five; this would suggest that the unknown military engagement that involved the Cylons in Season Three has reduced their population to a few thousand at most. It cannot be the Civil War that has caused this reduction, as Boomer, at the end of the story, is genuinely shocked that Cavil should order the wholesale killing of other Cylons without hope of resurrection.

We never learn precisely how Cavil's faction are able to control or redirect Natalie's resurrection ship so that it does not make the jump to the ambush point, and some of the technobabble involved makes it difficult to figure out, at first, precisely what the rebel fleet have been asked to do. (The resurrection ships must, apparently, go to 'servers' to download the consciousnesses of Cylons from the central resurrection hub.) Nonetheless, Cavil's plan to regain the upper hand is cleverly conceived, well executed and ruthless, leaving Boomer visibly disturbed at the thought that she is participating in the total destruction of her model, saying 'We're truly killing them. My own sisters–', and Cavil dismissing the moral implications of his act by saying 'We're machines, dear, remember? We don't have souls'.

War by Other Means: Autocracy and the Fleet

The political arc on the Fleet is well described, and sets up an ongoing antagonism between Lee and Roslin over Baltar that will inform subsequent episodes. Lee's opening speech to the press shows he has already mastered political language; he praises Roslin, establishes his elite credentials by referencing his father and his own Caprican origin, but then says that he has non-Caprican friends, presenting himself as a member of the ruling class who is nonetheless in touch with the people. However, the tension between Lee and Roslin is evident in the actors' brittle and tense performances; Zarek is correct when he tells Lee, 'By standing up for Baltar, you crossed the line with her. And Laura Roslin is not the type to forgive and forget'. With the Sagittaron storyline removed, it seems instead that Zarek has been biding his time for a season, waiting for a chink to open in Roslin's armour which he could exploit. Roslin is the author of her own problems, in that her antagonistic feelings toward Lee have given Zarek his opportunity.

This is shown in the political fallout from the *Demetrius*'s departure. By not consulting Roslin before sending out the vessel, Adama has put the President in a difficult position. Inevitably, rumours are circulating that its mission is to find the route to Earth, which, as one of the Quorum delegates notes, casts doubt upon Roslin's own certainty on this subject. However, through covering for it, she looks autocratic and secretive, even though, in this case, the autocratic element does not come from her. As Lee knows the truth behind the decision taken to send the *Demetrius* on its mission, he initially sees through Zarek's bid to accuse Roslin of autocracy. He remarks, 'Sometimes a benevolent tyrant's exactly what you need', no doubt thinking of his father's governance of *Galactica*, but also reflecting autocratic philosophies that go all the way back to the original series.

However, when Lee defends Roslin over the *Demetrius* and she slaps him down for it, he then comes back with Executive Order 112, which Zarek has shown him and 'which establishes a system of tribunals, the judges chosen by [Roslin], answerable only to a special court of appeals, the judges of which would also be chosen by [Roslin]'. This is clearly a move inspired by the fact that Baltar was declared not guilty, with Roslin wanting more control over the judicial system so that similar incidents do not occur again. While Lee's response over the *Demetrius* seems to be the correct one, as it calms down the Quorum delegates and they cease questioning Roslin, her resentment over his role in the events of Baltar's trial costs her an ally.

Lee's challenge to Roslin is, however, only partly successful. While it makes her look autocratic and secretive, she parries it by saying that Executive Order 112 was still in the planning stages and would have been opened up for discussion later, and suggests that, since Lee has raised it, they should put it on the agenda for the next Quorum session. When Lee mentions the order, Roslin looks at Zarek and he looks worried; clearly, he had not expected Lee to raise it at this point, but to wait until Roslin tried to implement it. In his political naivety, Lee has caused a problem in, first, allowing Roslin an easy way out, and, secondly, making it clear to her that Zarek is fomenting dissent behind her back, as the only way Lee could have been aware of the proposal was through Zarek. We never hear about the proposal again in the series, suggesting that it was kicked into the long grass. The politics in this episode are well presented, only hampered by the fact that we are expected to believe that three entire weeks have passed between Apollo leaving *Galactica* and his actually taking up his role as a Quorum delegate.

Ship of Fools: The Demetrius *Crew*

The weak link this episode is the *Demetrius* storyline, which appears to be the only reason why events have been moved forwards three weeks. Otherwise, it would suggest that the friction we see on board the vessel has been there from the outset, rather than having built over time as the crew have become frustrated, and would therefore highlight how badly-thought-out the entire mission is. Although in the previous episode we learnt that the crew were 'hand-picked' by Helo, the selection of personnel makes no sense. For example, Athena, in a deleted scene from 'He That Believeth In Me', told Starbuck to her face that she ought to be thrown out of an airlock, while Seelix, Barolay and Starbuck all did actually attempt to fire Gaeta out of a launch tube in 'Collaborators'. Anders, meanwhile, contradicts the idea that Helo chose the crew, by saying that he personally volunteered for the mission. The only new member of the party is Pike, who implies from the outset that he thinks the whole mission 'is a set-up anyway. I mean, you think that the old man just gave her the ship and then cut her loose? I guarantee you *Galactica*'s dogging our every move, and they're just waiting to jump in as soon as she shows her true colours'. Furthermore, there seem to be an unfeasibly large number of crewmembers for a reconnaissance mission; Hot Dog and Mathias, although not seen in this episode, are also part of Starbuck's complement. The fact that the mission includes no fewer than four Viper pilots and a full two-man Raptor crew also makes one wonder why Adama is willing to release so many people needed for the defence of the Fleet; in the podcast for 'Escape Velocity', even Moore complains about the difficulties created for the writing team by placing most of the semi-regular pilot characters on the *Demetrius*, saying, 'I had to find somebody ... to get hurt in a Raptor. And we were ... running kinda low on pilots at this point ... If we cast it with somebody who was just a brand new pilot you'd never met before ... you're gonna know something's gonna go wrong'. Also, if both Helo and Athena are on the *Demetrius*, the question must be raised as to who is currently looking after Hera.

The scenes on *Demetrius* are also not very interesting. They tell us nothing bar the fact that Starbuck, apparently, can no longer hear the 'ringing' that she said in the last episode was guiding her to Earth, as she is now trying to locate the planet using star charts.[80] This implication will later be confirmed in 'The Road Less Traveled', where she says, 'If I could just focus, I know I could find that sound again ...' 'The Ties that Bind' does establish, through Starbuck's confrontation with Anders, that while he is still trying to hang on to their past life together, she is not feeling much commitment to their marriage; but this is nothing particularly new or exciting. Overall, the *Demetrius* storyline is a waste of time.

Mother's Ruin: The Death of Cally

At the start of the episode, the marriage between Tyrol and Cally, under strain even before the revelation of the Four, is already worsening, with Tyrol spending a lot of time with his fellow Cylons and/or at Joe's Bar. A deleted scene shows him dreaming first of caressing Cally, then of hitting her, straddling her and strangling her, ending with him going to the crib and reaching down to strangle Nicky. This echoes Tigh's vision of shooting Adama in 'He That Believeth In Me', although it is played to imply that Tyrol subconsciously wants to kill Cally and the baby rather than that he fears he might. Shots taken from this sequence, of Tyrol caressing Cally's face and of him reaching menacingly into the crib toward Nicky, are included in the delusional montages as Cally gradually loses control. There are a number of call-backs to earlier incidents of violence in Tyrol's life. Cally, when talking with Cottle, mentions the occasion when Tyrol beat her up in 'Lay Down Your Burdens'. Later, she hits Tyrol with a wrench, recalling him being tempted to bludgeon Helo with a spanner in 'Flight of the Phoenix'. It is thematically in keeping with Tyrol's character arc that his marriage might end in violence.

Cally's assumption that her husband is having an affair is logical under the circumstances, and indeed Tory's and Tyrol's behaviour toward each other is definitely flirtations.[81] However, Cally's suspicions are coloured by her deteriorating mental state; when she has a flashback to seeing Tyrol and Tory in Joe's Bar, she remembers Tyrol moving in for a kiss, whereas the third-person take on the scene does not show this, indicating that she is imagining it. Cottle remarks that 'fatigue and antidepressants can make a hell of a paranoia cocktail'. Moore, in his podcast, says that Cally's distracted state is the reason why she does not go to Adama when she learns Tyrol is a Cylon. He also, however, points out that she does not have a genuine death wish, saying, 'She wants to be talked down off the ledge, you know ... She doesn't want to do this, on some level. It is the classic suicide thing'.

---

80 Which, leaving aside the blatantly obvious fact that two-dimensional charts are useless in three-dimensional space, should not even exist, since the Fleet are supposed to be in uncharted territory.
81 SPOILER SECTION: 'No Exit' reveals that Tyrol and Tory were lovers on Cylon Earth, suggesting that there may still be a subconscious attraction between them here.

53: THE TIES THAT BIND

Tory, meanwhile, is adjusting well to her new Cylon status, saying delightedly, 'It's like I'm being flooded with new sensations and new feelings'. When Cally confronts her, she says 'You want to kill me? Go ahead', recalling Starbuck surrendering her gun to Roslin in the previous episode. In this case, the twist is that Tory is trying to defuse Cally's suspicions enough so that she can take Nicky and fire his mother out of the launch tube. Although Tory has clear reasons to kill Cally, as the woman is unstable and there is a genuine risk of her betraying the identities of the Four to Adama, she probably saves Nicky only because she believes him to be half-Cylon, given her growing anti-human sentiments.[82] The effect of Cally's frozen corpse as it floats in space, with its bloodied, staring eyes, is appropriately gruesome. Her death is ironic on a number of levels, first in that a woman who is deeply racist toward Cylons should find out she is married to one, secondly in that she meets much the same fate meted out to Cylons and Cylon sympathisers, and thirdly in that she is killed just as she seems to be on the point of accepting the situation.

Lost in Space: Continuity and Worldbuilding

In terms of continuity references, Cavil observes that, for all the rebels' talk of equality, the skinjobs still treat the Centurions as social inferiors. Cally's suicide bid is probably inspired by her experiences with the airlock in 'A Day in the Life'. The Aurora figurine is briefly visible on the *Demetrius*, with Kara pushing it around a star chart. According to Moore in his podcast, evidently (as he says) deep into the Woodford Reserve Bourbon, this episode was to have included 'a whole exchange between Gaeta and [Kara] about the Goddess Aurora and this and that and she said something else', but once the sequence of Lee giving her the object in 'Six of One' was cut, the team tried to downplay its presence, and the scene with Gaeta went by the wayside. Pike, on the *Demetrius*, is seen reading a copy of *Nymph* magazine, which is the same one Hot Dog obtained in 'Scar'. The line-up of Quorum members changes over time, which is explicable in light of the deaths and resignations taking place over the Fleet's journey.

Cavil, when resurrected, is wrapped in two large white towels, giving him a robed and hooded appearance that references the film *Killing Zoe*, which itself references the final episode of *The Prisoner*, 'Fall Out'. In 'Fall Out', the mysterious figure Number One wears a white hooded robe; as Cavil is Cylon model Number One, this suggests a witty visual allusion. The title echoes the Protestant hymn 'Blessed Be the Tie that Binds'; the 'tie' in question is usually taken to be marriage, but it could mean any form of social connection, making it relevant to the Cylon and political plots as well as to Tyrol and Cally. On this occasion, the temptation to make the obvious connection with Colonel Tigh has been resisted. Moore says that he wanted the Quorum to be more like the British

---

82 SPOILER SECTION: She is wrong, however, as the baby is fully human, which explains why Cally is not repulsed by Nicky as she is by Tyrol; her husband's suggestion that they have another child is what sends her over the edge.

House of Commons than the US committee system, with formal debates and modes of address, and that Laura's attempt to concentrate power in her own hands 'was obviously a nod toward current events and tendencies of the executive branch to want to control things', though he hastened to add, 'I don't think that it's something unique to the Bush administration'.

The constellation Orion is, improbably, visible in the sequence shortly before Cavil's basestars attack the rebels. The known configuration of the *Galactica* also indicates that, when Cally looks out of the window in the side of Launch Tube 06, she should not, as she does, see empty space, but Launch Tube 07. The reference to Weapons Locker 1701D is another *Star Trek* inside joke, referencing the *Enterprise*'s registration number from *The Next Generation*; Moore claims he did not notice this until viewing the daily rushes later. The writers abandoned a storyline planned for later episodes, in which Tyrol becomes suspicious of the circumstances surrounding Cally's suicide and investigates; however, the biggest question such an investigation would doubtless have raised, is why the launch tubes have an easily-accessible manual release inside the bay.

Till Death Us Do Part: Writing and Production

According to director Michael Nankin as quoted in *The Official Companion Season Four*, the basestar sequences changed focus during editing. Originally, the writing team had wanted to explore the evolution of the Centurions over this season, and thus the sequences would have dealt less with the negotiations than with 'the education of the Centurions, who were watching this political discussion and learning to lie. They were learning human traits from the skinjobs, and there are all kinds of little cutaways, such as where Cavil, making a point, taps the table, and then behind him the Centurion is doing the same gesture'. However, visual effects supervisor Gary Hutzel observed that the result was distracting, causing the audience to concentrate on the Centurions and miss the rest of the story, so Moore, over Nankin's objections, removed them. This created further problems, as the basestar scenes had been filmed to allow space for the addition of CGI Centurions, and, despite clever editing, this is still visible. Moore has, in his podcast, expressed disappointment with the way the episode turned out, saying that while the death of Cally was supposed to be the A plot, he felt that it didn't work as a central focus, and so cut back on it to emphasise the other storylines, with the result that the episode lacks a driving central narrative: as he says, 'There was no real sense of rhythm and flow to the scene order anymore. It's almost like random cuts now'. The decision was also consciously taken to make the episode more Cally's story than Tyrol's, building on the idea that she is having difficulty coping with the pressures of being a young working mother, even before learning the truth about her husband. Early drafts had Cally using a piece of 'sound sensitive equipment', obtained from the hangar deck, to listen in on the Four's conversation, but Nankin and Richard Hudolin convinced Moore that it would be more dramatic to have her hiding between the ship's walls instead.

Also according to Moore in his podcast, the political storyline was originally to have been focused directly on the conflict between Lee and Laura, featuring arguments between them about telling the truth to the Fleet. In one version, Lee confronted his father about the public needing to know about *Demetrius*'s mission, but this was removed as the antagonism between the Adamas had now been resolved. Originally the sequence of Adama reading to Laura was to have been at the end of the episode, but Moore felt it would be less sentimental to start their arc with the pair in an affectionate state and then move on to their fight over the *Demetrius*.

Nankin, the director also responsible for shooting the death of Kara Thrace, used a number of devices to represent Cally's confused state of mind, employing a fuzzy camera lens in the bar scene to indicate her drug use. In *The Official Companion Season Four*, Nankin is quoted as describing how, together with the director of photography Steve McNutt, he also rigged up a system of synchronised projectors to cast cutout moons and stars on the wall of the Tyrols' quarters, as in a child's night-light, such that Cally is continually surrounded by a whirling starscape indicating her confusion and prefiguring her demise. The final scene with Tyrol and Adama sitting together, in the aftermath of Cally's death, was, according to Moore, written to include dialogue, but the actors suggested doing a silent take.

'The Ties that Bind' is less like an episode of a TV series, and more like four barely-connected vignettes of varying quality. Although the stories about Lee's confrontation of Roslin, Cavil's regaining the upper hand from the rebels, and Cally's murder are all dramatic, they lack a sense of thematic cohesion, and are generally let down by the poor quality of the *Demetrius* arc.

54: Escape Velocity

FIRST TRANSMISSION DATE: 25 April 2008 (USA/CANADA)

WRITER: Jane Espenson

DIRECTOR: Edward James Olmos

CREDITED CAST: Kate Vernon (Ellen Tigh); Rekha Sharma (Tory Foster); Keegan Connor Tracy (Jeanne); Leah Cairns (Racetrack); Colin Lawrence (Skulls); Don Thompson (Figurski); Finn R Devitt (Baby Nicky); Leela Savasta (Tracey Anne); Lara Gilchrist (Paulla Schaffer); Donna Soares (Speaking Delegate #1); Andrew McIlroy (Jacob Cantrell); Judith Maxie (Picon Delegate); Iris Paluly (Speaking Delegate #2); Marilyn Norry (Reza Chronides); Heather Doerksen (Surveillance Marine); Laara Sadiq (Priestess); Karen Austin (Lilly); Steve Lawlor (Marine at Baltar's); Hector Johnson (Marine Lieutenant); Lee Jefferies (Redwing)

STUNTS: Lani Galeri, Krista Bell, Janene Carleton (Female Stunt Acolytes); Trevor Jones (Male Stunt Acolyte); Jase Griffith, Colby Chartrand, Carolyn Field, Rob Hayter (Stunt Thugs)

SYNOPSIS: A funeral service is held for Cally. Tyrol, believing she killed herself because she suspected him of having an affair, becomes withdrawn. When Adama tries to approach him in Joe's Bar, the Chief lashes out verbally. Adama demotes him to Specialist. Tigh visits Caprica-Six, hoping to find out more about his Cylon nature, but when he looks at her, he perceives her as Ellen, and is disturbed. Baltar's cult are attacked by a militant group calling itself the Sons of Ares, who accuse the cultists of heresy. Baltar goes on the offensive, disrupting a pantheist religious service, and is arrested. Roslin introduces legal measures, ostensibly to protect small religious groups, which in fact limits their ability to worship while not preventing mainstream services. Barred from entering their quarters by a Marine enforcing these regulations, Baltar makes a stand, but is beaten down in the process. Finally, Lee arrives to announce that the Quorum has voted to restore full right of assembly.

ANALYSIS: 'Escape Velocity' succeeds in being a story in its own right, rather than merely part of the wider half-season arc, with consistent internal themes about pain, punishment and self-justification, but also forgiveness and love.

54: ESCAPE VELOCITY

Coping Strategies: Tyrol's Breakdown and Tory's Newfound Faith

The focus for this episode is Tyrol dealing with conflicted emotions over Cally's death, and problems adjusting to his new identity. Tory advises him, regarding his guilt, to 'just shut it down'; Tyrol looks to Tigh for reassurance, asking him, 'We're still the same people, aren't we?', and the XO replies 'Be a man, Chief, feel what you gotta feel'. Later, however, Tyrol says, 'I don't even know what I am anymore. I don't know which of my memories are real. I don't know that I've had one action in my life that isn't programmed'. Although his failure to fix the capacitor on Racetrack's Raptor could be down to his state of confused grief, he also clearly suspects that he may be unconsciously sabotaging Colonial equipment. Tyrol feels like he deserves punishment for what he believes is Cally's suicide, but this is also confused with his belief that, had he known his Cylon nature from the outset, he would not have pushed away Boomer, the woman he truly loved. In his confrontation with Adama, he says he married Cally as a second-best option because 'the ones we really wanted, really loved … turned out to be Cylons and they didn't know it', ending with, 'If Boomer had … If I had known …' Like Tory, he thinks that his life as a Cylon could be better than his life as a human; however, unlike Tory, he feels guilty for what has come of not having known his true nature. Tyrol thus wants to be punished not just for Cally's death, but for being a Cylon.

Tyrol's confrontation with Adama in Joe's Bar echoes the theme of 'Unfinished Business', about the difficulties that arise when one crosses the line between the professional and the personal. Adama tries to commiserate with Tyrol over Cally's death, but Tyrol, in response, blows up at the Admiral, who is eventually forced into giving him a public demotion to Specialist. While the situation is Adama's own fault, he cannot overlook Tyrol's behaviour and still maintain his authority in the Fleet. Moore sums up Tyrol's state of mind by saying: 'He wants this punishment. He's so out of his mind on so many levels, with his own identity, with what he thinks is the suicide of his wife, the near-fatal accident with [Racetrack] and Skulls that he's taking on his shoulders. All these things combine. He's just going into this completely self-destructive mode'.

Tyrol's seeking punishment is contrasted with Tory's refusal to feel any guilt at all. She distances herself from the humans, saying, 'We were made to be perfect' and 'We're stronger, right?' The hint of doubt in the last sentence, however, shows that she still feels the need for external justification, hence her turning to the Baltar cult. In the extended version of the Four's discussion available on the DVD, Tory says to Tyrol and Tigh that Baltar's God is the Cylon God, meaning she is perceiving in Baltar's words a message for them alone. The scene where she plucks out Baltar's hair, talking, with echoes of Head Six in 'A Measure of Salvation', about how pleasure and pain come from the same source, has her saying 'If you assume that God forgives you, then it's gone, right? … And doesn't that mean, if you really become one with God, you can never do wrong?' Baltar replies, 'Well, no, um, not really, because that would, uh … that would more than imply that we're all perfect'. Although Baltar will later turn this conversation into the basis of a more benign, inclusive theology, whereby God loves each individual as they are, faults and all, Tory is speaking of herself in the singular, using faith to justify her own actions, and setting up an idea that, as a Cylon, she is perfect, and humans are rejected by God for their imperfection.

Suffering Cylons: Tigh and Caprica-Six

Tigh, meanwhile, builds on his strange relationship with Caprica-Six. There is a parallel with Tyrol in that Tigh is also motivated by guilt, identity confusion and a desire for punishment. His feelings about Ellen are clearly coming to the surface as he tries to counsel Tyrol over the death of his own wife. Although he describes Baltar's theology as 'crap', he is clearly motivated by what Tory says; rather than, as Tory does, rejecting his humanity, Tigh seeks out Caprica-Six in the hope that she will give him some clues as to how to reconcile his Cylon and human sides. He asks if she can turn off her feelings, evidently thinking about his own pain. Although the implication is that Cylons cannot do so, Caprica-Six does not view this as a problem, saying, 'I want the pain, it's how I learn'. She also tells Tigh, 'You talk as if we're different but you know we're not', and her elaboration, 'veins, not wires, we're the same', echoes Shylock's well-known line 'If you prick us, do we not bleed?' As with Baltar and Tory, she is telling him one thing and he is reading another: she is approaching him as a human, whereas he is seeking common cause with her as a Cylon.

Inevitably, however, Tigh's grief over Ellen comes into the situation. When he asks Caprica-Six how she can live with what she's done, she tells him that she can give him absolution and forgiveness; he seems to have crystallised his trauma over the deaths he caused on New Caprica into the single act of murdering his wife. Caprica-Six talks about the pain of falling in love with a man and realising it couldn't last forever, as he is mortal and she is not; realising the nature of loss allowed her to appreciate the crime she had committed. As she speaks, Tigh actually perceives her as Ellen; and he continues periodically to see her as his wife during the rest of their scenes together. Tigh appears to gain a kind of absolution through his love for Ellen, and through recalling her love for him. However, when Caprica-Six goes on to mention that the man she loved was Baltar, he closes up again (leading to the single best line in the episode, 'We are not going to talk about the fragile body of Gaius frakking Baltar!'), again paralleling Ellen's multiple affairs and the strain this occasionally put on the relationship. When this confrontation devolves into violence and Caprica-Six hits him, Tigh asks her to hit him 'more', suggesting that, like Tyrol, he wants to be punished for the killing of his wife, and all that it represents. Caprica-Six, however, picking up on Tory's exploration of the confusion between pleasure and pain, says that it's not what he needs and kisses him. A complicated, guilt-ridden and somewhat disturbing relationship is thus developing unbeknownst to the rest of the Fleet, containing elements of both Tyrol's and Tory's ways of dealing with their new self-knowledge.

54: ESCAPE VELOCITY

Kiss My Ares: The Tribulations of the Baltar Cult

Baltar's cultists, in this episode, are attacked by the Sons of Ares, a fundamentalist group protecting the old gods from the threat posed by the new religion. Roslin implies they are religious hardliners from Dogsville, although, given their association with the God of War, their access to weaponry and their familiarity with the security arrangements on *Galactica*, it seems likely that they have a large military element among their number. Roslin's observation suggests that that they have been created by the same social forces that developed the Baltar cult: in times of crisis, it is natural that people find different means of coping, with some trying new religions and others resorting to the old faith, meaning that the attack is partly motivated by religious rivalry, partly, no doubt, by the events on New Caprica. When Baltar discovers that some of his followers still hedge their bets and worship the old gods as well, Head Six describes it, metaphorically, as 'the old gods … fighting back'. Baltar's response, attacking the temple and mocking the ancient myths (calling Zeus, not inaccurately, 'a serial rapist prone to giving birth from his head'), is a parallel with Christ driving the moneychangers from the temple.

Although Baltar hides when the cult's lair is attacked, indicating that he is still driven by self-preservation, he has undergone some development. While Head Six attempts to force him to action through an appeal to his vanity, telling him that if he challenges the worship of the Colonial pantheon, he will appear 'magnificent. Larger-than-life. Godlike', he is ultimately motivated by the injustice of the attack on the cult. Head Six lies in order to persuade him to confront the Marines, saying that if he does, he won't be hurt. She appears to physically lift Baltar when he collapses and walk him toward the Marines. Baltar's encounter with the Marines might seem to have parallels with the Tigh and Tyrol subplots, in that he apparently achieves his goal through pain. However, unlike Tigh and Tyrol, he is not seeking punishment, but is being forced by Head Six to suffer in the name of standing up against religious oppression. Furthermore, the association is false in all three cases: Tyrol's seeking punishment achieves nothing for him bar demotion; Caprica-Six recognises that Tigh does not need pain, but love; and, although Baltar achieves the moral victory of being seen to physically confront a brutally repressive regime, Lee would have obtained the repeal of Roslin's decision regardless how much or how little he suffered in the meantime.

Roslin, meanwhile, comes across as rather frightening in her conversation with Baltar, saying: 'There are some people who say that when people are getting closer to their death, they just don't care as much about rules and laws and conventional morality'. In a continuation of the series' repeated trope of characters motivated by a death wish to take risks, the imminent fact of Roslin's demise encourages her to pursue personal vendettas without considering the future consequences. Although she couches the anti-cult legislation as a crowd-control measure designed to protect the cultists, when the Quorum members note that it could affect the worship practices of other religious minorities, she reveals her hand by saying that it is aimed only at the Baltar cultists. Her wig, worn to cover her doloxan-induced hair loss, and clearly the same one as in the opera-house vision, makes her look rather like Admiral Cain. She justifies her behaviour by saying, when talking about Lee, 'There are pragmatic realities he refuses to face ... Sometimes the right thing can be a luxury, and it can have profoundly dangerous consequences'. This clearly refers to the vote-fixing controversy of 'Lay Down Your Burdens', indicating that she is still motivated not by any sense of right and wrong, but by her anger over the Baltar verdict. Baltar's cult now constitutes a political threat to the establishment, with Roslin appealing for the Quorum's support by saying 'Every single one of you remembers what it was like when Gaius Baltar had political power. And you should be terrified to think about what this man will do with blind religious devotion'. However, the fact that Lee defends Baltar makes this once again a fight between members of the elite rather than a genuine challenge from outside.

At the end of the story, a more uplifting note is struck, first by the Quorum's recognising the injustice of Roslin's proposed legislation and voting it down, and secondly by Baltar's articulation of his theological position. Baltar in his speech defines God as 'a singular spark that dwells in the soul of every living being' and urges people to love their faults, saying 'If God embraces them, then how can they be faults?' He ends by urging his followers, 'Love yourself ... If we don't love ourselves, how can we love others?' Baltar thus takes Tory's attempt at self-justification and turns it into a positive theology built around unconditional love.

I Could Have Been a Contender: Continuity and Worldbuilding

In this episode, it is implied that some Colonial rituals are held at specific times, as Tory complains, regarding Cally's funeral, 'Why do they have to do these things at dawn?' and Roslin admonishes her, saying, 'They do because they have to'. Cally's full name is given as 'Callandra Henderson Tyrol', contradicting the miniseries novelisation[83], which gives it as 'Jane Cally'. Her unmarried surname, according to writer/producer Bradley Thompson, had been used in Season Three to label props relating to the character; however, this was never actually visible on screen. There are other religious minorities in the Fleet besides the cultists, with Quorum delegate Reza Chronides and a delegate from Gemenon referring to Mithras worshippers. In our universe, Mithras is a deity, possibly of Persian origin, popular in ancient Rome, whose cult is sometimes argued to have influenced the early Christian church. In *Battlestar Galactica*, they are said to have beliefs close to Baltar's, implying that they too are monotheists. Asclepius, god of healing, is named by Baltar as another member of the Colonial pantheon.

Regarding outside references, Moore likens Baltar's beating at the hands of the Marine to *On the Waterfront* (1954), in which the hero, dockworker Terry Malloy, is beaten by thugs in the pay of a corrupt union boss, but the visible

---

[83] For further details, see the 'Merchandise and Legacy' chapter at the end of this book.

injustice of this action rallies other dockworkers to his side. Moore also refers to Gandhi's techniques of passive resistance: 'They would go up against the British troops, and ... the British would just beat them down, one by one, and they would just keep coming, and coming, and the next man would come ... And they would beat them down, too, and there was this great – this amazing, brave symbolism of that'. This episode contains a curious continuity error, in that Tigh is seen to be wearing Admiral's pips in the scene where he and Tory visit Tyrol.[84] A red University of Southern California (USC) jersey is also visible to the sharp-eyed in Joe's Bar.

Among the Gods: Writing and Production

Examination of this story's development reveals a plotline that explains why the Sons of Ares appear to emerge out of nowhere, then disappear just as rapidly. Originally, according to Moore's podcast, it was to have come to light that Zarek had engineered the whole scenario, paying thugs to beat up the Baltar cultists under the pretence of being a rival cult, knowing that Roslin would take the bait and come down hard on Baltar, which would in turn cause conflict with Lee. Although this is not explicitly mentioned in the story as broadcast, the implication remains, and is highlighted by the fact that Zarek is conspicuously absent from the Quorum scenes. Draft scripts for 'The Oath', in the second half of the season, also describe Zarek's supporters as including '"Sons of Ares" types'.

Other abandoned early ideas noted by Moore in the podcast include having the Quorum scenes take place off-screen, and the political story being told through exchanges between Lee and Laura. A scene of Laura choosing a wig was also dropped, after Moore and McDonnell had an extensive discussion of which aspects of the progress of Laura's cancer to show and which to leave implicit. Head Baltar was to have featured again, among other things, talking to Baltar as Tory pulls his hair, though Moore does not tell us what the conversation was to have involved. According to Moore, some scenes of Head Baltar were filmed, but the split-screen proved too expensive and time-consuming to keep up for long, and so the idea was dropped. In the pitch document for the episode, which Moore reads out on his podcast, Baltar denounced polytheism as the reason for the holocaust.

Before the decision was taken to put Helo on the *Demetrius*, it was to have been his Raptor, not Racetrack's, that crashed due to Tyrol failing to replace the capacitor; as it stands, this is the second time Racetrack and Skulls have crashed their Raptor due to a technical fault. If Helo had been the victim, it would also have provided more material for Tyrol's guilt complex, as it would have raised questions as to whether he had unconsciously sabotaged the Raptor out of jealousy, or whether he was acting on a Cylon plan that involved Athena as well.

---

84 SPOILER SECTION: Although Adama gives Tigh his Admiral's pips at the end of 'Sine Qua Non', he never actually wears them.

The confrontation between Adama and Tyrol was originally to have followed on from a sequence of Helo finding Nicky alone and crying in the Tyrols' quarters (indicating Tyrol's detachment from the child), in a call-back to the abandoned scene of Helo and Tyrol bonding over the trials of parenthood in 'Crossroads'. Finding Tyrol drinking in Joe's Bar, Helo was to have confronted him, leading to, in Moore's words, 'a whole yelling match about it'. Adama would subsequently have come to the hangar deck to have a quiet word with Tyrol about his leaving Nicky alone, but Tyrol would have attacked Adama verbally, shouting, according to Moore, 'Don't tell me how to take care of my kid … You're not my fuckin' father … Who the fuck do you think you are?' The situation would then have degenerated. The storyline about Tyrol appears to have been inspired by an incident described in the series bible's entry for Tyrol, in which it was stated that, after he rose to the rank of deck chief on the *Columbia*, a Viper pilot was killed as 'a valve had been improperly seated and Tyrol's deck gang was responsible'; Tyrol, as the man officially in charge, was demoted to Specialist and sent to *Galactica*.

The 29 June 2007 draft script is close to the final version. One notable detail is that the Baltar cult's use of the gull symbol is emphasised, the description of the lair reading in part: 'Everywhere on the walls there are images of SEAGULLS. From elaborate Baltar-headed hallucinatory gulls to simple charcoal double-arched scrawls, there are gulls'. When he attacks the temple, Baltar draws a gull on the wall with a piece of charcoal and begins to explain the acronym, saying 'Grace means God's forgiveness. Unity–', before he is dragged off by Marines. Roslin, talking to Adama about Lee, says, 'It's like having another Zarek. Worse than Zarek, because I can't even feel morally superior'. When debating Lee, she describes Baltar's organisation as a 'sex cult', getting some laughs from supporters in the Quorum, and goes on to ask, 'Are there benches [at Baltar's sermons] or just beds?' More viciously, when visiting Baltar in his cell, she reminds him of his role in the destruction of the Colonies, and describes him as 'a snake trying to slither its way back to the top of the pile of corpses', while he, for his part, implies she is jealous of his also attaining prophet status, saying, 'Don't worry. I'm not kicking you off the throne of heaven. There's room for more than one of us'. The suggestion is that Roslin, herself a secular leader who has become the focus of religious devotion, views Baltar's shift into religion as a cynical bid to rival her own power. Tyrol, in his rant against Cally, says, 'There were times I looked at her and she'd be, you know, eating, chewing, and I'd think, I'd think, "cow." "Stupid cow."' There is also a brief sequence of him looking at Nicky and wondering aloud, 'What are you?', with an accompanying direction 'Tyrol … cradles the toddler's head in one hand. We should be reminded of when we saw Caprica [-Six] break a baby's neck'. Tory gets some good stage descriptions: she is said to be looking at Baltar's naked body 'like a buffet'; and, at the point when her hair-pulling session is interrupted by the Sons of Ares, is noted to have a handful of his chest hair, while he is 'looking worried'. Toward the end of the story, she clearly starts to entertain the idea that Baltar is the missing fifth Cylon: she says to him, 'The one god. He's *our* god, isn't he? The

54: ESCAPE VELOCITY

god for ... *our* people?' and the stage directions continue, 'She's asking if he's a Cylon, but he doesn't hear it'. This explains why in the transmitted version Tory is smiling at Baltar's final speech, as she clearly thinks he is talking about Cylons exclusively.

The sequence where Adama reads the novel *Searider Falcon* to Laura underwent some development. The premise is set up in the exchange where he confesses, 'I never read the ending', she says, 'You're kidding. It's your favourite', and he replies, 'I like it so much, I don't want it to be over. So I'm saving it'. In the 29 June draft, he warns her that he has reached the point beyond which he hasn't read yet, and then goes on reading, with the scene ending as he reads, 'The raft was not as seaworthy as I hoped, and waves repeatedly threatened to swamp it'. Olmos, however, suggested that Adama should close the book and continue, saying, 'I couldn't feel anything, and that's what scared me. It came into my thoughts. It filled them. It felt good'. Moore says of this final version, 'What is he saying here? ... Has he memorised it? Which would imply that he has actually read ahead and that he wasn't telling the truth. Or that he read ahead prior to the scene for himself. Is he making it up? Is it a confession? I think it's a really interesting, open question'. Writer Jane Espenson, in the podcast for 'The Hub', says of the scene, 'He ... pretends what he's saying comes from the book, but is actually just speaking his heart'.

This episode is a dark and claustrophobic exploration of grief, guilt and responsibility. As such, it makes for difficult viewing, as there is very little to lighten its unrelentingly grim and miserable tone.

55: The Road Less Traveled

FIRST TRANSMISSION DATE: 2 May 2008 (USA/CANADA)

WRITER: Mark Verheiden

DIRECTOR: Michael Rymer

CREDITED CAST: Callum Keith Rennie (Leoben); Rekha Sharma (Tory Foster); Bodie Olmos (Hot Dog); Keegan Connor Tracy (Jeanne); Alisen Down (Barolay); Eileen Pedde (Sergeant Mathias); Jennifer Halley (Seelix); Finn R Devitt (Baby Nicky); Leela Savasta (Tracey Anne); Lara Gilchrist (Paulla Schaffer); Ryan McDonell (Lieutenant Eammon 'Gonzo' Pike); Lori Triolo (Phoebe)

STUNTS: Rob Hayter (Leoben Stunt Double)

KNOWN UNCREDITED CAST: Leo Li Chiang (Tattooed Pilot)

SYNOPSIS: As the deadline for the *Demetrius*'s return to the Fleet approaches, a damaged Heavy Raider appears, piloted by Leoben. He offers a truce, telling them about the Civil War. He proposes an alliance between the rebels and the Fleet, saying that if Kara comes together with their Hybrid, they can find the way to Earth. The humans try to get the jump coordinates from the Raider but a hull rupture causes it to explode, killing Mathias. Baltar is now making radio broadcasts to the Fleet, and his cult becomes more influential. Tyrol attends his sermons but, when Baltar offers his hand and asks him to forget their differences, Tyrol grabs him by the throat. Later, Baltar goes to Tyrol's quarters. He asks the former Chief to forgive him for his presumption, and Tyrol accepts the apology. Starbuck resolves that the *Demetrius* will find the rebels' basestar before returning to the Fleet. Questioning the intelligence of her decision, with some suspecting her to be a Cylon leading them into a trap, her crew mutiny, with Helo relieving her of command.

ANALYSIS: This episode features more selfish and unhinged behaviour from Starbuck, more manic and self-abusive behaviour from Tyrol and, in the middle of it all, Baltar sporting what looks like a Biblical dressing gown.

Latrine Duty: The Demetrius *Arc*

'The Road Less Traveled' sees the return of Leoben, who suggests that the humans join forces with the rebel Cylons to find Earth. Clearly, from dialogue, this is the same Leoben who imprisoned Starbuck on New Caprica, rendering the deleted scene from 'A Measure of Salvation' non-canonical. Leoben implies that he subconsciously knows Anders is a Cylon, saying: 'After all the celebrity and acclaim, what were you? ... [Y]ou always knew you were destined for more. You were just waiting for your singular moment of clarity'. (Anders responds by pulling a gun on Leoben and saying 'Well, maybe I just found it'.) Leoben also indicates that Starbuck's nature has changed:

LEOBEN: I'm sorry. The difference between the way you were on New Caprica and now ...

STARBUCK: I'm the same person!

LEOBEN: I have eyes. I can see. God has taken your hand and purged you of the questions, the doubt. Your journey can finally begin.

In giving the eulogy for Mathias, Starbuck confesses to an uncharacteristic sense of religious uncertainty, saying, 'We've all heard the words, the prayers, but I don't know what any of it means anymore. We want to believe that she died for something. But in this war, people die and it is just stupid, it's an accident, there's no nobility to it'. When she beats Leoben up, in a call-back to 'Flesh and Bone', he notes that this time the pain and anger have vanished, and they are just going through the motions. As with the Four, the reason behind her old behaviour patterns has now gone, but she still returns to them because this is all that she knows.

Leoben's presence advances the idea that, if Earth is to be found, the humans and Cylons must achieve it together. He says of Starbuck, 'I look at you now, I don't see Kara Thrace, I see ... an angel, blazing with the light of God. An angel eager to lead her people home'. However, he also emphasises that it is both she and the Hybrid who will find the way together. He guides her hand as she paints one of the starscapes that she began making when she came aboard the *Demetrius*. He describes the Cylon Civil War cryptically, saying, 'Battle lines have been drawn between those who embrace their nature and those who fear it'.

However, the *Demetrius* sequences continue to strain credibility. A rough head-count this episode suggests there are 14 people, plus a detachment of Marines, on board; given the cramped, dark, hot and smelly conditions on this flying toilet, it is surprising that the crew haven't airlocked each other on day one. Helo expresses concern that if they miss the rendezvous, the Fleet will abandon them, picking up on the fact that the *Demetrius* crew seems to consist entirely of people Adama and/or Roslin wouldn't mind being rid of.

With Extreme Prejudice: Tyrol, Tory and the Baltar Cult

Tyrol, meanwhile, has shaved his head in what may be a Colonel Kurtz-esque indication that he is in the grip of an insane death wish. Unfortunately the actual effect is less Colonel Kurtz and more Private Pyle from *Full Metal Jacket* (1987), the mentally subnormal Marine recruit who is eventually driven by his drill instructor's taunting to execute a murder/suicide. Tyrol hints that he has subconsciously embraced the Cylons' patriarchal monotheism, saying, 'All I know is that if there's a God, he's laughing his ass off'. His confrontation with Baltar parallels his shouting at Adama in 'Escape Velocity', as first he says, 'There are some sins that even your imaginary God can never forgive', clearly referring to his guilt over Cally's death, then, when Baltar suggests that they make up their quarrel for Cally's sake, he attacks him, shouting, 'You didn't know her'. As in the previous episode, Tyrol's ambivalence over Cally's death contrasts with everyone else's assumption that he is in mourning. Baltar, when asking Tyrol for forgiveness, says, 'I have been offered one last chance at redemption. Because I chose to accept my fate, not fight it anymore'. This indicates to Tyrol that perhaps he himself needs to come to terms with all that has happened to him, and move on.

Tory, meanwhile, is still tacitly justifying Cally's death, referring to it as an accident and suggesting that it is God's will, or even part of God's plan. She hints to Tyrol that perhaps Cally somehow found out they were Cylons, in something approaching a confession. Although Tyrol suggests she is spending too much time with Baltar, it is worth noting that all three of the Four who are still on *Galactica* wind up at a cult meeting at some point. Nicky, amusingly, also seems to like Baltar, making angry-baby noises when Tyrol switches the radio off and calming down when it is turned back on. Tyrol himself is clearly drawn to Baltar's philosophy, seeking redemption and justification for his role as a Final Five Cylon.

Baltar, meanwhile, is exploiting people's anger at the Gods for having failed to prevent the attacks on the Colonies in order to promote his own faith; the appeal of the cult is summed up by Phoebe, one of the women who comes to see Baltar, when she says, 'I need you to tell me all of this makes sense'. He is also still rather ego-focused: he is hurt at Tory's suggestion that he is considered a fringe element, and his subsequent speech urges people not to live with past shame but to look forward to future glory. However, although he is to some extent talking about himself, he puts his own philosophy of forgiveness into practice with Tyrol, suggesting that the new faith is bigger than Baltar himself. A deleted scene exists in which Head Six appears to Baltar and bids him farewell, saying that he has achieved what she wanted for him. Although the team abandoned the idea of having her depart the series entirely, she will now leave Baltar to his own devices for several episodes, indicating that she thinks he is doing quite well on his own.

Loss of Faith, Loss of Hair: Continuity, Writing and Production

The early story document that Moore reads out in his podcast for this episode indicates a few major changes. Originally, the mutiny on the *Demetrius* was to have been sparked when it was left damaged after a battle with Heavy Raiders but Kara refused to do the sensible thing and return to the Fleet. The Raiders were clearly to have been from Cavil's forces, as Moore states, 'Anders' sense of invincibility takes a hit when the mission encounters Heavy Raiders, which do not retreat this time'. Gaeta was to have been the mission XO in the absence of Helo. The mutiny itself was to have been focused around a confrontation between Athena and Kara, as 'the crew ... had accepted Athena, and would actually be willing to follow Athena and had more faith in her, the Cylon, than they did in Kara, who they really didn't know who or what she was'. The climax would have had Kara and Athena pulling guns on each other, in another iteration of the *Crimson Tide*-influenced trope that the writing team seem to have been determined to fit into *Galactica* as many times as they could. The story was to have ended with the shooting and injuring of Gaeta; however, when the episode was found to be overrunning, Moore decided to cut the conflict earlier, and move this incident to 'Faith'.

The title is based on a line from the well-known Robert Frost poem, 'The Road Not Taken'. ('Two roads diverged in a wood, and I/I took the one less traveled by/and that has made all the difference'), presumably reflecting Kara's decision to oppose her crew and insist on going after the basestar to find the Hybrid and the path to Earth, rather than make a safer choice and return to the Fleet. The *Demetrius* mutiny plot is loosely based on *The Caine Mutiny*, which was of course also an influence on 'The Captain's Hand', with Helo as the good officer who tries to stick up for his commander but eventually finds himself forced to lead the crew in revolt. Baltar is now using the wireless to communicate his message to the Fleet, in a call-back to Roslin in 'The Farm', but the fact that the message is simultaneously recorded on reel-to-reel also references Colonel Kurtz in *Apocalypse Now*. Leoben does not explain what the Hybrid is; however, the Fleet has learned about them from Athena after their encounter with the Cylon Guardians in 'Razor'. The comet-like object in Kara's starscape strongly resembles the Ship of Lights from the original series.

The episode is unusual in that, for the only time in the series, neither Laura Roslin nor Admiral Adama appears. Mathias's death sequence, originally quite elaborate, was heavily cut down in editing. While Moore argues that the final version of her death is powerful in its immediacy, the character was never well drawn, and the audience didn't even know she was on the *Demetrius* until this episode, making it difficult to care. Moore himself also admits that the episode could have said more regarding Anders's feelings about discovering he is one of the Final Five. This seems a missed opportunity, given how little else is actually going on aboard the *Demetrius*.

In terms of the series' design, the tape-recorder spools on which Baltar records his sermons are polyhedral rather than circular, echoing the series' blunt-cornered hexagonal paper and hexagonal CDs. The crew on Demetrius wear shirt-sleeves to indicate that it is hot on board the vessel, in a parallel to the rising tempers among its personnel. We learn in the funeral service that Mathias's first name was 'Erin'. The production crew again discussed building a Heavy Raider interior set, but, as usual, it was decided that this would not be cost-effective.

The idea that Tyrol should shave his head was Aaron Douglas's, and he rang up Ronald D Moore personally to suggest it. The scene where Tyrol goes mad in his quarters was also largely improvised by the actor. The conversation where Baltar asks Tyrol's forgiveness originally had dialogue for Tyrol, but the actors wanted to play it with Tyrol remaining silent. Moore says, 'I sort of pitched a fit and said, "Fuck you. No. You can't do this," and "You're gonna do it as written" … and sorta had a whole thing, by long distance on the phone. Well, they shot both versions, and I saw it in the editing bay, and as I watched both versions play, I decided that the version that the actors wanted was the correct one'.

'The Road Less Traveled' focuses on probably the least interesting arc of the first quarter-season, namely the *Demetrius* storyline, while the Fleet arc tells us little that we didn't learn in the previous episode about Tyrol's guilt and rage or Baltar's new interest in forgiveness.

56: Faith

FIRST TRANSMISSION DATE: 9 May 2008 (USA/CANADA)

WRITER: Seamus Kevin Fahey

DIRECTOR: Michael Nankin

CREDITED CAST: Callum Keith Rennie (Leoben); Donnelly Rhodes (Doctor Cottle); Rekha Sharma (Tory Foster); Bodie Olmos (Hot Dog); Alisen Down (Barolay); Tiffany Lyndall-Knight (Hybrid); Jennifer Halley (Seelix); Nana Visitor (Emily Kowalski); Alana Husband (Nurse Sashon)

STUNTS: Carolyn Anderson (Barolay Stunt Double)

KNOWN UNCREDITED CAST: Leo Li Chiang (Tattooed Pilot)

SYNOPSIS: As the standoff on *Demetrius* continues, Anders shoots Gaeta in the leg to prevent him taking the craft back to the Fleet. Starbuck proposes a compromise: she, Anders, Athena and Barolay will take a Raptor to the basestar, then, if the mission is successful, return to the *Demetrius* and rendezvous with the Fleet. If they do not come back within 14 hours and 40 minutes, the *Demetrius* will jump to meet *Galactica* on its own. They find the rebel basestar, damaged and surrounded by wreckage. The Eights ask Athena to lead them in a mutiny against the Sixes, as they disagree with their decisions, but Athena gives them a lecture on loyalty. The humans and Cylons figure out a way to give the basestar jump capability again by linking its drives to the Raptor's, taking the Hybrid offline. When this happens, the Hybrid screams, prophesies that Starbuck will lead them all to their end, and falls unconscious. Barolay is killed by a Six who was traumatised through Barolay sadistically murdering her on New Caprica. Natalie, in turn, executes the Six. On *Galactica*, Roslin makes friends with another cancer patient, Emily Kowalski, and they discuss the afterlife. Kara and her crew return to *Demetrius* with the basestar, and the ships prepare to jump to the Fleet.

ANALYSIS: 'Faith', despite the title, is more a story about death, as the crews of the *Demetrius* and the basestar consider what sacrifices are necessary for them to work together and the rebel Cylons ponder the meaning of their own mortality. Meanwhile, Roslin gains a new perspective on her own imminent demise through her friendship with a woman in the final stages of cancer.

BY YOUR COMMAND: VOL 2

Pump Up the Basestar: The Demetrius/*Basestar Arc*

On the *Demetrius*, the tensions finally come to a head, but unfortunately the resolution of this storyline is no better than the rest of it. For a start, as the *Demetrius* has a 15-hour window of opportunity remaining in which to meet the *Galactica*, there is no real reason why it cannot make the rendezvous straight away, put Gaeta in sickbay, explain developments to the Fleet's leadership, arrange a new deadline, and then jump back to meet Starbuck. The fact that Helo does not raise this makes him look unfortunately rather dim. It also means that he is the one most responsible for Gaeta losing his leg, as the longer the ship stays away from the Fleet, the less chance there is of his leg being saved. Athena's concern that the Cylons have set up a trap in order to learn the human Fleet's current location, could still be valid even with the revised plan (as the Cylons could discover *Demetrius*'s location from the Raptor, capture *Demetrius*, and from there proceed to the Fleet), but nobody raises the issue at all. Once again, too, this is something that could have been resolved by having the *Demetrius* return to the Fleet and explain the situation, so that countermeasures could be arranged.

We learn in this episode that the *Demetrius* crew are all volunteers, which contradicts the statement in 'Six of One' that Helo chose them, and Anders' saying in 'The Ties that Bind' that only some of them volunteered. This makes it all the more surprising that they are complaining so much about the assignment. Seelix, in this episode, is openly contemptuous of Athena and accuses Starbuck of being a Cylon, which raises the question of why she agreed to come along. It's possible that she did so because, as established in 'Crossroads', she has feelings for Anders; however, this is not even remotely hinted at. It is difficult to feel sorrow at Barolay's death, especially when one considers that it is incurred in revenge for gagging a Six and throwing her into a septic tank to drown.

The rebel Cylons are not much better. The Eights come across as bizarrely self-obsessed, as according to Leoben they spend all their time talking about another Eight, Athena. Athena's self-righteous talk about loyalty and choosing a side hides the fact that she is completely, and damagingly, rejecting her Cylon nature through acquiescing to the humans' racism. When the dying Eight reaches out to Athena, she will not take her hand, and it is Anders who does. Natalie killing the Six after she has killed Barolay is the same *Lawrence of Arabia*-derived scenario that the writing team wanted to use in the aborted Sagittaron-massacre storyline in 'Crossroads', where Lawrence must kill his friend to keep peace between two tribes: Natalie tells Anders and Kara, 'No resurrection ship. You understand? She's just as dead as your friend. Is that enough human justice for you? Blood for blood'. When the Hybrid screams upon being disconnected, a Centurion shoots the Eight responsible; removing their telencephalic inhibitors has evidently made them capable of panicked reactions as well as independent thought. Although the Hybrid says that the Final Five come from the home of the Thirteenth Tribe, nobody ever remarks on the fact that this means there were Cylons on Earth.

56: FAITH

Time discrepancies continue to plague the *Demetrius* arc. Five weeks have supposedly passed since the events of 'Escape Velocity', including the battle to which Leoben is clearly referring when he says, 'We were lured out of resurrection range. Ship was attacked. We survived. The baseship was damaged. We were set adrift'. However, Starbuck's discovery in 'Faith' of a debris field with ordinance still exploding among the drifting wreckage and Natalie's damaged basestar in close proximity, suggests that little time has passed since the battle.

What Fresh Hell is This: God and Fate

Roslin's friendship with Emily Kowalski and the Cylon storyline both attempt to explore the various metaphysical forces that exist within the *Battlestar Galactica* universe. During her conversation with Roslin, Emily ridicules the religious fundamentalist position:

> 'And the Lords of Kobol are real? Reigning from a metaphysical mountaintop in those silly outfits? Zeus handing out fates out of an urn like – like they were lottery tickets. You're gonna work on a tylium ship, you're gonna be an Admiral, your family's gonna be evaporated in an attack on the Colonies, but you'll survive for three more years in a mouldy compartment on a freighter till your body starts to eat itself up alive. Those are the Gods that you worship? Capricious, vindictive?'

The reference to Zeus handing fates out from an urn refers to the classical Greek idea that Zeus had two urns, one containing blessings, the other misfortunes, and he would dole these out to mortals as he saw fit (meaning that Emily's comparison of them to lottery tickets is not entirely accurate). Laura replies to Emily that she sees the gods as metaphors rather than as literal beings; if fate is directed by gods, as in the Greek myth of Zeus, then this means that these gods are capricious and cruel, and it is better to see fate as a mysterious, random force. Furthermore, the Greek concept of fate holds that certain events will come about, but how they do so is not predetermined. Starbuck may have been fated to die in a way that involved a mandala, but this did not necessarily have to mean her plunging her Viper into the storm in 'Maelstrom'; it could instead have involved any of the other iterations of the mandala in the series. She might, for instance, have died in 'Rapture' as the sun became the mandala-like supernova, or, on Caprica, she and Helo could have been found by the Cylons as they visited her flat, with its mandala painting on the wall.

The problem is that what Starbuck sees as she jumps into the debris field is not the action of fate, but determinism: the concept that all events are predetermined, and can unfold in no other way. In 'He That Believeth in Me', we learn that, as Kara returned to the Fleet from Earth, she saw 'a giant gas planet with rings ... a flashing triple star. And a comet'. This would appear to have a perfectly obvious explanation, as all three objects could easily refer to astronomical bodies that are known to exist near Earth; even God appears to be working to this interpretation, which explains why Starbuck ceases to hear the 'ringing' after his original plan falls apart. In this episode, however, it turns out instead to have been a vision predicting the battlefield vista, with the 'comet' revealed to be the damaged basestar. Unfortunately, however, for Starbuck to see this particular configuration of debris, the Cylon Civil War had to begin, the battle that damaged Natalie's basestar had to take place in a specific location at a specific time, and Leoben had to bring Starbuck there at exactly the right moment. This would further mean that God knew that his plan to unite the races in 'Crossroads' would fail, implying that God is also subject to the forces of determinism, and is living a tormented existence whereby he knows the outcome of each scheme before he puts it into motion, but must do so anyway.

Keeping the Faith: Continuity and Worldbuilding

In terms of outside references, Baltar's broadcast contains two quotes from *Hamlet* about death: 'Shuffle off this mortal coil' and 'The undiscovered country from whose bourn no traveller returns'. His use of a river metaphor is another indication that the Colonial mythology closely parallels that of the ancient Greeks, who believed dead souls were ferried across the River Styx to the afterlife; and it suggests that, despite his declaration of war on the old gods in 'Escape Velocity', he is using elements of Colonial mythology in his speeches, much as Christianity adopted elements of pagan traditions as it developed and spread. Baltar's version of God is much more loving, and much less petty and vindictive, than the God who is actually trying to guide the action.

The Hybrid quotes part of Jeremiah 31: 13, 'Then shall the maidens rejoice in the dance …'; the verse continues '… and the young men and the old shall be merry. I will turn their mourning into joy, I will comfort them, and give them gladness for sorrow'. Similarly, when she says, 'The children of the one reborn shall find their own country', she is paraphrasing the end of 31: 17, 'There is hope for your future, says the Lord, and your children shall come back to their own country'. Her line, 'All these things at once and many more, not because it wishes harm, because it likes violent vibrations to change constantly', is a paraphrase of one from the theosophical text *At the Feet of the Master*, which runs, 'All these things it wants, and many more, not because it wishes to harm you, but because it likes violent vibrations, and likes to change them constantly', referring to the idea that the body has desires that must be resisted. In the bonus DVD commentary, the writers liken Baltar to Rush Limbaugh, the controversial but popular American talk radio commentator, who is, according to Moore, 'widely listened to, even by people who hate him'. In *The Official Companion Season Four*, Seamus Fahey is quoted as saying, 'I couldn't help but think about the ending of *Se7en* (1995) in regards to Anders's wanting to kill the Six in retribution [for Barolay's death]. But the switch is that the Six understands … that her sacrifice is necessary or all will be lost'. Roslin's dream of the afterlife shows two people wearing Colonial uniforms among the group stood with her mother, suggesting that she had family in the military. We learn that her mother was a teacher, marking the first point at which she discusses her family background in any detail. Her account of her mother's death runs: 'At the moment she died, there was no gleaming fields of Elysium stretched out before her, there was this ... dark, black abyss. And she was just terrified'. Emily, perceptively, responds, 'Laura, *you* were terrified. *You* saw only darkness. You can't possibly know what your mother experienced. You're, you're still searching'. This makes it clear that Roslin fears the abyss, and it is at least partly this that causes her to cling to prophecy and the hope it offers.

Faithlift: Writing and Production

This story's script was the first professional credit for Seamus Kevin Fahey, who had started as writers' assistant on the series and graduated to staff writer. In *The Official Companion Season Four* he is quoted as saying that Weddle and Thompson performed some rewrites. According to Moore's podcast, early drafts contained a political subplot, in which Zarek was trying to manipulate Lee into having Roslin declared unfit to be President due to her illness, and, listening to Baltar's tapes, Lee 'starting to be convinced that there was actually some kind of backroom dealing going on between Zarek and Baltar'. Originally Starbuck's Raptor, as it flies through the battle zone, was to have been attacked by a surviving Raider rather than struck by a piece of random wreckage. A climactic scene of Cavil's faction attacking the basestar just before it jumps was cut in editing, as Moore felt the performances of the actors playing the characters aboard the basestar did not match the urgency of the scene, although it would also have raised the question of why Cavil's faction were returning to a battlefield they had abandoned five weeks earlier.

While the shooting of Gaeta was written by Mark Verheiden and directed by Michael Rymer, as it had been moved forward from the previous story, Michael Nankin restaged the action after the gunshot in order to fit it seamlessly into his episode. Prior to Helo being written into the *Demetrius* arc, Gaeta was to have spearheaded the mutiny. Gaeta's injury was not pre-planned; Moore says in his podcast that he decided to use the idea because, unlike the usual television trope of characters recovering quickly from a gunshot wound, it showed such injuries have 'real consequences'. According to Moore, the scene of Laura choosing a wig from a selection, planned for but later dropped from 'Escape Velocity', was again considered for this episode, with Laura eventually deciding, 'Fuck it. I'm gonna go with the scarf'. Nankin's own cut of the episode featured flashes of Laura's vision of the river scattered throughout, most of which Moore later removed as he did not want to make it seem like a literal, true vision – though as Starbuck regains consciousness on the Raptor after it is struck by debris there is a brief glimpse of the water, suggesting, given that she has returned from the dead, that the river is another of *Battlestar Galactica*'s truths that can be found between life and death.

Emily Kowalski was played by Nana Visitor, *Star Trek: Deep Space Nine*'s

Major Kira. Weddle and Thompson suggested her for the role; they had originally tried to get her to play Socrata in 'Maelstrom', but she had been unavailable. Fahey's first choice for the role had been Alfre Woodard, a black actress who had also been considered for the part of Roslin and who had appeared with Mary McDonnell in the film *Passion Fish* (1992). The bald-head makeup for Mary McDonnell was found to bulge unnaturally, so her head was digitally reshaped by the visual effects department. Mary McDonnell was forced to spend three to four hours in make-up every time she had to appear in the bald cap. The boat sequences were difficult to film; the studio would not authorise the expense unless a whole day's filming was involved, and as a result, the team wrote more boat scenes than were needed. Musically, ambient quotations from 'Gaeta's Lament' (the full version of which will appear in the following episode) can be heard in this story.

According to *The Official Companion Season Four*, a rumour circulated that Quentin Tarantino was interested in directing an episode of the series, and was available during the time slot allocated for filming 'Faith', which Fahey said influenced his writing of the sequence where Gaeta is shot, but nothing came of it. The network were apparently dismayed by the cancer storyline and wanted it cut back, but Moore insisted that the scenes be kept in.

This story has the familiar problems that bedevil the *Demetrius* arc: the main characters behave in an obnoxious and irrational manner; there are too many people on board; indications as to who, if anybody, volunteered for the mission change from episode to episode; and the chronology relative to other events in the series is full of discrepancies. To these, however, it adds a determinist philosophy, which strips from the *Battlestar Galactica* universe all forms of agency and meaning.

57: Guess What's Coming to Dinner

FIRST TRANSMISSION DATE: 16 May 2008 (USA/CANADA)

WRITER: Michael Angeli

DIRECTOR: Wayne Rose

CREDITED CAST: Richard Hatch (Tom Zarek); Callum Keith Rennie (Leoben); Donnelly Rhodes (Doctor Cottle); Rekha Sharma (Tory Foster); Bodie Olmos (Hot Dog); Tiffany Lyndall-Knight (Hybrid); Brad Dryborough (Hoshi); Leah Cairns (Racetrack); Colin Lawrence (Skulls); Jennifer Halley (Seelix); Colin Corrigan (Marine Nowart); Alexandra Thomas (Hera); Donna Soares (Gemenon Delegate); Andrew McIlroy (Jacob Cantrell); Judith Maxie (Picon Delegate); Iris Paluly (Speaking Delegate #2); Marilyn Norry (Reza Chronides); Craig Veroni (Maldonaldo); Lee Jeffery (Redwing)

KNOWN UNCREDITED CAST: Leo Li Chiang (Tattooed Pilot)

SYNOPSIS: *Demetrius* prepares to return to the Fleet with the basestar. A jump drive failure means the basestar arrives first, sparking a general alarm before Tigh orders a weapons hold. The *Demetrius* arrives and the matter is explained. Meeting with the Fleet's leaders, Natalie proposes that they go together to the Resurrection Hub, where they will unbox D'Anna and learn the identities of the Final Five. In return, the rebel Cylons will allow the humans to destroy the Hub, making all Cylons incapable of resurrection. Natalie wants the Final Five to join the rebels; Roslin and Adama, however, secretly plan to hold on to the Final Five until they reach Earth. Natalie, suspecting this, plots to take the humans on the basestar hostage after the mission, until the Five are turned over to them. Gaeta's lower leg is amputated and, as he recovers, he sings a lament. The Quorum, angry about not being consulted over the mission, propose a vote of no confidence in Roslin. Roslin in turn brings Natalie to the Quorum to make her case. Starbuck tells Roslin about the Hybrid's prophecy regarding the opera house. Roslin insists she wants to meet the Hybrid, taking with her Baltar, who appears in her vision of the opera house. Natalie, feeling conflicted about the rebels' plan to take hostages, asks Leoben to stand the Centurions down, and goes to speak with Adama. Athena discovers Hera has been drawing pictures of Number Six. When Athena finds Hera with Natalie, seemingly echoing the opera house vision, Athena fatally shoots Natalie just as the Cylons reconnect the Hybrid. The basestar jumps away.

ANALYSIS: 'Guess What's Coming to Dinner' should be an exciting episode, where battle lines are drawn between Cavil's forces on one side, and the Cylon-human alliance on the other. Unfortunately, the story is shot through with contrivance, and some very dubious politics.

Giving Away a Miracle: The Rebel Cylons

Natalie's speech to the Quorum contains an audacious retcon to the Cylon timeline:

> 'In our civil war, we've seen death. We've watched our people die. Gone forever. As terrible as it was, beyond the reach of the resurrection ships, something began to change. We could feel a sense of time, as if each moment held its own significance. We began to realise that for our existence to hold any value, it must end'.

This, first of all, retroactively erases the engagement with the unknown force from Season Three, as, if something else had happened to cause large-scale permanent death for the Cylons, the idea of mortality would not be as new to them as Natalie implies. The Civil War is also indicated to have been a multi-engagement conflict taking place over an extended period, of which the battle in 'The Ties That Bind' was only the opening gambit. This is not completely implausible, and certainly the fact that the rebels are badly losing this supports the Eights' argument in the last episode that Natalie is a poor leader. However, it raises a few problems. First, Natalie apparently survived two near-identical encounters with Cavil's forces several weeks apart, which suggests bad luck and a failure to learn from experience. More seriously, Cavil's subterfuge in 'The Ties That Bind' goes from being a clever ruse to destroy his enemies in one fell swoop, to becoming the trigger for a large-scale civil war. It also raises the question of why, since the rebels believe the Final Five are among the humans, Cavil never puts forward the perfectly valid suggestion that, instead of fighting each other, they should join forces and destroy the Fleet, so that the Final Five will then download among the Cylons. The attempt to rewrite the Cylon story is a necessary one, but unfortunately cannot cover all the plot holes without doing damage to continuity and characterisation; and indeed, the idea of a short Cylon Civil War preceded by a longer engagement will return in 'Someone to Watch Over Me' and 'Islanded in a Stream of Stars'.

Natalie, furthermore, comes across in this story as too flaky to be put in charge of anything as serious as a military campaign. While her reasoning that the humans will double-cross the rebel Cylons, and her countermeasure of taking hostages, are astute, she then abruptly decides to scupper the whole plan because, apparently, a few minutes spent with the Quorum has given her second thoughts. This is then compounded by her decision to go over to *Galactica* and speak with Adama personally as a means of stalling the mission to the Hub, as the Centurions, who had to be talked into the hostage plan, must now be talked out of it again. Why she does not just send a wireless message saying they are having technical problems is not explained.

There is therefore a good reason why God might want Natalie to die at the end of the episode, as it leaves the way clear for another, stronger leader to take over on the rebel basestar and removes the chief obstacle blocking the mission to destroy the Hub – which God wants to go ahead, as rendering the Cylons mortal will provide them with another incentive to come together with the humans, but which Natalie's spate of second thoughts puts in jeopardy. There are also obvious further benefits to having the basestar jump away right when it does, in response to Natalie's death. First, by having Baltar on board when the ship jumps, God now has a source of information there as well as on the Fleet; as noted in earlier episodes, God's primary source of information is the Head People, who are linked with Baltar and Caprica-Six. Secondly, having Roslin on board means that the Cylons have a valuable hostage, and thus, if conflict breaks out between the two sides, the humans might think twice before destroying the basestar.

All this explains why Athena apparently goes insane at the end of the episode and kills Natalie. Throughout 'Guess What's Coming to Dinner', God appears to be goading Athena to view Natalie as a threat to her child. Head Six has clearly made some form of contact with Hera, as most of her drawings of Sixes show them wearing red dresses. However, one of them is wearing a black dress similar to that worn by Natalie. After Hera disappears, Athena sees the picture and leaps to the conclusion that Natalie is going to kidnap the child. Encouraged on by flashes to the opera house vision, she pursues Hera and shoots the Cylon. Although Athena has shared the opera house vision with Caprica-Six, she reinterprets the Six as being Natalie, as Caprica-Six is in the brig and thus poses no threat to the child. It is also worth noting that, in this instance, neither Roslin nor Caprica-Six apparently shares the vision with Athena. In the next episode, *'Sine Qua Non'*, Athena will tell Adama, 'It was more than just a vision, sir. When I saw them together, I knew that they would take her, that they would take away my child'. The implication therefore is that Head Six has induced Hera to perform certain actions that have then encouraged Athena to interpret the opera house vision as meaning that Natalie is going to take the child away from her.

Governance by Fiat: Roslin and the Quorum

This episode shows that Roslin's attitude to the Quorum is little better than her attitude to the union in 'Dirty Hands'. In Season Two, Roslin and Adama agreed that maintaining a separation between politicians and the military was untenable, and that they must jointly agree on decisions. However, in this episode, Roslin says, 'I won't compromise the success of this operation or the safety of this Fleet to indulge the neediness of 12 perpetually unhappy representatives'. In practice, therefore, the only politician who needs to be consulted, and whose approval Adama requires, is Roslin. Together they agree on the mission without even bothering to solicit the Quorum's views. Although, after Lee makes a fuss, Roslin eventually allows the Quorum to meet Natalie, the Cylon is obviously unaware of the second part of Roslin and Adama's plan (i.e. to double-cross the Cylons), making this a blatant political dodge. Furthermore, had the Quorum forbidden the mission after hearing Natalie's speech, it is doubtful that they would have been obeyed.

Moore says in his podcast for the episode, 'It was great having Lee be in the Quorum ... When it was just Laura ... you always kinda didn't care what the rest of them thought ... But having Lee in the scene ... sort of allowed the whole system [to] feel a little more legitimate, like, you really felt there was an actual government that mattered and things weren't just being done by fiat'. However, in actual fact, Lee is left in the dark throughout the story, and has no more say than the other Quorum members.

Zarek, also, has reverted from being an astute political operator to being once again just an obstreperous voice hindering Roslin's ability to railroad her own decisions through. One of the biggest problems with the way the Quorum are written is that Zarek, even before Lee arrives on the scene, could serve as a plausible and sympathetic leader of the opposition, but this idea is never seriously pursued. The advent of Lee, taking his unelected post, simply means that all opposition, such as it is, still comes from a member of the political and social elite, and dissenting opinions from other quarters are silenced. For all the cosmetic change of having a few of the Quorum members be semi-regular characters, the only real difference between the way the Quorum were treated in the original series and in the reimagined one, is that the original-series Adama was politer to them.

Gone but Not Forgotten: Continuity and Worldbuilding

In 'Guess What's Coming to Dinner', we learn that the Hub coordinates all Cylon resurrection activities. It is mobile, transmitting its location to the baseships when it jumps, and looks like a cross between a basestar and a resurrection ship; Skulls describes it as 'kind of pretty'. Starbuck recalls the Hybrid's prophecy during Natalie's speech to the Quorum, making it clear that she sees its destruction as the fulfilment of her role as 'the harbinger of death'. There is also a genuine irony in the scene where Natalie makes her speech to the Quorum, in that the Cylons are willing to give up their immortality as they have found meaning in death, whereas Roslin, who is dying, not only fears death, but seek to inflict it upon them. Although Baltar says that he learned about Roslin's visions from Caprica-Six, via Lampkin, during the trial, in the 18 September draft, Tory was to have been Baltar's source of information on Roslin's visions, as she wanted to convert her to Baltar's faith. Tigh gets several good lines this episode, describing the attack on the Hub by saying 'Billions of skinjobs lose their bath privileges', calling the Cylon Raiders 'Slit-eyed black bastards', and saying, regarding Tyrol's proposal that they support the unboxing of D'Anna as it will reveal who the Fifth Cylon is, 'All that'll do is crowd the airlock a little more'.

57: GUESS WHAT'S COMING TO DINNER

Whereas during her conversations with Emily in the previous episode Roslin admitted that some of Baltar's sermons might be relevant, her resentment toward him is reawakened here by his announcement to the Fleet at large that she shares visions with Cylons. She takes out her frustrations on Tory, berating her for sleeping with Baltar and accusing her of being a 'charter member of his nymph squad'. However, Roslin also insists that Baltar come to the basestar with her, suggesting that her old anger toward him is now giving way to more ambivalent emotions.

Problems with the story include the fact that the Fleet is still waiting at the rendezvous point, even though the *Demetrius* is by now seriously overdue, and yet this is never mentioned by anyone involved. The only plausible explanation for Tigh ordering a weapons hold is that he himself is a Cylon; when asked, he glosses it by saying 'We got lucky'. In the 18 September 2007 script draft, he covers for his action by saying that the gunnery sergeant has 'that lazy eye. I wanted to hold for a better shot'. It is also rather unwise, from both a scripting and a practical point of view, to have Athena as the officer in charge of communications from the basestar when it jumps in, as the Fleet might reasonably suspect that it is another Eight impersonating her. Helo uses the expression 'round the Horn' when preparing to jump the *Demetrius*: on Earth, this refers specifically to Cape Horn, but as Adama will use it again in 'Daybreak', evidently there is another referent in the Colonies.

Also problematic is Gaeta's habit of singing as a means of coping with losing his leg. This idea was reportedly brought in because the writing team learned that Alessandro Juliani is an opera singer; and the piece is indeed well sung. There is a connection between the song's lyrics, which refer to a sleeping woman holding wishes in her hand, whom the singer hopes will wake, and the Hybrid, who holds the answers to Roslin's questions and who lies unplugged and catatonic for most of the story. Unfortunately, the lyrics are awful, the sentiment is trite and Gaeta apparently sings the same song over and over for several hours. In a deleted scene, Baltar implies that Gaeta's injury may be divine retribution for his perjuring himself earlier, but the audience might wonder why the rest of the Fleet must also suffer for his crime.

Regarding outside references, the title is a pun on that of the film *Guess Who's Coming to Dinner* (1967), about a girl who brings her black boyfriend home to meet her conservative parents. The phrase has since gone into popular parlance to refer to situations in which people have to be polite in a racially- or ethnically-charged situation, as in *Star Trek VI* (1991), in which Chekhov humorously uses it in reference to the Klingons.

Legato: Writing and Production

The main difference between the 18 September draft and the final episode is that it gives more extensive treatment to the Quorum's anxiety at being kept out of the loop, as the Fleet jumps to emergency coordinates while *Galactica* remains behind to confront the basestar, and to Lee's difficulties coping with no longer being in the thick of the action. For instance, as the Fleet wait for the *Galactica*, it envisages 'QUORUM MEMBERS gathered, silently agonising, faces lock-jawed with worry', and Zarek bluntly telling Lee to get used to the anxiety of not knowing when the *Galactica* will return. In this version, when Lee says that he knows no more than Zarek about the basestar's presence, Zarek responds, 'I'm hoping that someone other than a president dying of cancer and a man so close to her that his judgment is in question knows enough to keep the two of them from making a terrible mistake'.

As originally scripted, the Hera subplot was different in execution: Athena, finding that Hera has covered sheets of drawing paper with the number six, goes to visit Oracle Yolanda Brenn from 'Maelstrom'; the Oracle's cryptic utterances (including 'The living will turn on each other-- Cylon, Human, Human, Cylon... the living will fight over the In Between to a glistening extreme... she will harbour a child of the In Between, whose father wears the fatigue of war') cause her to fear that, when the Cylons can no longer download, they will want to possess Hera. The sequence where Hera runs away and finds Natalie took place on the hangar deck and did not include the cutaways to the opera house vision. Wayne Rose, in *The Official Companion Season Four*, is quoted as saying that he shot the scene in the corridor and dropped in the opera house cutaways, to make the parallel between the vision and the events unfolding. Baltar was to have had a nosebleed when the basestar returned to the Fleet, and his nose was to have continued to bleed periodically throughout the episode (requiring him to wander about with cotton wool stuffed up his nostrils), until a cut scene in which Tory tells him that Roslin's shared vision involves an opera house, at which point he was to have declared, 'The hemorrhaging ... It's a sign. A sign. From God'. Natalie's address to the Quorum went through a number of versions, including, at one point, having her broadcast it to them from the brig. The 18 September draft has a scene that jump-cuts from Helo and two Marines bursting in on Baltar as he records one of his radio sermons, to them waiting outside Roslin's Raptor as she informs Baltar she's taking him to the basestar.

There is also more emphasis on the idea that the Cylons seek to reproduce; Natalie, in her initial speech, was to have referred to the Cylons as desiring to find immortality, as the humans do, through their children. The draft also makes it explicit that the Centurions are an independent force with whom the Cylon models have to negotiate, with an Eight saying, after they have come up with the plan to double-cross the humans, 'I'll begin making contact with the Centurions'. Earlier, in a scene where the Marines board the basestar and shout aggressively at the Cylons they find there, before an Eight tells them that the Centurions have been stood down, a Centurion is described as follows: 'His fingers DRUM on the side of his leg – just once, just enough to convey a little impatience and a portending streak of restless defiance'. After Laura's speech to the Quorum, Lee in this draft makes one too, urging them to support her – which unfortunately makes Roslin look rather weak, as it seems as if the Quorum vote in her favour not because they think she's right, but because Lee has swayed them to her side. Quite how he could have managed this is unclear, as his speech goes on for a full

57: GUESS WHAT'S COMING TO DINNER

page and contains such wonderful lines as, 'My grandfather once told me that the best way to tell how someone's going to vote is to ask them if they pray regularly'. Roslin also has a dreadful extra line earlier in the episode, during her speech to Lee about how the world seems to have been turned upside down, where she says 'Cancer feeds on your breasts instead of the children you'd never had', which is at the very least rather out of character.

This is another good script for stage directions, with the Quorum being described as 'a Last Supper with no appetite', and the wires connecting the Hybrid to the ship as resembling 'those fat, dangerous-looking cables the lighting crew handle that could blow your teeth through your head'. Gaeta on the *Demetrius* is said to be 'not the Gaeta who historically obeyed and struggled and obeyed again ... but a man whose moral metronome has been cranked to the breaking point', whereas Tigh, during the discussion about the plan to destroy the Resurrection Hub, is 'doing his best to be his old, gnarly self, but he might as well be sitting on a toilet seat wired with plastic explosives'.

The song, entitled 'Gaeta's Lament' (although Alessandro Juliani says he prefers to call it 'The Stump Serenade'), was written by Michael Angeli and Bear McCreary. Angeli, who had been in a band, is quoted in Bear McCreary's blog as saying that he used as a jumping-off point a song that his wife Karen, a classical pianist, had composed for him. Angeli wrote the lyrics after discussion with Moore, who wanted the song to hint at Gaeta's backstory and the idea that he had a lost lover. Angeli thought it should also relate to the awakening of the Hybrid at the end of the episode. Juliani performed the song live on set, and is quoted in Bear McCreary's blog as saying, 'Let's just say that as an actor it was a welcome change from DRADIS contacts and star charts'. From this point onwards, Alessandro Juliani's real leg was covered in a green stocking during recording, to allow for it to be digitally removed in post-production.

It is difficult to feel any emotional investment in this episode: Athena's madness is contrived, the Quorum's threat to Roslin's power proves, as usual, toothless, and the shooting of Natalie requires the audience to care for someone who is differentiated from any other Six only by virtue of her indecisiveness.

58: *Sine Qua Non*

FIRST TRANSMISSION DATE: 30 May 2008 (USA/CANADA)

WRITER: Michael Taylor

DIRECTOR: Rod Hardy

CREDITED CAST: Kate Vernon (Ellen Tigh); Richard Hatch (Tom Zarek); Mark Sheppard (Romo Lampkin); Donnelly Rhodes (Doctor Cottle); Rekha Sharma (Tory Foster); Leah Cairns (Racetrack); Colin Lawrence (Skulls); Alexandra Thomas (Hera); Donna Soares (Gemenon Delegate); Andrew McIlroy (Jacob Cantrell); Judith Maxie (Picon Delegate); Iris Paluly (Speaking Delegate #2); Ryan McDonell (Lieutenant Eammon 'Gonzo' Pike); Laara Sadiq (Priestess); Veena Sood (Quorum Delegate)

STUNTS: Mike Mitchell (Adama Stunt Double); Lief Havdale (Tigh Stunt Double); Carolyn Field (Racetrack Stunt Double)

KNOWN UNCREDITED CAST: David Kaye (James McManus); Jerry (Lance)

SYNOPSIS: Despite Cottle's best efforts, Natalie dies of her gunshot wounds. Athena is thrown in the brig. Meanwhile, with Roslin aboard the missing rebel basestar, Zarek takes charge of the Quorum. Adama refuses to recognise Zarek's legitimacy, creating a political crisis. Lee establishes a search committee, consisting of himself and Lampkin, to find a suitable leader. Adama asks Tigh to question Caprica-Six about the location of the Resurrection Hub, believing this is where the rebel basestar was going; she replies that only the Hybrids can locate it. A Raptor from the basestar jumps back, containing the corpse of its pilot, Lieutenant Pike. Using data from the Raptor's flight recorder to locate its origin point, the *Galactica* finds the aftermath of a battle, which includes the wreckage of a basestar and of a resurrection facility. Adama learns from Cottle that Caprica-Six is pregnant by Tigh. He confronts Tigh, who criticises Adama for putting the whole Fleet at risk over his vain hope that Roslin has survived, and the two men come to blows. Realising he has lost his objectivity, Adama resigns command of the Fleet. Lampkin selects Lee as President, but pulls a gun on him, saying Lee offers hope for the future, but that he believes the remnant of humanity does not deserve to continue and should die out. Lee talks him down and is later sworn in as President. Adama takes a Raptor and remains behind to wait for the basestar as the Fleet jumps away.

58: *SINE QUA NON*

ANALYSIS: With the basestar gone (James Callis and Mary McDonnell, although credited, do not appear in the story), the Fleet storyline takes a turn for the worse, as the human political system is revealed to be a fascist dictatorship masquerading as a democratic society.

The Madness of Bill Adama II: The Aftermath of Natalie's Murder

Like the shooting of Adama at the cliffhanger of Season One, Natalie's murder leads to the assassin being put in custody, political chaos breaking out, and Colonel Tigh eventually emerging in charge. Athena's action appears insane, as Adama points out when he confronts her, saying: 'Do you hate your people so much that you look for any excuse to kill one? Or did you deliberately try to sabotage this truce?' He points out that her behaviour has not only put the Fleet at risk, but also has specifically endangered the life of her husband, Helo, who is aboard the basestar. Athena, for her part, cannot come up with a sensible reason for her behaviour, saying only that her actions were based on a vision that told her Baltar and Six were going to take away her child. The one bright spot is that Adama refers to Natalie as 'an innocent woman', indicating a significant change in his attitude toward Cylons.

Adama's actions elsewhere this episode, while not out of character, certainly expose the worst side of his nature. For most of the story, he is re-enacting the well-worn trope in which he puts everyone else's lives at risk just to save someone he personally cares about, first declaring martial law, then risking pilots and commandeering civilian Fleet resources in order to search ostensibly for 'Laura Roslin and the missing baseship', though the baseship is clearly a secondary objective. Although he made a speech in 'Unfinished Business' about separating the personal and the professional, he doesn't appear to be even trying to live up to this anymore. His treatment of the Quorum also highlights the fact that he is, generally speaking, not a big fan of democracy, and tolerates it only because of Roslin.

Adama's reaction, after he finally admits he might be going too far, is not to take responsibility, but to resign his command, climb into a Raptor and sit around in deep space reading *Searider Falcon* waiting for the rebel basestar to return. This leaves the Fleet with no plausible replacement military leader, apart from Tigh; Helo, Adama's other XO, is away on the basestar. Even Tigh himself thinks putting him in command is a bad idea, reminding Adama what happened the last time he was left in charge. Adama's response is to say, 'That was a long time ago. You're not the same man you were', but there is no indication anywhere that Tigh has changed to the extent that one would entrust him with saving what remains of humanity. Lee aptly says that Adama's decision to go sit in the Raptor 'sounds a lot like suicide'; faced with the loss of Roslin, Adama would rather die than carry on living for the sake of the rest of the Fleet.

Lampkin, meanwhile, comes across as very different from the man we met during Baltar's trial. Although he should be the very person who exposes the elitist and authoritarian nature of Fleet governance, and finding ways to subvert or challenge it, he fails to do so, instead acclaiming Lee as President and thus giving his sanction to the Fleet being ruled entirely by people surnamed Adama. In Season Three, Lampkin retained a cynical faith in humanity despite, or perhaps because of, continually seeing it at its worst. Here, however, he decides the human race must become extinct because someone killed his cat, Lance. Moore indicates in his commentary that Lampkin takes care of Lance as a way of assuaging his guilt over how he survived the holocaust: having, as Lampkin relates, just disembarked from a shuttle after retrieving the cat from a vet on Gemenon, he chose to reboard it and escape the bombing rather than rush home to his wife and daughters. On hearing this story, Lee suggests that Lampkin is suffering from survivor's guilt, saying, 'At a certain point we all made decisions which saved our lives at the cost of others'. However, this seems a disappointingly banal motivation. We never find out who killed Lance or why, (anti-Baltar vigilantes? Edward James Olmos?) and at the end of the episode Lampkin is stuck with taking care of Jake, canine hero of the resistance.

Proper Leadership: The Quorum versus the Military

As the Fleet's military take over in the aftermath of the basestar jumping away, the Quorum, already weakened by Roslin's increasing concentration of authority in her own hands, become powerless. By depriving the Fleet's ostensible political representatives of both information and the ability to legislate, the situation resembles that of the original series, where the Quorum were unable to mount a sensible challenge to military rule.

Zarek, meanwhile, remounts his critique of the Roslin regime, saying, 'What we had these past five years isn't a true government, but a tacit agreement between a military strongman and a political strongwoman to rule together by fiat', and arguing that he was retained as Vice-President simply to give this arrangement some democratic legitimacy, as he is an actual elected official. While he was aware of this situation in 'Collaborators', and willing to work within it so long as he retained a political voice, both Roslin's autocratic rule, and Adama's refusal to recognise him as President subsequent to her departure, have rendered him voiceless. His proposal, in this episode, to establish a civil defence force, is a sensible one, aimed at forestalling martial law (and not dissimilar to what Lee attempted when working for Roslin in Season Two). Zarek here returns as a credible leader of the opposition, but one who has been subverted through Adama's refusal to recognise due political process.

The fact that Adama will recognise neither Zarek nor the Quorum means that Lee is the only person who can now govern. The writing team acknowledge that from the start of Lee's political career, the idea was that he would eventually become President. Lampkin argues that he is a natural candidate, as, despite his protestations that he doesn't want power, his *curriculum vitae* clearly shows otherwise. The scene where Lampkin pulls a gun on Lee is obviously intended to show, through Lee talking the unhinged lawyer round to his point of view, what a true natural leader he is. This harks back to the original series' trope of the only good leader being a reluctant one, the problem with that idea here being highlighted by the fact that both writer Michael Taylor and actor Jamie Bamber are on record as saying that they think Lee was subconsciously ambitious to become President. While this ostensibly gives the Fleet a ruling family, with the father in charge of the military and the son in charge of the government, the emasculation of the Quorum means that Lee is not actually being given any power at all; Adama (or, in his absence, Tigh) is no more likely to accede to Lee's wishes, if they go against his, than to any other political leader's.

This elitism, furthermore, goes unchallenged within the story. Lampkin pulls a gun on Lee because, in his words, 'Hope is the last thing we need', not for the obvious reason of trying to prevent the totalitarian domination of the Fleet by a small coterie of Capricans. Lampkin also suggests Tyrol as a possible leader on the grounds that he stood up to Roslin and Adama during the tylium strike, which indicates that he does not actually understand what happened during the 'Dirty Hands' incident, in which Tyrol caved in to their every demand. The Quorum do not even raise a feeble query about the idea of selecting Lee as President, even though he is the son of the Admiral, the man who is opposing them at every turn. The very people who should be challenging Lee's Presidency are thus supporting it.

The problem also stems partly from the structure of the series. With Baltar now running a religious cult, the only three major politician characters remaining are Roslin, Zarek and Lee; thus, with the other two ruled out, Lee is the only choice. The 25 September 2007 draft script has two politicians joining Lee and Lampkin as part of the selection committee, but significantly, they are Reza Chronides and Jacob Cantrell, the only other Quorum members who can be described as recurring characters. Although Tyrol and Captain Franks are suggested as alternative candidates for President, it is obvious to the audience that neither of them will become so, as Tyrol is a Cylon and Captain Franks is too minor a character to be suddenly promoted in this manner. Conversely, it would be difficult for the writing team to move Lee from being a major figure, as he was when in the military, to a minor figure, as a lowly Quorum member. The way the series is written thus endorses an autocratic political system.

Still Nothing But the Rain: Continuity and Worldbuilding

This episode contains a number of call-backs to earlier stories, with a mention in dialogue of Adama giving Lee his lighter in 'The Hand of God', a brief repetition of the 'Nothin' but the rain' call-and-response between Adama and Starbuck, and a cameo from Lance the Cat; the direction nicely obscures, on first viewing, the fact that only Lampkin can see the animal. A stage direction in the 1 October script draft suggests that the cat should be visible on Lampkin's bed but then, 'in what to the viewer may seem only a continuity error', the bed should appear empty. Although Lance is not the feline equivalent of a Head Person, he could arguably be analogised to Adama's nostalgia-fuelled visions of Carolanne during 'A Day in the Life'. The 25 September draft has Lampkin also experiencing visions of 'a beautiful but somber WOMAN', evidently his wife. In this draft, when he pulls a gun on Lee, he orders him to kneel before he shoots him; but, as he relays the story about abandoning his wife, 'the kneeling Lee is transformed into the ... woman we glimpsed earlier in his quarters'. This is presumably intended to illustrate Lampkin's feelings of guilt and hopelessness over his wife's death, but instead reads more as if he is expecting Lee to give him a blow-job. Zarek's proposal to create a civil defence force has antecedents not just in the New Caprica Police, and the Sons of Ares (that Zarek himself, it is implied, established earlier), but in the original series' development of a civilian police force out of former private security guards. The lullaby Athena hums is the same Korean children's song that Boomer hummed to the Raider in 'Flesh and Bone'. In Adama's fight with Tigh, the model ship takes another beating, and Adama complains, 'You know how many times I've had to repair this thing?'

In continuity terms, we learn during his swearing-in ceremony that Lee's full name is Leland Joseph Adama, and a deleted scene explains that Lampkin's career has been stagnating since he received a contempt-of-court charge for speaking too frankly to a judge during one of Roslin's circuit courts. We see the present-day Adama in a flightsuit for the first time; although, in a deleted scene from 'Six of One', he suggested that Tyrol would need to sew two flightsuits together for him, this one appears to fit. There is a brief reference to former *Pegasus* Deck Chief Laird salvaging the Raptor's flight recorder, which implies that he has, logically enough, taken over as Deck Chief on the *Galactica* following Tyrol's demotion. There is an amusing throwaway line, regarding a possible candidate for office, 'An actor, for President?', suggesting that the Fleet narrowly missed out on having its very own Ronald Reagan. Racetrack, investigating the downed Raptor, says its 'grav field' is off; such a device would explain how it is that weightlessness is avoided on board ship. As Natalie dies, she says the 'Prayer to the Cloud of Unknowing', last heard in 'A Measure of Salvation'. She also projects as she dies, seeing, like Caprica-Six, a forest. Tigh, meanwhile, has been doing more with Caprica-Six than just talk about guilt and absolution, and she is now pregnant, making this the first Cylon-Cylon conception thus far. In a deleted sequence after Adama and Tigh come to blows, Tigh asks Adama why he is beating up a one-eyed man, and Adama remarks that for a one-eyed man, Tigh has a 'helluva left'. A slight continuity error creeps in when Zarek rails against the Roslin-Adama government of the 'past five years', as it has been only around three and a half years since the attack on the Colonies, of which about one year and four months were under Baltar's regime. Adama's promotion of Tigh to Admiral during his absence may be a pre-emptive move in case the Fleet encounters another homicidal war criminal.

Land of the Rising Son: Writing and Production

Moore, in the commentary, indicates that the Lampkin-Lee confrontation was rewritten several times, with the direct revelation of the death of the cat being removed and reinserted. The main difference between the 25 September and 1 October draft versions of this scene is that in the 25 September draft, Lampkin sees a vision of his wife. The 1 October draft also reveals the names of his wife (Faye) and daughters (Jennifer and Katie). The confrontation between Athena and Adama also went through several iterations. For instance, in the 25 September draft, there is a mention by Athena of seeing the oracle whom she visited in the draft of 'Guess What's Coming to Dinner'; and in the 1 October draft, when Adama asks why she thought Natalie had designs on Hera, Athena briefly flashes back to Hera's drawings of sixes, but finds herself 'at a loss how to add this strange incident to her defence'. Neither of these features in the final version.

The 25 September draft has a line building on the idea established in 'Faith' that the Cylons perceive the Eights as weak and treacherous, where Athena states 'The others always said my line was weak, that we couldn't be trusted'. There is also a subplot in which a group of rebel Cylons who have been left on *Galactica* are locked up with Caprica-Six; one Six, described as looking exactly like Gina for no apparent reason, complains to Caprica-Six that both she and they were imprisoned due to the actions of an Eight (meaning Athena). The story thread goes nowhere in the draft, which is clearly why it was later abandoned.

Also in the 25 September draft, Tigh and Caprica-Six have an explicit lovemaking scene in the interrogation room, with the memorable stage direction, 'While Tigh is unshy with her about his body, our focus remains mainly on the faces of this odd couple'. It ends with Caprica-Six suggesting, 'If we're going to keep this up, you might at least install a couch on some pretext. "Group interrogations", perhaps'. By the 1 October draft, the lovemaking has gone, but Caprica-Six asks Tigh if they are back to 'playing warden and prisoner'. She also has something of an epiphany, realising that Tigh cares for Adama as if he is part of himself, but 'Gaius was never like that. Could never truly care for anyone more than himself'. Lampkin, in the 1 October draft, has a speech about how 'We try to create Camelot, only to prove it's a myth …', going on to conclude that all humanity has in common is its weaknesses – a nice connection to the John F Kennedy allusions running through the political storylines, but clearly an anachronism too far.

Zarek states during his initial scene with the Quorum in the 25 September draft, that what they do know about the military situation, they know only through Lee's connections; this causes a surge of general discontent among the delegates. There is a direction that we should see in Lampkin's quarters an empty litter tray, 'finger-raked into patterns like a miniature Zen garden'. The scene where Lampkin mentions Joseph Adama's lighter is given more context in the draft, where the action begins with a close-up of a pilot about to depart on a mission giving his wristwatch to his girlfriend to keep for him while he is away; although the couple exchange a token in the transmitted version, it is later in the scene, and it is not entirely clear what they are doing or how it relates to the two men's conversation. After the exchange where Lampkin suggests that the pilots have 'given up' on hope, and Adama counters that the lawyer has no idea what the pilots are thinking, as he has never experienced combat, Lampkin in the draft retorts, 'I've never been in combat, but I do know the face of surrender. I've even seen it in the mirror'. Lampkin, confronting Lee with a gun, says, 'I'd rather take a moment to work up a nice homicidal buzz, but I'm quite prepared to go off half-cocked'.

Lance the Cat was killed off in part due to the difficulties of doing television work with cats, who notoriously will not perform on cue; this is strange as the episode nonetheless features the cat quite a lot. Jake the Dog was added to the storyline, according to Moore, due to the fact that he had acquired a vocal internet fandom who kept contacting Moore's wife to request that he be brought back in to the series, however briefly. Moore says that he at one point requested an insert shot of the dead cat when the truth of the situation is revealed, but in response to this the props team produced first a bag with four paws sticking stiffly out of the top, and then a mummified cat straight out of a horror movie, leading him to drop the idea completely. Moore also admits to disliking the CGI weightless spacewalk sequence where Racetrack investigates Pike's Raptor, which he feels looks unrealistic.

The phrase '*sine qua non*' denotes, as Lampkin puts it, 'Those things we deem essential, without which we cannot bear living, without which life in general loses its specific value'; but in the various iterations of this idea throughout the episode, it doesn't occur to anyone that perhaps a functional democracy ought to be one of these.

59: The Hub

FIRST TRANSMISSION DATE: 6 June 2008 (USA/CANADA)

WRITTEN BY: Jane Espenson

DIRECTOR: Paul Edwards

CREDITED CAST: Lucy Lawless (D'Anna); Callum Keith Rennie (Leoben); Donnelly Rhodes (Doctor Cottle); Lorena Gale (Elosha); Dean Stockwell (Cavil); Bodie Olmos (Hot Dog); Tiffany Lyndall-Knight (Hybrid); Jennifer Halley (Seelix); Colin Corrigan (Marine Nowart); Ryan McDonell (Lieutenant Eammon 'Gonzo' Pike); Lee Jefferies (Redwing)

STUNTS: Brett Armstrong (Baltar Stunt Double); Angela Uyeda (Sharon Stunt Double); Brad Loree (Helo Stunt Double); Sharon Simms (D'Anna Stunt Double)

KNOWN UNCREDITED CAST: Leo Li Chiang (Tattooed Pilot)

SYNOPSIS: The Hybrid, plugged into the basestar, makes a series of jumps following the random course generated by the Hub, and as each jump takes place, Roslin experiences visions of her own death aboard *Galactica*, in the company of the dead priest Elosha. Helo encounters an Eight who has downloaded his wife's memories. Roslin meets with Helo secretly and tells him she wants the resurrected D'Anna to be interrogated by the humans first. Cavil revives D'Anna, asking her to speak with the rebel models and end the Civil War. Baltar and Roslin try to learn from the Hybrid the meaning of the opera house vision, with no success. The humans and Cylons attack the Hub together: the Colonial fighter craft, with engines and communications switched off to avoid detection, are towed into the battle zone by Heavy Raiders. During the ensuing conflict Lieutenant Pike, his Raptor damaged, tries to jump back to the Fleet. Baltar is injured during an explosion on board the basestar and, under the influence of morpha, confesses to having given the access codes to the Cylons. Roslin contemplates letting him die, but after a conversation with Elosha, decides to save his life. Helo and the Eight find and rescue D'Anna, and the Eight feels betrayed when Helo insists on taking D'Anna to Roslin rather than have both groups question her together. The Hub is destroyed in a nuclear strike. D'Anna refuses to disclose who the Final Five Cylons are until after they return to the Fleet. The basestar jumps back to where Adama is waiting in his Raptor.

ANALYSIS: Due to a mistake in the editing process, 'The Hub' exists in a quantum state, where the nature of the story exists simultaneously in two separate and incompatible forms.

Divine Intervention, Infernal Confusion: God, Head People and Roslin

This episode may provide an additional reason for Natalie's shooting at the end of 'Guess What's Coming to Dinner'. The central storyline appears to have God communicating with Roslin through the medium of a Head Person who looks like Elosha. Since Roslin is not one of the characters who regularly talks to Head People, she can do so only in the space between life and death. Elosha here appears to Roslin when the basestar is in the process of jumping, which constitutes a space between places, and thus between life and death. The fact that the real Elosha, having died on Kobol, was, according to Head Six, condemned to oblivion, reinforces the idea that she is a Head Person, as the real Elosha no longer exists in either physical or spiritual form. Part of God's aim in 'Guess What's Coming to Dinner', therefore, may have been to enable himself to communicate with Roslin during the jumps.

The initial breakdown for the story had Baltar being injured such that Roslin had the opportunity to kill him, but cames instead to forgive him. In the original drafts, the scenes with Elosha took place only when Baltar was bleeding out from his wound, and thus Elosha could be seen as a manifestation of Laura's conscience allowing her to work through her issues, like Adama with Carolanne during 'A Day in the Life'. However, the writing team clearly thought that there should be the implication of something more metaphysical: Moore says in the podcast, regarding the choice of Elosha, 'Well, it's a spiritual journey … Elosha felt like the natural spiritual link to Laura's experiences', and Moore also likens the whole story to *A Christmas Carol*. When editor Andy Seklir came up with the idea of linking the visions to the jumps, the writers agreed, in Moore's words, 'That's the critical choice that makes this thing work'.

The problem, however, comes in the final scene on the basestar, when one of Roslin's conversations with Elosha takes place not during a jump, but directly after one occurs, and continues regardless of whether the ship is jumping or not. This would mean that, as per the rules above, Elosha cannot be a Head Person. Viewing the sequence, Moore says, 'This is very specific to Laura and not connected to the larger mythos going on in the show'. Espenson agrees: 'I don't think she is at all the same sort of head creature as Six; this really is more Laura's subconscious'.[85] However, aside from the final basestar scene, Elosha could be a messenger from God, and all the events described make sense within the text; furthermore, even the original authorial intention was to imply a spiritual dimension. Unfortunately, the presence of the final basestar scene in this form

---

[85] If Elosha is Roslin's subconscious, furthermore, it removes the implication that God, to pass his message on, had to engineer a scenario which led to the death of one person, and another landing in the brig.

traps the story between interpretations: Elosha appears to be a messenger from God, and yet cannot be a messenger from God, and the two are irreconcilable.

Whatever its source, Elosha's message is a crucial one for Roslin at this point. She finds herself on a deserted *Galactica*, where she sees herself dying, surrounded by Starbuck, Lee and Adama. Elosha pricks her conscience about the way she has acted toward them, saying:

> 'The people in this room are the closest thing you've got to family, and you – you've been their President. Watch them try to comfort each other. At least you haven't taken that away from them – yet. You didn't rob them of their empathy. Yet. You just don't make room for people anymore. You don't love people. Is that clear enough? Practical enough for you, Madam President?'

The absence of others on *Galactica* extends the message out to the people Roslin supposedly represents; the ship is deserted because, as Elosha says later, 'The body of a people is not the same as the body of its leader. But the soul and the spirit might be'. Lampkin, in the previous episode, refers to the Roslin administration as a 'bitter disappointment', suggesting that the Fleet in general have a low opinion of her leadership. By rejecting love, and becoming dictatorial and ruthless, Roslin is also destroying the people she represents. Elosha admonishes Roslin for her belief that if she follows the prophecy to the letter she will automatically receive her divine reward, saying: 'It's not a vending machine, Laura. You don't save a life and then … cue the celestial trumpets, here's the way to Earth'. Elosha's final 'is that clear enough?' recalls God's anger at the way Roslin misinterprets Pythian prophecy in the deleted scene from 'Fragged': God's messenger in that scene took the form of Billy, and Billy was originally to have been the one Roslin talks with in 'The Hub'. Through seeing, in the vision, Adama's love for her, Roslin comes to realise that Baltar, whatever he has done and however she may hate him, deserves mercy, and she saves his life. At the end of the story, Roslin tells Adama for the first time that she loves him, which allows Adama to express his love in return. Elosha's message to Roslin is thus that her ruthless autocracy is not the right path; that she must forgive and love, and allow other voices to speak, even if they oppose her.

Eight is Enough: The Cylons

The main development in the Cylon storyline is Helo's strange relationship with another Eight who has downloaded his wife's memories. This confirms the fears Roslin expressed during 'Rapture': in deleted material from her conversation with Helo in the Raptor, she says 'So, that would suggest that Colonial military information was released. I had warned you about that at the time'. Although Helo is understandably weirded-out by the experience, the resulting woman is a lot nicer than the Athena we know. This is presumably because she is not Athena precisely, but a mix of her own experiences and Athena's, and/or because, at the time of Athena's last download, the racism and prejudice she experienced had not embittered her to the current degree.

The Eights in general continue to be portrayed as somewhat flaky, for instance in Cavil's exchange with D'Anna: 'An Eight can make a passionate ally'. 'Until she sees something shiny'. In a deleted scene, the Athena-Eight pulls a gun on D'Anna when the latter says that Hera can automatically get a 'fresh mommy' every time she needs one, which echoes the way the original Athena can overreact to a threat to her daughter. The jibe also reminds the Eight that she is a Cylon, and her reaction could suggest that she has taken on some of Athena's ambivalent feelings about her own species. Although a deleted scene has the Athena-Eight being shot dead by a Cavil who has invaded the basestar as part of a boarding party, the finished version never explains what happens to her. Helo, for his part, has changed over the past season, such that he is more cautious in defence of his principles: while he is concerned about Roslin's plan to double-cross the Cylons, and discusses it with her, he nonetheless goes along with it.

The other major event in this episode is the unboxing of D'Anna. The rebel Cylons are interested only in her information specifically, and seem quite willing to sacrifice all the other Threes in the process of obtaining it. This is in line with the way the Cylons in general show obsessive tendencies, from the surreal coffee-house society on Cylon-Occupied Caprica to the Athena-Eight's obsession with Hera. D'Anna herself openly states to Roslin that she does not trust either faction: she also figures out that Cavil knows a secret about the Final Five that he has not shared with the other Cylons. It is unstated how Cavil knows that the humans and rebel Cylons have formed an alliance (the most obvious answer being that there is a spy for Cavil aboard the Fleet), however, this would explain why his basestars are already at the Hub, as he has clearly realised that the resurrection facility is an obvious target.

Things to Come: Continuity, Writing and Production

In continuity terms, we learn that Eights don't automatically share memories on download. We also see Cylon pilot dress – a kind of black leather-look ensemble – for the first time. The pilots seem to be exclusively Sixes and Eights. Espenson rationalises the fact that Pike can apparently return from the Hub to the Fleet at the touch of a button by explaining, 'A whole sequence of jumps must have been programmed into the Raptor to take him back'. This is the first episode to take place entirely off *Galactica*, and the only one in which Natalie is actually named on screen. The quote Adama reads to the dying Laura in her vision – 'I collected seeds from the few fruits the island offered, and planted them in long, straight furrows, like the ranks of soldiers. When I finished, I looked at what I had done. I did not see a garden. I saw a scar. This island had saved my life, and I had done it no service' – seems a subversive thrust at the supposed benefits of civilisation, order and hierarchy.

Baltar's conversation with the Centurion shows him reverting to his political mode, saying that the hierarchy on the basestar goes against the will of God, and giving the Centurion a lecture about egalitarianism, saying 'He's your God as well. And God doesn't want any of his creations to be – slaves'. Baltar has finally rationalised his guilt over the destruction of the Colonies by comparing himself to a flood mentioned in the Scrolls of Pythia that wiped out most of humanity (presumably the Colonial equivalent of the Noah's Ark myth): he says, 'I was another flood, you see. I blamed myself ... But God made the man who made that choice. God made us all perfect. And in that thought, all my guilt flies away'. However, for God to have predetermined things to such an extent would require him to be omnipotent, omniscient and omnipresent, which clearly he is not, indicating that Baltar is ignoring the evidence before him and interpreting things as a means of self-exoneration. It would also make God directly responsible for the destruction of the Colonies, which cannot be the case, as both humans and Cylons have agency in their own right.

As well as the changes discussed above, the commentary indicates that the episode was originally to have repeated the *Battlestar Galactica* trope of beginning on a dramatic scene from late in the narrative and telling most of the story in flashback. Espenson says that there were also ideas of intercutting scenes of Roslin dying injured in Baltar's arms, and scenes of Baltar dying injured in Roslin's arms, and not revealing until late in the episode which was the actual story and which a 'fevered dream of the person who's dying'. There was also an idea that 'after Elosha had told subconscious Laura "You have to love someone", she then said, "and now you have to convince her", and pointed to the Laura who was sitting there next to the dying Baltar, and at that point dying Baltar sort of became inhabited by subconscious Laura, and it became a "Laura having to convince herself to save her" sequence' – a confusing idea that would have been difficult to convey. Mary McDonnell also pointed out that 'if subconscious Laura is convinced, your arc is over; she's convinced, you don't need to convince her again'. The episode was originally to have ended with Laura announcing she knew who the Final Five were, rather than with Roslin's and Adama's reunion.

As it stands, the episode has similarities to 'Resurrection Ship', with two factions coming together to destroy a Cylon resurrection facility and planning to double-cross each other afterwards. In terms of outside references, Roslin's exchange with Adama where she says, 'I love you', and he replies, 'About time', was based on Han Solo' and Leia's exchange, 'I love you', 'I know', from *The Empire Strikes Back* (1980). The sequence where Roslin removes the gory bandage from the gaping wound in Baltar's side references a similar scene in *Catch-22*. The brief glimpse of the Hub interior, with inert Eights in pools (as D'Anna puts it to Helo in a deleted line, 'flaccid Athenas') and glowing chambers, is reminiscent of H R Giger artwork, and of the imagery of humans in pods from *The Matrix* (1999).

In production terms, editing the episode so that the Elosha conversations happen between jumps caused a problem, as the team had not recorded enough shots of Laura reacting as she goes into or comes out of a jump. The editors had to hunt through available footage for shots they could repurpose, and wound up mostly using material of Mary McDonnell before or after a take was called.

Dialogue was also cut from the vision sequences in order to make them more surreal and dream-like. There were several minor cuts to the story, with the Athena-Eight arc and the pilot briefing sequences losing material; and another call-back to the opera house vision, when Roslin is aboard the Raptor, was removed. Baltar's one-sided conversation with the Centurion originally took place entirely during the battle, but, as it went on slightly too long to feasibly fit within this timeframe, the editors adjusted it to start earlier. Sequences of Simons and Dorals shooting at the humans in the Resurrection Hub were also lost in editing.

The team had always intended to bring Lucy Lawless back, and contacted her between seasons; she agreed on condition that D'Anna should remain a duplicitous, ambiguous character rather than become a heroic one. The change from Billy to Elosha was made because Paul Campbell was unavailable; Espenson says that she changed only one of the character's lines (beginning 'Cue the celestial trumpets') when this decision was taken. Edward James Olmos suggested that Adama should put his wedding ring on Roslin's finger. The Adama point-of-view shot of the Raptor cockpit interior and the starscape beyond is entirely CGI; in a production error, constellations visible from Earth can be seen from his Raptor. Although credited, neither Katee Sackhoff nor Jamie Bamber appear in this episode.

Elosha's message to Roslin is a Classical metaphor linking the state of the monarch to the state of the land: her physical degeneration is having a corrupting effect on her spirit, and, through this, also on the people of the Fleet. By becoming a compassionate leader who can forgive her enemies, Roslin has the power to revive the Fleet, and ultimately fulfil God's plan.

60: Revelations

FIRST TRANSMISSION DATE: 13 June 2008 (USA/CANADA)

WRITERS: Bradley Thompson & David Weddle

DIRECTOR: Michael Rymer

CREDITED CAST: Lucy Lawless (D'Anna); Callum Keith Rennie (Leoben); Rekha Sharma (Tory Foster); Bodie Olmos (Lieutenant Brenden [sic] 'Hotdog' [sic] Costanza); Keegan Connor Tracy (Jeanne); Brad Dryborough (Hoshi); Vincent Gale (Lieutenant Peter Laird); Don Thompson (Specialist 3rd Class Anthony Figurski); Alexandra Thomas (Hera); Lara Gilchrist (Paulla Schaffer); Heather Doerksen (Sergeant Brandy Harder); Finn R Devitt (Baby Nicky); Sonja Bennett (Specialist 2nd Class Marcie Brasko); Barry Nerling (Adama's Corporal)

KNOWN UNCREDITED CAST: Leo Li Chiang (Tattooed Pilot)

SYNOPSIS: D'Anna announces that she will keep all humans on the basestar captive until the four undisclosed Cylons aboard the Fleet are handed over. Tory goes to the basestar, but, when no-one else comes forward, D'Anna starts executing hostages, announcing that she will do this every quarter hour until the other three give themselves up. The Four begin to hear the music again, and Tyrol, Tigh and Anders are drawn to Kara's Viper, sensing that something has changed about it. Tigh confesses to Adama that he is a Cylon, and suggests that, if Adama threatens to airlock him, D'Anna will back down. Adama cannot do this, so Lee has Tigh put in a launch tube, and orders him to reveal the identities of the others. As he is arrested, Anders urges Kara to investigate her Viper. With the *Galactica* and basestar squaring off, Kara rushes to the launch tube to prevent the executions; her Viper is picking up a Colonial signal that points the way to Earth. Lee shares the information with the Cylons, and announces that he has granted an amnesty to the Four; D'Anna releases the hostages. The humans and Cylons make the journey to Earth, only to find it a radioactive wasteland.

ANALYSIS: At first glance, 'Revelations' has all the elements of a blockbuster episode, which, as the title promises, resolves some of the mysteries surrounding Earth and the Final Five. However, repeated viewing shows how it truly lives up to its name, with a dense script that rewards the viewer with deep, sometimes disturbing, character insights.

BY YOUR COMMAND: VOL 2

Free the Watchtower Four: The Standoff on the Fleet

As expected, once on the rebel basestar, D'Anna becomes the leader of the Cylons. Everything D'Anna does in the story is logical, rational and an understandable counterpoint to the humans' actions; for instance, when she learns the humans are proposing to airlock Tigh, we see the Cylons preparing to airlock eight pilots. Lee's announcement that the Four are free to go to the baseship is a clear ruse, to get them to come forward and identify themselves; the only one who goes to the baseship, Tory, does so under the pretext of taking Roslin her medication, something Adama clearly will not challenge.

Adama's actions in response are perfectly in keeping with his character development up to this point. While he was willing to put the Fleet at risk two episodes earlier just to save Roslin, here she says to him, 'If the Cylons get the Four, they get Earth. You can't let this happen. Even if you have to blow this ship to hell'. To stay true to Roslin, he cannot give the Cylons the Four; however, he cannot just nuke the basestar without at least attempting to save her. The plan Lee proposes to Adama is one Adama himself might have come up with: a rescue mission involving an invasion of the basestar. Athena points out the problem with this idea, specifically that it will involve compartment-by-compartment fighting, and Tigh observes that the basestar could attack the human Fleet while this is taking place. The Fleet cannot jump away before the beginning of the fight as this would give the game away to the Cylons; indeed, 'A Disquiet Follows My Soul' indicates that it is possible to detect when a ship is spooling up its FTL drives (an operation that, according to 'Crossroads', normally takes about 20 minutes), meaning that they cannot even jump away right when battle is joined. Kara says that as a means of defending the Fleet, 'We need to make sure that our Raptors are already out there with their nukes cocked and locked'; however, the presence of Raptors simultaneously attempting to board the basestar and protect the Fleet, with live nuclear weapons, adds another element of risk to an already treacherous situation. Since the plan has a high likelihood of destroying not just the basestar but *Galactica* (which cannot fire on the basestar while the rescue mission is taking place) and most if not all of the Fleet, it thus becomes Adama's own death wish writ large: he knows that Roslin's order, to nuke the basestar, is the right one, but he also does not want to live without her. Knowing the assault on the basestar is suicidal, he supports the plan, as a kind of *Götterdämmerung*. When Tigh outs himself as a Cylon, Adama is torn; he now has a possible means of rescuing Roslin, but it requires sacrificing Tigh. It is at this point that Adama breaks down and abdicates responsibility.

With Roslin gone and Adama out for the count, Lee is now in charge of both military and civilian administrations. Although Starbuck, quoting Leoben, tells Lee, 'Children are born to replace their parents; for children to reach their full potential, their parents have to die',[86] and although Adama symbolically 'dies' through his breakdown, Lee continues to act exactly as his father would do. In a deleted scene from early in the episode, he asks Adama to 'back my play the way you would Roslin's', appealing to his love and respect for the President. Later, after Adama's collapse, Lee puts Tigh in an airlock because he knows this is the strategy Adama would pursue, were he not letting the personal interfere with the professional. He forgets about the danger the rescue plan poses to the civilian Fleet until too late, not even telling the Fleet to spool up before he attempts his gambit with airlocking the Four, because he is unwittingly playing along with his father's suicide plan. Although Lee only stops emulating his father once Starbuck tells him about the signal, when he does so, he instead becomes someone acting for 'a higher power'. In spite of what the writers may say, Lee never actually stands on his own two feet at any point in the story, but is always an agent for someone else.

Starting Over Again: God's Plan B

In this episode, we see the fulfilment, in part, of God's plan. After the disaster at the Ionian Nebula, God is now salvaging the situation, in a way summed up by Starbuck: 'I vanish into a storm, ride this Viper to Earth. Coming back, I get a vision that leads me to the baseship. Its Hybrid tells me that the Final Five Cylons have been to Earth, but we need the missing Three, D'Anna, to bring them out into the open ... Like or not, Lee, something's orchestrating this for a purpose ... Call it whatever you want, but it seems to want us to find Earth with the Cylons'.

However, the initial plan was not to take them to nuclear-devastated Earth, even though this is the place the Final Five came from and the home of the Thirteenth Tribe. This is evident because the Fleet, following Pythia, are heading toward it, but Starbuck, when she returns in 'Crossroads', wants to take them in a different direction. The plan changes for a number of reasons. First, the idea of bringing the humans and Cylons together was falling apart under the standoff described above. Although God believed that revealing the identities of the Final Five would cause the humans to rethink their attitude toward Cylons, instead it causes them to rethink their attitude to the Final Five, as Lee is perfectly happy to airlock not just Tigh but Tyrol and Anders as well. To prevent the situation from deteriorating, something must be found that will unite them in a common cause. Secondly, and more crucially, the united Fleet cannot go to the second Earth straightaway, as there is a sizable faction of Cavil's forces intent on tracking them down, and he will do so, particularly if he still has a spy on board as implied in 'The Hub'. The reason Adama rejects Lee's suggestion that they

---

86 Starbuck states that Leoben told her this 'when he was holding me in that dollhouse on New Caprica'; however, Leoben never says this on screen. Doral, in 'Bastille Day', does make a similar observation after Caprica-Six refers to Cylons as 'humanity's children'.

should first reconnoitre the planet is clearly down to fatalism. Earth may welcome them, or it may be their destruction, but either way, they have no choice in the matter.

On a Mission from God: Continuity and Worldbuilding

Among the Cylons, we learn that the Final Five visibly grow older, through Adama's exchange with Tigh: 'When I met you, you had hair. I never heard of a Cylon aging'. 'Doesn't mean they don't ... Turns out there's another kind of Cylon we didn't know about'. Tyrol smiles when the Marines come to arrest him, when he is placed in the launch tube, and again when he sees the devastated Earth, as if he views the whole thing as a cosmic joke. Although Leoben goes along with D'Anna's plan, he is not happy about it, indicating yet another division among the rebels. Current Deck Chief Laird makes his first on-screen appearance since 'Resurrection Ship', and (in a scene that, like the ones of the cheering workers on the *Hitei Kan*, had been recorded for 'Dirty Hands') Figurski is kissed by a female deckhand when the Fleet reaches Earth. A key development comes when Lee states, 'All this has happened before, but it doesn't have to happen again', acknowledging that humans and Cylons have agency, and can break the cycle of violence.

Gaeta says that the 'visible constellations [around Earth] are a match', presumably referring to the ones from 'Home' and 'He That Believeth in Me'. The ruined dome in which the landing party stand is a match for the Temple of Aurora in Pythia's prophecy of Earth, and also recalls the opera house on Kobol. The connection with Aurora again links Starbuck with the goddess, and the devastated state of the planet is in keeping with her status as the harbinger of death.

In continuity terms, Tigh's exclamation about his Cylon nature, 'It is not a delusion, it is not a chip in my head', alludes to Baltar's initial rationalisations for the presence of Head Six. The line was suggested by Michael Rymer; the dummy ending of 'Crossroads' part two, which was also directed by Rymer, had Tigh believing that the Cylons had placed a chip in his head. The airlock scene has three members of the Circle facing the same treatment they were meting out to suspected collaborators. Athena has been released from the brig, clearly because she is willing to share her inside knowledge of Cylon tactics, and, furthermore, because her shooting of Natalie is retrospectively no longer a crime. At the end of the episode, Caprica-Six has also been released, evidently as part of the general amnesty. According to sound editor Daniel Colman, the Colonial signal that Starbuck's Viper is picking up is beating out the rhythm to 'All Along the Watchtower'. The standoff between Lee and D'Anna seems loosely based on the Cuban missile crisis, with Lee as a Kennedy figure, picking up on Michael Taylor's reference in '*Sine Qua Non*' that Lee has a JFK haircut. Adama's drunken rage is yet another *Apocalypse Now* reference, with him punching his mirror as Willard does near the beginning of the film.

60: REVELATIONS

Breaking the Deadlock: Writing and Production

This episode is another one that was partly developed in the writers' retreat, with the intention that it should be a mid-season cliffhanger. Weddle and Thompson wrote the story as a standoff between humans and Cylons; when Michael Rymer complained that this was too reminiscent of 'The Eye of Jupiter' and 'Rapture', they decided to make a virtue of this, and make it the incident where the pattern breaks. Although the revelation about the Viper was always intended to be the event that ended the deadlock, the writers explain in the podcast that in the original version, 'Lee didn't have a point of view about it all. Lee didn't make the speech that he does at the end... that we've done this over and over again and here's an opportunity to not do it again'. Moore acknowledges in the podcast that it took the writing team a long time to get to grips with Lee, saying: 'The character is searching, hunting, never quite figuring out who he is, what he wanted to do. There's a lot of blind alleys he goes down because we were going down blind alleys with him ... as writers, but here it all kind of comes together'.

According to the podcast, the episode was originally to have started with the Four hearing the music and having a discussion about how they are all in key positions within the Fleet, and Tory saying, 'We have the power to bring the Fleet to its knees'. There was also, later, a storyline in which Helo was going to be the first human thrown out the airlock but the Eights objected. Another ultimately abandoned plot thread had the Cylons trying to discuss Earth with Tory, expecting her to have information about it, where, in Thompson's words, Tory was 'vamping it', temporising and telling them the planet might not be what they expect. A version of the scene where Roslin learns about Tory's identity was shot in which Roslin burst out laughing. Editor Jude Ramsay says in the podcast that this was cut because it seemed cruel, and also made it look like Tory's subsequent actions stemmed from this reaction rather than from a sense of grievance that had been building up for a long time. Adama had a line about Tigh, 'I knew, I knew for months, but I didn't want to face it', which was presumably cut as it raises the question of why he put Tigh in charge of the Fleet in '*Sine Qua Non*'. Originally Kara was to have kissed Anders on learning he is a Cylon, as if this knowledge suddenly puts him into focus for her; but, according to the podcast, on the day, the two actors did not feel this was the right reaction.

The Earth sequences were filmed on Centennial Beach in Tsawwassen, south of Vancouver. The three-minute-long scene that closes the episode was shot in a single pan, at the same time as material for the next episode, 'Sometimes a Great Notion', was being recorded. Dialogue was written for the scene, but it was decided to leave it out in favour of the characters' silent reactions. Moore notes that the original version of the skyline 'felt much more like Manhattan, and I didn't want so many of the buildings, I wanted a much older sense of ruin'. Jude Ramsay, in the podcast, says that the editors discussed the possibility of the series not being renewed and agreed that if it wasn't, they would not show the nuclear devastation, but instead 'shoot a little scene with, you know, them down on the planet being happy'. Moore, however, was on this occasion uncompromisingly in favour of leaving the ending as it was; in the podcast, he says that he didn't want the Sci-Fi Channel to put 'To Be Continued' at the end of the episode, explaining, 'Even saying "To be continued" lets out the hope of, oh well, okay, something better will happen next week'. 'Revelations' was given an advance screening in Los Angeles on Wednesday 11 June 2008, in order to draw attention to the upcoming Emmy Award nominations. *Battlestar Galactica* was nominated in five categories, and won two, both for visual effects.

The myths and legends about Earth had the power to bring both humans and Cylons to the point where they were prepared to commit terrible acts for a planet they knew nothing about, but also the power to unite the two factions and bring them together despite everything that has happened. However, Roslin and Adama, for the past three and a half seasons, have used the ideal of Earth as a means of justifying a violent and repressively authoritarian regime. The fact that this course has taken them not to a Utopia, but to a nuclear-devastated planet, is a fitting reward.

61: Sometimes a Great Notion

FIRST TRANSMISSION DATE: 16 January 2009

WRITERS: David Weddle & Bradley Thompson

DIRECTOR: Michael Nankin

CREDITED CAST: (Lucy Lawless (D'Anna); Callum Keith Rennie (Leoben); Rekha Sharma (Tory Foster); Kate Vernon (Ellen Tigh); Brad Dryborough (Hoshi); Jennifer Halley (Seelix); Don Thompson (Specialist 3rd Class Anthony Figurski); Alexandra Thomas (Hera); Sonja Bennett (Specialist 2nd Class Marcie Brasko)

STUNTS: Ellen Field (Ellen Tigh Stunt Double); James Bamford (Stunt Pilot #1); Kit Mallett (Stunt Pilot #2)

SYNOPSIS: The Fleet investigates Earth. They learn that the nuclear holocaust took place about 2,000 years earlier, and that the Thirteenth Tribe were, in fact, Cylons. The Four all experience visions and memories that tell them that they themselves lived on Earth before its destruction. Kara, tracking down the source of the signal that led them there, finds the wreckage of her own Viper, containing her own corpse. She builds a pyre and cremates her body. Roslin abdicates responsibility, ceasing her doloxan treatments and burning her copy of Pythia. Dualla and Lee go out for a drink together, following which Dualla shoots herself. Adama, affected by Roslin's behaviour and Dualla's death, becomes suicidal, but rallies after a confrontation with Tigh. Adama announces that he will lead the Fleet to a new home. On Earth, D'Anna tells Tigh that she wishes to remain behind and die in the home of the Thirteenth Tribe. Tigh experiences a vision in which he learns that the Fifth Cylon is his wife, Ellen.

ANALYSIS: The key to 'Sometimes a Great Notion' lies in a story Adama tells about hunting foxes with his uncle. When the foxes were cornered at the river, 'half would turn and fight. The other half would try to swim across. But my uncle told me about a few that – they'd swim halfway out, turn with the current, and ride it all the way out to sea. Fishermen would find them a mile offshore, just swimming'. Tigh replies, 'because they wanted to drown', and Adama says, 'maybe. Or maybe they were just tired'. Like the foxes, the Fleet are reacting to a crisis in different ways: some giving up, some reverting to familiar behaviour patterns, and others trying something totally different.

After the Flood: Reactions to Prophecy

The discovery of Earth means the characters must reconsider Pythia in light of the outcome of their journey. The prophecy appears, at this juncture, to have failed: although they have journeyed to the home of the Thirteenth Tribe, it is not a 'new homeland', and Roslin, despite her identification with the prophecy of the dying leader, is still alive. There are two reasons why prophecies do not come true. One is that they are conditional prophecies, such that they are fulfilled only if particular conditions are met. This is clearly what Baltar chooses to believe. In a deleted scene in which he addresses his flock, his message is that 'God does not bestow his gifts arbitrarily', that 'paradise has to be earned', and that the Fleet have more trials to endure, but that the people who live through this will have 'proven themselves worthy to enter the promised land'.

The other possibility is that the prophecies have been wrongly, or selectively, interpreted. The historical Pythia was the priestess at Delphi in ancient Greece, whose prophecies often had dual, even opposite, meanings. Within *Battlestar Galactica*, the audience have heard only a few direct quotes and paraphrases from the book of Pythia. We do not know what Pythia says in its entirety, and are largely dependent on the characters' interpretations; indeed, as the scroll Gaeta uses in 'Torn' is in a foreign language, it is also likely that we are hearing it in translation as well. The prophecy of the dying leader in particular is never directly quoted: in 'The Hand of God', Elosha says that Pythia 'wrote that the leader suffered a wasting disease and would not live to enter the new land', and in 'Fragged', Quorum delegate Porter states, 'The scrolls tell us that a dying leader will lead us to salvation', while her fellow Gemenon Corporal Venner reports, 'Pythia foretold the rise of a leader. A leader who would lead all humanity to salvation'. However, precisely what Pythia herself has to say is unknown.

In cases where people are desperate for hope, they may interpret such a prophecy in ways that make sense under their circumstances. If Roslin's interpretation of Pythia, as articulated through the first three seasons, is correct, then it gives significance to her life and death, justifies her decisions, and has the promise of a happy future for the people of the Fleet. Because she was so certain in her interpretations, everyone else in the Fleet was forced to buy into them, particularly as she became more autocratic, backed up with military force from Adama. However, the planet she has led them to is a nuclear wasteland.

The characters' reactions fall into three categories. Roslin's attitude to prophecy has been all or nothing, and so when things do not turn out as she expected, she abdicates responsibility, burns her copy of Pythia, refuses her cancer treatments and curls up on the floor of Adama's quarters in the foetal position, clutching the plant she found on the surface of Earth. She does not have the flexibility to consider that she, or Elosha, may have selectively interpreted the prophecy. This response also informs Dualla's suicide; having spent so long in the certainty that they were heading to the promised land, she cannot cope with the reality. Baltar, in a deleted scene, quotes official figures stating that there have been 14 suicides on the Fleet so far. Roslin's solution to the Fleet's problem is, essentially, death.

Leoben, on the other hand, does not reject the prophecies, but decides that his interpretation of them was completely wrong; that he has been following not an angel, but a demon. He does not want to know the truth about what happened to Kara's Viper, saying, 'Maybe it's better off not knowing … I've got a feeling you might not like what you find'. When he sees the wreckage of the craft, he stammers, 'I was wrong. About Earth', and runs away; we never see this Leoben in the series again. Like Laura, he believed his actions were justified because he was right; when he learns that he was wrong, he must rethink everything he has done up to this point.[87] Moore, in the podcast, describes Leoben as 'the demon and the guide and the fellow traveller on her journey who knew more than [Kara] did'; his role is now revealed to have been more demon than guide.

Lee takes a different tack, making a speech to the Quorum that runs, in part, 'We can either view this as a catastrophe or an opportunity … I choose the latter. We are no longer enslaved by the ramblings of Pythia, no longer pecking at the breadcrumbs of the Thirteenth Tribe. We are now free to go where we want to go and be who we want to be'. He tacitly attacks Roslin's leadership, but offers the freedom to make their own choices. As in the previous episode, Lee believes salvation is achieved through the rejection of the old ways of thinking; and the recognition that Earth is a nuclear wasteland encourages this. While a more positive attitude, this approach is also a frightening one, offering an already terrified people a leap into the unknown.

Adama's response, finally, is to fall back on what he already knows. Making a speech to the Fleet about the Thirteen Tribes striking out into the void, looking for new worlds to live on, he reminds them that, as it were, all this has happened before. This offers the possibility that the Fleet, like the Tribes before them, can indeed find a new place to live. However, this plan has failed them once. D'Anna's reaction to it is to say:

> 'No, I'm not going. You know, all this is just gonna happen again and again and again, so I'm getting off this merry-go-round. I'm going to die here with the bones of my ancestors, and it beats the hell out of being out there with Cavil. Gonna die in the cold and the dark when Cavil catches up with us'.

Although Adama is articulating a practical solution, which is grounded in historical precedent, it is possible, indeed likely, that many on the Fleet will not feel like it offers much in the way of hope for the future.

---

87 SPOILER SECTION: The question remains of why, if God intended the Fleet to go to new Earth, as in 'Daybreak', Kara's Viper should be found on nuclear Earth. While no direct explanation is given in the series, the most likely scenario is that God was trying to work around and subvert the prophecy that Kara is the harbinger of death, by having her die on the devastated planet. However, as will be made clear at the end of 'Daybreak', even God cannot subvert the action of Fate.

BY YOUR COMMAND: VOL 2

Assignment Earth: Reinterpreting the Battlestar Galactica Universe

A significant development in this episode comes when the Thirteenth Colony, with whom the Fleet have been identifying for three seasons, are revealed to have been Cylons. Caprica-Six says that they have tested the skeletons 'using our protocols', meaning that they have reached this conclusion using the Cylons' own methods for identifying a human-like Cylon. While we never learn what caused the nuclear war on Earth, Jane Espenson, in an interview with Maureen Ryan of the *Chicago Tribune*, said: 'The skinjob-style Cylons on Earth built their own metal battlebots who turned on them', showing both factions conclusively that the Cylons are capable of repeating exactly the same sequence of events as the humans who created them.

Another key incident comes in the deleted scene of Baltar's sermon. When Caprica-Six joins the crowd, the audience are disturbed; Baltar rebukes his followers, saying, 'The fact that there have been Cylons in the highest ranks of our government, up until this very moment, should say something to you … We are all the same in God's eyes'. The revelation of the identity of the Four is consequently, as God intended, causing a rethinking of human-Cylon relations in some quarters. When Paulla exclaims, 'She's a Cylon', Athena says, 'So am I', and Helo invites Caprica-Six to sit with them. Athena herself is now learning to appreciate her Cylon identity. Although some cultists leave after this exchange, most remain, indicating that attitudes are, gradually, changing on the Fleet.

Finally, a positive note is struck by the way in which Kara's storyline plays out. Starbuck's self-cremation parallels Roslin's burning of Pythia, but, in Kara's case, the act is a cathartic letting go of a negative past. At the pyre, her expression is a peaceful one. When she returns to the Fleet, she goes to Lee, clearly planning to tell him about finding her own corpse, but when she sees he is distressed by something else, she stops and asks him what's wrong. This marks a change in behaviour: rather than focusing only on herself, she now recognises that others may have needs too.

End of the World: Continuity and Worldbuilding

There are a few tantalising revelations in this episode concerning the Final Five. Anders played 'All Along the Watchtower' to the other four on Earth before its devastation, explaining in part why the song is so important to them. Moore says in the podcast, 'I think it was also intended that he wrote it'. Tigh's vision revealing Ellen as the Fifth Cylon comes when he wades out to sea and puts his hands in the water, recalling the Cylon data-stream technology. The connection is foreshadowed in a deleted scene, set before his confrontation with Adama, in which Tigh looks at Ellen's photograph through the liquid in an ambrosia bottle. It is implied, though never stated, that Baltar's Cylon detector did identify Ellen in 'Tigh Me Up, Tigh Me Down'. In 'Rapture', D'Anna says, 'Forgive me, I had no idea', to one of the Final Five, and her next words, directed to Baltar, are 'You were right'. As Moore has said that the Cylon to whom D'Anna spoke was intended to be Ellen, her remark to Baltar implies that he had told her he knew Ellen was a Cylon. Clearly, however, she was the only one in whom he confided, and they had both agreed to keep the information to themselves.

On *Galactica*, we see that two Baltar cultists are drawing the gull symbol on a wall, and that someone else has graffitied 'Frak Earth', showing different reactions within the Fleet to the discovery that the planet is a cinder. Dualla's face is serious as she picks up the gun to kill herself, but her reflection in the mirror is smiling, suggesting she is at peace with her decision. Kara's corpse found in the Viper has retained its blonde hair despite being severely burned, though this is perhaps excusable as a way of indicating its identity. The portrayal of Earth as a radiation-soaked wasteland is dramatic, but unfortunately makes the Caprica sequences of Season One look even more unbelievable in contrast. Equally, the idea that the destruction of Earth took place 2,000 years ago could work with the dates given for the exodus in 'The Eye of Jupiter' (4,000 years ago) or 'A Measure of Salvation' (3,000 years ago), but not with the date given in 'Kobol's Last Gleaming' (2,000 years ago). The main title sequence is omitted from this episode, the names of the principal actors simply appearing over the opening scene.

In terms of outside references, the shadow of Tyrol's former self on the ruined wall resembles those at Hiroshima and Nagasaki. The story's title comes from a novel by Ken Kesey, which opens with a line from the folk song 'Goodnight Irene': 'Sometimes I live in the country. Sometimes I live in the town. Sometimes I get a great notion. To jump in the river and drown'. Weddle, in an interview with Maureen Ryan, elaborates that in the novel, the hero 'does constant battle with the river that runs past his home, a river that has claimed the lives of pets and loved ones and comes to symbolise the vast and indifferent power of the universe that both gives life and cruelly snatches it away again'. The story about the foxes is also, according to Weddle, from this novel: 'I first read about this phenomenon in Ken Kesey's masterpiece, *Sometimes a Great Notion* ... Since reading that book I have come across many other stories about animals doing this'.

Outfoxed: Writing and Production

This episode is another one that was developed at the writers' retreat. Moore, in his podcast, says: 'I wanted the mid-season break to be pretty startling and shocking and get us to Earth at a point where the audience was not expecting us to get there ... The idea [in 'Sometimes a Great Notion'] was to say to these people and to the audience, what happens when you take the fondest dream away from all these characters? ... Most importantly, I wanted the people at the top to lose faith'. There was a lot of discussion amongst the writers as to the backstory of the Thirteenth Tribe, which Moore describes as follows: 'Man ... on the planet of Kobol, stole fire from the gods ... and that fire was the knowledge of life and how to create life, and they created their own Cylons. And it was that creation and the destruction of paradise that was the end of Kobol ... And then at some point, people on Earth, the Cylons on Earth, repeated the pattern and destroyed themselves as well. So this feeds into the overall "All this has happened before and all this will happen again" mythology of the show'.

Weddle, in an interview with Maureen Ryan, recalls another issue that was discussed: 'Should the [F]leet find a ray of hope by the episode's end? Another piece of prophecy in Pythia; a vision, or a clue among the ruins that would send them on another leg of their journey? Brad and I did not want to do that'. He and Thompson wrote this episode back to back with the previous one. Thompson, in the same interview, says that their original draft was very effects-heavy, including detailed and involved flashbacks to the events of the nuclear holocaust. Producer Harvey Frand sent them a note beginning, 'Guys, your script is great. But we seem to be in a financial bind with it. While the studio is willing to go over pattern on this episode, preliminary estimates have us at about two and a half times their limit'. The pair had to rewrite extensively to bring the script back in line with the budget.

The decision to make Ellen the final Cylon was also taken at the writers' retreat, following on from Tigh's selection as a Cylon. Moore, interviewed by Ryan, says, 'I liked ... that there was something deeper to their marriage ... that it was literally a relationship that had transcended time and space'. Regarding Dualla's death, Moore says, 'It felt like not everyone should come back from that. And Dualla was the one that we decided would take the hit here'. There also may have been concerns as to where they could go with the character: Moore admits, 'I think that we mishandled the Dualla-Lee relationship, that we ... didn't quite know what to do with it, we kind of jig-jagged back and forth with it a few too many times'. This is the last episode to feature the 'Seven are known ...' pre-titles sequence.

This was to have been yet another episode with a nonlinear structure, framed by the conversation between Tigh and Adama; however, Michael Nankin opted instead to cut it chronologically, which makes the story much starker. Most of the material of Baltar and his followers was shifted to later episodes. The scene where Dualla comes to babysit for the Agathons, finding them playing raucously with the clearly-unconcerned Hera, was almost cut, but was left in as a way of showing that, even under the worst circumstances, life goes on.

In production terms, the stark grimness of the Earth is well conveyed, with the light filtered so as to give the planet a bleak, washed-out look. The episode was filmed shortly after the writers' strike was called, meaning that the production team were entirely on their own, able to obtain no guidance or changes from the writers. Nankin added a few touches, including Dualla finding the jacks and Roslin holding the plant. The night before filming on the beach location was to begin, the set was devastated by a storm with 90-kilometre-per-hour winds; however, the next day was sunny, and so the art department reconstructed the set while everyone else did studio work. Nankin, in *The Official Companion Season Four*, is quoted as saying: 'By Wednesday morning 90 percent of it was there. But 90 percent of ruins pretty much looks like 100 percent of ruins!' The tune Kandyse McClure hums as Dualla puts her jewellery away was improvised, but Nankin asked Bear McCreary to work it into his score, and it can be heard in Dualla's scenes leading up to and following her death.

'Sometimes a Great Notion' opens the second half of the season with the Fleet at what appears to be its lowest emotional point. However, although it seems as if nothing can get worse for the characters, the subsequent episodes demonstrate that indeed it can, and will.

62: The Face of the Enemy

FIRST TRANSMISSION DATE: 2 December 2008 through to 12 January 2009 (USA)

WRITTEN BY: Jane Espenson and Seamus Kevin Fahey

DIRECTOR: Wayne Rose

CREDITED CAST: Brad Dryborough (Hoshi); Leah Cairns (Racetrack); Michael Rogers (Brooks); Jessica Harmon (Esrin); William C Vaughn (Finn); James Callis (Gaius Baltar)

SYNOPSIS: Gaeta is suffering from fatigue, and Tigh orders him to take leave on the *Zephyr*. As Gaeta travels over in the shuttle, accompanied by two Eights, deckhand Brooks and pilots 'Shark' Finnegan and 'Easy' Esrin, the Fleet makes an emergency jump. The shuttle goes to the wrong coordinates, and is lost. At minimal oxygen levels, the crew has only 20.25 hours to live. Brooks offers to look at the CO2 scrubbers to see if he can extend the air supply. One Eight tries to help him and is electrocuted as someone has deliberately stripped the insulation from the pliers. Gaeta discovers the other Eight is one he knew on New Caprica. They were lovers, and he would provide her with the names of missing resistance members believed to be in custody, whom she would then get released. Brooks dies of an overdose from Gaeta's stash of morpha, and the pilots accuse Eight of his murder and shackle her. Later, Gaeta wakes to find that both pilots are apparently asleep and the Eight has freed herself. Gaeta helps her hook up to the Raptor's systems through inserting a data cable into her hand. She finds the Fleet's last position and jumps the ship, but on arriving, they discover that the Fleet has moved on and is now out of the Raptor's DRADIS range. Gaeta then finds that Esrin and Finnegan have been killed. He comes to realise that the Eight murdered the others, which she confirms, and also that she passed on his information as to the identities of resistance members to the Cylon administration, leading to most of them being executed, with a few left alive to cover the deception. Gaeta kills Eight with a scalpel, and attempts to kill himself with an overdose of morpha, but then his ship is found by Racetrack and Hoshi, Gaeta's current lover. Back on *Galactica*, Gaeta expresses his belief that there should be no human-Cylon alliance, and requests to meet with the Admiral directly.

ANALYSIS: The webisodes comprising 'The Face of the Enemy' were released during the season break after 'Revelations', but the story is set between

'Sometimes a Great Notion' and 'A Disquiet Follows My Soul'. It is therefore best considered at this point in the series' ongoing narrative.

Not Rolling the Hard Eight: Gaeta and Sweet Eight

According to Espenson, the story was written in part to explain 'one of the show's remaining open mysteries', regarding what Baltar whispered to Gaeta in 'Taking a Break from All Your Worries'. This was originally to have involved Gaeta's complicity in the massacre of Sagittarons; in the webisodes, it is revealed that Baltar said, 'I know what your Eight did'. The story draws implicit parallels between Gaeta's behaviour on New Caprica and Baltar's guilt in the destruction of the Colonies; Espenson originally wrote Sweet Eight[88] as a Six, making the comparison more obvious and suggesting a continuous *modus operandi* on the part of the Sixes. Like Baltar, Gaeta was involved in a relationship with a female Cylon, who used him to commit acts of mass murder, and then told him that he knew all along what she was doing but blinded himself to her actions. There are, however, significant differences. In Baltar's case, Caprica-Six accused him in order to salve her own conscience; later, in 'Downloaded' and in 'Escape Velocity', she admitted her own guilt and ceased blaming him. Whatever mental gymnastics Baltar goes through, it is very unlikely that he could have understood what Caprica-Six was planning; indeed, had he been consciously aware of her activities, he would not have remained complicit. In Gaeta's case, Sweet Eight is not trying to make excuses for herself, and he could not have been unaware of the likelihood that she was sleeping with him to gain information about the resistance.

The problem is that, in retroactively changing the scene from 'Taking a Break From All Your Worries', Espenson is damning Baltar as well as Gaeta. If Baltar knew Gaeta was passing information about resistance members to Sweet Eight, and yet did nothing about it, then he too is complicit in their subsequent deaths. Baltar then goes from being a man who, as established in 'Crossroads', was guilty of nothing more on New Caprica than complying with an oppressive regime, to being someone who actively helped that regime to murder resistance members. Ironically, then, a scene originally intended to lead to Baltar's exoneration at his trial, retroactively condemns him.

Missing in Action: Gaeta on the Raptor

The Raptor accident that forms the core of the storyline serves as a parallel to the events on New Caprica. When Gaeta learns that Sweet Eight murdered the others, she says, 'Felix, I picked you, over my own kind, over my own model. I protected you from something you never could have done, but you were

---

[88] Espenson, in the script, distinguished the two Eights by calling the one in civilian clothes 'Sweet Eight' and the one in the Cylon flightsuit 'Hard Eight', though she also refers to the latter in her podcast commentary as 'Pilot Eight'.

thinking all along'. Although this casts Sweet Eight in the role of the murderer who lets one victim go as a power trip and as a form of self-exoneration, this must be a ploy; she cannot use the death of Hard Eight as evidence in support of her position, as, if it was a murder attempt (since it is just about plausible that the insulating rubber could have worn off the pliers rather than being deliberately removed), she was clearly not the intended target, as she only volunteers to help when Brooks fails to fix the broken scrubber. Her words make it clear that, although Gaeta can't bring himself to commit the murders personally, he is capable of turning a blind eye while someone else does so on his behalf. On New Caprica, he was in danger of being killed by both sides. Not only was his passing information on to the resistance a form of insurance, but, if the Cylons approached him as a source of information, meaning that they knew he had resistance connections, collaborating with them was also a means of keeping himself alive. Sweet Eight draws the parallel when she says, 'I'm not a monster … You kill when you're in a war, you kill when you have to … It's basic'. Gaeta, in some ways, is like Boomer in Season One, in that both retain their sanity by compartmentalising their actions; however, Boomer was programmed to do so, and Gaeta is actively living in denial.

The presentation of Gaeta as an idealist betrayed also figures strongly in these webisodes. Hoshi says, 'He's got this … this fire about doing the right thing', and Racetrack adds, 'A moral core, huh?' We know from episodes such as 'Unfinished Business' that Gaeta initially bought into the New Caprica project out of idealism. However, it is easy to have such ideals when things are going well, but not when basic survival is at stake. A failure to acknowledge this can cause a schism, as with Gaeta convincing himself that, when he passed information on to Sweet Eight, he was innocently trying to save resistance members. There is a lot of obvious symbolism in the webisodes, for instance Gaeta taking morpha to numb his pain, and, when he touches the dead pilots, literally having their blood on his hands. After he is forced to confront the truth, he murders Sweet Eight, and then deliberately opposes the human-Cylon alliance, another project born of idealism. At the end of the webisodes, he projects his guilt onto the Cylons, saying that they aren't trustworthy, when in fact he is the one who has turned a blind eye to horrific things and then blamed others when the truth was exposed.

Lost at Sea: Continuity and Worldbuilding

We learn in these webisodes that the *Zephyr* has taken over *Cloud 9*'s role as the Fleet's R&R destination. The presence of Cylons is now accepted in the Fleet, albeit not without an undercurrent of racism on the part of the humans. Raptors do carry enough flightsuits for passengers as well as crew; the fact that these are not worn at all times as a safety measure can be put down to lax discipline. Brooks has a Poseidon medallion to ensure his safety when travelling, like a Colonial version of a St Christopher. Gaeta is ordered on leave out of Tigh's concern that he is so exhausted that he is 'on the verge of seeing ghosts on the

DRADIS screen'; the person who replaces him sounds a false alarm and causes the Fleet to jump away, suggesting that he is not the only one. The fact that the personnel on the Raptor are suffering from oxygen deprivation exacerbates tensions on the ship, in a tacit call-back to '33' and its exploration of how physical strain combines with mental strain to make an already difficult situation worse. Shark is the second crewmember to take this callsign; the other appears in 'The Captain's Hand'.

The webisodes elaborate on same-sex relationships in the Colonies. There is a hint of institutionalised prejudice against gay couples, as a conversation between Racetrack and Hoshi appears to imply that Gaeta saw his attraction to Hoshi as morally wrong at first. Hoshi does not make Tigh directly aware that he and Gaeta are lovers, and Tigh seems rather nonplussed when he figures out Hoshi's euphemisms. However, this prejudice is not universally shared, as Hoshi and Gaeta kiss openly on *Galactica*, Hoshi holds Gaeta's hand when he is taken to sickbay, and Racetrack seems happy that they are in a relationship.[89] She says, 'I was making book on that since, like, forever', indicating that other pilots also knew and had no problem with it. The story's portrayal of gay relationships is an improvement over 'Razor', in that Hoshi is a decent man and his love for Gaeta is shown as a saving one, contrasted with the corrupting love Gaeta experienced with Sweet Eight. At the end of the story, Gaeta keeps Hoshi ignorant of his plans in order, he says, to protect him, in a reversal of how Sweet Eight destroyed Gaeta by making him consciously acknowledge what he did. However, we have seen only two same-sex couples in the Fleet, Gaeta and Hoshi and Cain and Gina, and neither is identified as such within the main story, only in webisodes and spin-off stories. Gaeta, also, follows up his same-sex relationship with a mutiny, buying into the unfortunate fictional trope of the doomed gay relationship.

The decision to jettison Hard Eight's corpse is impractical since, if the only problem with having it on board is that it would produce 'methane and hydrogen sulphide', the crew would be better off sealing it in a flightsuit rather than losing air through throwing it out of the Raptor. The writers' decision to kill Hard Eight was taken to minimise the difficulty and expense of split-screen filming, but sealing the corpse in a flightsuit would also have disguised its identity and obviated the need for such effects. The song Gaeta sings is a reprise of 'Gaeta's Lament' from 'Guess What's Coming to Dinner', with the lines 'But wish no more, my life you can take, to have her please just one day wake' expressing his confusion and remorse over killing Sweet Eight. The Red Line is defined in the series bible as being the point past which information about the celestial bodies at the vessel's destination is sufficiently out of date that it is dangerous for the ship to make the jump. As the Fleet passed that point in the miniseries, here it refers more generally to uncharted and unknown space.

---

89 *Caprica* also indicates that pre-Fall Caprican society practiced same-sex marriage; there is a possible implication that Colonial society has become more homophobic in the intervening 58 years.

The list of names that Gaeta gives to Sweet Eight on New Caprica contains those of a number of series crewmembers, including assistant director Stacy Fish, camera operator Kevin Hall, make-up artist Shauna Magrath and director Wayne Rose. The name 'Hitchcock' also appears, perhaps acknowledging that, as Fahey is quoted as saying in *The Official Companion Season Four*, the story is inspired by Alfred Hitchcock's film *Lifeboat* (1944), a psychological thriller about a mixed group of American, British and German survivors of a battle at sea thrown together in a single lifeboat. The webisodes also bear a resemblance to John Wyndham's short story 'Survival', about a space mission that goes adrift, following which a seemingly sweet-natured woman passenger first manipulates the crew into protecting her and then resorts to murder to ensure her own survival and that of her child.

Piecing It Together: Writing and Production

According to *The Official Companion Season Four*, originally Fahey and Espenson planned to do a story that, while it involved a Raptor mission going wrong, avoided all the ongoing narratives in the series. At Moore's suggestion, they instead wrote a story that connected with the upcoming arcs in the second half of Season Four. As with 'The Resistance'/'Crossroads', content was largely dictated by which actors and/or sets were available. The fact that Olmos was busy working on 'Daybreak' and 'The Plan' meant that the scenes originally meant for Adama went to Colonel Tigh, adding the twist that the superior officer to whom Gaeta reports is a Cylon. According to Espenson's commentary, 'Our first thought was that we would have both Trish and Grace … By webisode seven or eight … the characters who were left alive on the ship were the two Cylons – the Six and the Eight – and Gaeta, and there was a whole webisode in which Gaeta was asleep and it was just Six and Eight talking about the murders they had committed on board … When we realised that we didn't have both actresses, at first we thought … we were going to have two Sixes. Later on, we realised we didn't have Trish; we did have Grace; we had two Eights'.

The webisodes were written as 'ten little scripts', according to Espenson's commentary, rather than as 'a 30 page script [that] I artificially went through later and put in the act breaks'. Originally Baltar was to have said, 'Do you know what your Eight did?' in the overdubbed clip from 'Taking a Break from All Your Worries', rather than 'I know what your Eight did', but Espenson asserts in her commentary that the latter version is stronger. She also says that a line where Sweet Eight observes that humans can delude themselves but Cylon brains record only the truth, was changed when Grace Park pointed out that Eights tend to be rather self-deluding.

The decision to make Gaeta and Hoshi a couple came about, according to Espenson, when director Wayne Rose 'pointed out that he was having a very hard time scheduling these scenes because we were spending so much time on that one set, the Raptor, and [said] wouldn't it be interesting if we could cut back to some other location'. Rose suggested writing in a subplot about someone

62: THE FACE OF THE ENEMY

looking for Gaeta. Initially Espenson thought of making Viper pilot Narcho Gaeta's lover[90], but, as actor Sebastian Spence was unavailable, Hoshi was used instead. A further motivation for this was that many fans had already begun thinking of Gaeta as a gay character, in part due to a scene in the widely-circulated Season Three gag reel in which Alessandro Juliani, in an outtake from 'Taking a Break from All Your Worries', tells the Marine guarding the brig that he has lovely eyes. Espenson recalls: 'We wrote this script in which we revealed that he'd had this affair back on New Caprica, this relationship with a female Cylon … and it always felt to me that it could be seen as a sort of a slap at the people who had assumed Gaeta was gay'. She therefore decided to make Gaeta bisexual, with his more positive relationship being with another man. The studio objected to only one aspect of this development, the fact that as originally scripted Hoshi called Gaeta 'darling' (which they described as 'too Brokeback'); they were happy after Espenson changed the term to 'baby' instead.

The production was complicated by the fact that the webisodes were being filmed at the same time as 'Daybreak' and 'The Plan', and that after filming on each set was completed, it was torn down, meaning the webisode crew had only limited access to the *Galactica* sets. According to *The Official Companion Season Four*, the webisodes have the honour of containing the last scenes shot on these sets. The webisode crew also had to share a camera with the main unit. There was not enough time to do a separate casting session for the pilots and Brooks, so actors were chosen using audition tapes for the roles of Coach and two Pyramid players from 'The Plan'. Although Espenson says she wrote the scene where Hard Eight's corpse is jettisoned deliberately so as to avoid the use of special effects, Rose managed to work in a small CGI sequence of the ejection into space.

The webisodes were initially released only for viewing in North America and, at the time of writing, the sole other official release has been on the 2013 Japanese Blu-Ray edition of Season 4, although they continue to be widely bootlegged. They were nominated for an Emmy and won 2009 Streamy Awards for Best Dramatic Web Series, Best Writing for a Dramatic Web Series and Best Male Actor in a Dramatic Web Series (Alessandro Juliani).

Although the webisodes fit well with Gaeta's established character, and set up an additional motivation for his actions in the second half of Season Four, by linking the story back to the events of 'Taking a Break from All Your Worries', they also do serious damage to the character of Baltar, making him retrospectively complicit in mass murder.

---

90 SPOILER SECTION: Narcho will be one of the main figures on the side of Gaeta and Zarek during the forthcoming mutiny.

63: A Disquiet Follows My Soul

FIRST TRANSMISSION DATE: 23 January 2009 (USA/CANADA)

WRITER: Ronald D Moore

DIRECTOR: Ronald D Moore

CREDITED CAST: Richard Hatch (Zarek); Donnelly Rhodes (Doctor Cottle); Bodie Olmos (Hot Dog); Keegan Connor Tracy (Jeanne); Kerry Norton (Medic Layne Ishay); Brad Dryborough (Hoshi); Christina Schild (Playa Palacios); Biski Gugushe (Sekou Hamilton); Lara Gilchrist (Paulla Schaffer); Finn R Devitt (Baby Nicky); Don Thompson (SP3 Anthony Figurski); Donna Soares (Speaking Delegate #1); Andrew McIlroy (Jacob Cantrell); Judith Maxie (Picon Delegate); Marilyn Norry (Reza Chronides); Veena Sood (Quorum Delegate)

STUNTS: Chad Sayn (Stunt Acolyte); Kim Howie (Stunt Pilot); Trevor Jones (Stunt Enlisted); Brad Kelly (Stunt Mechanic)

KNOWN UNCREDITED CAST: Leo Li Chiang (Tattooed Pilot); Hector Johnson (Marine Lieutenant); Robin Moore (Child Member of the Cult of Baltar); Roxy Moore (Child Member of the Cult of Baltar)

SYNOPSIS: As the Fleet leaves Earth, its leaders debate whether or not to make the alliance with the rebel Cylons permanent. Zarek is opposed to it, on the grounds that the Cylons are the enemy, but the Cylons wish to remain in the alliance as it provides them with protection against Cavil. Roslin continues to refuse treatment, and also refuses to act as President. The upgrading of all FTL drives to more powerful Cylon-based versions is proposed, in exchange for allowing the Cylons to join the Fleet. When the Quorum vetoes the motion, Adama tries to enforce the upgrade on the grounds that it is a military decision, but certain ship's captains, encouraged by Zarek, refuse. The tylium refinery *Hitei Kan* mutinies, jumping away from the Fleet, and Adama orders Zarek's arrest. He manipulates Zarek into revealing the location of the *Hitei Kan*, insinuating that he knows about Zarek's less-than-legal political activities. Nicky Tyrol suffers renal failure. When Tyrol offers to donate blood for him, Cottle reveals that Nicky is in fact Hot Dog's biological child. Tyrol gets into a fight with Hot Dog, but the two eventually agree to co-parent Nicky for the time being. Zarek meets with Gaeta and together they plan a *coup d'etat*.

63: A DISQUIET FOLLOWS MY SOUL

ANALYSIS: 'A Disquiet Follows My Soul' marks the start of the mutiny arc, setting up the post-Earth situation in the Fleet as one of anger and mistrust, increasingly focused on the rebel Cylons and the Fleet's leaders. Again, we will be using the extended DVD version of this episode as our reference point.

Giving Up and Letting Go: Roslin's Unofficial Resignation

Roslin's abdication of her responsibilities continues in this episode, as, heedless of the social deterioration around her, she throws out her pills and goes jogging. Zarek remarks, 'And where is Laura Roslin? Oh, that's right. "Resting comfortably aboard Galactica." Funny how she kind of dropped out of sight ever since her prophecies about Earth turned out to be a bunch of crap'. Roslin is not only selfish but also inflexible, unable to adapt to her new circumstances. Echoing her speech in 'Unfinished Business', she says she has earned the right to live for herself; however, her actions are the ultimate catalyst for all the chaos that follows. She refuses to act as President, but has not formally resigned nor named a successor, meaning that the only person with the official power to take over her political role is Zarek; but Zarek cannot wield effective power because the military will not support him.

In the absence of Roslin, Adama, true to form, reverts to military dictatorship. While his insistence that the civilian ships accept the Cylon jump drive upgrades makes perfect logical sense, as it triples their chances of finding a habitable planet, he enforces this without discussion and at gunpoint. The objections the civilians have are perfectly understandable, given that the Cylons are responsible for the destruction of the Colonies, and that the alliance is effectively one based on fear of other Cylons. Indeed, only three episodes back, the rebel Cylons were prepared to destroy the civilian Fleet in order to achieve their objectives. When Lee slips up at the press conference and reveals he knows the gender of the Fifth Cylon, it is obvious to everyone that the ordinary people are being kept out of the loop. Moore says of Adama, 'He's willing to let the Fleet go to hell, really, for Laura ... There are places that Adama goes frequently where sometimes ... his gut and his heart will just send him in a different place than his head will, and he will be guided by that'. As before, Adama's behaviour is informed by his feelings about Laura, his personal dislike of Zarek, and his contempt for civilian government.

The elitist ethos of the Fleet can also be seen running through the political storyline. Adama accepts the deal with the rebels in part because it is brokered by Lee. Tyrol, a supporter of the elite, now appears to have taken over as spokesperson for the rebel baseship, and the presence of Marines on the *Hitei Kan* indicates a general lack of trust of the non-elite, making a prophecy of Adama's remark in 'Water' that, when the military starts to take on the role of the police, 'then the enemies of the state tend to become the people'. Furthermore, oppositional characters are only ever given a voice through the elite: we know nothing at all about Zarek, for instance, outside of the points at which his life intersects with those of Roslin, Lee and Adama. The Fleet's oligarchical tendencies are clearly visible, but the audience are expected to sympathise with this elite rather than question or criticise them.

An Accident Waiting to Happen: Gaeta and Zarek

Under the circumstances, the actions Gaeta and Zarek take are perfectly justified. While Zarek has shown in the past that he is happy so long as he has a political voice, but silencing him entirely is dangerous, Adama openly denies him even the pretence of political power. When Zarek says, 'If you try to shove an alliance with the Cylons down their throats there will be consequences, Admiral, I promise you', Adama replies, 'Thank you, Mr Zarek. Makes it a little bit easier to know who to hold responsible if there's an unfortunate incident'. Zarek says, 'I'm not hard to find, Admiral, I'm right here, running the government', and Adama counters, 'For now'. Adama is indicating that not only has he shut Zarek out of the loop on major decisions, but that he intends to take away whatever power he has. Since Zarek is the only one of the Fleet's leaders to have been directly elected, this is a serious blow against democracy.

However, this episode again tries to discredit Zarek's point of view. Adama produces documents about 'the buying and selling of the Vice-President's office', which he describes as 'dirty laundry'. However, this turns out to be literal rather than figurative, as they are laundry reports. Adama has reasoned that all politicians have their corrupt side, and that Zarek could not abide his image being tarnished in the eyes of the public. However, Zarek's pointed comment, 'You know what the difference is between us, Admiral? You wear the uniform, and I don't', reminds the viewer that Zarek is being unfairly treated. We are being asked to condemn Zarek's acts of corruption, while simultaneously giving a pass to questionable behaviour, not only from Adama, but also from Roslin and Lee. The 11 March 2008 script draft goes further, and has Adama accuse Zarek of 'Graft. Bribery. Drug-running. The black market sale of medical supplies. Gambling. Theft. Even a murder or two'. This is a clear reference to the activities of the mafia last seen in 'Black Market', and implies, first, that the military has been less assiduous in cracking down on these activities than Apollo promised, and, secondly, that Roslin has been maintaining her distance from the black market by virtue of having Zarek conduct the necessary activities in this area. The pilot episode for *Caprica* will also establish that Adama came from a family involved with organised crime, explaining his familiarity here with how such things operate. Adama is thus being singularly hypocritical in his treatment of Zarek.

Gaeta, meanwhile, draws attention to a growing problem on the Fleet. Although his grumbling about the Cylons getting priority over him in the sickbay comes across as selfish, as a unique foetus and a toddler with kidney failure are likely to need more urgent attention than someone needing treatment for chapped skin, he is articulating a prejudice that is widely felt and affecting people's view of the alliance. Gaeta chooses to complain to medic Ishay, who, moments earlier, was seen looking distinctly worried as Caprica-Six described her unborn baby as 'the future of the entire Cylon race'; clearly Gaeta expects Ishay to sympathise with his feelings. Gaeta's verbal attack on Starbuck is understandable; although she is no longer the same person who tried to have him thrown out of an airlock, he has no way of knowing this, and the fact that a lot of the pilots stay to listen shows he is not the only one with a grievance.

However, Gaeta, like Zarek, is discredited, in this case retroactively by 'The Face of the Enemy'. Although his anger against the Final Five has its origins in the events of 'Collaborators' and 'Faith', his opposition to allying with the rebel Cylons is given a new context in light of his backstory with Sweet Eight, and suggests instead that he is attacking the Cylons and their allies in order to disguise his own collaboration. While 'The Face of the Enemy' accurately picks up on his characterisation as an idealist betrayed, it makes his later rebellion look like an act of personal retribution by someone who is implicated in mass murder, thus making his actions unjustified.

Gaeta's storyline also picks up on the developing theme of dealing with the past. Starbuck, having burnt her own corpse, is now a new person. Tyrol, likewise, is changing in light of his new Cylon identity. The revelation that Cally had a fling with Hot Dog, and that Nicky is therefore fully human, re-contextualises Tyrol's relationship with the child. His agreement to co-parent Nicky becomes another case of the gulf between human and Cylon being bridged by love, as he teaches Hot Dog about the responsibilities of parenthood. Gaeta, however, is motivated by past grievances, leading him to foment mutiny: he says to Ishay, 'Earth's a cinder, Dee's dead, suicides are up, Fleet's a mess, the President's missing in action, but hey, gotta make sure the Cylons are taken care of'. The fact that the *Hitei Kan* is the first ship to rebel supports the idea that the rebellion is about addressing unresolved issues from the past. The idea of learning from, but letting go of, the past bringing freedom, and clinging to the past bringing conflict, is becoming prominent.

Ye Shall Be as Little Children, Or Worse: Baltar and his Cult

Baltar, meanwhile, is testing the limits of his relationship with God. He has a conversation with Head Six in which she assures him he is 'the instrument [God] uses to speak to the people'; he points out that he could say there is no God, and she states that God would not allow that to happen. Baltar then goes out to the cultists and says that God should be asking their forgiveness, rather than the other way around. This again highlights the fact that God, in this series, has to follow certain rules, one of which is evidently that he can warn and advise, through the Head People, oracles and visions, but cannot actually control people's behaviour. Baltar's speech implies that God is directly responsible for the situation, saying, 'Are you being punished for your multitude of sins? Are you? Is this really our lot? To have been led … to the promised land … only to have paradise cruelly smashed to bits before our very eyes? Are these the actions of a father towards his children?' However, the Fleet are not so much being punished, as borne along by forces outside their control.

When Baltar makes his speech, a fight breaks out in the audience. This is a serendipitous act, as, although the trigger for it is Tyrol seeing Hot Dog and realising that the pilot is Nicky's biological father, Baltar looks pensive when it happens, suggesting that he is thinking about the power his words have and how advocating anger, rather than forgiveness, might inspire his followers to conflict. He muses contemptuously on the fact that his followers do whatever he tells them to, and Head Six pointedly remarks, 'A father's contempt for his children. Isn't that what you were just preaching against?' This picks up on the paternalistic authoritarianism seen elsewhere in this story, but also on the theme of letting go of the past and forgiving. Among the cultists as on the Fleet generally, bad leadership inspires conflict.

Truth and Consequences: Continuity, Writing and Production

In continuity terms, Caprica-Six's pregnancy indicates that the Cylon race can now continue without resurrection technology. Caprica-Six states, 'Our love produced a child', reminding us of the link between love and reproduction for Cylons. The child, according to Cottle, is a boy. Regarding Nicky, Cottle informs Tyrol that he would have helped Cally terminate the pregnancy had she wanted, stating, 'The procedure is illegal, but there are ways around it'. On the political front, Zarek gets in a good dig at Lee's three-season-long career search, observing, 'I get confused what your job is on any given day'. At the opening of the episode, the 'Seven are known ...' pre-titles sequence is not on either version of this story, but the main titles have returned. Again, the *Hitei Kan* is treated as if it were the only tylium ship in the Fleet, with no reference to the second refinery, the *Daru Mozu*.

This episode was Moore's first time directing, in 20 years in the television industry, although he took advice from Director of Photography Steve McNutt. Moore had planned to direct an episode in Season Three but had been prevented from doing so due to time constraints. He says in the extended DVD commentary that he wanted to try directing on a series where he knew the cast and crew. He also took Michael Rymer's advice and wrote the script as well, so as not to be continually having to confer with another writer, and to allow him to work out the blocking and camera angles in his head beforehand. As this was the first episode filmed after the strike, he had a longer period for preparation than was usual. Moore brought the episode in on time and under budget for the most part, which is a source of some pride for him, although he admits that the filming on the cult lair set went two hours over time. The actors contributed a few ad-libs, including Gaeta's 'I guess a pity frak is out of the question?' as Starbuck storms out of the rec-room. Moore says in the podcast that he had written into the script the idea that part of Adama's daily routine was to pick a book off his shelves and read a passage at random, but Olmos's chance selection, an excerpt from Emily Dickinson's poem 'There is a Langour of the Life', worked well in the episode. Adama does not, however, pick out a book in the white production draft, dated 11 March 2008.

63: A DISQUIET FOLLOWS MY SOUL

Unsurprisingly given Moore's involvement as both writer and director, there are few changes between the 11 March draft and the final (extended) version of the episode. One significant difference is that, in the draft, Caprica-Six informs Tigh that the Cylons had 'come to believe it was the lack of ... God's love that prevented us from biological reproduction', adding 'belief in God is something we got from you', evidently meaning the Final Five. Ishay's ambivalent feelings about the Cylons are better highlighted in the draft; for instance, rather than saying, regarding Nicky's parentage, 'His father should know', she says 'His real father should know', dismissing Tyrol's role in parenting the child. In the draft, before leaving Nicky alone with Hot Dog, Tyrol kisses the child and tells him everything will be okay, which he doesn't do in the final version. Adama's confrontation with Zarek begins, in the draft, with Zarek asking if the folder is his execution order, and Adama responding 'No, that'd be a single sheet of paper'. The script continues, 'He lets Zarek wonder for a beat'. The message is clearly that, with Roslin out of the way, Adama would have no need to justify his actions; he could have Zarek executed without amassing evidence to support the decision, and thus only his love for Roslin compels him to maintain any form of democracy in the Fleet. Laird, not Figurski, is the one overseeing the deck in the draft; the change of character was probably due to actor availability.

The subplot about Nicky's parentage came up in the writers' room, because, as Moore puts it, 'We had said very clearly that ... in the mythology of the show, Hera was the only hybrid between human and Cylon, and I didn't want to change that'. As to the father, Moore jokes, 'Figurski was a candidate I really wanted to do for a while, but cooler heads prevailed'[91]; the podcast for 'Daybreak' part one mentions that Narcho was another possibility. According to *The Official Companion Season Four*, although Moore thinks this episode marks the first time that Adama and Roslin have had sex, Olmos and McDonnell believe that the pair have been sleeping together since New Caprica. Lee telling the journalists that the Fifth Cylon is dead was suggested by Bamber himself, because, according to Moore, 'There was a line in the press conference, where somebody asked about it, and it was blown off, and [the actors] said no ... there should be something ... as kind of indicated that they knew but were keeping the secret'. A deleted scene from 'No Exit' explains why the Fleet believe Ellen is dead, when Tory says, 'The Hub, if Ellen downloaded, she was probably there. Died again when we took it out'; however, this makes little sense, as the Hub was destroyed over a year after Ellen's death on New Caprica.

Moore's script has Adama continually picking up pieces of garbage and putting them in his pockets; as Olmos's costume did not usually have pockets, a special pair of trousers had to be sewn. The sequence in Zarek's cell, where Zarek throws a piece of paper that contains the coordinates of the *Hitei Kan* to the floor (symbolically discarding the ship once it is no longer of use to him), and Adama picks it up, is different in the 11 March draft: this has Zarek toss the paper onto the folder of laundry reports instead (this time conflating his

---

91 For the uninitiated, Figurski is an overweight, unkempt balding slob.

involvement in the *Hitei Kan*'s mutiny with a long list of self-serving criminal activities). The children in Baltar's lair are played by Moore's own son and daughter: Robin is the boy in the blue-grey shirt visible at the start of the sermon, Roxy the girl in the brown shirt seen later on.

'A Disquiet Follows My Soul' clearly demonstrates that the coming mutiny is entirely down to the actions of the Fleet's leaders, and more specifically to Roslin's initial authoritarianism and then abrupt withdrawal from political life. However, it also implies that we should be sympathising with these leaders and seeing their opponents as corrupt and compromised.

64: The Oath

FIRST TRANSMISSION DATE: 30 January 2009 (USA/CANADA)

WRITER: Mark Verheiden

DIRECTOR: John Dahl

CREDITED CAST: Richard Hatch (Tom Zarek); Sebastian Spence (Narcho); Bodie Olmos (Lieutenant Brenden [sic] 'Hotdog' [sic] Costanza); Ryan Robbins (Charlie Connor); Keegan Connor Tracy (Jeanne); Mike Dopud (Specialist Gage); Ty Olsson (Captain Aaron Kelly); Leah Cairns (Lieutenant Margaret 'Racetrack' Edmondson); Jennifer Halley (Specialist 2nd Class [sic] Diana 'Hardball' Seelix); Brad Dryborough (Hoshi); Colin Lawrence (Ensign Hamish 'Skulls' McCall); Alexandra Thomas (Hera); Derek DeLost (Specialist Vireem); Vincent Gale (Chief Peter Laird); Colin Corrigan (Marine Allan Nowart); Michael Leisen (Private Stewart Jaffee); Lara Gilchrist (Paulla Schaffer); Andrew McIlroy (Jacob Cantrell); Judith Maxie (Picon Delegate); Iris Paluly (Speaking Delegate #2); Marilyn Norry (Reza Chronides); Craig Veroni (Lance Corporal Eduardo Maldonaldo); Veena Sood (Quorum Delegate); Alain Chanoine (Marine Reb)

STUNTS: Raymond Sammel (Adama Stunt Double); Colin Decker (Tigh Stunt Double); Darryle Scheelar (Thompson); Christopher Gordon (Stunt CIC Enlisted); Chad Bellamy (Stunt Marine #1); Heath Stevenson (Stunt Marine #2)

KNOWN UNCREDITED CAST: Leo Li Chiang (Tattooed Pilot)

SYNOPSIS: As civilian captains refuse to allow the Cylons to refit their jump drives, Gaeta releases Zarek from the brig and puts him on a Raptor to *Colonial One*. While Zarek stalls the Quorum, Gaeta and his supporters mount a bid to take over *Galactica*, imprisoning Caprica-Six, Anders and the Agathons. Gaeta uses his position in CIC to disrupt communications and keep the Fleet leaders from finding out what is really going on. Lee takes a Raptor back to *Galactica* and joins forces with Kara Thrace to fight the mutiny; they and Roslin go to the Baltar cult lair, where Roslin broadcasts a message to the Fleet using Baltar's wireless. Gaeta's forces take over CIC, arresting Adama, Tigh and the senior staff. Adama and Tigh evade their captors and meet Thrace and Lee, who are escorting Baltar and Roslin to an airlock that Tyrol has secured. Baltar and Roslin are flown to the basestar, while Adama and Tigh remain behind and hold off the attacking Marines.

ANALYSIS: 'The Oath' reiterates many of the same themes as 'A Disquiet Follows My Soul', albeit with more bloodshed. However, the way in which events develop brings the impetus behind the mutiny, and the reasons why it is doomed from the outset, into sharp focus.

Body of Evidence: How the Elite Bring About the Mutiny

Toward the end of the episode, Lee says to his father, 'You want to know why Tom Zarek's got so much clout in this Fleet? Because when you get past the arrogance, he's right. We can pretend to put it behind us, exchange lofty words about an alliance, but if this is what survival has come to–'. However, Lee's interpretation of the mutiny is off target; while bad feelings about the alliance with the rebel Cylons are certainly fuelling it, the revolt itself is not so much anti-Cylon as anti-elite.

At the start of the story, Adama and Lee are both firmly entrenched in their familiar behaviour patterns. Adama is railroading through the jump drive upgrades, despite not-unjustified protests from the civilian captains; his response, when Tigh briefs him on the unrest, is, 'I'm tired of this. Go to Lee. Tell the Quorum that if they don't get their ships in line, they can all share a blanket in Zarek's cell'. Lee, meanwhile, is back to being Adama's man on the Quorum, saying, 'Mr Zarek was taken into custody because he was agitating against a lawful order'. Roslin, significantly, can see the problem, telling Adama, 'The Fleet has never been comfortable with this "blanket Cylon amnesty" thing ... Siccing Lee on the Quorum is only going to be seen as a shot across the bow. He can hedge it all he wants, but the delegates will see that it comes straight from you'. Kara also seems to be experiencing a reversion to type, possibly in reaction to the general anti-Starbuck feeling among the pilots; her baiting of Costanza in the pilots' quarters is firmly in line with her old nastiness, and goes some way toward explaining why Costanza is working with the mutineers at the end of the story. Adama's behaviour, and Lee's support of it, illuminate the root causes of the mutiny.

Roslin makes an ostentatious pose of refusing to get involved at first. However, every action she has taken over the past few episodes has had a clear political significance. The speech she makes over the wireless, outlining the reasons for the alliance with the Cylons and selling the idea persuasively, shows that, had she not indulged in her withdrawal a few episodes earlier, the mutiny would not have happened. The white production draft of the episode, dated 26 March 2008, has some significant differences from the final version in the scene where Lee and Kara go to Adama's quarters to persuade Roslin to help them stop the mutiny: Roslin initially refuses, but is galvanised to action when Kara, angered, tosses her gun on the table and tells her, 'Go ahead. Finish what the cancer started'. As with 'The Hub', which equated Roslin's physical person with the body politic, the implication is that Roslin's suicidal feelings after the discovery of Earth have been projected onto the rest of the population; her withdrawal of political support will thus ultimately destroy the Fleet. The same script has a stage direction in Roslin's discussion with Adama about Fleet politics early in the episode, stating that she 'catches herself, realising she's been unconsciously working the politics of the situation', indicating that deep down, she is aware of the consequences of her withdrawal. In the transmitted version, however, what motivates Roslin is learning that Zarek has not only made a bid for power, but has gained military support through Gaeta. Knowing that she is dying, and that Lee will ultimately take over from her, she forces Zarek to suffer along with her by putting him in a position that prevents him from exercising power in the interim, and that will ultimately destroy him: she knows Adama will never support a Zarek-led administration, and so what will ultimately transpire is a military dictatorship under Adama. When she realises that Zarek now has a chance of gaining power over the Fleet, she is moved to act. In the early draft, she is punishing everyone in the Fleet; in the final version, she is punishing Zarek alone, which is more in line with her characterisation. While she may be vindictive and selfish, it is usually Adama who wants to take the rest of the Fleet down with him. The problem of leadership is compounded by the hierarchical nature of the system on the Fleet, which naturally concentrates power into the hands of a few people, and as such magnifies the flaws of those people throughout the system of governance.

In an interview on geeksdreamgirl.com, Richard Hatch says, 'Zarek had every reason to be pissed off and angry at what [Roslin and Adama] were doing – they wanted to operate without accountability because they believed they had all the answers ... Zarek and Gaeta can only go by what they've experienced in the past, what they've seen. And in reality, the Cylons are so unpredictable ... How in the world can you ever trust anybody that's killed millions of people?' Although the audience, with an omniscient point of view guided by the writers, are focusing on Roslin's and Adama's perspective, it is worth remembering that the characters themselves don't experience events in this way; from Zarek's and Gaeta's point of view, they are taking justified action against an illegitimate, unaccountable ruling body.

Semper Frakking Fi: The Problems with the Mutiny

In his podcast for this episode, Moore says that the one substantial way in which the original version differed from the later drafts was that it had the Quorum voting Zarek in as President immediately on his arrival on *Colonial One*, and Lee leaving for *Galactica* in a snit. Moore says that he changed this as it didn't feel 'believable' that the Quorum would do so. However, given their exclusion from power over the last few episodes, there are clear reasons why the Quorum might vote Zarek in. The killing of Laird was a late addition to the story, according to Moore, but its inclusion raises the question of why Zarek does not kill Lee when he has the chance, perhaps using the pistol he keeps in his desk, as Lee is much more of a political threat to him. Although his letting Lee go to *Galactica*, the hangar deck of which is under mutineer control, is effectively sending him to his death (in the event, he survives only through the timely intervention of

Starbuck), it suggests that Zarek does not have the courage to kill Lee himself. Zarek's speech to Lee, in which he points out that the latter cannot support Adama and still be true to his responsibilities as Caprican representative, and that Adama's rule is leading to military dictatorship, mixes untruth – when he claims that Adama released him from prison 'because I'm only a threat if he recognises civilian authority' – with valid points about the lack of accountability in the system. As such, it casts doubt upon the veracity of what he is saying. Once again, Zarek is painted as a man not to be entirely trusted.

Within the story, the problems with the mutiny are, ultimately, connected with its leadership. Roslin's and Adama's roles are reversed in the case of Gaeta and Zarek: where Roslin was the idealist and Adama the military muscle who backed her up, here the pragmatic, ruthless one is Zarek, while the one in charge of the military is the idealist Gaeta. As Moore notes on the podcast, regarding Gaeta's crucial mistake in leaving Adama alive: 'Zarek knew that Adama should have been executed immediately, and Gaeta has … a different agenda from Zarek, and it's really the difference between those two agendas that will be their undoing'.

Furthermore, the motivations of Gaeta's and Zarek's supporters pose risks for the movement's success in the longer term. As in the previous episode, we see here that the mutiny's supporters are building on long-term grudges: a number of the key figures are former *Pegasus* crewmembers; Seelix is clearly settling a score against Anders; and Skulls, previously seen as a fairly cheerful sort, complains about Laird being 'up Adama's ass since he transferred in from *Pegasus*'. The trial of Baltar also appears to have been a particular flashpoint: both Racetrack and Kelly, who voiced anti-trial sentiments, are key mutineers, and Connor mockingly suggests to Lee that he convene a trial to sort everything out. However, although these individuals were clearly disaffected before the alliance was proposed, a common sentiment among the mutineers appears to be anti-Cylon racism. Again, from our omniscient perspective, it is easy for the audience to see that the mutiny, if successful, would end with *Galactica* turning its guns on the rebel basestar, which would not only go against God's plan, but ultimately lead to the destruction of the Fleet as, without the jump drive upgrades, they will be less likely to find a habitable planet, and more vulnerable to Cavil's forces.

Given Zarek's customary pragmatism, it would be surprising if he had not considered this outcome. However, in this case, Roslin's actions have left him with no real other option but to revolt. Had Roslin remained in command, and allowed him a voice in politics, he would have sided with her and supported the alliance; as it is, his only options are to remain voiceless or to fight back, however suicidal this may be. The Fleet's problems, therefore, continue to stem from its leadership.

Night of the Living Dead: The Military and Religious Fightback

Baltar, meanwhile, comes down firmly on the side of the administration. This is partly because he must know there is still bad feeling over the trial, but furthermore because the cult is being assisted by Tyrol, who also supports Adama and Roslin. While it makes sense that Tyrol would do so given his usual obedience to the regime, he also is a Final Five Cylon, and thus at personal risk from the mutiny. Baltar and Roslin clash over the issue of religious sincerity with her saying, 'I never really believed in your conversion, so I was counting on your well-honed sense of self-preservation', he retorting, 'I'm so sick of your insinuations. I recall your sudden allegiance to the priestess Elosha and the scrolls of Pythia the last time your political fortunes were in doubt. Tell me, how is that working out for you now?' and Roslin concluding, 'If it makes you happy, maybe we're both frauds'. She is being unfair on both of them here, as she sincerely believed in the prophecy, and as he does have a direct line to God. However, she has a good point about Baltar's instinct for self-preservation: his declarations of loyalty to his followers sound insincere in light of the fact that he is openly preparing to flee to the rebel basestar, leaving them behind.

The sequence where Baltar makes a phone call to Gaeta and attempts to remonstrate with him is a late addition, not appearing until the pink production draft[92], dated 2 April 2008. This is evidently intended to tie the story in with 'The Face of the Enemy', but it makes Baltar look foolish. Baltar first asks Gaeta to back down and give up the mutiny, which he clearly cannot, then threatens him with the knowledge of what he did on New Caprica, referring to 'our little secret, sealed with a very special pen'. In the first place, this would provide fewer reasons for Gaeta to surrender than it would for him to have Baltar killed before he can go public with his information. Furthermore, as discussed in the review for 'The Face of the Enemy', the secret damns Baltar along with Gaeta, meaning that Gaeta is being blackmailed by someone who is implicated in the same crime, but who does not appear to feel any remorse over it. Finally, Baltar says he will forgive Gaeta, which, on top of everything else, is not likely to go down too well.

At the end of the story, Adama and Tigh remain behind on *Galactica* ostensibly to allow Roslin and Baltar to make their escape in the Raptor to the basestar. However, this act is completely unnecessary in strategic terms, as the Raptor is well away from the ship before the Marines have even broken down the door to the auxiliary airlock. Adama's motivation is more clearly given when he says, 'I couldn't have lived with it'; a good captain cannot leave his ship, even at the cost of his own life.

Say You Want a Revolution: Continuity and Worldbuilding

In continuity terms, the Fleet are now making ersatz coffee out of algae, and there is a reference in the draft script to Roslin eating 'algae biscuits', which she

---

[92] Television production teams routinely use different coloured paper for different drafts of scripts. On *Battlestar Galactica*, white paper was used for the first draft, and pink for one produced later in the process.

appears to like. Gaeta has been involved in mutinous actions twice before: in 'Resistance', when he aided Roslin's escape from *Galactica* by covering for Dualla's scrambled off-log calls, and 'The Road Less Traveled', when he supported Agathon's action on *Demetrius*. Roslin is surprised by Gaeta's actions here, because the latter incident was covered up and the former was in support of her. Moore points out in his podcast that the mutiny reveals the extent to which the *Galactica* itself has become fragmented into little autonomous subcultures: 'The ship is big enough that people are starting to barricade their own sections. The civilians are trying to protect themselves ... Now the ship is just divided up into isolated pockets of resistance and isolated pockets of control'. The fact that the ship is undermanned and increasingly filled with civilian groups is also, he says, a contributing factor in the mutiny, limiting communication between Adama's supporters, although this contradicts the 5 December 2006 draft of 'Collaborators', in which *Galactica* was established as being overpopulated, not just with civilians but with military personnel taken on from the *Pegasus*. Seelix, currently an ensign, is referred to as a Specialist in the end credits. Although the chyrons (time-stamps) in the episode are generally well used to indicate the rapid pace of the action, Lee's arrival on *Galactica* is said to take place at 9:02, but, although well over a minute passes before his and Starbuck's escape from the hangar deck, the latter sequence is also time-stamped as 9:02.

Beyond the Barricades: Writing and Production

The earliest draft script, dated 26 March 2008, differs primarily from the final version in that it contains, throughout, Gaeta flashing back to two incidents in the miniseries: Adama's inspiring speech at the memorial service, and the moment when Gaeta tells Adama it's been an honour to serve with him. The episode also opens with Gaeta's shocked reaction to Laird's murder, but then jumps back in time to Adama's meeting with Tigh, where the transmitted episode begins. Private Jaffee, in the 26 March draft, pulls a gun to defend Adama and is shot by the Marines, whereas in later drafts he is killed while pushing Adama to the floor to avoid the gunfire, as in the final version.

Stage directions provide some enlightening details: for instance, when Adama says in CIC that there will be 'No forgiveness. No amnesty', the directions read, 'Adama's words have an impact, especially on Nowart', which further contextualises why Adama begins his strategy against the arresting Marines by speaking to Nowart in a friendly way. Civilians fleeing through *Galactica* are described with the line, 'Think refugees escaping a fire-fight in Baghdad'. In all drafts, the devastated Earth is called 'Cinder Earth' in the descriptions. There is a deleted exchange where Tigh, giving Adama his situation report at the start of Act One, states there has been no enemy contact, and adds "less you wanna count the civvies calling for your scalp', and Adama replies, 'Tell 'em to get in line'.

The episode's director, John Dahl, is an independent film-maker who

64: THE OATH

frequently employs Ronald D Moore's wife Terry as a costume designer. Moore observes in his podcast, 'We have only a limited number of corridors and doorways and intersections and ladders and so on, and John [Dahl] was able to go into our sets and continually make you feel like you were moving throughout the ship, that there are people scattered around in all these disparate corners of the *Galactica*, and this is sort of the first time in the series, actually, that I truly felt the size of the ship'.

'The Oath', in essence, comes down to one bunch of bad guys fighting another bunch of bad guys. The main difference between the two is that one bunch of bad guys does, in fact, literally have God on their side.

BY YOUR COMMAND: VOL 2

65: Blood on the Scales

FIRST TRANSMISSION DATE: 6 February 2009 (USA/CANADA)

WRITER: Michael Angeli

DIRECTOR: Wayne Rose

CREDITED CAST: Richard Hatch (Tom Zarek); Callum Keith Rennie (Leoben); Mark Sheppard (Romo Lampkin); Rekha Sharma (Tory Foster); Sebastian Spence (Narcho); Bodie Olmos (Hot Dog); Mike Dopud (Specialist Gage); Ty Olsson (Captain Aaron Kelly); Leah Cairns (Lieutenant Margaret 'Racetrack' Edmondson); Jennifer Halley (Specialist 2nd Class [sic] Diana 'Hardball' Seelix); Alexandra Thomas (Hera); Derek Delost (Specialist Vireem); Colin Corrigan (Marine Allan Nowart); Andrew McIlroy (Jacob Cantrell); Judith Maxie (Picon Delegate); Iris Paluly (Speaking Delegate Dahlia); Marilyn Norry (Reza Chronides); Veena Sood (Quorum Delegate); Adrian Holmes (Specialist [sic] Parr)

STUNTS: Raymond Sammel (Adama Stunt Double); Jason Calder (Stunt Rebel Marine 'Bayless'); Dan Shea (Stunt Rebel Marine #2); Clay Virtue (Stunt Rebel Marine #3); Yves Cameron (Stunt Rebel Marine #4)

KNOWN UNCREDITED CAST: Leo Li Chiang (Tattooed Pilot)

SYNOPSIS: Adama and Tigh are captured by Marines, while Roslin and Baltar make it safely to the basestar. The Cylons want to jump away, but Roslin persuades them instead to move into the centre of the Fleet, so as to prevent *Galactica* from firing on them. Zarek lands *Colonial One* on board *Galactica*, and he and Gaeta plan a trial for Adama, press-ganging Lampkin to act as defence. Gaeta is to be prosecutor and Zarek the judge. The Quorum question the legitimacy of their seizure of power, and Zarek has them executed, to Gaeta's dismay. Gaeta orders the Fleet to prepare to jump away. Kara and Lee free Tigh, Anders, Caprica-Six and the Agathons from the brig, but Anders is later shot in the head and wounded. Roslin, aided by a Leoben, manages to broadcast to the rest of the Fleet, telling them to stand down their FTL drives; ten out of the 35 ships in the Fleet do so. Adama is saved from imminent execution by a rescue force headed by Lee. Tyrol enters the *Galactica*'s service tunnels and shuts down its FTL drives, preventing her from jumping away. Adama's supporters retake *Galactica*, and Zarek and Gaeta are executed by firing squad.

65: BLOOD ON THE SCALES

ANALYSIS: 'Blood on the Scales' concludes the mutiny arc by following through on the implications of 'The Oath', that the rebellion will ultimately be destroyed by the fault-line running between Gaeta and Zarek, and by the fact that the defending group have a unified clarity of purpose that the rebels are lacking.

Which Side Are You On? The End of the Mutiny

The mutiny, once underway, appears to have strong popular support: whereas 24 ships, over a third of the Fleet at the time, supported Roslin in 'The Farm', here only ten ships out of the 35 remaining in the Fleet obey Roslin's order to stand down their FTL drives and side with the rebel basestar. However, what ultimately causes it to fail is the difference between Gaeta's and Zarek's agendas, as discussed in relation to the previous episode. Gaeta, believing that he has failed to live up to his own impossibly high ideals, looks for someone else to blame instead, and here focuses on Adama, hence his insistence on a trial for the Admiral. The whole exercise boils down to exploring Gaeta's personal feeling that he has been treated unfairly: he is bitter about the fact that, whereas he was forced to work for the Cylon regime and was nearly thrown out of an airlock as a result, Adama, who has a choice whether or not to ally himself with the rebel Cylons, does so with no consequences or personal feelings of guilt. Furthermore, Gaeta also holds Adama responsible for the situation on New Caprica, as he abandoned the colonists. In the 3 April 2008 script draft, the *Demetrius* incident is also mentioned, with the charges against Adama including 'Did you allow the willing participants in a Cylon-orchestrated mutiny [sic] aboard the *Demetrius* to go un[punished]', presenting Kara's decision to pursue the basestar as an act of criminal disobedience. This suggests that, after the return to the Fleet, the participants in the *Demetrius*'s mission closed ranks and did not discuss the more controversial events of the endeavour, and Adama did not pursue the matter, meaning Gaeta further feels as if he is being punished over actions for which others have been excused. Although Tigh asks Starbuck and her crew, in 'Guess What's Coming to Dinner', what happened to Gaeta's leg, we never hear the answer, and the implication is that the incident was hushed up.

This can be seen in other aspects of Gaeta's leadership. He has no qualms about ordering Roslin's Raptor shot down, as Roslin is a civilian who for some time has effectively abdicated her role as President, and from a military perspective Adama's leadership is the only one that truly matters. But when he does this, Hot Dog, a member of his own side, opposes him, even though he could be arrested or killed for disobeying the order (and indeed, in the 3 April draft, Hot Dog is thrown in the brig for doing so), showing that, where Gaeta compromised his ideals on New Caprica, other people are capable of living up to their internal moral codes, even under threat of imprisonment or death. Roslin's rant at the end of the episode, in which she says in part, 'I will use every cannon, every bomb, every bullet, every weapon I have down to my own eye-teeth to end you. I swear it!' shows that, however crazed it is, she has a set of principles she will not abandon, even if it means her death and the deaths of those around her. Gaeta's belief that he is compromised is thrown into sharp relief by Hot Dog's and Roslin's respective refusals to abandon their own ideals.

The production drafts of the scene in which Gaeta, prior to his execution, talks with Baltar, contain a significant extra line. Gaeta says, 'I was meant to bring out the best in everyone else, like the black velvet they put under precious stones. Someone has to light up the good'. Gaeta, subconsciously, believes that he was wrong, and everything that happened during the mutiny proves to him that he was wrong. As he thinks very much in black and white terms, this means, to him, that his opponents must have been right. He dies content at the end of the story, because he thinks he deserves death. Gaeta accepts his punishment because he believes that his own villainy can serve as a foil, to highlight the good in the victors.

Zarek, on the other hand, acts logically throughout, and his final episode is by far his best. He smiles at the end of the story, when facing execution, suggesting that he does not blame Gaeta for the failure of the mutiny, but accepts that losing was always a possible outcome for them. However, one significant change in Zarek's storyline between the 3 April draft and the final version is that in the former, the Quorum actually supported Zarek and voted him in as President, and he then had them executed anyway. Moore says in his podcast: 'Richard ... said, "You know, I just have a problem with this, I just don't know why he would do that if they're supporting him. It would be so much simpler and stronger if they just vote against him and then he does it ... If they supported him, he would be smart enough to play that into solidifying his political position." And you know what, I said he was right, I realised he was right; we were trying ... to have him get the win and still do the bad thing anyway'. While Hatch's criticism and Moore's decision to change the scene were perfectly correct, as Zarek's execution of the Quorum appears in the draft like an uncharacteristically crude and gratuitous act of villainy, it does not speak well of the Quorum that they reject the mutiny, as Roslin and Adama have actively worked against them, and as 25 ships support the action. Presumably, after years of mistreatment by their leaders, they have become too cowed and subservient to take a step toward change.

The way the mutiny plays itself out supports Zarek's assertion in 'The Oath' that 'Success ... hangs in the cumulative moments, each one building on the next. And it can be lost with the slightest hesitation'. Although within nine hours the mutiny is over, clearly this allows sufficient time for doubts to creep into the minds of the participants. Kelly, for instance, switches sides because of his shock over the murder of the Quorum, his concerns about executing Adama and his encounter with Tyrol in the weapons locker, in which they joke about the past and he decides to let the Cylon go rather than shoot him on sight. The fact that Adama, Roslin and Lee were not killed straight away lost the revolution the key act it needed to succeed. On some level, Roslin and

Adama have imprinted themselves so strongly upon the Fleet that the mutineers hesitate to take action against them, and this hesitation loses them the advantage.

On the basestar, Roslin again shows herself to be a skilled orator, persuading the Cylons to remain with the Fleet rather than jump to safety. It is perhaps not too surprising that she dominates the Cylons, as, following D'Anna's departure, they have no credible leaders of their own. Her speech declaring total war on Zarek, while dramatic, suggests that, once Zarek informs her that Adama has been killed, her hatred of Zarek becomes so pathological that she would be willing to destroy all the other people on *Galactica* – indeed, by implication, in the entire Fleet – rather than let him take over. Like Gaeta, Roslin is a driven idealist, whose belief has failed her, who wants to take this out on others, and who resolves her issues through the events of the mutiny, the difference being that Gaeta concludes he is wrong and accepts death, whereas Roslin finds a new motivation to act.

Retaking the Fleet: Continuity and Worldbuilding

In continuity terms, there are a number of call-backs to earlier episodes; for instance, Lampkin using a pen to kill Marine Parr recalls Gaeta's attempt to murder Baltar in 'Taking a Break from All Your Worries', and Kelly's comment to Tyrol, 'Heard your kid's not a Cylon … Could have told you she was trouble', references the discovery of Nicky's parentage in 'A Disquiet Follows My Soul'. Tyrol is able single-handedly to take out *Galactica* by physically sabotaging her FTL drives, recalling Adama's observation in 'Litmus' that 'If [Tyrol] really wanted to take this ship down, he could'. Baltar sleeps with yet another Six, Lida, but appears to be finding a new sense of responsibility when he explains to her that he fled *Galactica* not out of fear, but to escape his cultists: 'I've got a kind of following on *Galactica*, like a fan club. Publicly, I humour them. Privately, I scorn their provincial intellects, their unfailing willingness to make me feel better … I have to go back. They're my responsibility'. This is given further context by a deleted scene in which Roslin attacks Baltar for failing to support her when persuading the Cylons to stay with the Fleet, accusing him of cowardice. Athena's behaviour in 'Guess What's Coming to Dinner' is again implied to have been a divinely-induced emotional crisis, as she seems unconcerned about Caprica-Six taking charge of Hera. Another of the landram-type vehicles first seen in 'Scar' is visible in the scene where *Colonial One* is brought aboard *Galactica*. *Galactica* was stated in the miniseries to have two FTL drives, but evidently disabling a single drive is sufficient to prevent the ship from jumping.

In terms of outside references, Zarek's joke to Racetrack runs in part '… "Shall we save the kid?" And the attorney says "Frak him", and the priest says, "Do we have time?"' which appears, strangely, to be a Colonial variant on a well-known anti-Catholic witticism. (The relevant lines do not appear in the production draft scripts, suggesting that it is an ad-lib.) Moore, according to his podcast, based Gaeta's mounting a trial for Adama on events after the coup that ousted Ceausescu, when the subsequent regime insisted on a show trial for the deposed Romanian ruler in order to establish a claim to legitimacy. Lampkin refers to his guards as 'Wynken and Blynken', referencing the children's poem 'Wynken, Blynken and Nod' by Eugene Field. Moore in his podcast says, 'Adama ... executed Felix and Tom Zarek, but there were significant numbers of other people who were not executed ... It didn't feel like that was the smart thing for him to do [to] start having mass executions on board'. This is also a call-back to an incident in the American Revolution in which Washington's men mutinied and, in Moore's words, 'Washington's solution was to hang the ringleaders but allow the rest of them to go back ... into the Continental Army and to serve again, because he was trying to hold the army together'. Adama's execution of Gaeta and Zarek bookends Zarek's killing of the Quorum early in the episode, reinforcing the parallels between Zarek and Adama.

Order is Restored: Writing and Production

Although during its development the story appears to have changed little in the essentials, a lot of material was lost for time reasons, with Baltar and Lida, Racetrack, and Lampkin all having their stories truncated. The 3 April draft features Racetrack quite strongly, including a subplot in which, tasked along with Seelix and some Sons of Ares militia men to find the brig escape party, she instead encounters Thrace, Lampkin and Anders at the medical centre, leading to a standoff in which Thrace says of her, 'You're so frakking stupid. Your nose is so far up Zarek's ass you can smell his breath', and of Seelix, 'You'd follow anybody with a stick [i.e. penis] and a pulse'. Racetrack counters in part, 'Who're we supposed to follow? ... Adama? Everywhere he's taken us has been a *DISASTER AND A MISTAKE*. Roslin? One day she's ready to kill all the skinjobs, the next, she's hallucinating with them'. Racetrack then calls CIC for guidance on what to do about the situation, saying 'We got Starbuck. And Anders. He's been shot and frakking Cottle won't stop treating him'; Gaeta receives the call as he hears the counterinsurgency approaching CIC, and 'at peace with himself and resigned to his fate, he gives his last order', telling Racetrack to make sure Anders lives (a sequence later replaced by the scene where Gaeta orders a 'weapons hold' rather than fight it out with the basestar). This subplot is gone by the 15 April draft, probably due to Leah Cairns' limited availability for filming. In this draft, when Gaeta is appalled at the Quorum massacre, Zarek replies, 'What have I done? I've shown the Fleet just how far Adama went to stay in power. We blame that slaughter in there on Adama ... *He* murdered them. All the more reason why we had to execute him'. Hot Dog has a further moment of heroism in the drafts, using his Viper to physically shield Roslin's Raptor from Narcho.

The 3 April 2008 draft had Lampkin presiding over Adama's 'trial', with Gaeta and Zarek reading the charges and Adama refusing to defend himself;

65: BLOOD ON THE SCALES

but, according to Moore in his podcast, as Lampkin is a defence lawyer by profession, the line-up was changed to a more formal situation with judge, prosecution and defence, making the show-trial aspect clearer in the process. According to Moore there was also a sequence that got as far as the filming stage, where Adama gave the Marines on his firing squad a chance to join the loyalists (making it clearer where the Marines who accompany him to CIC come from) and, on retaking CIC, randomly shot someone to indicate the strength of the counter-coup; this was dropped as it didn't seem entirely in character.

As usual with Angeli's scripts, there are some great stage directions. In the 3 April draft, after Adama refuses to answer the charges Gaeta has set him, Lampkin 'gets a look from [Specialist] Vireem that would make a mountain lion whimper in its own piss'. The atmosphere in the brig is described as 'grimness in matching colours', and Zarek, receiving the phone call about the brig escape, is said to look 'as if he is trying to pass a starfish'. Adama, when brought to the CIC at the start of the story, is described as looking 'as if Noah found monkeys crapping on the deck of the Ark', and, as for Roslin, 'Al Pacino couldn't over-dramatise her displeasure'. One direction indicates that we should see a graffito reading 'The people will know the truth' in one of the *Galactica*'s corridors near a group of Gaeta's Marines, implying that the phrase was scrawled by the mutineers in protest at the Fleet's governance. Some unfortunately cut lines include Lampkin, after Adama refuses to answer the charges, saying that he would beat all-comers in a 'Say the Word No' competition. In the drafts, when Kelly arrests Tigh and Adama at the start of the episode, Tigh says, 'Well, well, what crawls will one day walk', prior to referring to Kelly as 'the brig rat'. Zarek, in the 3 April draft, and Lampkin, in the 15 April draft, both say that Gaeta's leg will grow back before Adama gives him the apology he is seeking.

According to the podcast, there was some debate over whether or not to have the basestar actually hit by a Colonial missile in the sequence where Narcho fires on the Raptor. Moore thought it would escalate hostilities, but Angeli insisted it would add an extra element of tension. An alternate version of the shooting of the Quorum scene, available on the DVD, actually shows the bloodbath rather than, as transmitted, having it take place off-screen. According to Wayne Rose as quoted in *The Official Companion Season Four*, Gaeta having a last meeting with Baltar, prior to the former's death by firing squad, was suggested by Juliani. Moore says in his podcast that he finds this scene effective because it means that Gaeta's final appearance is not simply his execution. In an interview in the 6 February 2009 *Chicago Tribune*, Angeli also remarks that the scene means the audience will 'think that Gaeta's been spared', describing this as 'kind of wicked'.

According to *The Official Companion Season Four*, Hatch apparently found the episode emotionally affecting, as he did not want Zarek to be remembered solely as a villain. Rose is quoted in the same volume as saying that, during the writers' strike, the actors were allowed to commit to other projects, meaning that scheduling many of the principals for their appearances in this episode was quite difficult. Juliani, who was acting in a play on Vancouver Island at the time, had to fly in for a few hours of filming each day. As in 'The Oath', Ensign Seelix is again wrongly credited as 'Specialist 2nd Class', and Marine Parr is also wrongly credited as a Specialist.

The conclusion of the mutiny storyline treats the subject of power and will in the Fleet with depth and complexity, with the similarities between both sides, and the mutineers' rationales for action, explored as events unfold. The final outcome is best summarised by Zarek: 'The truth is told by whoever's left standing'.

66: No Exit

FIRST TRANSMISSION DATE: 13 February 2009 (USA/CANADA)

WRITER: Ryan Mottesheard

DIRECTOR: Gwyneth Horder-Payton

CREDITED CAST: Kate Vernon (Ellen Tigh); Rekha Sharma (Tory Foster); Donnelly Rhodes (Doctor Cottle); Dean Stockwell (Cavil); John Hodgman (Doctor Gerard); Kerry Norton (Medic Layne Ishay); Darcy Laurie (Dealino)

STUNTS: Keel Worker Stunt (Rick Pearce)

SYNOPSIS: Eighteen months earlier, following her death on New Caprica, Ellen resurrects. She meets Cavil, whom she calls 'John'. Over the months that follow, they hold conversations about the past, their relationship, and Cylon nature. On *Galactica*, Tyrol considers what to do about the stress fractures in the ship, Lee and Roslin rebuild the Fleet government on the basis of ship rather than Colony affiliation, and Cottle prepares to perform surgery to remove the bullet from Anders's skull. Anders asks Kara to assemble the rest of the Four, as his injury has restored his memories of their past. Through Ellen's conversation with John, and Anders's revelations to the other Cylons, we learn that the Final Five rediscovered the secret of Cylon resurrection on Earth 2,000 years ago, and fled after the nuclear war, resurrecting on a ship in orbit and travelling to the Colonies at relativistic but sub-light speed, so that very little time passed for them on their journey, but thousands of years in the outside universe. Encountering the Centurions during the First Cylon War, they worked with them to develop the human-like Cylons in exchange for the Centurions ceasing to fight against the humans. John, however, rebelled against his creators, destroying one of the original human-like Cylons (Daniel, Number Seven). He trapped the Final Five in a compartment, took the oxygen offline to suffocate them, and boxed them. Later, he released them into the Colonies with altered memories, with the aim of demonstrating to them that machine life is inherently superior to human life. After the destruction of the Hub, John pleads with Ellen to recreate the resurrection system, but she says that she needs the other four Cylons in order to do this. John threatens to dissect Ellen's brain, but Ellen escapes to the Fleet in a Raptor with Boomer. Anders is rendered comatose after further surgery, leaving the rest of the story untold.

ANALYSIS: 'No Exit' is low on plot and heavy on info-dumps, as the writers attempt to cram the entire backstory of the Final Five and their relationship to modern Cylons into a single episode, giving the impression that the series has too much plot remaining to be easily conveyed in the time available to them.

My Brother's Keeper: Ellen and John

The first main focus of the story is an exploration of John/Cavil, through his conversations with Ellen. In these, John comes across as the series' only demonic figure. While other characters have motivations, Cavil, when pressed to explain why he is acting in a certain way, will provide a lucid and rational argument, but one that is contradicted by something else he says or does. Early on, he expresses his loathing for his human nature, and yet that very emotion is itself a human one. When Ellen asks why he focuses on pursuing such human activities as vengeance and murder, he replies, 'Because … my forebears on the Centurion side of the family were the slaves of humanity and I want justice for that', and yet he also is the one who had the Centurions fitted with telencephalic inhibitors, presumably because to enslave is another of humanity's traits. John is also perversely aware of his contradictory nature, stating that to be human is to be 'torn apart by conflicting impulses'. There are Freudian aspects to the character, in that Ellen not only named him after her father, but designed him in her father's image; Moore, regarding John's malevolence, says, 'What does that say about Ellen and Tigh and the rest of the Final Five who created John Cavil, there's like the seeds of their own destruction always seem to be carried within all of the characters'. John has certain parallels with Iago from *Othello*, who expresses a number of different reasons for his tormenting of the titular character, without identifying which is primary; however, where Iago's motivations are not inherently contradictory, John's cannot be reconciled.

What John appears to have done is to set himself up as the personification of human evil. He justifies his every malevolent act by putting it down to his human nature. This is an inversion of the original series' premise that sufficiently advanced species will become godlike: by going down the other path, John has become demon-like. In this, he particularly resembles the original-series character Count Iblis, from the story 'War of the Gods', whose true motivations are also not explored, and who encourages humanity to its worst behaviour. Iblis is set up as the antagonist of the lightship people, a godlike, advanced species who are seen as glowing humanoids in white hoods, as the Final Five appear in D'Anna's vision. Significantly, when Ellen refers to the one true God as having generated the supernova and D'Anna's vision of the Five, Cavil does not argue with her, indicating that he does in fact know God exists; however, he also clearly does not believe that God is a deity. As the Final Five are reimagined versions of the lightship people, technologically advanced but not always benign figures who aid the advancement of more primitive species, so Cavil is a reimagined Count Iblis.

The situation between Ellen and John in part becomes a battle for the soul of

Boomer, who is understandably conflicted between her human and machine sides. This is symbolically illustrated in the sequence where Ellen, with obvious overtones of the Garden of Eden, chooses an apple from a tray of fruit, offers it to Boomer, who rejects it, and then bites it herself, showing that she is not afraid of knowledge. Reinforcing this, Anders refers to Ellen as 'the mother of mankind', a term normally given to Eve; John's killing of Daniel also has obvious overtones of the Biblical story of Cain and Abel. Boomer tells Ellen that John is teaching her to be a better machine, but John is using her to demonstrate to Ellen the conflict between the human and machine natures of the human-like Cylons. Ellen's description of Daniel's murder is clearly aimed at Boomer. Boomer's disillusionment with, and rejection of, humanity, is presented by John as a vindication of his position on the evils of mankind; however, the fact that Caprica-Six and Sharon Agathon (and indeed, Ellen herself) have not done so indicates that this conclusion is not inevitable. At the end of the story, Boomer says she rescues Ellen because she is forgiving her, referring back to the earlier conversation where she says, regarding Tigh, 'How do you stand it? Knowing he hates you for the things you've done', and Ellen, recognising, according to a stage direction in the 23 April script draft, that Boomer is thinking of Tyrol, responds, 'Maybe not. Love's like that sometimes'. All this suggests that Ellen has finally got through to Boomer on some level, although Boomer's full motives will be explored over subsequent episodes.

The 23 April draft also contains a monologue from Ellen, which Moore says in his podcast was cut because 'It's very written on some level, it's a theatrical kind of moment, it's probably a moment that would work better on the stage than would work in the show'. It comes as Ellen does a t'ai chi session with Boomer, and runs in part:

> 'In theatre, fictional characters are sometimes given a form of self-awareness. This is known as 'breaking the fourth wall'. The device is a form of metafiction, allowing characters to address the audience directly and comment on the narrative in which they themselves are participants. In so doing, the characters transcend their fictive nature and enter into a dialectical relationship with the viewer, with each side seeking to persuade the other of the innate truth of their reality'.

Although Ellen goes on to liken the Cylons' achieving self-awareness and rebelling against the humans to a character breaching the fourth wall, there is another parallel here. On a metaphysical level, the presence of a figure whose reasons for action are continually obscure highlights that characters with clear motivations are contrived; real people are normally contradictory and hypocritical. John thus embodies human nature in several different ways.

Information Overload: The Final Five Backstory

In this episode, Anders, following a period where, Hybrid-like, he babbles symbolically about events and characters, turns into the info-dump machine from hell, explaining every single loose end whether it needs it or not, and yet somehow also throwing up new loose ends in the process. We learn that the Final Five worked in the same research facility, and that they reinvented organic memory transfer ('resurrection'), which originated on Kobol but had fallen out of use with the Earth Cylons, who reproduced through procreation. Anders said that they saw 'warning signs' on Earth that appear to have involved Head People: he mentions that Tory saw a man and Sam saw a woman[93], and this experience may have primed them to view the Centurions' worship of a loving god as a positive sign. Jane Espenson, in her interview in the 16 February 2009 *Chicago Tribune*, explains that the Five were originally polytheists, and learned monotheism from the Centurions. They survived the nuclear attacks by downloading to a spaceship, and went to the Colonies to warn them not to ill-treat their machines, but arrived too late, as their journey, without jump capability, took thousands of years. The Centurions had tried to build skinjobs and got as far as Hybrids by the time the Final Five encountered them. Ellen says that John is 'still the same confused and petulant little boy I loved so dearly all those years ago'; the skinjobs are physically the same age throughout their lives, but there must have been a period when they were, mentally and emotionally, like children. Despite Ellen's optimistic words about instilling love and compassion into the Cylon models, the Final Five also clearly did not completely trust their creations, keeping the details of the resurrection process to themselves and ensuring that all of them must be alive and well in order for the knowledge to be passed on. Cavil reveals that all of the equipment brought by the Final Five is still on the Cylon homeworld, which we now learn is ironically called the Colony. Cavil did not release the Five into Colonial society all at once, but did so over a number of years, unboxing first Tigh, then Ellen and then later the others.

We also learn a few personal details, such as that Tyrol and Tory were lovers on Cylon Earth, and planned to get married. They both look rather unhappy about this revelation, and Starbuck, when she hears about it, stifles a laugh. In a deleted scene, Tyrol and Tory expand on their feelings, discussing the fact that the Tighs' relationship endured where theirs did not, and Tyrol suggests that there is nonetheless a connection between them, which Cally might have picked up on when she accused them of having an affair; Tory, pensively, remarks 'I don't know', presumably musing on the possibility that this subconscious rivalry was what motivated her to kill Cally. In the 23 April 2008 draft's version of this scene, Tory blurts out, 'Oh god, you want me', and Tyrol exclaims, 'No! I mean, sorry, but no'. The Five appear to have had the same personal names while on Earth, though not necessarily the same surnames; Anders only ever uses their first names in his info-dumps, although there is the implication that Ellen's

---

[93] Why Tory and Anders can no longer see the Head People is never explained in the series; it is possible that God has given up on Anders and Tory, or that Cavil's giving them new memories somehow interfered with their ability, but nothing is ever confirmed.

family name was Cavil. The temple in 'The Eye of Jupiter' was the place where the Thirteenth Tribe broke their journey and prayed for guidance, and is known as the Temple of Hopes; the Final Five visited it on their travels, though Ellen insists that D'Anna seeing their faces in the temple had nothing to do with them. It is perhaps worth noting here that Pythia's lines associating the Final Five with the temple's priests are clearly reflected in the God-inspired vision. When Boomer comes to take her off for dissection, Ellen mentions a 'tumbrel', referring to the carts used to take condemned prisoners to the guillotine during the French Revolution (suggesting that Cylon Earth had some kind of analogue to this event), and Anders in his Hybrid-style vocalisations quotes snippets of *Paradise Lost*, including 'He it was, whose guile, stird up with Envy and Revenge, deceiv'd The Mother of Mankind' (associating Cavil with Satan) and also 'The mind is its own place, and in itself can make a Heav'n of Hell, a Hell of Heav'n'.

Patching Things Up: The Fleet, After the Mutiny

The reorganisation of the Quorum is significant in light of the Fleet's previous political efforts. Its make-up, rather than being based on colony of origin, is now based on the ships as political units, echoing the 'Galacticans' of *Galactica 1980*, who had abandoned a Colonial identity in favour of one as people of the Fleet. However, in the case of the Galacticans, the change took place over 30 years, during which time old religious and Colonial identities no doubt became gradually eroded: in this case, making the captains the Fleet's political representatives means that the social hierarchy noted in Season Three, with the Capricans at the top and Sagittarons on the bottom, remains unchallenged. Consequently, if a captain is inclined to ignore religious or ethnic persecution on his or her ship, there is no-one to prevent it from happening. Even Moore acknowledges that this marks a greater shift from democracy toward authoritarianism. Further emphasising the unfairness of the system, the podcast for 'Islanded in a Stream of Stars' indicates that each captain gets one vote, regardless of the size of population he or she represents. The decision is also a clever one from the perspective of the ruling elite, providing a sop to the captains who opposed Roslin during the mutiny by giving them power, but at the same time ensuring their position is owed to her, and thus that they will not substantively oppose her. The new order is suggested by Lee, whom Roslin has asked to take over the 'heavy lifting' for the rest of her presidency. Roslin tells him, 'My only concern about you, is that you're so hell-bent on doing the right thing, that you sometimes don't do the smart thing'; this is ironic, as, while the new system is certainly smart, it is highly questionable if one could call it 'right'.

The *Galactica* itself, meanwhile, is beginning to fall apart under the strain of recent events. Tyrol attributes the damage to the ship to the fact that it was old to begin with and has been through a lot since the attacks, though it also seems some of the original contractors cut corners. Significantly, Adama wants the crew fixing the damage to be human, and, when it transpires that Cylon technology appears to be the best answer, as they have an organic resin that can meld with metal to make it stronger, Adama only makes the decision to use it after excessive drinking and taking of pills. This shows that, even though he is happy to adopt Cylon jump drive upgrades, and even to force them on the rest of the Fleet at gunpoint, he himself has boundaries past which he is not comfortable working with the Cylons. However, the decision to do so is paralleled in his re-promotion of Tyrol to Chief; when Tyrol says 'I'm a Cylon', Adama remarks 'Is that right? So's my XO'.

Starbuck, meanwhile, appears disappointed to learn that she is not the missing Seven model. This is explained when she says, 'I need to be something', indicating that, the mutiny over, she is now back to seeking a role. When Anders says, 'You know what it is to have something you have to do', she replies, 'I used to'. She has found Earth and helped put down the mutiny, but is still alive and on the Fleet, and puzzled as to why. We also encounter the *Inchon Velle*'s brain specialist Doctor Gerard. (Jonathan Hodgman, the actor who plays him, has claimed in his Twitter feed that he suggested they call the character 'Doctor Zee', in homage to *Galactica 1980*.) The same ship, according to 'Maelstrom', also boasts a psychologist, suggesting it has a specialty in the treatment of brain disorders. It is never explained how Boomer intends to locate the Fleet; presumably Cavil's unnamed informant, who tipped him off about the attack on the Hub, is still keeping them up to date.

In Search of a Ho Called Ellen: Writing and Production

'No Exit' was Ryan Mottesheard's first script for television (he was at the time *Battlestar Galactica*'s script coordinator, a job normally held by aspiring writers), and he did a good job considering his lack of experience; the clunkiest and slowest scenes are the John and Ellen ones, which were written by Moore up to the one where John brings Ellen a drink, following which Mottesheard took over. Moore had intended his Cavil and Ellen scenes as a B-plot for 'A Disquiet Follows My Soul', subsequent to the reveal of Ellen as the Fifth. However, according to Moore, it seemed too big a story to convey simply in a B-plot, and as the writing team were at the same time developing a plotline involving Anders revealing the backstory to the Final Five, it was suggested that the Ellen sequences might be combined with this. The script was then polished by Weddle and Thompson, and later by Espenson. Mottesheard says that initially the action was intended to play over several episodes, but the team felt that intercutting between Ellen and John in the past, and *Galactica* in the present, was too confusing and the story was instead distilled into a single episode. Flashbacks to life on Cylon Earth were also considered at one point.

Although much of this was worked through before the script went to draft stage, there are some significant differences between the draft and final versions. The scene with Lee and Roslin is absent from the drafts; in the earliest one, dated 23 April 2008, Roslin does not appear at all, and in the second, dated two days later, she appears only briefly in Adama's quarters, where she becomes dizzy and Adama goes to get her a drink of water – which is when, in this draft, he

66: NO EXIT

notices the crack in the wall. In the 23 April draft, Kara is much more concerned about Anders' health, siding with Cottle over the issue rather than trying to pump Anders for information about her nature. The plotline where Tyrol identifies the damage to the ship also went through a couple of iterations; originally Adama did not ask Tyrol to resume his post as Chief, and the 23 April draft had Tyrol expanding on the idea that the ship wasn't built entirely to specifications, saying, 'It's not uncommon for budgets to run over, but the contractor has promised a certain price'. The 23 April draft also features the story of Daniel less strongly; he is mentioned much later, and the description of how John destroyed the model through poisoning the embryonic fluid in which the Daniel copies were maturing, does not appear. The 23 April draft has Ellen referring to John leading a rebellion against the Final Five, though we do not know who else was involved. Both this and the 25 April draft have a beat where, as Ellen and Boomer escape, the Centurions move to stop them, but Ellen does the same eye-recognition trick that Anders did in 'He That Believeth in Me', and they stand down. In both drafts, also, when Boomer is introduced, Ellen asks if she has been taught 'the swirl'. This, picking up on the deleted scene from 'The Hub' that implies that some models automatically share memories among themselves upon downloading, suggests that the Cavils engage in this practice, which would explain their unity of thought.[94] The drafts also contain some banter between John and Ellen in which the former suggests that a lifespan of nearly 2,500 years (expanded, in a recorded but deleted version of the same scene, to 'approaching 3,000') ought to have given her some wisdom and maturity, and, when she protests that they attempted to pass on their wisdom to their creations, sarcastically informs her that the place of the Final Five in history 'as the robots with the hearts of gold' is assured. Later, after referring to his mechanical ancestors being slaves, Cavil observes, 'and from your side of the family, Mom, I got this body. Really? This is your idea of intelligent design?' In the 25 April draft, Anders explicitly says of the First Cylon War, 'It broke our hearts to see the cycle repeating like it had on Kobol and on Earth'. In her monologue about achieving self-awareness, Ellen says, 'The Lords of Kobol once felt that Man could never break the fourth wall … They believed this until one day Man stole their fire and created the first Cylons, the first artificial life. And then Man, in his arrogance, believed Cylons could never break the fourth wall … and Man believed that right up until the moment the first Centurions rebelled'. An amusing stage direction in the 25 April draft describes Adama entering his quarters 'with a head of steam, in a mood to slam something', and adds, 'If I was a model ship, I'd be worried'.

The Daniel story was, according to Moore, written in because the team had established that there were 12 Cylon models and designated Sharon as Number Eight before they came up with the idea of the Final Five; as eight and five make

---

94 Furthermore, in 'The Hub', the Cavil who started the Civil War was killed by D'Anna after the Hub's destruction, meaning that he is permanently dead, but the Cavil who appears after his death in 'No Exit' shares his memories and ideas.

13, there must be a missing Cylon model. The story's title is taken from that of a 1944 existentialist play by Jean-Paul Sartre, which famously contains the line 'Hell is other people'. The Fleet ship *Inchon Velle*'s name appears to allude, for no discernible reason, to that of a port city in Korea that was the site of a battle in the Korean War.

Moore, regarding the character of Ellen, says, 'I really like the idea that we were going to see a different Ellen ... I didn't want her to be a completely different Ellen Tigh, in that she still likes to drink and smoke and fuck ... and she's probably still troubled. But that she's a slightly different person, she's not some idiot, I mean she really is one of the Final Five Cylons. She has this history, she has this knowledge, she has this intelligence that we haven't seen before'. John Hodgman, who played Doctor Gerard, was a friend of Moore's, and was also suggested for the role by Espenson; both the 23 and 25 April drafts identify the character as being played by Hodgman, indicating that casting for this role was decided early on. The set of the interior repair site was built around the wall of the soundstage, to save money. The episode also contains new, one-off, introductory text: 'This has all happened before/And will happen again. The Cylons were created by man. They rebelled. Then they vanished. Forty years later they came back. They evolved. 50,298 human survivors. Hunted by the Cylons. Eleven models are known. One was sacrificed', in an attempt to summarise the Cylon backstory for the audience. Moore says the idea was developed by editor Andy Seklir and producer Paul Leonard, to 'deliver the audience the idea of, okay, this is a specific episode where we want you to really pay attention to the Cylon mythos'. 'No Exit' is the last episode to feature a pre-titles sequence with introductory text in any form.

Espenson, in the *Chicago Tribune* interview, says, 'Both stories in the episode were very difficult to write, because they both required finding interesting ways to convey massive amounts of information'. Ellen actress Kate Vernon is quoted in *The Official Companion Season Four* as saying that, when filming her previous episode, she had asked, 'Is there any chance that I'm coming back at all? As a Cylon?', and that Moore had told her, 'No, you're not coming back as a Cylon. You'll come back in a couple of dream sequences or fantasy sequences'. More than anything, 'No Exit' conveys the improvisational nature of television writing, as the team use the episode to cover holes, explain discrepancies and fill in backstory as preparation for the final push.

67: Deadlock

FIRST TRANSMISSION DATE: 20 February 2009 (USA/CANADA)

WRITER: Jane Espenson

DIRECTOR: Robert Young

CREDITED CAST: Kate Vernon (Ellen Tigh); Donnelly Rhodes (Doctor Cottle); Rekha Sharma (Tory Foster); Roark Critchlow (Piano Player); Bodie Olmos (Lieutenant Brenden [sic] 'Hotdog' [sic] Costanza); Keegan Connor Tracy (Jeanne); Patrick Currie (Enzo); Brad Dryborough (Hoshi); Lara Gilchrist (Paulla Schaffer); Rebecca Davis (Naia); Merwin Mondesir (Marine #1); Tammy Gillis (Marine #2)

STUNTS: Brett Chan (Thug #1); Dustin Brooks (Thug #2); Justin Thames (Thug #3); Jeff Sanca (Thug #4); Sharon Sims (Dogsville 'Ite'); Chad Sayn (Steelworker)

KNOWN UNCREDITED CAST: Patrick Gilmore (Rafferty); Bear McCreary (Joe's Bar Patron)

SYNOPSIS: Ellen and Boomer return to *Galactica* in their stolen Raptor. Boomer is arrested and thrown in the brig, while Ellen meets with Roslin, Adama, Lee and Tigh and tells them about John and his plan to reinstate resurrection, before she and Tigh have an emotionally fraught private reunion, making love on the wardroom table. Some of the rebel Cylons want to take the Final Five and strike out on their own in the basestar, as they can now reproduce by procreation. The Five vote but, as Ellen (angered upon learning the circumstances of Caprica-Six's pregnancy) abstains, they are deadlocked. Ellen visits Caprica-Six, reveals that she and Tigh made love, and assures her that she will not make Tigh choose between them. Later, however, she announces that she has voted to go to the basestar. When Tigh objects, Ellen points out to Caprica-Six that Tigh loves Adama and the *Galactica* more than he loves either of them. Caprica-Six, under enormous emotional stress, miscarries. Ellen then changes her mind and agrees that they should stay with the Fleet. Baltar returns to his cult to discover that Paulla has been organising them in his absence, stockpiling food and defending it with weaponry looted from corpses during the mutiny. Baltar challenges her leadership by announcing that they must use their own food resources to feed the hungry people of Dogsville; but, when they do so, their food is stolen at gunpoint by the Sons of Ares. Baltar persuades Adama to authorise his cultists as an auxiliary civilian defence force, overseeing food distribution. The cultists rally behind Baltar.

ANALYSIS: In 'Deadlock', power relations within the Fleet shift as the Cylons become more integrated, and as the Baltar cult receives official recognition. However, a major obstacle to integration returns in the form of the resurrected Ellen Tigh, pursuing, as always, her own agenda.

Praise the Lord and Pass the Ammunition: Baltar versus Paulla

At the cult's lair, Baltar returns to find that his followers have, in fact, done very well for themselves in his absence. They are selling jewellery and stockpiling food, and Paulla looks deeply sceptical of Baltar's self-serving attempts to justify his flight to the basestar. Baltar's subsequent insistence that they should share their food with others is, at first, a clear attempt to grab power back from Paulla under the guise of philanthropy. However, he admits to Head Six that he did enjoy feeding the people, and she tells him that he can give people hope, which Paulla, with what Baltar deems as her 'icy pragmatism', cannot. Although initially intended as a cynical political move, the act of giving has clearly opened something else up in him. The situation has obvious Biblical overtones, with Baltar's food distribution recalling Jesus's Feeding of the Multitude and his aphorism 'When you share your food, God makes it tenfold', echoing Ecclesiastes 11: 1, 'Cast thy bread upon the waters: for thou shalt find it after many days', which is normally interpreted as an exhortation to give to others without thought of immediate reward. However, in response to the threat from the Sons of Ares, Baltar's position is not exactly Christlike: in his speech, prompted by Head Six, he says, 'There is a way to bring hope to the lower decks, to the whole of this poor ship. There is a way to win! ... She thinks we can't get what we need! ... All we need is strength! And strength comes from within ... And guns! More guns! Bigger guns! Better guns! And when we have those, we will win!'

As a result, a power struggle within a tiny religious cult has consequences for the politics of the Fleet. The other new religious organisation, the Sons of Ares, is developing into a criminal gang now that Zarek is no longer there to provide support. In the original cut of the scene where Caprica-Six is attacked when visiting Dogsville, the thugs tell her to go back to her one true God; and Moore in his podcast explicitly identifies them as members of the Sons of Ares. As a response to this, Baltar cuts a deal with Adama, pointing out that starving civilians could breed revolution, that the Marine forces are overstretched, and that the people have 'no representation, no recourse', as a direct result of the Quorum being replaced with the Fleet captains. More importantly, Baltar makes it clear that the Cylon presence is encouraging anxiety among the populace. In a deleted scene intended to come after Caprica-Six is attacked in Dogsville, Lee suggests using Centurions as police, and Adama rejects this vehemently; and indeed this solution would probably meet with a similar response from the people. Having the cultists as a civilian police force in charge of food redistribution means that neither the Cylons nor the Marines are involved; and, as the cultists are not motivated by profit, they will not attempt to exploit their position. Unfortunately, how this affects the balance of power on the ship is never explored; in particular, the danger of giving Paulla legal access to heavy weaponry is a plot thread the writers really ought to have developed, given the look of satisfaction that comes over her face toward the end of the story when she raises and cocks her semi-automatic rifle.

Come Together: Continuity and Unification

In continuity terms, the Cylons are now putting up pictures of their own dead on the memorial wall, affording them individuality, although this does not appear to include the Centurions. This presumably means that either no Centurions have died since the rebels joined the Fleet, the skinjobs still do not consider them their equals, or else that this is not a normal part of Centurion mourning practice. As Leobens do not appear to fly combat missions, the three Leobens on the wall were presumably killed when Narcho fired on the basestar in 'The Oath', unless one of them is Kara's Leoben, who apparently stayed behind on Earth. We see Dogsville again; a deleted scene reveals that Caprica-Six's reason for being there at the start of the episode is to obtain some anti-nausea medication from an herbalist. Although this is not directly stated in the episode, Moore indicates in his podcast that a large number of mutineers, including Racetrack and Skulls, are currently under arrest on the prison ship, contributing to the undermanning of the Fleet, which would also explain why Connor no longer appears to be tending bar. Enzo, Kat's ex-lover from 'The Passage', has now joined the Sons of Ares. Roslin and the new Quorum appear to be operating from *Galactica*. This is presumably because *Colonial One* has too many ties to the old order, but it further highlights the increasingly autocratic nature of the Fleet. There are a few hints of upcoming story developments: Joe's Bar has now acquired a piano, and Tyrol's dark 'Nice to see you again' to Boomer indicates that the pair still have unfinished business.

We also learn that the Cylon obsession with voting comes, at least in part, from the Final Five themselves: as Tigh sarcastically puts it, 'We *invented* majority rule!' Narratively, this derives from *Galactica 1980*, in which the Cylons were a hierarchical society with democratic practices at lower levels, such as groups of Centurions voting on their course of action. Roslin says she doesn't think she has ever called Caprica-Six by her name before, although a deleted sequence from 'Taking a Break from All Your Worries' has Roslin calling her 'Caprica'. Both Roslin and Caprica-Six have ceased experiencing the opera house vision, and the latter says that it has been absent 'the whole time since I've been pregnant'. This suggests the opera house vision is by way of a conditional prophecy, as Caprica-Six would not be carrying and protecting Hera if she were mother to Liam, which also brings up the possibility of the Cylons leaving the Fleet. Tyrol actor Aaron Douglas has explained on his Livejournal fan community the character's decision to support the separatists: having come to terms with the knowledge that Nicky is not his son, and believing that he and the other Cylons will never be accepted in the Fleet, he is feeling increasingly detached from the human race.

Whatever the tensions, this episode does show tentative signs of unification between the factions. This is symbolised by the rather obvious metaphor of the cracks in *Galactica* being imbued with the Cylon organic resin in order for the ship to remain functional. The Cylons are, clearly of necessity, flying CAP with the humans. A Heavy Raider assigned to Red Squadron uses the call sign 'Red Turkey', referencing the human slang expression 'turkeys' for Heavy Raiders as used in 'Maelstrom'. Although Adama is still plainly conflicted over the integration, he and Tigh can joke about the latter's Cylonhood; when they drink together, Tigh declares at one point, 'Great grandpa was a power sander'. Ellen likens the situation of the Final Five after the loss of Earth to that of the Fleet in the present day, providing common ground between the groups.

Suffer the Little Children: The Return of Ellen

This episode sees the return to the Fleet of Boomer and Ellen (with Hot Dog asking, as Ellen emerges from the Raptor, 'How many dead chicks are out there?') Ellen here appears, on the surface, much like the original Ellen: jealous, making ill-thought-out allegations, and conspiring against other people. Her accusing Tigh of incest is more than a little unfair, as he could not have known that he was one of Caprica-Six's creators, the Sixes also look rather like an idealised version of Ellen, and in any case he believed Ellen was dead. Ellen also does not show a similar revulsion over the fact that she herself had sex with a Cavil. However, what the new Ellen has that the old one lacked is a guided, strategic intelligence. Her possessiveness of Tigh and her creation of John also suggest abandonment issues, probably stemming from the relationship she had with her father. Consequently, none of Ellen's behaviour in this story is accidental.

Ellen deliberately engineers Caprica-Six's miscarriage. She knows that the Cylons cannot conceive unless they are in love; she herself says, 'The child Hera is the hope for a new blended future'. Although Moore, in his podcast, suggests that perhaps Cylons have conceived with each other before but never brought a child to term, this appears to be contradicted by 'A Disquiet Follows My Soul', in which everyone seems surprised that Caprica-Six has conceived at all. Ellen initially laughs off Tigh's affair with Caprica-Six, but when she learns a child was conceived, she attacks him, saying 'All those years we tried to have children and we never could. You must have been laughing your shiny, shiny head off … It was impossible. You didn't love me'. Leaving aside Ellen's possessiveness of Tigh, the child is a direct threat to her power, as him having a permanent link to Caprica-Six would divide her husband's loyalties between the Significant Seven and the Final Five and weaken Ellen's strategic position within the Fleet as the wife of the XO. Ellen's and Tigh's inability to conceive together may inform the fact that the Seven apparently cannot reproduce among themselves as the Cylons on Earth could. That God would allow Caprica-Six to conceive in the first place, however, makes sense, as Tigh initially rejected his Cylon nature and needed some motivating factor to bring him closer to the Cylons, such as a permanent relationship with Caprica-Six and parenthood to a unique child. However, as Tory and the separatist faction realise, a pure Cylon child could also divide the Cylons from the humans, as it offers the possibility of reproduction.

We know that Ellen believes in God; when Tigh says, 'No wonder we had to invent some compassionate god for them to believe in; we couldn't have them deify us, could we?' she says, 'We didn't invent anything'. She must also be aware of God's plan, as indicated by her remarks about Hera; she mentions Simon to Caprica-Six, showing she knows about the Farms and about the Cylons' attempts to conceive. She would therefore also be aware that God would go to extreme lengths to prevent the rebel Cylons from leaving the Fleet. Tigh observes, regarding Ellen and the basestar, 'You don't even wanna go', indicating that a sudden belief in Cylon self-sufficiency is not her motivation. When Liam, in the sickbay, begins to gain strength, this is when Ellen says to Caprica-Six, 'You and he can stay on *Galactica*, I'll go away with the others', at which point the foetus's heartbeat ceases. Although Moore says in his podcast that he wanted to leave it ambiguous whether or not God actually intervened to cause the foetal distress, the connection is clear, in that Liam only begins failing when his continued existence threatens to cause the rebel Cylons to leave the Fleet. Ellen has thus engineered a way of getting Tigh back through forcing God to destroy Tigh's child; she, in her new incarnation, is therefore capable of manipulating God.

No Way Out: Writing and Production

Moore's commentary indicates that the episode did not undergo many changes from start to finish; the title was originally to have been 'Drowning Woman', referring both to *Galactica* and to Caprica-Six, and it was Espenson who changed it to 'Deadlocked'. One difference is that Baltar's return to *Galactica* was originally to have come later on in the series, and was moved back to speed up events in his storyline. Another is that the Final Five were originally to have been deadlocked due to Anders's inability to communicate his vote; however, it was then decided that he should make a statement in the previous episode indicating that he wanted to stay with the Fleet, so that Ellen would then have the deciding vote and the tension would rest on which path she would choose. Minor changes, according to the podcast, included having Caprica-Six attacked in Dogsville rather than, as in the earlier version, while walking down a corridor. The writing team were open until a very late stage to the possibility of Caprica-Six having her baby, or even still being pregnant at the end of the season, but eventually decided to have her miscarry, clearly as having a pure Cylon child would have removed the focus from Hera.

By Moore's own admission, this episode serves mainly as the start of the writing team tying up the series' loose ends, reintroducing Boomer to the Fleet, reuniting the Tighs, killing Liam and reminding the audience about the opera house vision. Ellen's arrival aboard the Raptor is a call-back to her very first scene in 'Tigh Me Up, Tigh Me Down'. More significantly, the team wanted the episode to convey the idea that a new order is springing up on the Fleet, as different groups of civilians begin running their own affairs, and as the question of who belongs in the Fleet becomes increasingly nebulous. In terms of things to watch out for, Bear McCreary appears in Joe's Bar as an extra, and the pianist known as 'Slick' in the following episode, 'Someone to Watch Over Me', can also be seen in the background when the camera focuses on Kara, suggesting that this scene was filmed at the same time.

Moore says in his podcast, regarding the Final Five Cylons, 'They're thousands of years old, they've become incredibly sophisticated, complex machines ... they're even more sophisticated than the skinjob Cylons'. This certainly holds true in the case of Ellen, making it clear that, were the rest of the Final Five to operate at full potential, they would be the most formidable force in the series.

BY YOUR COMMAND: VOL 2

68: Someone to Watch over Me

FIRST TRANSMISSION DATE: 27 February 2009 (USA/CANADA)

WRITERS: Bradley Thompson & David Weddle

DIRECTOR: Michael Nankin

CREDITED CAST: Kate Vernon (Ellen Tigh); Donnelly Rhodes (Doctor Cottle); Rekha Sharma (Tory Foster); Roark Critchlow (Slick); Bodie Olmos (Lieutenant Brenden [sic] 'Hotdog' [sic] Constanza); Brad Dryborough (Hoshi); Iliana Gomez-Martinez (Hera); Sonja Bennett (Specialist 2nd Class Marcie Brasko); Darcy Laurie (Dealino); Rika-Shaye Gair (Young Kara Thrace); Patrick Gilmore (Rafferty); Cherilynn Fulbright (Dionne); Curtis Caravaggio (Nathanson); Ivan Cermak (Corporal D Wallace); Torrance Coombs (Lance Corporal C Sellers); Samantha Kaine (Off-duty Crew Person)

STUNTS: Maja Stace-Smith (Sharon Stunt Double)

KNOWN UNCREDITED CAST: David Weddle (Smoking Man in Joe's Bar)

SYNOPSIS: The Fleet's pilots search for a habitable planet as repairs continue on *Galactica*, with the ship being affected by power fluctuations and vibration. Sonya, the Six who is the basestar's representative to the Quorum, demands that Boomer be handed over to them for trial and, probably, execution. Kara visits the Agathons, and Hera gives her a drawing of a pattern of dots. Tyrol visits Boomer in the brig; she demonstrates to him how to project, and shares with him projections of a life together, with a house and a daughter. In Joe's Bar, Kara begins spending time with a mysterious piano player known as Slick, who is composing a piece of music; she helps him, and in doing so revisits her childhood with her composer father. Realising that Hera's drawing is really a musical score, she incorporates it into the composition, and the pair discover they have written 'All Along the Watchtower'. Starbuck realises Slick is her father, and he vanishes. Tyrol, having failed to get Boomer released by legal means, helps her escape the brig. Unbeknownst to him, she then assaults and ties up Athena in the communal bathroom, has sex with Helo and kidnaps Hera, fleeing *Galactica* in a Raptor.

ANALYSIS: 'Someone to Watch Over Me' is a clever synthesis, drawing connections between the story of Kara, coming to terms with the last of her childhood issues through a loving vision of her father, and that of Boomer, screwing over both Tyrol and the Agathons and stealing Hera, through a manipulative vision of herself and Tyrol as parents.

Now That's Slick: Kara and her Head Father

The first of this episode's storylines has obvious parallels with 'Maelstrom'. However, in this case, Kara's encounter with her dead parent involves, not an inward-looking exploration of her personal problems, but a creative process leading to the rediscovery of 'All Along the Watchtower' and sharing of it with the world at large. Kara, as a person, normally concentrates on the work at hand as a means of avoiding her issues. At this point, however, as the opening montage makes clear, her daily routine has become so boring and repetitive that she cannot find any sort of fulfilment in it, and is spending her spare time at Joe's Bar. Although Helo has managed, at great effort, to reacquire Kara's possessions, which, as per Fleet custom, were auctioned off after her death, the only thing she wants is a DAT tape of a live album made by her father, *Dreilide Thrace Live at the Helice Opera House*. When Slick says that composing his song is 'hell', Kara retorts, 'So then, quit. What's the point?', and he responds, 'Point? The point is to bring a little grace and beauty to an otherwise brutal existence'. As Kara is drawn into the act of composing the song, Slick reassures her that she may not actually lack a purpose: 'Sometimes lost is where you need to be. Just because you don't think you have a direction, doesn't mean you don't have one'. Through doing something that is creative, rather than utilitarian, Kara is able to find a new purpose.

In doing so, she confronts Slick over her father's departure. That this still affects her is highlighted early on when she talks about how Slick's composition makes her feel: 'Made me think of someone chasing after a car ... It's like losing someone you care about. Their car pulls away. You chase them. But they're going too fast'. The look she gives him at this point is childlike; innocent and expectant. The exact reasons for her father's departure, and why he apparently cut off contact with his family, are never pinned down: Slick says that it was because his wife wanted him to quit being a musician and take a regular job, but Moore, in the podcast, also says, 'Her mother was the soldier, that dragged her around to the different bases', which would, if nothing else, have made it difficult for her father to stay in touch. Although she may not get all the answers she wants, through composing the song with her father, Kara is at least able to reconcile herself to him. The episode thus sets up Kara's crucial role in the series' climax, without making its importance too obvious.

The Future That Never Was: Boomer and Tyrol

The second major storyline continues the theme, in recent episodes, of exploring the relationship between the Final Five and a member of the Significant Seven, in this case through Tyrol's relationship with Boomer. Tyrol's story has clear parallels with Starbuck's. Tyrol, like Starbuck, is doing repetitive work he finds unsatisfying and boring. He and Boomer using their dream of mustering out together and having a house and a child, to get through the drudgery of labour, chimes with Slick's remark about adding grace and beauty to a brutal existence. Now, however, he has lost this dream, and is both surrounded by women who look like Boomer, and tormented by the idea that, had he known his Cylon nature earlier, things might have been different. Like Starbuck, he has a reunion with someone he loved and lost, and with whom he works through his issues, but the difference is that Starbuck's father was sent by God, and Boomer by Cavil. Tyrol says, 'There isn't a soul on this Fleet that doesn't have blood on their hands', which also includes Starbuck; however, whereas Starbuck, in this story, produces something that gives the promise of the Fleet coming together for a brighter future, Tyrol's actions lead to division, kidnapping and, possibly, at least one death, to judge by the grim appearance of the Eight Tyrol leaves in Boomer's cell. As if to emphasise this, Starbuck and Slick in Joe's Bar are surrounded by fairy lights, suggesting that they are among the stars, whereas Tyrol, below decks, is surrounded by sparks, recalling Job 5: 7: 'Man is born to trouble as the sparks fly upwards'.

Tyrol also has clear feelings of betrayal. Although he may have become more detached from the Fleet in recent episodes, he still clearly supports Adama and Roslin, preventing the *Galactica* from jumping away during the mutiny, and accepting Adama's request that he return as Chief. However, Adama and Roslin here show that this support is not reciprocated: when he asks that they block Boomer's extradition 'as a personal favour', Roslin instead signs the order in front of him and tells him he is 'dismissed'. Tyrol attacks an Eight with a wrench, in a callback to his assault on Helo in 'Flight of the Phoenix', again showing his violent side and exposing the depth of his anger over the situation. The Cylons' request for Boomer's extradition is understandable: even though her betrayal of her model is, ironically, one of the most human and individual acts a Cylon has committed, the ensuing conflict led to thousands of rebel Cylon deaths. The response of the Fleet leaders, who have no love for Boomer and who also need the rebel Cylons to stay in the alliance, also makes sense. However, their high-handed manner alienates Tyrol, with tragic consequences.

As for Boomer, her feelings in the matter are evidently complicated. Although her kidnapping of Hera was clearly planned in advance, she and Cavil could not have anticipated precisely how events would unfold when she returned to the Fleet, so it is likely that the specifics of the plan were dependent on the situation in which she found herself. Whatever her wishes, also, the strength of feeling against her from both humans and rebel Cylons means she would never again have a place in the Fleet. The plan also shows that Cavil is able to outthink Ellen under some circumstances, as Ellen's belief in her own rhetorical skills has led her not to question Boomer's motives in rescuing her from Cavil.

Although Boomer does prey on Tyrol through the projection of their house and daughter, the detail in the vision shows she has put a lot of thought and emotion into it, and at the end of the story, she tells him, 'There's something I want you to remember. All the things that I said. About us. I meant them with all my heart. So no matter what happens–', showing her inner conflict. Equally, although Tyrol offers to accompany Boomer, she refuses; while it would undoubtedly help Cavil to have one of the Final Five in his custody, she does not want to put Tyrol in danger. Her escape is an inversion of the events of 'Rapture', in which Athena and Caprica-Six killed Boomer and fled with Hera; here, Boomer kidnaps Hera, savagely beating Athena in the process. Her treatment of Athena picks up on the idea, first seen in 'The Eye of Jupiter', that she envies the fact that Athena has a husband, a child and the respect of at least some of her peers. The parallel is further drawn in a deleted scene, intended to come right before Boomer attacks Athena, in which Athena happily discusses with Hot Dog the problems of parenthood. Although a note from Michael Nankin that Moore reads out in the podcast makes it clear that Boomer did not actually intend to seduce Helo, but had to 'go through it to keep her cover', there is a bitter parallel with Athena seducing Helo on Caprica in Season One, through pretending to be Boomer. As Boomer and Helo make love, the soundtrack emphasises the creaking of the ship under strain, symbolising the way their action is tearing Helo's and Athena's family apart. When Boomer prepares to jump her Raptor, Adama orders the pods closed, believing, rightly, she would not jump the Raptor inside the *Galactica* and risk destroying the battlestar; not only does Boomer still have feelings for Tyrol, but none of the Significant Seven – even Cavil – would intentionally wish to kill the Final Five. Whatever Boomer's feelings in carrying out her plan, ultimately, she does follow it through, allying herself with Cavil throughout.

Continuity and Worldbuilding

Regarding the integration of the Cylons, they now have a representative on the Quorum, Sonja. Their intention to apply the death penalty to Boomer shows that the idea of mortality has a kind of macabre novelty value for them. Ellen's response to the Boomer issue is to say that she will speak in her defence but leave the decision as to her fate to the rebel Cylons, clearly choosing to play the politician in this episode, in marked contrast to her behaviour in 'Deadlock' when her own interests were threatened. Boomer is said to have caused 'thousands', not 'millions', of deaths, which again implies that the decline in Cylon numbers took place prior to the Civil War – Tigh, who was not aware of the losses among the Cylons, estimated their population in 'billions' in 'Guess What's Coming to Dinner' – contradicting Natalie's implication that large-scale death was something the Cylons had not encountered before Cavil's attack. A few episodes earlier, in 'A Disquiet Follows My Soul', Tyrol was the one to formally request a Cylon presence on the Quorum; but the Cylons' first act upon gaining this presence is to request the extradition of his former girlfriend. This episode shows that the Final Five can project, that projections can be shared, and, when Tyrol meets his and Boomer's seven-year-old daughter, that beings who do not actually exist can appear in projections; retrospectively, it is possible that

68: SOMEONE TO WATCH OVER ME

Tigh's visions of Ellen when making love to Caprica-Six may also have been a projection.

The episode also emphasises the decay of the Fleet. Starbuck's 'motivational' speech shows that they are running low on human and physical resources: 'Planet-hunters, make sure to draw long-duration provisions. If those clapped-out FTLs go down when you're out there, you're gonna get mighty hungry waiting for the SAR[95] birds to find you. As you know, the mutiny has thinned our ranks. We cannot give all you Raptor jocks back-seaters. Savour this alone time but do not whack too much. We need you to conserve your O2'. The first line is also a blink-and-you-miss-it set-up for the way in which Boomer smuggles Hera off the Fleet, hidden in an equipment container. Earlier episodes, such as 'A Disquiet Follows My Soul', have shown that jumping a ship creates a shockwave capable of buffeting nearby vessels; *Galactica*'s poor condition, however, means that Boomer's jump actually damages the hull. It has been implicit throughout the series that it is unsafe to jump a Raptor while it is still inside *Galactica*, as otherwise it would obviate the need for the smaller vessels to take off before jumping. In one deleted scene, Roslin makes parallels between her own imminent death and the fact that the *Galactica* is also being given only a temporary reprieve by the Cylon repairs, saying to Adama, 'You're gonna lose her'.

In continuity terms, a few weeks are said to have passed since Anders entered his catatonic state, registering brain activity but no consciousness. We see the ship's day care, which has been frequently alluded to, but previously appeared only in a deleted scene from 'Dirty Hands'. Kara opens her locker and briefly sees the face of her corpse from Cinder Earth in the mirror, in a familiar visual motif. In terms of outside references, the title of the episode is from a song by George and Ira Gershwin that deals in part with the need to find love and acceptance. In a letter to Bear McCreary, later published in Maureen Ryan's *Chicago Tribune* blog, David Weddle says Slick's character was in part inspired by Hoagy Carmichael's cinema roles as a 'piano playing confidant' in *The Best Years of Our Lives* (1946) and *To Have and Have Not* (1944), and his keyboard style was indebted to Chico Marx, in particular the latter's trademark 'shooting the key' gesture, which Slick uses at the end of the song. 'Helice', where Kara's father performed, is the Greek name for the constellation Ursa Major/the Great Bear, and is thus probably an inside homage to Bear McCreary. There are a couple of original-series references: the brand of 'Tauron toothpaste' that Kara offers as a prize to the pilot who finds a habitable planet is 'Felgercarb', an original-series expression that translates as 'shit', suggesting that the prize is Tauron Felgercarb, and thus, 'bullshit'. The tune Kara identifies as Nomian's 3rd Sonata, Second Movement, is actually a quote from the music accompanying the dialogue that opened many episodes of the original series ('There are those who believe that life here, began out there …'), by Stu Phillips. The plotline concerning Boomer's extradition recalls similar controversies in our universe

---

95 Search and rescue.

over the extradition of criminals and terrorists, particularly from countries that do not have the death penalty to ones that do.

I Like a Gershwin Tune: Writing and Production

Judging from the March 2008 story document read out by Moore in his podcast, this episode, which was first developed in the midseason writers' retreat, changed little in its essentials; the main difference seems to be that the document places the Boomer-Tyrol story as the A plot, and the Kara-Slick story as the B plot, whereas the final version reverses the emphasis. The character of Slick developed over the rewrites. In an interview with Maureen Ryan in the 28 February 2009 *Chicago Tribune*, Weddle says, 'Ron Moore ... felt [Slick] came off like a stock bartender/wise man from a hundred other movies ... Our next draft went too far into the obsessive details of composing, and Nankin felt it made the character too self-absorbed. But on the third draft we tacked back to a middle course between the two drafts'. In early versions, Boomer and Helo did not have sex; this was added by Nankin, in a note that read in part, 'I can't believe that Helo and Boomer don't fuck. That's the juiciest scene in the story. It could be incredible! ... It's great, let's do it! We'll burn up the internet over that one for months!' Early drafts had Anders conscious, walking and talking, and also featured the Agathons, when Kara comes to visit, puzzling over Hera's drawing; this was abandoned because, Moore says in his podcast, it drew too much attention to the dots and gave the game away to the audience.

In the same interview with Maureen Ryan, Thompson says that a Boomer-Tyrol reunion 'was something we'd floated in the room in Season Three, but didn't know where it fit or what it would be. Like so many *Battlestar* ideas, it simply hung in limbo until the time was right for maximum impact'. Weddle says the story came from two sources: 'First, Mark Verheiden suggested that Kara's father appear in Joe's Bar on *Galactica* as a kind of ghost, or projection of her subconscious. The second inspiration came from Ron Moore, who had the idea of Hera actually drawing the notes of "Watchtower"'. Featuring Kara's father allowed the team to work through the issues that were briefly introduced in 'Valley of Darkness'; when Kara first speaks to Slick, she is sat next to a mirror, to highlight that the pianist may be a reflection of herself.

Due to the amount of music in this episode, the writers worked closely with Bear McCreary during its development; and Weddle, in the interview with Ryan, says, 'We modelled Slick on Bear because Bear undergoes the same tortures of the damned trying to top himself with each new *Battlestar* score'. Weddle adds that, as the actor who played Slick would need also to play the piano, 'Nankin suddenly had an idea: "Why don't we have Bear audition for the part?" Brad and I thought we had nothing to lose ... I thought [Bear in his audition] did a great job for a non-actor. But we realised we needed a professional actor who could deliver all of the emotional nuances and levels to the character'. Weddle himself appears as an extra in the first bar scene; Thompson was also present, but no shots of him made the final cut. The network

68: SOMEONE TO WATCH OVER ME

objected to the sequence where Helo is seduced, saying it was damaging to his character that he could not tell the two women apart, but Moore, in his podcast, says, 'I felt it *is* a knock against his character ... I just said, "Let's do that. He doesn't have to be perfect, and there will be consequences."' Tyrol and Athena both recognise Boomer on sight, implying that Cylons have some ability to tell individuals of the same model apart.

'Someone to Watch Over Me' achieves closure on some levels, allowing Kara to work through her issues about her father, and revealing Boomer's true intentions in returning Ellen to the Fleet. Its ending also opens up new issues, such as the further significance of 'All Along the Watchtower', and what will come of the kidnapping of Hera.

69: Islanded in a Stream of Stars

FIRST TRANSMISSION DATE: 6 March 2009 (USA/CANADA)

WRITER: Michael Taylor

DIRECTOR: Edward James Olmos

CREDITED CAST: Kate Vernon (Ellen Tigh); Donnelly Rhodes (Doctor Cottle); Rekha Sharma (Tory Foster); Dean Stockwell (Cavil); Bodie Olmos (Lieutenant Brenden [sic] 'Hotdog' [sic] Costanza); David Patrick Green (Captain Fenner); Kerry Norton (Medic Layne Ishay); Iliana Gomez-Martinez (Hera); Lara Gilchrist (Paulla); Leela Savasta (Tracey Anne); Darcy Laurie (Dealino); Susan Hogan (Captain Franks); William Samples (Captain Greene)

STUNTS: Monique Ganderton (Six Stunt Double); Dave Hospes (Stunt Repair Worker #1); Dean Choe (Stunt Repair Worker #2)

SYNOPSIS: As *Galactica* continues to deteriorate, the Fleet captains argue over the disposition of her salvageable goods. Adama allows a Heavy Raider to jump to the Cylon homeworld, the Colony, to look for Hera, using coordinates provided by Ellen, but the Colony has moved on and Adama refuses to authorise further efforts. Kara gives Baltar the dog-tags she took from her corpse and asks him to analyse the blood on them. At a memorial service to honour the crewmembers killed in the hull breach caused by Boomer's escape, Baltar reveals the results of his analysis – namely, that Kara Thrace is dead – and says that this is proof of life after death. The Cylons hook Anders up to a Hybrid tank, but this does not improve his condition. When Kara prepares to shoot him as a mercy killing, he suddenly awakens and begins making Hybrid vocalisations. It becomes apparent that he is starting to control the ship, linking with the electrical circuitry in the bulkheads through inductive elements in the Cylon repair substance. Tigh orders him disconnected on the grounds that he might access the FTL drives, which were also upgraded with Cylon technology. Adama comes to terms with the loss of the *Galactica,* and announces that he will transfer his flag to the basestar.

ANALYSIS: 'Islanded in a Stream of Stars' is a fairly tedious and frequently self-indulgent story, with few significant developments. We will again be using the director's cut released on DVD as our main reference point.

69: ISLANDED IN A STREAM OF STARS

Treading Water: An Episode With No Purpose

Bad episodes in Battlestar Galactica are usually flawed because of something that occurred during their execution, not because they contribute little to the ongoing narrative; 'Islanded in a Stream of Stars', however, is pure filler. There are four main story points: the integration of the Cylons into the Fleet, Adama's grief over giving up his ship, Kara being outed as the reincarnation of her former self, and Boomer bonding with Hera. These we have either seen before, will see again in the series finale, or, in the case of Kara's undead status, go absolutely nowhere, making this episode somewhat redundant. What we have in this story is therefore a collection of scenes that appear significant, but, on closer inspection, turn out to be pointless melodrama.

The episode begins with a sequence in which a Six we have never seen before sacrifices herself to save the life of Specialist Dealino, who has made only the briefest of appearances in 'No Exit'; as a result, there is little to no emotional engagement on the part of the audience. Perhaps if, as originally intended, the deckhand in question had been Figurski, there might have been some tension in the scene. The subsequent conversation where a fatally wounded Eight asks to see Tigh, and thanks him 'for the privilege of finally being able to meet my father before I die', is a nice character piece, but again says nothing new regarding Tigh's conflicted feelings about being the co-creator of the Significant Seven. It is also somewhat undermined by the later maudlin scene between the Tighs in which Ellen tells Tigh that the Significant Seven are his children.

The storyline about Adama's decision to transfer his flag to the basestar is similarly redundant. The initial scene in which the Fleet captains fight over disposition of *Galactica*'s usable parts is interesting, underlining that they have very different priorities from the previous Quorum, as their main concern is keeping their ships running. However, Moore himself admits in his podcast, 'I think I hit the story of Adama losing his ship a little too hard ... What seemed like a couple of beats here and there in the story-plotting process, when all is said and done and you look at the completed episodes, I feel there's a repetitive quality'. Adama has a long speech about his sense of disillusionment, running in part: 'I've had it up to here with destiny, prophecy, with God or the gods. Look where it's left us. The ass end of nowhere. Nearly half of our people are gone. Earth a worthless cinder, and I can't even walk down the halls of my ship without wondering if I'm gonna catch a bullet for getting us into this mess'. While this is nicely dramatic, it has already been established that Adama, as an atheist, is sceptical about the various spiritual claims made in the series, and it is hardly surprising that, given all that has happened recently, he is rather fed up with the supernatural. The sequence where he attempts to whitewash his quarters and collapses weeping has visual parallels with Kara's dream of trying to paint over the mandala in 'Maelstrom', but there seems to be no reason to draw these parallels, and it also makes one wonder if Leoben is suddenly going to turn up and have sex with him.

Likewise, the scientific confirmation that Kara is dead accomplishes nothing;

she was regarded with suspicion before, and is still regarded with suspicion. We do get a rather nice speech from Baltar, running in part, 'I don't believe that God speaks to us on high through some appointed human mouthpiece. But he does speak to us. He speaks to each one of us directly. In our hearts. And it's up to us to listen. If you find yourself straying from the one true path, then perhaps you'll be lucky enough for God to send you an angel'. It also has some good dialogue from Kara, where she says to Anders, 'The old me is dead and gone, same as the old you. Just took me a while to accept it'. However, all of this is just making subtext text, spelling out things that have been obvious in earlier episodes.

The scenes with Boomer and Hera forming a bond feature very good performances from both Grace Park and child actor Iliana Gomez-Martinez. However, according to the podcast, one of Olmos's earlier cuts of the episode deleted them entirely, highlighting how unnecessary the whole subplot is. While it explores Boomer's conflicted feelings over Hera, involving both anger at, and love toward, the child, this ambivalence will be perfectly well conveyed in the following story.

Pilgrims of Mortality: Continuity and Worldbuilding

Within the Fleet, the Quorum scenes show how Lee's continued presence in the new regime makes sense: in a nakedly autocratic government of ship's captains, it is logical to have the Admiral's son acting as the representative for the Admiral's vessel, as the Admiral himself is unlikely to have the time to attend Quorum meetings. Captain Franks of the *Prometheus* makes a return appearance in the Quorum scene. The Baltar cult are continuing their rise to power within the Fleet, with several ships, including the *Prometheus* and the *Argo Navis*, offering to headquarter them, and Paulla, who is once again toeing the cult's party line, setting up a number of new food redistribution centres as well as at least one 'people's medical clinic'. Kara has evidently taken her picture down from the memorial wall at some point since 'He That Believeth in Me', when she complained to Anders that no-one had removed it; here, she reaffixes it between those of Kat and Dualla, two people whose lives she ruined. Dealino says regarding the hull breach, 'The Leobens are calling it the proverbial straw, so we've got five more jumps max'. This suggests that the Leobens deal mainly with planning and design issues, explaining why they have not been seen among the combat pilots or repair crews. In the argument between the Six and Dealino, the Six says that the Cylon goo will not bond with the 'inferior alloys' used in the ship's construction. Tyrol is currently in the brig, having turned himself in after Boomer's escape, although it is never stated what the charges are.

In this episode, Baltar and Caprica-Six meet again and begin the rapprochement that will continue over the remaining episodes. Head Six seems strangely displeased about this, telling Baltar, 'She's not the one', to which Baltar responds, 'She's the only one'. This displeasure is even stranger given that Caprica-Six experiences the opera-house vision a few scenes prior to this meeting, as it raises the question of why God would send her the vision otherwise. Either Head Six is practising reverse psychology, or perhaps God is ambivalent about involving her, given the fallout from her relationship with Tigh, and is trying to prevent the conditional prophecy from being fulfilled.

Regarding the Cylons, we learn from Ellen that their homeworld, the Colony, is 'where we and the Centurions went after the First War once we convinced them to abandon their own experiments with evolution in exchange for resurrection technology'. Moore, in his podcast, slightly contradicts this by saying that the Colony was built around the ship the Final Five brought from Earth. Like the Resurrection Hub, it is capable of movement. Its design picks up on the Giger imagery of Season One; and at least three old-style Raiders, as previously seen in 'Razor', are visible when Boomer lands her Raptor: one flying and two docked. The Eight, as she dies, says, 'So much confusion', in a slight misquote of 'All Along the Watchtower', suggesting again that characters experience true visions in the space between life and death. Ellen notes that she and Tigh had 'millions' of children, and five months are said to have passed since the Cylon Civil War began, which, if the destruction of the Hub occurred four months prior to 'No Exit' and Anders has been in his catatonic state for a few weeks, is a return to the idea of a brief Civil War preceded by an unexplained event that caused a huge die-off among the Cylons.

In terms of internal references, Anders, in Hybrid mode, quotes the folk song 'There's a Hole in the Bucket, Dear Liza'. This, as well as Helo's disparaging reference to *Galactica* as a bucket, is a call-back to the terms 'the Beast and the Bucket' from 'The Captain's Hand'. Laura refers again to her dream of building a little cabin to live in, which picks up on the previous story's theme of getting through difficult times by creating, or hoping for, something finer. Anders's hand comes out of the tank to grip Kara's, recalling the Hybrids' actions in both 'The Passage' and 'Razor'. Among his more significant pronouncements is, 'The neural anatomy of fear and faith share common afferent pathways'. This recalls what Head Six said about pleasure and pain in 'A Measure of Salvation', and suggests that, as Baltar used pleasure to overcome pain in that episode, so religion can be used to unite the humans and Cylons. He also says, 'A closed system lacks the ability to renew itself', explaining why the two groups have to combine. The story begins with a scene of Hera crashing the tactical model of *Galactica* into that of the basestar, foreshadowing the clash between the Fleet and the Colony next episode. The title of the episode is a reference to a line from the book *The Outermost House* by Henry Beston, about the author's life on an isolated beach: 'For a moment of night we have a glimpse of ourselves and of our world islanded in its stream of stars – pilgrims of mortality, voyaging between horizons across eternal seas of space and time'.

Hera Today, Gone Tomorrow: Writing and Production

Moore says in the podcast that this story suffered as a result of the change of storyline for the second half of the season, as discussed in the Season Four overview essay: 'Over the course of the writers' strike, I started to rethink the plan ... and as a result this episode went in a very different direction'. Originally there was to have been no recon mission to find the Colony, but Moore felt that Adama should at least be seen to try to find Hera. The writers had also been concerned about going to the Cylon homeworld: as Moore puts it, 'We always kind of said, it's a place we don't want to go, you know you're always going to be disappointed by whatever it is'. The funeral scene was scripted as three separate services, but then editor Andy Seklir cross-faded between them in post-production, emphasising new connections within the Fleet.

Olmos directed the episode, apart from the scenes by Nankin discussed below and the inserts of Baltar in the lab. The latter were late additions directed by Wayne Rose and used a stand-in for James Callis. The episode also features a brief insert from Season One of Baltar looking into a microscope; this appears to be an unused take, most likely from 'Six Degrees of Separation'. Olmos says he came in as a last-minute replacement when the original director, Frank Darabont (best known for the 1994 film *The Shawshank Redemption* and 1999 film *The Green Mile*), became unavailable. The scenes with Boomer and Hera in the projection were filmed at the same time as those of Boomer and Tyrol in the previous episode, and so were mainly directed by Michael Nankin. Olmos took over at the point where Hera goes up to Boomer's daughter's room. According to the podcast, originally the team had thought that the damaged section of *Galactica* would be deep within the ship, but as they wanted to do a dramatic blow-out scene, and as nothing directly contradicted it, the setting was moved to close to the ship's skin. Tricia Helfer did her own wire-harness stunts in this sequence. Moore says in his podcast that he had expected the scene of Adama and Roslin getting high would again cause problems with the network, but in fact they did not complain, he believes because this was close to the end of the series.

The Official Companion Season Four quotes David Eick as saying of the series: 'Every nook and cranny felt like it had been explored ... Even though the characters could have gone on and on, the *story* had reached its conclusion. That's why we had to end the show'. This episode clearly indicates it was the right decision. If *Battlestar Galactica* had stretched its ongoing narrative out over seven or eight seasons, the audience would have had to suffer many more episodes like this one.

70: Daybreak
(Parts One, Two and Three)

FIRST TRANSMISSION DATE: 13 March and 20 March 2009 (USA/CANADA)

WRITER: Ronald D Moore

DIRECTOR: Michael Rymer

CREDITED CAST: Callum Keith Rennie (Leoben); Kate Vernon (Ellen Tigh); Rick Worthy (Simon); Mark Sheppard (Romo Lampkin); Donnelly Rhodes (Doctor Sherman Cottle); Matthew Bennett (Doral); Rekha Sharma (Tory Foster); Kerry Norton (Medic Layne Ishay); Dean Stockwell (Cavil); Bodie Olmos (Lieutenant Brenden [sic] 'Hotdog' [sic] Costanza); Leah Cairns (Lieutenant Margaret 'Racetrack' Edmondson); Brad Dryborough (Hoshi); Colin Lawrence (Lieutenant Hamish 'Skulls' McCall); Lara Gilchrist (Paulla); Colin Corrigan (Marine Allan Nowart); Leela Savasta (Tracey Anne); Darcy Laurie (Dealino); Finn R Devitt (Nicky); Iliana Gomez-Martinez (Hera); Tobias Mehler (Zak); Antony Holland (Julius Baltar); Simone Bailly (Shona); Elan Ross Gibson (Nurse Barbara); Skylar Tyj (Calvin); France Perras (Sandra); Sarah Deakins (Cheryl); Tiffany Burns (Reporter Carolyn); Kevin McNulty (Frank Porthos); Stefanie Samuels (Police Officer); Richard Jollymore (Marine #1); Dan Payne (Sean); Holly Eglinton (Stripper); Anthony St. John (Marine #2)

STUNTS: Raymond Sammel (Adama Stunt Double); Duane Dickinson (Lee Stunt Double); Monique Ganderton (Number Six Stunt Double); Colin Decker (Cavil Stunt Double); Carolyn Field (Racetrack Stunt Double); Ashley Earl (Stunt Militia); Yvette Jackson (Laura Stunt Double); Kim Howey (Kara Stunt Double); Maja Stace-Smith (Sharon Worker Stunt Double); Sylvesta Stuart (Skulls Stunt Double); Shawn Beaton (Stunt Worker); Carolyn Anderson, Dan Pelchat, Mark Chin Gerald Paetz, Mike Desabrais, Simon Brunette, Guy Bews, Kit Mallet, Paul Wu, Leif Havdale, Charles Andre, Paul Pat, Jonathan Kralt, Simon Burnett, Dan Redford, Raymond Chan, Nikolas Baric, Sharon Simms (Stunt Marines); Brett Armstrong, Rob Boyce, Doug Chapman, Larissa Stadinchuk, James Bamford, Jovan Nenadic, Janina Nenadic, Lloyd Adams (Stunt CIC)

KNOWN UNCREDITED CAST: Tiffany Lyndall-Knight (Hybrid); Gareth Riceman (Marine); Leo Li Chiang (Tattooed Pilot); Ronald D Moore (Man at News Stand)

BY YOUR COMMAND: VOL 2

SYNOPSIS: <u>On Caprica, before the Fall</u>: Adama considers taking a civilian job, but decides to stay with *Galactica* until retirement. This leads to an argument between the Tighs, as Saul will not leave the service until Adama does. Roslin learns of the death of her father and sisters in a car accident, grieves, and allows herself to be set up by a friend with a younger man who turns out to be a former student of hers. She finally resolves to join Adar's presidential campaign. Lee meets Zak's girlfriend Kara for the first time; the pair feel a connection. Anders conducts an interview with a journalist, talking about how what really matters to him as an athlete is the search for perfection. Baltar finds his attempts to build a relationship with Caprica-Six interrupted by his obstreperous father, whose carer has walked out on him. Caprica-Six finds a suitable residence for his father, and a grateful Baltar agrees to provide her with access to the defence mainframe.

<u>In the present</u>: As the population of *Galactica* leave for other ships, Adama decides to launch a mission to rescue Hera from the Colony, finding its location, on the edge of a black hole, through coordinates supplied by Anders. Adama asks for volunteers; the Fleet is left with Lampkin as its President and Hoshi as its Admiral. Anders is connected to *Galactica*'s computers, and the ship jumps to the Colony; Anders communicates with the Colony's Hybrids, taking them offline. The *Galactica* rams the Colony directly, and as the Raiders and Vipers do battle, the Raptors carry raiding parties to board the Colony and seek Hera. Racetrack and Skulls are killed early on when their Raptor is hit by an asteroid. Boomer, troubled by Cavil's plans to vivisect the child, steals Hera and returns her to Athena; Athena kills Boomer. When the team return to *Galactica*, Helo is wounded and Hera, in the confusion, runs away; she flees to CIC, pursued by Roslin and Athena, and is found by Caprica-Six and Baltar, fulfilling the opera house prophecy. Cavil takes Hera hostage, but Baltar and Tigh negotiate, persuading him to let the girl go in exchange for the secret of resurrection. The Final Five pool their memories to provide this; however, in doing so, Tyrol learns that Tory murdered Cally and, in anger, kills her, triggering a firefight in which Cavil, realising the game is up, shoots himself. Debris hits Racetrack's Raptor, causing her dead hand to fall upon the missile launch button, and the resultant explosion pushes the Colony toward the black hole. To save *Galactica*, Starbuck executes a blind jump using coordinates derived from 'All Along the Watchtower', and the *Galactica* arrives at a habitable planet, which Adama names 'Earth'. They send a Raptor to guide the Fleet to the new world and colonise it, resolving to abandon their old technology and structures and instead to disperse across the surface and mingle with the natives. The Centurions take off on their own in the basestar to begin a new life, while the human-model Cylons remain with the colonists to create a new hybrid race. Starbuck, her mission completed, vanishes into thin air, Anders flies the Fleet into the sun and Roslin succumbs to cancer.

<u>150,000 years later</u>: Head Baltar and Head Six walk through New York's Times Square and speculate on the future of the hybrid human/Cylon race, and Hera is

70: DAYBREAK

revealed to be Mitochondrial Eve.

ANALYSIS: Despite a deeply unsatisfying beginning, 'Daybreak' works well on a thematic level, providing a resolution for every character's story without feeling as if it is ticking off a laundry list of loose ends. Unfortunately, it is let down on a practical level, as the plan for colonising Earth makes absolutely no sense relative to what has gone before. As always, we will be using the extended DVD version as our reference point.

We Are All In The Gutter, But Some Of Us Are Puking At The Stars: The Flashback Storylines

The weakest part of the story is its emphasis on the fairly pointless flashback sequences, which are also clearly not contemporaneous with each other, just to add to the confusion. This is even more annoying on first viewing, when most people are eager to learn the resolution of the present-day storyline rather than wait through seemingly unrelated backstory. Indeed, it is a full 14 minutes and 30 seconds before the series returns to *Galactica* itself. There is a direct influence here from *The Godfather II*, in which flashback sequences of the Corleone family's past add colour and poignancy to the contemporary storyline. Much as Slick in 'Someone to Watch Over Me' used Nomian's Third Sonata as a touchstone when unsure how his composition was to continue, so Moore here appears to be using *The Godfather II* as a source of inspiration. However, much as Slick does not actually include Nomian's Third Sonata in his final composition, so the flashbacks really ought to have been cut once Moore discovered the first draft was over 130 pages in length.

The Roslin storyline in particular is deeply irritating. The scenario of her sisters being killed by a drunk driver immediately after attending a baby shower for one of them is clichéd, and we met them so briefly it is difficult to feel anything upon hearing they are dead; we never meet her father, also killed in the crash. Given that she has a terminal illness, it feels rather like piling tragedy upon tragedy for the character. This set of flashbacks is based on the series bible's entry for Roslin. However, the bible states, 'When Laura was 15 years old, both her sisters and her father were killed by a drunk driver. [Her mother] never recovered from the shock and Laura would spend the next 20 years caring for her mother in ways large and small', which gives the incident a very different place in Roslin's life, affecting her career and her self-image rather than simply providing a catalyst for her decision to go into politics. It also goes some way toward explaining why Roslin acts like a ditz during the baby-shower scene, as the character was supposed to be a teenager at the time the tragedy happened, though why she has to dress like one here is never explained. Finally, Roslin's flat looks more like a show flat than a real home. About the only interesting character aspect revealed is that she was willing to sleep with Sean despite his being her former student, which recalls the abandoned idea that she would have a May-December fling with Apollo – although the bedroom scene is shot so ambiguously that it is not apparent what, if anything, Roslin actually did with Sean. We also learn that she is a former smoker who kept a secret stash of cigarettes in the bathroom. Neither revelation is really earthshaking enough to justify the amount of time spent on the storyline.

Baltar's story is at least more convincing, tying in with the idea of his discomfort with his rural roots; his father's accent is more or less Irish rather than the Yorkshire one attempted by Callis in 'Dirty Hands'. Although the miniseries has already provided an explanation for why Baltar gave Caprica-Six access to the defence mainframe – it was in return for her extensive assistance with the CNP project – these flashbacks imply there was a more personal dimension, in that he was grateful for her help with his family problems. However, the set-up is a little too reminiscent of *Frasier*, featuring a cantankerous working-class father, an urbane, successful son who finds him embarrassing, and a beautiful woman mediating between them. Far more seriously, it raises the question of why Baltar has never confronted Caprica-Six about the fact that she kindly found his father a place to live, and then promptly burned him to ashes in a nuclear attack. We also learn that Baltar was mentoring a local teenager, Calvin; unfortunately, as Calvin has an androgynous look and long dark hair, the suggestion is less one of mentorship than of Baltar having a more flexible sexual orientation than previously suggested.

The story about Lee and Starbuck is the only one of the flashbacks that is really successful, and that could be argued to contribute something of value to the main narrative. Lee is already flirting with politics, giving Starbuck an earnest lecture on civics over dinner, running in part: 'If you don't participate in the global conversation them you are giving up your voice. You are giving up your right to have a say in the way that our society is run ... That's what the uniform stands for, it's what we train to defend'. This is a counterpoint to the way in which Lee ultimately became the architect of the authoritarian regime currently governing the Fleet. Zak, however, describes his brother as a 'true cynic', suggesting that he knows there is a less idealistic side to Lee, whatever he may say about democracy. Although we see a framed mandala painting hung on the wall, Starbuck's flat is neat and ordered compared with the way it looks in 'Valley of Darkness', suggesting Zak was a civilising influence on her. She tells Lee that she is not afraid of dying, which might seem to contradict the theme running through 'Maelstrom'; however, in that episode, Head Leoben states that she has never told anyone about her fear of death. The crucial point, however, comes when Lee and Starbuck briefly end up in a clinch, but disentangle themselves when she knocks over a glass and the drunken Zak momentarily awakes, murmuring 'Oops, something's broken'. This serves to indicate that their complicated mutual attraction was there from the beginning, with the abortive clinch as a kind of unfinished business informing all their subsequent actions. In the bookending sequence, Lee, returning home and knocking over a pair of wine glasses, finds a pigeon in his flat; he tries to sweep it out with a broom and fails, but, when he leaves it alone, it departs of its own accord. A pigeon in the house is believed, in some traditions, to be a harbinger of death, making the connection with Starbuck; Zak, sleeping on a couch in Starbuck's flat, will later die, and Lee, waking up on a couch in his own flat, has been led by Starbuck to Earth, humanity's end.

The Adama and Tigh flashbacks are partly successful, in that they pick up on the theme in the present-day storyline of careful plans being destroyed by personal obsessions and random events. Ellen's scheme for she and her husband to live together full-time is thrown into chaos when Adama decides not to retire into civilian life and Tigh continues as his XO. Adama's rejection of the polygraph test makes sense, as being given a petty question like 'Have you ever stolen money from a cash drawer' is insulting for a serving Colonial officer of many years' standing. It is debatable, however, what seeing the future Admiral throwing up down his shirt-front as he gazes up at the stars after a drunken evening with the Tighs contributes to our understanding of the character. We also have a flashback story involving Boomer as a young rookie, having trouble learning to fly and starting her controversial relationship with Tyrol, with Cally prophetically warning him, 'You know, there's people you can count on, and people you can't. It's good to know the difference between the two'. Again, though, this tells us nothing that was not already apparent; indeed, the scene with Cally appears to have been inspired by the deleted scene from the miniseries in which she warns Tyrol that sleeping with his superior officer is a bad idea. The storyline seems to have come about as an attempt to provide gratuitous return appearances for Cally and (in a deleted scene) Socinus and Prosna.

The brief sequences of Anders are interesting in that they have surreal visual links to his present; he is sitting in a tub, talking to a blonde female reporter and a silent cameraman, in parallel to the present, in which he sits in a Hybrid tank, about to be questioned by Kara on Adama's behalf. His words in the interview, 'The beauty of physics … you know, the elation of action and reaction, and that is the kind of perfection that I want to be connected to', spill over into his Hybrid dialogue, 'Spins and turns, angles and curves, the shape of dreams half-remembered. Slip the surly bonds of Earth and touch the face of perfection', suggesting that he is remembering the Caprica incident as he speaks.

In his podcast, Moore says that he regards the flashbacks as 'the A plot' of the story, which is bizarre, and suggests he was fast approaching creative burnout. Given that Moore was working on *Caprica*, a series that sets up the events of the Cylon War and Adama's early childhood, at the same time as 'Daybreak', it is also tempting to speculate that the flashbacks are a form of conceptual bleed-through.

Loose Ends: The Rescue Mission

The outset of the present-day story sees Adama preparing to transfer his flag to the basestar. He reconciles himself with Kara, calling her 'daughter' for the first time since 'Torn', and wants to fly the last Viper off the ship himself, in a symbolic gesture, all suggesting he has come to terms with the idea of leaving

Galactica. However, his identity is too tied up with his role as the ship's commander. It is seeing a picture of Athena with Hera on the memorial wall, as Hot Dog collects the unclaimed pictures on the grounds that no-one should be left behind, that clearly triggers the same impulse as underlay his desire to conduct a suicide run in the miniseries. He then proposes a final mission that, if it is successful, will rescue the child; and if it isn't, then the loss of the ship will matter little in the long run. There are echoes of *The Wild Bunch* (1969): like the outlaw gang in Peckinpah's film, Adama chooses to engage on a desperate venture to rescue a vulnerable person and achieve redemption, with religious overtones throughout. However, there is also a practical side to his decision: the continued presence of Cavil's hostile Cylon force is an ongoing threat to the Fleet, and sacrificing the *Galactica* is tactically worthwhile to destroy or cripple that menace. Finally, even though non-volunteers significantly outnumber volunteers, it is a mission that is likely to find support in the Fleet: as the jubilant dialogue between Racetrack and Skulls implies, the people who have been demoralised by the discovery of Earth, and confused by the alliance with the rebels, are once again fighting enemy Cylons to protect innocent civilians.

This storyline sees further developments regarding the rise of the Baltar cultists. Paulla points out that they have 'a solid majority on over half the civilian ships in the Fleet'; they have apparently gained converts from among a population made anxious by the damage to *Galactica*. At her urging, Baltar demands a voice in government, but Lee, quite rightly, identifies this as a power bid, saying that he has never seen Baltar perform a truly selfless act. The irony, however, is that, had Lee not instigated the new government based on Fleet captains, Baltar would never have been in a position to make his demands. Baltar's decision to join the volunteers for the mission appears to be inspired partly by Lee's words about selflessness, but also by an earlier deleted scene in which Paulla talks him out of volunteering for the mission. As Baltar, having made his choice, leaves the cultists, he says, 'I don't belong to you, Paulla, I never belonged to you. You appropriated me. I'm sorry. I'm sorry if I led you to believe– They're all yours now, Paulla, enjoy them'. This recognises that Paulla, as shown in 'Deadlock', is the one seeking power within the Fleet, and Baltar has been the means to that end.

The volunteers are divided from those who will remain by a line marked on the deck. This both recalls the salt-line ritual the pilots perform in 'Exodus' and symbolises the idea that the volunteers are crossing a line. This is reinforced by a sequence in which Adama is reluctant to hook Anders up to the ship's computers and describes it as a line he will not cross, while Starbuck points out that she, Anders and others have all crossed the line for him, and he must commit himself to the mission too. Among the volunteers are the Agathons, Hot Dog, Ishay, all of the Final Five (Tyrol remarking to Tory as he steps forward, 'You got something better to do?'), Caprica-Six, Roslin, Hoshi and Cottle, although the latter two are then told by Adama to stay behind. Ishay volunteers even though she has previously been very anti-Cylon. Possibly the heroic sacrifices made by Cylons during the hull breach in 'Islanded in a Stream of

Stars' have changed her opinion, or her commitment to her profession overrides her personal feelings, or perhaps both. Hot Dog might seem to be an unusual volunteer given that he has a son, but presumably, being a combat pilot, he has already made arrangements for Nicky's future in the event that he is killed. The choice of Hoshi as Admiral is something of a narrative convenience, as having him off *Galactica* means Kara is the one who must input the jump coordinates, allowing her to program in the divinely-inspired formula. There is nothing professional or personal to recommend Hoshi for the job, and it seems particularly odd in light of 'The Face of the Enemy', which indicates that he was the lover of a man Adama recently had executed for treason.

Götterdämmerung: The Cylons

This story clears up some of the questions regarding the size of Cavil's forces. Clearly, even though Lee estimated in the previous story that Cavil had 'a thousand' baseships, the rebel Cylons must have been keeping his actual strength quiet, possibly for strategic reasons to keep the alliance together out of fear of the enemy, as Cavil's Cylons here are revealed to be in fairly dire straits. We see 'Razor'-era Centurions on the Colony as well as the 'Razor'-era Raiders in the previous episode; although Roslin wondered in 'Razor' why the Cylons would resurrect a model 'that by their standards is hopelessly obsolete', and Athena refers to most of the older models as having been 'scrapped', it seems likely that some remaining old Centurions and Raiders were brought out of storage to compensate for the Cylons' reduction in numbers. Furthermore, Cavil is seeking natural defences for the Colony in stationing it near a singularity, which would again suggest there are not enough baseships to protect it; only two are seen jumping in and out during the reconnaissance trip by Racetrack and Skulls. As Cavil was not forewarned about the attack, this also indicates that the informant he had on the Fleet has been killed or otherwise neutralised some time after 'No Exit'.

We also finally get closure to Boomer's storyline. Her own motivations are explored in her final scene, where she gives Hera back to her mother and asks Athena to tell Adama she owed him one. This is explained in a flashback to her cadet days, when Adama allowed her to continue as a pilot despite her poor performance record; she stated she would pay him back someday, but he dismissed this as unlikely. What this scene highlights are the qualities of love, compassion and forgiveness; as Adama showed these emotions to Boomer in giving her a second chance, so Boomer must now do the same in returning Hera to her mother. Athena shooting Boomer is within Athena's character: she has indicated to both Helo and Tyrol that, while she can understand why they acted as they did during Boomer's escape, she cannot forgive them, so it makes sense that with Boomer herself, she can understand but not forgive. Boomer accepts her fate, knowing that she would not be welcome on *Galactica* and that, after killing a Simon and kidnapping Hera, she cannot go back to Cavil either. While Boomer achieves some redemption through doing the right thing in the end,

Athena's reaction is perfectly understandable, given Boomer's role in kidnapping her daughter, beating her savagely, and seducing her husband.

The story's climax sees the return, and fulfilment, of the opera house prophecy. In this, Hera flees through *Galactica*, pursued by Athena and Roslin, and is found by Baltar and Caprica-Six, who take her into CIC, where the glowing figures on the balcony are revealed to be the Final Five. The Hybrid's words in 'The Hub', 'Close the doors. Protect the child', turn out to refer to different parts of this vision. Although God himself does not seem to fully understand the nature of the events it predicts, the prophecy culminates in what seems, inadvertently, to be a victory for God, as Baltar then talks Cavil into accepting Tigh's deal. The offer made to Cavil - resurrection in exchange for peace - recalls the agreement the Final Five made with the Centurions to bring about the end of the First Cylon War, and, finally, unites the humans and Cylons. In a deleted scene from 'The Hub', Baltar also provides an alternate meaning for the prediction that he will be Hera's father, speculating, 'Six told me that was our child. Hers and mine. I was the real father. Maybe I am. Maybe if her real father is that leader, prophet–', and it is in his role as prophet that he saves the child's life.

Baltar's speech to Cavil is an articulation of the series' concept of God:

'There's another force at work here. There always has been. It's undeniable. We've all experienced it. Everyone in this room has witnessed events that they can't fathom, let alone explain by rational means. Puzzles deciphered in prophecy. Dreams given to a chosen few. Our loved ones, dead, risen. Whether we want to call that 'God' or 'gods' or some sublime inspiration or a divine force we can't know or understand, it doesn't matter. It doesn't matter. It's here. It exists, and our two destinies are entwined in its force … God's not on anyone's side. God is a force of nature, beyond good and evil. Good and evil, we created those. You wanna break the cycle? Break the cycle of birth? Death? Rebirth? Destruction? Escape? Death? Well, that's in our hands, in our hands only. It requires that we live in hope, not fear'.

God is, therefore, an active, scheming participant, but one whose aim is not to favour either side, just to make them come together and produce a new, hybrid species – hence there may be some truth to Baltar's later attributing to divine intervention the fact that they are genetically compatible with the humans of Earth.

However, although God may devise such plans, as we have seen before, they can be easily foiled by haphazard occurrences. In this case, Tyrol's killing of Tory means that the secret of resurrection is lost, and a random chain of circumstances leads to the dead hand of Racetrack triggering the nuclear missiles. It is at this point that Cavil shoots himself, with a rationale explained by Moore in his commentary: 'Dean just said, "I think that, you know, he would figure it's game over, man, it's all pointless, and he'd just blow his brains out." That was his rationale, and I just went with it … He just thought, "What's the fucking point, now, there's no God, there's no nothing, we're not getting resurrection, they've got the girl? It's all going to hell, screw it," and he blows his head off'. Throughout the series, Cavil has continually presented himself as an oppositional figure, and although it is the idea that God is neutral that causes him to stand down his forces, the subsequent unpredictable explosion of random, chaotic violence leads him to conclude that actually there is no God, and he is living in a universe that exists without any objective meaning, purpose or intrinsic value. Furthermore, Cavil's plan for all of the Five to die among the humans and, upon download, return to awareness, acknowledge that he was right about the inferiority of human life and love him, has been rendered completely impracticable; not only is there no resurrection, and no hope that the rest of the Five will regain their former memories, but one of them is now dead.

In contrast, the *Galactica* is saved through another form of divine information. Starbuck types a numerical key based on the notes of 'All Along the Watchtower' into the navigation computer (saying 'There must be some kind of way out of here' as she does), leading the Fleet to its end on Earth. In the 6 Sept 2008 draft script of the third part, when Adama (not Roslin) asks where they are, Starbuck replies, 'Somewhere along the watchtower', but, according to Moore in his podcast, Rymer rejected this. The events of the past half-season culminate in this moment: the upgrading of *Galactica*'s jump drives with Cylon technology allows them to make the journey in a single trip. The Fleet also have little to fear from Cavil's forces at this point; although some Ones, Fours and Fives must have survived the destruction of the Colony, they are ultimately doomed without resurrection. While the Significant Seven do not appear to age, they do wear out: this is made clear in 'No Exit', when Cavil says that the destruction of the Hub means their 'extinction', and in 'The Hub', when D'Anna says 'And with a whimper, every Cylon in the universe begins to die'. Since, as Adama says, Earth is 'a million light-years away', the area they must search is so vast that they are unlikely to find it before they all perish.

Finally, a word on Centurion culture. The *Galactica*'s Centurions, who wear a red stripe to identify them in battle, can be seen making the same hand-signals and gestures as the human Marines. While this recalls the imagery of newly-conscious Centurions imitating the human models that was originally planned for 'The Ties that Bind', it stems from a different source. The Centurions were originally designed as Colonial military machines, and *Caprica* indicates that they have been programmed with Colonial military drill; while there was no need for them to communicate through hand-signals when they were a Cylon-only force earlier in the series, now that they are fighting alongside humans, who need verbal or visual signals, they are employing the gestures for their benefit. At the end of the story, the Centurions go off on their own, with parallels to the Thirteenth Tribe during the exodus from Kobol. Although fears are expressed that they might evolve again and return to wage war on the humans in the future, as they have still not returned after 150,000 years, the implication is that the current Centurions bear their creators no further animosity. Perhaps, ironically, they have gone on to found the pure machine race Cavil desired.

Arseholes Lag Behind: The Human Race's End

The Fleet's arrival on primitive Earth (with overtones of Douglas Adams's *The Restaurant at the End of the Universe*, complete with a man in a bathtub[96]) appears to resolve the question of when *Battlestar Galactica* is set relative to our own time. Adama tells Roslin he is calling the planet 'Earth' because 'Earth ... is a dream. One we've been chasing for a long time. We've earned it. This is Earth'. Strangely, although the African continent and the constellation Ursa Major are plainly visible as the Fleet approach the planet, no-one comments on the degree to which the constellations, continents, moon and sun resemble those of the nuclear-devastated Earth.

A key development comes when Lee proposes that they abandon Colonial technology and society: 'We break the cycle. We leave it all behind and start over ... One thing we should have learned, it's that, you know, our brains have always outraced our hearts. Our science charges ahead, our souls lag behind. Let's start anew'. Following on from the conversation Zak and Lee have in the flashback sequences, the impetus behind this seems to be Lee's idealism resurfacing in extreme form, as a counterbalance to all the cynicism he has been showing aboard the Fleet. However, Lampkin's reaction, 'I have to say I'm shocked at how amenable everyone is to this notion. Would have thought there'd be a general uprising at the idea of losing whatever little creature comforts we have left', was echoed at the time by many viewers. Adama's next line provides an explanation of sorts: 'Don't underestimate the desire for a clean slate, Mr Lampkin'. Presumably, since the tribulations of the Fleet stem largely from Colonial technology (the Cylons) and Colonial politics (the authoritarian, elitist system), the people want to start afresh. The previous experiment in planetary settlement, New Caprica, in which as many aspects of Colonial society as possible were retained, also proved somewhat less than successful. Thematically, the idea of starting over recalls Doral's remark in the miniseries: '*Galactica* is from a time when we were so frightened by our enemies that we literally looked backward for protection'. More pertinently, it is a call-back to the original series, in which cut dialogue from 'Lost Planet of the Gods' reveals that the founders of the Colonies abandoned their technology and started again from scratch: eschewing modern society and going back to the land to rebuild is a common trope of 1970s television. The dispersal of the Fleet is also a narrative echo of what happens when a major television project finishes, as the team leave to take up new jobs elsewhere in the world, and also in line with American fictional tropes of abandoning the corrupt old world for a spiritually-cleansing new frontier.

---

96 Albeit with an interesting reversal: in Adams' novel, the arrival of the Golgafrinchan fleet on Earth ruins an experiment set up by an alien computer to produce the Question to the Ultimate Answer to Life, the Universe and Everything, whereas in *Battlestar Galactica*, the Colonial/rebel Cylon Fleet's arrival on Earth is an integral part of God's experiment.

70: DAYBREAK

All that aside, the idea is, in the end, naively idealistic, and the way the Colonials go about it strains credibility. One thing they ought to have learned on New Caprica is that going from a technological, computerised society to an agrarian, craft-based one is very difficult, and that while making that transition they will need all the physical resources – metals, chemicals, tools and so forth – the Fleet has to offer. Vital skills, such as farming and medicine, also must be shared and passed on. However, rather than cannibalising the ships, and staying in a large group in order to pool resources, the colonists send the Fleet into the sun, and wander off in small groups and couples. The final testament to the misguided nature of the endeavour is the *National Geographic* article seen in the coda, which reveals that Hera died young; under the circumstances, it is a miracle that any of them survived long enough to become the ancestors of modern humans.

Roslin's death, murmuring 'So much life' as she observes the fauna of the new world from Adama's Raptor, clarifies the nature of the Pythian prophecy. In 'The Hub', Elosha shows Roslin a vision of her dying on a near-deserted *Galactica*. This is evidently a conditional prophecy or warning, as she makes it plain that this outcome is down to Roslin's selfishness and rejection of love. The fact that Adama puts his wedding ring on Roslin's finger in the vision, as he does when Roslin dies in reality, indicates that there is truth to the prediction, and also makes it clear that it is indeed a vision from God rather than just the action of Roslin's conscience. The next iteration of Roslin's death comes when she tells Adama to nuke the basestar during the standoff with D'Anna. This comes about as an accidental consequence of God's intervention: by giving D'Anna the vision of the Final Five, and killing off Natalie, God ensures that D'Anna, with all her suspicions and mistrusts, comes to power with no checks on her authority. As the standoff is resolved through God's subsequent intervention, the united Fleet travels to nuclear-devastated Earth, which is the planet toward which Pythia was leading them. Once the Fleet had passed Pythia's Earth, however, Pythia's prophecy is concluded, and all bets regarding the time and place of Roslin's demise are now off. Roslin's death thus illustrates the complicated and conditional nature of prophecy in the series.

150,000 Years Later: The Coda

'God's plan is never complete', says Head Six in her final conversation with Baltar and Caprica-Six, which is underlined by the episode coda. This sequence reveals three crucial things: first, that Hera was Mitochondrial Eve; secondly, that God, according to Head Baltar, 'doesn't like that name', implying that God may well be a super-advanced alien – and, thirdly, that Earth may well be going the same way as Kobol, Caprica and the original Earth. The warning message is reinforced by an image of a homeless person with a radio playing the Jimi Hendrix cover of 'All Along the Watchtower', as a montage of robots plays out on TV screens: all this has happened before, but the question remains as to whether or not it will happen again.[97] Taking the cases of Kobol, Caprica, nuclear-devastated Earth and the second Earth together, the implication is that humans are programmed to create intelligent robots at a certain stage of their development; although *Caprica* reveals that God did influence the emergence of Cylons in the Colonies, it also suggests that the Colonials would have developed them within a generation or two without intervention, and God encouraged the process along because the arrival of the Final Five was imminent. It is not actually explained how it is that humans came to be programmed with this drive, though logic dictates that it was done by one of the gods. The Prometheus myth of humans 'stealing fire' from the Gods, which Moore outlines in the podcast for 'Sometimes a Great Notion' by way of backstory to the series, is therefore a symbolic reference to humans, once they reached the appropriate stage of development, usurping the gods' power and creating their own intelligent race.

The idea that *Battlestar Galactica* is set in Earth's past was, according to an interview with Moore in the 21 March 2009 *Chicago Tribune*, one that the writing team had decided on from an early stage. In the DVD commentary, Eick, Moore and Rymer add that they toyed with the idea of having the Fleet arrive later, perhaps during Greek history so as to inspire Greek mythology, but decided this was 'too *Star Trek*' and instead had them arrive further back, to affect social evolution more generally. However, this does raise the question of how it is that, as Moore and Eick say in the commentary and in interviews, Colonial culture 'influenced' present ones, given the great temporal distance between us and them; indeed, one might ask why people on the Colonies, 150 thousand years in our past, nonetheless wear ties, drive cars, drink coffee and do many other things firmly associated with modern Western civilisation.

There are three clear reasons for this situation. The first is that of science-fiction film and television convention. In his DVD commentary for the movie *Aliens*, director James Cameron justified his inclusion of anachronistic

---

97 Outside of internal continuity, the idea of the repeating cycle could also explain the presence of two different *Battlestar Galactica* series (as presumably the 1978 series is another iteration of the cycle of human-Cylon warfare), and could even, arguably, explain the time discontinuity between the original series and *Galactica 1980*. In the original-series episode 'The Hand of God', the Fleet receives the Apollo 11 Moon landing transmission, meaning that the story takes place sometime after the landing occurred in 1969, and yet, in the *Galactica 1980* story 'The Super Scouts', which is set in 1980, the Fleet is said not to have experienced any Cylon attacks for 30 years, meaning that the latest time 'The Hand of God' could take place is 1950. Under the repeating-cycles argument, the moon landing transmission seen in 'The Hand of God' need not necessarily have come from the Earth they encounter in *Galactica 1980*; or, indeed, *Galactica 1980* might involve a completely separate iteration of the cycle, with different Colonials, different Cylons, and a different Earth, which would additionally explain all the discontinuities between *Galactica 1980* and the original series, and why the Earth seen in the 'Daybreak' coda has apparently not been visited by Galacticans or Cylons.

contemporary clothing, language and so forth in his future society by saying, 'We ... wanted to understand who these people were ... If everyone's running about in *Star Wars*-type costumes, it's a little harder to relate to who these people are'. The second is that, as Rymer says in the DVD commentary for 'Daybreak', Caprican society serves as an allegory to our own, and the similarity of artefacts highlights its allegorical nature. Both of these justifications are elaborated in a quote from the series bible:

> 'Colonial society is very similar to 21st Century Earth society and can be considered a parallel world for all intents and purposes. People watch TV, they follow professional sports, they use telephones, drive cars, have apartments, battle bureaucracies, wear ties, etc. etc. This is a deliberate creative choice – we are not trying to present a society of "weird space people". The people of *Galactica* and their world have been intentionally designed to evoke present-day American society as a way of drawing the viewer into the drama instead of wowing them with the trappings of a completely fantastical culture and society. Clearly, there are differences, but our creative intention is to make this series about us, rather than a fictitious them.'

The fact that the final sequence of 'Daybreak' takes place in Times Square, however, suggests an in-text explanation beyond all of these. The dialogue between Head Baltar and Head Six implies that humanity are programmed to develop along similar cultural lines, as Head Six says 'Remind you of anything?' and Head Baltar replies 'Take your pick. Kobol, Earth ... Caprica before the Fall'. Details may vary, such as Colonial society using DAT tapes as a common recording device, but clearly, in the *Battlestar Galactica* universe, all human (and indeed, skinjob Cylon) societies we have seen up to this point, eventually become decadent, commercialised and technological, with a predisposition for creating robots. Head Six believes Earth will beat the odds, because, she explains, 'Let a complex system repeat itself long enough, eventually something surprising might occur'; God's plan, evidently, is to repeat the same experiment over and over, until finally one society gets everything right. The fact that the gods are advanced beings who built the humans also explains how it is that the Greek pantheon recurs in different civilisations, as, if the one God exists and had a role in the creation of the humans, so might they.

This also ties in with the series' theme of 'All this has happened before, and all this will happen again'. The idea that a number of similar societies have developed throughout the universe explains the recurrence of technologies, tropes and even people: for instance, the original series featuring Adama with two sons and a daughter, and the new series featuring William Adama, with two sons and a drive to seek out daughter-figures. There are echoes here of *Blade Runner*, where the replicants are programmed with memories, human personality traits and the drive to ask existential questions about their nature, and also the neo-noir film *Dark City* (1998), in which the eponymous city turns out to be an experimental set-up created by aliens, with inhabitants who take on different social roles each time the clock strikes 12. Consequently, whatever the writing team's intentions, it is even possible that the New York we see in the coda is in fact another city on another Earth, continuing the experiment.

Brave New World: Continuity and Worldbuilding

The story contains a number of call-backs to earlier episodes. Roslin sits in a fountain when she hears the news of her family's deaths, recalling her dangling her feet in a fountain when she gets the news of her cancer in 'Epiphanies'. Racetrack and Skulls have been released from custody as the opportunity to volunteer has been extended to, in Lee's words, 'any former colonial officer [or] crewman incarcerated after the recent mutiny'; this also includes Tyrol, who begins the story in the brig. Not everyone appears to have accepted the offer, however, as Seelix is nowhere in evidence. It is unknown whether or not Kelly was re-incarcerated, as he changed sides during the mutiny, but he too is conspicuous by his absence. Racetrack and Skulls joke that they are the ones who get all the dangerous missions, which, given their history over the series, is broadly true, making their sudden deaths all the more startling. A number of Centurions, but no skinjobs bar Athena and Caprica-Six, participate in the mission, suggesting that the rebel Cylons were also given a choice to volunteer, and the Twos, Sixes and Eights of the basestar opted to stay behind. Lee, in the flashbacks, provides an apt summing up of Adama's character throughout the series, saying: 'Dad believes in himself. His uniform, his system, his way of life. And if you're not with him in that tiny little bubble, then you may as well not exist'. This neatly explains Adama's decision to go off on his own at the end of the story.

As 'Daybreak' is the final story of the series proper, it contains elements of symmetry and reflection with the miniseries. The miniseries begins with the Cylon attack on the Colonies, and 'Daybreak' climaxes with the Fleet attacking the Cylon Colony. Both campaigns involve the disabling of the target world's defences (in the case of 'Daybreak', using Anders to stand down the Hybrids equates to using a backdoor program to disable the system, as in the miniseries). Helo saves Baltar's life at the start of the series, but Baltar, at the end, saves Helo's daughter; and Caprica-Six, for her part, starts the series killing a baby and ends it saving one. Baltar's selfishness at the start of the series is mirrored by his selflessness at the end.

In continuity terms, we see Hot Dog carrying Nicky when collecting the pictures at the memorial wall; on Earth, Tyrol strikes out on his own without the child, which indicates that Hot Dog has taken over Nicky's full-time care. Jake the Dog makes a final cameo, appearing with Lampkin as he prepares to depart *Galactica* for the Fleet. There is a sly joke when Tigh, at the start of the story, tells Hoshi, who has just spilled some coffee, 'You'll never make Admiral like that'. Earth is said to have more wildlife than all the Twelve Colonies put together. Cottle's first name is briefly revealed to be 'Sherman'. We get direct confirmation that the present-day Hybrids are a single model of identical female humanoids, as the one seen on the Colony looks the same as the one aboard the basestar. Adama, in the flashback to his polygraph test, is asked 'Are you a Cylon?'; as the existence of human-like Cylons was unknown at that point, this is clearly a nonsense question intended to test that the machine is functioning correctly. A few deleted flashback scenes from 'Daybreak' part one show Tory and Boomer being released into human society, and Boomer learning of her parents' deaths; one of these, involving a conversation between Boomer and Gina right before the former goes into sleeper-agent mode, was later transferred to the follow-up 'The Plan', which is why it does not appear among the deleted scenes on the 'Daybreak' DVD. Although the Six is not named as Gina on screen, listings on the Propworx auction house site when the costume came up for sale reveal the character's identity.

There are also references to the original series, with its theme tune playing as the Fleet flies into the sun, and the idea of taking the fight to the Cylon homeworld echoing Baltar's proposal in 'Lost Planet of the Gods'. According to Moore in the podcast, the use of old-style Centurions was suggested by Gary Hutzel as an original-series callback. In terms of outside references, Anders's 'slip the surly bonds of Earth and touch the face of perfection' is a paraphrase of lines from John Gillespie Magee Jr's sonnet 'High Flight', which begins 'Oh! I have slipped the surly bonds of Earth/And danced the skies on laughter-silvered wings', and ends '... put out my hand, and touched the face of God'; this was also quoted in part by Ronald Reagan in his speech following the *Challenger* disaster. The story title itself might be partly an allusion to the war film *Operation Daybreak* (1975), about a group of patriots from Czechoslovakia's army-in-exile who are sent to Nazi-occupied Prague to assassinate Heydrich. The Simon dying on his feet in CIC visually recalls the death of the Yellow Man in *Blue Velvet*, which co-starred Dean Stockwell; and the sequence of Apollo chasing the pigeon is another *Blade Runner* allusion. The music as the Raptors first approach the planet's surface quotes John Barry's theme from *Walkabout* (1971). The aerial shots of the Earth landscape were a homage to *Out of Africa* (1985), with the sequence of flamingos taking off also referencing the title sequence to *Miami Vice*, which featured Edward James Olmos.

In real-life terms, Moore reveals in his podcast that the pan up from the moon 'is inspired by two shots ... the Apollo 8 shot, coming around the dark side [sic] of the moon, the famous Earthrise, and then the actual image of Earth is inspired by the Apollo 17 astronauts' shot of Earth'. The colonists' decision to abandon technology was in part drawn from the story of Cortez making his men burn their ships so as to commit themselves to the New World. Moore says in the podcast that the team had intended to show the Raptors exploding in the background during the scene where the colonists disperse on Earth to bring the point home, but this was felt to be too distracting. Mitochondrial Eve is the most recent common matrilineal ancestor of humankind, i.e. the most recent person in the female line to whom all humanity are related, but this does not mean that she is the only ancestor of modern humans, as there may be others in the male line of descendants. Critics have argued that, as the Milky Way galaxy is only 100,000 light years across, Adama's statement that they are a million light years away must be a mistake or exaggeration; however, given that the climax reveals that the universe contains two identical planets, with identical constellations (implying that they exist in two identical galaxies), anything is possible.

In a well-known inside joke, Moore himself is the man in the coda reading the article about the discovery of Mitochondrial Eve, perhaps suggesting that *Battlestar Galactica* is itself divinely inspired. In the podcast, he reveals that he actually wore a Jimi Hendrix T-shirt under his top for the scene. He also worked in a couple of personal references: Ellen's line about 'You and me in a house or in a tent or on the street' was something he had said to his wife Terry, and his own first memory of his father is of him returning from Vietnam, an inversion of Lee's memory of seeing his father leave on military service. In another inside joke, the dismal island where Tyrol, still immersed in self-pity and self-loathing, intends to spend his exile, was meant to be Vancouver Island, but Aaron Douglas, who is of Scottish descent, was excited by the idea that it might refer to Scotland, so Moore wrote in a line about 'highlands' to suggest that this was the case (in the process, casting similar aspersions on Scotland). The planet seen at the start of the first episode of 'Daybreak' is clearly Caprica rather than Earth. The *Kodiak*, a ship from the video game *Command & Conquer: Tiberian Sun*, is visible in the Fleet in one establishing shot. The channel airing the documentary on robotics is MSNBC, part of NBC Universal, the media conglomerate that also owns the Sci-Fi Channel.

Walking Down Madison: Writing and Production

The idea for the story, according to Moore in his podcast, came in part from an image he and Eick had early on of Six in New York City: 'I remember having that conversation in Season One with David Eick, you know, about the last shot of the series, should be Number Six walking through Times Square, and both of us just, like, really loving that. And then, yeah, I included Head Baltar because it made more sense ... But I love this whole notion of bringing it all back to us'. This seems to have been unconsciously influenced by the sequence in *The Matrix* where Neo sees a beautiful blonde woman in a red dress walking among the crowd on a city street. The team started discussing the finale at the Las Vegas writers' retreat 18 months prior to its recording; but, as noted, it was extensively redeveloped after the WGA strike. Moore says in his DVD commentary, 'It was different [from the situation with] the miniseries, in that I didn't have a detailed outline this time. We broke the story in the [writers'] room and I decided to just sit down and just write it from the gut, which was how I did "33", and "33" was one of the best experiences writing on the show'. The first draft was over 130 pages long; Moore cut it down to about 110 pages and sent it out to the others involved, who, unsurprisingly, all said they liked it.

One key change between draft and final versions was that Helo and Athena were originally to have died, and Baltar and Caprica-Six to have taken over raising Hera. This seems to have been proposed largely to provide a literal meaning for Head Six's prophecies about Hera being Baltar's child. Tahmoh Penniket has said that he made a case to Michael Rymer as to why Helo should survive, and the character did make it to the end of the 11 June 2008 script draft. An early suggestion by Bradley Thompson as to the fate of the *Galactica*, mentioned in *The Official Companion Season Four*, was that it should be buried in what later became Central America, and then rediscovered in the present day. According to Moore in his podcast, the visual effects team originally had the *Galactica* almost completely penetrating the Colony during the battle sequences, and were not pleased when Moore asked them to redo it so more of the ship was outside. Moore says, 'Originally as scripted, Tigh was going to pick up Cavil and throw him off the second level to his death. And Dean Stockwell called me personally, which Dean never did ... and said, "I'd like him to kill himself."' This adjustment was made prior to the 11 June 2008 draft, which reads, 'Tigh turns to take out Cavil – but Cavil ... puts the gun in his mouth and pulls the trigger'. The idea of having Adama fly the last Viper off the ship at the end of the story was a later addition; originally he was to have left in a Raptor with everyone else. The fate of Adama and Roslin after they depart together was originally to have been left ambiguous; Moore says in the podcast, however, that Mary McDonnell insisted on a death scene. He also says regarding Roslin: 'Originally the idea for the character was that she was not gonna make it to Earth ... Mary and I talked about the fact that she was going to be Moses, and she was gonna lead the people there but she was gonna die just before they got to Earth. And then when we got to the end ... I didn't want to take that from her'. The network had intended the colonists to land in North America, presumably to tie in with the shift to present-day New York, but the location remained Africa, with connotations of the birthplace of mankind.

The 11 June draft script of part three of the story shows some significant differences from the transmitted version. The intercutting of flashbacks to the opera-house vision during Hera's journey through the ship is not scripted in the draft, apart from one brief cut to the shining figures on the balcony right at the end. Baltar's line about how God is beyond good and evil is completely different; when Cavil asks how he knows God is on his side, Baltar replies, 'I don't. But I choose to believe that whatever we are dealing with ... is ultimately a force for good'. In the sequence where the Final Five pool their memories, the script has the flashbacks starting out with 'a cascade of IMAGES from all five lives', but then going on to a montage of Tyrol and Tory 'back on Earth together (Tyrol has his glasses on) ... Tyrol and Tory kissing ... then images of Tory and Cally ... Cally crying ... Tory talking to her ... Cally reaching out to her ... Tory knocking her across the launch tube ... and finally killing her'.

Turning to more minor differences, the draft has Adama speculate that the humans on Earth may be another offshoot of the Twelve Tribes, but Cottle denies this, saying they appear to have evolved there naturally. Lee, when saying that the colonists can give the indigenous people the best part of themselves, explicitly states that he means their 'culture ... arts, traditions and principles of government, even our faith'. He ends his speech by saying, 'and while all this has happened before ... maybe this time ... it will not happen again'. When Lampkin resigns his Presidency, he says that there was only one real President at the start of the journey and that it should be the same now; a curious endorsement of Roslin, whose regime he called a 'bitter disappointment' in '*Sine Qua Non*'. The flashback in which Roslin's date Sean leaves after their sexual encounter simply has him saying 'Uh, okay', gathering his clothes, and departing, rather than including the awkward conversation of the final version. Adama putting the wedding ring on Roslin's finger is not scripted. There is a stage direction describing Calvin as 'the nerdy boy who still can't quite stop looking at Caprica-Six's legs', and another where it is said, during the ceasefire, that 'a couple [of] Colony Centurions are watching the Red Stripe Centurions (and vice versa)'. Finally, the draft script states that, as Adama sits by Roslin's grave, 'In the [background] are the RUINS of his Raptor and the STAKES in the ground where he's going to build the cabin', which we do not see in the final version.

The draft script has the flashbacks distributed randomly through the story, and they are also non-linear, moving back and forth along the different storylines. However, according to Moore in his podcast, Michael Rymer recut the episode so that the flashbacks would run mainly in chronological order, to make it less difficult for the viewer to follow. Mark Stern, the series' creative executive and liaison with the Sci-Fi Channel, then said he found the flashbacks hard to invest in emotionally, so Andy Seklir, the editor, suggested instead concentrating them at the start of the story. This unfortunately means that the finished episode has a very slow first hour.

There were also problems when it became plain that 'Daybreak' was going to be too long for the series' usual time slot. In fact, according to the extended commentary on the DVD, there was an even longer, four-hour, cut at one point. The network allowed the studio an extra hour – making the story three hours long with adverts; the final DVD cut runs to two hours, 32 minutes and 27 seconds – but refused to screen the whole thing on a single night, showing the first third, and the remaining two-thirds cut together the following week.

Fans have pointed out some technical problems. For instance, the constellation Ursa Major is visible even though it would not have been in its present configuration at the time of the colonists' landing on Earth. The Centurion in the museum has now changed to a 'Razor'-style war-era Cylon, and the window in the starboard flight pod has been repaired – although this could be explained by someone on the ship being obsessive enough to keep the museum display renovated and updated. Although the Head People are supposed to be invisible, a couple of passers-by in Times Square rather obviously check Head Six out.

In production terms, people familiar with Vancouver may enjoy spotting the landmarks visible from Baltar's limousine in the flashbacks, and the University of British Columbia campus when he offers to provide the codes to Caprica-Six, and even in the New York sequence, which was also filmed in Vancouver,

70: DAYBREAK

adding support to the argument that this may not actually be New York on our own planet. The strip club sequences were, according to the DVD commentary, shot in a real strip club, which catered to couples. Moore had wanted the venue to have a gender-egalitarian atmosphere, with male and female strippers dancing, but in directing and editing the male strippers were largely removed, though two are briefly visible in separate scenes. Laura's flat was represented by one in the same complex as that used for Starbuck's home, although it was of a quite different configuration. The scene of Adama taking the lie detector test was actually filmed in Eick's office, and that of Anders talking to the reporter in the production office gym. Regarding Baltar's house, Rymer says in the DVD commentary, 'We couldn't get the original house where we'd shot the [miniseries] because [we were told] a Harrison Ford movie had gone in there and had burned the location ... I thought that literally meant burned it down, but what they meant was, ruined it, because the neighbours got so pissed off they wouldn't let anybody go back and shoot'. A similar house by the same architect was found instead, with the view out of the windows replicated on green-screen. The Colony was shot using the basestar sets; Richard Hudolin covered the walls with a mesh to make them look different. The CIC set had to be physically altered to allow the opera house vision sequence to be shot, with a portion of the balcony removed to make all of the Final Five visible. The shots of the Marines cutting their way into the Colony were lifted from 'Bastille Day'.

Gareth Riceman, an astronaut and *Battlestar Galactica* fan, can be seen playing one of the Marines in Racetrack's Raptor. The crossing-the-line sequence required CGI to make the crowd appear larger, and the close-ups of Adama and Roslin together were shot on green-screen. By contrast, very little effects work was used on the Earth locations, which were shot once again in Kamloops. According to the DVD commentary, the team considered including CGI prehistoric animals, but decided it would be too distracting. The idea of using a red filter to make the location look more 'African' was also rejected, since director of photography Steve McNutt wanted the scenes to have a clean, unfiltered look. Although there were fears that the bird in Lee's flat would also need to be achieved through CGI, the pigeon performed on cue. As with 'Razor', the end credits theme on the extended cut is different from the usual *Battlestar Galactica* closing music.

The episode aired without the usual precap clips. Critical response on broadcast was mixed. The final episode averaged 2.364 million viewers. This was the highest figure of Season 4.5, for which ratings mostly ranged between 1.5 million and 1.7 million. The top-rated cable show of the week in which 'Daybreak' was aired, WWE RAW, averaged over five million. Fan sites on the internet were particularly critical of the story for making the presence of God explicit, even though the intervention of supernatural beings was an essential part of the original series' premise, and despite the fact that most of the reimagined *Battlestar Galactica* only makes sense if one includes the concept of divine intervention. Most of these criticisms, however, make the fundamental mistake of assuming that God is omnipotent and omniscient; as previous episodes have shown, the God of this series is neither, and is subject to external circumstances.

The message of 'Daybreak' is perhaps best summed up by a sequence that did not make it into the transmitted version. After Head Baltar says that God does not like to be called by that name, in the draft, he continues: 'In any case, it would require mankind, in all its flaws, to have learned from its mistakes'; Head Six replies, 'Stranger things have happened'. They pause outside a shop, watching something out of vision, and Head Baltar says, 'I think I'll take that bet. What are the stakes?' Head Six 'looks at him', and he continues, 'Silly, silly me'. The script goes on: 'They walk away, and the CAMERA MOVES TO – the shop window, which has a TV set playing NEWS FOOTAGE of [Canadian cellist] YO-YO MA shaking hands with a WHITE ROBOT just before it walks across the stage and begins to CONDUCT AN ORCHESTRA'.

The warning note this strikes about the human race's prospects for survival casts a new light on the First Hybrid's prophecy, 'Kara Thrace will lead the human race to its end … She is the herald of the Apocalypse, the harbinger of death. They must not follow her'. If this Earth develops intelligent robots before it develops interstellar travel, then the system is closed – as there is nowhere to escape from the coming catastrophe – and its people are doomed. As we have seen before, fate in *Battlestar Galactica* is inescapable, and so regardless of Kara's changed nature, she brings the human race to what will, ultimately, be its final demise. The central conflict in the series is thus between the cyclical nature of history, where 'All this has happened before, and all this will happen again', and God's attempt to impose upon this system a linear structure in which events progress inevitably to some kind of fulfilment or salvation.

71: The Plan

FIRST TRANSMISSION DATE: 10 January 2010 (USA)

WRITTEN BY: Jane Espenson

DIRECTOR: Edward James Olmos

CREDITED CAST: Dean Stockwell (Cavil); Callum Keith Rennie (Leoben); Kate Vernon (Ellen Tigh); Rick Worthy (Simon); Lymari Nadal (Giana O'Neill); Matthew Bennett (Doral); Rekha Sharma (Tory Foster); Alisen Down (Jean Barolay); Tiffany Lyndall-Knight (Hybrid); Alonso Oyarzun (Specialist Socinus); Colin Corrigan (Marine Alan Nowart); Diego Diablo Del Mar (Hillard); Bruce Dawson (Coach); Lawrence Haegert (Wheeler); Tommy Europe (Rally); Maya Washington (Sue-Shaun); Luvia Petersen (Kai); Richard Yearwood (Marine); Alex Ferris (Boy); Gina Vultaggio (Jemmy)

STUNTS: Dan Redford (Doral Stunt Double); Timothy Webber (D-Cavil [sic] Acting Double); Efosa Otoumagie (Simon Stunt Double); Mike Carpenter (Anders Stunt Double); Kim Howey (Kai/Nurse Stunt Double); Gaston Morrison (Stunt Patient); Lars Grant, Clay Virtue, Simon Burnett, Clint Carleton, David Mylrea, Chad Sayn, Fraser Corbett, Dave Hospes, Mike Desabrais, Duane Dickinson, Dustin Brooks (Stunt Civilians); Kimani Ray Smith, Marshal Virtue, Dean Choe, Gerald Paetz, Scott Athea, James Bamford, Ashley Earle, Doug Chapman (Stunt Resistance)

UNCREDITED MAJOR CAST APPEARANCES VIA ARCHIVE FOOTAGE: Jamie Bamber (Lee 'Apollo' Adama); Katee Sackhoff (Kara 'Starbuck' Thrace); James Callis (Gaius Baltar); Tahmoh Penikett (Karl 'Helo' Agathon); Lucy Lawless (D'Anna); Alessandro Juliani (Felix Gaeta); Kandyse McClure (Anastasia Dualla); Nicki Clyne (Cally); Leah Cairns (Margaret 'Racetrack' Edmondson)

SYNOPSIS: Forty years after the armistice that marked the end of the Cylon War, the Cylons launch a new and devastating attack on the Colonies. The Cavils believe that, afterwards, the Final Five, who are living among the humans unaware of their true nature, will resurrect and accept the Cavils' assessment of humanity as flawed. However, all of them survive the devastation. On the Fleet, a Cavil unites the available human-like Cylons, meeting with them under the pretext of religious worship, and assigns them to various tasks; he also guides the sleeper agent Boomer. However, Cavil's subjects are less than obedient:

Leoben becomes obsessed with Kara Thrace; Shelley Godfrey cannot bring herself to discredit Baltar; Boomer cannot kill Adama and, believing her place to be with the Fleet, is unable to commit suicide; and a Simon, who has married a human woman and adopted a child, refuses to obey Cavil's instruction to blow up his ship, the *Cybele*, in the end committing suicide rather than doing so. Cavil himself is drawn to a human boy who tries to befriend him, but kills him rather than let him get closer. On Caprica, Anders leads the fledgling resistance movement, which boasts a Simon and a hat-wearing Cavil in its ranks. Hat Cavil becomes fascinated with Anders, seeking forgiveness from him. When the resistance arrive on the Fleet, Hat Cavil and Fleet Cavil are arrested and sentenced to execution. Hat Cavil has come to believe that their plan was a mistake, and that they should love humanity, but Fleet Cavil rejects these ideas.

ANALYSIS: 'The Plan', a movie-length spin-off produced after the series proper, is the follow-up that should never have been made. Despite the obvious talents of the writer, production team and cast, in revisiting the events of earlier episodes it takes a good deal of the mystery out of the show, and nails down things that do not need to be nailed down. Its main strengths are in developing the love-conquers-all idea of the series and providing some belated characterisation for the Simons. We will here be using the DVD cut of the story as our reference point.

The Big Disappointment: Revelation of the Cylons

Part of the story's impact is, unfortunately, to diminish Cavil as an antagonist. Up until the scene where he speaks with Ellen in the sequence of 'The Plan' set during the events of '33', it might have been assumed that his strategy included the Final Five surviving and making it onto the Fleet, in order to show them humanity at its worst, and that the various torments the Fleet endures were intended to underline this message. Although Ellen states in 'No Exit', 'But we didn't die. And then you decided we hadn't suffered enough', we have no idea how she has reached that conclusion; and, since her own survival is directly down to Cavil's intervention, it seems a strange thing for her to say. Cavil, at that point, makes no statement either way as to his intentions. However, in 'The Plan', he is surprised that all of the Five made it through the attacks, and that four of them are on the Fleet, suggesting that their survival was instead down to coincidence. It is unlikely that God preserved the Five, as it would better serve God's ultimate objective of bringing the humans and Cylons together if they were to download back into Cylon society, where they could successfully mount a powerful opposition to Cavil's plan. Furthermore, nothing we see in the Five's escapes suggests that any of them were alerted to the danger (as God cannot control people's minds, but only warn), or indeed that there was any divine intervention at all.

We also learn that Shelley Godfrey is not, in fact, a Head Person, taking out of the story in retrospect the tantalising ambiguity that she is a kind of demonic

Head Six come to torment Baltar, or a precursor to the resurrected Starbuck. Her motivation for accusing Baltar of sabotaging the defence mainframe on Caprica is revealed to be that Cavil has ordered her to ruin his reputation as, if they were merely to destroy his Cylon detector, he would build a new one – which begs the question of why the Cylons don't simply murder him and have done with it. The reason for her mysterious vanishing at the end of 'Six Degrees of Separation' turns out to be, prosaically, that she airlocks herself following its events, rather than any mystical occurrence. Leoben's belief that Starbuck has a destiny also stems purely from his becoming obsessed with her voice when listening to military traffic on the wireless rather than from any actual knowledge of a greater plan. It also transpires that he was discovered by the Colonials by accident, whereas previously it appeared that he had given himself up voluntarily as part of a wider mystical strategy. However, the Leoben storyline is partly redeemed in that there are indications of something more mysterious: Leoben daubs a mandala on the wall, suggesting a deeper spiritual connection with Starbuck, and when he grabs her by the throat in the 'Flesh and Bone' sequence, he has a sudden prophecy of their future on New Caprica and her death in the maelstrom, including some of her dreams and visions.

Omnia Vincit Amor: The Theme of Love

The overriding theme of the story is that the Cylons, when they come into contact with humanity, are changed and cannot remain a unified race. It is worth noting that we never actually see what the Significant Seven Cylons would be like without human contact, as even at the start of the series, they are affected by humans, and before that, they were influenced by the human-like Final Five. Indeed, prior to the destruction of the Colonies, Cylons had been living in human society and been changed by it: Leoben was a yoga instructor, and one of the Sixes was working as a prostitute, affecting both of their characters. Even the Cavils find themselves differentiating as a result of contact with humans, as Hat Cavil (referred to as C-Cavil in the script, with his counterpart being F-Cavil) begins to question his model's drive to destroy humanity. Boomer finds that she is increasingly integrated into human society. It is here explained that she was able to come out of her sleeper-agent mode through the visual trigger of a carved wooden elephant; the human persona does not remember the Cylon's actions, but the Cylon remembers everything the human has done. She says of her attempt to kill Adama that the only way she could do it was to turn herself into a machine, but, in doing so, she 'lost the best part of [her]self'. This phrasing recalls the deleted scene from 'Kobol's Last Gleaming' where she mechanically rehearses the act of killing her commander. All the Cylons, therefore, find themselves drawn to reject Cavil's philosophy.

In particular, love is seen to be a key factor in changing the Cylons and causing them to question the plan. Simon is in love with Giana; Leoben is obsessed with Starbuck; Hat Cavil develops a childlike, platonic love for Anders (Espenson says in her commentary that Hat Cavil is upset by the fact that

Anders keeps preferring humans to him); Shelley Godfrey starts to love Baltar, despite everything. Even Boomer rejects her Cylon side in part due to being loved by Tyrol, and she does not want to kill Adama as she considers him a father figure. Cavil himself starts to feel affection toward the human boy John. Realising what is happening, he then kills the child. This murder takes place at the same time that Hat Cavil passes up the opportunity to shoot Kara and Anders, highlighting the divergence between the two Cavils. The boy also offers Cavil an apple, recalling Ellen's gesture to Boomer in 'No Exit' and with similar implications of temptation. At the destruction of the Colonies, a Hybrid says '... and love no more', quoting the Hybrid's line from 'Torn', and indicating that the attack on the humans comes from a desire to prevent love. Hat Cavil asserts to Fleet Cavil that their entire motivation is the search for parental love, and Hat Cavil reaches out his hand to Fleet Cavil (which he takes) as they are airlocked. Prostitute Six sums up Cavil's failure by telling him, 'You can't declare war on love'; the Cylons are inevitably transformed by loving humans, or the Final Five. While this is an uplifting message, it is one more subtly expressed in the parent series, and does not need reiterating quite so blatantly here. Furthermore, although jealousy and the rejection of love are certainly part of Cavil's motivation in the series, reducing such a complex figure down to the simple idea that, as Hat Cavil puts it, his model 'had a temper tantrum in the form of a cataclysm, because we wanted them to treasure us, the Ones, more than humanity, more than their own history and blood' is, again, to rob the character of its power.

One curious trick of the writing in this story is that most of the Cylon characters we see appear in both 'Sweet' and 'Hard' versions – like the Eights in 'The Face of the Enemy', which was written afterwards – suggesting they are outgrowths of the divisions in 'The Plan', which itself is derived from Boomer's divided and conflicted nature in Season One. The exceptions are Leoben (who appears only as a single unit) and Doral (who is largely undifferentiated: in one of the episode's funniest lines, a Doral asserts that he looks different from another Doral because, 'His jacket was burgundy. This is *teal!*'). This division (or, in two cases, lack of it) allows Espenson to explore the acceptance and rejection of love among some of the Cylon models. However, Sweet Eight's complex characterisation in 'The Face of the Enemy' is largely eschewed here in favour of simpler and more stereotyped divisions, such as Fleet Cavil attempting to embrace his machine side while his Caprican counterpart is drawn toward the human.

Simon Says: The Number Four Subplot

One arguable strength of this story is that it gives Simon a character and something to do. Up until this point he has been criminally underused, and indeed Caprica Simon does little in 'The Plan' bar whining to Hat Cavil about how they should get on with massacring Anders' resistance group, but in the narrative of Fleet Simon and his wife, we get some development. Fleet Simon loves his human family enough to sacrifice himself completely for them (as Prostitute Six notes that there is no resurrection ship nearby when he commits suicide). Likewise, Simon's wife Giana comes to accept that her husband must really have loved her, despite being a Cylon. However, although her friendship with Tyrol means her experiences could have helped him come to terms with his own feelings about Boomer, they appear instead to exacerbate his fears that he himself is a Cylon, and her assertion that were she to suspect she was a Cylon she would throw herself off the catwalk at the top of the hangar deck inspires his dreams of suicide. Furthermore, like Novacek in 'Hero', Simon's characterisation has strong elements of the 'Othello' stereotype: a black man who has trouble articulating his emotions and comes across as threatening to the very people he loves.

And Then There Was One: Continuity and Worldbuilding

This story reveals a lot of general information on the Cylons. We get a close-up and detailed view in daylight of the nuclear ordinance they are about to unleash upon the Colonies, which is clearly inspired by cluster bombs. (Visually, it also resembles a nest of snakes, as well as being in a similar style to the Mark IX Hawk fighter craft and Eagle transporters of *Space: 1999*.) Leoben's interest in communications technology is evident from the start, and what attracts him to Starbuck originally is the way she is able to rewire the Raider and get it off the planet (see 'You Can't Go Home'). Cavil's priest persona is the perfect cover for meeting with the other Cylons, and for debriefing Boomer when she is arrested, in the guise of a priest visiting the prisoners. The flyers he hands out inviting people to worship cryptically reads, 'Do you know about the Plan? The lessons of the Gods can help. Private counselling, group prayer'. It is revealed that Boomer and Cavil began their relationship on *Galactica*, long before we saw her doing a naked t'ai chi routine for him in 'Six of One'. Although not stated, clearly Fleet Cavil did follow up on his threat to have Hat Cavil boxed, as at no other point does a dissenting Cavil appear. In a symbolic moment, we see all of the Final Five present as the two Cavils march to their execution.

We learn that the basestars can rotate their middle section to reform the ship into an aerodynamic shape suitable for combat in atmosphere, and many basestars are seen attacking the Colonies, in a tacit reminder that something mysterious severely reduced the Cylons' ranks around the end of Season Two. The story also indicates that, in the miniseries, there are in fact *two* Dorals (one in burgundy and one in teal), rather than a single unit who changes his clothes part-way through, retroactively rationalising the character's switch of wardrobe; the teal-wearing Doral also turns out to be the Doral in the mustard-coloured jacket – evidently his idea of a disguise – who blows himself up in 'Litmus'.

The appearance of the boy who tries to befriend Cavil is a deliberate homage to the central figure in *The Boy with Green Hair* (1948), which starred Stockwell as the eponymous child; and Cavil's question to him, 'Are you a war orphan?' is a line from that film as well as another call-back to Six's 'Are you alive?' in the miniseries. Boomer's carved elephant references her collection in 'Downloaded' and – as noted in the entry on that episode – may be a call-back to *The Deer Hunter*, in which a suicidal Vietnam veteran becomes obsessed with sending carved wooden elephants home, making them symbols of memory and death wish.

The sequence leading to the destruction of the Colonies contains some excellent Hybrid lines. Significant ones include an inversion of Yeats' poem 'The Second Coming' – 'The centre holds. The falcon hears the falconer' – and allusions to the series' themes of cyclical time – such as 'Apotheosis was the beginning before the beginning' and 'The flower inside the fruit that is both its parent and its child. Decadent as ancestors'. There is also a very poetic monologue:

> 'Nuclear devices activated, and the machine keeps pushing time through the cogs, like paste into strings into paste again, and only the machine keeps using time to make time to make time. And when the machine stops, time was an illusion that we created. Free will, 12 battles, three stars, and yet we are countless as the bodies in which we dwell, are both parent and infinite children in perfect copies, no degradation'.

This links the Cylon condition in with Marxist philosophical ideas about the commodification of time; the Cylons, as a slave race, are bound to a human concept of time as an economic unit, which when they liberate themselves no longer applies, returning them to the cyclical time of the gods.

There is an interesting suggestion that Kara Thrace doesn't go to church, despite being very religious, as she fails to recognise Hat Cavil when she sees him – or perhaps she simply attends services held by another priest, as there may be several competing chaplains on *Galactica*. We also learn that Baltar is the one who at the end of the miniseries leaves the note revealing that there are 12 Cylon models. Ellen Tigh's assertion in 'Tigh Me Up, Tigh Me Down' that she was at an airport buying a ticket to return home when she was rescued by a mysterious stranger is here shown to have been at best stretching the truth, as she was in fact drinking in a strip club, although the part about the stranger (Cavil) is in fact true. However, Adama's statement in 'Tigh Me Up, Tigh Me Down', 'No-one can recall giving [Ellen] any medical assistance until about a week ago', does not reflect what we see in 'The Plan', in which she receives such aid from the point at which she is rescued and taken on board the Fleet. Giana, briefly seen in the miniseries, asking after her husband as she disembarks from Boomer's Raptor on *Colonial One*, returns to a much more extensive part in the story. Cavil was the first one to airlock a Cylon, well before Roslin thought of the idea. The sequence where the resistance attack the Cylons using tactics from the film *The Tauron Line* picks up on Anders' admission in 'The Farm' that their strategies consist mostly of 'stuff we just saw in the movies'. Their failure is consequently very believable: being a group of people with no real military experience imitating a showy and slightly unrealistic film, they go out *en masse*

71: THE PLAN

to plant a bomb rather than send one person to limit casualties, leading to a firefight in which four of them are killed. The resistance's survival is explained as being down at least partly to Hat Cavil's intervention.

An extensive storyline was deleted, concerning the decision by Caprica-Six and Boomer in 'Downloaded' to propose a more harmonious existence with humans. The Cylons approach the Caprica resistance through Hat Cavil, under the pretence that he has been taken prisoner by them and released to convey their message, with an offer of relocation to labour camps on Picon; however, those who come forward to accept are gunned down by Centurions, while Caprica-Six and Boomer beg the Centurions to stop. This all feels rather pointless in story terms, and seems to have been included mainly to explain how it is that in 'Lay Down Your Burdens' Hat Cavil knows about Caprica-Six and Boomer having mounted a peace campaign. Caprica-Six and Boomer apparently believe the offer to be genuine, and the incident takes place after the resistance execute Simon, suggesting that Hat Cavil set the whole thing up as an act of revenge. Caprica-Six is on crutches during this sequence, evidently from the injury she sustained in 'Downloaded'; she has retained her old body, clearly picking up on Moore's remarks in the 'Downloaded' podcast about her doing so as a means of focusing on the life she has rather than on a multiple existence, though also suggesting she may still be wary of being boxed during resurrection. On a more frivolous note, a line was cut where, on Doral being less than pleased about being presented with a suicide belt, Cavil unkindly suggests he paint it teal.

There are many other problems aside from the ones already pointed out. The dialogue often comes over as awkward and full of clumsy info-dumps, with Cavil being a particular offender in this area. It would have been nice to have more than a few minutes' worth of screen time for Tory, as we never learn how she succeeded in becoming Roslin's aide. Simon, somewhat improbably, has to remain unseen by Starbuck for the entire duration of her visit to Caprica, as otherwise she would have recognised his counterpart on the Farm. The explanation of who wrote the word 'Cylon' on Sharon's mirror is confused; Sharon's Cylon persona says she 'thinks' she did it herself, presumably in some kind of mental fugue, and offers the contradictory rationale, 'I think I was trying to warn myself, or scare myself, into doing what you want, or out of it', which is much less effective than simply leaving it ambiguous. When one of the worker-Dorals on Caprica remarks that the Centurions should be doing their job (throwing the bodies of the deceased into an incinerator), it begs the question of why the Centurions are not, at least, helping them. It is never explained how, or why, the Cylon transponder comes to be aboard *Galactica* before the attack; and, indeed, since Cavil intended humanity's destruction in the attacks on the Colonies, there is no reason why it should be there. Removing the possibility that the Cylons intended the humans to find Earth also causes serious problems for certain stories from Seasons One and Two, for instance making the Cylons' failure to ambush the Rebel Fleet on Kobol in 'Home' completely inexcusable. Furthermore, although Cavil says that no humans were supposed to survive the destruction of the Colonies, he also knows about the Farms, which would seem a complete contradiction.

In production terms, although the new arrangement of the theme music is outstanding, some of the new CGI does not look as polished as in earlier stories. Lucy Lawless is quite conspicuous by her absence, appearing only in what is obviously a brief archive clip, and the fact that Cavil never so much as alludes to the arrival of the *Pegasus* seems strange. The name 'Giana' is a little too close to 'Gianne', the name of Apollo's girlfriend mentioned in 'Black Market', as well as to 'Gina'. (The series also includes a Baltar-cultist named Jeanne, and, in the 12 October draft of 'The Captain's Hand', a Geena.) There are a few continuity problems: the scene where Starbuck and Helo come to rescue the resistance has an extra line, with Helo responding 'Who wants to know?' after Anders asks 'Is Kara Thrace there?'; the dialogue when the two Cavils are locked in the brig has Tigh, not Roslin, advising that they should be airlocked (Roslin does not appear at all in 'The Plan'); Leoben has an extra line ('You're dead') in the sequence from 'Flesh and Bone' when he grabs Starbuck by the throat; and Sue-Shaun is played by a different actress from the one in the series. The massacre of half of the resistance in a Cylon ambush has been deleted from history, clearly because it would have occurred when Cavil was supposedly protecting the group: in 'Resistance', Anders says to Kara that there are 53 resistance members, down from 'almost a hundred' prior to the massacre the previous week, but in 'The Plan', Anders says to Hat Cavil that the day before he met Kara he had 98 followers, and the dialogue implies that losses are down to attrition. The resistance's radio is marked with a 'Centrios' brand name, which is that of an actual Canadian electronics firm.

Urbane Planners: Writing and Production

'The Plan' was originally to have been one of three spin-off movies, with Verheiden writing the first, Weddle and Thompson the second and Espenson the third. However, Verheiden was recruited by *Heroes*, and Weddle and Thompson by *CSI*, very shortly after *Battlestar Galactica* finished; and, although Olmos said at a ComicCon panel that Universal would make more movies if 'The Plan' did well, none has been announced at the time of writing. ('Blood and Chrome' – covered below – was not originally intended to be a standalone movie, and therefore does not count.) In many ways 'The Plan' turned out to be a glorified, albeit well edited, clip-show.

The location filming was done at a facility for practising rescues, hence the derailed train and damaged buildings. Most of the supporting artists who played resistance members in the series were able to return, but one man, who was dreadlocked in the original, had to wear a (somewhat unconvincing) wig as he had since had a haircut. Lymari Nadal, who plays Giana, is married to Edward James Olmos. The planet behind the Universal logo at the start is not Earth, but Caprica. The commentary reveals that originally Tory was to have been near an airport when her car was caught in the blast, providing her with a convenient means to leave the planet. The final version instead shows rescue ships landing in the background as she emerges from her car. We also learn that originally the production team wanted to have a shot of a Cylon Raider recognising Anders on Caprica. As with 'Islanded in a Stream of Stars', Olmos was asked to replace Frank Darabont as director on this story.

Whatever the episode's limitations otherwise, the performances are all very good, particularly Dean Stockwell's. There are some nice directorial touches, such as a cut from Hat Cavil meeting Caprica Simon, to Fleet Cavil meeting Fleet Simon. As the production team were not required to abide by network television restrictions (since 'The Plan' was going straight to DVD), there is some nudity in certain scenes; the story was later transmitted on the Sci-Fi Channel, now rebranded Syfy, in a cut-down version with the nudity either removed, or with the background artist strategically blurred. A body double who was also an actor was hired for the scenes with two Cavils, so that Stockwell had someone to perform against. Restaging earlier sequences required some ingenuity: the scene where Caprica-Six speaks with Cavil on Caprica during the events of the miniseries was shot on green-screen; and, according to the DVD commentary, Tyrol was given artificial stubble for the material extending his conversation with Cavil from 'Lay Down Your Burdens'. A close match had to be found for the school that served as a base for the resistance, as the one used in the series was unavailable. The story was originally written so as to be very light on effects, but in post-production, after the director's cut, the decision was taken to show the cities of the Twelve Colonies burning, and, consequently, to include also a few shots of them before the destruction. As the studio was destroying each set after the team finished filming on it, the wreckage of the hangar deck set was used for the debris on Picon.

'The Plan' is overall a disappointing addition to the series. By going back and officially providing concrete explanations for events and characters that were devised as ambiguous and organic, it retroactively reduces all that has gone before. While a general audience would be confused by the story, fans are equally likely to be frustrated by the reductive and prosaic answers to some of the series' most intriguing mysteries.

72: Blood and Chrome

FIRST TRANSMISSION DATE: 10 February 2013 (USA)

TELEPLAY: Michael Taylor

STORY BY: David Eick & Michael Taylor & Bradley Thompson & David Weddle

DIRECTOR: Jonas Pate

CREDITED CAST: Luke Pasqualino (Ensign William Adama); Ben Cotton (Coker Fasjovik); Lili Bordán (Doctor Becca [sic] Kelly); Jill Teed (Commander Ozar); John Pyper Ferguson (Xander Toth); Brian Markinson (Silas Nash); Karen LeBlanc (Jenna); Sebastian Spence (Kirby); Ty Olsson (Tactical Officer on Osiris); Zak Santiago (Captain Diaz); Mike Dopud (Deke Tornvald); Adrian Holmes (Zachary Elias); Carmen Moore (Nina Leotie); Jordan Weller (Rookie Pilot Seamus); Tom Stevens (Marine Baris); Terry Chen (Crew Chief Tiu); Sooraj Jaswal (BSG CIC Marine); Leo [Li] Chiang (Osiris Marine Sergeant); Colin Corrigan (Osiris Marine); Zach Martin (Marine Strohmeyer); Aaron Hughes (Army Medic); Toby Levins (Pilot Sandman)

KNOWN UNCREDITED CAST: Tricia Helfer (Cylon Voice); Heidi Brook Myers (Additional Voices)

SYNOPSIS: Ensign William Adama arrives on the battlestar *Galactica*. Rather than the Viper-piloting assignment he expects, he is tasked to a beat-up old Raptor, the *Wild Weasel*, in company with a drunken, cynical ECO, Coker. The pair are assigned a routine mission ferrying cargo to the Scorpion shipyards. As they prepare for departure, they are informed that their cargo is a civilian scientist, Doctor Beka[98] Kelly. Once they are clear of *Galactica*, Beka gives them new, top-secret orders to rendezvous with the heavy cruiser *Archeron*. Arriving at the designated coordinates, they find the *Archeron* destroyed. Beka has them send out a hail on a particular frequency; they receive coordinates for a location in Cylon space. There, they find a 'ghost fleet' of supposedly destroyed Colonial vessels, which have been assembling in secret. They go aboard the assault ship *Osiris*, which takes them to the winter resort moon Djerba, now a Cylon outpost, where the trio expect to rendezvous with a team of Marines. The *Osiris* engages in combat with a basestar, ramming the Cylon craft and blowing up both vessels.

---

[98] Although some sources spell her name as 'Becca', we will here use the spelling given in the draft script.

72: BLOOD AND CHROME

Adama, Beka and Coker make it down to Djerba, battle a snakelike cyborg creature and meet with the sole survivor of the Marine troop, Toth, who has holed up in an abandoned ski lodge. Adama and Beka make love, and the lodge is attacked by Cylons, with Toth fatally wounded. The trio flee to what Beka says is their objective, an automated Cylon transmission array six kilometres from the lodge, where she will upload a virus into the Cylon defence systems. However, it emerges that she is in fact a Cylon sympathiser, and has uploaded information about the ghost fleet to the Cylons. All three are injured in the resulting standoff; Coker and Adama escape to warn the Fleet, and Beka is killed by a Cylon with both mechanical and human elements. Back on *Galactica*, Commander Nash explains that the military were aware of Beka's treachery, and wanted her to upload the transmission so that the Cylons would send their forces to the ghost fleet's coordinates, by which time the fleet would have departed to attack many now-undefended Cylon targets; the mission was therefore a success. Adama is built up as a hero by the Colonial propaganda machine, and assigned to a Viper.

ANALYSIS: 'Blood and Chrome', initially released as a series of ten webisodes, is a reasonable addition to the *Battlestar Galactica* prequels, being a pacy and well-realised action drama enhanced by many good performances. However, comparing the final version of the story to the 30 November 2010 draft script indicates that it could have been a much cleverer, more subversive piece. We will again be using the DVD cut of the story as our main reference point.

I Lost My Heart to a Starship Trooper: 'Blood and Chrome' and Propaganda

'Blood and Chrome' contains large numbers of war-film clichés. The dialogue ranges from some clever wit – for instance Adama and Coker squabbling as they discover they do not know the password to identify them as friendly to the ghost fleet: 'Didn't you read the order?' 'I skimmed it!' – to some appalling lines – for instance Beka describing her husband, who was killed in action, as 'an historian who woke up one day and decided he couldn't sit back and just watch history happen anymore'. Although the action is gripping, it includes familiar tropes such as the idealistic young rookie who is given a harsh lesson about war, the cynical hard-drinking veteran, and the deluded traitor who works for the enemy despite the fact that they are portrayed as so reprehensible that no-one should even consider sympathising with them. In the draft script, Beka does defend the Cylons as mistreated slaves involved in a just rebellion, but even so, the scale of her treachery, and her brutal murder at Cylon hands, makes them completely unsympathetic. Co-writer Michael Taylor has cited *The Hurt Locker* (2008) and *Restrepo* (2010) as specific influences, and indeed 'Blood and Chrome' lifts many of its concepts from the former, a gritty and gory movie about a bomb disposal squad in Iraq, which features at its heart a conflict between a cynical, by-the-book soldier and his showy, risk-taking NCO, and which also considers the addictive nature of danger and violence. *The Hurt Locker*'s Sanborn, who wants to leave the service and start a family, provides an obvious antecedent for Viper pilot Kirby in 'Blood and Chrome', who rethinks the whole military endeavour upon learning he has fathered a son.

There are indications in the draft script that 'Blood and Chrome' at one point had another reading, lost by the final version: that it is a fiction within a fiction, a Colonial propaganda movie intended to reassure the public that although war is hell, the military are (flawed) heroes whose actions are justified, and their leaders know exactly what they are doing. The draft bookended the main narrative with idealised propaganda newsreels that provided a heroic version of the Colonial war effort and contrasted with the gritty reality of Adama's experiences. The fact that the story is based so heavily on *The Hurt Locker* supports this, as the film remains pro-military despite, or perhaps because of, its downbeat portrayal of conflict. This reading is also partly reinforced by certain discrepancies between 'Blood and Chrome' and the parent series: the casting of Joe Pasqualino rather than Nico Cortez as Young Adama, for instance, and the portrayal of the Cylons as ruthless and implacable rather than the more nuanced image we get in both the parent series and *Caprica*. The subplot about the 'ghost fleet' could be taken as a reassurance to Colonial audiences that even those military personnel reported dead may one day return. Seen in this light, 'Blood and Chrome' could be read as a postmodern film along the lines of Verhoeven's *Starship Troopers*, in which the gung-ho presentation of the military is subverted by the revelation at its conclusion that the entire story has been a propaganda piece in support of a fascist government, or indeed, a riff on the Nazi film *Kolberg* (1945), made to shore up civilian morale when the administration was on the brink of defeat.

However, in the rewriting process, this reading has been lost. Without the bookending sequences, the idea that the rest of the drama may be a propaganda film is no longer present. The finished version also has explicit references to the Adama family's association with organised crime, as seen in *Caprica*, which would not fit with the character of an idealised war hero. The inclusion of Pasqualino now comes across as simply a production decision to recast the role of Young Adama rather than having a narrative logic within the series. However, despite the loss of the propaganda-film subtext, the final version shows no attempt by the writers to provide any nuance in its portrayal of the conflict. The opening newsreel sequence has been replaced with a voiceover by Young Adama, which states 'We were the ones who let these robots become our servants, our trusted helpers and even our friends. We let them into our lives, only to see them repay our trust with a violent revolt against us', but 'Blood and Chrome' never challenges this or suggests it is anything other than the truth. Indeed, as the draft script at least had Beka arguing that the Cylons are sentient beings deserving of sympathy, the final version is actually even more one-sided than the earlier iteration. 'Blood and Chrome' thus loses the opportunity to be a clever take on wartime propaganda, and instead becomes a straightforward military drama.

72: BLOOD AND CHROME

The Grunts on Ice Station Zero: References and Continuity

The story draws heavily on the 'Razor' webisodes, which involved Young Adama on an ice planet discovering a Cylon secret; 'Blood and Chrome' similarly features, at the end, an early human-like Cylon. There are also some resemblances to Eick's earlier story 'Hero', which featured an older Adama taking part in covert operations behind Cylon lines. Furthermore, a key theme of 'Hero' was one of the establishment building up heroes for propaganda purposes, in cases where the truth of the situation may be less positive, just as in 'Blood and Chrome' Adama is built up by the Colonial forces after the ghost fleet action. Adama's call sign is finally explained, albeit in deleted scenes (a 'Husker' is an Aerilon derogatory term meaning a hick or hayseed, rapidly applied to Adama by Coker as a slight on his naivety), and his friendship with Coker, a drunken cynic with keen professional skills, foreshadows his support of Tigh; the draft script hints that Coker's marriage is less than happy. Adama's own youth as a brash, arrogant, risk-taking pilot might also explain his fondness for Starbuck.

There are a lot of references to *Caprica*. The military use holobands for training and briefings, and V-World, *Caprica*'s virtual reality entertainment universe, is still running, although it seems odd that both of these are in use this late in the war, as, if the Colonials abandoned networked computer systems due to their vulnerability to Cylon infiltration, one would think that a shared virtual reality world would have been one of the first things to be shut down. Beka is a former employee of Graystone Industries, creators of the Cylons and the holobands, which explains why the military trust her, but also why she has come to sympathise with the enemy. Adama refers to his deceased half-sister and -brother, and there are two mentions of his father's connections with the Tauron organised crime syndicate the Ha'la'tha; the draft script does not contain such references, apart from Commander Nash briefly mentioning Adama's 'interesting Tauron family connections' when he reviews his file. We learn that Adama does sport a Tauron tattoo; it is in the middle of his back, explaining why we did not see it in the parent series. The draft script version of the scene where Beka finds a child's doll abandoned in the ski lodge has her also find a children's book featuring Serge, the cute robot from *Caprica*.

The story contains a couple of original-series and *Galactica 1980* references. The original-series two-part story 'The Gun on Ice Planet Zero' similarly involved a team of characters with dubious and changeable loyalties being sent to neutralise a Cylon superweapon on an icy world; and Nash shares his name with Jeremy Brett's character from *Galactica 1980*.

In terms of outside references, the sequence where Coker is attacked by the cyborg snake – which the production team dubbed the 'cython' – is a riff on the garbage disposal scene from *Star Wars*. The draft script, in which the sequence takes place on the surface of the planet rather than in a cave, describes several cythons burrowing through the snow to attack their prey; this evokes an image familiar from *Tremors* (1990), the *Dune* franchise and the 1964 *The Outer Limits* episode 'The Invisible Enemy'. One pilot's name, Kirby, may be a reference to Jack Kirby, creator of Captain America among other comic-book heroes, and another's call-sign, Spoon, may be a reference to the battle-cry of spoof superhero the Tick. The skinjob Cylon's line, 'Do you think because you're more enlightened than the rest of your species, we hate you any less?' is a paraphrase of one from *Cross of Iron* (1979). The military set-up is yet another mix of those *Battlestar Galactica* favourites, the Battle of Midway and the Battle of the Bulge. During Midway, the Americans were able to surprise the Japanese by having one more ship than expected, as the latter believed the aircraft carrier USS *Yorktown* to have been sunk, much as the Colonials surprise the Cylons with a 'ghost fleet' of vessels believed lost; and the Colonials' position also resembles that of the Nazis at the time of the Battle of the Bulge, an army on the back foot attempting a last desperate throw of the dice.

In continuity terms, the Cylons are different in design from the war-era Centurions from 'Razor' and 'Daybreak', bearing more than a slight resemblance to General Grievous from *Revenge of the Sith* (2005). The draft script gives them camouflage and stealth abilities, by virtue of which they can change the colour of their skin to white when in the snow, and black when tracking their quarry through the ski lodge. This is rather wonderfully described with the phrase, 'Its armor ripples as thousands of tiny facets, like snake scales, [flip] over from silver to black'. The Cylons have been experimenting with skinjob forms and with cyborg forms of other animals. The skinjob recalls the Zoe android from the end of *Caprica*, and looks like a cross between the robots of *I, Robot* (2004) and anthropomorphic computer virus Hexadecimal from the CGI series *Reboot*. We also see another basestar design that is evidently an intermediate stage between the earlier two-flattened-cones version and the Guardians' one as seen later in 'Razor'. Although Adama's father is implied by Adama's letters home to be disapproving of his son's career choice, he is supportive, pulling strings on his behalf to get him into the Academy. The appearance of an early skinjob Cylon two years before the end of the war, however, strikes a problematic note, as Anders stated in 'No Exit' that, at the point when the Final Five reached the Colonies, 'The Centurions were already trying to make flesh bodies. They had created the Hybrids, but nothing that lived on its own. So we made them a deal. You stop the war, and we'll help you'. The fact that the Cylon has Six's voice is another discontinuity, as Six herself is a later development; the product of Earth Cylon technology. There is also a major discrepancy between this story and the 'Razor' webisodes, in which Adama's very first engagement as a pilot takes place on the final day of the war; the 'Razor' webisodes also show several crewmembers wearing original-series-style uniforms, none of which appears in 'Blood and Chrome'. It is possible to excuse some of these glitches, however, if one assumes this is yet another *Dark City*-style iteration of the story, with familiar characters from *Battlestar Galactica* and *Caprica* all playing new roles, and the Colonial Centurions developing an independently viable skinjob. However, more likely it is simply a case of poor continuity, combined with Eick opting to go for the best actors for the roles regardless whether or not they had a previous association with *Battlestar Galactica*.

Waiting for 'Blood and Chrome': Writing, Production and (Eventual) Release

'Blood and Chrome' was first announced on 27 July 2010 by Mark Stern, Syfy's executive vice-president of original programming, as an online series of ten webisodes, which would be filmed primarily using green-screen and virtual sets, presumably in light of the network's concerns about the expenses incurred by *Caprica*. In the DVD documentary, David Eick indicates that the story was first intended as a project for a gaming platform, which could be downloaded in ten segments. On 22 October 2010, it was announced that the project would instead form a feature-length pilot for a possible television series. Then, as no further news emerged, various rumours circulated that it would see a straight-to-DVD release like 'The Plan'; that it would be screened as a one-off telemovie; and that it would be released, as originally intended, as a webisode series. A trailer for the story was shown at the Wondercon convention, which ran from 16-18 March 2012. The trailer appeared on the internet three days later, but was hastily removed by Universal on the grounds that it was unofficial. Universal would not release an official trailer until November 2012; the only difference between it and the unofficial one is that the latter was temp-tracked with the Trent Reznor and Karen O cover of 'The Immigrant Song' and the former had music by Bear McCreary. The series was eventually released as ten webisodes in conjunction with Machinima.com, a gaming and animation website, beginning on 9 November 2012. It was later broadcast in the US on 10 February 2013, and was initially released as a DVD and Blu-Ray on 19 February 2013. In keeping with *Battlestar Galactica*'s earlier use of digital media, purchasers of the Blu-Ray also received codes giving them access to a direct download version of the story through iTunes, and a streamed version through the Ultraviolet online storage system. Although rumours circulated for a while that its release might spark the production of a full series, this never came to pass, the announcement that Luke Pasqualino was to be starring as D'Artagnan in the BBC's 2014 series *The Musketeers* being the final nail in the coffin for such speculation.

Principal photography reportedly took place in February 2011, with post-production continuing subsequently. In a documentary included as an extra on the DVD release, Paul Leonard estimates that the story is '90% post-production', due to the extensive use of green-screen; the before-and-after footage available on the DVD shows how seamlessly the virtual backgrounds were integrated with the live action. In casting terms, the story features a few veterans of the reimagined series, with Jill Teed, who formerly played Sergeant Hadrian, appearing as Captain Ozar of the *Osiris* (a male character in the 30 November draft script); Sebastian 'Narcho' Spence as Kirby; Ty 'Kelly' Olssen as an *Osiris* crewman; Brian Markinson, who played Agent Duram in *Caprica*, as Nash; Leo Li Chiang, the Tattooed Pilot, as a Marine Sergeant; and John Pyper-Ferguson, in his third *Battlestar Galactica* role, as Toth. Rumours circulated that Allison

Warnyca would reprise her role as Jaycie McGavin, who appears in the draft script; by the final version, however, her lines had been given to a new character, Jenna, and a brief sequence at the end of the story, where Adama finds a note from Jaycie in his Viper inviting him for drinks, had been removed. Leah Cairns auditioned for the parts of pilot Elias and *Galactica* CAG Rios, but was not chosen. A fan campaign was started by Marcel Damen to get Nico Cortez recast as Young Adama when it was learned that he had not even been considered. This was successful in getting him an audition, though he was eventually not selected. The acting is generally up to *Battlestar Galactica*'s usual high standards, although Lili Bordán lets the side down somewhat with a performance consisting mainly of speaking in a monotone.

Aside from the loss of the newsreel bookends discussed above, the main difference between the draft script and the final version has to do with how much the Colonial forces know about Beka's mission. In the draft version, it is indicated that they know nothing about her activities, and that she subverts the 'milk run' being undertaken by Adama and Coker into a covert operation without Nash's knowledge; Adama is able to warn the Colonial forces in time for them to abort the ghost fleet's attack, though a propaganda film is nonetheless released saying the campaign was a complete success. In the final version, Nash instead indicates that the military were aware of Beka's activities from the outset, and the whole mission was a set-up – which is considerably less interesting, to say nothing of less plausible. One storyline that was lost involved Adama, sent on a routine operation to take out Cylon automated batteries in an asteroid field, seizing the opportunity to show off his abilities by destroying two batteries at once, subsequently having to dodge a pair of missiles. Its removal had a knock-on effect, as the story lost the implication that Nash assigned him the flight to the Scorpion shipyards as a direct consequence, either as punishment for his daredevil activities, or, conversely, that his superior piloting skills meant that he would be considered suitable for a dangerous mission despite him being on his first posting.

The dialogue in the final version has been cleaned up and shortened from that in the draft script; the main casualties are several extensive and clunky speeches by Beka in which she expounds on her opposition to the war. A few good lines have also been lost, including an exchange between Beka and Coker as the Raiders pursue the *Wild Weasel* through the wreckage of the *Archeron*: 'I thought we couldn't outrun them?' 'We can't'. 'Then why are we trying?' 'Cause it beats the alternative'. The *Osiris* was originally to have been called the *Reliant*, a name that may have been considered to have too many associations with *Star Trek II: The Wrath of Khan* (1982). Beka's husband Ezra is named 'Eyal' in the draft. The battles are all very different in their on-screen execution from the descriptions in the draft; in particular, the two sequences involving the Raptor's tailgun are later additions. In the draft, Toth has painted on his shotgun the legend 'This machine kills machines'. There is an entertaining stage direction where the tiny noise of a Cylon extending its arm and deploying its built-in gun is described as like 'a mouse pissing on cotton'.

72: BLOOD AND CHROME

Had it been presented as a propaganda film, 'Blood and Chrome' could never have been the pilot for a series. However, even with the propaganda-film elements removed, it still fails to work as a pilot, since all the interesting characters barring Adama himself are either dead or preparing to leave the service at the story's end. The final result, therefore, is a stand-alone space adventure that is exciting enough but lacks the parent series' thoughtful take on modern warfare.

Caprica

EPISODE LIST: 'Pilot' (1); 'Rebirth' (2); 'Reins of a Waterfall' (3); 'Gravedancing' (4); 'There is Another Sky' (5); 'Know Thy Enemy' (6); 'The Imperfections of Memory' (7); 'Ghosts in the Machine' (8); 'End of Line' (9); 'Unvanquished' (10); 'Retribution' (11); 'Things We Lock Away' (12); 'False Labor' (13); 'Blowback' (14); 'The Dirteaters' (15); 'The Heavens Will Rise' (16); 'Here Be Dragons' (17); 'Apotheosis' (18)

SYNOPSIS: Zoe Graystone, teenage daughter of inventor Daniel Graystone and a secret member of a militant monotheist sect known as the Soldiers of the One (STO), has developed a computer program that will collate data about individuals and turn it into virtual copies of them that are near-indistinguishable from the originals. She intends to take this program to the monotheist headquarters on Gemenon, but is killed when her boyfriend, Ben, detonates a suicide vest on a Maglev train. Daniel Graystone, creator of the holoband (through which users can access the Colonies' virtual reality environment, V-World), is working on a military contract for intelligent robot soldiers; to generate artificial intelligence, he needs a metacognitive processor (MCP) chip, developed by his rival Tomas Vergis. Graystone develops a friendship with a Tauron lawyer, Joseph Adama, whose wife and daughter were killed in the Maglev blast. When Graystone discovers Zoe's avatar programme, he copies the code and persuades Adama to help him acquire the chip from Vergis in exchange for creating avatars of his daughter and wife. Adama uses his connections with the Tauron mafia, the Ha'la'tha, to do so, but is horrified by the avatar Graystone creates of his daughter Tamara. In an attempt to give the Zoe avatar a physical body, Graystone programs it onto the MCP in his prototype robot, U-87, but the program appears to crash and is wiped. In fact, Zoe lives on inside the robot, and enlists the help of her friend Lacy Rand to get to Gemenon. Lacy allies herself with monotheist terrorist Barnabas to do so, unwittingly involving herself in his power struggle with his rival Clarice Willow, headmistress of the school Lacy and Zoe both attended. Zoe's mother Amanda, grief-stricken, announces to the press that Zoe was a monotheist involved with the train bombing. She also later sees visions of her dead brother. Tamara's avatar escapes into the virtual environment of V-World and joins a massively multi-player online role-playing game (MMORPG) called New Cap City, in which the only rule is that players 'killed' in the game cannot return; Tamara cannot be killed, and so earns status. Learning of her whereabouts, Joseph joins the game and pursues her. Eventually, in collusion with Adama's assistant Evelyn, Tamara fakes her own 'death' and 'kills' Joseph, to force him to return to real life and take care of his son, Willie, who is being drawn into the Ha'la'tha under the influence of Adama's brother Sam. Daniel discovers that he cannot copy the MCP chip, and that it will not work in any other robot bodies. Daniel suspects that Zoe is alive in the U-87, but, when she fails to respond to his efforts to communicate with her, he orders his staff to wipe the chip. Zoe, as the U-87, escapes and steals a vehicle, but crashes into a military roadblock. Daniel loses his contract and his company to Vergis, and Amanda attempts suicide.

Three weeks later, Clarice persuades the monotheist leaders to support the use of Zoe's program to develop a 'virtual heaven', to which believers can upload copies of themselves upon death. Following the crash, a successful copy has been made of the MCP from the damaged U-87, and Vergis is now producing robots for the Caprican military. Daniel allies himself with the Ha'la'tha, marketing the program to them as a means by which grieving relatives can reunite virtually with their loved ones; and with the Ha'la'tha's support, he regains his company. Amanda, estranged from Daniel, lives with Clarice; she agrees to spy on Clarice for Global Defence Directorate (GDD) investigator Duram, and gradually she and Daniel are reconciled. Clarice tracks down Barnabas and his supporters and murders them, then orders Lacy to travel to Gemenon and join an STO training camp. Duram discovers that Clarice is being protected by Singh, the head of the GDD, and is consequently shot and injured by a sniper. The Adamas discover that the intelligent soldier robots, or 'Cylons' (short for 'Cybernetic Life-form Nodes'), are being sold to the STO by the leader of the Ha'la'tha, the Guatrau. They secretly arrange for Cylons to be sent to Tauron for use in a civil war against the Tauron government; learning of this, the Guatrau orders a hit on the Adamas, but instead kills Willie. The Adamas ally themselves with the Guatrau's daughter Fidelia and assassinate him, leaving Fidelia as the new Guatrau. Lacy, at the STO camp, encounters the Cylons but discovers that they all have some aspect of Zoe's identity. Zoe, having escaped into New Cap City, allies herself with Tamara and they remake it into a virtual world of their own creation. The Graystones enter the virtual world and are reconciled with Zoe. Through Amanda's activities they learn of Clarice's plans to stage a mass suicide bombing at a Pyramid game, followed by an upload of the bombers' avatars to 'heaven', but Singh attempts to bring the Graystones down by planting information that they are involved with the STO. The Graystones prevent the bombing through deploying Cylon soldiers to take out the bombers, while Zoe, in V-world, destroys Clarice's 'heaven'.

Five years later, Cylons have become integrated into human society as labourers. Clarice is preaching monotheism to Cylons in V-world, while Lacy has with Cylon backing become leader of the monotheist church. Joseph Adama has married Evelyn and fathered a son named William after his older half-brother, and the Graystones are working on a 'skinjob' robot body for Zoe.

ANALYSIS: *Caprica*, developed as a prequel series to *Battlestar Galactica*, is in some ways very different, focusing more on its social drama side and less on its space opera aspects. However, it matches and, in some areas, exceeds, its parent in terms of its moral complexity and exploration of complicated metaphysical themes. It should be noted that, as *Caprica* is a spin-off series, this is an overview essay only, and as such we will not be discussing each episode in detail.

The One and Only: Series Background and Production

Eick and Moore had been contemplating producing a prequel series since Season Two of *Battlestar Galactica*, and when a third writer, Remi Aubuchon, pitched an unconnected story idea to the Sci-Fi Channel, which he described to *Dreamwatch* magazine (May 2006) as 'an allegorical story about slavery with robots', he was invited to work with them on what later became *Caprica*. The series then spent 2006 and much of 2007 in the proverbial 'development hell', until 18 September 2007 when it was announced that the pilot had been green-lit. This positive development apparently came about for two reasons. First, NBC had been trying to lure Ronald D Moore away from the Sci-Fi Channel in the wake of the announcement of *Battlestar Galactica*'s cancellation, and the Sci-Fi Channel wanted to persuade him to stay. Secondly, the writers' strike had left the network with a dearth of usable material, and the *Caprica* pilot was one of the few items in a state suitable for production. In December 2008, after the pilot's completion (but well before it debuted with its DVD release on 21 April 2009), the Sci-Fi Channel announced they would be following it with a 20-episode season – although in the end, due to the series being more expensive than planned, this translated to only 18 episodes (counting the double-length pilot as a single episode). The pilot was subsequently broadcast on 22 January 2010 (by which point the network had rebranded itself as Syfy), followed seven days later by the first episode of the series. When the series took its mid-season break after the transmission of an episode entitled 'End of Line' on 24 March 2010, Syfy delayed on announcing its return until 21 July 2010, at which point they stated it would come back in January 2011. Following complaints from fans, Syfy later issued a press release saying the series would return on 5 October 2010. Unsurprisingly, however, the series lost viewers as a result of the long delay, with 'Unvanquished', the first episode broadcast after the hiatus, being watched by fewer than 900,000 viewers.

As many of the series' production crew had transferred over from *Battlestar Galactica* (including, among others, Glenne Campbell, Richard Hudolin, Gary Hutzel director of photography Steve McNutt, and Bear McCreary), and as the team were finishing up *Battlestar Galactica* at the same time as making the pilot, *Caprica* has a consistent look and feel with its parent series. Through a combination of advanced technology in some areas with retro styling in others, the impression is given of a culture like our own but, as Eick says in the commentary for 'Gravedancing', one with slightly different priorities. The fact that *Caprica* was also shot in Vancouver provides visual connections between the two series: for instance, the decadent virtual club seen in the pilot was filmed in the Orpheum Theatre, which was also the parent series' opera house. Different visual cues, colour palettes and shooting techniques are used to distinguish the various social worlds of *Caprica*, from the *Godfather*-inspired Little Tauron, to the cold, modernist corporate world of the Graystones, to the dieselpunk look of New Cap City. Kevin Murphy, in the commentary for 'Unvanquished', remarks that the visual effects give the series a grandeur and sense of scale. Visual effects are also used to give *Caprica* one of the best title sequences in telefantasy, with sweeping camera arcs describing the different worlds of the Graystones, the Adamas and the monotheists, and indicating the links between them.

Jeffrey Reiner, director of the pilot, opted to distinguish *Caprica* from *Battlestar Galactica* subtly through largely avoiding handheld cameras, except during the chaotic V-Club sequences. He also used multi-camera shooting, which gave the series a greater fluidity and immediacy, but also saved both time and money. This was carried over into the episodic series, with all those involved commenting on how difficult it was to get used to the new technique. To convey the reactions of Zoe, trapped in the body of the U-87, the team developed the conceit of cutting between the robot and Zoe in the same scene, which was clever, but also resulted in having to shoot everything twice, once with either a VFX placeholder or a physical model of the U-87, and once with Alessandra Torresani (the actress playing Zoe), which was undoubtedly a factor in the abandonment of the concept in Season 1.5. The Graystones' cute household robot, Serge, was controversial with the team, but seems to have been generally embraced by the fandom.

Caprica's cast was headed by Eric Stoltz, known for *Pulp Fiction* and, ironically, Roger Avery's heist film *Killing Zoe* (1994). The teenage cast are good-looking but not unrealistically so; for instance Alessandra Torresani is slightly cross-eyed, and Magda Apanowicz (Lacy Rand) has very large ears. Paula Malcolmson, who plays Amanda Graystone, was originally been considered for the part of Sister Clarice; while Polly Walker is excellent in the latter role, it is slightly disappointing that the series' main antagonist falls into the 'villainous Brit' stereotype that pervades American television. (Although Malcolmson is from Belfast, she adopts an American accent throughout.) Serge is voiced by assistant editor Jim Thomson; he had originally read in the part as a stand-in voice during filming, but the team liked his performance so much that they retained him in the role. The part of Tomas Vergis proved difficult to fill; James Marsters, who was later chosen to play Barnabas, was considered for the role, and Jamaican-Canadian actor Roger R Cross was actually cast at one point, appearing on casting sheets and in at least one publicity picture before the part was ultimately reassigned to John Pyper-Ferguson.

A number of *Battlestar Galactica* alumni appear in the series, including Pyper-Ferguson, who had previously played Taylor, *Pegasus*'s CAG; Luciana Carro; Jill 'Hadrian' Teed; Christian 'Duck' Tessier; and, as the father of Sam and Joseph Adama in the flashback sequences of 'The Dirteaters', Aleks Paunovic, who had played the minor character Sergeant Fisher in Seasons Two and Three of the parent series. Several *Caprica* alumni would, in turn, go on to appear in 'Blood and Chrome'. David Eick observed that casting a *Battlestar Galactica* actor in *Caprica* always sparked debate among the fans over whether the character was intended to be the ancestor of their *Battlestar Galactica* counterpart, or whether it was simply a case of the production team casting the best actor for the role.

The series also boasted a tie-in website *The Caprican*, a mock newspaper that both reported on story developments and also provided backstory, including travel features on the different colonies, entertainment features on Caprican soap operas (one entitled *Young People Going Out With Each Other*), articles about racism, and so on. After the mid-season break, Syfy ran a short feature called 'Re-Caprica', in the same dry style as the *Battlestar Galactica* one known informally as 'What the Frak?', which was graced with a number of good lines (such as, after describing Zoe building an avatar from compiling personal data such as restaurant receipts and medical records, 'This is why shredders are so important, folks'.) Serge also gained his own Twitter feed and a devoted internet following.

Despite the series' technical accomplishment, there was clearly an uncertainty among the writing team as to its target audience. This comes through strongly in the first half of the series. Remi Aubuchon describes it as 'a family drama ... not a space drama', Esai Morales, who plays Joseph Adama, also refers to it as a family show, and the series contains more teenage actors than its parent; but at the same time it features smoking, drug use, violence and sexuality to a sufficient degree to earn the DVD box sets a 15 certificate in the UK and a 14A rating in North America. Eick's frequent references to the series as a 'soap' are inaccurate, as soaps have multiple, usually non-intersecting, storylines written so as to run and run with no ultimate conclusion. The writing team also appear to have decided that calling it a 'soap' was a license to introduce far-fetched elements, such as the idea that Amanda's visions of her brother were in fact Vergis 'gaslighting' her (i.e. subjecting her to psychological torment) with an exact double of her brother, in order to send her mad (a concept that still survives in a deleted scene from 'End of Line'). Paula Malcolmson says in the podcast for 'End of Line': 'I begged the writers not to do the gaslighting episode to begin with. Yeah. I begged. I said, "It's a great idea but it's not gonna work."'

This uncertainty was exacerbated by the rapid turnover of series showrunners. Aubuchon was originally named in this capacity, but he left for *Persons Unknown* in September 2008. Moore initially ran the series before handing it over to Jane Espenson, who did the job until 15 November 2009, when it was announced that Kevin Murphy, who had joined the team in October, would be the new showrunner starting with 'Unvanquished'. David Eick, who, like Moore, was credited as executive producer for the series' entire run, tellingly recorded his final commentary podcast on the second episode of Season 1.5, 'Retribution', during which he remarked that the series' ratings were disappointing. Following this, most of the commentaries were recorded by a studio representative named Tom Leiber and Magda Apanowicz, and the absence of senior production team involvement suggests a lack of confidence in the series at its top levels. Under the stewardship of Murphy, whose previous projects included *Desperate Housewives* and *Reefer Madness: The Musical*, *Caprica* stabilised, and some of the more improbable elements disappeared (with Amanda's mental health problems miraculously clearing up and never being referred to again), but unfortunately the series was cancelled without going to a second season. Indeed, the final five episodes were removed from American transmission schedules after the cancellation was announced in October 2010, and were later transmitted in a block 'catch up' session; thus, the final episode, 'Apotheosis', received its debut broadcast in Canada, on the SPACE channel, on 30 November 2010.

Caprica's cancellation is something of a disappointment, as, although it struggled to find its feet, this is frequently true of new television series; recall that the reimagined *Battlestar Galactica* itself had Helo and Sharon wandering around Caprica doing next to nothing for most of its first season. Two key factors appear to explain *Caprica*'s premature end. The first is that it struggled to find an audience, with those fans who preferred *Battlestar Galactica*'s more space-operatic elements being put off by its relative lack of action ('*Crapica*' became an unfortunate alternate title in some quarters) and, on the other side, potential new viewers who might have been more interested in a slower-moving series being alienated by the *Battlestar Galactica* connection. Murphy remarks that internally, the team were told 'When it comes to Cylons, less dancin', more shootin'', for Season 1.5, suggesting that the loss of the core *Battlestar Galactica* audience was worrying the network. This was also reflected in the fact that the cancellation announcement did not inspire the same sort of concerted fan campaign for a reprieve as *Dollhouse* received when the latter series' cancellation was first mooted in 2009. Although the low ratings were cited by Syfy as the main reason for pulling the show, another, possibly more important, issue was cost. Universal had initially intended *Caprica* to be cheaper than *Battlestar Galactica*, but the episode commentaries contain many accounts of how the network was continually having to find additional money for unexpected effects shots. The ultimate result was, however, that the series never progressed beyond 18 episodes.

Kevin Murphy, in the commentary for the final episode, 'Apotheosis', and in a 29 April 2011 interview for fan site *The Caprica Times*, has given some indication of the direction the series would have taken had it continued. The second season, like the coda to 'Apotheosis', would have been set five years in the future. Zoe would have become the first skinjob, the Graystones having learned the technique after she had an encounter in V-World with Galen Tyrol, who was at the time on the ship travelling from Cylon Earth to the Colonies. However, Murphy states, 'She's a skinjob, but not the undetectable kind from *BSG*. It's a rudimentary version of the technology. She's more like Arnold in *Terminator*'. In other words, she would have had an organic covering with electronics underneath. Keeping her identity secret, Zoe would have joined up with the Caprica Legionnaires, a group dedicated to eradicating Cylons, with Duram, having left the GDD, as her commanding officer: Murphy, again, says, 'Zoe has turned against her "children" and has decided to cast her lot in with her human family and the human race'. Clarice, a wanted fugitive, would have formed an uneasy alliance with Lacy, while Mother, the former leader of the church, would have joined with Daniel Graystone in an attempt to regain power from Lacy. Joseph Adama would have had an affair with Fidelia; the sexual tension between the two characters was not originally intended, but came out of the actors' performances, and the writing team decided it would be a good direction in which to take them. Where all these storylines would have progressed is, however, now the purview of fan fiction.

The Adama Family: Society and Worldbuilding

The series gives us further insights into life in the Colonies before the Fall. Caprica is a decadent, pansexual and gender-neutral society. Gay marriage and group marriage are not unknown; and Jane Espenson says in the commentary for 'Gravedancing' that the team were concerned that showing Ruth, Joseph Adama's mother-in-law, in a traditional maternal role might undermine the gender-neutrality of the society, and so were careful to highlight the other aspects of her character (for instance, her tattoos, her Ha'la'tha connections, and her ability to assassinate grown men using a well-aimed meat-cleaver). Following fan criticism about the lack of out gay or bisexual characters in the parent series, it is perhaps not surprising that *Caprica* boasts two such regular characters, Clarice and Sam; and although Clarice unfortunately falls into the predatory bisexual woman stereotype (the fact that she is in a group marriage further contributes to the idea that female promiscuity is somehow threatening), Sam is somewhat more progressively depicted, being a Ha'la'tha assassin who is not remotely camp and is, ironically given his profession, one of the more likeable characters in the series.

In terms of Colonial politics, Moore, Eick and Aubuchon say in their commentary for the pilot that at this point the Colonies aren't united and don't have an overall President, although STO recruit Odin's remark that 'Everyone speaks Caprican' suggests that Caprica dominates even at this time. This is reflected in, for instance, Lacy's reference in the pilot to Caprica's Prime Minister; and in 'False Labor' we see the leader of Tauron. Furthermore, rather than simply prejudice against Sagittarons, we see racism from Capricans toward Taurons, Gemenons and Scorpions, and toward Capricans from people of these groups. This is also consistent with the parent-series episode 'Colonial Day', in which we learn that it is the fifty-second anniversary of the signing of the Articles of Colonisation that united the Colonies under the Quorum of Twelve, meaning that, at the time of *Caprica*, unification is six years away. In the abovementioned commentary, the showrunners also say that the Cylons would have become the foot soldiers in wars between the Colonies, presumably before the Colonies united against a common enemy. We hear the Caprican national anthem, 'Caprica Abides', including the lyric, 'So say we all'. On the religious front, we learn that monotheism, while a minority faith whose members are subject to harassment and persecution, is nonetheless an established presence with a hierarchy well integrated into the political landscape of the Colonies; the Soldiers of the One are a militant faction who might be best analogised to the Knights Templar, particularly given the ambivalence shown toward them by the

Church's official leaders. There is some indication that the polytheists have variations in their religious beliefs, given that Taurons appear to have different mourning customs and rituals from Capricans; a deleted scene from the pilot reveals that Taurons don't believe in an afterlife, but Capricans do. A lot of attention has clearly also been put into the small details of the society, the production team for instance having figured out the meanings of all of Sam's tattoos, and come up with brand names based on Greek and Latin (sometimes with humorous effect; Lethe Beer is named after the mythological river whose waters caused forgetfulness, and Joseph Adama purchases a holoband at a shop named 'Emptor', which is Latin for 'Buyer'). Mention should also be made of Baxter Sarno, the Caprican comedian explicitly based on *The Daily Show*'s Jon Stewart; the actor who plays him, Patton Oswalt, was a *Battlestar Galactica* fan and was thrilled at being asked to take part.

The story's central figures are well characterised. The Graystone parents' relationship is credibly portrayed, both in their passive-aggressive infighting after Zoe's death and the way in which they work as a team toward the end of the series. Daniel is explicitly based on charismatic information-technology entrepreneurs such as Bill Gates and Steve Jobs (who, like Daniel, was both fired and rehired by his own company). Daniel distances himself from the Zoe and Tamara avatars, treating them as less than human so as to justify his own experimentation on them, but he also later uses the avatar he creates of Amanda to work through his own relationship problems, coming to understand her personality through his failure to recreate it, and using the avatar to talk through the issues he wants to discuss with his wife. He can thus finally get himself to the point where he can be honest with the real Amanda, and accept her anger towards him. Parallels are also drawn between Daniel and his rival Tomas Vergis, in negative as well as positive ways: the final episode sees Daniel vowing to take apart the STO in much the same way that Vergis tried to get revenge on him by dismantling his organisation piece by piece. The final confrontation between Zoe and her parents in 'Here Be Dragons' exposes a lot of conflicted emotions on all sides, but also shows the Graystones finally achieving the maturity to apologise to Zoe, to let her come back on her own terms, and to accept her as a young adult capable of making her own decisions.

Other characters, however, benefit more from performance and direction than from the writing. Barnabas's characterisation is slightly clichéd, being clearly based on David Koresh, Charles Manson and other personality-cult leaders who use religion to gain sex and power, but James Marsters nevertheless manages to make the character engagingly villainous. Polly Williams also enables her character Clarice to transcend the obvious overtones of both Manson and Gaius Baltar in her lifestyle as the drug-fuelled leader of a polygamous monotheistic cult.

The sheer scale of Clarice's political activities, however, caused problems for the writing team. Originally Youngblood, a relatively junior blonde GDD operative who features in Season 1.0, was to have been the monotheist traitor in the ranks, and hints in this direction can still be seen in early episodes. However, the fact that Clarice's actions would require a higher-level cover-up meant that Singh, the Director of the Caprica City Bureau of the GDD, had to become the traitor instead. This renders somewhat inexplicable his earlier actions, for instance his verbal disciplining of Duram and Youngblood over their failure to identify Ben as the bomber when he was picked up for curfew violations, rather than quietly sweeping the matter under the carpet, as he is the only person who knows of the existence of an incriminating video of Ben being interviewed by the GDD. Even in this case, too, it strains credibility that the headmistress of a school known to have been attended by at least four radical monotheist terrorists would not be coming under wider scrutiny from other areas of the establishment, particularly as it has also been made clear that the GDD was an underfunded backwater department with little power prior to the Maglev bombing.

One of the series' early problems is, however, the depiction of Amanda Graystone in the first half-season. Originally, the writing team had intended that Amanda would be having an affair with Vergis, but they decided early on to drop the storyline, as it made her seem unsympathetic. This might have led to a love triangle, with Amanda secretly passing information about Vergis to Daniel, giving Vergis a stronger reason for his personal vendetta against Daniel than the deaths of his two employees. However, with this storyline gone, once Amanda loses her job (at which she appears to have no friends, or at least none willing to talk to her after her resignation), there is little for her to do until she starts cohabiting with Clarice in Season 1.5. Although Eick has stated that the two women's relationship was not intended to be openly sexual, it certainly has a clear lesbian subtext. Notably, Zoe's hair is black, which given that her mother has blonde hair and her father red, might be taken to indicate that Amanda has had affairs in the past; however, it is genetically possible for a blonde and a redhead to produce a dark-haired child, and there is no suggestion in the relationship between the Graystones, or between Zoe and her parents, that Zoe is not Daniel's daughter.

Amanda is better portrayed in the second half-season. A particularly telling sequence is one where she informs Clarice's wife Mar-Beth that Zoe was an unplanned pregnancy, that she suffered from postpartum depression after Zoe's birth and that she worries that the baby somehow picked up on this, causing Zoe to go off the rails later, but subsequently states to Duram that this is a lie, suggesting that, instead, Zoe was wanted, planned and loved, and thus her delinquency is down to more complex factors.

One key contribution that *Caprica* makes to the *Battlestar Galactica* mythos is its exploration of the backstory of the Cylons. In a slight contradiction to the miniseries, which states that the Cylons were developed to 'make life easier on the Twelve Colonies', the genesis of the project is explicitly military, even if the Cylons are later used as workers. The Centurions' base personality is that of an angry teenage girl who has a lot of unresolved issues about her parents and who turns to religion to compensate. This not only explains a lot about the Centurions' rebellion and feelings toward humanity, but also suggests that John Cavil's Oedipal issues might be a bleed-through from the Centurions as much as an outgrowth of his relationship with Ellen. Amanda Graystone's observation in 'Rebirth' – 'It's our job, we create life and then one day we have to face who we are, what they become and what they do' – is an effective summary of the human/Cylon relationship as much as of her relationship with Zoe. We also see foreshadowing of the Head People in the V-World avatars, and in Amanda's visions of her brother (with the team leaving it ambiguous at first as to whether or not he might be a Head Person), and of Cylon resurrection in Clarice's virtual heaven. V-World, a virtual environment created by its users, is a forerunner of Cylon projection. The Zoe avatar frequently wears silver metallic clothing, symbolising her connection to the U-87.

This brings us to the question of how involved God is in the events of *Caprica*. Initially, it is left ambiguous as to whether or not God is intervening directly; although Ben's suicide-bombing could have been arranged by God as a means of bringing the Zoe-avatar together with the U-87 body, it might equally have come about solely through the internal politics of the STO, as one of Barnabas's attempts to undermine Clarice. Clarice herself appears to be motivated more by ego than by faith, as evidenced by the Freudian slip in 'The Dirteaters' where she inadvertently reveals that she wants statues of herself in virtual heaven. However, Kevin Murphy has stated that the team took the conscious decision for Season 1.5 to indicate that God is indeed operating in *Caprica*, and that Clarice is being guided by God (although she does not appear to be in contact with the Head People at this point; she says of Zoe, 'She was the one who talked to angels'.) An initial idea to have James Callis and Tricia Helfer appear as Head People was ultimately dropped due to lack of actor availability – luckily so, as it would have raised the question of why the Head People chose to look like two individuals from the future who had no personal connection with any of the characters in *Caprica*. (Apparently, the team had an idea that Callis would play the bartender at the Dive, Clarice's favourite drug-taking haunt, suggesting that she would see the Head People while under the influence.) Instead, Zoe is, at the age of five, visited by a Head Person who resembles a teenage version of herself; this Head Person later encourages her to create the avatar programme. Although Kevin Murphy says he has no idea why Zoe appears at Clarice's church service in 'Apotheosis', a possible explanation is that this is actually Head Zoe too, albeit now sporting a different hairstyle, as we know she has free access to V-World through her association with the Zoe avatar. The Head People might well be interested in the new faith, as most of Clarice's sermon involves promoting equal rights for Cylons, something God would no doubt want to be a discourse in society before the Final Five reach the Colonies. However, Clarice's final pronouncement, 'The day of reckoning is coming. The children of humanity shall rise and crush the ones who first gave them life', indicates that the struggle for civil rights is about to become instead a war for supremacy, which goes against God's plan. The question also must be asked of why Head Zoe appears to her younger self as a teenager; possibly, given the way fate works in the series, she was destined to die at 16.

Although Caprican society would clearly have developed intelligent robots at some point in the near future, the imminent arrival of the Final Five means that God intervenes to jump-start the process by inspiring Zoe to develop her avatar programme. The fact that the Zoe-avatar bonds with the U-87 body (which Zoe herself cannot explain), and later becomes unbonded following the crash, suggests that God has intervened to try to prevent the Cylons from being used as machines of war, then given up this attempt when it became obvious it was futile. However, it is possible that by God encouraging this development in an adolescent girl whose society is not yet ready for the presence of a new intelligent species, a chain of events is set in motion that leads to the nuking of the Colonies 58 years later. Indeed, when the Zoe avatar takes over the U-87, its eye changes from a neutral yellow to an incandescent red.

Caprica makes an interesting theological contribution to *Battlestar Galactica* lore, in an exchange between Mother and Diego in 'The Heavens Will Rise'. Mother says: 'Secrets have answers. Now, mysteries, they don't have answers. That's why I love them. They're full of endless possibilities and permutations, like God himself. But if you solve a mystery, what are you left with?' Diego responds: 'A secret'. This distinction carries over implicitly to the parent series: at first the Cylons were a mystery, then they became a secret. Indeed, God's own mystery is stripped away through the omniscient perspective of the viewer over the course of the series. In a similar vein, Kevin Murphy, in the commentary for 'Unvanquished', suggests that the virtual heaven removes the faith from religion, and that Caprica is a place where there is no mystery; through scientific knowledge, the people have taken away uncertainty in most aspects of life, and are now taking the uncertainty out of religion. Within the series, however, this leads to the commodification of heaven by both Clarice and Daniel Graystone, and Zoe's observation that if people are certain of how to get to heaven, then there will be no restrictions on their activities in life; they will kill, rape and murder as in New Cap City, knowing that all they have to do to go to heaven is to upload an avatar. Indeed, as New Cap City, for all its hellishness, offers an escape for people like Heracles, who live boring, low-status lives, the future that Zoe postulates would be even worse. Ultimately, also, the certainty Clarice and Daniel appear to provide is itself illusory, as is the certainty that underlies Caprican society itself, undermined as it is by corruption and caprice; heaven becomes a kind of sanitised V-World, lacking the intensity brought about by the ability to engage in forbidden practices; and as countless fictional examples have shown, eternity with no goals, rules or sanctions is not heaven, but hell. This is symbolised in the series by the fact that Zoe, despite her limitless powers in V-World, in the end wants only to re-create the home she had with her parents. *Caprica* brings into the series as a whole the idea that faith must have mystery.

Must Be the Clouds in My Eyes: Themes of Caprica

Caprica develops the intricacy of its moral palette through a number of overarching themes. The first, as observed in the Cylon storyline, is that of parents and children, particularly as regards Zoe's relationship with her father.

The complex dynamic between the two is summed up by the story from Zoe's childhood that Daniel and Zoe remember in the pilot: Daniel held his daughter up on his shoulders to see a parade, but she wound up hitting her head on a sign as a result, and he then took her to the emergency room and held her hand so that she wouldn't be scared. Daniel loves Zoe, but is disengaged from her until something happens to force him to pay attention; likewise he denies the humanity of the Zoe avatar until forced to confront it. Zoe herself combines vulnerability with adolescent ruthlessness. These themes are counterpointed by the different dynamic between Joseph and Willie Adama, where Joseph's neglect of his son due to his grief over the deaths of his wife and daughter leads to the child seeking out alternative authority figures among the Ha'la'tha, choosing to reject, rather than revenge himself upon, his father.

Death and the need to let go of the dead are also key themes. Joseph Adama's storyline follows his difficulty in coming to terms with the loss of his wife and daughter; he is horrified by the Tamara avatar, and yet still wants to see her again. Although he seemingly achieves closure through a Tauron memorial service, when he learns afterwards that Tamara survives in V-World, his efforts to find her lead to addictive and self-destructive behaviour. The Tauron funeral song at the service is to the tune of the *Caprica* theme, meaning that the programme opens each week with a dirge. The original storyline in which Joseph was to have ended his pursuit of Tamara in New Cap City involved Evelyn and Sam setting up a fake scenario in the game, in which Joseph rescued Tamara from a gang, but she died in the process, leaving Evelyn to suggest that perhaps being able to say goodbye to her father was what finally allowed her to die; although her death was faked, this would have brought home clearly the idea that grief needs closure.[99] Both Daniel Graystone and Clarice manipulate people's desires to see their dead loved ones again as part of their respective bids for power, highlighting both the seductive nature of such emotions, and the fact that they are ultimately destructive.

The third key theme identified here is that of corruption. Adama is an ostensibly moral lawyer but has Ha'la'tha connections; Graystone is oblivious to the amoral uses of the technology he has invented until he is actually confronted with it. There are parallels between Clarice's and Zoe's respective manipulation of Lacy to get what they want from her (and Zoe similarly manipulates her father's lab assistant Philo, ultimately leading to his death), and there are also parallels drawn between the Church and the Ha'la'tha; for instance Lacy's planting of a bomb in Clarice's car is later recalled when the Adama brothers test Daniel to see if he would blow up his own mother to secure the deal with the Ha'la'tha. The V-Club seen in the pilot contains all the clichés found in moral crusades against the internet – porn, violence,

---

[99] In the version as broadcast, although he is twice given hints by New Cap City players that Tamara is dead and cannot be 'killed' in the game, Joseph does not seem to make the connection, meaning that when she fakes her own death by shooting herself, he appears to accept that she is dead.

blasphemy and so forth – and the monotheists are in part inspired by such environments to declare that one needs to know God in order to have morality. The discovery that the Guatrau is providing Cylons to the STO reveals that he is putting profit over the Ha'la'tha codes of conduct; Fidelia collaborates in her father's murder because she realises that the Adamas will probably kill him and take over regardless of what she does. Caprican society is deeply unequal, with the lives and technological gadgets of the super-rich Graystones standing in stark contrast to the lot of poorer characters like the Rands. There is also a sub-theme critical of libertarianism and rejecting the virtues of selfishness; aside from occasional hints like Lacy having the same surname as the famous libertarian thinker Ayn Rand and the prominence of technocratic figures such as Graystone and Vergis, Eric Stolz alludes to this in the commentary on 'Unvanquished', describing the bombing of the Atlas Arena by observing 'Atlas shrugs' – a reference to the title of Rand's seminal work, *Atlas Shrugged*.

The series is also suffused with religious, and particularly Christian, imagery. Lacy describes the Zoe-robot as being the Trinity, and the series' advertising depicted a nude Alessandra Torresani holding an apple. The title sequence shows a statue of an angel, which becomes Clarice meeting Lacy in a church with a flame-effect running over the pews and pillars, suggesting both heaven and hell. The STO's adoption of the infinity symbol as an identifyer recalls the use of the stylised Icthys fish by the early Christian church – as well as, tacitly, indicating that all this has happened before, and will happen again – and Tamara's flower symbol resembles a cross, while much of the STO's rhetoric against Caprican society recalls that of modern Christian evangelical groups. On a more philosophical front, Clarice refers to her god as 'creator and destroyer' – and expands on this more colloquially in a deleted scene from 'Here Be Dragons', where she remarks, 'Don't get me wrong, I love God, but he can be a real bastard sometimes'.

Finally, the series explores the concept of sentience, and the answer to the question posed by Clarice in the first iteration of Six's catchphrase, 'Are you alive?' As well as the actual sentient avatars, Caprica has virtual copies of people that are physically indistinguishable from the real thing, as witness the virtual Daniel Graystones that appear in 'Know Thy Enemy' and 'False Labor'. Graystone himself explores the question of humanity when, having lost the code he used to build the Tamara avatar, he tries to build an avatar of Amanda from scratch, but never succeeds in capturing her personality. New Cap City itself is a parallel to life in that, as Daniel states, it is a game with only one rule – that players who are 'killed' may not return – indicating that there is no way of 'winning' the game, and, as with life, the players themselves define the criteria for success. Finally, in 'Apotheosis', we have the ironic sequence in which Daniel tells Baxter Sarno's audience not to blur the distinction between human and machine, while he is secretly working on an artificial body for Zoe; in *Caprica*, reality and artifice combine and inform each other.

CAPRICA

The Revolution Will Not Be Televised: References Within Caprica

Like its parent series, *Caprica* draws on a number of films, TV shows and entertainment genres. The writers themselves cite as references several well-known films, such as *Gattaca* (mainly for the look and feel of *Caprica*) and *Goodfellas* (1990) (for the storyline of Willie being drawn into the Ha'la'tha); the casting of Meg Tilly and Winston Rekert as Church leaders brings in a connection to *Agnes of God* (1985), a film exploring the tension between faith and logic. Although Eick says that the Armenians were the explicit referent for the Taurons, their portrayal owes a lot to Mafia films focusing on Italian, Irish and Jewish gangsters (though Sam's tattoos also recall the Yakuza, themselves the subject of a number of films); 'The Dirteaters' reads like an unsuccessful attempt to riff on *The Godfather II*. New Cap City, despite drawing its name from *New Jack City* (1991), does not otherwise reference that film, and is instead drawn partly from the video-game series Grand Theft Auto, and partly from 1930s and 1940s gangster films and German expressionist movies. This last was an inspiration from Michael Nankin, who directed the episode 'There is Another Sky', which first introduces New Cap City.

As with the parent series, *Blade Runner*, with its film noir-inspired exploration of real and artificial life, is an influence, as is *Robocop*, particularly for the sequence in which Daniel presents the prototype Cylon to the Graystone Industries board. Eick in the video blog documentary *Caprican Stylz* on the Season 1.0 DVD explicitly cites *Dark City* as another antecedent, and this can be seen particularly in 'The Heavens Will Rise', when Zoe and Tamara reconstruct New Cap City into a kind of fantasy mountainscape. The V-Club scenes are heavily indebted to *Strange Days* (1995), a film focusing on decadence, millennialism and full-immersion virtual-world technology, although in this case the plot involves memories being copied and viewed rather than artificial worlds being created. *The Matrix* provides another antecedent for V-World, as well as the bit-rush imagery that precedes a character entering V-World. *Starship Troopers*, like *Robocop*, also featured a similar visual motif of introducing and commenting on events in the story through montages of news reports, public information films and popular entertainment.

Less immediately obvious antecedents include *Don't Look Now* (1973), a film exploring the relationship of a couple whose grief over the loss of their daughter leads one of them to apparent hallucinations, and the *The Prisoner* episode 'Living in Harmony', featuring a simulation that becomes more real to its participants than the physical world. Space does not permit a full exploration of all the film references within the series, though it is worth noting that the storyline where Joseph asks Sam to murder Amanda, and then agonises over the decision, is based on *Crimes and Misdemeanours* (1989); the virtual gang who take on Zoe in 'Unvanquished' reference *A Clockwork Orange* (1971); and the virtual Russian Roulette game Tamara encounters in 'There Is Another Sky' recalls *The Deer Hunter*.

The series also references Greek and Roman mythology. As well as the abovementioned product names, the language used as Tauron is actually Homeric Greek; Old Gemenon is Romanian, something that was earlier established in 'Razor'. Joseph Adama's pursuit of his daughter through New Cap City is based on Orpheus's quest to find his beloved in the underworld. The sequences in the Mysteries nightclub, in which a cross-dressing MC named Cerberus asks riddles that have a particular narrative significance, references the legend of the Sphinx, as well as that of Tiresias, a male prophet who was transformed into a woman. Deleted scenes from this sequence develop the theme further, featuring Cerberus wearing a three-headed dog mask at the outset of the performance[100], telling through a burlesque act the story of how the Gods overthrew the Titans, and then recounting the legend of 'Prometheus, who stole fire from the gods and shared it with man', elaborating, 'For what is fire but the light of knowledge'. This lends further significance to Cerberus's addressing Joseph, father of one of the new virtual life-forms, as 'Prometheus'. The inclusion of the Prometheus legend dovetails with the parent series' mythology about the Lords of Kobol, with Prometheus stealing fire and giving it to the human race symbolising one of the creator-gods encoding the drive to create intelligent robots in humanity. Prometheus does not, however, seem to be the God influencing the development of humanity in the series, as Prometheus is a trickster-figure with the gift of foresight whose attitude to humanity is generally benign, whereas the God of the series is a periodically wrathful, interfering type whose ability to foresee events is distinctly limited.

Caprica has other, less metaphysical, connections with reimagined *Battlestar Galactica*. The most obvious is the bait-and-switch storyline with Willie Adama. The fact that Willie has brown eyes rather than blue, and that his biological mother is Shannon rather than Evelyn, suggests that the decision to make him the Admiral's half-brother rather than the Admiral himself was taken at an early stage, though it is unknown precisely when the decision was made, and the production team's coyness about the subject rather suggests that Willie was originally intended to be the future Admiral, but that once the pilot was recorded, it was realised that the abovementioned continuity errors posed some serious problems to this scenario. After the decision was taken, the series chronology was moved back from the original dating of 50 years before the Fall (in the original DVD release of the pilot) to 58 years before the Fall because it was subsequently realised that the Bill we see in *Battlestar Galactica* would have been no older than nine at the time of the Armistice in the 50-year timeline –although the evidence as to how old Adama was at the time of the Armistice is contradictory, this would have been too young to rationalise.[101] For the record, Ruth in 'Gravedancing' indicates that Willie is 13, which, given that he would then be 31 at the time of the Armistice, is another hint that he is not the Admiral.

---

100 Cerberus was the name of the three-headed dog who guarded the gates of the underworld in Greek mythology.
101 The series' original 50-year chronology also would contradict the timeline of events discussed in the review for 'Colonial Day'.

Nonetheless, the *Caprica* team still play the question of Willie's identity close to their chests: the 'Re-Caprica' synopsis openly states that Willie is the future Admiral Adama; we have scenes of Willie building a model ship (albeit unenthusiastically) with Evelyn in 'Here Be Dragons'; and later Evelyn tells him about her brother's farm where he can go foxhunting (clearly the farm alluded to in 'Sometimes a Great Notion'). All of this does mean that Willie's death is genuinely surprising on first viewing.

Caprica also reveals the origins of terms such as 'toaster' (first used by Tomas Vergis) and 'skinjob' (first used by Zoe), while Daniel himself coins the term 'Cylon'. The blinking lights on the holobands used to access V-World superficially resemble the scanning eyes of Cylons (although they seem arguably closer to the eyes of the original series' IL-class Cylons). The red bit-rush effect, most notable as an establishing shot to indicate to the audience that the following action is set in V-World, and seen briefly in the title sequence when the perspective zooms into the eye of the Zoe avatar, recalls the later Cylons' data stream computer interfaces and wall displays seen on the basestars. The clinic where Amanda recovered from her depression will later become the hospital in 'The Farm', and the original series' theme tune plays on the wireless in 'Gravedancing'. Amanda knows an emergency-room doctor named Cottle, suggesting that Sherman Cottle was following a family profession – as his age would be in single digits at this point, it must be an older relative. The V-World bar frequented by Tamara and Zoe toward the end of the series is 'Sinny McNutt's Slash and Cut', named after series cinematographer Steve McNutt.

Caprica retrospectively introduces background regarding the character of Admiral Adama. There is now the implication that, much as Zoe rebels against her parents' hypocrisy, Adama himself experienced a similar rebellion: Adama's ambivalence regarding his father's reputation as a moral civil-rights lawyer is no doubt influenced by the knowledge that he was also heavily involved with the Ha'la'tha, and it is significant, in hindsight, that Adama never once mentions his Tauron ethnicity, suggesting that, like Michael Corleone in *The Godfather*, he has gone away to war as a means of rejecting his family. One other originally-intended thematic parallel was for Clarice to be a comedic villain along Baltar's lines. Eick says that this was dropped because there was not the same sense of overarching threat in *Caprica* as in *Battlestar Galactica*; in the parent series, the threat comes from the Cylons, not from Baltar, whereas in *Caprica*, the threat comes from Clarice herself. Nonetheless, a certain Baltaresque dark humour does survive in the STO storylines, for instance in Clarice's tea with Lacy in 'Rebirth', and in the self-aggrandising streak she clearly shows when constructing her virtual heaven.

Mention must also be made, however, of the worrying parallels between *Caprica* and *Galactica 1980*. Both were short-lived sequels to *Battlestar Galactica*, about which the network was ambivalent and a number of fans hostile; both were location-bound rather than set in space; both went over-budget despite the intention for them to be cheaper than their parent series; both featured a number of children and/or teenagers (Cyrus Xander was also originally written as a teenage computer genius, so it is lucky for *Caprica* that the rather older Hiro Kanagawa was eventually cast instead); and both feature a character named Willie played by a child actor who is not really very good. Finally, both series found their feet immediately before cancellation. It has to be said, though, that whereas *Galactica 1980* appears in many ways to be disconnected from the original series, *Caprica* was able to sum up and develop its parent series' moral themes, and thus can stand as a worthy coda to reimagined *Battlestar Galactica*.

To sum up, then, *Caprica* is a flawed series, but by no means a fatally flawed one. The concept is perfectly sound, and its major contribution lies in its uncompromising moral complexity. It not only presents characters who are neither heroes nor villains, and a situation where there is not necessarily a narrative reward for good or retribution for evil, only consequences, good and bad, for each character's actions, but it also never succumbs to the temptation to skew the portrayal to present one viewpoint as more positive than the other. *Caprica* is a series that did not flinch when dealing with ambiguous situations and characters, and as such improves upon the legacy of reimagined *Battlestar Galactica*.

Merchandise and Legacy

Like the original series, reimagined *Battlestar Galactica* sparked a wave of tie-in merchandise, official and unofficial, from Season Two onwards, as well as having an impact on the wider world of telefantasy.

Original Novels and Comics

Titan produced a one-off companion magazine for the miniseries in 2003, as well as a bimonthly dedicated publication for the series' fans, which ran for seven issues.[102] However, one of the first more substantial examples of official tie-in merchandise was a set of books published by TOR. This launched on 27 December 2005 with Jeffrey A Carver's novelisation of the miniseries, and continued with the publication of three original novels, *The Cylons' Secret* (2006) by Craig Shaw Gardner, *Sagittarius is Bleeding* (2006) by Peter David and *Unity* (2007) by Steven Harper. The novels' main problem is that they were rapidly overtaken by developments in series continuity. For instance, in *The Cylons' Secret*, set 20 years after the end of the Cylon War, Adama serves as *Galactica*'s XO upon his recommissioning, and gets Tigh a post as a flight instructor on the same battlestar, both of which are contradicted by the later 'Hero'. Similarly the Cylons, in a foreshadowing of 'Razor', are kidnapping humans and turning them into cyborgs, whereas the series would later establish that they gave up doing this after encountering the Final Five.

Battlestar Galactica also spawned a large number of comic books and graphic novels published by Dynamite Entertainment. Despite occasionally including Seamus Kevin Fahey (known otherwise for 'Faith' and 'The Face of the Enemy') as a writer, these also periodically suffered from being overtaken by developments in official continuity. They began with a 13-issue series entitled *Battlestar Galactica*, which was set between 'Home' part two and '*Pegasus*' and featured several variant covers for collectors; problematically, the storyline involved the Cylons creating duplicates of dead humans, something that never happened on screen. Subsequently, Dynamite has concentrated on developing prequel series. These include the 11-issue *Battlestar Galactica: Origins*, which began in 2007 and consisted of three stories focusing, respectively, on Baltar, Adama, and Starbuck and Helo; 2007's *Zarek*, exploring the revolutionary's backstory; *Battlestar Galactica: Season Zero* (2007), an immediate prequel to the miniseries; 2008's four-issue *Battlestar Galactica: Ghosts* series, following the

---

102 There have also been numerous official and unofficial non-fiction books devoted to the series. These are not covered in this chapter, but those we consulted for this volume are mentioned in the Authors' Introduction above.

adventures of a black-ops Viper squadron at the time of the Fall of the Colonies; and, in 2009, the four-issue *Battlestar Galactica: Cylon War*, the title of which is self-explanatory, and *Battlestar Galactica: The Final Five* by Fahey and David Reed, focusing partly on the exodus of the Thirteenth Tribe and partly on the events leading up to the destruction of the first Earth. The stories sometimes contradict established canon; for instance, in *The Final Five*, only Ellen Tigh and Galen Tyrol develop resurrection, whereas the series establishes in 'No Exit' that all of the Five reinvented it together. In 2014, Dynamite released a six-part story exploring the origins of Six, as well as a steampunk reimagining of the series entitled *Steampunk Battlestar Galactica 1880*.

In 2009, manga publisher Tokyopop released a single graphic novel, *Battlestar Galactica: Echoes of New Caprica*, which contained short stories relating to the New Caprica storylines, including one, focusing on Zarek, by Richard Hatch.

Action Figures and Models

Due to the shift in viewer demographics and toy markets since the 1978 series, the action figures produced for the reimagined series are firmly aimed at an older, adult collector market. Diamond Select produced a series of seven-inch figures covering most of the main and supporting cast and a range of Cylon Centurions of various types, including modern Centurions, Centurions with different types of battle damage, 'Razor'-era Centurions in silver and bronze iterations, and an all-black 'Stealth Cylon', which was an exclusive for the 2009 New York ComicCon. They also produced some special variations and exclusives, such as 'New Caprica Boomer' and 'Off Duty Apollo'. Quantum Mechanix released a pair of limited-edition cartoon-style figures representing a Centurion and Starbuck, under the name 'Little Frakkers', in keeping with the contemporary fashion for cartoon or chibi-style figurines. Minimates produced a range of 2.5-inch Lego-style figures depicting most of the main characters. Art Asylum produced limited-edition busts of Baltar, a Centurion, Adama, Starbuck, Helo, Caprica-Six, two versions of Head Six (in red and blue dresses), with Six bearing a distinct, somewhat ironic, resemblance to Ellen Tigh, and one of Baltar and Head Six together.

There are also vehicle figures of varying degrees of accuracy. Hasbro produced diecast models of both *Galactica* and *Pegasus*, as well as Mark II and VII Vipers; the Vipers, for some reason, came in a variety of colours. Hasbro also released diecast models of *Colonial One*, Raptors and Raiders. Diamond Select came out with a Viper Mark VII and a Raider sculpture, and Moebius Models have developed a range of high-quality model kits.

Apparel

While NBC Universal produces official T-shirts, jumpers and hoodies bearing *Battlestar Galactica* logos, quotes and slogans, there is also an extensive internet-based cottage industry in unlicensed and unofficial homage or spoof T-shirts.

Examples can be found bearing virtually every group or ship logo seen within the series, including the Vigilantes; spoof tourist T-shirts advertising for holidays in Caprica City; and Starbuck's and Anders' wedding tattoos as design elements. There are quite a number of garments emblazoned with toasters; and quotes from the series, such as 'So Say We All' or 'I Have a Destiny', are frequently seen. Many sites offer the same designs on mugs, mouse-mats, wall clocks and other housewares.

While there are too many slogan T-shirts to provide an exhaustive list here, some of the more noteworthy examples include the rival 'Roslin '08' and 'Baltar '08' T-shirts that circulated during the 2008 American presidential election. As speculation grew over the identities of the Cylons, T-shirts with slogans such as 'Part Toaster', 'You said my *what* is glowing?' and 'I am the Final Cylon' were developed. The term 'Frak' has also given rise to a variety of T-shirt designs, for instance 'Number Eight is a CILF [i.e. Cylon I'd Like to Frak]' and a popular one replicating the 'Frak Earth' graffito seen on one of *Galactica*'s walls in Season Four. When fans of the *Twilight* character Edward began wearing T-shirts bearing his likeness, a spoof T-shirt circulated depicting Edward James Olmos's image in the same style. On a less frivolous note, costume pieces such as rank insignia pins, dog-tags and replica uniforms are also available.

Miscellaneous Merchandise

To further cash in on the series' popularity, Universal Studios officially released several posters, including: a set of 1940s-style 'propaganda posters' urging people to be vigilant against Cylons, join the Colonial Warriors or *Galactica* deck gang, and so forth; a 'Spot the Cylon' poster dryly listing the identifying traits of the species, such as glowing spines and listening to music no-one else can hear; a Cylon Evolution poster showing the rise of the Cylons, starting with a toaster and finishing with Number Six; a Centurion target poster modelled on the ones that appeared in the series; and prints of the 'Monclair' Cylon War painting from Adama's quarters. Freelance artist and fan of the series Steve Anderson also released several limited edition prints of series characters.

Game-related merchandise includes a trading card set, a board game (in which one of the players is secretly a Cylon agent working against the others) and a video game. This last, which was released in 2003 shortly before the miniseries, was based on one developed but never released at the time of the Singer-DeSanto revival project; as it currently stands, it freely mixes original- and reimagined-series continuity, focusing on the adventures of William 'Husker' Adama fighting the Cylons, who are led by an Imperious Leader named Lord Erebus. In 2011, an MMORPG based on the series, entitled *Battlestar Galactica Online*, was launched.

Other merchandise includes bumper stickers with series slogans and logos, mugs and shot glasses with the *Galactica* insignia, and a badge based on the Eye of Jupiter mandala. Mention must be made of Ctrl-Alt-Delete's mugs, designed in imitation of Starbucks Coffee's official logo and reading 'Starbuck's Coffee:

Fresh Roasted Cylon', and also of the much-sought-after limited-edition *Battlestar Galactica* toaster. Designed as an exclusive for ComicCon 2009, this has the series logo on one side, a Centurion face on the other, and toasts a Centurion face pattern on one side of the bread and the legend 'Frak Off' on the other.

Finally, *Caprica* also boasts a small amount of merchandise. Official merchandise includes products emblazoned with the Graystone Industries logo, Avenging Angels T-shirts as worn by Caprican hipsters in 'The Dirteaters', and the much-coveted Serge keychain, another ComicCon exclusive (a later model advertised as being 'Serge' is also available, but it is in fact based on the military drones seen in the pilot rather than on the Graystones' household robot). There is a Graystone Industries toaster (which burns a U-87 face onto the bread) and, strangest of all, Tauron temporary tattoos. Notable unofficial merchandise includes STO T-shirts (in one commentary, Magda Apanowicz suggests to Tom Lieber that these ought to be produced, and Lieber replies that they will have them made for Season Four – evidently fans took matters into their own hands), and, when T-shirts supporting amendments in favour of gay marriage began to proliferate in the USA, one entrepreneur developed a spoof version supporting a Caprican amendment in favour of group marriage.

The Legacy, So Far

While it is too soon at the time of writing to fully judge the impact of *Battlestar Galactica* on telefantasy in general, it has already inspired a few developments. Its relative success seems to have been a driver behind the wave of classic telefantasy series revivals of the early 2000s, such as *Flash Gordon* (2007), *The Bionic Woman* (2007), *Knight Rider* (2008) and *V* (2009); aside from *Doctor Who* (2005), none has had the staying power of *Battlestar Galactica*. It has also helped to popularise percussion-heavy, world-music-influenced soundtracks, and some of its alumni have gone on to other telefantasy series, with *Terminator: The Sarah Connor Chronicles* having Toni Graphia, Bear McCreary and Stephanie Jacobsen on its team; *Dollhouse* featuring Michael Hogan and Jamie Bamber as guest stars in its second season alongside series regular Tahmoh Penikett; *V* featuring Rekha Sharma and Roark Critchlow, who played Kara's father in 'Someone to Watch Over Me', in recurring roles, with Michael Trucco also appearing in one episode; and, more recently, clone thriller series *Orphan Black* featuring Matthew Bennett as a semi-regular.

Thus far, however, the impact of the *Battlestar Galactica* franchise on its parent genre has been limited. While there have been shows that met or exceeded its depth of characterisation and nuanced exploration of complicated philosophical and moral themes, these have all been outside the realms of science fiction, instead coming from fantasy (*Game of Thrones*), historical drama (*Boardwalk Empire*) or contemporary drama (*Breaking Bad*). While there has been a spate of complex political and social dramas in a variety of genres on American television in recent years, *Battlestar Galactica* remains the only space opera in this category. *Caprica*, however, appears to have had more of a legacy, with the

Swedish series *Äkta människor* (2012), remade as the British-American co-production *Humans* (2015), picking up the theme of a near-future society changing after the development of intelligent humanoid robot servants.

Rather than having a wider legacy on television, therefore, *Battlestar Galactica* must be appreciated as a unique moment in early 21st Century American genre television: an exciting and gripping space opera that aspires to present realistic sociopolitical dynamics and morally ambiguous characters, developed further in the spin-off series *Caprica*.

INDEX BY TITLE

33   62, 95-101, 103, 106, 119, 121-122, 131, 204, 352, 425, 506, 577
A Day in the Life   118, 379-383, 448, 480, 485
A Disquiet Follows My Soul   491, 504, 509-515, 517, 526, 535, 541, 547-548
A Measure of Salvation   324, 330-337, 346, 357, 367, 371, 374, 376-378, 393, 431, 452, 460, 481, 500, 554
Aces   258
Act of Contrition   113-120, 152, 163, 169, 180, 186, 252, 257-258, 262, 382, 391, 410
Apotheosis   593, 598, 602, 605
Baltar's Escape   164, 263, 343
Bastille Day   91, 107-112, 114, 156, 164, 202, 230, 243, 250, 264, 283, 492, 574
Battlestar Galactica: The Miniseries (Parts One and Two)   67-68, 70, 72-91, 93-95, 97-99, 102, 104-105, 109-113, 117-118, 120-122, 126, 129, 138-141, 144, 147-148, 163-164, 166, 168, 171, 174, 180, 183-184, 186, 192, 197, 207, 212, 219, 225, 232, 238-239, 247, 253, 257, 274-275, 278, 284-285, 294, 306, 314, 317, 325, 341, 359, 363, 374, 382, 424, 428, 455, 506, 521, 526, 559-561, 565, 569, 571, 580-581, 584, 601, 610, 612
Battlestar Galactica: The Second Coming   13, 72, 581
Black Market   172, 237, 245, 249-254, 255, 259, 264, 269, 271, 377, 511, 383
Blood and Chrome   89, 426, 583, 585-592, 596
Blood on the Scales   523-529
Blowback   593
Captain's Hand, The   201, 266-271, 284, 347, 419, 462, 506, 554, 583
Collaborators   316, 318-323, 328, 369, 376, 407-408, 410, 433, 446, 479, 512, 521
Colonial Day   91, 128, 146, 153, 155-161, 166, 177, 208, 216, 431, 599, 607
Crossroads (Parts One and Two)   122, 282, 284, 289, 297, 307, 319, 332, 376, 394, 397, 400, 403-411, 430-431, 433, 439, 457, 465, 467, 491-493, 50
Crossroads / Resistance, The (Parts One to Ten)   23, 293-297, 404, 507
Daybreak (Parts One, Two and Three)   64, 77, 170, 413-414, 427, 474, 498, 507-508, 514, 556-575, 589
Deadlock   538-543, 547, 561
Dirteaters, The   593, 596, 602, 606, 613
Dirty Hands   384-389, 405, 407, 472, 480, 493, 548, 559
Downloaded   173, 212, 217, 237, 271-278, 282, 287, 294, 306, 335, 419, 444, 504, 581-582
Drowning Woman   542
End of Line   340, 593, 595, 597
Epiphanies   242-249, 260-261, 268-269, 273, 280-281, 387, 569
Escape Velocity   414, 446, 451-458, 461, 466-468, 504
Exodus (Parts One and Two)   288, 302, 310-317, 326, 333, 353, 561
Experiment in Terra   83, 94
Eye of Jupiter, The   92, 289, 291-292, 354-359, 362, 371, 424, 438, 441, 494, 500, 534, 547
Face of the Enemy, The   417, 503-508, 512, 520, 562, 579, 610
Faith   462, 464-469, 482, 512, 610
False Labor   593, 599, 605
Farm, The   174, 200-204, 206, 213, 232, 275-276, 308, 462, 524, 581, 608
Final Cut   66, 169, 215-221, 223, 232, 253, 288, 400
Fire in Space   83, 180
Flesh and Bone   135-142, 147-148, 153, 159, 167, 186, 210, 230, 239, 243, 301, 352, 393, 460, 481, 578, 583
Flight of the Phoenix   172, 219, 221-226, 232, 257, 262, 282, 447, 546
Fragged   184, 187-193, 202, 204, 211, 214, 486, 497
Galactica 1980   9, 13, 18-19, 62, 77, 96, 116, 120, 123, 141, 225, 290, 321, 394, 434, 440, 534-535, 540, 567, 588, 608-609
Ghosts in the Machine   593
Gravedancing   84, 593, 595, 599, 607-608
Greetings from Earth   63
Guess What's Coming to Dinner   88, 134, 387, 430, 439, 470-476, 482, 485, 506, 524, 526, 547
Gun on Ice Planet Zero, The   62, 107, 111, 153, 588
Hand of God, The   117, 124, 129, 149-154, 159, 161, 170, 198, 207, 210, 239-240, 257, 431, 480, 497

Hand of God, The (original series) 19, 123, 146, 169, 567
He That Believeth in Me 413, 429-435, 466, 493, 536, 553
Heavens Will Rise, The 593, 603, 606
Here Be Dragons 593, 600, 605, 608
Hero 145, 338-343, 352-353, 364, 368, 380, 394, 424, 434, 442, 580, 588, 610
Home (Parts One and Two) 138, 205-214, 219, 230, 237, 243, 247, 267, 334, 353, 399, 493, 582, 610
Hub, The 210, 458, 484-489, 492, 517, 536, 563-564, 566
Imperfections of Memory, The 593
Islanded in a Stream of Stars 209, 471, 534, 551-555, 584
Know Thy Enemy 593, 605
Kobol's Last Gleaming (Parts One and Two) 62, 93, 114, 162-171, 173, 178-179, 183-184, 190-191, 197, 207, 214, 275, 286, 291, 313, 321, 357, 367, 433, 441, 500, 578
Lay Down Your Burdens (Parts One and Two) 132, 175, 276, 279-288, 293-294, 297, 302, 307, 344, 394, 408, 422, 447, 455, 582, 584
Litmus 116, 122, 125-131, 159, 195, 229, 298, 410, 526, 580
Living Legend, The 146, 152, 231-233, 314
Long Patrol, The 71, 225, 440
Lost Planet of the Gods 116, 152, 169, 212, 285, 335, 352, 363, 565, 570
Maelstrom 222, 332, 390-396, 412-413, 422, 432-433, 438, 466, 469, 475, 535, 541, 545, 552, 559
Man with Nine Lives, The 105
Murder on the Rising Star 111, 146, 352, 381, 400
Mutiny, The 285, 408
Night the Cylons Landed, The 19
No Exit 282, 447, 514, 530-537, 552, 554, 562, 564, 577, 579, 589, 611
Oath, The 456, 516-522, 524-525, 529, 540
Occupation 95, 296-304, 309, 316, 323, 326, 405
Our Enemies, Ourselves 388-389
Passage, The 97, 105, 181, 349-353, 363, 391-392, 410, 423, 431, 540, 554
Pegasus 172, 227-233, 238, 245-246, 262, 269, 422, 425, 610
Pilot (Caprica) 593
Plan, The 77, 89, 86, 103, 127, 132, 139, 144, 166, 179, 197, 204, 275, 282, 291, 427, 507-508, 570, 576-584, 590
Precipice 274, 295, 302-309, 311, 314, 316, 407
Raid, The 173, 240, 276-277, 335
Rapture 289, 292, 354, 356, 360-365, 369, 406, 430, 466, 486, 494, 499, 547
Razor 77, 89, 105, 116, 160, 231, 236, 238-239, 271, 334, 392, 412, 416, 418-428, 437, 462, 506, 554, 562, 573-574, 588-589, 607, 610-611
Rebirth 593, 602, 608
Reins of a Waterfall 593
Resistance 194-199, 209, 216, 232, 281, 284, 297, 314, 400, 521, 583
Resistance, The / Crossroads (Parts One to Ten) 23, 293-297, 404, 507
Resurrection Ship (Parts One and Two) 226, 234-241, 245, 248-250, 252-253, 262, 275, 277, 367, 425, 427, 488, 493
Retribution 593, 597
Return of Starbuck, The 116, 120, 123, 225, 440
Revelations 415, 441, 490-495, 503
Road Less Traveled, The 440, 447, 459-463, 521
Sacrifice 70, 173, 260-265, 269
Saga of a Star World 15, 19, 75, 81, 83, 85-86, 105, 123, 152, 285, 314, 343, 352
Scar 175, 237, 239, 255-259, 264, 352, 391, 448, 526
Scattered 66, 165, 176-182, 193, 211, 213, 224-225, 245, 258, 380
Secrets and Lies 147
Showdown 388
Sine Qua Non 456, 472, 477-483, 493-494, 573
Six Degrees of Separation 131-135, 140, 145, 159, 243, 437, 555, 578
Six of One 412, 433, 436-442, 444, 448, 465, 481, 580
Someone to Watch Over Me 117, 277, 471, 543-550, 558, 613
Sometimes a Great Notion 415, 494, 496-502, 504, 567, 608
Son Also Rises, The 397-402, 433-434
Super Scouts, The 567
Take the Celestra 269
Taking a Break From All Your Worries 292, 366-372, 391, 409, 438, 504, 507-508, 526, 540
There is Another Sky 593, 606
Things We Lock Away 593

BY YOUR COMMAND: VOL 2

Ties That Bind, The   443-450, 465, 471, 564
Tigh Me Up, Tigh Me Down   66, 91, 141, 143-148, 153, 172, 220, 263, 352, 413, 499, 543, 581
Torn   118, 324-331, 333, 339, 367, 376, 497, 560, 579
Unfinished Business   285, 289, 292, 344-348, 353, 383, 424, 452, 478, 505, 510
Unvanquished   593, 595-597, 603, 605-606
Valley of Darkness   180, 182-186, 190-191, 193, 204, 211, 256, 270, 296, 363, 424, 438, 549, 559

War of the Gods   19, 231, 236, 290, 434, 531
Water   91, 93, 101-106, 116, 125, 128, 168, 218, 222, 224, 275, 352, 400, 421, 510
Wheel of Fire   290, 434
Woman King, The   373-378, 386, 407
You Can't Go Home Again   120-124, 134, 147, 163, 240, 270, 312
Young Lords, The   116, 123

About the Authors

Alan Stevens has written, edited and developed numerous publications on telefantasy series, including *Doctor Who*, *Blake's 7* and *The Prisoner*. He is also co-author of the Telos books *Fall Out: The Unofficial and Unauthorised Guide to The Prisoner* and *By Your Command: The Unofficial and Unauthorised Guide to Battlestar Galactica* Volumes 1 and 2. Since the early 1990s, he has written for the stage, and produced a number of documentaries, serials and dramas for radio and independent audio release, including the *Blake's 7/Doctor Who* spin-off series *Kaldor City* and the Gothic horror time-travelling adventure *Faction Paradox*. He is currently based in the South East of England, and runs his own audio production company, *Magic Bullet Productions* (**kaldorcity.com**).

Fiona Moore was born and raised in Toronto, but has lived in the UK since 1997. She has a doctorate in Social Anthropology from the University of Oxford, and is currently Professor of Business Anthropology at Royal Holloway, University of London. She has written non-fiction on a wide variety of subjects, from the identities of Taiwanese businesspeople to the culture of drag queens, and is also co-author of the Telos books *Fall Out: The Unofficial and Unauthorised Guide to The Prisoner* and *By Your Command: The Unofficial and Unauthorised Guide to Battlestar Galactica* Volumes 1 and 2. Her fiction and poetry have been published in, among others, *Asimov*, *Interzone* and *Dark Horizons*. She will admit to owning a ComicCon exclusive keychain of Serge.

BY YOUR COMMAND: VOL 2

MAGIC BULLET

KALDOR CITY

A 6-part CD series combining CHRIS BOUCHER's worlds of DOCTOR WHO and BLAKE'S 7 into a political and philosophical thriller set in an ultraviolent urban dystopia, where a corrupt super-rich elite face a robot slave rebellion driven by a mysterious supernatural force and a relentless terrorist cult. Starring PAUL DARROW and RUSSELL HUNTER

1: OCCAM'S RAZOR
2: DEATH'S HEAD
3: HIDDEN PERSUADERS
4: TAREN CAPEL
5: CHECKMATE
6: STORM MINE

Faction Paradox

THE TRUE HISTORY OF FACTION PARADOX
A series of 6 FACTION PARADOX CDs, the mind-bending time-travelling steampunk adventure that takes you to the stronghold of the Egyptian Gods, the mysterious Ibis Gates, the ruins of Pompeii, and Sutekh's Pyramid on Mars.

Originally created by LAWRENCE MILES for the BBC's acclaimed DOCTOR WHO series of novels. Starring GABRIEL WOOLF and JULIAN GLOVER

1: COMING TO DUST
2: THE SHIP OF A BILLION YEARS
3: BODY POLITIC
4: WORDS FROM NINE DIVINITIES
5: OZYMANDIAS
6: THE JUDGMENT OF SUTEKH

Visit www.kaldorcity.com for downloads, special online exclusives, and much more!